THE
POLITICAL
ECONOMY
Readings in the
Politics and Economics of
American Public Policy

THE POLITICAL ECONOMY

Readings in the
Politics and Economics of
American Public Policy

Edited by
THOMAS FERGUSON
and JOEL ROGERS

M. E. Sharpe, Inc.
Armonk, New York
London, England

Copyright © 1984 by M. E. Sharpe, Inc.
80 Business Park Drive   Armonk, New York 10504

Available in the United Kingdom and Europe from M. E. Sharpe
Publishers, 3 Henrietta Street, London WC2E 8LU.

Library of Congress Cataloging in Publication Data

The political economy

   Includes bibliographical references.
   1. United States—Politics and government—Addresses, essays, lectures.
2. United States—Economic policy—Addresses, essays, lectures. 3. Power
(Social sciences)—Addresses, essays, lectures.   I. Ferguson, Thomas,
1949–   . Rogers, Joel, 1952–
JK21.P65 1984   361.6′1′0973   84-3111
ISBN 0-87332-276-2
ISBN 0-87332-272-X (pbk.)

Printed in the United States of America

Contents

Introduction

Nothing is more striking in the recent development of professional political science than the emergence of political economy as a distinct and rapidly growing discipline subfield. Benefiting from the eclipse of pluralism as an accepted description of the exercise of power in America, sharp policy debates over the proper role of government in an era of economic instability and decline, the resurgence of libertarian, Marxist, and other heterodox traditions of analysis, the continuing vitality of institutional economics, and the proliferation of neoclassically based economic interpretations of voting behavior, public administration, and private law—political economy is booming. It is now increasingly recognized as a critical ingredient of political science curricula at both graduate and undergraduate levels. It has been institutionalized through the spectacular growth and popularity of such professional associations as the Conference Group on the Political Economy of Advanced Industrial Societies. And it continues to generate work that cuts across and invades the traditional discipline subfields of political theory, comparative politics, international relations, urban politics, and, above all, American politics.

But while political economy is thriving, a bottleneck is clearly emerging in the dissemination of the new research. With the continued dominance of American politics as the central study of those within the profession, there has been a need for a book of readings that integrates important works done from a political economy perspective into an accessible overview of the American political system as a whole.

As teachers of American government, we have felt this need for some time. This book is our effort to meet it.

The richness and variety of current studies in political economy makes it impossible to specify a single methodological approach that dominates and defines the field. Political economy may nevertheless be usefully understood as reflecting a general set of concerns and assumptions about the nature of economic and political power that are highlighted by the rise of the interventionist state and the advent of what has been variously denoted as "modern," "political," "welfare," or "organized" capitalism. Here what has newly gained acceptance within political science are the elementary propositions that political institutions and decisions critically affect the conditions of economic activity, and that the structure and articulation of economic interests determine much of what once passed as pristine political process. Acceptance of these propositions not only implies a need to understand state–market relations in far more detail than that approached by conventional social science, but the need as well to reconceptualize the inner terms of those relations, namely states and markets themselves.

Most basically, then, and whatever its varied expression, the political economy perspective rejects any presumption of a sharp separation between economic and political power. It abandons the claim, canonized within classical liberalism and carried over into much mainstream social science, that through institutional design modern capitalist societies can and do succeed in segregating the domains of public authority and private coercion.

In this collection we bring together several sorts of writings within the political economy perspective, thus broadly understood, that relate to American politics. We are not promoting any particular "school" of political economy, but instead aim to present in as accessible a form as possible as wide a variety as possible of important and representative work within the field. Further, since we are chiefly concerned with facilitating student confrontation with this work, and not our own interpretation of it, we have kept the editorial apparatus to a minimum, and that largely confined to abstracting the articles for first-time readers.

The articles gathered here are organized into three large sections. These sections derive their coherence from the problem and topic clusters considered, rather than the approaches to those problems.

The articles in the first section, "Structure: Markets, Politics, and the Constraints of Capitalist Democracy," highlight the basic economic constraints on the exercise of state power in advanced industrial states such as the United States. Topics include the competing ranges and rationales of public and private decision making; the conditioning of political action by economic calculation; the "political business cycle"; and the critical requirement that the state ensure private accumulation, both as a source of its own funding and as a precondition for obtaining levels of welfare necessary to regime stability.

Articles in the second section, "Conduct: Processes, Institutions, and Group Bargaining," focus on the structure of political competition and the management of poltical demand in the United States. Here the text approaches many of the mainstream concerns of studies of American politics. Topics include the processes of formal politics, including voting behavior and party competition; informal coalition building; the patterning of demands for economic and social regulation; and the evolution of central institutions of formal government, including Congress, the executive bureaucracy, and law.

Finally, in the third section, "Performance: Policies, Outcomes, Directions," the focus extends to consideration of the results of the political-economic bargaining process, particularly in the area of state–market relations. Discussion ranges over the shape of the political demand in the United States. Here the text approaches many of the mainstream action in international arenas to secure satisfaction of domestic market interests; the production of public goods; and other supplementations or partial replacements of the market mechanism. The section concludes with speculation on the near-term future of advanced capitalist democracies.

Implicit in the political economy perspective is an account of strategic behavior exercised within a framework of multiple constraints. These constraints have to do both with the most general requirements of accumulation and stability within advanced industrial states ("Structure") and with the more particular institutional settings within which those requirements are addressed ("Conduct"). Both sets of constraints are, of course, contingent products of previous strategic action, but they nevertheless critically shape the dimensions and content of political expression, conflict, and result ("Performance"). In our organizational scheme for the book we have thus made this implicit framework explicit. Our purpose, again, is to make the materials that follow accessible to the widest possible student audience. Of that audience itself we assume only an interest in understanding how the world works, and offer the materials collected here as one important set of attempted explanations.

A Note to Students and
the General Reader

With few exceptions, the essays in this collection have been specially edited to make them accessible to you. Texts have been shortened or condensed to make their main argument clearer and many footnotes have been pruned. We have also prefaced each essay with a headnote that introduces each article's leading points or puts its argument in context. We would strongly urge you to read these headnotes before tackling the articles, since they might help you through a few occasionally difficult or obscure passages.

Once you are confident you have understood a particular piece, it is our hope that you will then go on and evaluate it. At this stage you may find it helpful to compare its analysis with the arguments of other essays in the book that treat the same broad subject, or with some other work you are reading for class or for pleasure. When you do this, however, you should remember that the essays in this book by no means represent the same point of view, and that no human being could possibly agree with all of them. Since we consider the ability to think critically one of the most important values of an educated person, we hope that you not only are not disturbed by this but actually come to enjoy it. However you feel about it, this state of affairs accurately reflects a fact that you must inevitably come to terms with: that violently clashing views about the relation of economics and politics pervade American politics, and that you have to make up your own mind. When you do, we hope you find the essays in this book helpful.

Acknowledgments

Many people helped us to prepare this book, and it is a pleasure to be able to thank them here.

Students helped by suggesting articles and, especially, by giving us their candid impressions of the pedagogical value of different essays. At MIT, Gregory Nowell provided exceptionally capable research assistance.

The authors and copyright holders of the essays made our job much easier than it might have been. All responded quickly to our requests for permissions. Many of the authors also cheerfully helped with the always unpleasant task of editing previously published works to fit the space constraints of an anthology of this sort.

Finally, we owe a special debt to Patricia Kolb, our editor at M. E. Sharpe. Widely read in this literature herself, her expert advice has proven invaluable at all stages of the project. Without her enthusiasm, the book would probably not have been begun. Without her guidance, it almost surely would not have been completed.

Thomas Ferguson
and Joel Rogers

1

STRUCTURE

Markets, Politics, and the Constraints of Capitalist Democracy

The essays in this section all deal with the basic structures governing political power and conflict in advanced industrial market societies. Charles Lindblom explores the different logics of decision making and control in market and public arenas. Anthony Downs highlights the rationality of the ordinary citizen's abstention from political activity. Michal Kalecki points out the barriers to achieving full employment within a capitalist economy. Finally, Fred Block attempts to identify the structural mechanisms that shape the workings of the capitalist state.

The Market as Prison

CHARLES E. LINDBLOM

Charles E. Lindblom takes up a topic "ordinarily brushed aside as an embarrassing feature of ostensibly democratic systems," namely the degree to which public policy is blunted and constrained by the peculiar demands and structure of market systems. While the behavior of public officials is susceptible to direction through commands, Lindblom argues, the behavior of market actors can, by definition, be directed only through inducements. This difference produces an important and self-enforcing asymmetry in the distribution of power within market systems. Unless market actors can be enticed to do something, they simply will not do it. But if, as is commonly the case, market actors wield important decision-making authority, and they choose not to do something (e.g., invest, hire workers, curb industrial pollution), the consequences of their choice can easily undermine the authority of the public system of decision making, as well as the welfare of the society as a whole. The position of powerful private market actors is thus different from the position of all other participants in the political economy. It is specially privileged, and this privilege may be thought of as a wide dispersion to the business community of veto power over the decisions of public policy. But Lindblom goes on to argue that the incarcerating effect of market structures, their "automatic punishing recoil" against disfavored public policy, would persist (though it might be mitigated) even within regimes featuring public ownership of the productive apparatus. He concludes with remarks on an additional imprisoning effect of market structures particularly appropriate to the beginning of this volume: that which their bare existence seems to exert on conventional social science thinking about the nature and distribution of political power.

Suppose—just to limber up our minds—that we faced the fanciful task of designing a political system or a political/economic system that would be highly resistant to change. How to do it? One way that can be imagined—but only imagined—is to design institutions of such excellence as would satisfy us without further amendment and would do so under all possible circumstances in a rapidly changing world. To identify such a possibility is to discard it as hopelessly visionary. Another possibility might be somehow to place all power in the hands of a despot or oligarch, who would thereafter deny citizens any capacity for changing the system. But doing so would of course enable the elites to change the system, and we know that some elites are more eager for change than some masses.

Another possibility is simple and fiendishly clever. It is to design institutions so that any attempt to alter them automatically triggers punishment. By "automatic" I mean that

Reprinted with permission from *The Journal of Politics*, Vol. 44, No. 2 (May 1982), pp. 324-36. Copyright © 1982 by the Southern Political Science Association. This essay is based on an informal talk by Professor Lindblom.

the punishment follows from the very act intended to change the system. Punishment does not wait for anyone's deliberation on whether the change is acceptable or not. Such a change-repressing system would be all the more effective if the punishments were strong; if they took the form of over-responses, like the tantrums of a spoiled child raging at even mild attempts at parental control.

How fanciful is that possibility? It is not at all clear how such a simple concept could be made effective in actual practice. Consider some of our institutions. There seems to be no way to make such a mechanism work in the case of schools. We are indeed sometimes punished in our attempts to improve them in that the attempts sometimes fail and make the situation worse. But that is not a built-in feature of the school system or of our attempts to improve it. There may be no way, even if we sought one, to build in an automatic punishing recoil. The same seems to be true for labor unions. Unions possess a capacity for retaliatory punishment through strikes, but it is a weapon they must use sparingly. And it is a weapon rarely used to punish attempts of society to change the institutional role of unions but is instead largely an adjunct to bargaining over terms of employment for members. There appears to be no easily perceived possibility for automatically punishing ourselves every time we try to legislate on unions.

If we go down the line of social institutions, the possibilities for repressing change through an automatic punishing recoil appear to be either nonexistent or impossible to imagine. For the church, the family, or the various institutions of government, for example, unpunished change continues in fact from year to year even if, again, we may sometimes construe a failure in reform as a punishment. No method for guaranteeing automatic punishment is in evidence.

When we come, however, to that cluster of institutions called business, business enterprise, or the market, just such a mechanism is in fact already operating. Many kinds of market reform automatically trigger punishments in the form of unemployment or a sluggish economy. Do we want businesses to carry a larger share of the nation's tax burden? We must fear that such a reform will discourage business investment and curtail employment. Do we want business enterprises to reduce industrial pollution of air and water? Again we must bear the consequences of the costs to them of their doing so and the resultant declines in investment and employment. Would we like to consider even more fundamental changes in business and market—worker participation in management, for example, or public scrutiny of corporate decisions? We can hardly imagine putting such proposals as those on the legislative agenda so disturbing would they be to business morale and incentive.

In the town in which I live, a chemical plant discharges something into the atmosphere that carries both a bad odor and irritants to the eyes. Town and state governments are both reluctant to put an end to the problem for fear that the plant will find it advantageous to move to a new location in another state. Nationally, we have recently seen that a re-invigorated Federal Trade Commission has been crippled by new restrictive legislation and presidential instructions for fear that effective regulation of monopoly by the Commission will undercut business incentives to invest and provide jobs.

All this is familiar. One line of reform after another is blocked by prospective punishment. An enormous variety of reforms do in fact undercut business expectations of profitability and do therefore reduce employment. Higher business taxes reduce profitability. Bearing the costs of pollution control reduces profitability. Building safer automobiles reduces profitability. Countless reforms therefore are followed immediately— swiftly—by the punishment of unemployment.

Change is repressed, not wholly stopped. Businessmen sometimes learn to live with reforms. Sometimes also we escape the punishment because we attach to the reforms new offsetting benefits to business to keep up their incentives to provide jobs. To a growing number of environmental controls over business we attach new tax benefits or, as in the case of Chrysler, new loan guarantees. But the conflict between reform and its adverse effects on business that punish us through unemployment is a long standing and real repressant of change. As for the ubiquity of punishment, its swiftness and severity, there is nothing like it elsewhere in the social system. Nowhere else is there so effective a set of automatic punishments established as a barrier to social change.

Business people often exaggerate the conflict. Chrysler, for example, argued that its financial difficulties, for which it sought relief from government, were largely caused by environmental regulations, which is almost certainly not the case. And business people often predict dire consequences from regulations that they know they can accept if they must. Nevertheless, change in business and market institutions is drastically repressed by the frequency with which change will in actual fact produce unemployment. This is a familiar phenomenon as old as markets themselves.

Punishment is not dependent on conspiracy or intention to punish. If, anticipating new regulations, a businessman decides not to go through with a planned output expansion, he has in effect punished us without the intention of doing so. Simply minding one's own business is the formula for an extraordinary system for repressing change.

The mechanism that accounts for this extraordinary state of affairs is the same one that I referred to in *Politics and Markets*[1] to explain the related phenomenon of the privileged position of business in the political system of all market oriented societies. In all market oriented societies, the great organizing and coordinating tasks are placed in the hands of two groups of responsible persons, functionaries, or leaders. One group consists of government officials at sufficiently high levels. The other group consists of business people. The tasks assigned to business people are of no less importance than those assigned to government officials. To business people is assigned the organizing of the nation's work force, and that task in itself is perhaps the largest and most basic specific problem in social organization faced by any society. Businessmen direct capital accumulation, income distribution, and resource conservation, as well as discharge more particular tasks such as organizing the production of steel, bicycles, armaments, pots and pans, and housing. Businessmen also undertake specific coordinating tasks as, for example, the bringing of farm products to urban consumers.

The defining difference between a government official and a business entrepreneur is not that one discharges important functions and the other only secondary functions, for both perform major and essential services for society. The difference is that one is directed and controlled through a system of commands while the other is directed and controlled by a system of inducements. Why societies use both systems of direction and control is a long story that we shall not undertake. But a market society is one that makes heavy use of an inducements system for directing and controlling many of its major leaders. Market systems are inducement systems. Put out of your minds the question of whether or not societies ought to use inducement systems for controlling and directing top leadership. The fact is that some do, and that is what market systems are.

Playing their roles in a command system, government officials can be commanded to perform their functions. Playing their roles in an inducement system, business people cannot be commanded but must be induced. Thus inducement becomes the nub of the automatic punishment system. Any change in their position that they do not like is a disincentive, an anti-inducement, leading them not to perform their function or to perform it with less vigor. Any change or reform they do not like brings to all of us the punishment of unemployment or a sluggish economy.

Again, the system works that way not because business people conspire or plan to punish us, but simply because many kinds of institutional changes are of a character they do not like and consequently reduce the inducements we count on to motivate them to provide jobs and perform their other functions.

The result is that across the entire array of institutional changes that businessmen themselves do not like, an automatic punishing recoil works to repress change. In that broad category, change—and often even the suggestion of change—adversely affects performance, hence adversely affects employment. Anticipations of change are enough to trigger unemployment.

Children may sulk when they do not like the way they are being treated. Professors may grumble. Workers may slow their work. But their responses differ from the responses of dissatisfied businessmen in a critical way. The dissatisfactions of these other groups do not result in disincentives and reduced performance that impose a broad, severe and obvious penalty throughout the society, which is what unemployment does. A generalized gradual slowdown of workers, if it were to occur, would ordinarily be neither measurable nor observable. Any general business slowdown is measurable and hurtful in jobs lost, and almost everyone is aware of it. A specific localized work slowdown or stoppage—say, a decision of trainmen to work by the rule-book so assiduously as to paralyze rail traffic—can be a felt injury to millions of people. But it is a tactic that can only now and then be mobilized. Instead, the penalty of unemployment is visited on us by business disincentives in any situation in which business people see themselves adversely affected, because business people are major organizers and coordinators.

Business people do not have to debate whether or not to impose the penalty. They need do no more—as I said before—than tend to their own businesses, which means that, without thought of effecting a punishment on us, they restrict investment and jobs simply in the course of being prudent managers of their enterprises.

Do I need to point out how broadly business disincentives injure a population? The unemployed suffer—that is obvious. So also do young prospective entrants into the labor force, who find that they cannot obtain jobs when business is slack. So also do businessmen themselves, large and small, as production is reduced. So also do stockholders, whose earnings decline. So also do farmers—businessmen themselves—who find markets for their outputs depressed.

What about government officials? It is critical to the efficacy of automatic punishment that it be visited on them. For it is they who immediately or proximately decide to persist in policy changes or to withdraw from such initiatives. The penalty visited on them by business disincentives caused by proposed policies is that declining business activity is a threat to the party and the officials in power. When a decline in prosperity and employment is brought about by decisions of corporate and other business executives, it is not they but government officials who consequently are retired from their offices.

That result, then, is why the market might be characterized as a prison. For a broad category of political/economic affairs, it imprisons policy making, and imprisons our attempts to improve our institutions. It greatly cripples our attempts to improve the social world because it afflicts us with sluggish economic performance and unemployment simply because we begin to debate or undertake reform.

In his *Great Transformation*, Karl Polanyi makes the point that early English experience with policy designed to soften the harshness of the market system in 18th century England demonstrated how easily regulation of the market could derange the economy. But he did not go so far as to argue that market systems imprison or cripple the policy-making process and indeed thought that more intelligent policy making could succeed where earlier attempts failed. I am arguing that the crippling of policy making in a market society may be more serious than he thought.

You may be tempted to believe that the real obstacle to social change is—as we often carelessly assert—a kind of social inertia or a tendency of societies to remain as they are. But it is not at all clear that inertia of that kind exists in the social world. Many people constantly try to change the social world. An explanation of their failure more plausible than that of inertia is to be found in the great number of other people who are vigorously trying to frustrate social change. My analysis points to a social mechanism that frustrates it. It is a highly selective mechanism, you should note, that permits change of some kinds and imposes powerful obstacles to other kinds.

Clearly, if we look at different areas of social life, ease of change varies greatly from area to area. In recent years we have seen large changes in sexual mores, for example, as well, of course, as multiple changes pressed on us by technological development. In political/economic life, society all over the world has gone through or is now going through one of the world's greatest social revolutions—the organization of almost every form of social cooperation through formal organization, especially bureaucratic organization. The bureaucratic revolution is enough to testify to the capacity of society for political and economic change. It is all the more impressive that there exists a mechanism of automatic punishing recoil that successfully retards or represses change in other aspects of political and economic life.

In just what aspects of political/economic life that mechanism operates I have not yet said, except to note that the included aspects are all those in which businessmen—or any large or critical number of them—see change as hurtful to their own prospects. You can fill in what those aspects are. They include institutions and policies that protect the decision-making authority of businessmen in their own businesses, and the customary prerogatives of management, including rights to self recruitment into corporate elites. They include policies that maintain the existing distribution of income and wealth, along with institutions and policies that hold the labor movement in check. The efficacy of the recoil mechanism is evidenced by the continuing historical failure of equalitarian aspirations to achieve a significant change in the distribution of wealth and income among social strata, and by the continuing autonomy of corporate management in a world in which increasing numbers of thoughtful people are arguing, on environmental and other grounds, that no group of leaders can be allowed to exercise so autonomous a control over our lives. A new study of corporate power by Herman opens our eyes to the extent in which business autonomy has been sustained despite decades of apparent growth in the regulation of it.[2]

It is also the case that in so far as policy has successfully pushed into areas of which business people disapprove, it has often had to be offset by new benefits or supports to business. When that happens, policy is imprisoned not in the sense that it cannot break out of its confinement but in the sense that to release it we must pay ransom. Where there are prisons, however, there are also jailbreaks. Again, therefore, I do not argue that the market is escape-proof.

The imprisoning of institutions and policy making in market-oriented society is, I think, ordinarily brushed aside as an embarrassing feature of ostensibly democratic systems. We are not comfortable in acknowledging that popular control is crippled in these systems by an automatic punishing recoil. In the U.S. today, however, in the

Reagan administration we now hear remarkably candid acknowledgements that we must learn to be happy in our prison. The new administration tells us boldly and badly that we cannot have growth, cannot have price stability, and cannot have full employment unless we stop undermining business incentives. Hence, they have told us that we cannot have an effective Federal Trade Commission, its recent energy having harmed business. Nor can we persist in recent programs of automobile safety, which must now be relaxed. Nor can we protect the landscape against strip mines. One after another of our recent reforms are being curtailed so far as the administration can achieve the result, on the grounds that our economic system—the market system—does not allow such reforms if we are to enjoy prosperity. We cannot even hold to a policy of human rights abroad. As David Rockefeller early announced and members of the Reagan administration have repeated since, our policy of protecting human rights abroad has to be subordinated to our needs for foreign markets, with which it has been an interference.

The Reagan administration is trying to make the automatic recoil mechanism even more obstructive to social change than it need be. But I credit the administration with understanding that such a mechanism exists in any market system. They are right in appreciating that policy making is imprisoned, even without their efforts to build the walls higher.

Finally, take note that my argument is that policy is imprisoned in market oriented systems, which is a broader generalization than if I had said that it is imprisoned in private enterprise systems. The feature of market systems that is at the core of the recoil mechanism is the inducement system that we use to motivate one great category of organizers and coordinators to do their work. If we were to operate a market system composed exclusively of government owned and operated market enterprises, the recoil mechanism would still operate. The inducements necessary to get the required perform-ance out of public managers might be fewer or less; hence the problem of automatic punishing recoil might be reduced. But it would not be eliminated unless we abandoned the inducement system in favor of a command system, thus removing the socialized enterprise from a market system of inducements.

One of the causes, I believe, of Soviet abandonment of their attempts in the 1960's to introduce more market elements into the Soviet economy is that their earliest moves were abruptly perceived as requiring top political leadership to sit on its hands, that is, not to interfere with market stimulated managerial decisions. At least dimly, they perceived that the growth of the market implied constrictions on their own ability to make policy. They, top Soviet authorities, would be imprisoned by their commitment to the market.

Some of you will hear my remarks today as constituting an argument for getting rid of the market system so that policy can escape from its prison. But that would be putting words in my mouth. I do believe that the fact that the market system imprisons policy through an automatic punishing recoil is a serious disadvantage of market systems. I would not want to deprecate, minimize or obscure that inference. We pay a big price for the use of a market system. But whether the market ought to be maintained or abandoned calls for a weighing of its advantages and disadvantages. And that task I am not undertaking today.

In any case, the relation between democracy and market is more complex than we hear it to be from classical liberals like Hayek and Friedman. No democratic nation state has ever arisen anywhere in the world except in conjunction with a market system—surely a historical fact of enormous importance. But, according to my argument today, no market society can achieve a fully developed democracy because the market imprisons the policy-making process. We may be caught in a vise. For minimal democracy, we require a market system. For fuller democracy, we require its elimination. But its elimination might pose more obstacles to a fuller democracy than does its continuing imprisoning of policy making. It may therefore be that a fuller democracy is never to be ours. Or, if it can be achieved, it will come only when we discover how to provide, without a market system, those minimal supports for democracy which, so far in history, only market systems have provided. Our dilemma or difficulties are extraordinary—and are not clarified for us by the current state either of market theory or democratic theory.

For Americans and many Western Europeans the market is a prison in another sense as well. Both as an institution and as an intellectual concept, it seems to have imprisoned our thinking about politics and economics.

For me, an early and memorable demonstration of imprisoned thought was many of the reviews of *Unions and Capitalism*, a book based on my doctoral dissertation and published in 1949. In it I had argued that certain incompatibilities between two major institutions of our society—collective bargaining, on one hand, and the market system, on the other—would in the future produce serious problems, including simultaneous unemployment and inflation. Not knowing what to do about the problem, I simply offered a diagnosis without a remedial prescription, naively assuming that the diagnosis implied that something had to give either on the side of collective bargaining or on the side of the market system. Almost all reviewers, however, simply took it for granted that my purpose was to make a case against collective bargaining or a case for its restriction. At least conventional academic reviewers seemed unable to contemplate the possibility that a conflict between two institutions raised questions about both of them and, *a priori*, no more about the one than the other.

Having been sensitized by that early experience, I have noted ever since that the standard formulation of one of our economic problems is that union pressure on wages causes inflation or restriction of job opportunities in the immediately affected industrial firm. *Given* a market system, that is probably true. But let me suggest the other possible formulation: given the inevitable and understandable desire of workers to increase their share of national income, a market system will produce inflation or unemployment. The second proposition is no less true than the first. The limited capacity of our thinking is revealed in our commitment in habit of mind to the first proposition to the neglect of the second. We have come to think not of human need and aspiration but of the market system as the fixed element in the light of which we think about policy. We find it difficult to think of the market as the variable.

Much of our thinking in other policy areas is similarly imprisoned, as, for example, our thinking on environmental protection. That policy made in Congress and in the White House sacrifices environmental protection to the needs of market enterprises is one thing. That those academics and other scholars, analysts, and critics who are trying to think constructively about the options open to us often themselves cannot see the market as a variable but treat it as the fixed element around which policy must be fashioned is another thing. The latter is what I mean by imprisoned thought.

A more striking example is the state of thinking about television. One of the great shapers of contemporary culture and politics is commercial broadcasting, especially television. You have all heard what once would have been thought of as astonishing figures on the number of hours adults and children spend watching and hearing what commercial advertisers and their clients decide we will see and hear. That in the United States we have permitted or chosen a broadcasting system that confers such authority on people whose motives are to sell something to us; that we accept frequent urgent interruptions in almost all programs so that we can be exhorted to buy; that we must also hear a steady diet of praise for the corporate institutions that exhort us to buy; that we grant without charge broadcasting rights to those fortunate enough to gain the enormously profitable broadcast licenses; and that we do not even ask in exchange for significant use of broadcast time for educational purposes—all these features of American broadcasting are as plausible evidences of insanity as they are of intelligence in public policy.

For a wealthy society that can afford any of a variety of superior systems—and for a society that in any case pays all the costs of the present system—one might think that political scientists and other analysts would attend to the merits and demerits of commercial broadcasting, that so critical a shaper of politics and culture would be on the agenda for spirited debate. It is not. Our thought is imprisoned. We cannot venture intellectually—a few exceptions aside—beyond what seems normal and natural. We uncritically accept what the market provides. For American social science it is a scandal that it remains silent on so great an issue. And—to make the point precisely—it is not that commercial television is unacceptable. That is not the point. The point is that whether it is or not is a great issue on which we are incapable of thought, so imprisoned are our minds.

You will note that I am saying—and here I make it explicit—that the prison is strong enough to incarcerate not only popular thought but professional thinking in the social sciences. Further evidence lies in the controversy over pluralism in the last fifteen or so years. Dominant pluralist thought in American political science describes all policy making as a result of vectors, each vector often consisting of the influence of some group. All groups who wish to be admitted are, according to pluralist thought, admitted to the process. The attack on pluralist thought that eventually emerged argued—successfully, I think—that in some policy areas or for certain kinds of policy issues the pluralist competition of groups did not work and that class influences, traditional biases in the political culture, or processes called "mobilization of bias" made certain policy positions dominant and others impossible to advance. But on the whole these critics missed the phenomenon I am describing—the extent to which policy making has to be and is constrained by the peculiar characteristics of an inducement system in a market system. Pluralism at most operates only in an unimprisoned zone of policy making. Hence the continuing debate on pluralism, although it has greatly improved our understanding of politics, is still significantly constrained or imprisoned.

Even today interest-group theory for the most part treats business interests as symmetrical with labor and other interests bearing on policy making. It has not yet generally recognized that business interests occupy a special place in imprisoned policy making.

More indirectly the market has taken hold of our thinking in social science in ways that cripple us, though a more complete account of what has happened to us would have to acknowledge the influence of professional economics as itself a major influence. For example, in regarding the market system as a piece of social machinery for organizing the nation's resources in response to individual wants expressed through purchases, economists have drifted into an ethics of preference. In so far as possible, all ethical issues are settled by reference to individual preferences taken as given. Is x good or is x bad? All depends on the patterns of individual preferences.

Impressed both by the market as an institution and by the tidyness of economists' interpretation of it, many political scientists have adopted the ethic of preferences taken as given. Is this policy a good one? It depends on the patterns of individual political preferences, whatever they are. Is democracy a good thing? Yes, because it is a system for letting individual preferences, whatever they are, govern policy making. Democracy is a political market. Or as Schumpeter, who is a major source of this current thought, put it: democracy is competitive politics.

What is wrong in this version of democracy as a market-like process in which individual preferences ideally prevail, as in an ideal market, is that the powerful and all-pervasive effect of politics on the formation of preferences is ignored. From at least Mill on to just before Schumpeter, so massive and persistent a process of preference formation as is constituted by the political system itself was never ignored. In allowing the market to dominate our political thought since then, we have simplified our political theories, with some gains in clarity. But we have impoverished our thought by imprisoning it in an unsatisfactory model of preferences taken as given.

My main point, however, has been that market systems imprison policy. Those of us who live in those market oriented systems that are called liberal democratic exercise significantly less control over policy than we have thought. And we are also less free than we may have thought. Such are the inevitable consequences of imprisonment. That our thinking is itself imprisoned is a separate phenomenon of importance. Given, however, the complexity of human thought and the impossibility of disentangling its sources, this second phenomenon cannot be so confidently argued as the first.

Again, I would like to leave a caution about inferences. What I have described constitutes serious disadvantages in making use of a market system. But the case for and against markets is extraordinarily complex, and my analysis is a long way from a case either for or against. It is also a long way from an answer to any question about what is to be done if the problems posed by my analysis are accepted as significant ones.

Notes

1. Charles E. Lindblom, *Politics and Markets* (New York: Basic Books, 1977).

2. Edward S. Herman, *Corporate Control, Corporate Power* (New York: Cambridge University Press, 1981).

An Economic Theory of Political Action in a Democracy

ANTHONY DOWNS

Nothing is as central to political science as analysis of the conditions under which people seek to gain, control, or restructure political power. The benefits of possessing political power seem so great that it is difficult to understand why, in a democracy such as our own, so few voters take the trouble to exercise their power at the polls. Pluralist models in particular interpret voter abstentionism as a sign of contentment with the status quo. In this path-breaking analysis by Anthony Downs, however, incentives to participate, barriers to entry into the political arena, and information costs are shown to have an impact on the structure of political life. High information costs, the number of parties in a political system, and the mode of representation are all determining elements that affect such behavior as voter turnout, party platforms, and elite relations with constituencies.

I

In spite of the tremendous importance of government decisions in every phase of economic life, economic theorists have never successfully integrated government with private decision-makers in a single general equilibrium theory.[1] Instead they have treated government action as an exogenous variable, determined by political considerations that lie outside the purview of economics. This view is really a carry-over from the classical premise that the private sector is a self-regulating mechanism and that any government action beyond maintenance of law and order is "interference" with it rather than an intrinsic part of it.[2]

However, in at least two fields of economic theory, the centrality of government action has forced economists to formulate rules that indicate how government "should" make decisions. Thus in the field of public finance, Hugh Dalton states:

> As a result of [the] operations of public finance, changes take place in the amount and in the nature of the wealth which is produced, and in the distribution of that wealth among individuals and classes. Are these changes in their aggregate effects socially advantageous? If so the operations are justified; if not, not. The best system of public finance is that which secures the maximum social advantage from the operations which it conducts.[3]

A similar attempt to differentiate the operations "proper" to government from those "proper" to private agents has been made by Harvey W. Peck, who writes: "If public

Reprinted with permission from *The Journal of Political Economy* 65 (1957), pp. 135–50 (with deletions). Copyright ©1957 by The University of Chicago Press.

operation of an enterprise will produce a greater net social utility, the services rendered by this enterprise should belong in the category of public goods."[4] In addition, several welfare economists have posited general principles to guide government action in the economy. For example, Abba P. Lerner indirectly states such a rule when he says: "If it is desired to maximize the total satisfaction in a society, the rational procedure is to divide income on an equalitarian basis."[5]

Admittedly, this list of examples is not very long, primarily because overt statements of a decision rule to guide government action are extremely rare in economic theory. However, it does not unduly distort reality to state that most welfare economists and many public finance theorists implicitly assume that the "proper" function of government is to maximize social welfare. Insofar as they face the problem of government decision-making at all, they nearly all subscribe to some approximation of this normative rule.

The use of this rule has led to two major difficulties. First, it is not clear what is meant by "social welfare," nor is there any agreement about how to "maximize" it. In fact, a long controversy about the nature of social welfare in the "new welfare economics" led to Kenneth Arrow's conclusion that no rational method of maximizing social welfare can possibly be found unless strong restrictions are placed on the preference orderings of the individuals in society.[6]

The complexities of this problem have diverted attention from the second difficulty raised by the view that government's function is to maximize social welfare. Even if social welfare could be defined, and methods of maximizing it could be agreed upon, what reason is there to believe that the men who run the government would be motivated to maximize it? To state that they "should" do so does not mean that they will. As Schumpeter, one of the few economists who have faced this problem, has pointed out:

> It does not follow that the social meaning of a type of activity will necessarily provide the motive power, hence the explanation of the latter. If it does not, a theory that contents itself with an analysis of the social end or need to be served cannot be accepted as an adequate account of the activities that serve it.[7]

Schumpeter here illuminates a crucial objection to most attempts to deal with government in economic theory: they do not really treat the government as part of the division of labor. Every agent in the division of labor has both a private motive and a social function. For example, the social function of a coal-miner is removing coal from the ground, since this activity provides utility for others. But he is motivated to carry out this function by his desire to earn income, not by any desire to benefit others. Similarly, every other agent in the division of labor carries out his social function primarily as a means of attaining his own private ends: the enjoyment of income, prestige, or power. Much of economic theory consists in essence of proving that men thus pursuing their own ends may nevertheless carry out their social functions with great efficiency, at least under certain conditions.

In light of this reasoning, any attempt to construct a theory of government action without discussing the motives of those who run the government must be regarded as inconsistent with the main body of economic analysis. Every such attempt fails to face the fact that governments are concrete institutions run by men, because it deals with them on a purely normative level. As a result, these attempts can never lead to an integration of government with other decision-makers in a general equilibrium theory. Such integration demands a positive approach that explains how the governors are led to act by their own selfish motives. In the following sections, I present a model of government decision-making based on this approach.

II

In building this model, I shall use the following definitions:

1. *Government* is that agency in the division of labor which has the power to coerce all other agents in society; it is the locus of "ultimate" power in a given area.[8]

2. A *democracy* is a political system that exhibits the following characteristics:

(a) Two or more parties compete in periodic elections for control of the governing apparatus.

(b) The party (or coalition of parties) winning a majority of votes gains control of the governing apparatus until the next election.

(c) Losing parties never attempt to prevent the winners from taking office, nor do winners use the powers of office to vitiate the ability of losers to compete in the next election.

(d) All sane, law-abiding adults who are governed are citizens, and every citizen has one and only one vote in each election.

Though these definitions are both somewhat ambiguous, they will suffice for present purposes.

Next I set forth the following axioms:

1. Each political party is a team of men who seek office solely in order to enjoy the income, prestige, and power that go with running the governing apparatus.[9]

2. The winning party (or coalition) has complete control over the government's actions until the next election. There are no votes of confidence between elections either by a legislature or by the electorate, so the governing party cannot be ousted before the next election. Nor are any of its orders resisted or sabotaged by an intransigent bureaucracy.

3. Government's economic powers are unlimited. It can nationalize everything, hand everything over to private interests, or strike any balance between these extremes.

4. The only limit on government's powers is that the incumbent party cannot in any way restrict the political freedom of opposition parties or of individual citizens, unless they seek to overthrow it by force.

5. Every agent in the model—whether an individual, a party or a private coalition—behaves rationally at all times; that is, it proceeds toward its goals with a minimal use of scarce resources and undertakes only those actions for which marginal return exceeds marginal cost.[10]

From these definitions and axioms springs my central hypothesis: political parties in a democracy formulate policy strictly as a means of gaining votes. They do not seek to gain office in order to carry out certain preconceived policies or to serve any particular interest groups; rather they formulate policies and serve interest groups in order to gain office. Thus their social function—which is to formulate and carry out policies when in power as the government—is accomplished as a by-product of their private motive—which is to attain the income, power, and prestige of being in office.

This hypothesis implies that, in a democracy, the government always acts so as to maximize the number of votes it will receive. In effect, it is an entrepreneur selling policies for votes instead of products for money. Furthermore, it must compete for votes with other parties, just as two or more oligopolists compete for sales in a market. Whether or not such a government maximizes social welfare (assuming this process can be defined) depends upon how the competitive struggle for power influences its behavior. We cannot assume a priori that this behavior is socially optimal any more than we can assume a priori that a given firm produces the socially optimal output.

I shall examine the nature of government decision-making in two contexts: (1) in a world in which there is perfect knowledge and information is costless and (2) in a world in which knowledge is imperfect and information is costly.

III

[. . .] However, I shall not explore party strategies in a perfectly informed world, because nearly all the conclusions that could be drawn are inapplicable to the imperfectly informed world in which we are primarily interested. Only one point should be stressed: in a world where perfect knowledge prevails, the government gives the preferences of each citizen exactly the same weight as those of every other citizen. This does not mean that its policies favor all citizens equally, since strategic considerations may lead it to ignore some citizens and to woo others ardently or to favor some with one policy and others with another. But it never deliberately eschews the vote of Citizen A to gain that of Citizen B. Since each citizen has one and only one vote, it cannot gain by trading A's vote for B's, *ceteris paribus*. In short, the equality of franchise is successful as a device for distributing political power equally among citizens.

IV

Lack of complete information on which to base decisions is a condition so basic to human life that it influences the structure of almost every social institution. In politics especially, its effects are profound. For this reason, I devote the rest of my analysis to the impact of imperfect knowledge upon political action in a democracy.

In this model, imperfect knowledge means (1) that parties do not always know exactly what citizens want; (2) that citizens do not always know what the government or its opposition has done, is doing, or should be doing to serve their interests; and (3) that the information needed to overcome both types of ignorance is costly—in other words, that scarce resources must be used to procure and assimilate it. Although these conditions have many effects upon the operation of government in the model, I concentrate on only three: persuasion, ideologies, and rational ignorance.

V

As long as we retain the assumption of perfect knowledge, no citizen can possibly influence another's vote. Each knows what would benefit him most, what the government is doing, and what other parties would do if they were in power. Therefore, the citizen's political taste structure, which I assume to be fixed, leads him directly to an unambiguous decision about how he should vote. If he remains rational, no persuasion can change his mind.

But, as soon as ignorance appears, the clear path from taste structure to voting decision becomes obscured by lack of knowledge. Though some voters want a specific party to win because its policies are clearly the most beneficial to them, others are highly uncertain about which party they prefer. They are not sure just what is happening to them or what would happen to them if another party were in power. They need more facts to establish a clear preference. By providing these facts, persuaders can become effective.

Persuaders are not interested *per se* in helping people who are uncertain become less so; they want to produce a decision that aids their cause. Therefore, they provide only those facts which are favorable to whatever group they are supporting. Thus, even if we assume that no erroneous or false data exist, some men are able to influence others by presenting them with a biased selection of facts.

This possibility has several extraordinarily important consequences for the operation of government. First, it means that some men are more important than others politically, because they can influence more votes than they themselves cast. Since it takes scarce resources to provide information to hesitant citizens, men who command such resources are able to wield more than proportional political influence, *ceteris paribus*. The government, being rational, cannot overlook this fact in designing policy. As a result, equality of franchise no longer assures net equality of influence over government action. In fact, it is irrational for a democratic government to treat its citizens with equal deference in a world in which knowledge is imperfect.

Second, the government is itself ignorant of what its citizens want it to do. Therefore it must send out representatives (1) to sound out the electorate and discover their desires and (2) to persuade them it should be re-elected. In other words, lack of information converts democratic government into representative government, because it forces the central planning board of the governing party to rely upon agents scattered throughout the electorate. Such reliance amounts to a decentralization of government power from the planning board to the agents.[11] The central board continues to decentralize its power until the marginal vote-gain from greater conformity to popular desires is equal to the marginal vote-loss caused by reduced ability to co-ordinate its actions.

This reasoning implies that a democratic government in a rational world will always be run on a quasi-representative, quasi-decentralized basis, no matter what its formal constitutional structure, as long as communication between the voters and the governors is less than perfect. Another powerful force working in the same direction is the division of labor. To be efficient, a nation must develop specialists in discovering, transmitting, and analyzing popular opinion, just as it develops specialists in everything else. These specialists are the representatives. They exercise more power, and the central planning board exercises less, the less efficient are communication facilities in society.

The third consequence of imperfect knowledge and the resulting need for persuasion is really a combination of the first two. Because some voters can be influenced, specialists in influencing them appear. And, because government needs intermediaries between it and the people, some of these influencers pose as "representatives" of the citizenry. On one hand, they attempt to convince the government that the policies they stand for—which are of direct benefit to themselves—are both good for and desired by a large portion of the electorate. On the other hand, they try to convince the electorate that these policies are in fact desirable. Thus one of their methods of getting government to believe that public opinion supports them is to create favorable opinion through persuasion. Though a rational government will discount their claims, it cannot ignore them altogether. It must give the influencers more than proportional weight in forming policy, because they may have succeeded in creating favorable opinions in the silent mass of voters and because their vociferousness indicates a high intensity of desire. Clearly, people with an intense interest in some policy are more likely to base their votes upon it alone than are those who count it as just another issue; hence government must pay more attention to the former than the latter. To do otherwise would be irrational.

Finally, imperfect knowledge makes the governing party susceptible to bribery. In order to persuade voters that its policies are good for them, it needs scarce resources, such as television time, money for propaganda, and pay for precinct captains. One way to get such resources is to sell policy favors to those who can pay for them, either by campaign contributions, favorable editorial policies, or direct influence over others. Such favor buyers need not even pose as representatives of the people. They merely exchange their political help for policy favors—a transaction eminently rational for both themselves and the government.

Essentially, inequality of political influence is a necessary result of imperfect information, given an unequal distribution of wealth and income in society. When knowledge is imperfect, effective political action requires the use of economic resources to meet the cost of information. Therefore, those who command such resources are able to swing more than their proportional weight politically. This outcome is not the result of irrationality or dishonesty. On the contrary, lobbying in a democracy is a highly rational response to the lack of perfect information, as is government's submission to the demands of lobbyists. To suppose otherwise is to ignore the existence of information costs—that is, to theorize about a mythical world instead of the real one. Imperfect knowledge allows the unequal distributions of income, position, and influence—which are all inevitable in any economy marked by an extensive division of labor—to share sovereignty in a realm where only the equal distribution of votes is supposed to reign.

VI

Since the parties in this model have no interest per se in creating any particular type of society, the universal prevalence of ideologies in democratic politics appears to contradict my hypothesis. But this appearance is false. In fact, not only the existence of ideologies, but also many of their particular characteristics, may be deduced from the premise that parties seek office solely for the income, power, and prestige that accompany it.[12] Again, imperfect knowledge is the key factor.

In a complex society the cost in time alone of comparing all the ways in which the policies of competing parties differ is staggering. Furthermore, citizens do not always have enough information to appraise the differences of which they are aware. Nor do they know in advance what problems the government is likely to face in the coming election period.

Under these conditions many a voter finds party ideologies useful because they remove the necessity for relating every issue to his own conception of "the good society." Ideologies help him focus attention on the differences between parties; therefore, they can be used as samples of all the differentiating stands. Furthermore, if the voter discovers a correlation between each party's ideology and its policies, he can rationally vote by comparing ideologies rather than policies. In both cases he can drastically reduce his outlay on political information by informing himself only about ideologies instead of about a wide range of issues.

Thus lack of information creates a demand for ideologies in the electorate. Since political parties are eager to seize any method of gaining votes available to them, they respond by creating a supply. Each party invents an ideology in order to attract the votes of those citizens who wish to cut costs by voting ideologically.[13]

This reasoning does not mean that parties can change ideologies as though they were disguises, putting on whatever costume suits the situation. Once a party has placed its ideology "on the market," it cannot suddenly abandon or radically alter that ideology without convincing the voters that it is unreliable. Since voters are rational, they refuse to support unreliable parties; hence no party can afford to acquire a reputation for dishonesty. Furthermore, there must be some persistent correlation between each party's ideology and its subsequent actions; otherwise voters will eventually eschew ideological voting as irrational. Finally, parties cannot adopt identical ideologies, because they must create enough product differentiation to make their output distinguishable from that of their rivals, so as to entice voters to the polls. However, just as in the product market, any markedly successful ideology is soon imitated, and differentiation takes place on more subtle levels.

Analysis of political ideologies can be carried even further by means of a spatial analogy for political action. To construct this analogy, I borrow and elaborate upon an apparatus first used by Harold Hotelling in his famous article "Stability in Competition."[14] My version of Hotelling's spatial market consists of a linear scale running from zero to one hundred in the usual left-to-right fashion. To render it politically meaningful, I make the following assumptions:

1. The political parties in any society can be ordered from left to right in a manner agreed upon by all voters.

2. Each voter's preferences are single-peaked at some point on the scale and slope monotonically downward on either side of the peak (unless it lies at one extreme of the scale).

3. The frequency distribution of voters along the scale is variable from society to society but fixed in any one society.[15]

4. Once placed on the political scale, a party can move ideologically either to the left or to the right up to but not beyond the nearest party toward which it is moving.[16]

5. In a two-party system, if either party moves away from the extreme nearest it toward the other party, extremist voters at its end of the scale may abstain because they see no significant difference between the choices offered them.[17]

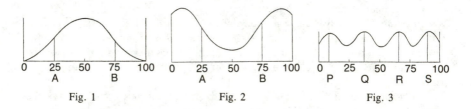

Fig. 1   Fig. 2   Fig. 3

Under these conditions Hotelling's conclusion that the parties in a two-party system inevitably converge on the center does not necessarily hold true. If voters are distributed along the scale as shown in Figure 1, then Hotelling is right. Assuming that Party A starts at position 25 and Party B at 75, both move toward 50, since each can gain more votes in the center than it loses at the extremes because of abstention. But, if the distribution is like that shown in Figure 2, the two parties diverge toward the extremes rather than converge on the center. Each gains more votes by moving toward a radical position than it loses in the center.

This reasoning implies that stable government in a two-party democracy requires a distribution of voters roughly approximating a normal curve. When such a distribution exists, the two parties come to resemble each other closely. Thus, when one replaces the other in office, no drastic policy changes occur, and most voters are located relatively close to the incumbent's position no matter which party is in power. But when the electorate is polarized, as in Figure 2, a change in parties causes a radical alteration in policy. And, regardless of which party is in office, half the electorate always feels that the other half is imposing policies upon it that are strongly repugnant to it. In this situation, if one party keeps getting re-elected, the disgruntled supporters of the other party will probably revolt; whereas if the two parties alternate in office, social chaos occurs, because government policy keeps changing from one extreme to the other. Thus democracy does not lead to effective, stable government when the electorate is polarized. Either the distribution must change or democracy will be replaced by tyranny in which one extreme imposes its will upon the other.

Hotelling's original model was limited to the two-firm (or two-party) case, because, when three firms existed, the two outside ones converged on the middle one, which then leaped to the outside to avoid strangulation. Since this process repeated itself endlessly, no stable equilibrium emerged. But, in my model, such leaping is impossible, because each party has to maintain continuity in its ideology. Hence this model can be applied to multiparty systems without resulting in disequilibrium.

Multiparty systems are most likely to exist when the distribution of voters is multimodal, as shown in Figure 3. A separate party forms at each mode, and each party is motivated to stay at its mode and to differentiate itself as completely as possible from its neighbors. If it moves to the left so as to gain votes, it loses just as many votes to the party on its right (or loses them because of abstention if it is an extremist party at the right end of the scale), and vice versa. Thus its optimal course is to stay where it is and keep other parties from approaching it. In a multiparty system, therefore, we find conditions exactly opposite to those in a viable two-party system. Whereas in the former each party links itself to a definite ideological position and stresses its differences from other parties, in the latter both parties move toward the political center so as to resemble each other as closely as possible.

This conclusion implies that voters in multiparty systems have a wider range of choice than voters in two-party systems and that each choice in this range is more definitely linked to some ideological position. Thus it appears that the electorate exercises a more significant function in a multiparty system than in a two-party system, because only in the former does it make much difference which party gets elected.

However, appearances are deceiving in politics, because in fact the government in a multiparty system is likely to have a less definite, less coherent, and less integrated program than the government in a two-party system. This paradoxical outcome arises from the necessity in most multiparty systems of forming coalition governments. Since voters are scattered among several modes, only rarely does one party obtain the support of a majority of those voting. Yet, in most democracies, the government cannot function without at least the indirect support of a majority of voters. Even in systems in which the legislature selects the government, a majority of its members must support the coalition chosen to govern before the coalition can take office. If we assume that representation in the legislature is "fair"—that each member represents the same number of citizens—then even a coalition government must receive the indirect support of a majority in order to govern.

Such support can be maintained only if the government implements at least some policies that appeal to—are ideologically near—each cluster of voters whose support it needs. If a majority of voters are massed in one relatively narrow band on the left-right scale, then the government can choose all its policies from within this band. Hence its policies will form a fairly cohesive set embodying the ideological viewpoint associated with that area of the scale. This outcome is typical of a two-party system.

But in a multiparty system there are many modes scattered across the whole scale. Therefore, in order to appeal to a majority of voters, the government must be a coalition of parties and must include in its policy-set some policies espoused by each party in the coalition. In this manner it "pays off" voters at each cluster in return for their support. However, the result is that its program contains policies reflecting a wide variety of ideological viewpoints, so that no real cohesion or integration about any one *Weltanschauung* is possible. This outcome necessarily occurs whenever the distribution of voters along the scale is so scattered that only a very wide band can encompass a majority.

Consequently, a multiparty system offers voters an ostensible choice between definite, well-integrated policy-sets in each election, but only rarely does one of these sets actually govern. Usually a coalition governs, and its policies are likely to be less definite and less well integrated than those of the government in a two-party system. This is true even though voters in the latter are offered only two relatively unintegrated alternatives which closely resemble each other. No wonder politics often seems confusing.

Whether a political system has two or more parties depends on the distribution of voters along the scale and on the electoral rules governing the system. To demonstrate this dual dependence, I use the concept of "political equilibrium." A state of political equilibrium exists when no new parties can successfully be formed and when no existing party is motivated to move away from its present position.

The limit to the number of new parties that can be formed successfully springs from my definition of success as ability to gain the income, power, and prestige that go with office; that is, as ability to get elected. If the constitution calls for the election of a legislature by proportional representation and the subsequent formation of a government by the legislature, then many parties can be formed, because any given party can get at least some of its members elected by winning the support of only a small proportion of the citizens. Once elected, these members have a chance to share in the fruits of office by joining a coalition government. Hence it follows from my hypothesis about party motivation that many parties are likely to exist in a proportional representation system. Their number is limited only by the number of seats in the legislature and by the necessity of formulating ideologies sufficiently different from those of existing parties to attract votes away from them.[18] New parties continue to form until the distribution of voters is "saturated"—until there is not enough ideological "room" between existing parties to support others significantly different from them.

In an electoral system in which a plurality is necessary for victory, the limit on successful party formation is much more stringent. Since the only way to insure a plurality against all opponents is to win a majority of votes, small parties tend to combine until two giants are left, each of which has a reasonable chance of capturing a majority in any given election. Where these two parties are located on the ideological scale depends upon the distribution of voters, as explained before.

Actually, the policy position and stability of the government in a democracy are relatively independent of the number of parties; they follow primarily from the nature of the distribution of voters along the left-right scale.[19] If a majority of voters are massed within a narrow range of that scale, democratic government is likely to be stable and effective, no matter how many parties exist. As noted earlier, the government can formulate a policy-set which appeals to a majority of voters and yet does not contain policies embodying widely disparate points of view. But, if the government can win the support of a majority only by adopting a scattering of policies chosen from a broad range of viewpoints, these policies tend to cancel each other out, and the government's net ability to solve social problems is low. Thus the distribution of voters—which is itself a variable in the long run—determines whether or not democracy leads to effective government.

VII

When information is costly, no decision-maker can afford to know everything that might possibly bear on his decision before he makes it. He must select only a few data from the vast supply in existence and base his decision solely upon them. This is true even if he can procure data without paying for them, since merely assimilating them requires time and is therefore costly.

The amount of information it is rational for a decision-maker to acquire is determined by the following economic axiom: It is always rational to perform any act if its marginal return is larger than its marginal cost. The marginal cost of a "bit" of information is the return forgone by devoting scarce resources—particularly time—to getting and using it. The marginal return from a "bit" is the increase in utility income received because the information enabled the decision-maker to improve his decision. In an imperfectly informed world, neither the precise cost nor the precise return is usually known in advance; but decision-makers can nevertheless employ the rule just stated by looking at expected costs and expected returns.

This reasoning is as applicable to politics as it is to economics. Insofar as the average citizen is concerned, there are two political decisions that require information. The first is deciding which party to vote for; the second is deciding on what policies to exercise direct influence on government policy formation (that is, how to lobby). Let us examine the voting decision first.

Before we do so, it is necessary to recognize that in every society a stream of "free" information is continuously disseminated to all citizens. Though such "free" data take time to assimilate, this time is not directly chargeable to any particular type of decision-making, since it is a necessary cost of living in society. For example, conversation with business associates, small talk with friends, reading the newspaper in a barber shop, and listening to the radio while driving to work are all sources of information which the average man encounters without any particular effort to do so. Therefore, we may consider them part of the "free" information stream and exclude them from the problem of how much information a decision-maker should obtain specifically to improve his decisions.

The marginal return on information acquired for voting purposes is measured by the expected gain from voting "correctly" instead of "incorrectly." In other words, it is the gain in utility a voter believes he will receive if he supports the party which would really provide him with the highest utility income instead of supporting some other party. However, unless his vote actually decides the election, it does not cause the "right" party to be elected instead of a "wrong" party; whether or not the "right" party wins does not depend on how he votes. Therefore, voting "correctly" produces no gain in utility whatsoever; he might as well have voted "incorrectly."

This situation results from the insignificance of any one voter in a large electorate. Since the cost of voting is very low, hundreds, thousands, or even millions of citizens can afford to vote. Therefore, the probability that any one citizen's vote will be decisive is very small indeed. It is not zero, and it can even be significant if he thinks the election will be very close; but, under most circumstances, it is so negligible that it renders the return from voting "correctly" infinitesimal. This is true no matter how tremendous a loss in utility income the voter would experience if the "wrong" party were elected. And if that loss is itself small—as it may be when parties resemble each other closely or in local elections—then the incentive to become well informed is practically nonexistent.

Therefore, we reach the startling conclusion that it is irrational for most citizens to acquire political information for purposes of voting. As long as each person considers the behavior of others as given, it is simply not worthwhile for him to acquire information so as to vote "correctly" himself. The probability that his vote will determine which party governs is so low that even a trivial cost of procuring information outweighs its return. Hence ignorance of politics is not a result of unpatriotic apathy; rather it is a highly rational response to the facts of political life in a large democracy.

This conclusion does not mean that every citizen who is well informed about politics is irrational. A rational man can become well informed for four reasons: (1) he may enjoy being well informed for its own sake, so that information as such provides him with utility; (2) he may believe the election is going to be so close that the probability of his casting the decisive vote is relatively high; (3) he may need information to influence the votes of others so that he can alter the outcome of the election or persuade government to assign his preferences more weight than those of others; or (4) he may need information to influence the formation of government policy as a lobbyist. Nevertheless, since the odds are that no election will be close enough to render decisive the vote of any one person, or the votes of all those he can persuade to agree with him, the rational course of action for most citizens is to remain politically uninformed. Insofar as voting is concerned, any attempt to acquire information beyond that furnished by the stream of "free" data is for them a sheer waste of resources.

The disparity between this conclusion and the traditional conception of good citizenship in a democracy is indeed striking. How can we explain it? The answer is that the benefits which a majority of citizens would derive from living in a society with a well-informed electorate are indivisible in nature. When most members of the electorate know what policies best serve their interests, the government is forced to follow those policies in order to avoid defeat (assuming that there is a consensus among the informed). This explains why the proponents of democracy think citizens should be well informed. But the benefits of these policies accrue to each member of the majority they serve, regardless of whether he has helped bring them about. In other words, the individual receives these benefits whether or not he is well informed, so long as most people are well informed and his interests are similar to those of the majority. On the other hand, when no one else is well informed, he cannot produce these benefits by becoming well informed himself, since a collective effort is necessary to achieve them.

Thus, when benefits are indivisible, each individual is always motivated to evade his share of the cost of producing them. If he assumes that the behavior of others is given, whether or not he receives any benefits does not depend on his own efforts. But the cost he pays does depend on his efforts; hence the most rational course for him is to minimize that cost—in this case, to remain politically ignorant. Since every individual reasons in the same way, no one bears any costs, and no benefits are produced.

The usual way of escaping this dilemma is for all individuals to agree to be coerced by a central agency. Then each is forced to pay his share of the costs, but he knows all others are likewise forced to pay. Thus everyone is better off than he would be if no costs were borne, because everyone receives benefits which (I here assume) more than offset his share of the costs. This is a basic rationale for using coercion to collect revenues for national defense and for many other government operations that yield indivisible benefits.[20]

But this solution is not feasible in the case of political information. The government cannot coerce everyone to be well informed, because "well-informedness" is hard to measure, because there is no agreed-upon rule for deciding how much information of what kinds each citizen "should" have, and because the resulting interference in personal affairs would cause a loss of utility that would probably outweigh the gains to be had from a well-informed electorate. The most any democratic government has done to remedy this situation is to compel young people in schools to take courses in civics, government, and history.

Consequently, it is rational for every individual to minimize his investment in political information, in spite of the fact that most citizens might benefit substantially if the whole electorate were well informed. As a result, democratic political systems are bound to operate at less than maximum efficiency. Government does not serve the interests of the majority as well as it would if they were well informed, but they never become well informed. It is collectively rational, but individually irrational, for them to do so; and, in the absence of any mechanism to insure collective action, individual rationality prevails.

VIII

When we apply the economic concept of rationality to the second political use of information, lobbying, the results are similarly incompatible with the traditional view of democracy. In order to be an effective lobbyist, a citizen must persuade the governing party that the policies he wants either are already desired by a large number of other citizens or are sufficiently beneficial to the rest of the electorate so that it will, at worst, not resent the enactment of these policies. To be persuasive, the would-be lobbyist must be extremely well informed about each policy area in which he wishes to exert influence. He must be able to design a policy that benefits him more than any other would, to counter any arguments advanced by opposing lobbyists, and to formulate or recognize compromises acceptable to him. Therefore, being a lobbyist requires much more information than voting, since even well-informed voters need only compare alternatives formulated by others.

For this reason, the cost of acquiring enough information to lobby effectively is relatively high. A lobbyist must be an expert in the policy areas in which he tries to exert influence. Since few men can afford the time or money necessary to become expert in more than one or two policy areas (or to hire those already expert), most citizens must specialize in a very few areas. Such behavior is rational even though policies in many areas affect them to some extent. Conversely, only a few specialists will actively exert pressure on the government in any one policy area. As a result, each need not heavily discount his own impact because of the large number of other persons influencing the decision, as he does in regard to voting. On the contrary, for those few lobbyists who specialize in any given area, the potential return from political information may be very high—precisely because they are so few.

The men who can best afford to become lobbyists in any policy area are those whose incomes stem from that area. This is true because nearly every citizen derives all his income from one or two sources; hence any government policy affecting those sources is of vital interest to him. In contrast, each man spends his income in a great many policy areas, so that a change in any one of them is not too significant to him. Therefore, men are much more likely to exert direct influence on government policy formation in their roles as producers than in their roles as consumers. In consequence, a democratic government is usually biased in favor of producer interests and against consumer interests, even though the consumers of any given product usually outnumber its producers. Tariff legislation provides a notorious example of this bias.

It should be stressed that such systematic exploitation of consumers by producers acting through government policy is not a result of foolish apathy on the part of consumers. In fact, just the opposite is true. Government's anticonsumer bias occurs because consumers rationally seek to acquire only that information which provides a return larger than its cost. The saving a consumer could make by becoming informed about how government policy affects any one product he purchases simply does not recompense him for the cost of informing himself—particularly since his personal influence on government policy would probably be slight. Since this is true of almost every product he buys, he adopts a course of rational ignorance, thereby exposing himself to extensive exploitation. Yet it would be irrational for him to act otherwise. In other words, lobbying is effective in a democracy *because* all the agents concerned—the exploiters, the exploited, and the government—behave rationally.

IX

Clearly, rational behavior in a democracy is not what most normative theorists assume it to be. Political theorists in particular have often created models of how the citizens of a democracy ought to behave without taking into account the economics of political action. Consequently, much of the evidence frequently cited to prove that democratic politics are dominated by irrational (non-logical) forces in fact demonstrates that citizens respond rationally (efficiently) to the exigencies of life in an imperfectly informed world.[21] Apathy among citizens toward elections, ignorance of the issues, the tendency of parties in a two-party system to resemble each other, and the anticonsumer bias of government action can all be explained logically as efficient reactions to imperfect information in a large democracy. Any normative theory that regards them as signs of unintelligent behavior in politics has failed to face the fact that information is costly in the real world. Thus political theory has suffered because it has not taken into account certain economic realities.

On the other hand, economic theory has suffered because it has not taken into account the political realities of government decision-making. Economists have been content to discuss government action as though governments were run by perfect altruists whose only motive was to maximize social welfare. As a result, economists have been unable to incorporate government into the rest of economic theory, which is based on the premise that all men act primarily out of self-interest. Furthermore, they have falsely concluded that government decision-making in all societies should follow identical principles, because its goal is always the maximization of social welfare. If my hypothesis is true, the goal of government is attaining the income, power, and prestige that go with office. Since methods of reaching this goal are vastly different in democratic, totalitarian, and aristocratic states, no single theory can be advanced to explain government decision-making in all societies. Nor can any theory of government decision-making be divorced from politics. The way every government actually makes decisions depends upon the nature of the fundamental power relation between the governors and the governed in its society; that is, upon the society's political constitution. Therefore, a different theory of political action must be formulated for each different type of constitution.

I conclude that a truly useful theory of government action in a democracy—or in any other type of society—must be both economic and political in nature. In this article I have attempted to outline such a theory. If nothing else, the attempt demonstrates how much economists and political scientists must depend on each other to analyze government decision-making, which is the most important economic and political force in the world today.

Notes

1. The argument presented in this article [is] developed further in my book, *An Economic Theory of Democracy*, published by Harper & Bros.

2. See Gerhard Colm, *Essays in Public Finance and Fiscal Policy* (New York: Oxford University Press, 1955), pp. 6–8.

3. *The Principles of Public Finance* (London: George Routledge & Sons, Ltd., 1932), pp. 9–10.

4. *Taxation and Welfare* (New York: Macmillan Co., 1925), pp. 30–36, as quoted in Harold M. Groves (ed.), *Viewpoints in Public Finance* (New York: Henry Holt & Co., 1948), p. 551.

5. *The Economics of Control* (New York: Macmillan Co., 1944), p. 32.

6. *Social Choice and Individual Values* (New York: John Wiley & Sons, 1951).

7. Joseph A. Schumpeter, *Capitalism, Socialism, and Democracy* (New York: Harper & Bros., 1950), p. 282.

8. This definition is taken from Robert A. Dahl and Charles E. Lindblom, *Politics, Economics, and Welfare* (New York: Harper & Bros., 1953), p. 42. However, throughout most of my analysis the word "government" refers to the governing party rather than the institution as here defined.

9. A "team" is a coalition whose members have identical goals. A "coalition" is a group of men who co-operate to achieve some common end. These definitions are taken from Jacob Marschak, "Towards an Economic Theory of Organization and Information," in *Decision Processes*, ed. R. M. Thrall, C. H. Coombs, and R. L. Davis (New York: John Wiley & Sons, 1954), pp. 188–89. I use "team" instead of "coalition" in my definition to eliminate intraparty power struggles from consideration, though in Marschak's terms parties are really coalitions, not teams.

10. The term "rational" in this article is synonymous with "efficient." This economic definition must not be confused with the logical definition (i.e., pertaining to logical propositions) or the psychological definition (i.e., calculating or unemotional).

11. Decentralization may be geographical or by social groups, depending upon the way society is divided into homogeneous parts.

12. I define "ideologies" as verbal images of "the good society" and of the chief policies to be used in creating it.

13. In reality, party ideologies probably stem originally from the interests of those persons who found each party. But, once a political party is created, it takes on an existence of its own and eventually becomes relatively independent of any particular interest group. When such autonomy prevails, my analysis of ideologies is fully applicable.

14. *Economic Journal*, XXXIX (1929), 41–57.

15. Actually, this distribution may vary in any one society even in the short run, but I assume it to be fixed in order to avoid discussing the complex of historical, sociological, psychological, and other factors which cause it to change.

16. It cannot go beyond the adjacent parties, because such "leaping" would indicate ideological unreliability and would cause its rejection by the electorate.

17. This is equivalent to assuming elastic demand along the scale, as Smithies did in his elaboration of the Hotelling model (see Arthur Smithies, "Optimum Location in Spatial Competition," *Journal of Political Economy*, XLIX [1941], 423–39).

18. The number of sufficiently different parties as system can support depends upon the shape of the distribution of voters along the scale.

19. However, because the preferences of rising generations are influenced by the alternatives offered them, the number of parties is one of the factors that determine the shape of the distribution of voters.

20. See Paul A. Samuelson, "The Pure Theory of Public Expenditures," *Review of Economics and Statistics*, XXXVI (November, 1954), 387–89.

21. In this sentence the word "irrational" is not the opposite of the word "rational," as the synonyms in parenthesis show. Admittedly, such dual usage may cause confusion. However, I have employed the word "rational" instead of its synonym "efficient" throughout this article because I want

to emphasize the fact that an intelligent citizen always carries out any act whose marginal return exceeds its marginal cost. In contrast, he does not always make use of logical thinking, because, under some conditions, the marginal return from thinking logically is smaller than its marginal cost. In other words, it is sometimes rational (efficient) to act irrationally (non-logically), in which case an intelligent man eschews rationality in the traditional sense so as to achieve it in the economic sense. This is really what is meant by the sentence in the text to which this footnote is attached.

1.3

Political Aspects of Full Employment

MICHAL KALECKI

The following essay, originally published by Michal Kalecki in 1943, is a succinct and prescient analysis of the political business cycle. Analyzing the political business cycle, as opposed to the business cycle pure and simple, requires an integrated approach to political and economic behavior that includes such diverse phenomena as worker behavior on the shop floor and business elites' attitudes toward macro-level economic intervention by the national government. Nonetheless, the fundamental motivations of major groups within an economy, however complex in their day-to-day manifestations, can often be outlined with persuasive clarity when underlying sectoral and class interests are made explicit. This is the great virtue of Kalecki's essay.

There are, however, two points that contemporary readers should bear in mind. First, Kalecki's affirmation that full employment does not adversely affect profits represents a radical departure from the classical Marxist theoretical tradition within which he wrote. Kalecki's view is at best controversial and has been refuted by authors otherwise sympathetic to his work. Indeed, the argument that profits undergo a wage-induced decline during an economic upswing actually reinforces Kalecki's basic thesis that full employment is not generally in the interest of business. Second, Kalecki did not foresee the degree to which an international debt and liquidity crisis could impinge on traditional interventionist tools, as happened during the 1980–83 depression. The remarkable incoherence of fiscal policy in the United States today may in large part be attributed to the fact that the nationally based policies and instruments of economic intervention are at variance with the requirements of an integrated world economy. Kalecki's analysis of the means and motivations for economic intervention at the national level should therefore be understood as describing only a part of the forces at work in the economic upheavals of the 1980s.

The maintenance of full employment through government spending financed by loans has been widely discussed in recent years. This discussion, however, has concentrated on the purely economic aspects of the problem without paying due consideration to political realities. The assumption that a Government will maintain full employment in a capitalist economy if it only knows how to do it is fallacious. In this connection the misgivings of big business about maintenance of full employment by Government spending are of paramount importance. This attitude was shown clearly in the great depression in the thirties, when big business opposed consistently experiments for increasing employment by Government spending in all countries, except Nazi

Reprinted with permission from Michal Kalecki, *The Last Phase in the Development of Capitalism*, pp. 75–85. Copyright ©1972 by Monthly Review Press. Reprinted by permission of Monthly Review Press.

Germany. The attitude is not easy to explain. Clearly higher output and employment benefits not only workers, but businessmen as well, because their profits rise. And the policy of full employment based on loan financed Government spending does not encroach upon profits because it does not involve any additional taxation. The business-men in the slump are longing for a boom; why do not they accept gladly the "synthetic" boom which the Government is able to offer them? It is this difficult and fascinating question with which we intend to deal in this article.

I

1. The reasons for the opposition of the "industrial leaders" to full employment achieved by Government spending may be subdivided into three categories: (i) the dislike of Government interference in the problem of employment as such; (ii) the dislike of the direction of Government spending (public investment and subsidizing consumption); (iii) dislike of the social and political changes resulting from the *maintenance* of full employment. We shall examine each of these three categories of objections to the Government expansion policy in detail.

2. We shall deal first with the reluctance of the "captains of industry" to accept Government intervention in the matter of employment. Every widening of State activity is looked upon by "business" with suspicion, but the creation of employment by Government spending has a special aspect which makes the opposition particularly intense. Under a *laisser-faire* system the level of employment depends to a great extent on the so-called state of confidence. If this deteriorates, private investment declines, which results on a fall of output and employment (both directly and through the secondary effect of the fall in incomes upon consumption and investment). This gives to the capitalists a powerful indirect control over Government policy: everything which may shake the state of confidence must be carefully avoided because it would cause an economic crisis. But once the Government learns the trick of increasing employment by its own purchases, this powerful controlling device loses its effectiveness. Hence budget deficits necessary to carry out Government intervention must be regarded as perilous. The social function of the doctrine of "sound finance" is to make the level of employment dependent on the "state of confidence."

3. The dislike of the business leaders of a Government spending policy grows even more acute when they come to consider the objects on which the money would be spent: public investment and subsidizing mass consumption.

The economic principles of Government intervention require that public invest-ment should be confined to objects which do not compete with the equipment of private business, e.g. hospitals, schools, highways, etc. Otherwise the profitability of private investment might be impaired and the positive effect of public investment upon employment offset by the negative effect of the decline in private investment. This conception suits the business men very well. But the scope of public investment of this type is rather narrow, and there is a danger that the Government, in pursuing this policy, may eventually be tempted to nationalize transport of public utilities so as to gain a new sphere in which to carry out investment.[1]

One might therefore expect business leaders and their experts to be more in favor of subsidizing mass consumption (by means of family allowances, subsidies to keep down the prices of necessities, etc.) than of public investment; for by subsidizing consumption the Government would not be embarking on any sort of "enterprise." In practice, however, this is not the case. Indeed, subsidizing mass consumption is much more violently opposed by these "experts" than public investment. For here a "moral" principle of the highest importance is at stake. The fundamentals of capitalist ethics require that "You shall earn your bread in sweat"—unless you happen to have private means.

4. We have considered the political reasons for the opposition against the policy of creating employment by Government spending. But even if this opposition were overcome—as it may well be under the pressure of the masses—the *maintenance* of full employment would cause social and political changes which would give a new impetus to the opposition of the business leaders. Indeed, under a regime of permanent full employment, "the sack" would cease to play its role as a disciplinary measure. The social position of the boss would be undetermined and the self assurance and class conscious-ness of the working class would grow. Strikes for wage increases and improvements in conditions of work would create political tension. It is true that profits would be higher under a regime of full employment than they are on the average under *laisser-faire*; and even the rise in wage rates resulting from the stronger bargaining power of the workers is less likely to reduce profits than to increase prices, and thus affects adversely only the *rentier* interests. But "discipline in the factories" and "political stability" are more appreciated by the business leaders than profits. Their class instinct tells them that full employment is unsound from their point of view and that unemployment is an integral part of the normal capitalist system.

II

1. One of the important functions of fascism, as typified by the Nazi system, was to remove the capitalist objections to full employment.

The dislike of Government spending policy as such is overcome under fascism by the fact that the State machinery is under the direct control of a partnership of big business with fascist upstarts. The necessity for the myth of "sound finance" which served to prevent the Government from offsetting a confidence crisis by spending, is removed. In a democracy one does not know what the next Government will be like. Under fascism there is no next Government.

The dislike of Government spending, whether on public investment or consump-tion, is overcome by concentrating Government expenditure on armaments. Finally, "discipline in the factories" and "political stability" under full employment are main-tained by the "new order," which ranges from the suppression of the trade unions to the concentration camp. Political pressure replaces the economic pressure of unemployment.

2. The fact that armaments are the backbone of the policy of fascist full employment has a profound influence upon its economic character.

Large-scale armaments are inseparable from the expansion of the armed forces and the preparation of plans for a war of conquest. They also induce competitive rearmament of other countries. This causes the main aim of the spending to shift gradually from full employment to securing the maximum effect of rearmament. The resulting scarcity of resources leads to the curtailment of consumption as compared with what it could have been under full employment.

The fascist system starts from the overcoming of unemployment, develops into an "armament economy" of scarcity, and ends inevitably in war.

III

1. What will be the practical outcome of the opposition to "full employment by Government spending" in a capitalist democracy? We shall try to answer this question on the basis of the analysis of the reasons for this opposition given in section I. We argued

that we may expect the opposition of the "leaders of industry"on three planes: (i) the opposition on principle against Government spending based on a budget deficit; (ii) the opposition against this spending being directed either towards public investment—which may foreshadow the intrusion of the state into the new spheres of economic activity—or towards subsidizing mass consumption; (iii) the opposition against *maintaining* full employment and not merely preventing deep and prolonged slumps.

Now, it must be recognized that the stage in which the "business leaders" could afford to be opposed to *any* kind of Government interventions to alleviate a slump is rather a matter of the past. The necessity that "something must be done in the slump" is agreed to; but the conflict continues, firstly, as to what should be the direction of Government intervention in the slump, and secondly, as to whether it should be used merely to alleviate slumps or to secure permanent full employment.

2. In the current discussions of these problems there emerges time and again the conception of counteracting the slump by stimulating *private* investment. This may be done by lowering the rate of interest, by the reduction of income tax, or by subsidizing private investment directly in this or another form. That such a scheme should be attractive to "business" is not surprising. The businessman remains the medium through which the intervention is conducted. If he does not feel confidence in the political situation he will not be bribed into investment. And the intervention does not involve the Government either in "playing with" (public) investment or "wasting money" in subsidizing consumption.

It may be shown, however, that the stimulation of private investment does not provide an adequate method for preventing mass unemployment. There are two alternatives to be considered here: (*a*) The rate of interest or income tax—or both—is reduced sharply in the slump and increased in the boom. In this case both the period and the amplitude of the business cycle will be reduced, but employment not only in the slump but even in the boom may be far from full, i.e. the average unemployment may be considerable, although its fluctuations will be less marked; (*b*) The rate of interest or income tax is reduced in a slump but *not* increased in the subsequent boom. In this case the boom will last longer but it must end in a new slump: one reduction in the rate of interest or income tax does not, of course, eliminate the forces which cause cyclical fluctuations in a capitalist economy. In the new slump it will be necessary to reduce the rate of interest or income tax again and so on. Thus in not too remote a time the rate of interest would have to be negative and income tax would have to be replaced by an income subsidy. The same would arise if it were attempted to *maintain* full employment by stimulating private investment: the rate of interest and income tax would have to be reduced continuously.

In addition to this fundamental weakness of combating unemployment by stimulating private investment, there is a practical difficulty. The reaction of businessmen to the measures described is uncertain. If the down-swing is sharp they may take a very pessimistic view of the future, and the reduction of the rate of interest or income tax may then for a long time have little or no effect upon investment, and thus upon the level of output and employment.

3. Even those who advocate stimulating private investment to counteract the slump frequently do not rely on it exclusively but envisage that it should be associated with public investment. It looks at present as if "business leaders" and their experts—at least part of them—would tend to accept as a *pis aller* public expenditure financed by borrowing as a means of alleviating slumps. They seem, however, still to be consistently opposed to creating employment by subsidizing consumption and to *maintaining* full employment.

This state of affairs is perhaps symptomatic of the future economic regime of capitalist democracies. In the slump, either under the pressure of the masses, or even without it, public investment financed by borrowing will be undertaken to prevent large-scale unemployment. But if attempts are made to apply this method in order to maintain the high level of employment reached in the subsequent boom a strong opposition of "business leaders" is likely to be encountered. As has already been argued, lasting full employment is not at all to their liking. The workers would "get out of hand" and the "captains of industry" would be anxious to "teach them a lesson." Moreover, the price increase in the up-swing is to the disadvantage of small and big *rentiers* and makes them "boom tired."

In this situation a powerful block is likely to be formed between big business and the *rentier* interests, and they would probably find more than one economist to declare that the situation was manifestly unsound. The pressure of all these forces, and in particular of big business would most probably induce the Government to return to the orthodox policy of cutting down the budget deficit. A slump would follow in which Government spending policy would come again into its own.

This pattern of a "political business cycle" is not entirely conjectural; something very much like that happened in the U.S.A. in 1937-8. The breakdown of the boom in the second half of 1937 was actually due to the drastic reduction of the budget deficit. On the other hand, in the acute slump that followed, the Government promptly reverted to a spending policy.

Note

1. It should be noticed here that investment in a nationalized industry can contribute to the solution of the problem of unemployment only if it is undertaken on principles different from these of private enterprise. The Government may have to be satisfied with a lower net rate of return than private enterprise and must deliberately time its investment so as to mitigate slumps.

1.4

The Ruling Class Does Not Rule: Notes on the Marxist Theory of the State

FRED BLOCK

Within Marxist theoretical discussion the 1970s were clearly "the decade of the state."
This discussion was endlessly complicated, involving innumerable positions and count-
less controversies, but broadly speaking there were two main competing interpretations of
state behavior: (1) "instrumental" theories, which saw the state as expressing the will—or
being the relatively blunt "instrument"—of the dominant class or class fraction, and (2)
"structuralist" theories, which understood the state to be engaged in the task or function of
reproducing, or maintaining, a given set of power relations among classes. As Fred Block
notes in the essay here, much of the early discussion was muddled. Instrumental accounts
were baffled by many things. A critical problem was their inability to explain or even
make sense of marginal improvements in the positions of subordinate classes within
continuing relations of dominance. In addition, instrumental theorists often made
implausibly strong assumptions about the conscious unity and coordination of dominant
groups. Structuralist accounts, at least as articulated in the seminal work of Nicos
Poulantzas, relied on an essentially functionalist conception of state activity that charac-
teristically failed to account for where the state's "functions" came from, why they are
fulfilled in the way they are fulfilled, or indeed why they are fulfilled at all. While
superficially closer to the structuralist camp, Block breaks with both of these interpreta-
tions. In his account, the state is constantly responding to the shifting positions of capital
and labor, although it does so within a specific institutional framework and under a
specific set of constraints imposed by the demands of private accumulation (chief among
the latter is the need to secure sufficient "business confidence" that capitalists will
continue to invest). Such an approach permits consideration of a number of more
explicitly political issues, including the degree to which advances and defeats of worker
power have consequences for state organization, the dynamics of reform struggles, and
problems associated with transitions beyond capitalism.

T he Marxist theory of the state remains a muddle despite the recent revival of interest in the subject.[1] Substantial progress has been made in formulating a critique of orthodox Marxist formulations that reduce the state to a mere reflection of economic interests. However, the outlines of an adequate alternative Marxist theory are not yet clear. This is most dramatically indicated by the continued popularity in Marxist circles of explanations of state policies or of conflicts within the state that are remarkably similar to

Reprinted from *Socialist Revolution*, Number 33 (Vol. 7, No. 3), pp.6–28. © 1977 by Agenda Publishing
Company. Reprinted with permission from the Center for Social Research and Education.

orthodox formulations in their tendency to see the state as a reflection of the interests of certain groups in the capitalist class. Many Marxists, for example, were drawn to interpretations of Watergate that saw it as a conflict between two different wings of the capitalist class.[2] This gap between theory and the explanation of actual historical events demonstrates that the critique of orthodox Marxist formulations has not been carried far enough. These earlier formulations—even when they have been carefully criticized and dismissed—sneak back into many current analyses because they remain embedded in the basic concepts of Marxist analysis.

This essay proposes two elements of an alternative Marxist theory of the state. The first element is a different way of conceptualizing the ruling class and its relationship to the state. This reconceptualization makes possible the second element—the elaboration of a structural framework which specifies the concrete mechanisms that make the state a capitalist state, whereas other structural theories have tended to analyze structures in an abstract and mystifying way.[3]

Although these two elements do not provide a complete Marxist theory of the state, they do provide a new way of thinking about the sources of rationality within capitalism. Contemporary Marxists have been forced to acknowledge that despite its fundamental irrationality, capitalism in the developed world has shown a remarkable capacity to rationalize itself in response to the twin dangers of economic crisis and radical working-class movements.[4] Since the present historical period again poses for the left the threat of successful capitalist rationalization, the understanding of the sources of capitalism's capacity for self-reform is of the utmost political importance. The traditional Marxist explanation of capitalist rationality is to root it in the consciousness of some sector of the ruling class. In this light, capitalist reform reflects the conscious will and understanding of some sector of the capitalist class that has grasped the magnitude of the problem and proposes a set of solutions. The alternative framework being proposed here suggests that the capacity of capitalism to rationalize itself is the outcome of a conflict among three sets of agents—the capitalist class, the managers of the state apparatus, and the working class.[5] Rationalization occurs "behind the backs" of each set of actors so that rationality cannot be seen as a function of the consciousness of one particular group.

This argument and its implications will be traced out through a number of steps. First, I intend to show that critiques of orthodox Marxist theory of the state are flawed by their acceptance of the idea of a class-conscious ruling class. Second, I argue that there is a basis in Marx's writing for rejecting the idea of a class-conscious ruling class. Third, I develop a structural argument that shows that even in the absence of ruling-class class consciousness, the state managers are strongly discouraged from pursuing anti-capitalist policies. Fourth, I return to the issue of capitalist rationality and describe how it grows out of the structured relationship among capitalists, workers, and state managers. Finally, I briefly analyze the implications of this argument for capitalism's current difficulties in the United States.

The Critique of Instrumentalism

The major development in the Marxist theory of the state in recent years has been the formulation of a critique of instrumentalism. A number of writers have characterized the orthodox Marxist view of the state as instrumentalism because it views the state as a simple tool or instrument of ruling-class purposes. First, it neglects the ideological role of the state. The state plays a critical role in maintaining the legitimacy of the social order, and this requires that the state appear to be neutral in the class struggle. In short, even if the state is an instrument of ruling-class purpose, the fact that it must appear otherwise indicates the need for a more complex framework for analyzing state policies. Second, instrumentalism fails to recognize that to act in the general interest of capital, the state must be able to take actions against the particular interests of capitalists. Price controls or restrictions on the export of capital, for example, might be in the general interest of capital in a particular period, even if they temporarily reduced the profits of most capitalists. To carry through such policies, the state must have more autonomy from direct capitalist control than the instrumentalist view would allow.

The critics of instrumentalism propose the idea of the relative autonomy of the state as an alternative framework. In order to serve the general interests of capital, the state must have some autonomy from direct ruling-class control. Since the concept of the absolute autonomy of the state would be un-Marxist and false, the autonomy is clearly relative. However, the difficulty is in specifying the nature, limits, and determinants of that relative autonomy. Some writers have attempted to argue that the degree of autonomy varies historically, and that "late capitalism" is characterized by the "autonomi-zation of the state apparatus." But these arguments have an ad hoc quality, and they share an analytic problem derived from the phrase "relative autonomy from ruling-class control."

The basic problem in formulations of "relative autonomy" is the conceptualization of the ruling class. Relative autonomy theories assume that the ruling class will respond effectively to the state's abuse of that autonomy. But for the ruling class to be capable of taking such corrective actions, it must have some degree of political cohesion, an understanding of its general interests, and a high degree of political sophistication. In sum, the theory requires that the ruling class, or a portion of it, be class-conscious, that is, aware of what is necessary to reproduce capitalist social relations in changing historical circumstances. Yet if the ruling class or a segment of it is class-conscious, then the degree of autonomy of the state is clearly quite limited. At this point the theory of relative autonomy collapses back into a slightly more sophisticated version of instrumentalism. State policies continue to be seen as the reflection of inputs by a class-conscious ruling class.

The way out of this theoretical bind, the way to formulate a critique of instrumental-ism that does not collapse, is to reject the idea of a class-conscious ruling class. Instead of the relative autonomy framework the key idea becomes a division of labor between those who accumulate capital and those who manage the state apparatus. Those who accumu-late capital are conscious of their interests as capitalists, but, in general, they are not conscious of what is necessary to reproduce the social order in changing circumstances. Those who manage the state apparatus, however, are forced to concern themselves to a greater degree with the reproduction of the social order because their continued power rests on the maintenance of political and economic order. In this framework, the central theoretical task is to explain how it is that despite this division of labor, the state tends to serve the interests of the capitalist class. It is to this task—the elaboration of a structural theory of the state—that I will turn after a brief discussion of the division of labor between capitalists and state managers.

Division of Labor

The idea of a division of labor between non-class-conscious capitalists and those who manage the state apparatus can be found in Marx's writings.[6] Two factors, however, have obscured this aspect of Marx's thought. First, Marx did not spell out the nature of the structural framework in which that division of labor operated, although he hinted at the existence of such a framework. Second, Marx's discussion of these issues is clouded by his polemical intent to fix responsibility for all aspects of bourgeois society on the ruling class. Even when Marx recognizes that the ruling class lacks class consciousness, he still formulates his argument in such a way as to imply that the ruling class as a whole is in conscious control of the situation. Marx used the idea of a conscious, directive ruling class as a polemical shorthand for an elaboration of the structural mechanisms through which control over the means of production leads to control over other aspects of society.

The tension in Marx's formulations is clearest in *The Eighteenth Brumaire* when he is explaining why the bourgeoisie supported Louis Napoleon's coup d'état against the bourgeoisie's own parliamentary representatives. He writes:

> The *extra-parliamentary* mass of the bourgeoisie, on the other hand, by its servility towards the President, by its vilification of parliament, by the brutal maltreatment of its own press, invited Bonaparte to suppress and annihilate its speaking and writing section, its politicians and its *literati*, its platform and its press, in order that it might then be able to pursue its private affairs with full confidence in the protection of a strong and unrestricted government. It declared unequivocally that it longed to get rid of its own political rule in order to get rid of the troubles and dangers of ruling.[7]

The passage suggests a division of labor and a division of interest between the extra-parliamentary mass of the bourgeoisie, primarily interested in accumulating profits, and the parliamentary and literary representatives of that class, whose central concerns are different. Marx uses the notion of representation as a substitute for specifying the structural relationship that holds together the division of labor.

In an earlier passage, in a discussion of the petite bourgeoisie, he states what is involved in the idea of representation:

> Just as little must one imagine that the democratic representatives are all shopkeepers or enthusiastic champions of shopkeepers. According to their education and their individual position they may be separated from them as widely as heaven from earth. What makes them representatives of the petty bourgeoisie is the fact that in their minds they do not go beyond the limits which the latter do not go beyond in life, that they are consequently driven theoretically to the same tasks and solutions to which material interest and social position practically drive the latter. This is in general the relationship of the *political and literary representatives* of a class to the class that they represent.[8]

Marx here rejects the simple reductionism so common among his followers. For Marx, representation was an objective relationship—one did not need to be of a class, to be its representative. And, in fact, representatives and their classes did not always see eye to eye, since their different positions could lead to different perspectives. In sum, representatives are *not* typical members of their classes, and it is a mistake to attribute to the class as a whole, the consciousness that parliamentary or literary representatives display.

Marx's idea of representation suggests the general structural links between the capitalists and those who manage the state apparatus. Marx recognized that those in the state apparatus tended to have a broader view of society than the capitalists, although their view is still far short of a general understanding of what is necessary to reproduce the social order. After all, the state managers' preoccupation with the struggle for political power distorts their understanding. This is the source of the "parliamentary cretinism" that made Louis Napoleon a better defender of the bourgeoisie's interests than that class's own representatives. But if neither the ruling class nor its representatives know what is necessary to preserve and reproduce capitalist social relations, why then does the state tend to do just that? The answer is that such policies emerge out of the structural relationships among state managers, capitalists, and workers.

Subsidiary Structural Mechanisms

When Marxists put forward a radical critique of instrumentalist views of the state, they usually do so to justify reformist socialist politics. When one argues that the ruling class is diffused, lacks class consciousness and political sophistication, it seems to follow that if socialists could gain control of the levers of the existing state, they would be able to use the state to effect the transition to socialism. The logic is impeccable—if the state is not inherently a tool of the ruling class, then it can be turned into a tool of the working class. This reformist view shares with instrumentalism a personalistic reductionism—either the ruling class controls the state personally and directly or it does not control it at all, in which case the state can be used for other purposes. Neither view recognizes the structural mechanisms that make the state serve capitalist ends regardless of whether capitalists intervene directly and consciously. However, once these mechanisms are understood, it is possible to construct a critique of socialist reformism that is far more powerful than the critiques derived from the instrumentalist tradition.

Before considering the major structural mechanisms, it is necessary to consider a number of subsidiary mechanisms. The first of these includes all the techniques by which members of the ruling class are able to influence the state apparatus directly. Even though the members of the ruling class lack class consciousness, they are acutely aware of their immediate interests as capitalists and of the impact of the state on those interests. Capitalists, individually and in groups, apply pressure on the state for certain kinds of lucrative contracts, for state spending in certain areas, for legislative action in their favor, for tax relief, for more effective action to control the labor force, and so on. Needless to say, the pursuit of these various interests does not add up to policies in the general interest of capital. Even in the area of control of the labor force, where the common interest among capitalists is strongest, the policies that the capitalists demand might not even be in their own long-term best interest. Nevertheless, capitalists attempt to assure responsiveness by the state through various means, including campaign contributions, lobbying activities, and favors to politicians and civil servants. While these techniques are primarily used for increasing the state's receptivity to the special interests of particular capitalists or groups of capitalists, the overall effect of this proliferation of influence channels is to make those who run the state more likely to reject modes of thought and behavior that conflict with the logic of capitalism.

Included in the category of influence channels is the recruitment of ruling-class members into government service, and in recent years, into participation in various private policy-making groups that have a powerful impact on the formulation of government policies. Instrumentalists tend to see such individuals as typical members of their class, and their impact on the state is viewed as the heart of capitalist class rule. In the perspective being advanced here, this direct ruling-class participation in policy formation is viewed differently. For one thing, ruling-class members who devote substantial energy to policy formation become atypical of their class, since they are forced to look at the world from the perspective of state managers. They are quite likely to diverge ideologically from politically unengaged ruling-class opinion. More important, even if there were no politically engaged ruling-class members, there is still every reason to believe that the state and policy-making groups would advance policies that are in the interests of the ruling class. Marx's formulation cited earlier makes clear that one does not need to be of the ruling class to "represent" it politically; when there are no ruling-class individuals around, individuals from other social classes will eagerly fill the role of ruling-class "representatives."

All of the techniques of ruling-class influence, including direct participation, constitute a structural mechanism of subsidiary importance. The influence channels make it less likely that state managers will formulate policies that conflict directly with the interests of capitalists. But it is a subsidiary mechanism because, even in the absence of these influence channels, other structural mechanisms make it extremely difficult for the state managers to carry through anti-capitalist policies. While instrumentalists argue that influence is the core of ruling-class control of the state, it is really more like the icing on the cake of class rule.

The same cannot be said of a second subsidiary mechanism—bourgeois cultural hegemony. The relevant aspect of cultural hegemony is the widespread acceptance of certain unwritten rules about what is and what is not legitimate state activity. While these rules change over time, a government that violates the unwritten rules of a particular period would stand to lose a good deal of its popular support. This acts as a powerful constraint in discouraging certain types of state action that might conflict with the interests of capital. However, simply invoking the existence of bourgeois cultural hegemony begs the problem of explaining how that hegemony is generated. Here, too, there must be specific structural mechanisms that operate to make "the ruling ideas" consistent with class rule. However, the task of explaining these structural mechanisms is beyond the scope of this essay.

Major Structural Mechanisms

A viable structural theory of the state must do two separate things. It must elaborate the structural constraints that operate to reduce the likelihood that state managers will act against the general interests of capitalists. An understanding of these constraints is particularly important for analyzing the obstacles to reformist socialist strategies. But a structural theory must also explain the tendency of state managers to pursue policies that are in the general interests of capital. It is not sufficient to explain why the state avoids anti-capitalist policies; it is necessary to explain why the state has served to rationalize capitalism. Once one rejects the idea of ruling-class class consciousness, one needs to provide an alternative explanation of efforts at rationalization.

Both tendencies can be derived from the fact that those who manage the state apparatus—regardless of their own political ideology—are dependent on the maintenance of some reasonable level of economic activity. This is true for two reasons. First, the capacity of the state to finance itself through taxation or borrowing depends on the state of the economy. If economic activity is in decline, the state will have difficulty maintaining its revenues at an adequate level. Second, public support for a regime will decline sharply if the regime presides over a serious drop in the level of economic activity, with a parallel rise in unemployment and shortages of key goods. Such a drop in support increases the likelihood that the state managers will be removed from power one way or another. And even if the drop is not that dramatic, it will increase the challenges to the regime and decrease the regime's political ability to take effective actions.

In a capitalist economy the level of economic activity is largely determined by the private investment decisions of capitalists. This means that capitalists, in their collective role as investors, have a veto over state policies in that their failure to invest at adequate levels can create major political problems for the state managers. This discourages state managers from taking actions that might seriously decrease the rate of investment. It also means that state managers have a direct interest in using their power to facilitate investment, since their own continued power rests on a healthy economy. There will be a tendency for state agencies to orient their various programs toward the goal of facilitating and encouraging private investment. In doing so, the state managers address the problem of investment from a broader perspective than that of the individual capitalist. This increases the likelihood that such policies will be in the general interest of capital.

Constraints on State Policies

This is, of course, too simple. Both sides of the picture—constraints and rationalization—must be filled out in greater detail to make this approach convincing. One problem, in particular, stands out—if capitalists have a veto over state policies, isn't this simply another version of instrumentalism? The answer to this question lies in a more careful analysis of the determinants of investment decisions. The most useful concept is the idea of business confidence. Individual capitalists decide on their rate of investment in a particular country on the basis of a variety of specific variables such as the price of labor and the size of the market for a specific product. But there is also an intangible variable— the capitalist's evaluation of the general political/economic climate. Is the society stable; is the working class under control; are taxes likely to rise; do government agencies interfere with business freedom; will the economy grow? These kinds of considerations are critical to the investment decisions of each firm. The sum of all of these evaluations across a national economy can be termed the level of business confidence. As the level of business confidence declines, so will the rate of investment. Business confidence also has an international dimension when nations are integrated into a capitalist world economy. Multinational corporations, international bankers, and currency speculators also make judgments about a particular nation's political/economic climate which determine their willingness to invest in assets in that nation. This, in turn, will affect the internal level of business confidence and the rate of productive investment.

Business confidence is, however, very different from "ruling-class consciousness." Business confidence is based on an evaluation of the market that considers political events only as they might impinge on the market. This means that it is rooted in the narrow self-interest of the individual capitalist who is worried about profit. Business confidence, especially because of its critical international component, does not make subtle evaluations as to whether a regime is serving the long-term interests of capital. When there is political turmoil and popular mobilization, business confidence will fall, and it will rise when there is a restoration of order, no matter how brutal. It was business confidence that responded so favorably to Louis Napoleon's coup d'état, because he promised to restore the conditions for business as usual, despite negative implications for the political rights of the bourgeoisie. The crudeness of business confidence makes capitalism peculiarly vulnerable to authoritarian regimes that are capable of acting against the general interests of capital.[9]

The dynamic of business confidence as a constraint on the managers of the state apparatus can be grasped by tracing out a scenario of what happens when left-of-center governments come to power through parliamentary means and attempt to push through major reforms. The scenario distills a number of twentieth-century experiences including that of Chile under Allende. From the moment that the left wins the election, business confidence declines. The most important manifestation of this decline is an increase in speculation against the nation's currency. Reformist governments are always under suspicion that they will pursue inflationary policies; a higher rate of inflation means that the international value of the nation's currency will fall. Speculators begin to discount the currency for the expected inflation as soon as possible.

This association between reformist governments and inflation is not arbitrary. Reformist policies—higher levels of employment, redistribution of income toward the poor, improved social services—directly or indirectly lead to a shift of income from profits toward the working class. Businesses attempt to resist such a shift by raising prices so that profit levels will not be reduced. In short, price inflation in this context is a market response to policies that tend to benefit the working class. The reformist government, faced with the initial speculative assault on its currency, has two choices. It can reassure the international and domestic business community, making clear its intention to pursue orthodox economic policies. Or, it can forge ahead with its reform program. If it pursues the latter course, an increased rate of inflation and an eventual international monetary crisis is likely.

The international crisis results from the combination of continued speculative pressure against the currency and several new factors. Domestic inflation is likely to affect the nation's balance of trade adversely, leading to a real deterioration in the nation's balance-of-payments account. In addition, inflation and loss of confidence in the currency leads to the flight of foreign and domestic capital and increased foreign reluctance to lend money to the afflicted nation. The initial speculative pressure against the currency could be tolerated; the eruption of an acute international monetary crisis requires some kind of dramatic response. The government may renounce its reformism or cede power to a more "responsible" administration.

But if the government is committed to defending its programs, it will have to act to insulate its economy from the pressures of the international market by imposing some combination of price controls, import controls, and exchange controls.

Escalation in the government's attempt to control the market sets off a new chain of events. These new controls involve threats to individual capitalists. Price controls mean that firms lose the ability to manipulate one of the major determinants of profit levels. Import controls mean that a firm may no longer be able to import goods critical to its business. Exchange controls mean that firms and individuals no longer are able to move their assets freely to secure international havens. The fact that assets are locked into a rapidly inflating currency poses the possibility that large fortunes will be lost.

These are the ingredients for a sharp decline in domestic business confidence. Why should business owners continue to invest if they must operate in an environment in which the government violates the fundamental rules of a market economy?

A sharp decline in business confidence leads to a parallel economic downturn. High rates of unemployment coexist with annoying shortages of critical commodities. The popularity of the regime falls precipitously. The only alternative to capitulation—eliminating controls and initial reforms—is sharp forward movement to socialize the economy. The government could put people back to work and relieve the shortages by taking over private firms. However, the political basis for this kind of action does not exist, even where the leaders of the government are rhetorically committed to the goal of socialism. Generally, the reformist government has not prepared its electoral supporters for extreme action; its entire program has been based on the promise of a gradual transition. Further, the government leaders themselves become immersed in the political culture of the state apparatus, militating against a sharp break with the status quo.

The outcome of this impasse is tragically familiar. The government either falls from power through standard parliamentary means—loss of an election, defection of some of its parliamentary support—or it is removed militarily. Military actions that violate constitutionality meet formidable obstacles in liberal capitalist nations, but when economic chaos severely diminishes the legitimacy of a regime, the chances of a military coup are enhanced. When the military intervenes, it does not do so as a tool of the ruling class. It acts according to its own ideas of the need to restore political order and in its own interests. Naturally, the removal of the reformist government leads to a rapid revival of business confidence simply because order has been restored. However, it should be stressed that this revival of business confidence might not be sustained, since there can be substantial conflicts between the interests of the military and the capitalists.

The key point in elaborating this scenario is that the chain of events can unfold without any members of the ruling class consciously deciding to act "politically" against the regime in power. Of course, such a scenario is usually filled out with a great deal of editorializing against the regime in the bourgeois press, much grumbling among the upper classes, and even some conspiratorial activity. But the point is that conspiracies to destabilize the regime are basically superfluous, since decisions made by individual capitalists according to their own narrow economic rationality are sufficient to paralyze the regime, creating a situation where the regime's fall is the only possibility.

Rationalization

The dynamic of business confidence helps explain why governments are constrained from pursuing anti-capitalist policies. It remains to be explained why governments tend to act in the general interests of capital. Part of the answer has already been suggested. Since state managers are so dependent upon the workings of the investment accumulation process, it is natural that they will use whatever resources are available to aid that process. In administering a welfare program, for example, they will organize it to aid the accumulation process, perhaps by ensuring certain industries a supply of cheap labor. Unlike the individual capitalists, the state managers do not have to operate on the basis of a narrow profit-maximizing rationality. They are capable of intervening in the economy on the basis of a more general rationality. In short, their structural position gives the state managers both the interest and the capacity to aid the investment accumulation process.

There is one major difficulty in this formulation—the problem of explaining the dynamic through which reforms that increase the rationality of capitalism come about. Almost all of these reforms involve an extension of the state's role in the economy and society, either in a regulatory capacity or in the provision of services. The difficulty is that business confidence has been depicted as so short-sighted that it is likely to decline in the face of most efforts to extend the state's role domestically, since such efforts threaten to restrict the freedom of individual capitalists and/or increase the tax burden on capitalists. If the state is unwilling to risk a decline in business confidence, how is it then that the state's role has expanded inexorably throughout the twentieth century?

Most theorists escape this problem by rejecting the idea that the capitalists are as short-sighted as the idea of business confidence suggests. Even if many members of the class share the retrograde notions implicit in the idea of business confidence, there is supposed to be a substantial segment of the class that is forward-looking and recognizes the values of extending the state's power. Theorists of corporate liberalism have attempted to trace many of the major extensions of state power in twentieth-century America to the influence of such forward-looking members of the ruling class. However, the position of these theorists ultimately requires an attribution of a high level of consciousness and understanding to the ruling class or a segment of it, and assumes an instrumental view of the state where state policies can be reduced to the input of certain ruling-class factions. [10]

There is, however, an alternative line of argument, consistent with the view of the ruling class and the state that has been advanced in this paper. It depends on the existence of another structural mechanism—class struggle. Whatever the role of class struggle in advancing the development of revolutionary consciousness, class struggle between proletariat and ruling class in Marx's view has another important function. It pushes forward the development of capitalism—speeding the process by which capitalism advances the development of the productive forces. This is conservative in the short term, but progressive in the long term; it brings closer the time when capitalism will exhaust its capacity to develop the productive forces and will be ripe for overthrow. Class struggle produces this result most clearly in conflict over wages. When workers are able to win wage gains, they increase the pressure on the capitalists to find ways to substitute machines for people. As Marx described the cycle, wage gains are followed by an intense period of mechanization as employers attempt to increase the rate of exploitation; the consequence is an increase in the size of the industrial reserve army, as machines replace workers. This, in turn, diminishes the capacity of workers to win wage gains, until the economic boom again creates a labor shortage. While this description applies particularly to competitive capitalism, the point is that workers' struggles—in Marx's theory—play an important role in speeding the pace of technological innovations. *Class struggle is responsible for much of the economic dynamism of capitalism.*

This pattern goes beyond the struggle over wages. From the beginning of capitalism, workers have struggled to improve their living conditions, which also means upgrading their potential as a labor force. For example, unbridled early capitalism, through child labor and horrendously long working days, threatened to destroy the capacity of the working class to reproduce itself—an outcome not in the long-term interests of capitalists. So working people's struggles against child labor, against incredibly low standards of public health and housing, and for the shorter day, made it possible for the class to reproduce itself, providing capitalism a new generation of laborers. In each historical period, the working class struggles to reproduce itself at a higher level of existence. Workers have played an important role, for example, in demanding increased public education. Public education, in turn, helped create the educated labor pool that developing capitalism required. Obviously, not every working-class demand contributes to the advance of capitalism, but it is foolish to ignore this dimension of class struggle.

In its struggles to protect itself from the ravages of a market economy, the working class has played a key role in the steady expansion of the state's role in capitalist societies. Pressures from the working class have contributed to the expansion of the state's role in the regulation of the economy and in the provision of services. The working class has not been the only force behind the expansion of the state's role in these areas. Examples can be cited of capitalists who have supported an expansion of the state's role into a certain area either because of narrow self-interest—access to government contracts, or because government regulation would hamper competitors, or because of some far-sighted recognition of the need to co-opt the working class. However, the major impetus for the extension of the state's role has come from the working class and from the managers of the state apparatus, whose own powers expand with a growing state.

Once working-class pressures succeed in extending the state's role, another dynamic begins to work. Those who manage the state apparatus have an interest in using the state's resources to facilitate a smooth flow of investment. There will be a tendency to use the state's extended role for the same ends. The capacity of the state to impose greater rationality on capitalism is extended into new areas as a result of working-class pressures. Working-class pressures, for example, might lead to an expansion of educational resources available for the working class but there is every likelihood that the content of the education will be geared to the needs of accumulation—the production of a docile work force at an appropriate level of skill. Or similarly, working-class pressures might force the government to intervene in the free market to produce higher levels of employment, but the government will use its expanded powers of intervention to aid the accumulation process more generally.

This pattern is not a smoothly working functional process, always producing the same result. First, working-class movements have often been aware of the danger of making demands that will ultimately strengthen a state they perceive as hostile. For precisely this reason, socialist movements have often demanded that expanded social services be placed under working-class control. However, working-class demands are rarely granted in their original form. Often, the more radical elements of the movement are repressed at the same time that concessions are made. Second, there can be a serious time lag between granting concessions to the working class and discovering ways that the extension of the state's power can be used to aid the accumulation process. There might, in fact, be continuing tensions in a government program between its integrative intent and its role in the accumulation process. Finally, some concessions to working-class pressure might have no potential benefits for accumulation and might simply place strains on the private economy. If these strains are immediate, one could expect serious efforts to revoke or neutralize the reforms. If the strains occur over the long term, then capitalism faces severe problems because it becomes increasingly difficult to roll back concessions that have stood for some time.[11]

These points suggest that the tendency for class struggle to rationalize capitalism occurs with a great deal of friction and with the continuous possibility of other outcomes. Nevertheless, the tendency does exist because of the particular interests of the state managers. Where there is strong popular pressure for an expansion of social services of increased regulation of markets, the state managers must weigh three factors. First, they do not want to damage business confidence, which generally responds unfavorably to an expansion of the government's role in providing social services or in regulating the market. Second, they do not want class antagonisms to escalate to a level that would endanger their own rule. Third, they recognize that their own power and resources will grow if the state's role is expanded. If the state managers decide to respond to pressure with concessions,[12] they are likely to shape their concessions in a manner that will least offend business confidence and will most expand their own powers. These two constraints increase the likelihood that the concessions will ultimately serve to rationalize capitalism.

Major Reforms

This argument suggests that while some concessions will be made to the working class, the threat of a decline in business confidence will block major efforts to rationalize capitalism. Since business confidence is shortsighted, it will oppose even pro-capitalist reform programs if such programs promise a major increase in taxes or a major increase in the government's capacity to regulate markets. This leaves the problem of explaining the dramatic increases in the state's role that have occurred in all developed capitalist nations during the course of this century. The explanation is that there are certain periods—during wartime, major depressions, and periods of postwar reconstruction—in which the decline of business confidence as a veto on government policies doesn't work. These are the periods in which dramatic increases in the state's role have occurred.

In wars that require major mobilizations, business confidence loses its sting for several reasons. First, international business confidence becomes less important, since international capital flows tend to be placed under government control. Second, private investment becomes secondary to military production in maintaining high levels of economic activity. Third, in the general patriotic climate, it would be dangerous for the business community to disrupt the economy through negative actions.[13] The result is that state managers have the opportunity to expand their own power with the unassailable justification that such actions are necessary for the war effort. Some of these wartime measures will be rolled back once peace returns, but some will become part of the landscape.

In serious depressions and postwar reconstruction periods, the dynamics are somewhat different. Low levels of economic activity mean that the threat of declining business confidence loses its power, at the same time that popular demands for economic revival are strong. In such periods, the state managers can pay less attention to business opinion and can concentrate on responding to the popular pressure, while acting to expand their own power. However, there are still constraints on the state managers. Their continued rule depends on their capacity to revive the economy. As government actions prove effective in reducing unemployment, redistributing income, or expanding output, the political balance shifts. Pressure from below is likely to diminish; business confidence re-emerges as a force once economic recovery begins. In short, successful reforms will tilt the balance of power back to a point where capitalists regain their veto over extensions of the state's role.

The increased capacity of state managers to intervene in the economy during these periods does not automatically rationalize capitalism. State managers can make all kinds of mistakes, including excessive concessions to the working class. State managers have no special knowledge of what is necessary to make capitalism more rational; they grope toward effective action as best they can within existing political constraints and with available economic theories.[14] The point is simply that rationalization can emerge as a by-product of state managers' dual interest in expanding their own power and in assuring a reasonable level of economic activity. The more power the state possesses to intervene in the capitalist economy, the greater the likelihood that effective actions can be taken to facilitate investment.

Not every extension of state power will survive beyond those periods in which state managers have special opportunities to expand the state's role. After a war, depression, or period of reconstruction, the business community is likely to campaign for a restoration of the *status quo ante*. State managers in these new periods will be forced to make some concessions to the business community in order to avert a decline in business confidence. However, the state managers also want to avoid the elimination of certain reforms important for the stabilization of the economy and the integration of the working class. Self-interest also leads them to resist a complete elimination of the state's expanded powers. The consequence is a selection process by which state managers abandon certain reforms while retaining others. In this process, reforms that are most beneficial for capitalism will be retained, while those whose effects are more questionable will be eliminated.[15] Again, the ultimate outcome is determined by intense political struggle.

Conclusion

The purpose of this essay has been to argue that a viable Marxist theory of the state depends on the rejection of the idea of a conscious, politically directive, ruling class. By returning to Marx's suggestions that the historical process unfolds "behind the backs" of the actors (including the ruling-class actors), it is possible to locate the structural mechanisms that shape the workings of the capitalist state. These mechanisms operate independently of any political consciousness on the part of the ruling class. Instead, capitalist rationality emerges out of the three-sided relationship among capitalists, workers, and state managers. The structural position of state managers forces them to achieve some consciousness of what is necessary to maintain the viability of the social order. It is this consciousness that explains both the reluctance of state managers to offend business confidence, and their capacity to rationalize a capitalist society. However, the fact of consciousness does not imply control over the historical process. State managers are able to act only in the terrain that is marked out by the intersection of two factors—the intensity of class struggle and the level of economic activity.

This framework has implications for a wide range of theoretical and political questions. One of the most critical of these concerns capitalism's capacity to overcome its current economic difficulties. Analysts on the left have predicted that the forward-looking segment of the American ruling class will favor a further extension of the state's role in regulating the economy as a means to solve the problems of stagflation.[16] This perspective exaggerates the capacity of capitalism to reform itself in "normal" periods, and is unable to account, for example, for the inability of British capitalism to rationalize itself during the long period of decline since the nineteen-fifties. The framework developed here predicts that while the working class and the state managers themselves might favor an expansion of state intervention, business confidence will effectively veto such changes. It is therefore quite possible that the American economy will continue in its present state of crisis for many years to come.

Notes

1. For two surveys of recent Marxist work on the state—one polemical and the other dispassionate—see Alan Wolfe, "New Directions in the Marxist Theory of Politics," *Politics and Society*, vol. 4, no. 2 (1974), and David Gold, Clarence Y. H. Lo, and Erik Olin Wright, "Recent Developments in Marxist Theories of the Capitalist State," parts 1 and 2, *Monthly Review*, October and November 1975.

2. For critiques of such interpretations of Watergate, see Steve Weissman, "Cowboys and Crooks," in Steve Weissman, ed., *Big Brother and the Holding Company: The World behind Watergate* (Palo Alto, Calif.: Ramparts Press, 1974), pp. 297-310; and Stephen Johnson, "How the West Was Won: Last Shootout for the Yankee-Cowboy Theory," *Insurgent Sociologist*, Winter 1975, pp. 61-93.

3. My analysis has been influenced by the arguments of Nicos Poulantzas, particularly in his "Problems of the Capitalist State," *New Left Review* 58 (November-December 1969). However, my analysis differs from Poulantzas' in two important respects. He tends to attribute consciousness to particular fractions of the ruling class and he fails to explain adequately the mechanisms by which the state is structurally a capitalist state. In this regard, my position is closer to that of Claus Offe in a number of articles, including "Structural Problems of the Capitalist State," in Klaus von Beyme, ed., *German Political Studies* (Beverly Hills, Calif.: Sage Publications, 1976); and Claus Offe and Volker Ronge, "Theses on the Theory of the State," *New German Critique* 6 (Fall 1975).

4. By "rationalization" and "capitalist reform," I am referring primarily to the use of the state in new ways to overcome economic contradictions and to facilitate the integration of the working

class. Rationalization must be distinguished from strategies of forcing the working class to bear the costs of economic contradictions through dramatic reductions in living standards combined with severe political repression.

5. Each of these categories requires some definition: "Capitalist class" or "ruling class" is used to refer to the individuals and families that own or control a certain quantity of capital. The cut-off point would vary by country or period, and it would necessarily be somewhat arbitrary, but the point is to distinguish between small businesses and large capitalist firms. The "managers of the state apparatus" include the leading figures of both the legislative and executive branches. This includes the highest-ranking civil servants, as well as appointed and elected politicians. "Working class" is being used in the broad sense. It includes most of those who sell their labor for wages, unwaged workers, and the unemployed.

6. In *The German Ideology*, Marx and Engels talk about a division of labor and of interests between capitalists and the producers of bourgeois ideology: ". . . so that inside this class one part appears as the thinkers of the class (its active, conceptive ideologists, who make the perfection of the illusion of the class about itself their chief source of livelihood), while the others' attitude to these ideas and illusions is more passive and receptive, because they are in reality the active members of this class and have less time to make up illusions and ideas about themselves." In Robert C. Tucker, ed., *The Marx-Engels Reader* (New York: Norton, 1971), pp. 136-37. This suggests an analogous division of labor between capitalists and state managers. In both cases, however, treating ideologists or state managers as part of the ruling class violates the idea that class is determined by one's relation to the means of production. In short, Marx and Engels in this passage are using the notion of the ruling class in a polemical sense.

7. "The Eighteenth Brumaire," in ibid., p. 502.

8. Ibid., p. 502.

9. It is beyond the scope of this essay to explore the dynamics of authoritarian rule in capitalist societies. However, it is important to give some content to the familiar Marxist thesis that authoritarian rule is a second-best solution for capitalism, as compared to parliamentarism, and is only resorted to when the threat of revolution is serious. Part of the answer is that authoritarian regimes are less reliable in serving the general interests of capital because the structural mechanisms described here do not operate in the same way in the absence of parliamentarism.

10. For a critique of corporate liberal theory, see Fred Block, "Beyond Corporate Liberalism," *Social Problems*.

11. An obvious example here is the commitment to maintaining "full employment." This was a concession granted to the working class in the aftermath of the Great Depression, but it has proved increasingly costly for the developed capitalist nations.

12. They also have the option of responding to pressures through severe repression. The choice between concessions and repression is made by the state managers on the basis of their perceptions of the general environment and their political orientations.

13. These arguments all assume that some significant degree of national mobilization has occurred. In this sense, the business confidence veto was far stronger during Vietnam than during Korea. (In fact, it can be argued that the Johnson administration's desire to continue escalating in Vietnam ran afoul of declining business confidence.) In some cases, the business community's lack of enthusiasm for a war can prevent mobilization efforts from getting off the ground in time. This was clearly an element in the French collapse during World War II. But how does business confidence evaluate wars? I would suggest that the answer lies in terms of short-term considerations rather than an evaluation of the nation's long-term international position. In conditions of weak demand, the outbreak of major wars generally leads to a decline in business confidence.

14. This was the case with the New Deal. The Roosevelt administration simply stumbled on some of the elements necessary for a rationalization of the economy. The open-ended nature of the process is indicated by the fact that full recovery was not achieved until the mobilization for World War II.

15. This kind of selection process was carried out by the Conservative government that came to power in Britain in 1951 after Labour had presided over postwar reconstruction. The dangers

involved in the selection process are indicated by the fact that Britain's long-term prospects as a capitalist nation might have been improved by the retention of more of the Labour reforms.

16. See, for example, Stanley Aronowitz, "Modernizing Capitalism," *Social Policy*, May-June 1975; and James Crotty and Raford Boddy, "Who Will Plan the Planned Economy?" *The Progressive*, February 1975. Such analyses tend to assume that the contradictions of advanced capitalism can be solved or effectively eased through state action. The possibility exists that this is not the case. While it is virtually impossible to reach a conclusion on that issue, one can debate whether such expanded state intervention will even be attempted.

2

CONDUCT

Institutions, Processes, and Group Bargaining

The basic demands and constraints discussed in the last section may be met through a variety of institutional forms. These more particular institutional settings additionally shape political bargaining, conflict, and the exercise of public and private power. In this section the essays focus on this institutional and "process" aspect of the American political economy, sometimes highlighting the distinctiveness of the American case by its comparison with other states. Theodore J. Lowi introduces the section with an overview of the philosophy of American public policy. George J. Stigler, James Q. Wilson, and Kathleen Kemp analyze the pattern of state regulation of the economy. Samuel Popkin, John W. Gorman, Charles Phillips, and Jeffrey A. Smith expand on the work of Downs and others to develop an "investment" theory of voting. Walter Dean Burnham and Martin Shefter chronicle the long-term decay of the American electoral system and Benjamin Ginsberg examines the effects of changing trends in campaign finance. Finally, Samuel P. Huntington looks at changes in the U.S. Congress, Richard B. Stewart reviews the shifting justifications given for administrative law, and Morris P. Fiorina considers the prospects for reform.

The New Public Philosophy:
Interest-Group Liberalism

THEODORE J. LOWI

Surveying American public policy in the 1960s and 1970s, Theodore J. Lowi argues that meaningful adversarial political proceedings between liberals and conservatives have given way to a merely "administrative, technical, and logrolling" form of politics. Whatever the symbolic rhetoric of opposition and debate, the old liberal–conservative dialogue has been overtaken by consensus on the need for positive government and an affirmative state. But within this consensus there is virtually no consideration given to the proper purposes of government action. Politics has ceased to pose a "question of morality" and now is only a "question of equity." Public policies identified as "liberal" or "conservative" no longer seem to correspond, respectively, to the furtherance of social change or the preservation of the status quo. Political parties are distinguishable only upon inventory of the different special interests to which they most closely ally themselves, and the force and legitimacy of law has been drastically undermined by the vast confused discretion of the modern administrative state. Within this universe, politics is no longer debate about the ends of social life, nor even debate of conviction about the permissible means of achieving social goals. There is "no substance. Neither is there procedure. There is only process."

The "new public philosophy" of this denatured politics, Lowi argues, is "interest group liberalism." The philosophy holds, inter alia, that organized interests are adequately representative of the distribution and strength of citizen concerns, and that the proper role of government should be limited to facilitating the bargaining and contestation of these competing interests (by ensuring their access to government) and ratifying the scrambled results of their competition. Closely resembling the pluralist theories of society advanced by political scientists, and offering a group-bargaining correlate to neoclassical economists' notions of market equilibrium, interest group liberalism makes the strong claim that through the mere facilitation of the self-correcting group-bargaining process, the coercion of both private and public authorities can be effectively overcome. Lowi declares faith in this claim an illusion, and a disastrous one.

Why Nineteenth-Century Liberalism Declined

The decline of capitalist ideology as the American public philosophy took the form of a dialogue between a private and a public view of society. This dialogue, between a new liberalism and an old liberalism (redefined as conservatism) comprises the constitutional epoch immediately preceding our own, ending in 1937. During this period there was no prevailing public philosophy but rather two bodies of competing ideology. Liberal and conservative regimes derived their specific uses of government and policy from their general positions, and differences between the two national parties were for the most part clear within these terms. The perennial issue underlying the dialogue was the question of the nature of government itself and whether expansion or contraction of government best produced public good. Expansion of government was demanded by the new liberalism as the means of combating the injustices of a brutal world that would not change as long as we passively submitted ourselves to it. The mark of the new liberalism was its assumption that the instruments of government provided the means for conscious inducement of social change and that outside the capacity for change no experimentation with new institutional forms would be possible. Opposition to such means, but not necessarily to the proposed forms themselves, became the mark of contemporary conservatism.

Across all disagreements there was unanimity on the underlying criteria. These basic criteria were attitude toward government and attitude toward social change. There was also agreement, which persists today, that these two attitudes are consistent and reinforcing, both as guides for leaders in their choices among policies and as criteria for followers in their choices among leaders. For example,

> Conservatism is committed to a discriminating defense of the social order against change and reform (liberalism) . . . . by the Right, I mean generally those parties and movements that are skeptical of popular governments, oppose the bright plans of the reformers and dogooders, and draw particular support from men with a sizable stake in the established order. By the left, I mean generally those parties and movements that demand wider popular participation in government, push actively for reform, and draw particular support from the disinherited, dislocated and disgruntled. As a general rule, to which there are historic exceptions, the Right is conservative or reactionary, the Left is liberal or radical.[1]

These two criteria arose out of a particular constitutional period, were appropriate to that period, and provided a mutually reinforcing basis for doctrine during that period. After 1937, the Constitution did not die from the Roosevelt revolution, as many had predicted, but the basis for the liberal-conservative dialogue did die. Liberalism-conservatism as the source of public philosophy no longer made any sense. Once the principle of positive government in an indeterminable but expanding political sphere was established, criteria arising out of the very issue of expansion became irrelevant.

Liberalism–Conservatism: The Empty Debate   The old dialogue passed into the graveyard of consensus. Yet it persisted. Old habits die hard. Its persistence despite its irrelevance means that the liberal-conservative debate has become almost purely ritualistic. And its persistence even in ritualistic form has produced a number of evil effects among which the most important is the blinding of the nation to the emergence of a new and ersatz public philosophy. The coexistence of a purely ritualistic public dialogue and an ersatz and unrecognized new public philosophy has produced most of the political pathologies of the 1960s and 1970s. The decline of a meaningful dialogue between a liberalism and a conservatism has meant the decline of a meaningful adversary political proceedings in favor of adminstrative, technical, and logrolling politics. In a nutshell, politics became a question of equity rather than a question of morality. Adjustment comes first, rules of law come last, if at all. The tendency of individuals to accept governmental decisions simply because these decisions are good has probably at no time in American history, save during the Civil War, been less widely distributed and less intensely felt. Cynicism and distrust in everyday political processes have never been more widespread. The emerging public philosophy, interest-group liberalism, has sought to solve the problems of public authority in a large modern state by defining them away. This has simply added the element of demoralization to that of illegitimacy. Interest-group liberalism seeks to justify power by avoiding law and by parceling out to private parties the power to make public policy. A most maladaptive political formula, it was almost inevitably going to produce a crisis of public authority even though its short-run effects seem to be those of consensus and stabilization.

A brief look at a few cases will expose the emptiness of the old liberal-conservative dialogue and the kinds of pathology it was likely to produce. Table 1 shows at a glance how irrelevant the old criteria are to present policies.[2] In the table there are a number of public policies and private policies (or widely established private practices) that have been arranged according to the two fundamental dimensions of liberalism-conservatism. Above the line is the public sphere containing public policy; below the line are the policies and established group practices associated with the private sphere. This vertical dimension is a simple dichotomy; therefore, the "liberal" dimension is supposedly above the line and the "conservative" dimension is below the line. The horizontal axis is a continuum whereupon each policy or practice is placed along the line from left to right roughly according to its probable impact upon the society. To the left is the liberal direction, where policies are placed if they are likely to produce a direct social change. To the right is the conservative direction because the policies and practices placed there are thought to militate against change and to support the status quo.[3]

If the two dimensions—attitude toward government and attitude toward change—were consistent, and if together they described and justified all public policy, then liberal policies would be concentrated in the upper left corner and conservative policies in the lower right. In reality these policies range all across the continuum, below and above the line. Little reflection is necessary to perceive the fact that policy-makers are being guided by criteria very different from those underlying Table 1. Obviously the liberal-conservative dialogue made no sense after the principle of positive government was established.[4]

Liberalism–Conservatism: The Public Policies   Although the distance above or below the line on Table 1 is not meant to convey addition information about the degree of public involvement, it is worthwhile to consider that dimension. This can be done by cross-tabulating each of the public policies according to the actual degree of government involvement against the probable degree of social change likely to be produced by the policy (Table 2). This particular look at government should be most unsettling to those who have assumed that political power is all one needs in order to achieve important humanitarian goals. Note especially how many government policies seem to congregate in cells labeled with a minus sign (hypothesized as likely to "militate against change"). Note also that government's relation to social change does not appear to increase as government involvement increases from one to two to three pluses. On the contrary, there almost seems to be an inverse relationship, suggesting that *government is most effective and most frequently employed when something in society has been deemed worthy of preservation.* This is why the notion of "maintaining public order" is more suitable than humanitarianism or egalitarianism as the initial hypothesis for an inquiry into the nature of contemporary government.

Table 1

Selected Public and Private Policies Arranged According to Probable Effect on Society

Graduated income tax (potential)	Luxury taxes	Growth fiscal policies	Countercyclical fiscal policies	Social Security programs based on insurance principles (U.S.)	Existing farm programs	High and rigid farm price supports
Social Security programs based on graduated income tax	Real antitrust	Graduated income tax (United States)	Sales taxes	Direct regulation (e.g., FCC, ICC, CAB, etc.)	Restraint of competition (NRA, fair trade, antiprice discrimination)	High tariffs Import quotas Utilities
Civil rights package	"Yardstick" regulation (TVA)		Aids to small business	Antitrust by consent decree	Tax on colored margarine	Group representation on boards
Low tariffs						Strict gold standard with no bank money
Competition in agriculture	Competitive business	Oligopoly with research competition	Oligopoly without competition (steel, cigarettes)		Trade associations	Monopoly
New interest groups	Corporate philanthropy		Brand names		Pools	Old interest groups (NAM, AFL-CIO, TWU, etc.)
	Merit hiring and promotion		Ethnic appeals of political campaigns		Basing points	
					Price leadership	
					Fair trade policies	
					Union unemployment and automation policies	

Above the line Public policies ("liberal").

Below the line Private policies or practices ("conservative").

Toward the left side Policies likely to produce change ("liberal").

Toward the right side Policies likely to maintain existing practices ("conservative").

Table 2

Selected Public Policies, Tabulated by Degree of Social Change and Degree of Government Involvement

Degree of government involvement	Impact of Policy: Likelihood of Significant Social Change				
	Change very likely +++	++	Change probable +	—	Militates against change ———
++ Sustained and active intervention	Title VI of 1964 Civil Rights Act; Civil Rights Act 1965; Fully progressive Income Tax (Hypothetical)	Walsh-Healy; Civil Rights Act, 1964; Reciprocal Trade	TVA; 1964 Tax cuts	Countercyclical fiscal policy; Manpower Training; Tax Revision 1961-62 Tax Cuts	FTC; Area Redevelopment; Nationalized industry; Defense construction; Public Housing; Farm Parity; Old tariff; ICC; Utilities
++ Substantial involvement	1962 Trade Act	Aid to Education	COMSTAT; Appalachia	Patents; Urban redevelopment	FCC; CAB; Social Security; French & Italian public corporations; War on Poverty; Farm extension; NRA codes; Robinson-Patman of FTC; Monopolies
+ Low but measurable involvement	Head Start; Free trade (Hypothetical)	Education grants-in-aid; Title I Housing; Research Subsidy			SEC

Analysis of the real or potential impact of public policies shows how incomplete is the fit between the old liberal-conservative public philosophies and the policies they were supposed to support and justify. The analysis reveals that those who espouse social change in the abstract, especially government-engineered social change, are seldom favoring policies that would clearly effect any social change. Conversely, the analysis shows that those who harangue on principle against government and against social change are frequently in real life supporting policies that would give us strong doses of both. If the guiding criteria do not really guide the leadership, they can certainly offer no plausible justification to the intelligent follower. A few examples will show why.

The income tax. All taxes discriminate. The political question arises over the kind of discrimination to choose. The graduated or progressive income tax is capable of effecting drastic changes in the relationships between social classes and between individuals and their property. According to the two dimensions governing Table 1, a steeply progressive income tax is "liberal" both because it is governmental and because it effects social change. Our own income tax can be called only mildly progressive because of the varieties of exemptions written into the law. It is generally understood that the effective ceiling on taxes is not 91 percent or 75 percent but a good deal less than 50 percent, with many large corporations not paying any taxes at all. And taking all our taxes together, from the local property taxes to the federal luxury and inheritance taxes, it seems fairly clear that they are a bastion against rather than a weapon for fluidity among economic classes in the society. This is not an argument in favor of one tax structure or the other but rather an attempt to assess the general tendency as an illustration of the virtual irrelevance of old liberal-conservative principles. With virtually every new administration, there is vigorous talk of tax reform, but the interests in maintaining the present structure seem always to be too strong to be overcome.[5]

The Social Security system. This is a bundle of policies, and an accurate account would require classification of each program. On balance, however, Social Security programs in the United States are "liberal" only because they are governmental. Otherwise they are quite conservative in their impact on the social structure and upon the behavior of individual clients. If the general welfare is promoted by our Social Security system it is only because a basically conservative policy *can* promote welfare. Nevertheless these programs are conservative in at least two senses of the term. First, welfare policies are fiscal policies and as techniques of fiscal policy they are countercyclical; that is to say, they are automatic stabilizers that work systematically to maintain demand, and therefore existing economic relationships, throughout the business cycle. Second, Social Security programs are techniques of social as well as economic control. Government's role is essentially paternalistic. For those basic Social Security programs that depend upon employee contributions, the government is saying in essence, "This much of your income we will not trust you to spend but will hold it for you until you really need it." The discretionary and noncontributory social welfare programs are also paternalistic to the extent that they are making judgments about the relative need of each applicant and whether the family situation deserves governmental assistance.[6]

Farm policy. Farm programs provide an equally good case of the irrelevance of actual policies to the old criteria. High price supports with crop controls—the central feature of farm policy for a generation—are supported by so-called liberals despite the fact that the basic purpose of these programs has been to restore or maintain a pre-1914 agriculture in the face of extremely strong contrary economic developments. So-called conservatives have made it a point to oppose these programs despite the fact that the quick elimination of price supports would probably revolutionize the agriculture industry.[7]

The private sector. It is equally bizarre to rate as "conservative" support on principle of practices in the private sector. Competitive business enterprise is a highly dynamic force that usually makes change normal, innovation necessary, and influence by ordinary individuals over economic decisions possible. For these reasons many forms of competitive enterprise should warrant the support of real liberals. However, except for occasional martyrs, such as Thurman Arnold, who have sought vainly to use government to decentralize industry, the net impact of attitudes toward business from conservatives as well as liberals has been to put restraints on the most dynamic aspects of the private sphere. One could say that the only difference between old-school liberals and old-school conservatives is that the former would destroy the market through public means and the latter through private means.

As shown on Table 1, organized competition in the private sphere is highly dynamic and is one of the most important sources of change in society. But it is of equal importance to stress that holding companies, pools, market sharing, nonprice competition, and trade associations are strongly opposed to change; indeed they are usually organized for the purpose of resisting change. On the other hand, they are in no way functionally distinguishable from such government policies as basing-point laws, fair-trade laws, fair-competition laws, industrial-safety codes, and monopoly-rate regulation. Note also that interest groups have been placed on Table 1. Although they are not policies, strictly speaking, interest groups, especially trade associations and unions, are formed and supported as a matter of policy by entrepreneurs and corporations. Putting old groups on the right and new groups on the left suggests a very important political tendency, which is that new groups, regardless of their program, tend to have a very innovative effect on society while all established interest groups tend to be conservative.[8]

The old public philosophy, drawn from the liberal-conservative dialogue, became outmoded in our time because elites simply no longer disagree whether government should be involved. Therefore, they neither seek out the old criteria for guidance through their disagreements, nor do they really have need of the criteria to justify the mere governmental character of their policy proposals. But this does not mean that public leaders are free of ideology. Leaders need ideology because they need guidance, and more importantly in a democratic society, they need rationalization. If they are no longer governed by their old public philosophy, it is highly probable that another one is emerging to take its place but may not be clearly enough formulated to be fully appreciated by themselves or by the public at large.

Interest-Group Liberalism

The frenzy of governmental activity in the 1960s and 1970s proved that once the constitutional barriers were down the American national government was capable of prompt response to organized political demands. However, that is only the beginning of the story, because the almost total democratization of the Constitution and the contemporary expansion of the public sector has been accompanied by expansion, not contraction, of a sense of distrust toward public objects. Here is a spectacular paradox. It is as though each new program or program expansion had been an admission of prior governmental inadequacy or failure without itself being able to make any significant contribution to order or to well-being. It is as though prosperity had gone up at an arithmetic rate while expectations, and therefore frustrations, had been going up at a geometric rate—in a modern expression of Malthusian Law. Public authority was left to grapple with this alienating gap between expectation and reality.

Why did the expansion of government that helped produce and sustain prosperity also help produce a crisis of public authority? The explanation pursued throughout this volume is that the old justifications for expansion had too little to say beyond the need for the expansion itself. An appropriate public philosophy would have addressed itself to the purposes to which the expanded governmental authority should be dedicated. It would also have addressed itself to the forms and procedures by which that power could be utilized. These questions are so alien to public discourse in the United States that merely to raise them is to be considered reactionary, apolitical, or totally naïve.

Out of the emerging crisis of public authority developed an ersatz political formula that bears no more relation to those questions than the preceding political formula. The guidance the new formula offers to policy formulation is a set of sentiments that elevated a particular view of the political process above everything else. The ends of government and the justification of one policy or procedure over another are not to be discussed. The *process* of formulation is justified in itself. As observed earlier it takes the pluralist notion that government is an epiphenomenon of politics and makes out of that a new ethics of government.

There are several possible names for the new public philosophy. A strong candidate would be *corporatism*, but its history as a concept gives it several unwanted connotations, such as conservative Catholicism or Italian fascism. Another candidate is *syndicalism*, but among many objections is the connotation of anarchy too far removed from American experience. From time to time other possible labels will be experimented with, but, since the new American public philosophy is something of an amalgam of all of the candidates, some new terminology seems to be called for.

The most clinically accurate term to capture the American variant of all of these tendencies is *interest-group liberalism*. It is liberalism because it is optimistic about government, expects to use government in a positive and expansive role, is motivated by the highest sentiments, and possesses a strong faith that what is good for government is good for the society. It is interest-group liberalism because it sees as both necessary and good a policy agenda that is accessible to all organized interests and makes no independent judgment of their claims. It is interest-group liberalism because it defines the public interest as a result of the amalgamation of various claims. A brief sketch of the working model of interest-group liberalism turns out to be a vulgarized version of the pluralist model of modern political science: (1) Organized interests are homogeneous and easy to define. Any duly elected representative of any interest is taken as an accurate representative of each and every member.[9] (2) Organized interests emerge in every sector of our lives and adequately represent most of those sectors, so that one organized group can be found effectively answering and checking some other organized group as it seeks to prosecute its claims against society.[10] And (3) the role of government is one of insuring access to the most effectively organized, and of ratifying the agreements and adjustments worked out among the competing leaders.

This last assumption is supposed to be a statement of how a democracy works and how it ought to work. Taken together, these assumptions amount to little more than the appropriation of the Adam Smith "hidden hand" model for politics, where the group is the entrepeneur and the equilibrium is not lowest price but the public interest.[11]

These assumptions are the basis of the new public philosophy. The policy behavior of old liberals and old conservatives, of Republicans and Democrats, so inconsistent with the old dialogue, is fully consistent with the criteria drawn from interest-group liberalism: *The most important difference between liberals and conservatives, Republicans and Democrats, is to be found in the interest groups they identify with. Congressmen are guided in their votes, presidents in their programs, and administrators in their discretion*

by whatever organized interests they have taken for themselves as the most legitimate; and
that is the measure of the legitimacy of demands and the only necessary guidelines for the
framing of the laws.

It is one thing to recognize that these assumptions resemble the working methodology of modern political science. But it is quite another to explain how this model was
elevated from a hypothesis about political behavior to an ideology about how our
democratic polity ought to work.

The Appeals of Interest-Group Liberalism   The important inventors of modern
techniques of government were less than inventive about the justifications for particular
policies at particular times. For example, Keynes was neither a dedicated social reformer
nor a political thinker with an articulated vision of the new social order.[12] Keynes helped
discover the modern economic system and how to help maintain it, but his ideas and
techniques could be used to support a whole variety of approaches and points of view:

> Collective bargaining, trade unionism, minimum-wage laws, hours legislation,
> social security, a progressive tax system, slum clearance and housing, urban
> redevelopment and planning, education reform, all these he accepted but they
> were not among his preoccupations. In no sense could he be called the father of
> the welfare state.[13]

These innovators may have been silent on the deeper justification for expanding
government because of the difficulty of drawing justification from the doctrines of popular
government and majority rule. Justification of positive government programs on the basis
of popular rule required, above all, a belief in and support of the supremacy of Congress.
The abdication of Congress in the 1930s and thereafter could never have been justified in
the name of popular government; and, all due respect to members of Congress, they
made no effort to claim such justification. Abdication to the Executive Branch on
economic matters and activism in the infringement of civil liberties produced further
reluctance to fall back upon Congress and majority rule as the font of public policy
justification. Many who wished nevertheless to have majority rule on their side sought
support in the plebiscitary character of the presidency. However, presidential liberals have
had to blind themselves to many complications in the true basis of presidential authority,
and their faith in the presidency as a representative majority rule came almost completely
unstuck during the late 1960s and thereafter.[14]

This is precisely what made interest-group liberalism so attractive. It had the
approval of political scientists because it could deal with so many of the realities of power.
It was further appealing because large interest groups and large memberships could be
taken virtually as popular rule in modern dress. And it fit the needs of corporate leaders,
union leaders, and government officials desperately searching for support as they were
losing communal attachments to their constituencies. Herbert Hoover had spoken out
eloquently against crass individualism and in favor of voluntary collectivism. His belief in
this kind of collectivism is what led him to choose, among all his offers, to be Secretary of
Commerce in 1921.[15] And the experts on government who were to become the
intellectual core of the New Deal and later Democratic administrations were already
supporting such views even before the election of Franklin D. Roosevelt. For example,

> [The national associations] represent a healthy democratic development. They
> rose in answer to certain needs. . . . They are part of our representative system.
> . . . These groups must be welcomed for what they are, and certain precaution-

ary regulations worked out. The groups must be understood and their proper place in government allotted, if not by actual legislation, then by general public realization of their significance.[16]

After World War II, the academic and popular justifications for interest-group liberalism were still stronger. A prominent American government textbook of the period argued that the "basic concept for understanding the dynamics of government is the multi-group nature of modern society or the modern state."[17] By the time we left the 1960s, with the Democrats back in power, the justifications for interest-group liberalism were more eloquent and authoritative than ever. Take two examples from among the most important intellectuals of the Democratic Party, writing around the time of the return of the Democrats to power in 1960. To John Kenneth Galbraith, "Private economic power is held in check by countervailing power of those who are subjected to it. The first begets the second."[18] Concentrated economic power stimulates power in opposition to it, resulting in a natural tendency toward equilibrium. This is not merely theoretical for Galbraith, although he could not possibly have missed its similarity to Adam Smith; Galbraith was writing a program of positive government action. He admitted that effective countervailing power was limited in the real world and proposed that where it was absent or too weak to do the job, government policy should seek out and support it and, where necessary, create the organizations capable of countervailing. It should be government policy to validate the pluralist theory.

Arthur Schlesinger summarized his views for us in a campaign tract written in 1960. To Schlesinger, the essential difference between the Democratic and Republican Parties is that the Democratic Party is the truly multi-interest party:

> What is the essence of multi-interest administration? It is surely that the leading interests in society are all represented in the interior processes of policy formation—which can be done only if members or advocates of these interests are included in key positions of government.[19]

Schlesinger repeated the same theme in a more sober and reflective book written after John Kennedy's assassination. Following his account of the 1962 confrontation of President Kennedy with the steel industry and the later decision to cut taxes and cast off in favor of expansionary rather than stabilizing fiscal policy, Schlesinger concludes,

> The ideological debates of the past began to give way to a new agreement on the practicalities of managing a modern economy. There thus developed in the Kennedy years a national accord on economic policy—a new consensus which gave hope of harnessing government, business, and labor in rational partnership for a steadily expanding American economy.[20]

A significant point in the entire argument is that the Republicans would disagree with Schlesinger on the *facts* but not on the *basis* of his distinction. The typical Republican rejoinder would be simply that Democratic administrations are not more multi-interest than Republican. In my opinion this would be almost the whole truth.

The appeal of interest-group liberalism is not simply that it is more realistic than earlier ideologies. There are several strongly positive reasons for its appeal. The first is that it helped flank the constitutional problems of federalism that confronted the expanding national state before the Constitution was completely democratized. A program like the Extension Service of the Department of Agriculture got around the restrictions of the

Interstate Commerce clause by providing for self-administration by a combination of land-grant colleges, local farmer and commerce associations, and organized commodity groups. These appeared to be so decentralized and permissive as to be hardly federal at all. With such programs we begin to see the ethical and conceptual mingling of the notion of organized private groups with the notions of local government and self-government. Ultimately, direct interest-group participation in government became synonymous with self-government; but at first it was probably a strategy to get around the inclination of the Supreme Court to block federal interventions in the economy.

A second positive appeal of interest-group liberalism, strongly related to the first, is that it helped solve a problem for the democratic politician in the modern state where the stakes are so high. This is the problem of enhanced conflict and how to avoid it. The contribution of politicians to society is their skill in resolving conflict. However, direct confrontations are sought only by so-called ideologues and outsiders. Typical American politicians displace and defer and delegate conflict where possible; they face conflict squarely only when they must. Interest-group liberalism offered a justification for keeping major combatants apart and for delegating their conflict as far down the line as possible. It provided a theoretical basis for giving to each according to his claim, the price for which is a reduction of concern for what others are claiming. In other words, *it transformed access and logrolling from necessary evil to greater good*.

A third and increasingly important positive appeal of interest-group liberalism is that it helps create the sense that power need not be power at all, control need not be control, and government need not be coercive. If sovereignty is parceled out among groups, then who is out anything? As a major *Fortune* editor enthusiastically put it, government power, group power, and individual power may go up simultaneously. If the groups to be controlled control the controls, then "to administer does not always mean to rule."[21] The inequality of power and the awesome coerciveness of government are always gnawing problems in a democratic culture. Rousseau's General Will stopped at the boundary of a Swiss canton. The myth of the group and the group will is becoming the answer to Rousseau and the big democracy. Note, for example, the contrast between the traditional and the modern definition of the group: Madison in *Federalist 10* defined the group ("faction") as "a number of citizens, whether amounting to a majority or minority of the whole who are united and actuated by some common impulse of passion, or of interest, *adverse to the right of other citizens, or to the permanent and aggregate interests of the community*" (emphasis added). Modern political science usage took that definition and cut the quotation just before the emphasized part.[22] In such a manner pluralist theory became the handmaiden of interest-group liberalism, and interest-group liberalism became the handmaiden of modern American positive national statehood [. . .].

Evidence of the fundamental influence of interest-group liberalism can be found in the policies and practices of every Congress and every administration since 1961. The very purpose of this book is to identify, document, and assess the consequences of the preferences that are drawn from the new public philosophy. President Kennedy is an especially good starting point because his positions were clear and because justification was especially important to him. His actions were all the more significant because he followed the lines of interest-group liberalism during a period of governmental strength, when there was no need to borrow support from interest groups. But whatever he did in the name of participation, cooperation, or multi-interest administration, and whatever President Johnson did in the name of "maximum feasible participation" and "creative federalism," so did President Eisenhower and Presidents Nixon and Ford do in the name of "partnership." This posture was very much above partisanship, and that is precisely what makes it the basis of what we can now call the Second Republic. *Fortune* could rave its approval of the theory of "creative federalism," despite its coinage by Lyndon Johnson, as "a relation, cooperative and competitive, between a limited central power and other powers that are essentially independent of it . . . a new way of organizing Federal programs . . . [in which simultaneously] the power of states and local governments will increase; the power of private organizations, including businesses, will increase; the power of individuals will increase."[23] Similarly, one of the most articulate officials during the Kennedy-Johnson years could speak glowingly of the Republican notion of partnership: "To speak of 'federal aid' simply confuses the issue. It is more appropriate to speak of federal support to special purposes . . . [as] an investment made by a partner who has clearly in mind the investments of other partners—local, state and private."[24]

In sum, leaders in modern, consensual democracies are ambivalent about government. Government is obviously the most efficacious way of achieving good purposes, but alas, it is efficacious because it is coercive. To live with that ambivalence, modern policy-makers have fallen prey to the belief that public policy involves merely the identification of the problems toward which government ought to be aimed. It pretends that through "pluralism," "countervailing power," "creative federalism," "partnership," and "participatory democracy" the unsentimental business of coercion need not be involved and that unsentimental decisions about how to employ coercion need not really be made at all. Stated in the extreme, the policies of interest-group liberalism are end-oriented but ultimately self-defeating. Few standards of implementation, if any, accompany delegations of power. The requirement of standards has been replaced by the requirement of participation. The requirement of law has been replaced by the requirement of contingency. As a result, the ends of interest-group liberalism are nothing more than sentiments and therefore not really ends at all.

The Flawed Foundation of Interest-Group Liberalism: Pluralism   Everyone operates according to some theory or frame of reference, or paradigm—some generalized map that directs logic and conclusions, given certain facts. The influence of a paradigm over decisions is incalculably large. It helps define what is important among the multitudes of events. It literally programs the decision-maker toward certain kinds of conclusions. People are unpredictable if they do not share some elements of a common theory. Pragmatism is merely an appeal to let theory remain implicit, but there is all too much truth in Lord Keynes's epigram . . .:

> . . . the ideas of economists and political philosophers, both when they are right and when they are wrong, are more powerful than is commonly understood.
> . . . Practical men, who believe themselves to be quite exempt from any intellectual influences, are usually the slaves of some defunct economist. Madmen in authority, who hear voices in the air, are distilling their frenzy from some academic scribbler of a few years back.

Interest-group liberals have the pluralist paradigm in common and its influence on the policies of the modern state has been very large and very consistent. Practices of government are likely to change only if there is a serious reexamination of the theoretical components of the public philosophy and if that reexamination reveals basic flaws in the theory. Because they guide so much of the analysis of succeeding chapters, contentions about the fundamental flaws in the theory underlying interest-group liberals ought to be made explicit here at the outset. Among the many charges to be made against pluralism, the following three probably best anticipate the analysis to come.

1. The pluralist component has badly served liberalism by propagating the faith that a system built primarily upon groups and bargaining is self-corrective. Some parts of this faith are false, some have never been tested one way or the other, and others can be confirmed only under very special conditions. For example, there is the faulty assumption that groups have other groups to confront in some kind of competition. Another very weak assumption is that people have more than one salient group, that their multiple or overlapping memberships will insure competition, and at the same time will keep competition from becoming too intense. This concept of overlapping membership is also supposed to prove the voluntary character of groups, since it reassures us that even though one group may be highly undemocratic, people can vote with their feet by moving over to some other group to represent their interests. Another assumption that has become an important liberal myth is that when competition between or among groups takes place the results yield a public interest or some other ideal result. As has already been observed, this assumption was borrowed from laissez-faire economists and has even less probability of being borne out in the political system. One of the major Keynesian criticisms of market theory is that even if pure competition among factors of supply and demand did yield an equilibrium, the equilibrium could be at something far less than the ideal of full employment at reasonable prices. Pure pluralist competition, similarly, might produce political equilibrium, but the experience of recent years shows that it occurs at something far below an acceptable level of legitimacy, or access, or equality, or innovation, or any other valued political commodity.

2. Pluralist theory is also comparable to laissez-faire economics in the extent to which it is unable to come to terms with the problem of imperfect competition. When a program is set up in a specialized agency, the number of organized interest groups surrounding it tends to be reduced, reduced precisely to those groups and factions to whom the specialization is most salient. That almost immediately transforms the situation from one of potential competition to one of potential oligopoly. As in the economic marketplace, political groups surrounding an agency ultimately learn that direct confrontation leads to net loss for all the competitors. Rather than countervailing power there is more likely to be accommodating power. Most observers and practitioners continue to hold on to the notion of group competition despite their own recognition that it is far from a natural state. Galbraith was early to recognize this but is by no means alone in his position that "the support of countervailing power has become in modern times perhaps the major peace-time function of the Federal government."[25] Group competition in Congress and around agencies is not much of a theory if it requires constant central government support.

3. The pluralist paradigm depends upon an idealized conception of the group. Laissez-faire economics may have idealized the enterprise and the entrepreneur but never more than the degree to which the pluralist sentimentalizes the group, the group member, and the interests. We have already noted the contrast between the traditional American or Madisonian definition of the group as adverse to the aggregate interests of the community with the modern view that groups are basically good things unless they break the law or the rules of the game. To the Madisonian, groups were a necessary evil much in need of regulation. To the modern pluralist, groups are good, requiring only accommodation. Madison went beyond his definition of the group to a position that "the regulation of these various interfering interests forms the principal task of modern legislation." This is a far cry from the sentimentality behind such notions as "supportive countervailing power," "group representation in the interior processes of . . . ," and "maximum feasible participation."

The Costs of Interest-Group Liberalism   The problems of pluralist theory are of more than academic interest. They are directly and indirectly responsible for some of the most costly attributes of modern government: (1) the atrophy of institutions of popular control; (2) the maintenance of old and the creation of new structures of privilege; and (3) conservatism in several senses of the word. [. . .]

1. In *The Public Philosophy*, Walter Lippmann was rightfully concerned over the "derangement of power" whereby modern democracies tend first toward unchecked elective leadership and then toward drainage of public authority from elective leaders down into the constituencies. However, Lippmann erred if he thought of constituents as only voting constituencies. Drainage has tended toward "support-group constituencies," and with special consequences. Parceling out policy-making power to the most interested parties tends strongly to destroy political responsibility. A program split off with a special imperium to govern itself is not merely an administrative unit. It is a structure of power with impressive capacities to resist central political control.

When conflict of interest is made a principle of government rather than a criminal act, programs based upon such a principle cut out all of that part of the mass of people who are not specifically organized around values salient to the goals of that program. The people are shut out at the most creative phase of policy-making—where the problem is first defined. The public is shut out also at the phase of accountability because in theory there is enough accountability to the immediate surrounding interests. In fact, presidents and congressional committees are most likely to investigate an agency when a complaint is brought to them by one of the most interested organizations. As a further consequence, the accountability we do get is functional rather than substantive; and this involves questions of equity, balance, and equilibrium, to the exclusion of questions of the overall social policy and whether or not the program should be maintained at all. It also means accountability to experts first and amateurs last; and an expert is a person trained and skilled in the mysteries and technologies of that particular program.[26]

Finally, in addition to the natural tendencies, there tends also to be a self-conscious conspiracy to shut out the public. One meaningful illustration, precisely because it is such an absurd extreme, is found in the French system of interest representation in the Fourth Republic. As the Communist-controlled union, the Confédération Générale du Travail (CGT), intensified its participation in postwar French government, it was able to influence representatives of interests other than employees. In a desperate effort to insure that the interests represented on the various boards were separated and competitive, the government issued a decree that "each member of the board must be *independent of the interests he is not representing.*"[27]

2. Programs following the principles of interest-group liberalism tend to create and maintain privilege; and it is a type of privilege particularly hard to bear or combat because it is touched with a symbolism of the state. Interest-group liberalism is not merely pluralism but is *sponsored* pluralism. Pluralists ease our consciences about the privileges of organized groups by characterizing them as representative and by responding to their "iron law of oligarchy" by arguing that oligarchy is simply a negative name for organization. Our consciences were already supposed to be partly reassured by the notion of "overlapping memberships." But however true it may be that overlapping memberships exist and that oligarchy is simply a way of leading people efficiently toward their interests, the value of these characteristics changes entirely when they are taken from the context of politics and put into the context of pluralistic government. The American Farm Bureau Federation is no "voluntary association" if it is a legitimate functionary within the extension system. Such tightly knit corporate groups as the National Association of Home

Builders (NAHB), the National Association of Real Estate Boards (NAREB), the National Association for the Advancement of Colored People (NAACP), or the National Association of Manufacturers (NAM) or American Federation of Labor-Congress of Industrial Organizations (AFL-CIO) are no ordinary lobbies after they become part of the "interior processes" of policy formation. Even in the War on Poverty, one can only appreciate the effort to organize the poor by going back and pondering the story and characters in *The Three Penny Opera*. The "Peachum factor" in public affairs may be best personified in Sargent Shriver and his strenuous efforts to get the poor housed in some kind of group before their representation was to begin.

The more clear and legitimized the representation of a group or its leaders in policy formation, the less voluntary its membership in that group and the more necessary is loyalty to its leadership for people who share the interests in question. And, the more widespread the policies of recognizing and sponsoring organized interest, the more hierarchy is introduced into our society. It is a well-recognized and widely appreciated function of formal groups in modern society to provide much of the necessary everyday social control. However, when the very thought processes behind public policy are geared toward these groups they are bound to take on the involuntary character of *public* control.

3. The conservative tendencies of interest-group liberalism can already be seen in the two foregoing objections: weakening of popular control and support of privilege. A third dimension of conservatism, stressed here separately, is the simple conservatism of resistance to change. David Truman, who has certainly not been a strong critic of self-government by interest groups, has, all the same, provided about the best statement of the general tendency of established agency-group relationships to be "highly resistant to disturbance":

> New and expanded functions are easily accommodated, provided they develop and operate through existing channels of influence and do not tend to alter the relative importance of those influences. Disturbing changes are those that modify either the content or the relative strength of the component forces operating through an administrative agency. In the face of such changes, or the threat of them, the "old line" agency is highly inflexible.[28]

If this already is a tendency in a pluralistic system, then agency-group relationships must be all the more inflexible to the extent that the relationship is official and legitimate.

[. . .] Old and established groups doing good works naturally look fearfully upon the emergence of competing, perhaps hostile, new groups. That is an acceptable and healthy part of the political game—until the competition between them is a question of "who shall be the government?" At that point conservatism becomes a matter of survival for each group, and a direct threat to the public interest. Ultimately this threat will be recognized.

The New Representation: A Second Republic?

If ambivalence toward government power is a trait common to all democracies, American leaders possess it to an uncommon degree. Their lives are dedicated to achieving it, and their spirits are tied up with justifying it. They were late to insist upon the expansion of national government, and when the expansion finally did begin to take place, it only intensified the ambivalence. *With each significant expansion of government during the past century, there has been a crisis of public authority. And each crisis of public authority has been accompanied by demands for expansion of representation.*

The clearest case in point is probably the first, the commitment by the federal government beginning with the Interstate Commerce Act of 1887, to intervene regularly in the economic life of the country. The political results of the expansion were more immediate and effective than the economic consequences of the statutes themselves. The call went out for congressional reform of its rules, for direct election of senators, for reform in nominating processes, for reform in the ballot, for decentralization of House leadership, and so on. The results were dramatic, including "Reed's Rules" in the House, direct election of senators, the direct primary movement, the Australian ballot, and the "Speaker Revolt." This is also the period during which some of the most important national interest groups were organized.

Expansion of government during the Wilson period was altogether intertwined with demands by progressives for reform and revision in the mechanisms of representation: female suffrage (Nineteenth Amendment), the short ballot, initiative, referendum and recall, great extensions of direct primaries, the commission form of city government, and the first and early demands for formal interest representation—leading to such things as the formal sponsorship of the formation of Chambers of Commerce by the Commerce Department, government sponsorship of the formation of the Farm Bureau movement, the establishment of the separate clientele-oriented Departments of Labor and Commerce, and the first experiments with "self-regulation" during the World War I industrial mobilization.

The Roosevelt revolution brought on more of the same but made its own special contribution as well. Perhaps the most fundamental change in representation to accompany expanded government was the development and articulation of the theory and practice of the administrative process. Obviously the more traditional demands for reform in actual practices of representation continued. Reapportionment became extremely important; demands for reform produced the Administrative Procedure Act and the congressional reforms embodied in the 1946 LaFollette–Monroney Act. But probably of more lasting importance during and since that time has been the emergence of interest-group liberalism as the answer to the problems of government power. The new jurisprudence of administrative law is a key factor, to me the most important single factor. The new halo words alone indicate the extent to which new ideas of representation now dominate: *interest representation, cooperation, partnership, self-regulation, delegation of power, local option, creative federalism, community action, maximum feasible participation,* Nixon's *new federalism,* and even that odd contribution from the 1960s New Left— *participatory democracy.*

In whatever form and by whatever label, the purpose of representation and of reform in representation is the same: to deal with the problem of power—to bring the democratic spirit into some kind of psychological balance with the harsh reality of government coerciveness. The problem is that the new representation embodied in the broad notion of interest-group liberalism is a pathological adjustment to the problem. Interest-group liberal solutions to the problem of power provide the system with stability by spreading a *sense* of representation at the expense of genuine flexibility, at the expense of democratic forms, and ultimately at the expense of legitimacy. Prior solutions offered by progressives and other reformers built greater instabilities into the system by attempting to reduce the lag between social change and government policy. But that was supposed to be the purpose of representation. Flexibility and legitimacy could only have been reduced by building representation upon the oligopolistic character of interest groups, reducing the number of competitors, favoring the best organized competitors, specializing politics around agencies, ultimately limiting participation to channels provided by preexisting groups.

Among all these, the weakest element of interest-group liberalism, and the element around which all the rest is most likely to crumble, is the antagonism of interest-group liberal solution to formalism. The least obvious, yet perhaps the most important, aspect of this is the antagonism of interest-group liberalism to law. Traditional expansions of representation were predicated upon an assumption that expanded participation would produce changes in government policies expressed in laws that would very quickly make a difference to the problems around which the representation process had been activated. Since the "new representation" extends the principle of representation into administration, it must either oppose the making of law in legislatures or favor vague laws and broad delegations of power that make it possible for administrative agencies to engage in representation. This tends to derange almost all established relationships and expectations in a republic. By rendering formalism impotent, it impairs legitimacy by converting government from a moralistic to a mechanistic institution. It impairs the potential of positive law to correct itself by allowing the law to become anything that eventually bargains itself out as acceptable to the bargainers. It impairs the very process of administration itself by delegating to administration alien material—policies that are not laws and authorizations that must be made into policies. Interest-group liberalism seeks pluralistic government, in which there is no formal specification of means or of ends. In a pluralistic government there is, therefore, no substance. Neither is there procedure. There is only process.

Notes

1. Clinton Rossiter. *Conservatism in America* (New York: Knopf, 1955), pp. 12, 15. The term *conservative* came to be attached to nineteenth-century liberals because they favored the government and social order that had become the established fact of the nineteenth-century United States. There is other conservatism in America—racial, aristocratic, ethnic, perhaps even monarchic and feudalistic. But the major part of it is nineteenth-century liberalism grown cold with success. This already suggests the narrow span of the ideological gamut in the United States.

2. The method of analysis is drawn from R. A. Dahl and C. E. Lindblom, *Politics, Economics, and Welfare* (New York: Harper & Brothers, 1953), Chapter 1, although the two of them may not necessarily agree with the particular uses here.

3. Placement along the continuum is gross and informal. However, it is very doubtful that any placement of these policies could reduce the spread from left to right. Moreover, differences of opinion as to the effect of a policy upon society would lead to the very kind of policy analysis political scientists need to get involved in.

4. Some readers will argue that there is still another dimension of difference, attitudes toward equality and welfare. Adding a third dimension to a diagram of this sort would overly complicate matters, but some response to this kind of objection can be made textually: (1) The equality dimension is already implicitly present in the sense that the policies to the left of the continuum tend to produce "change toward equality." However, (2) "equality" is a tendency produced by some private policies as well as public policies. Furthermore, (3) many public policies *reduce* the forces of equality (as well as change). Those in the upper right quadrant of the chart serve as examples. Welfare is no better a basis for distinguishing positions. (1) No definition of welfare could put it strictly within the province of the public or of the private sphere. And (2), no definition of "effect on welfare" would eliminate the enormous spread of public policies from left to right along the continuum.

5. For an effort to assess dispassionately the economic significance of tax exemptions and the political difficulties of reforming the tax structure, see Stanley S. Surrey, *Pathways to Tax Reform* (Cambridge, Mass.: Harvard University Press, 1973). For a lively account of some of the same problems, see Philip M. Stern, *The Rape of the Taxpayer* (New York: Random House, 1973).

6. Many more details will be found in *The End of Liberalism*, Chapter 8. For an independent but related critique, see Francis Piven and Richard Cloward, *Regulating the Poor* (New York: Pantheon, 1971).

7. See *The End of Liberalism*, Chapter 4.

8. This particular tendency is pursued elaborately in a book of mine, *The Politics of Disorder* (New York: Basic Books, 1971), see especially Chapters 1 and 2.

9. For an excellent inquiry into this assumption and into the realities of the internal life of organized interests, see Grant McConnell, *Private Power and American Democracy* (New York: Knopf, 1966); S. M. Lipset et al., *Union Democracy* (New York: Anchor, 1962); and Raymond Bauer et al., *American Business and Public Policy* (New York: Atherton, 1963).

10. It is assumed that countervailing power usually crops up somehow, but when it does not, government ought help create it. See John Kenneth Galbraith, *American Capitalism* (Boston: Houghton Mifflin, 1952). Among a number of excellent critiques of the so-called pluralist model, see especially William E. Connolly, ed., *The Bias of Pluralism* (New York: Atherton 1969).

11. See *The End of Liberalism*, Chapters 2 and 11.

12. Alvin H. Hansen, *The American Economy* (New York: McGraw-Hill, 1957), p. 152.

13. Ibid., pp. 158–59. Keynes himself said, "the Class War will find me on the side of the educated bourgeoisie" (Ibid., p. 158).

14. For a critique of the majoritarian basis of presidential authority see Willmoore Kendall, "The Two Majorities," *Midwest Journal of Political Science* 4 (1960): 317–45. The abdication by Congress to the Executive Branch will come up again and again throughout this volume.

15. For an account of Herbert Hoover's political views and his close relationship to the New Deal, see Grant McConnell, *Private Power*, pp. 62 ff; and Peri Arnold, "Herbert Hoover and the Continuity of American Public Policy," *Public Policy* (Autumn 1972).

16. E. Pendleton Herring, *Group Representation before Congress* (Baltimore: Johns Hopkins Press, 1929), p. 268. See his reflections of 1936 in Chapter 2 of that book.

17. Wilfred Binkley and Malcolm Moos, *A Grammar of American Politics* (New York: Knopf, 1950), p. 7. Malcolm Moos became an important idea man in the Eisenhower Administration.

18. Galbraith, *American Capitalism*, p. 118.

19. Arthur Schlesinger, Jr., *Kennedy or Nixon—Does It Make Any Difference?* (New York: Macmillan, 1960), p. 43.

20. Arthur Schlesinger, *A Thousand Days*, as featured in the *Chicago Sun-Times*, January 23, 1966, section 2, p. 3.

21. Max Ways, " 'Creative Federalism' and the Great Society," *Fortune*, January 1966, p. 122.

22. David Truman, *The Governmental Process* (New York: Knopf, 1951), p. 4.

23. Ibid., p. 122. See also *Wall Street Journal*, March 16, 1966, for another positive treatment of creative federalism.

24. Francis Keppel, while assistant secretary for education, quoted in *Congressional Quarterly, Weekly Report*, April 22, 1966, p. 833.

25. *American Capitalism*, p. 136.

26. These propositions are best illustrated by the ten or more separate, self-governing systems in agriculture, in *The End of Liberalism*, Chapter 4.

27. Mario Einaudi et al., *Nationalization in France and Italy* (Ithaca: Cornell University Press, 1955), pp. 100–101. (Emphasis added.)

28. *The Governmental Process*, pp. 467–68.

The Theory of Economic Regulation

GEORGE J. STIGLER

In this classic article, University of Chicago economist George J. Stigler outlines a theory of the supply and demand for economic regulation that was sharply at odds with then prevailing "public interest" views. Instead of maintaining that regulation is supplied in response to public outcry over inefficient or inequitable market practices, Stigler argues that "as a rule, regulation is acquired by [an] industry and is designed and operated primarily for its benefit." Economic regulation is seen here as an explicit attempt to shield firms from competition. It may take many different forms, of course, but in Stigler's view the incidence of any of those forms follows from the straightforward hypothesis that "every industry or occupation that has enough political power to utilize the state will seek to control entry." Regulation is thus one way to achieve the many benefits of cartelization, and the decision to pursue the regulatory route to such benefits is shaped chiefly by prudent calculation of the offsetting costs of obtaining regulatory legislation. On this account, regulation often implies shifting (sometimes enormous) losses onto the consumers of a given good. The costs of achieving regulation within a majoritarian liberal democracy might thus be thought to be extremely high. But Stigler argues that the wide discretion of elected representatives and the prevalence of the "uninterested" voter significantly reduce these potential costs. Coalitions of voters united only in their opposition to particular instances of regulatory largesse are rarely able to punish representatives who heed industry requests. On the other hand, those same representatives commonly do derive tangible rewards for their compliance from the affected industries.

One of the great merits of the Stigler "economic theory" of economic regulation is that it is more amenable to empirical testing than are competing accounts. In addition to stating the rudiments of his approach, in the excerpt below Stigler reports on some attempts to test the theory.

T he state—the machinery and power of the state—is a potential resource or threat to every industry in the society. With its power to prohibit or compel, to take or give money, the state can and does selectively help or hurt a vast number of industries. That political juggernaut, the petroleum industry, is an immense consumer of political benefits, and simultaneously the underwriters of marine insurance have their more modest repast. The central tasks of the theory of economic regulation are to explain who will receive the benefits or burdens of regulation, what form regulation will take, and the effects of regulation upon the allocation of resources.

Reprinted with permission from *The Bell Journal of Economics and Management Science*, Vol. 2, No. 1 (Spring 1971), pp. 3-21 (with deletions). Copyright 1971, The American Telephone and Telegraph Company.

Regulation may be actively sought by an industry, or it may be thrust upon it. A central thesis of this paper is that, as a rule, regulation is acquired by the industry and is designed and operated primarily for its benefit. There are regulations whose net effects upon the regulated industry are undeniably onerous; a simple example is the differentially heavy taxation of the industry's product (whiskey, playing cards). These onerous regulations, however, are exceptional and can be explained by the same theory that explains beneficial (we may call it "acquired") regulation.

Two main alternative views of the regulation of industry are widely held. The first is that regulation is instituted primarily for the protection and benefit of the public at large or some large subclass of the public. In this view, the regulations which injure the public—as when the oil import quotas increase the cost of petroleum products to America by $5 billion or more a year—are costs of some social goal (here, national defense) or, occasionally, perversions of the regulatory philosophy. The second view is essentially that the political process defies rational explanation: "politics" is an imponderable, a constantly and unpredictably shifting mixture of forces of the most diverse nature, comprehending acts of great moral virtue (the emancipation of slaves) and of the most vulgar venality (the congressman feathering his own nest).

Let us consider a problem posed by the oil import quota system: why does not the powerful industry which obtained this expensive program instead choose direct cash subsidies from the public treasury? The "protection of the public" theory of regulation must say that the choice of import quotas is dictated by the concern of the federal government for an adequate domestic supply of petroleum in the event of war—a remark calculated to elicit uproarious laughter at the Petroleum Club. Such laughter aside, if national defense were the goal of the quotas, a tariff would be a more economical instrument of policy: it would retain the profits of exclusion for the treasury. The nonrationalist view would explain the policy by the inability of consumers to measure the cost to them of the import quotas, and hence their willingness to pay $5 billion in higher prices rather than the $2.5 billion in cash that would be equally attractive to the industry. Our profit-maximizing theory says that the explanation lies in a different direction: the present members of the refining industries would have to share a cash subsidy with all new entrants into the refining industry.[1] Only when the elasticity of supply of an industry is small will the industry prefer cash to controls over entry or output.

This question, why does an industry solicit the coercive powers of the state rather than its cash, is offered only to illustrate the approach of the present paper. We assume that political systems are rationally devised and rationally employed, which is to say that they are appropriate instruments for the fulfillment of desires of members of the society. This is not to say that the state will serve any person's concept of the public interest: indeed the problem of regulation is the problem of discovering when and why an industry (or other group of like-minded people) is able to use the state for its purposes, or is singled out by the state to be used for alien purposes.

1. What Benefits Can a State Provide to an Industry?

The state has one basic resource which in pure principle is not shared with even the mightiest of its citizens: the power to coerce. The state can seize money by the only method which is permitted by the laws of a civilized society, by taxation. The state can ordain the physical movements of resources and the economic decisions of households and firms without their consent. These powers provide the possibilities for the utilization of the state by an industry to increase its profitability. The main policies which an industry (or occupation) may seek of the state are four.

The most obvious contribution that a group may seek of the government is a direct subsidy of money. The domestic airlines received "air mail" subsidies (even if they did not carry mail) of $1.5 billion through 1968. The merchant marine has received construction and operation subsidies reaching almost $3 billion since World War II. The education industry has long shown a masterful skill in obtaining public funds: for example, universities and colleges have received federal funds exceeding $3 billion annually in recent years, as well as subsidized loans for dormitories and other construction. The veterans of wars have often received direct cash bonuses.

We have already sketched the main explanation for the fact that an industry with power to obtain governmental favors usually does not use this power to get money: unless the list of beneficiaries can be limited by an acceptable device, whatever amount of subsidies the industry can obtain will be dissipated among a growing number of rivals. The airlines quickly moved away from competitive bidding for air mail contracts to avoid this problem.[2] On the other hand, the premier universities have not devised a method of excluding other claimants for research funds, and in the long run they will receive much-reduced shares of federal research monies.

The second major public resource commonly sought by an industry is control over entry by new rivals. There is considerable, not to say excessive, discussion in economic literature of the rise of peculiar price policies (limit prices), vertical integration, and similar devices to retard the rate of entry of new firms into oligopolistic industries. Such devices are vastly less efficacious (economical) than the certificate of convenience and necessity (which includes, of course, the import and production quotas of the oil and tobacco industries).

The diligence with which the power of control over entry will be exercised by a regulatory body is already well known. The Civil Aeronautics Board has not allowed a single new trunk line to be launched since it was created in 1938. The power to insure new banks has been used by the Federal Deposit Insurance Corporation to reduce the rate of entry into commercial banking by 60 percent.[3] The interstate motor carrier history is in some respects even more striking, because no even ostensibly respectable case for restriction on entry can be developed on grounds of scale economies (which are in turn adduced to limit entry for safety or economy of operation). [. . .]

We propose the general hypothesis: every industry or occupation that has enough political power to utilize the state will seek to control entry. In addition, the regulatory policy will often be so fashioned as to retard the rate of growth of new firms. For example, no new savings and loan company may pay a dividend rate higher than that prevailing in the community in its endeavors to attract deposits.[4] The power to limit selling expenses of mutual funds, which is soon to be conferred upon the Securities and Exchange Commission, will serve to limit the growth of small mutual funds and hence reduce the sales costs of large funds.

One variant of the control of entry is the protective tariff (and the corresponding barriers which have been raised to interstate movements of goods and people). The benefits of protection to an industry, one might think, will usually be dissipated by the entry of new domestic producers, and the question naturally arises: Why does the industry not also seek domestic entry controls? In a few industries (petroleum) the domestic controls have been obtained, but not in most. The tariff will be effective if there is a specialized domestic resource necessary to the industry; oil-producing lands is an example. Even if an industry has only durable specialized resources, it will gain if its contraction is slowed by a tariff.

A third general set of powers of the state which will be sought by the industry are those which affect substitutes and complements. Crudely put, the butter producers wish to suppress margarine and encourage the production of bread. The airline industry actively supports the federal subsidies to airports; the building trade unions have opposed labor-saving materials through building codes. We shall examine shortly a specific case of inter-industry competition in transportation.

The fourth class of public policies sought by an industry is directed to price-fixing. Even the industry that has achieved entry control will often want price controls administered by a body with coercive powers. If the number of firms in the regulated industry is even moderately large, price discrimination will be difficult to maintain in the absence of public support. The prohibition of interest on demand deposits, which is probably effective in preventing interest payments to most non-business depositors, is a case in point. Where there are no diseconomies of large scale for the individual firm (e.g., a motor trucking firm can add trucks under a given license as common carrier), price control is essential to achieve more than competitive rates of return.

Limitations upon Political Benefits   These various political boons are not obtained by the industry in a pure profit-maximizing form. The political process erects certain limitations upon the exercise of cartel policies by an industry. These limitations are of three sorts.

First, the distribution of control of the industry among the firms in the industry is changed. In an unregulated industry each firm's influence upon price and output is proportional to its share of industry output (at least in a simple arithmetic sense of direct capacity to change output). The political decisions take account also of the political strength of the various firms, so small firms have a larger influence than they would possess in an unregulated industry. Thus, when quotas are given to firms, the small firms will almost always receive larger quotas than cost-minimizing practices would allow. The original quotas under the oil import quota system will illustrate this practice (Table 1). The smallest refiners were given a quota of 11.4 percent of their daily consumption of oil,

---

Table 1

**Import Quotas of Refineries as Percent of
Daily Input of Petroleum
(Districts I–IV, 1 July—31 December 1959)**

Size of Refinery (thousands of barrels)	Percent Quota
0–10	11.4
10–20	10.4
20–30	9.5
30–60	8.5
60–100	7.6
100–150	6.6
150–200	5.7
200–300	4.7
300+	3.8

Source: Hearing, Select Committee on Small Business, U.S. Congress, 88th Cong., 2nd Session, August 10 and 11, 1964 [12], p. 121.

and the percentage dropped as refinery size rose.[5] The pattern of regressive benefits is characteristic of public controls in industries with numerous firms.

Second, the procedural safeguards required of public processes are costly. The delays which are dictated by both law and bureaucratic thoughts of self-survival can be large: Robert Gerwig found the price of gas sold in interstate commerce to be 5 to 6 percent higher than in intrastate commerce because of the administrative costs (including delay) of Federal Power Commission reviews [5].

Finally, the political process automatically admits powerful outsiders to the industry's councils. It is well known that the allocation of television channels among communities does not maximize industry revenue but reflects pressures to serve many smaller communities. The abandonment of an unprofitable rail line is an even more notorious area of outsider participation.

These limitations are predictable, and they must all enter into the calculus of the profitability of regulation of an industry.

An Illustrative Analysis   The recourse to the regulatory process is of course more specific and more complex than the foregoing sketch suggests. The defensive power of various other industries which are affected by the proposed regulation must also be taken into account. An analysis of one aspect of the regulation of motor trucking will illustrate these complications. At this stage we are concerned only with the correspondence between regulations and economic interests; later we shall consider the political process by which regulation is achieved.

The motor trucking industry operated almost exclusively within cities before 1925, in good part because neither powerful trucks nor good roads were available for long-distance freight movements. As these deficiencies were gradually remedied, the share of trucks in intercity freight movements began to rise, and by 1930 it was estimated to be 4 percent of ton-miles of intercity freight. The railroad industry took early cognizance of this emerging competitor, and one of the methods by which trucking was combatted was state regulation.

By the early 1930's all states regulated the dimensions and weight of trucks. The weight limitations were a much more pervasive control over trucking than the licensing of common carriers because even the trucks exempt from entry regulation are subject to the limitations on dimensions and capacity. [. . .] Sometimes the participation of railroads in the regulatory process was incontrovertible: Texas and Louisiana placed a 7000-pound payload limit on trucks serving (and hence competing with) two or more railroad stations, and a 14,000-pound limit on trucks serving only one station (hence, not competing with it).

We seek to determine the pattern of weight limits on trucks that would emerge in response to the economic interests of the concerned parties. The main considerations appear to be the following:

(1) Heavy trucks would be allowed in states with a substantial number of trucks on farms: the powerful agricultural interests would insist upon this. The 1930 Census reports nearly one million trucks on farms. One variable in our study will be, for each state, trucks per 1000 of agricultural population.[6]

(2) Railroads found the truck an effective and rapidly triumphing competitor in the shorter hauls and hauls of less than carload traffic, but much less effective in the carload and longer-haul traffic. Our second variable for each state is, therefore, length of average railroad haul.[7] The longer the average rail haul is, the less the railroads will be opposed to trucks.

(3) The public at large would be concerned by the potential damage done to the

highway system by heavy trucks. The better the state highway system, the heavier the trucks that would be permitted. The percentage of each state's highways that had a high type surface is the third variable. Of course good highways are more likely to exist where the potential contribution of trucks to a state's economy is greater, so the causation may be looked at from either direction.

We have two measures of weight limits on trucks, one for 4-wheel trucks (X_1) and one for 6-wheel trucks (X_2). We may then calculate two equations,

$$X_1 \text{ (or } X_2) = a + bX_3 + cX_4 + dX_5,$$

where

X_3 = trucks per 1000 agricultural labor force, 1930,
X_4 = average length of railroad haul of freight traffic, 1930,
X_5 = percentage of state roads with high-quality surface, 1930.

The three explanatory variables are statistically significant, and each works in the expected direction. The regulations on weight were less onerous; the larger the truck population in farming, the less competitive the trucks were to railroads (i.e., the longer the rail hauls), and the better the highway system.

The foregoing analysis is concerned with what may be termed the industrial demand for governmental powers. Not every industry will have a significant demand for public assistance (other than money!), meaning the prospect of a substantial increase in the present value of the enterprises even if the governmental services could be obtained gratis (and of course they have costs to which we soon turn). In some economic activities entry of new rivals is extremely difficult to control—consider the enforcement problem in restricting the supply of domestic servants. In some industries the substitute products cannot be efficiently controlled—consider the competition offered to bus lines by private car-pooling. Price fixing is not feasible where every unit of the product has a different quality and price, as in the market for used automobiles. In general, however, most industries will have a positive demand price (schedule) for the services of government.

2. The Costs of Obtaining Legislation

When an industry receives a grant of power from the state, the benefit to the industry will fall short of the damage to the rest of the community. Even if there were no deadweight losses from acquired regulation, however, one might expect a democratic society to reject such industry requests unless the industry controlled a majority of the votes.[8] A direct and informed vote on oil import quotas would reject the scheme. (If it did not, our theory of rational political processes would be contradicted.) To explain why many industries are able to employ the political machinery to their own ends, we must examine the nature of the political process in a democracy.

A consumer chooses between rail and air travel, for example, by voting with his pocketbook: he patronizes on a given day that mode of transportation he prefers. A similar form of economic voting occurs with decisions on where to work or where to invest one's capital. The market accumulates these economic votes, predicts their future course, and invests accordingly.

Because the political decision is coercive, the decision process is fundamentally different from that of the market. If the public is asked to make a decision between two transportation media comparable to the individual's decision on how to travel—say, whether airlines or railroads should receive a federal subsidy—the decision must be abided by everyone, travellers and non-travellers, travellers this year and travellers next year. This compelled universality of political decisions makes for two differences between democratic political decision processes and market processes.

(1) The decisions must be made simultaneously by a large number of persons (or their representatives): the political process demands simultaneity of decision. If A were to vote on the referendum today, B tomorrow, C the day after, and so on, the accumulation of a majority decision would be both expensive and suspect. (A might wish to cast a different vote now than last month.)

The condition of simultaneity imposes a major burden upon the political decision process. It makes voting on specific issues prohibitively expensive: it is a significant cost even to engage in the transaction of buying a plane ticket when I wish to travel: it would be stupendously expensive to me to engage in the physically similar transaction of voting (i.e., patronizing a polling place) whenever a number of my fellow citizens desired to register their views on railroads versus airplanes. To cope with this condition of simultaneity, the voters must employ representatives with wide discretion and must eschew direct expressions of marginal changes in preferences. This characteristic also implies that the political decision does not predict voter desires and make preparations to fulfill them in advance of their realization.

(2) The democratic decision process must involve "all" the community, not simply those who are directly concerned with a decision. In a private market, the non-traveller never votes on rail versus plane travel, while the huge shipper casts many votes each day. The political decision process cannot exclude the uninterested voter: the abuses of any exclusion except self-exclusion are obvious. Hence, the political process does not allow participation in proportion to interest and knowledge. In a measure, this difficulty is moderated by other political activities besides voting which do allow a more effective vote to interested parties: persuasion, employment of skilled legislative representatives, etc. Nevertheless, the political system does not offer good incentives like those in private markets to the acquisition of knowledge. If I consume ten times as much of public service A (streets) as of B (schools), I do not have incentives to acquire corresponding amounts of knowledge about the public provision of these services.[9]

These characteristics of the political process can be modified by having numerous levels of government (so I have somewhat more incentive to learn about local schools than about the whole state school system) and by selective use of direct decision (bond referenda). The chief method of coping with the characteristics, however, is to employ more or less full-time representatives organized in (disciplined by) firms which are called political parties or machines.

The representative and his party are rewarded for their discovery and fulfillment of the political desires of their constituency by success in election and the perquisites of office. If the representative could confidently await reelection whenever he voted against an economic policy that injured the society, he would assuredly do so. Unfortunately virtue does not always command so high a price. If the representative denies ten large industries their special subsidies of money or governmental power, they will dedicate themselves to the election of a more complaisant successor: the stakes are that important. This does not mean that every large industry can get what it wants or all that it wants: it does mean that the representative and his party must find a coalition of voter interests more durable than the anti-industry side of every industry policy proposal. A representative cannot win or keep office with the support of the sum of those who are opposed to: oil import quotas, farm subsidies, airport subsidies, hospital subsidies, unnecessary navy shipyards, an inequitable public housing program, and rural electrification subsidies.

The political decision process has as its dominant characteristic infrequent, universal (in principle) participation, as we have noted: political decisions must be infrequent and they must be global. The voter's expenditure to learn the merits of individual policy proposals and to express his preferences (by individual and group representation as well as by voting) are determined by expected costs and returns, just as they are in the private marketplace. The costs of comprehensive information are higher in the political arena because information must be sought on many issues of little or no direct concern to the individual, and accordingly he will know little about most matters before the legislature. The expressions of preferences in voting will be less precise than the expressions of preferences in the marketplace because many uninformed people will be voting and affecting the decision.[10]

The channels of political decision-making can thus be described as gross or filtered or noisy. If everyone has a negligible preference for policy A over B, the preference will not be discovered or acted upon. If voter group X wants a policy that injures non-X by a small amount, it will not pay non-X to discover this and act against the policy. The system is calculated to implement all strongly felt preferences of majorities and many strongly felt preferences of minorities but to disregard the lesser preferences of majorities and minorities. The filtering or grossness will be reduced by any reduction in the cost to the citizen of acquiring information and expressing desires and by any increase in the probability that his vote will influence policy.

The industry which seeks political power must go to the appropriate seller, the political party. The political party has costs of operation, costs of maintaining an organization and competing in elections. These costs of the political process are viewed excessively narrowly in the literature on the financing of elections: elections are to the political process what merchandizing is to the process of producing a commodity, only an essential final step. The party maintains its organization and electoral appeal by the performance of costly services to the voter at all times, not just before elections. Part of the costs of services and organization are borne by putting a part of the party's workers on the public payroll. An opposition party, however, is usually essential insurance for the voters to discipline the party in power, and the opposition party's costs are not fully met by public funds.

The industry which seeks regulation must be prepared to pay with the two things a party needs: votes and resources. The resources may be provided by campaign contributions, contributed services (the businessman heads a fund-raising committee), and more indirect methods such as the employment of party workers. The votes in support of the measure are rallied, and the votes in opposition are dispersed, by expensive programs to educate (or uneducate) members of the industry and of other concerned industries.

These costs of legislation probably increase with the size of the industry seeking the legislation. Larger industries seek programs which cost the society more and arouse more opposition from substantially affected groups. The tasks of persuasion, both within and without the industry, also increase with its size. The fixed size of the political "market," however, probably makes the cost of obtaining legislation increase less rapidly than industry size. The smallest industries are therefore effectively precluded from the political process unless they have some special advantage such as geographical concentration in a sparsely settled political subdivision.

If a political party has in effect a monopoly control over the governmental machine, one might expect that it could collect most of the benefits of regulation for itself. Political parties, however, are perhaps an ideal illustration of Demsetz' theory of natural monopoly [4]. If one party becomes extortionate (or badly mistaken in its reading of effective desires), it is possible to elect another party which will provide the governmental services at a price more closely proportioned to costs of the party. If entry into politics is effectively controlled, we should expect one-party dominance to lead that party to solicit requests for protective legislation but to exact a higher price for the legislation.

The internal structure of the political party, and the manner in which the perquisites of office are distributed among its members, offer fascinating areas for study in this context. The elective officials are at the pinnacle of the political system—there is no substitute for the ability to hold the public offices. I conjecture that much of the compensation to the legislative leaders takes the form of extra-political payments. Why are so many politicians lawyers?—because everyone employs lawyers, so the congressman's firm is a suitable avenue of compensation, whereas a physician would have to be given bribes rather than patronage. Most enterprises patronize insurance companies and banks, so we may expect that legislators commonly have financial affiliations with such enterprises.

The financing of industry-wide activities such as the pursuit of legislation raises the usual problem of the free rider.[11] We do not possess a satisfactory theory of group behavior—indeed this theory is the theory of oligopoly with one addition: in the very large number industry (e.g., agriculture) the political party itself will undertake the entrepreneurial role in providing favorable legislation. We can go no further than the infirmities of oligopoly theory allow, which is to say, we can make only plausible conjectures such as that the more concentrated the industry, the more resources it can invest in the campaign for legislation.

Occupational Licensing   The licensing of occupations is a possible use of the political process to improve the economic circumstances of a group. The license is an effective barrier to entry because occupational practice without the license is a criminal offense. Since much occupational licensing is performed at the state level, the area provides an opportunity to search for the characteristics of an occupation which give it political power.

Although there are serious data limitations, we may investigate several characteristics of an occupation which should influence its ability to secure political power:

(1) *The size of the occupation*. Quite simply, the larger the occupation, the more votes it has. (Under some circumstances, therefore, one would wish to exclude noncitizens from the measure of size.)

(2) *The per capita income of the occupation*. The income of the occupation is the product of its number and average income, so this variable and the preceding will reflect the total income of the occupation. The income of the occupation is presumably an index of the probable rewards of successful political action: in the absence of specific knowledge of supply and demand functions, we expect licensing to increase each occupation's equilibrium income by roughly the same proportion. In a more sophisticated version, one would predict that the less the elasticity of demand for the occupation's services, the more profitable licensing would be. One could also view the income of the occupation as a source of funds for political action, but if we view political action as an investment this is relevant only with capital-market imperfections.[12]

The average income of occupational members is an appropriate variable in comparisons among occupations, but it is inappropriate to comparisons of one occupation in various states because real income will be approximately equal (in the absence of regulation) in each state.

(3) *The concentration of the occupation in large cities*. When the occupation

organizes a campaign to obtain favorable legislation, it incurs expenses in the solicitation of support, and these are higher for a diffused occupation than a concentrated one. The solicitation of support is complicated by the free-rider problem in that individual members cannot be excluded from the benefits of legislation even if they have not shared the costs of receiving it. If most of the occupation is concentrated in a few large centers, these problems (we suspect) are much reduced in intensity: regulation may even begin at the local governmental level. We shall use an orthodox geographical concentration measure: the share of the occupation of the state in cities over 100,000 (or 50,000 in 1900 and earlier).

(4) *The presence of a cohesive opposition to licensing.* If an occupation deals with the public at large, the costs which licensing imposes upon any one customer or industry will be small and it will not be economic for that customer or industry to combat the drive for licensure. If the injured group finds it feasible and profitable to act jointly, however, it will oppose the effort to get licensure, and (by increasing its cost) weaken, delay, or prevent the legislation. The same attributes—numbers of voters, wealth, and ease of organization— which favor an occupation in the political arena, of course, favor also any adversary group. Thus, a small occupation employed by only one industry which has few employers will have difficulty in getting licensure; whereas a large occupation serving everyone will encounter no organized opposition.

An introductory statistical analysis of the licensing of select occupations by states is summarized in Table 2. In each occupation the dependent variable for each state is the year of first regulation of entry into the occupation. The two independent variables are

(1) the ratio of the occupation to the total labor force of the state in the census year nearest to the median year of regulation,

(2) the fraction of the occupation found in cities over 100,000 (over 50,000 in 1890 and 1900) in that same year.

We expect these variables to be negatively associated with year of licensure, and each of the nine statistically significant regression coefficients is of the expected sign.

The results are not robust, however: the multiple correlation coefficients are small, and over half of the regression coefficients are not significant (and in these cases often of inappropriate sign). Urbanization is more strongly associated than size of occupation with licensure.[13] The crudity of the data may be a large source of these disappointments: we measure, for example, the characteristics of the barbers in each state in 1930, but 14 states were licensing barbers by 1910. If the states which licensed barbering before 1910 had relatively more barbers, or more highly urbanized barbers, the predictions would be improved. The absence of data for years between censuses and before 1890 led us to make only the cruder analysis.[14]

In general, the larger occupations were licensed in earlier years.[15] Veterinarians are the only occupation in this sample who have a well-defined set of customers, namely livestock farmers, and licensing was later in those states with large numbers of livestock relative to rural population. The within-occupation analyses offer some support for the economic theory of the supply of legislation.

A comparison of different occupations allows us to examine several other variables. The first is income, already discussed above. The second is the size of the market. Just as it is impossible to organize an effective labor union in only one part of an integrated market, so it is impossible to regulate only one part of the market. Consider an occupation—junior business executives will do—which has a national market with high mobility of labor and significant mobility of employers. If the executives of one state were to organize, their scope for effective influence would be very small. If salaries were raised

Table 2

Initial Year of Regulation as a Function of
Relative Size of Occupation and Degree of Urbanization

Occupation	No. of states licensing	Median census year of licensing	Regression coefficients (and t-values)		R^2
			Size of occupation*	Urbanization**	
Beauticians	48	1930	—4.03 (2.50)	5.90 (1.24)	0.125
Architects	47	1930	—24.06 (2.15)	—6.29 (0.84)	0.184
Barbers	46	1930	—1.31 (0.51)	—26.10 (2.37)	0.146
Lawyers	29	1890	—0.26 (0.08)	—65.78 (1.70)	0.102
Physicians	43	1890	0.64 (0.65)	—23.80 (2.69)	0.165
Embalmers	37	1910	3.32 (0.36)	—4.24 (0.44)	0.007
Registered Nurses	48	1910	—2.08 (2.28)	—3.36 (1.06)	0.176
Dentists	48	1900	2.51 (0.44)	—22.94 (2.19)	0.103
Veterinarians	40	1910	—10.69 (1.94)	—37.16 (4.20)	0.329
Chiropractors	48	1930	—17.70 (1.54)	11.69 (1.25)	0.079
Pharmacists	48	1900	—4.19 (1.50)	—6.84 (0.80)	0.082

Source: The Council of State Governments, "Occupational Licensing Legislation in the States," 1952 [3] and *U.S. Census of Population* [15], various years.

*Relative to labor force.

**Share of occupation in cities over 50,000 for 1890 and 1900; otherwise, cities over 100,000.

above the competitive level, employers would often recruit elsewhere so the demand elasticity would be very high.[16] The third variable is stability of occupational membership: the longer the members are in the occupation, the greater their financial gain from control of entry. Our regrettably crude measure of this variable is based upon the number of members aged 35–44 in 1950 and aged 45–54 in 1960: the closer these numbers are, the more stable the membership of the occupation. The data for the various occupations are given in Table 3.

The comparison of licensed and unlicensed occupations is consistently in keeping with our expectations:

(1) the licensed occupations have higher incomes (also before licensing, one may assume),

(2) the membership of the licensed occupations is more stable (but the difference is negligible in our crude measure),

Table 3

Characteristics of Licensed and Unlicensed
Professional Occupations, 1960

Occupation	Median age (years)	Median educ. (years)	Median earnings (50-52 wks)	Instability of mbrshp*	% not self-empl.	% in cities over 50,000	% of labor force
Licensed:							
Architects	41.7	16.8	$9,090	0.012	57.8	44.1	0.045%
Chiropractors	46.5	16.4	6,360	0.053	5.8	30.8	0.020
Dentists	45.9	17.3	12,200	0.016	9.4	34.5	0.128
Embalmers	43.5	13.4	5,990	0.130	52.8	30.2	0.055
Lawyers	45.3	17.4	10,800	0.041	35.8	43.1	0.308
Prof. nurses	39.1	13.2	3,850	0.291	91.0	40.6	0.868
Optometrists	41.6	17.0	8,480	0.249	17.5	34.5	0.024
Pharmacists	44.9	16.2	7,230	0.119	62.3	40.0	0.136
Physicians	42.8	17.5	14,200	0.015	35.0	44.7	0.339
Veterinarians	39.2	17.4	9,210	0.169	29.5	14.4	0.023
Average	43.0	16.3	8,741	0.109	39.7	35.7	0.195
Partially licensed:							
Accountants	40.4	14.9	6,450	0.052	88.1	43.5	0.698
Engineers	38.3	16.2	8,490	0.023	96.8	31.6	1.279
El. schl.teachers	43.1	16.5	4,710	(a)	99.1	18.8	1.482
Average	40.6	15.9	6,550	0.117(b)	94.7	34.6	1.153
Unlicensed:							
Artists	38.0	14.2	5,920	0.103	77.3	45.7	0.154
Clergymen	43.3	17.0	4,120	0.039	89.0	27.2	0.295
Col. teachers	40.3	17.4	7,500	0.085	99.2	36.0	0.261
Draftsmen	31.2	12.9	5,990	0.098	98.6	40.8	0.322
Reporters, editors	39.4	15.5	6,120	0.138	93.9	43.3	0.151
Musicians	40.2	14.8	3,240	0.081	65.5	37.7	0.289
Nat. scientists	35.9	16.8	7,490	0.264	96.3	32.7	0.221
Average	38.3	15.5	5,768	0.115	88.5	37.6	0.242

*1–R, where R = ratio: 1960 age 45–54 to 1960 age 35–44.

[a]Not available separately; teachers N.E.C. (incl. secondary school and other) = 0.276.

[b]Includes figure for teachers N.E.C. in note a.
Source: *U.S. Census of Population* [15], 1960.

(3) the licensed occupations are less often employed by business enterprises (who have incentives to oppose licensing),

(4) all occupations in national markets (college teachers, engineers, scientists, accountants) are unlicensed or only partially licensed.

The size and urbanization of the three groups, however, are unrelated to licensing. The inter-occupational comparison therefore provides a modicum of additional support for our theory of regulation.

3. Conclusion

The idealistic view of public regulation is deeply imbedded in professional economic thought. So many economists, for example, have denounced the ICC for its pro-railroad policies that this has become a cliché of the literature. This criticism seems to me exactly as appropriate as a criticism of the Great Atlantic and Pacific Tea Company for selling groceries, or as a criticism of a politician for currying popular support. The fundamental vice of such criticism is that it misdirects attention: it suggests that the way to get an ICC which is not subservient to the carriers is to preach to the commissioners or to the people who appoint the commissioners. The only way to get a different commission would be to change the political support for the Commission, and reward commissioners on a basis unrelated to their services to the carriers.

Until the basic logic of political life is developed, reformers will be ill-equipped to use the state for their reforms, and victims of the pervasive use of the state's support of special groups will be helpless to protect themselves. Economists should quickly establish the license to practice on the rational theory of political behavior.

Notes

1. The domestic producers of petroleum, who also benefit from the import quota, would find a tariff or cash payment to domestic producers equally attractive. If their interests alone were consulted, import quotas would be auctioned off instead of being given away.

2. See [7], pp. 60 ff.

3. See [10].

4. The Federal Home Loan Bank Board is the regulatory body. It also controls the amount of advertising and other areas of competition.

5. The largest refineries were restricted to 75.7 percent of their historical quota under the earlier voluntary import quota plan.

6. The ratio of trucks to total population would measure the product of (1) the importance of trucks to farmers, and (2) the importance of farmers in the state. For reasons given later, we prefer to emphasize (1).

7. This is known for each railroad, and we assume that (1) the average holds within each state, and (2) two or more railroads in a state may be combined on the basis of mileage. Obviously both assumptions are at best fair approximations.

8. If the deadweight loss (of consumer and producer surplus) is taken into account, even if the oil industry were in the majority it would not obtain the legislation if there were available some method of compensation (such as sale of votes) by which the larger damage to the minority could be expressed effectively against the lesser gains of the majority.

9. See [2].

10. There is an organizational problem in any decision in which more than one vote is cast. If because of economics of scale it requires a thousand customers to buy a product before it can be produced, this thousand votes has to be assembled by some entrepreneur. Unlike the political scene,

however, there is no need to obtain the consent of the remainder of the community, because they will bear no part of the cost.

11. The theory that the lobbying organization avoids the "free-rider" problem by selling useful services was proposed by Thomas G. Moore [8] and elaborated by Maneur Olson [9]. The theory has not been tested empirically.

12. Let n = the number of members of the profession and y = average income. We expect political capacity to be in proportion to (ny) so far as benefits go, but to reflect also the direct values of votes, so the capacity becomes proportional to $(n^a y)$ with $a > 1$.

13. We may pool the occupations and assign dummy variables for each occupation; the regression coefficients then are:

> size of occupation relative to labor force: —0.450 $(t = 0.59)$
> urbanization   : —12.133 $(t = 4.00)$.

Thus urbanization is highly significant, while size of occupation is not significant.

14. A more precise analysis might take the form of a regression analysis such as:

> Year of licensure = constant

$+ b_1$ (year of critical size of occupation)
$+ b_2$ (year of critical urbanization of occupation),

where the critical size and urbanization were defined as the mean size and mean urbanization in the year of licensure.

15. Lawyers, physicians, and pharmacists were all relatively large occupations by 1900, and nurses also by 1910. The only large occupation to be licensed later was barbers; the only small occupation to be licensed early was embalmers.

16. The regulation of business in a partial market will also generally produce very high supply elasticities within a market: if the price of the product (or service) is raised, the pressure of excluded supply is very difficult to resist. Some occupations are forced to reciprocity in licensing, and the geographical dispersion of earnings in licensed occupations, one would predict, is not appreciably different than in unlicensed occupations with equal employer mobility. Many puzzles are posed by the interesting analysis of Arlene S. Holen in [6], pp. 492-98.

References

1. Association of American Railroads, Bureau of Railway Economics. *Railway Mileage by States*. Washington, D.C.: December 31, 1930.

2. Becker, G. S. "Competition and Democracy." *Journal of Law and Economics*, October 1958.

3. The Council of State Governments. "Occupational Licensing Legislation in the States." 1952.

4. Demsetz, H., "Why Regulate Utilities?" *Journal of Law and Economics*, April 1968.

5. Gerwig, R. W. "Natural Gas Production: A Study of Costs of Regulation." *Journal of Law and Economics*, October 1962, pp. 69-92.

6. Holen, A. S. "Effects of Professional Licensing Arrangements on Interstate Labor Mobility and Resource Allocation." *Journal of Political Economy*, Vol. 73 (1915), pp. 492-98.

7. Keyes, L. S. *Federal Control of Entry into Air Transportation*. Cambridge, Mass.: Harvard University Press, 1951.

8. Moore, T. G. "The Purpose of Licensing." *Journal of Law and Economics*, October 1961.

9. Olson, M. *The Logic of Collective Action*. Cambridge, Mass.: Harvard University Press, 1965.

10. Peltzman, S. "Entry in Commercial Banking." *Journal of Law and Economics*, October 1965.

11. *The Motor Truck Red Book and Directory*, 1934 Edition, pp. 85-102.

12. U.S. Congress, Select Committee on Small Business. *Hearings*, 88th Congress, 2nd Session, August 10 and 11, 1964.

13. U.S. Department of Agriculture, Bureau of Public Roads. *Public Roads*. Washington, D.C.: U.S. Government Printing Office, December 1932.

14. U.S. Department of Commerce, Bureau of the Census. *United States Census of Agriculture, 1930*, Vol. 4. Washington, D.C.: U.S. Government Printing Office, 1930.

15. ———. *United States Census of Population*. Washington, D.C.: U.S. Government Printing Office, appropriate years.

16. ———, Bureau of Foreign and Domestic Commerce. *Statistical Abstract of the U.S., 1932*. Washington, D.C.: U.S. Government Printing Office, 1932.

17. U.S. Interstate Commerce Commission. *Annual Report*. Washington, D.C.: U.S. Government Printing Offfice, appropriate years.

18. ———. *Statistics of Railways in the United States, 1930*. Washington, D.C.: U.S. Government Printing Office, 1930.

2.3

The Politics of Regulation

JAMES Q. WILSON

In an intended corrective to the economic theory of regulation just considered, James Q. Wilson insists on the importance of a distinct, albeit often messy, politics of the regulatory process. He traces the role of political motives and institutions in shaping the mobilization of demand for regulation, in finally determining the circumstances under which regulation is achieved, and in influencing the design and administration of regulatory programs, along with the conditions of business "capture." Along the way, Wilson provides an extensive review of existing literature and debates.

Two points are of special importance. The first is Wilson's typology of cost–benefit distribution and regulatory forms. Here he starts from the presumption that political actors are generally more "threat-oriented" than "opportunity-oriented," or more inclined to take political action upon a prospective showing of increased costs and decreased benefits than increased benefits and decreased costs. He then argues that, given this general propensity, different patterns in the concentration and diffusion of costs and benefits of government intervention encourage different sorts of regulatory forms, objects, and coalition structures and participants. The second point flows out of this typology, namely the apparent improbability of regulatory action being taken where the benefits of that action are diffuse but the costs are concentrated on a limited number of individuals or groups. Such a distribution of costs and benefits, Wilson argues, is typical of much of the "new" or "social" regulation of the 1960s and early 1970s—such as environmental or auto-safety regulation—but would never be predicted by conventional interest group accounts of widely dispersed veto powers within a political system driven by elite consensus. Wilson concludes, therefore, that the conventional account is no longer adequate to explain economic regulation.

Whenever government in the United States has sought to introduce social objectives or constraints into the management of business enterprise, it has usually done so by administrative regulation or regulation combined with direct or indirect cash subsidies.[1] The public authorities have largely forgone the major alternative device for altering business behavior—namely, changing the structure of the economy by means of public ownership or management. Though experiments have been made from time to time with varying degrees of ownership or control over railroads and atomic energy production, and though there are at the local and regional level a substantial number of publicly owned utilities, the United States, more than almost any other advanced industrial society, has left the ownership and management of enterprise in private hands even in those industries—transportation, broadcasting, and telephone and telegram communication—that have been most frequently nationalized in other countries.

It is increasingly recognized that the U.S. public regulatory agencies do not select optimal regulatory policies.[2] This may be because in the nature of things no such policy can exist. It is impossible, for example, to devise a "correct" or "optimal" criterion by which to choose among competing applicants for a broadcast license if the choice depends on measuring the value of what an applicant will broadcast; for that is largely a matter of taste over which consumers will differ. Or the difficulty may arise because a legislature has required that an economically inefficient policy be pursued, as when Congress enacted the Federal Water Pollution Control Act Amendments of 1972 requiring that the discharge of all effluents into the nation's waters end by 1985, whatever the cost (it will be vast) and however illusory the benefit (many waterways can easily handle, at no significant loss of water quality, some effluent discharge). Or the problem may result from the constellation of political forces in which the agency is caught. Strong arguments have been made, for instance, that cable b. adcasting deserves at least a reasonable chance to compete in large cities with over-the-air broadcasting, but the political influence of the television stations and networks is so great and that of the cable companies and allied consumer groups so weak that the cable rules adopted by the Federal Communications Commission (FCC) are prohibitively restrictive.[3]

That regulation is subject to these difficulties does not mean there should never be regulation. We often prefer the imperfect benefits of a regulatory system to the imperfections of the market, as when we ask the government to determine the prices that can be charged by "natural monopolies" such as the telephone company. It is remarkably difficult to decide what those prices should be and to revise them in a timely and equitable way as costs change, but the alternative is to allow the company to set its own monopoly prices or to place it under government ownership.

Much, probably most, regulation in the United States is not concerned with avoiding the evils of monopoly, however. Various levels of government regulate railroads, trucking companies, airlines, broadcasters, pharmaceutical firms, dry cleaners, savings banks, and automobile manufacturers, not because these industries are immune from effective competition and thus in a position to charge monopoly prices, but because we wish them to serve objectives other than, or in addition to, the objective of selling their products at the lowest price. In some cases we regulate them to ensure that they will *not* engage in price competition, because we believe the "health" of the industry (and presumably, the well-being of the country) is served by prices being set higher than market forces would allow. In other cases we regulate to protect the consumer from fraud, misrepresentation, or hazard. In still other cases we regulate to prevent market transactions from imposing uncompensated costs on third parties, as when a factory pours noxious fumes into the air or a household sends untreated sewage into a river that cannot absorb it.

Some of these regulatory objectives, such as that of avoiding price competition in the transportation industry, are questionable; others, such as that of reducing pollution, unexceptionable. And some laudatory objectives could perhaps be served as well or better by nonregulatory devices, such as negotiating contractual agreements, levying appropriate taxes, or imposing compensatory charges for wear on the environment. It is not the purpose of this chapter, however, to evaluate the worth of a regulatory objective or to consider alternative means to reach a given objective. Rather, the purpose here is to explain, insofar as available facts permit, the circumstances under which regulation becomes politically possible, the pattern of regulation that is likely to emerge from a given political context, and the forces that will influence how a regulatory agency does its job.

The reason for this approach is simple. Whenever we want business to act in ways other than as self-interest would require, we rarely content ourselves for long with urging businessmen to examine their consciences or to attend conferences on their social responsibilities. If the problem is sufficiently bothersome or a political constituency opposed to a certain practice can be readily mobilized (not necessarily the same thing), we ask the government to direct businessmen to stop doing certain things and to start doing something else. Often businessmen themselves are in the forefront of those making these demands. If we turn so often to government regulation to achieve what self-interest cannot, we ought to have a better understanding than we do of what is necessary to enact such regulatory legislation and how the process of its enactment and the imperatives of agency management will affect the regulatory policy that emerges. Such an analysis may help us decide under what circumstances government regulation is an efficient and fair means to realize public objectives and under what circumstances it is not, and therefore it may help us decide the larger question of when the imperfections of government action are preferable to the imperfections of the market and when they are not. The world being as it is, a choice between imperfect alternatives is usually the best that can be hoped for.

The Sources of Regulation

The political circumstances under which business regulation occurs must be distinguished from those economic factors that may or may not make such regulation desirable. Sometimes, to be sure, the economic reasons for regulation are so compelling that, sooner or later, the political capacity for regulation is developed. The existence of "natural monopolies" is usually regarded as a case in point: when a firm, such as a telephone company, can realize substantial returns to scale because of continuously falling average costs, it has a powerful incentive to drive out or buy up competitors. Only by government regulation or government ownership can such a firm be prevented from charging a monopoly price (assuming there are no ready substitutes for its services). Every country places such natural monopolies under some form of public control.

But in most cases, there is no overwhelming reason why business regulation must occur—it may be desirable or undesirable, but it is not inevitable. For example, instead of regulating drug companies to prevent them from making harmful medicines, the government might facilitate the recovery of damages by injured parties.

There have been, in general, two main theories of the political causes of regulation. According to the first one, regulation results when legislators, mobilized by a broad social movement or energized by a dramatic crisis, enact laws designed to prevent a firm or industry from carrying on certain practices. This is the "public interest" theory of regulation. The other, currently more in fashion among many scholars, is that regulation results when an industry successfully uses its political influence to obtain legal protection for itself or to impose legal burdens on its rivals. This is the "self-interest" theory of regulation. The origins of many regulatory laws are hotly disputed between adherents of the one theory and adherents of the other. The act that created the Interstate Commerce Commission is believed by some scholars to have been in large part a governmental response to the interests of farmers and other shippers who were aggrieved by monopoly rates being charged on short-haul railroad lines. Other scholars contend, on the contrary, that the creation of the ICC was a response to the demands of railroad companies eager to reduce price competition and create or preserve cartel arrangements.[4]

The view taken here is that regulatory laws can have a variety of political causes and that it is necessary, in order to understand why regulation occurs, to specify the circumstances under which one or another cause will be operative.

These circumstances can be classified by examining the distribution of the perceived costs and benefits of the proposed regulation. A cost may be perceived to be widely distributed (as when it is paid for through a general tax levy or a general price increase) or narrowly concentrated (as when it is met with a fee or impost charged to a particular industry, firm, or locality). Similarly a benefit, real or imagined, may be widely distributed (as with lower prices or taxes, improved products and services or reductions in the degree of fraud and deception tried on the public); or a benefit may be narrowly concentrated (as when a subsidy is paid to a particular industry or occupation or a license is granted for the operation of a particular valuable facility). Not everyone will agree on the distribution of costs and benefits, opinions about any particular distribution often change over time, and occasionally beliefs can be made to change by skillful political advocacy.

The distribution of costs and benefits affects regulatory politics in two ways. First, individuals and groups are politically more sensitive to sudden or significant *decreases* in their net benefits than they are to increases in net benefits. That is, they are more sensitive to, and thus more easily mobilized for political action about, circumstances that make costs seem likely to go up or benefits to go down than they are when they foresee a chance to reduce costs or enhance benefits. They are, in short, more *threat*-oriented than opportunity-oriented.

This is, of course, a sweeping generalization, but it is on the whole consistent with such evidence as we have regarding how persons compare expected utilities and expected disutilities in experimental situations.[5] It fits with what we know about the behavior of economic organizations in legislative struggle over tariff legislation.[6] It is in line with the circumstances under which various trade associations have emerged.[7]

Most of the governmental regulatory agencies designed to control the behavior of single industries or organizations were created in response to serious economic instability in that industry: price wars among long-haul railroads and price increases to shippers served by short-haul railroads contributed to the creation of the Interstate Commerce Commission; acute signal interference led to the formation of the Federal Radio Commission (later the Federal Communications Commission); depressed conditions in the coal industry gave rise to the National Bituminous Coal Commission (later abolished); the financial crises of the airlines and accompanying scandals with respect to the awarding of subsidies for carrying mail by air led to the creation of the Civil Aeronautics Authority (later the Civil Aeronautics Board); extreme fluctuations in the money supply stimulated the organization of the Federal Reserve Board; the insecurity of labor organizations gave rise to demands for the Wagner Act and the establishment of a National Labor Relations Board; the uncertainty of the congressional licensing system for hydroelectric power plants led to the creation of the Federal Power Commission; and the competition of foreign shipbuilders and the sudden increases in the cost of shipping occasioned by World War I led to the formation of the Shipping Board (superseded by the U.S. Maritime Commission).

Interest-group activity intensifies when the associations confront a visible, direct, and immediate threat to their values. The National Association of Manufacturers (NAM) has typically waxed (in size, budget, and energy) during "anti-business" Democratic administrations and waned during "pro-business" Republican ones. The AFL-CIO has been more active in attempting to defeat the Taft-Hartley Act, to repeal section 14(b) of that act after it was passed, and to defeat state "right-to-work" laws than in arguing for new wage-and-hours legislation. Conservation groups are more easily mobilized by a threat to an existing forest or a particular marshland than by proposals to create new forests or new bird sanctuaries.

In addition to serving as a source of assumed threats or deprivation, there is a second way in which costs and benefits affect regulatory politics, and that has to do with the extent to which they are concentrated. When the cost to be avoided or the benefit to be maintained is specific to a certain sector of society conscious of its special identity, political action is easier to stimulate than when costs or benefits fall on a large, diverse group with no sense of special identity and no established patterns of interaction. Partly this is simply a matter of size: in a small group each member's contribution is sufficiently significant so that it may help to attain the organization's goal and sufficiently visible so that its presence will be noted and rewarded by other members.[8] As a result, members of small organizations often find it more satisfying to contribute time, money, and effort to a common cause than do members of a large one. By itself, a feeling of deprivation does not necessarily lead to a political effort.

The greater ease of organizational activity in response to concentrated costs and benefits is also the result of the greater homogeneity of interest and belief among sectors of society that are clearly defined along lines of occupation, industry, or locality. People are less likely to be divided by a proposed policy that serves their common interests as members of an organization than they are by a policy that cuts across their various interests either as individuals or as members of society in general. For example, an organization representing firms making watches will be more aroused by a proposed tariff reduction on imported watches than will an organization representing businessmen generally, some of whom buy and others of whom sell watches. Of course, organizations purporting to speak for very large sectors are often active in regulatory politics, but in many cases the positions they take are either highly general (so as to avoid antagonizing any element of a diverse membership) or unrepresentative (because they are responsive to the interests and beliefs of an activist minority rather than to those of a broad constituency).

So far as degree of concentration is concerned, costs and benefits may fall into any of several distribution patterns. The main patterns are worth looking at one by one for their different consequences. *

Concentrated Benefits, Diffused Costs   Any proposed policy that confers highly concentrated costs or benefits will be more likely to stimulate organized activity by a fully representative group than will a policy that confers widely distributed costs and benefits. When the benefit is entirely concentrated on a single group but the cost is diffused, an organization will quickly form to propose a regulatory arrangement to institutionalize the benefit; and that proposal, except under special conditions to be noted below, will not be seriously challenged. At the behest of the Florida Dairy Products Association, the Florida Milk Commission was created in 1939 to eliminate "overproduction" and "predatory" price-cutting. The benefits to the producer of a guaranteed minimum price were great; the cost to the average consumer was relatively small.[9] Over seventy-five occupations in the United States require state licenses; there is an average of twenty-five such laws per state. A typical one is the 1939 law that created the Oklahoma State Dry Cleaning Board,

*After the publication of this essay Professor Wilson provided a revised statement of the theory, which can be found in chapters 14 and 15 of James Q. Wilson, *American Government: Institutions and Policies* (Lexington, MA: D.C. Heath & Co., 1983). In that version what is here called "concentrated benefits, diffused costs" is referred to as "clientele politics"; what is described as "concentrated benefits, concentrated costs," is called "interest group politics," and what is described as "diffused benefits, concentrated costs" is called "entrepreneurial politics." A fourth category, called "majoritarian politics," is added, which involves those circumstances in which there are both diffused benefits and diffused costs.

charged with many duties, including the prevention of fires, but over the years concerned chiefly with eliminating price competition.[10] The regulation of, and limitations on, the number of taxicab licenses in cities is a well-known example of a competitive industry using legal enactments, usually defended in terms of eliminating fraud, enhancing safety, or maintaining quality of service, in order to restrict entry and set minimum prices.[11]

Thus regulatory constraints often arise out of a political situation in which a small, relatively homogeneous beneficiary group can make substantial gains by imposing unobstrusive costs on large numbers of others. Constraints arising under such conditions tend to have the following characteristics: (1) they will involve the elimination or reduction of price competition within the affected industry; (2) entry to the industry will be restricted or at least made more expensive; (3) the organized beneficiary will strongly influence the regulatory agency that administers the policy; (4) the industry and its agency will strive to maintain a position of low visibility to avoid stimulating the formation of an organization representative of those who bear the costs of the regulation; and (5) should the regulation become controversial, it will be defended by attempting to show the eliminating price competition is an appropriate means for ensuring safety, ending fraud, and promoting amenity (correcting evils allegedly caused by price cutters, who will be termed "fly-by-night operators").

Concentrated Benefits, Concentrated Costs   Some regulatory constraints arise, not out of the unopposed aggrandizement of a single beneficiary, but out of competition between two or more organized opponents. This occurs when a historical development or a proposed policy creates both concentrated benefits and concentrated costs. The struggle between labor and management over union recognition and union security agreements is the most obvious instance. The conflict between wholesalers and retailers and between large chain stores and small independent ones over resale price maintenance is another, and the battle between the railroads and the truckers when the former were regulated and the latter were not is a third. The union-management issue led to three major federal laws (the Wagner Act, the Taft-Hartley Act, and the Landrum-Griffin Act) and the creation of a regulatory body (the National Labor Relations Board) which has been a cockpit for continuing organized struggle. Resale price maintenance issues were won by the small retailers who obtained passage of the Robinson-Patman Act (1936), the Miller-Tydings Act (1937), and the McGuire Act (1952). The transportation conflict was temporarily resolved, not by deregulating railroads but by extending rate regulation, through the Motor Carrier Act of 1935, to truckers.

Regulatory constraints arising out of a political situation in which two clearly defined, undifferentiated sectors of the economy contend over the allocation of costs and benefits tend to have these characteristics: (1) a "charter" will be adopted that contains a definition of the competing rights and obligations of each party; (2) no one organized sector will be able to dominate permanently the administrative arrangements created to implement the charter; (3) there will be continuing efforts to renegotiate or amend the charter; and (4) the visibility of the issue will be relatively high because there is conflict, because each party to it will attempt to enlist allies (for example, business groups will try to enlist the American Farm Bureau Federation against labor, while labor will try to enlist the National Farmers Union), and because there will be frequent appeals to the courts.

Diffused Benefits, Concentrated Costs   Finally, regulatory constraints may impose highly concentrated costs on some in order to obtain widely distributed benefits for others. Politically, this implies that a small group, faced with the immediate prospect of increased burdens, is unable to defeat a proposal brought on behalf of large numbers of (inevitably unorganized) persons, each of whom may benefit, if at all, only in the future. Such an eventuality strikes some political scientists as so unlikely that they have argued that it will almost never occur barring a major crisis (a depression or a war) or a fundamental political realignment. In fact, regulatory constraints embodying concentrated costs and distributed benefits have been imposed, and with increasing frequency in recent years. The Sherman Antitrust Act of 1890, the Pure Food and Drug Act of 1906, the Meat Inspection Act of 1906, the Food, Drug, and Cosmetic Act of 1938, and the Public Utility Holding Company Act of 1935 are familiar examples from the early decades of this century and before. In the 1960's the number of such laws, especially in the consumer and environmental protection fields, increased dramatically. Congress passed twenty consumer bills between 1962 and 1970—bills aimed against postal fraud, flammable fabrics, unwholesome meat and poultry, radiation, automobile and highway dangers, unsafe toys, exploitative credit practices, deceptive package labeling, and inadequate testing of drugs. In the ecology area, Congress enacted the Water Quality Act and the Motor Vehicle Air Pollution Control Act in 1965, the Clean Water Restoration Act of 1966, the Air Quality Act of 1967, the National Environmental Policy Act of 1969, the Water Quality Improvement Act of 1970, and the 1970 amendments to the Clean Air Act.

Some of these bills were the products of major scandals: the early food and drug and meat inspection acts followed upon public exposures of unsavory conditions in these industries; the 1938 drug laws were prompted by the deaths caused by elixir of sulfanilamide; the National Traffic and Motor Vehicle Safety Act of 1966 was helped along by public disclosure of a General Motors investigation of Ralph Nader; and the 1962 amendments to the drug laws were aided in their passage by the thalidomide disaster. Similarly, the crisis conditions of the Depression facilitated public utility and stock exchange control legislation. Yet it is easy to exaggerate the importance of any one set of critical events.[12] The Kefauver drug probe leading to the 1962 legislation was under way well before thalidomide was a public issue. Most of the environmental legislation was unrelated to any particular crisis or disaster, and the "truth-in-lending" and "truth-in-packaging" bills developed slowly in Congress without benefit of scandal.

One of the striking aspects of the politics of consumer and ecology legislation is the important role Congress—or, more accurately, key congressmen and congressional committees—plays in their initiation. The usual assumption (an assumption increasingly questioned by scholars) that the executive proposes and the legislature disposes seems not to hold for consumer and environmental bills.[13] Senator Abraham A. Ribicoff formulated the auto safety bill, Senator Estes Kefauver the 1962 drug amendments, Senator Paul Douglas the truth-in-lending bill, Senator Phillip A. Hart the truth-in-packaging bill, and Senator Edmund S. Muskie most of the water and air pollution bills. Furthermore, even when a president has submitted his own bills in these fields, consumer and ecological activists have usually judged them to be "weaker"; and when a president has endorsed an existing bill, his support has been slow in coming. President John F. Kennedy, for example, was reluctant to support the truth-in-lending bill until several years after it was first introduced, and he backed a prescription drug bill less stringent than that initiated by Senator Kefauver. President Lyndon Johnson moved more cautiously on auto safety than Senator Ribicoff. President Richard Nixon opposed much of the pollution legislation emanating from the so-called Muskie subcommittee and offered several alternatives.

The importance of Congress in issues of this sort is in part a result of the relative newness of consumer and environmental enthusiasms: the White House, along with much of the rest of the country (including, to their chagrin, auto manufacturers, credit institutions, and other affected industries), at first underestimated the salience and appeal of these legislative initiatives. Had a president guessed sooner that such issues were politically important, he no doubt would have acted sooner and by so doing preempted the field. But legislative leadership has also been the result of the symbiotic political relationship between certain congressmen and various "public interest" activists. As Paul Halpern observes in his study of auto safety legislation, many congressmen are continuously surveying their political horizons in search of issues with which they can become personally identified and which can become the basis of subcommittee chairmanships, highly publicized hearings, and state or national visibility.[24] This is especially true of senators, who not only must appeal to larger, harder-to-reach constituencies but who, unlike representatives, can take advantage of televised hearings. Senators Ribicoff and Warren G. Magnuson, for example, deliberately sought out auto safety as an issue with which they could make their mark, as Senator Kefauver before them had done, first with organized crime and then with prescription drugs. In becoming the source of regulatory legislation, a senator of course does not act alone: he is only the central figure in a constellation of staff assistants, newspapermen, organizational representatives, and political celebrities (such as Ralph Nader).

Regulatory proposals emerging from this process are likely to have certain distinctive features. First, in order to ensure vital publicity and develop political momentum in the competition for attention in and around Congress, the bills will focus attention on an "evil," personified if possible in a corporation, industry, or victim. Second, the proposal will be "strong"—that is, there will be little incentive in the developmental process to accommodate conflicting interests and thus little incentive to find a politically acceptable formula which all affected parties can live with. (To compromise the proposal would be to sacrifice the capacity of the bill to mobilize support by its moralistic appeal.) Third, though few *substantive* bargains will be struck, many procedural ones will, especially ones that recognize the central structural fact of the American Congress—namely, that it is a federal institution based on state and district representation. Concessions will often be made to recognize existing state programs or to provide incentives for states to develop new programs. Finally, the proposed solution to the problematic business practice will be shaped as much by the political process by which the proposal is generated as by an analysis of the problem itself. The consequences for a regulatory strategy of the political gestation it undergoes is discussed in the next section. It should be recognized, of course, that the tendencies latent in congressionally initiated regulatory programs with widely distributed benefits and concentrated costs are only tendencies: the final shape of the bill will be affected by the legislative struggle itself. It is worth noting, however, that many of the major consumer and environmental bills were passed by extraordinary majorities, especially during the 1960s, and that the number of floor amendments adopted was typically rather small.

The Nature of Regulation

Economists and others frequently complain that the regulations imposed on American businesses are not optimal and in some cases may even be unnecessary. Academic journals and books are filled with detailed analyses of why much regulatory policy is wrong and how it might be corrected. Few of these suggestions are acted upon by the government.

This political indifference to professional opinion may in part result from the arcane language in which the professionals address each other, but in large part it is the result of the imperatives of the political and administrative processes. When government regulation fails to compel businesses to serve socially desirable objectives, it is not usually because of the incompetence or venality of the regulators but because of the constraints placed on them by the need to operate within the political system. When the regulation arises out of the desire to alleviate widely distributed burdens (say, auto accidents, water pollution, hidden interest charges), then assigning blame becomes virtually a political necessity in order to get the issue on the public agenda and move it through the legislative obstacle course. If the regulation arises out of a desire to confer highly concentrated benefits (stabilized prices, lessened competition, restricted entry), then the "needs" of the industry must be dramatized, the "failures" of the economic system emphasized, and an administrative alternative to that system devised. If the regulation is the result of the momentary political supremacy of one organized interest over another (as with the victory of labor over management or retailers over wholesalers), then the constraints employed will be devised to protect the politically stronger group from the politically weaker. The protection conferred, however, will rarely be complete, for the adversary will look for new ways to organize for political action. As the political tides change, counterattacks occur, and new constraints are imposed to redress the effects of old ones.

In all three cases, the result is the multiplication of detailed constraints, sometimes in the form of rules, sometimes by way of the exercise of ad hoc administrative discretion undefined by rule. In the case of a widely shared burden such as pollution, the administrative agency charged with alleviating that burden will (provided it retains the capacity for independent action, a matter discussed in a later section) consider that it was created to constrain the wicked or self-seeking behavior of a firm, industry, or group and thus that it has a mandate to do whatever it legally can to eliminate abuses (and not merely the particular abuse to which it owes its existence). In the case of concentrated benefits such as reducing price competition, the agency will believe that it has general responsibility for ensuring the health and well-being of a firm, industry, or group and thus will seek not merely to eliminate a particular problem but generally to reduce uncertainty and protect firms against failure. In the case of organized interests struggling for political advantage over each other, rules will multiply and discretionary authority expand as a consequence of the seesaw battle for agency domination between two or more organized sectors of the economy whose interests are at stake.

These tendencies can be illustrated with a few important examples. Many economists argue that the control of noxious effluents from fixed sources, as with the discharge of sewage from a pipe into streams or the emission of gaseous pollutants into the air from factory smokestacks, is best handled by forcing those who discharge undesirable wastes to bear the cost of doing so. This can be accomplished by levying an effluent tax or discharge fee that increases with the amount emitted. The result is to increase the cost to the producer of using the heretofore "free" environment as a dump and to induce him to economize by finding ways of reducing his output of effluents, by recycling his waste products in order to use them in the productive process, or by reducing his production of high-waste products in favor of producing more low-waste products.[15] Such a strategy would lead the producer to find the least-cost solution to a waste problem but would leave him free to select among various technologies for achieving this. If technology is unavailing, the producer will be led either to pass the cost of effluents on to the consumer, thereby reducing demand and thus production, or, if competitive conditions do not permit him to increase prices, to accept lower profits, which would discourage new investment in the industry.

The actual legislation aimed at air and water pollution uses quite different strategies—generally a combination of fixed standards (regarding the absolute level of pollutants that may be discharged) with financial incentives (such as accelerated depreciation of investment in anti-pollution equipment or cash subsidies to municipalities building sewage treatment plants). The most extreme form of what might be termed a directive strategy, as distinct from an incentive strategy, is the Federal Water Pollution Control Amendments of 1972 that would ban *all* effluent discharge into the nation's waters by 1985, however great the cost of achieving the ban and however small the benefits from preventing the last quantum of discharge.

A second example is in the area of air pollution caused by motor vehicles. The Motor Vehicle Air Pollution Control Act of 1965 set some emission standards; the 1970 amendments to the Clean Air Act made the standards more severe. They required auto manufacturers to reduce hydrocarbon emissions by 90 percent by 1975 and nitrous oxide emissions by the same amount by 1976. Though some may disagree with these standards as inadequate, the chief difficulty with the approach is that any such standards, imposed within a short time, almost certainly require the industry to commit itself to seeking improvements in the present technology (namely, the internal combustion engine) and provide no serious incentive to explore theoretically more promising alternatives involving other technologies (for example, external, continuous combustion engines, as in steam engines, gas turbines, or electric drives).[16] Adapting the internal combustion engine to minimal-pollution operation is quite difficult, and maintaining such an engine in proper tune or inspecting it to ensure that it remains in tune would be expensive and easily evaded by both motorists and repairmen. Furthermore, without a major development of alternative technologies, the government agency enforcing the 1975/1976 emission standards was forced to choose between stopping auto production (politically unthinkable) or relaxing the standards to accord with whatever level of improvement the industry has been able to attain. So far, the government has been inclined to relax the standards marginally.

A third instance of political rather than economic solutions can be found in the area of consumer credit. Various studies have suggested that "the poor pay more" for various items, especially furniture and major appliances.[17] Some part of these higher prices results from steep finance charges. The upshot is that a significant proportion of the poor in the city are heavily in debt as purchasers of low-quality household furnishings, and many of these persons have their wages garnisheed when they default on the payments. Ostensibly to deal with this problem, the Consumer Credit Protection Act of 1968 (the "truth-in-lending bill") was passed, providing that there must be full disclosure of all interest and finance charges in consumer transactions, that "loan sharking" is a federal crime, and that wages can be garnisheed only up to 25 percent of a person's weekly paycheck after exemption of the first $48 earned. Interest-charge disclosure, the most hotly debated of the bill's provisions, has apparently had almost no effect on the evils it was intended to cure and probably cannot even in principle have much of an effect. The prior Massachusetts truth-in-lending law was reportedly without impact, and this fact was known before the federal law was passed.[18] The ineffectual nature of such regulatory devices arises from the nature of both the demand and the supply of consumer goods. Poor persons are not comparison shoppers and display little interest in the size of a finance charge, though considerable interest in the size of the total weekly or monthly payments. If these latter figures are kept small enough, the consumer will buy with little regard for interest rates. And those firms that supply such persons can, if regulation lowers finance charges, recapture profits by either raising the price or lowering the quality of the merchandise sold. Furthermore, owing to the higher cost of doing business in poor neighborhoods (resulting from credit losses, theft, and the like), retailers in these areas, though they have higher markups, do not have higher profit levels than similar retailers in middle-class areas.[19] If the "problems" of consumer credit can be solved by government at all, easier access to chain stores that sell good merchandise at reasonable prices might be arranged for the poor (which in turn would require investment subsidies and credit guarantees to induce such stores to locate in the poorest neighborhoods); or else the amount of debt low-income persons can run up might be restricted (by, for example, requiring large down payments such as were in effect during the Second World War). Throughout the debate on the truth-in-lending legislation, the discussion of the problems of poor consumers bore almost no relationship to the provisions of the bill.

A fourth example concerns the regulation of prices in competitive industries. Most economists who have examined the air passenger and freight transport industries have concluded that prices charged to most (though not all) consumers by federally regulated airlines and truckers are higher than they would be without regulation and that deregulation would not substantially effect other important values (such as safety).[20] There is substantial evidence that the regulation of the field prices of natural gas, though it may have kept gas prices down for some present-day consumers, will eventually lead to higher prices owing to the absence of any market incentive to explore and develop additional gas reserves.[21]

In these four cases, the government sought either to protect an industry (as in the regulation of air fares and truck and rail rates) or to set for industry a standard that was impossible of attainment (as with the ban on effluent discharges into waterways), irrelevant to the objective being sought (as with the disclosure of finance charges), or likely to produce unwanted side effects (as with the auto emission standards). These examples are not necessarily representative of all regulatory policies, but they are important cases that affect the behavior of thousands of firms and the expenditure of many millions of dollars. To obtain any regulation at all, it was necessary in each case to get legislators to take the problem seriously, to forge a winning coalition among legislators with diverse interests and perceptions, and to overcome the arguments and influence of opponents. Accomplishing this in a representative government requires the recitation of powerful arguments, the evocation of horror stories, or the mobilization of a broad political movement. Political inertia is not easily overcome, and when it is overcome, it is often at the price of exaggerating the virtue of those who are to benefit (a defrauded debtor, a sick industry) or the wickedness of those who are to bear the burden (a smog-belching car, a polluting factory, a grasping creditor).

These political constraints on economic regulation may exist in all governments, or they may be especially pervasive in American government. Without a study comparing regulation in several regimes, that question cannot be answered, and scarcely any such studies exist. It is a plausible hypothesis, however, that American government is not powerful enough to impose radical solutions for problems of business behavior (by nationalizing firms or sectors); but neither is it powerful enough to ignore demands for political solutions (by deliberately choosing free market arrangements). In short, the U.S. government may own fewer businesses but regulate more business practices than most other democracies. This is because political power in the United States is sufficiently localistic in its sources to be responsive to demands for change and sufficiently diffuse in its institutional forms to be incapable of extreme actions. The result is piecemeal regulation made possible by either quiet bargaining on behalf of benefited interests or populistic appeals on behalf of larger publics.

Regulatory Administration

Business regulation is affected not only by its political origins but by its administrative embodiment. Sometimes this takes the form of rule making, as when the Federal Reserve Board sets the discount rate, the Environmental Protection Agency sets allowable automotive emission standards, or the ICC sets freight rates. Sometimes administration consists of adjudicating claims, as when the FCC awards a television license or the National Labor Relations Board (NLRB) hears a complaint about employment practices. Sometimes administration takes the form of attacking an alleged ill, as when the Department of Justice Antitrust Division prosecutes under the Sherman Act or the Federal Trade Commission (FTC) orders an advertiser to cease and desist.

For all agencies with less than precise standards for their actions and conspicuous boundaries to their authority, regulatory management will consist of efforts to enlarge the domain and specificity of regulation. One reason for this is the continuing effort of the agency to decide, in the absence of a clear standard, what it wants to accomplish. If "public interest, convenience, and necessity" cannot guide automatically the licensing process of the FCC, the FCC will begin elaborating, on a case-by-case basis, an opinion, not always consistent or enduring, as to what this phrase entails. It will suggest, for example, that the phrase requires local ownership of broadcast stations, a limit on the number of stations under a single ownership, and a commitment to "public service" broadcasting at least some of the time. A case can be made for these rules, though they are hardly without drawbacks (for example, local ownership inhibits the development of regional broadcast services with some attendant economies of scale) or always mutually consistent (the smaller the ownership interest, the fewer the resources for public service broadcasting). But these standards, detailed though they seem, are insufficient to settle all contests for licenses or even to narrow the field down very much. Hence further criteria, generally a good deal less plausible and even less likely to remain intact from one case to the next, are invented—whether the prospective licensee is of "good character," whether he will conduct a survey of "community groups" to ensure that he is meeting their "needs," and so on. One does not have to go very far down this road before one has enough "standards" to permit one to make virtually any decision one wants—which is to say, to act arbitrarily. The result is a state of affairs that both outrages the critics of broadcasting (who find the FCC too close to the regulated industry) and dismays the broadcasters themselves (who find the FCC constantly meddling in decisions about the content of broadcasting and generally keeping them on tenterhooks).

A second reason for the efforts to enlarge the domain of regulation can be found in what James W. McKie has called the "tar-baby effect."[22] This occurs when an agency applies a regulation, perhaps a quite clear and defensible one, to some single aspect of an enterprise (for example, the rate a utility may earn) only to discover that the effect of its regulation is not what it hoped; as a consequence, it then seeks to regulate additional aspects of the enterprise in order to make the initial regulation "come out right." Suppose, to use McKie's example, one sought to regulate the rate of return on investment to prevent a utility from making monopoly profits. Theoretically, such a strategy meets most of the requirements of an economizing approach: a single key variable is regulated; the regulation takes the form of an unambiguous quantitative constraint; and the public purpose is clear and easily justified. But once the rate of return is set, the utility's managers lose much of their incentive to keep costs down and produce efficiently: they will get their allowable earnings whatever the costs. (One appealing way to let costs go up is to inflate managerial salaries.) If the allowed rate of return is higher than the cost of capital, there may be a tendency to overinvest in capital-intensive innovations (the so-called Averch-Johnson effect, the empirical existence of which is debatable). The utility may charge very high prices to customers whose demand for the utility's product is inelastic and much lower prices for the same product to those whose demands are highly elastic, and all this will appear to be unjust price discrimination. In response, the regulatory agency will endeavor to issue new directives controlling executive salaries, licensing new capital investment, and setting prices for various classes of users. In counter-response, the utility may let the quality of its service deteriorate to those customers for whom the agency has set prices lower than what the utility would have charged. In counter-counter-response, the agency will issue quality-of-service directives. And so on.[23] This sort of friction occurs even if the regulated monopoly faces no competition. Competition frequently exists, however (as between electricity and gas as a source of power), and of course multiplies the problems.

An especially interesting example of the unintended effect is found in the attitude of public utility commissions toward the charitable contributions of regulated utilities. Because the commissions see their task as keeping rates down, they typically will not allow utilities to charge as business expenses any educational or charitable contributions. These must instead be shown as deductions from net income. As a result, utilities contribute, on the average, a much smaller percentage of their before-tax income to charity than do industries not subject to rate regulation. Here, the existence of regulation, designed originally to achieve one social objective, prevents the development of "social responsibil-ity" among businessmen.[24]

A third reason for the tendency to increase the domain of regulation arises out of the fact that a regulatory agency is a *public* body and thus is the natural locus for public expectations that "problems" involving the affected industry will be solved. If a group feels that television programs are silly or dull or show too much violence, it is only necessary that there be an FCC for it to become the object of a campaign aimed at requiring broadcasters to show programs that are sophisticated, entertaining, and nonviolent (by somebody's standards). Never mind that the FCC has no idea how to achieve these results and, given the economics of over-the-air broadcasting, that perhaps they cannot be achieved at all. The agency will either resist the demands (a risky course now that plaintiffs increasingly obtain court orders compelling action), or it will conduct studies and issue notices of proposed regulations. In due time new rules will emerge—for example, restricting the number of hours of prime time that can be preempted by networks—but who can say whether the programs will improve?

If passenger rail service is declining in quality or appears on the verge of going out of existence altogether, it is only necessary that there be an ICC for suburban middle-class commuters, in their own interest, to find a plausible target. If two small cities wish to acquire air service between them, it is only necessary that the Civil Aeronautics Board (CAB) exist and have the power to award air routes and approve fares; in time Jonesville and Toonerville will get air service, and the cost of this uneconomic arrangement will be passed on to those who fly on self-sustaining routes. Richard A. Posner has offered a theory that summarizes many of these tendencies: regulation has, as one of its functions, the performance of taxation and subsidization chores normally (but with greater difficulty) performed by the legislature.[25] Other examples of this process include the requirement that auto insurers accept high-risk drivers at rates that produce a loss to the company, that AT&T provide free interconnections for the National Educational Television network, that electric utilities give discounts to hospitals, and (until recently) that magazine publishers be allowed to mail at rates below the postal service's marginal cost.

Some of these subsidies may be desirable, others may not be. But all create great difficulties for the rational management of public regulation inasmuch as there is neither a criterion for balancing costs and benefits nor any incentive to reveal publicly who is getting how much from whom. There are also difficult questions of equity. For example, even if one ought to subsidize uneconomic air or train service, should the cost fall wholly on other passengers or shippers? Finally, if the cost of the subsidy is not fully recovered by the affected industry, it will have a powerful incentive to cheat by allowing service to deteriorate. This, of course, produces more consumer complaints and a further round of regulatory intervention.

A fourth reason why regulation expands is that an agency may wish to increase its power over an industry. The agency may wish to improve its prospects for accomplishing its substantive objectives, perhaps by increasing its bargaining power so as to get better settlements than the rote application of policy would produce. Or (a motive rare among federal agencies but not so rare among state and local ones) the agency may wish to increase its nuisance value and thus what its members can charge the industry in graft or favors. The Antitrust Division brings many cases it probably cannot win but through which it may influence business behavior via consent-decree proceedings. The Securities and Exchange Commission (SEC) can use its right to approve or disapprove new security registrations to exact changes in corporate arrangements. The FCC can use the vagueness of its policies and the fact that broadcast licenses are issued for only three years at a time to get changes (or promises of changes) in broadcast content even though in the end hardly any license is ever revoked and despite the fact that the governing legislation specifically forbids the regulation of content.

Finally, as a matter of bureaucratic politics, agency officials often wish to hold the initiative. The existence of an unchanging policy or set of substantive rules makes more predictable the behavior of an agency in various circumstances; the more predictable the behavior, the more it can be taken for granted, and the less discretionary influence the agency can wield.[26] Furthermore, as studies of bureaucratic administration have shown, if a rule specifies the minimum expected behavior for a person, then his actual behavior will tend to conform to—and in some cases decline to—that minimum.[27] Thus recurrent changes are necessary to break the pattern.

We have no direct and systematic measure of the extent to which an agency's domain of directive regulation expands for the reasons suggested here. Roger G. Noll has argued, after reviewing historical data on selected agency budgets, that many agencies use additional money to increase regulatory domain rather than to improve performance.[28] In any event, the argument that expansive tendencies cannot possibly prevail because the regulatory agencies are always starved for funds is clearly false. After World War II and again in the 1950s and early 1960s, agency appropriations increased dramatically (in the latter period, they tripled). George J. Stigler has observed that "economic regulation is clearly a prosperous calling: the average federal regulatory agency doubles its dollar expenditures each eight to ten years."[29]

There will, of course, be exceptions to the general tendencies discussed above. Some agencies administer legal rules so exact and under grants of authority so inflexible that reinterpreting those rules or extending the boundaries of that authority is virtually impossible. The minimum wage and maximum hours legislation enforced by a bureau of the Department of Labor seems to be of this character. To many readers, however, the chief defect with the expansion theory offered here is that it neglects the principal determinant of the growth and function of business regulation—the interests and preferences of the regulated businesses.

Business "Capture" of Regulatory Agencies

Commentators as otherwise different as George Stigler and Gabriel Kolko have argued that administrative regulation will not succeed in constraining business firms to act in accordance with socially valuable objectives because the agencies that administer these regulations will be "captured" by or otherwise serve the interests of the affected industries. Professor Stigler in particular has offered as a general theory the proposition that government regulation is "acquired by the industry and is designed and operated primarily for its benefit."[30] Beneficial regulation can take several forms: direct money subsidies (as for airlines or the merchant marine), control over entry (as with airline certification, bank charters, protective tariffs, or oil import quotas), the control of substitute products and processes (as with restrictions on oleomargarine to benefit butter producers or on labor-saving devices to protect the craft unions), and price fixing (as with freight rates).

To the extent regulation takes this form, its use as a means of inducing business to serve socially desirable objectives is obviously quite limited, even trivial, unless one can argue that the anticompetitive interests of a particular industry are coincident with the broader interests of society.

The analysis earlier in this chapter regarding the political sources of regulation should provide some clues as to the circumstances under which the regulated industry will become the client of the regulatory agency. When a potential government policy promises to confer concentrated (i.e., high per capita) benefits on a small, organizable sector of society and impose only widely distributed (i.e., low per capita) costs on a large, hard-to-organize segment of society, then (a) the proposed policy will probably be adopted and (b) those who implement the policy will seek to serve the group requesting it. It is now generally understood, for example, that those agencies which have in the past been most solicitous of the welfare of the industries they regulate—the CAB and the airlines, the FCC and the broadcasters—were not "captured" by those industries but were created at the industries' request or at least with their active support. To serve these industries was only to obey a clear legislative mandate. Domestic airlines complained of the "chaos" caused by "destructive competition," and broadcasters confronted acute problems of signal interference. Both turned, with varying degrees of unanimity and enthusiasm, to the government for help.[31]

Regulatory agencies that were created out of the conflict between two organized sectors of society under circumstances such that the benefits to one were costs to the other are less likely to adopt a serving-the-client attitude. If favoritism develops, it will represent an unstable equilibrium of forces, and the balance will shift from time to time. The National Labor Relations Board began as the patron of organized labor, became pro-business under the Eisenhower administration, shifted back toward labor under Kennedy, and so on. The railroads' position as the favored clients of the ICC declined after the truckers were brought under ICC control in the 1930s.

Regulations created to impose costs on organizable sectors of the economy in order to obtain diffused benefits for the society offer the key test of the "capture" hypothesis. When government attempts to prevent restraint of trade, to keep impure food and harmful drugs off the market, to improve auto safety, to eliminate unsafe toys, to end false and misleading advertising, to reduce air and water pollution, or to maintain a minimum wage, it is in effect defying an industry or even all industry. There are two ways industry can fight back: block passage of the legislation or (failing that) influence its administration.

In the past, blocking legislation entirely has been the most successful strategy, though in truth little "strategy" was involved because until fairly recently legislators did not take most "consumer" bills seriously. Today, the advent of consumer and ecology movements, combined with the publicity rewards and the increased opportunities for presidential nominations now available to senators who can find and capitalize on a popular issue, have reduced significantly (but not eliminated) the chances of industry blockage of such legislation.

Such legislation can be emasculated. The case most frequently mentioned (though the accounts thus far available have scarcely been dispassionate) is that of the Food and Drug Administration (FDA), which allegedly adopted for many years a solicitous and benign attitude toward the pharmaceutical manufacturers. This attitude was rewarded, it is claimed, by giving lucrative or prestigious jobs in the drug industry to former members of the agency. Assuming that the worst was true, what is striking is how easily the situation was reversed by the appointment in 1966 of a new, more vigorous administrator. A comparable degree of activism was instilled in the Federal Trade Commission by the appointment of new commissioners. Whether these new ways of acting will persist remains to be seen. And the behavior of the newer agencies in the fields of auto safety and pollution abatement is too recent to be assessed.

Before one supposes that the laxity of the old Federal Drug Administration and perhaps of the old FTC was entirely the result of industrial capture, it is important to consider other explanations consistent with the same facts. The Department of Agriculture must inspect every piece of meat slaughtered for shipment across state lines; under the Wool Products Labeling Act of 1939, the FTC examined in a recent year 25 million products in 12,000 establishments, thereby discovering 14,000 violations. Postal inspectors are supposed to prevent the mailing of materials intended to defraud, the amount of which must be staggering; the FDA is empowered to inspect any establishment processing or storing foods, drugs, or cosmetics, but there are 85,000 such establishments, the total output of which is vast. The FTC is charged with preventing false and misleading advertising, an ambiguous criterion that must (in theory) be applied to hundreds of thousands of commercial announcements.[32] In short, part of the problem of using regulation to confer widely distributed benefits is that the transactions to be regulated are almost as numerous and as widely distributed as the benefits to be had from them. This often means that what is in fact controlled is not all such transactions but a sample of them somehow drawn—by lot, by complaint, or by design. And where in fact all such transactions are controlled, as is the case in meat inspection, the number of persons who must be employed is very large and the circumstances under which they work give little visibility to, and thus impede control over, their activity.

Regulation on behalf of consumers creates very large problems of discretion among lower-ranking personnel, just as attempts to enforce traffic laws and vice laws create such problems for police departments.[33] How the members of a large organization will manage that discretion depends on a number of factors, of which influence from the affected industry is only one, and may not be the most important. We know very little—indeed, next to nothing—about the day-to-day management of these regulatory tasks. (By comparison, assessing the behavior of the more industry-oriented agencies is relatively easy: each year the FCC handles six hundred to seven hundred commercial broadcast license applications, and the CAB takes on perhaps five thousand or six thousand economic enforcement cases.) We can here only speculate on the factors that will make for better or worse agency discretion.

One is the extent of the sampling problem. Bias can enter into any situation in which one can claim he "didn't have time" to consider a particularly nettlesome problem. The FTC has been in this position, to its great regret. The Antitrust Division of the Justice Department, by contrast, is in the happy position of being able to investigate *every* plausible case presented to it. As Suzanne Weaver has shown, clues as to possible violations of the Sherman Act arise in manageable numbers each year, and the division has enough lawyers to look closely at all but the most farfetched or trivial.[34]

Another factor behind agency perfomance is the presence or absence of an external, more or less objective measure of success. For the Antitrust Division, this is found in the decisions of judges before whom Sherman or Clayton Act cases are brought: the division does not *decide* cases; it *prosecutes* them. Requiring conformity to an explicit monetary figure is the essence of wage regulation in the Labor Department.[35] On the other hand, there is no objective measure or third-party judgment for the FTC or the FCC.

Sometimes there is no objective test of the rightness of an agency decision but there are strong professional norms maintained by outside reference groups which can serve much the same function. Suzanne Weaver's research suggests the importance to the laywers of the Antitrust Division of the good opinion of the "antitrust bar," and not merely because a number of division lawyers will someday join that bar on the side of the defense—the respect of professional colleagues, earned by bringing "good cases," is valued even by those attorneys who spend their lives in the division.[36] By contrast, examiners who conduct hearings for some of the regulatory agencies may have to make important decisions without generally accepted and professional norms to guide them. And the meat inspectors of the Department of Agriculture, though they perform semiprofessional tasks for which one might be expected to know a good deal of medicine, anatomy, bacteriology, and law, are in fact low-paid civil servants with a rudimentary knowledge of such matters and are required to work in the unpleasant, sometimes hostile environment of a slaughterhouse. Recently several inspectors went on trial in Boston for allegedly accepting gratuities from a meatpacker (though the facts of the case do not indicate clearly whether there was any substantial wrong-doing).[37] Meat inspectors are in a situation very much like big-city policemen: the wonder is that they can do their jobs as well as they do. The about-face in the posture of the FDA came about, it seems, in large part because a new administrator was able to hire new personnel and instill in the old personnel a sense that the governing standards of their work in drug testing should be those of academic and research-oriented chemists and doctors rather than those of medical practitioners and commercial chemists.

The existence of strong professional norms is not an unmixed blessing. What is a desideratum to some will be a bias to others. The Antitrust Division, for example, has succeeded in institutionalizing the ethos of the lawyer, or more exactly of the prosecuting attorney, in a field in which one might wish for the application of economic analysis as well. From time to time economic guidelines have been suggested for antitrust work (in order, for example, to gauge the likelihood of workable competition or predict the market effect of a divestiture order), but these have been ignored. Few organizations, and especially few successful ones, can tolerate having more than a single governing ethos: the need for morale, for a sense of mission and of distinctive competence, and for standard operating procedures means that competing norms will be suppressed, ignored, or isolated.[38]

A partial and temporary substitute for professional norms is missionary zeal. An agency in its formative years, especially one created on a wave of public expectations or as a result of an ideological struggle, will attract as pioneer staff members persons who believe in the cause and who are adventurous enough to attract public attention during the early years. This was true of the Bureau of Chemistry (predecessor agency of the FDA) under Dr. Harvey Wiley and of the National Highway Safety Bureau (predecessor of the National Highway Traffic Safety Administration—NHTSA) under Dr. William Haddon, Jr. The zeal of the FDA soon began to decline, a slowdown caused as much by presidential opposition as by industry "capture" or internal complacency: Wiley made the mistake of describing saccharin as perhaps harmful to health at a time when President Theodore Roosevelt was using it every day. Roosevelt retaliated by appointing a board to review (and in effect to overturn) many bureau decisions.[39] The fate of the NHTSA remains to be seen.

The nature of the rules being administered will influence the exercise of discretion and the degree of industry compliance. If compliance with a rule is highly visible, costs little, and entails no competitive disadvantage, that rule will be more easily enforced than one with the opposite characteristics. Thus scarcely any administrative effort will be required to get cigarette manufacturers to print a health warning on their packages: the printed message costs little, its absence would be quickly noted, and no brand is likely to sell better because the warning is left off. By contrast, great effort will be needed to ensure proper meat inspection: it is expensive and arduous work, the consumer cannot readily detect falsely certified meat, and meat packaging is so competitive and the profit margins so thin that the sale of substandard or adulterated products could be quite profitable.

There is evidence that compliance is more readily obtained from large, prosperous firms than from small, marginal ones. This was the conclusion of Robert Lane in his study of the economic regulation of New England businessmen, and there is some support for this in George Katona's study of business observance of wartime price controls.[40] If this difference between firms exists, one reason may be that large firms are more visible and politically more vulnerable (i.e., they make more inviting targets for critical politicians) than smaller ones. The New York City Department of Consumer Affairs, for example, has found that large retail stores will often yield to adverse publicity whereas the smaller stores must be taken to court to achieve the same result. Another reason may be that a big firm is likely to have a large, specialized bureaucracy to handle compliance with rules just as it has specialized bureaucracies to handle other aspects of its business.

Finally, solicitousness toward industry is sometimes promoted by the requirements of due process. As Richard E. Caves observed in his study of air transport regulation, a perfectly autonomous and (from an economic point of view) efficient regulatory agency would be one that was free to act without constraint—which is to say, to act without giving notice, holding hearings, considering evidence, receiving petitions, or rendering opinions.[41] Not only does political reality often conflict with an economizing approach to regulation; so also do the rule of law and the requirement of adversary proceedings. The interests of the producer are often taken into account because, at a hearing, he makes a persuasive case that they *ought* to be. And when an adversary hearing is held—for example, when two airlines are competing for a particular route—the agency's attention is inevitably drawn away from fundamental issues. (Should the route be regulated at all? What service would competition produce?) From the start, the question is narrowed down to that of who should provide a given service. In any case, how could an agency *not* be "industry-oriented" when the only parties to hearings are *firms*. [. . .]

Some Preconditions of Effective Regulation

The administrative management and economic effect of regulatory agencies vary with the kind of rules enforced and the kind of industry regulated. Other things being equal, a program adopted as the result of the successful effort by one organized economic interest to impose constraints on another organized interest will be more effective than one adopted in response to efforts to confer benefits on large numbers of diverse and unorganized beneficiaries. The reason for this is that in the former case market power reinforces political power. For example, legal requirements to disclose the composition and quality of insecticides, fungicides, seeds, animal serums and toxins, caustic poisons, fabrics, and wool products are ordinarily obeyed because the "consumers" to whom the information is disclosed are to a significant degree not individual users but economic producers—farmers, clothing and furniture manufacturers, and importers. They purchase in large quantities and by specifications rather than by brand names, and they have trade associations that monitor business behavior and report violations.

If the beneficiaries of a regulation are large numbers of individual consumers, the regulation is most likely to be obeyed when compliance is readily visible and no firm suffers a competitive disadvantage by obeying (e.g., by printing proof numbers on liquor bottles or health warnings on cigarette labels). When noncompliance is easily concealed in ways that confer an economic advantage, compliance will be greatest among the largest firms and least among the smallest: a few large firms are easier to inspect than many small ones, and large firms are more likely to be internally bureaucratic to a degree that leads to the routinization of compliance. For example, compliance with many of the requirements of the Occupational Safety and Health Act or with various mine safety regulations seems to be greater among large firms that have the specialized competence to devise, acquire, and maintain the necessary equipment and for whom monetary costs of compliance represent a smaller proportional increase in overhead.

Regulations that stipulate a clear and timely standard for compliance such that all improper behavior can be specified or reasonably inferred in advance will be more effective than those that do not. A package-labeling requirement that calls for a full statement of the contents of the package will be routinely obeyed; a regulation barring "false and misleading advertising" will not. Though some advertising statements clearly contrary to fact can be made the subject of effective administrative actions, the myriad ways by which claims, including false ones, can be suggested or implied can never be anticipated in advance nor ended before there has been an opportunity for economic gain from their use. Furthermore, claims proscribed from nationally circulated advertising can be shifted from the media to the point of sale and from printed statements at the point of sale to oral representations made by store clerks responding, perhaps, to special rebates or other incentives.

The institutional arrangements defining an enforcement agency's powers and jurisdiction will influence its effectiveness. An agency monitoring all commerce will be less influenced by industry claims than one monitoring a particular sector. An agency that prosecutes suspected offenders will be inclined to judge its own performance by how many cases it wins; an agency with the power to examine goods or investigate conditions will judge its behavior by how many inspections it carries out and at what cost. Neither test may be meaningful in terms of larger social objectives. In the first instance, the cases won by the agency's prosecutors may be trivial rather than important, have adverse rather than beneficial economic effects, and represent empty victories if there is no means for ensuring continuing compliance among the parties to the proceedings. In the second instance, the number of inspections executed tells one nothing about the fairness and propriety of the inspections, the existence or absence of corruption among the inspectors, or the value to the consumer of the inspected as opposed to the uninspected product. At a minimum, prosecutorial agencies seem less likely to be "captured" by an industry than inspectional ones.

Both business firms and regulatory agencies act on the basis of a common principle: maintain the organization. For the firm, that means creating and managing an income stream in a way that pleases union leaders, boards of directors, and institutional investors. For the public agency, that means creating and managing services (or a public image of services) that please key congressmen, organized clients, and the news media. From time to time that pattern is interrupted by an Upton Sinclair or a Ralph Nader, but there are not yet grounds for concluding that the functions of the crusader and the watchdog can be institutionalized.

Notes

1. For help in gaining an overview of American business regulation, I would like to acknowledge the research assistance of Frances Francis, Marc Landy, and Paul Quirk and the useful comments on earlier drafts of this paper by Richard A. Posner and Suzanne Weaver, by my colleagues in the Faculty Seminar on the Politics of Regulation at the Institute of Politics at Harvard, by members of the Workshop on Industrial Organization at the University of Chicago, and by my associates in the Brookings project on the social responsibilities of business.

2. See, for example, Paul W. MacAvoy (ed.), *The Crisis of the Regulatory Commissions* (Norton, 1970).

3. Roger G. Noll, Merton J. Peck, and John J. McGowan, *Economic Aspects of Television Regulation* (Brookings Institution, 1973), Chaps. 6-7.

4. Compare Gabriel Kolko, *Railroads and Regulation, 1877-1916* (Princeton University Press, 1965), with John A. Garraty, *The New Commonwealth, 1877-1890* (Harper and Row, 1968), and Edward A. Purcell, Jr., "Ideas and Interests: Businessmen and the Interstate Commerce Act," *Journal of American History*, Vol. 54 (December 1967), pp. 561-78.

5. Howard Raiffa, *Decision Analysis: Introductory Lectures on Choices under Uncertainty* (Addison-Wesley, 1968), pp. 91-94; Frederick Mosteller and Philip Nogee, "An Experimental Measurement of Utility," *Journal of Political Economy*, Vol. 59 (October 1951), pp. 371-404.

6. Raymond A. Bauer, Ithiel de Sola Pool, and Lewis Anthony Dexter, *American Business and Public Policy* (Atherton, 1963), pp. 139-42.

7. James Q. Wilson, *Political Organizations* (Basic Books, 1973), Chaps. 8, 10.

8. Mancur Olson, Jr., *The Logic of Collective Action: Public Goods and the Theory of Groups* (Harvard University Press, 1965), pp. 48-50, 126-28.

9. Harmon Zeigler, *The Florida Milk Commission Changes Minimum Prices* (University of Alabama Press for the Inter-University Case Program, 1963).

10. Charles R. Plott, "Occupational Self-Regulation: A Case Study of the Oklahoma Dry Cleaners," *Journal of Law and Economics*, Vol. 8 (October 1965), pp. 195-222.

11. Edmund W. Kitch, Marc Isaacson, and Daniel Kasper, "The Regulation of Taxicabs in Chicago," *Journal of Law and Economics*, Vol. 14 (October 1971), pp. 285-350.

12. I draw here on Mark V. Nadel, *The Politics of Consumer Protection* (Bobbs-Merrill, 1971), pp. 18, 143.

13. See ibid., pp. 252-43; Ronald C. Moe and Steven C. Teel, "Congress as Policy-Maker: A Necessary Reappraisal," *Political Science Quarterly*, Vol. 85 (September 1970), pp. 443-70; John R. Johannes, "When Congress Leads" (Ph.D. dissertation, Harvard University, 1970).

14. Paul J. Halpern, "Consumer Politics and Corporate Behavior: The Case of Automobile Safety" (Ph.D. dissertation, Harvard University, 1972).

15. A. Myrick Freeman III and Robert H. Haveman, "Clean Rhetoric and Dirty Water," *Public Interest* (Summer 1972), pp. 51-65. See also, in Selma Mushkin (ed.), *Public Prices for Public Products* (Urban Institute, 1972), the chapter by Allen V. Kneese, "Discharge Capacity of Waterways and Effluent Charges," pp. 133-51, and Paul H. Gerhardt's chapter on "Air Pollution Control: Benefits, Costs and Inducements," pp. 153-71.

16. I am indebted here to Henry D. Jacoby and John Steinbruner, "Salvaging the Federal Attempt To Control Auto Pollution," *Public Policy*, Vol. 21 (Winter 1973), pp. 1-48, and to

Steinbruner, "Toward an Analysis of Policy Implementation: The Case of Mobile Source Air Pollution" (paper prepared for the 1971 annual meeting of the American Political Science Association; processed).

17. See, for example, David Caplovitz, *The Poor Pay More* (Free Press, 1963).

18. Homer Kripke, "Gesture and Reality in Consumer Credit Reform," *New York University Law Review*, Vol. 44 (March 1969), pp. 7-9.

19. This is the finding of Federal Trade Commission, *Economic Report on Installment Credit and Retail Sales Practices of District of Columbia Retailers* (1968).

20. Regarding the airlines, see Richard E. Caves, *Air Transport and Its Regulators: An Industry Study* (Harvard University Press, 1962), Chap. 18: William A. Jordan, *Airline Regulation in America* (Johns Hopkins Press, 1970). On freight transportation, see John R. Meyer et al., *The Economics of Competition in the Transportation Industries* (Harvard University Press, 1959); Merton J. Peck, "Competitive Policy for Transportation?" in Almarin Phillips (ed.), *Perspectives on Antitrust Policy* (Princeton University Press, 1965), pp. 244-72. A synthesis of much of the recent evidence on both industries can be found in William A. Jordan. "Producer Protection, Prior Market Structure, and the Effects of Government Regulation," *Journal of Law and Economics*, Vol. 15 (April 1972), pp. 151-76.

21. Paul W. MacAvoy, *Price Formation in Natural Gas Fields: A Study of Competition, Monopsony, and Regulation* (Yale University Press, 1962), Chap. 8: MacAvoy, "The Regulation-Induced Shortage of Natural Gas," *Journal of Law and Economics*, Vol. 14 (April 1971), pp. 167-99; Edward W. Erickson and Robert M. Spann, "Supply Response in a Regulated Industry: The Case of Natural Gas," *Bell Journal of Economics and Management Science*, Vol. 2 (Spring 1971), pp. 94-121.

22. McKie, "Regulation and the Free Market: The Problem of Boundaries," *Bell Journal of Economics and Management Science*, Vol. 1 (Spring 1970), p. 9.

23. The work of the New York Public Commission serves as a case in point. At one time that agency had under way eight separate investigations into the pricing and service levels of the New York Telephone Company, *New York Times*, August 24, 1972.

24. Council for Financial Aid to Education, *Educational Contributions by Public Utilities and Other Regulated Industries as an Allowable Operating Expense for Rate-Making Purposes* (New York, 1972), p. 15. The figures used by the CFAF are from 1967 tabulations of corporate income tax returns. See also Henry G. Manne, "The Social Responsibility of Regulated Utilities," Wisconsin Law Review No. 4 (1972), pp. 995-1009.

25. Posner, "Taxation by Regulation," *Bell Journal of Economics and Management Science*, Vol. 2 (Spring 1971), pp. 22-50.

26. Michel Crozier, *The Bureaucratic Phenomenon* (University of Chicago Press, 1964), pp. 156-59; James Q. Wilson, "The Dead Hand of Regulation," *Public Interest*, No. 25 (Fall 1971), pp. 39-58.

27. Alvin W. Gouldner, *Patterns of Industrial Bureaucracy: A Case Study of Modern Factory Administration* (Free Press, 1954), Chap. 9.

28. Noll, *Reforming Regulation: An Evaluation of the Ash Council Proposals* (Brookings Institution, 1971), p. 88.

29. Stigler, "The Process of Economic Regulation," *Antitrust Bulletin*, Vol. 17 (Spring 1972), pp. 216, 218.

30. Stigler, "The Theory of Economic Regulation," *Bell Journal of Economics and Management Science*, Vol. 2 (Spring 1971), p. 3.

31. On the airlines, see Robert Burkhardt, *The Federal Aviation Administration* (Praeger, 1967); on railroads, see Kolko, *Railroads and Regulation*, and Garraty, *The New Commonwealth*; on broadcasters, see Robert E. Cushman, *The Independent Regulatory Commissions* (Oxford University Press, 1941), and *Regulation of Broadcasting*, a study for the House Committee on Interstate and Foreign Commerce, 85 Cong. 1 sess. (1958). After a period in which public interest theories of the origins of regulation were unquestioningly accepted, we have now entered a period in which self-interest theories are uncritically substituted. In most cases, the matter is more complex than either theory admits. Railroaders were divided about the Interstate Commerce Act. Furthermore, the act

specifically denied the railroads what they most wanted—legally binding "pooling" (i.e., cartel) agreements. The Radio Act of 1927, strongly supported by the broadcasting industry, was also supported by spokesmen for a public that was upset by poor radio reception. A full discussion of these matters is beyond the scope of this paper.

32. See Clair Wilcox, *Public Policies toward Business* (rev. ed., Irwin, 1960), p. 204.

33. See James Q. Wilson, *Varieties of Police Behavior: The Management of Law and Order in Eight Communities* (Harvard University Press, 1968), Chap. 2.

34. Suzanne Weaver, "Decision-Making in the U.S. Antitrust Division" (Ph.D. dissertation, Harvard University, 1973).

35. See Peter M. Blau, *The Dynamics of Bureaucracy: A Study of Interpersonal Relations in Two Government Agencies* (University of Chicago Press, 1955), Chaps. 7-11. The agency analyzed by Blau is not identified by him, but I have it on excellent authority that he in fact studied the office in the Department of Labor that administers the Fair Labor Standards Act.

36. Weaver, "Decision-Making in the U.S. Antitrust Division."

37. Peter Schuck, "The Curious Case of the Indicted Meat Inspectors," *Harper's*, Vol. 245 (September 1972), pp. 81-88.

38. The perspective is that of Philip Selznick, *Leadership in Administration* (Row, Peterson, 1957).

39. Nadel, *Politics of Consumer Protection*, p. 24.

40. Robert E. Lane, *The Regulation of Businessmen* (Yale University Press, 1954), pp. 95, 103; George Katona, *Price Control and Business: Field Studies among Producers and Distributors of Consumer Goods in the Chicago Area, 1942-44* (University of Indiana Press, 1946), p. 241.

41. Caves, *Air Transport and Its Regulators*, p. 297.

2.4

Industrial Structure, Party Competition, and the Sources of Regulation

KATHLEEN KEMP

Although political campaigns are usually full of rhetoric concerning the "good of the country" or the "national interest," it is important to remember that to participate in politics requires both time and money. It therefore follows that the majority of partici-pants in the electoral process will, as a rule, be those who have strong incentives for participation. The man on the street may crudely formulate this opinion when he says that politics is for "the rich," a view that is often given a sophisticated echo by those who decry the influence of "big business." The true state of affairs, however, seems to be this: Politics as an arena is open to anyone able to overcome the entry barriers of time, money, and incentives, and it is generally the case that business can cross these barriers more readily than other interest groups can.

However, business, far from representing a homogenous set of interests, is comprised of highly competitive groups, large and small, with quite specific and often conflicting objectives, for whom influence with the government can mean the difference between success or failure. Election rhetoric, on the other hand, usually reflects pocketbook issues in the most general terms, as in "the interests of the farmers" or "the importance of the steel industry"; specific corporate interests and political objectives can be culled only by careful examination of newspapers, financial journals, and campaign contributions. In this essay, Kathleen Kemp provides a lucid overview of party–industry relations over the last century.

There is a growing body of research linking industrial sectors and types of economic structures with particular political parties and party systems. Cameron (1978), for the most relevant example, studied eighteen nations for the 1960–1975 period and found that countries with industrialized, open economies tended to have strong left-wing parties and extractive, redistributive macroeconomic policies. Kurth (1979), Gershenkron (1943), and Gourevitch (1977) have developed the relation between the dominance of particular economic sectors (agriculture, textiles, heavy steel-based manufacturing) and types of political structures for earlier historical periods. There has been little systematic research on American political parties and economic interests; however, there have been numerous observations of economic groups aligned with particular political parties. Salamon (1975), for example, found a Democratic coalition of homebuilders, savings institutions, and northern big city mayors aligned with the Democratic controlled Commerce Committees and HUD in the mid-1970s. And Knapp (1956) has described the Farm Bureau–Democratic congressional coalition in its battle with the Republican dominated Agriculture Department in the 1950s. In the only work focused specifically on party–industry coalitions, Ferguson (1983) presents convincing evidence that the Democratic New Deal coalition was based on capital-intensive, high-technology industries with significant world markets.

The Basic Hypothesis and Assumptions

The basic hypothesis of this essay is that political parties comprised in part of coalitions of industrial groups are significant in explaining regulatory policy formulation and the level of support given regulatory agencies by Congress and the President. The argument is based on three assumptions. The first assumption is that the economic groups of greatest importance are not atomized units as described in much of the pluralist literature; rather, economic groups are seen as coalescing in relatively invariant structures depending upon their amount of market power and market interdependence.

The second assumption is that regulatory policies, regardless of how broadly based their benefits may appear to be, directly or indirectly benefit some industry or group of firms within an industry. This is most obvious with protective policies such as the 1938 Civil Aeronautics Act, which limited market entry and price competition for the newly emerging commercial airline industry, and the Robinson–Patman Act of 1936, which protected the independent retailers against the chain stores. The benefits of policies such as the Occupational Safety and Health Administration Act (1970) and the Equal Employment Opportunity Act (1970) are less obvious. However, some of the largest corporations did benefit when their standard operating procedures in safety and hiring were made mandatory for their smaller, more marginal and labor-intensive competitors. IBM and other high-technology firms decreased rather than increased their costs of production because of clean air laws. And Southern Railway, "discoverer" of the infamous snail darter, stood to maintain its market position had environmentalists succeeded in preventing the construction of the Tellico and Tenn–Tomm waterway projects; the maritime industry would have lost out.

The third assumption is that the party affiliation of economic groups is not a matter of partisan identification on the part of individual corporate officials. Rather it refers to on-going relations between businessmen acting as corporate representatives and elected officials of one party. The distinction is nicely illustrated by Donald T. Regan, Secretary of the Treasury in the Reagan Administration. Although a Republican in terms of partisan identification, Regan revealed in his book, A View From the Street, that as chief operating officer of Merrill Lynch brokerage firm, he maintained "very productive" long-term relations with Democratic officials such as Senator and Vice President Edmund Muskie and Senators Cannon and Kennedy. The basis of the relation was Regan's interest in security regulations; he expressed dismay at President Nixon's lack of understanding of the securities industry's need for governmental regulation.

Finally, corporate policy preferences concerning regulation cannot be assumed to be manifested in advertising extolling the virtues of "free enterprise." As Galbraith (1952) has pointed out, it is in the best interests of corporate officials to maintain the myth of free enterprise, in order to deny not only their market power but also their dependence on the government for maintaining their market position.

Industries, Parties, and Institutions

The theory of regulatory policy formulation and agency support has two dimensions. The first dimension is that of alliances between particular political parties and industries and firms. The second dimension is the differentiation between the parties in the two major policy-making institutions—the presidency and Congress.

Market Power and Political Access: "Ins" and "Outs"   At any given time, particular sectors of the economy may contain an industry with substantial market power and also disadvantaged industries with less. For example, in the 1920s and 1930s the railroads dominated the transportation sector to the disadvantage of trucking and air transport; in the 1970s and 1980s oil and natural gas dominated the energy sector relative to solar power and synfuels. Moreover, within a particular industry, one or a few firms may have so large a share of the market that they control prices, wages, and the quantity of goods and services produced. For example, AT&T currently dominates telecommunications in terms of market shares and IBM controls the computer market. Often the dominant industry group has obtained and/or maintained market power through favorable public policies and protective regulation, although economic factors, such high capital-investment requirements for market entry, product differentiation, and mergers, may explain or contribute to market dominance. These dominant industry firms, the "ins," tend to be aligned with the dominant political party and to use their political influence to maintain their market power.

The best known example of an "in" industry is the House of Morgan, which developed an alliance with the Republican Party in the late nineteenth century. U.S. Steel, J. P. Morgan's creation, was large at the time of incorporation in 1906. It could not, however, have achieved its dominant market position without the support of the Republican Party, which was the dominant party from 1886 through 1932. President Theodore Roosevelt's blessing of U.S. Steel as a "good trust" made it immune from antitrust action, as Standard Oil and American Tobacco were not. This alliance continued though the 1970s with U.S. Steel doing poorly under Democratic presidents, as evidenced by Truman's attempt to seize the steel mills in 1952 and Kennedy's "jawboning" of the corporation's attempt to raise prices in 1962. The Republican years of White House control were more beneficial to U.S. Steel, although it was often compelled to give in to Eisenhower's secretary of the Treasury, George Humphrey, "for the good of the party" (Kolko, 1963; Blough, 1975; McConnell, 1963).

"Outs" develop and define themselves as political groups as a result of losing market power, such as occurred in the 1880s with skilled labor and in the 1920s with the independent retailers in their battle with chain and discount stores. "Outs" also develop as a result of the creation of new industries because of technological innovations, such as aeronautics in the 1930s, or because of new opportunities for market entry, as occurred in the oil industry in the 1920s when new discoveries in East Texas created the "independent" producers. As Galbraith (1952) has pointed out, the "outs" seek *political* power to compensate for their lack of *market* power. They are, however, limited to seeking access to political institutions through the minority party or a minority faction within the dominant party. After a critical realignment in which the minority party becomes dominant or after a deviating election in which the minority party temporarily assumes control of the presidency and Congress (Campbell, et. al., 1960; Pomper, 1967), the "outs" are able to obtain policies giving them market advantages or what Galbraith referred to as "countervailing power."

The adoption of federal regulatory laws has tended to occur during those periods when control of political power shifts from one party to another. The first federal regulatory law directly constraining business decision making—that creating the Interstate Commerce Commission—was passed in 1887 when the Democrats for a brief period controlled the White House and the House of Representatives during the long period of Republican hegemony stretching from 1860 to 1932. The Sherman Antitrust Act of 1890, the first federal government attempt to influence market structure, was passed when the Republicans had regained control of the White House and the House. Their hold was tenuous, however, with Republicans comprising only 51 percent of both the House and the Senate. The first period of rapid growth in the number of laws passed was during the Wilson administration, 1912–1920, when the Democrats again obtained control of both the presidency and Congress. The New Deal realignment of 1932, which changed the relative positions of the two parties, giving the Democrats dominance for the next fifty years, was the next period of rapid growth in federal regulation. The greatest growth, however, occurred in 1966–1976. This period is more difficult to explain. The growth in adoptions began after the 1964 election, which Pomper (1967) among others has labeled a realigning election in that the electoral composition of the dominant Democratic party changed. However, the largest number of laws (71) were passed after the deviating election of 1968, when the Republicans controlled the presidency and the Democrats controlled Congress.

Not all shifts in party control enable "outs" to become "ins," as evidenced by the critical realignment of 1896 and the deviating election of 1952, which were not followed by the adoption of new regulatory laws. For economic policy shifts to follow political change, the latter must be associated with severe dislocations or declines in either the national economy as a whole or in particular markets. These economic disruptions must also be widely interpreted to be the failure of specific industries or business in general. And there must be a public willingness, if not a demand, for changes in federal economic policies. Severe economic depressions preceded the critical realignments of 1896 and 1932. However, anti-business sentiments in 1896 were limited to the populist–agrarian wing of the Democratic Party, whose negative "Cross of Gold" platform had little meaning for the urban working and middle classes of the northeast. There were dislocations and price changes associated with the deviating elections of 1884, 1912, and 1968, but not in the early 1950s.

The economic dislocations associated with political power shifts can facilitate the adoption of policies that accommodate "outs" because they foster both a willingness to try new ideas and an antipathy to any further catering to the "ins," who may be perceived as being either responsible for the economic problems or incompetent to solve them. For example, when the business cycle is at the trough, as in 1914 and 1935, there is a need for new investment opportunities. In this circumstance the "outs," if they are new industrial groups in their capital-formation years, can easily advance the argument for a weakening of protection for old industrial groups and the adoption of new regulatory policies that will assure them market stability and investment protection.

During the New Deal, "outs" such as commercial broadcast radio, aeronautics, public brokerage firms, and the regional stock exchanges sought and obtained government access and protection through the Democratic Party (the Republican Party had been aligned with the print media, the railroads, investment banking, and the New York Stock Exchange). Ferguson has argued that the New Deal coalition that emerged in 1935 was largely comprised of young, capital-intensive industries with international markets that were opposed to the Republicans' restrictive trade policies while being not unduly threatened by the Democrats' labor policies. He has also amassed considerable evidence that the coalition behind the New Deal's Glass–Steagall Act, which required the separation of investment from commercial banking, was comprised of smaller regional banks and investment houses that were seeking to weaken the control of the House of Morgan over the major capital markets.

Current policies of deregulation can be explained as an attempt on the part of technologically innovative industry groups, such as world-wide electronic banking and satellite-based telecommunications, to eliminate the advantages of older segments of their industries and obtain their own governmental guarantees of market stability and access.

Often new agencies are created to accommodate the new "ins." Older, established agencies that might appropriately assume administrative responsibility for the new policies are perceived as "captured" by the old "in" industries and the now minority party, while new agencies can be staffed with activists from the new controlling party and those supportive of the party's position on the industry. Thus, the new agencies not only serve the interests of the dominant party's industry groups but also provide opportunities for patronage. The old agencies are permitted to exist, though with severely reduced resources unless they are able to shift their industrial alliances and goals significantly, as the Federal Trade Commission was able to do in the 1930s (Hawley, 1966; Stone, 1977). New agencies staffed with intense partisan loyalists are particularly vulnerable to purges should there be a partisan shift in control of Congress and the White House shortly after their establishment (Meier and Kramer, 1980). This is most likely to affect agencies established after deviating elections, such as the ICC in 1887 and the FTC in 1914, both of which went into decline after the Republicans regained control in the elections of 1896 and 1920 respectively.

Congressional and Presidential Constituencies   The two major parties are not cohesive monoliths. James MacGregor Burns (1963) has argued that both major parties actually consist of two wings, the congressional and the presidential. According to Burns, this division has been the result of a number of historical and institutional factors, the most important being the difference in the electoral constituencies of Congress and presidency. Because of the bias in favor of the larger states in the Electoral College, for example, the presidential wings of both parties have had to respond to the liberal demands of labor and minority groups in the large industrial states of the northeast. Burns also argued somewhat more vaguely that the presidential wings of both parties have been internationalist and interventionist because presidents of both parties have been recruited from large northeastern "bureaucracies," such as large corporations and law firms, universities and state governments.

Although Burns did not comment on this, it is significant that the economic base of the large industrial states of the northeast has consisted mainly of the large national and multinational corporate-structured industries with world markets, requiring an internationalist government committed to free trade policies. The electoral power shift in the 1970s to the south and west would only reinforce an interventionist, free-trade orientation, for the Sunbelt's economic base is also comprised of multinational corporations in oil, aeronautics, and computers, food-based conglomerates, and multinational construction companies such as Brown and Root and Bechtel. These companies all trade in world markets and are dependent upon them. Because world markets are extremely unstable and unpredictable, corporations with international markets have been eager to have the government assume an active role in providing subsidies (agricultural programs, Export-Import Bank), insurance for capital exporters (AID, Commodity Credit Corporation), regulations putting a floor under prices and guaranteeing domestic profit (Civil Aeronautics Board and the National Maritime Commission), and also welfare programs to cushion the impact of intermittent workforce reductions. For our purposes, then, we can assume that the presidential wings rather than the congressional wings of the two parties will provide the access and channels of influence for the large national and multinational corporations.

In contrast, Burns argued that the congressional wings of the two parties have been oriented toward small-town parochial interests because of the smaller electoral districts and also because the seniority system in Congress has given disproportionate influence to congressmen from noncompetitive rural distircts. Powerful congressmen have disproportionately been small independent businessmen, small-town lawyers, local law-enforcement officials and state legislators. According to Burns, their interests are local and biased in favor of small businesses and their ideology is states'-rights-oriented, conservative on labor and welfare issues, isolationist and protectionist on trade issues. While this view of congressmen as "small-town boys" has been challenged (e.g., Aberbach and Rockman, 1977), there is evidence that congressmen have been particularly influenced by small businessmen and their associational representatives, such as the Chamber of Commerce, the National Association of Manufacturers and the more regionally based trade associations. This influence has been more pronounced in nonurban districts without diversified industrial bases and where small businessmen speak for "business" and the economic welfare of the districts. Roger Davidson (1977) has described how congressmen compete to serve on the House Select Committee on Small Business although it has no lawmaking authority.

Palamountain (1955) has described how support for independent retailers in their battle against the chain stores in the 1930s came primarily from the House of Representatives. There was less support in the Senate, where the chain stores were able to obtain significant concessions in the formulation of the Robinson–Patman Act which prohibited certain forms of price competition. The Roosevelt administration did not support the act and neither did congressmen from urban districts in the northeast. According to Bailey and Samuel (1952), for another example, the weakening and eventual defeat of rent control after the second world war was accomplished largely by congressmen who were amenable to the arguments of small landlords and real-estate dealers. Proponents of rent control were President Truman and senators from northeastern urban states. From the 1930s through the 1960s representatives continually sponsored bills designed to control the growth of the largest banks and bank holding companies. These bills were sought by small bankers whose market position was threatened. According to Salamon, support for the small bankers "was most prominent in the House, where these small bankers have traditionally enjoyed the most strength" (1975:107).

If small businessmen have any influence on policy, and they have had successes from time to time, their influence must come through Congress and particularly the House of Representatives. There is little evidence that the White House has been a point of access for small businessmen. The exception may have been Eisenhower, who frequently opposed legislation favoring large businesses in order to protect smaller firms. For instance he successfully fought new securities regulation throughout his two terms because he believed that it would hurt small brokers (Kemp, 1982). He also resisted airline mergers approved by the CAB, because of their effect on competition (Behrman, 1980). This posture can be explained by the cross-cutting dimensions of party–industry coalitions. Both the large public brokerage firms seeking new legislation and the airlines wanting merger approvals had become "ins" during the New Deal and had primary access through the Democratic Party.

Summary

The two dimensions of the theory can now be briefly summarized. Weak firms and industries in terms of market power will obtain political access and favorable regulatory policies when a minority party becomes a majority party. Cutting across party affiliation is the size and market of the firm or industry. In general, the presidency will provide greater access and protection for large corporations with world markets and those industries most important to the economy. Congress, and particularly the House of Representatives, will provide greater access for small business. Both the congressional and presidential wings will, however, give greater access to industries within their parties' coalitions.

References

Aberbach, Joel and Rockman, Bert. A. (1976) "Clocking Beliefs Within the Executive Branch: the Nixon Administration Bureaucracy," *American Political Science Review* 70 (June): 46-468.

Bailey, Stephen and Samuel, Howard (1952) *Congress at Work* (New York: Holt).

Behrman, Bradley (1980) "Civil Aeronautics Board," pp. 75-122 in James Q. Wilson (ed.) *The Politics of Regulation* (New York: Basic Books).

Blough, Roger (1975) *The Washington Embrace of Business* (Pittsburgh: Carnegie-Mellon Press).

Burns, James MacGregor (1963) *The Deadlock of Democracy* (Englewood Cliffs: Prentice-Hall).

Cameron, David (1978) "The Expansion of the Public Economy: A Comparative Analysis," *American Political Science Review* 72 (December): 1243-1261.

Campbell, Angus (1960) "A Classification of the Presidential Elections," pp. 531-538 in Campbell, Phillip E. Converse, Warren E. Miller and Donald Stokes, *The American Voter* (New York: Wiley).

Davidson, Roger H. (1977) "Breaking Up Those 'Cozy Triangles': An Impossible Dream?" pp. 30-53 in Susan Welch and John G. Peters (eds.) *Legislative Reform and Public Policy* (New York: Praeger).

Ferguson, Thomas (forthcoming) *Critical Realignment: The Fall of the House of Morgan and the Origins of the New Deal* (New York: Oxford University Press).

———— (1983) "From Normalcy to New Deal: Industrial Structure, Party Competition, and American Public Policy in the Great Depression," *International Organization* (Winter 1983-84).

Galbraith, John Kenneth (1952) *American Capitalism* (New York: Houghton Mifflin).

Gerschenkron, Alexander (1943) *Bread and Democracy in Germany* (Berkeley: University of California Press.

Gourevitch, Peter Alexis (1977) "International Trade, Domestic Coalitions, and Liberty: Comparative Responses to the Crisis of 1873-1896," *Journal of Interdisciplinary History*, VIII:2 (Autumn): 281-313.

Hawley, Ellis W. (1966) *The New Deal and the Problem of Monopoly* (Princeton: Princeton University Press).

Kemp, Kathleen (1983) "Instability in Budgeting for Federal Regulatory Agencies," *Social Science Quarterly* 63 (December): 643-660.

———— (1982) "Accidents and Political Support for Regulatory Agencies. Prepared for the 1982 Annual Meeting of the Midwest Political Science Association Meeting, Milwaukee, Wisconsin.

———— (1981) "Symbolic and Strict Regulation in the American States," *Social Science Quarterly* 62 (September): 516-526.

Knapp, David (1956) "Congressional Control of Agricultural Conservation Policy," *Political Science Quarterly* 71 (June): 257-281.

Kolko, Gabriel (1970) *Railroads and Regulation: 1877-1916* (New York: Norton).

———— (1963) *The Triumph of Conservatism* (New York: Free Press).

Kurth, James (1979) "The Political Consequences of the Product Cycle," *International Organization* (Winter 1979-80).

McConnell, Grant (1966) *Private Power and American Democracy* (New York: Knopf).
———— (1963) *Steel and the Presidency—1962* (New York: Norton).
Palamountain, Joseph C. (1955) *The Politics of Distribution* (Cambridge: Harvard University Press).
Pomper, Gerald (1967) "Classification of Presidential Elections," *Journal of Politics* 29 (August); 535-566.
Regan, Donald T. (1972) *A View From the Street* (New York: New American Library).
Salamon, Lester (1975) *The Money Committee* (New York: Grossman).
Stone, Alan (1977) *Economic Regulation and the Public Interest* (Ithaca, N.Y.: Cornell University Press).

The Appearance and Disappearance of the American Voter

WALTER DEAN BURNHAM

A striking feature of the United States when compared with other industrial democratic states is its lack of strongly organized political parties. This has not always been the case. During the nineteenth century party discipline, affiliation, and electoral mobilization reached levels that made the United States one of the most active and participatory polities in the world. However, with the "crackup" of 1896, electoral participation declined sharply to record-low levels. Although a partial upswing occurred during the New Deal era, the dominant trend in the twentieth century has been toward demobilization of the U.S. electorate, while exactly the opposite trend has been characteristic in Western Europe. These changes in voting behavior did not occur in a vacuum, but were rather closely associated with the profound economic, social, and political changes that were a part of the complex processes of industrialization.

This essay by Walter Dean Burnham examines the historical evolution of the American voting universe. Making extensive use of voting statistics, Burnham vividly traces the complex interaction of social class, economic power, and mass voting in American history. Particularly interesting because of the way it links political parties to voter mobilization, Burnham's essay raises a provocative question: Have American political parties become so atrophied that the American voter is now becoming a vanishing species?

The American case deviates in many crucial respects from [political] developmental models based on Western European historical experience. These models suggest a cumulative penetration and organization of the society by increasingly elaborate partisan structures, and thus a long-term trend toward the maximization of electoral participation. In the United States, on the other hand, saturation was reached a century ago. Since then, electoral demobilization has occurred in several waves, and is still going on. Thus, we may speak of the appearance and disappearance of the American voter. Such an extraordinary peculiarity requires both documentation and explanation.

We begin with several propositions. Firstly, electoral mobilization of the mass electorate in pluralistic political systems is contingent on the competition between and organizational vitality of political parties. The one cannot be understood in isolation from the other. Secondly, one widely and rightly used index of democratization in a political system is the proportion of the potential electorate that actually votes. Thirdly, by this

Reprinted with the permission of the American Bar Association from *The Disappearance of the American Voter* (1979), pp. 35-73 (with deletions).

criterion, the United States is significantly less democratized today than any other polity of consequence holding more or less free elections. This is the more striking in view of the enormous aggregate American advantage in wealth, education and the like, which normally increase the comparative level of mass mobilization.

There are two features of American electoral participation particularly worthy of note. For one thing, turnout in contemporary American elections is very much concentrated in the middle and upper classes. For another, long-term trends in American participation run exactly counter to historical developments in other Western countries. [1] The American shift toward functional disfranchisement—especially of the lower classes—is an anomaly historically as well as comparatively. It implies that the less wealthy and well-educated the population was (at least back to the middle of the last century), the higher were the participation rates. Moreover, the disappearance continues: by 1978, the non-Southern regions of the country showed the smallest participation rate (about 38 percent for House races) since data was first compiled in 1824.

An extensive polemical and analytical literature has grown up on the subject of American electoral participation during the past decade. [2] Some has attempted to discount the anomalously high nineteenth-century participation rate by arguing that it was grossly inflated by the kind of electoral corruption known as ballot-box stuffing. [3] No one doubts the occasional appearance of these abuses, but neither the work of the present author nor the judgment of leading historians of the period lends credence to the view that this was overwhelmingly common. [4]

A good deal of effort has gone into the analysis of the influence of specifically American rules governing access to the ballot box—particularly the personal-registration statute—upon depressing and skewing turnout, both in the 1900–1920 period of initial decline and in the contemporary era. [5] In a recent article, Rosenstone and Wolfinger estimate that removal of these peculiarly American legal barriers would lead, ceteris paribus, to an increase of slightly more than nine percent in the participation rate. [6] On the whole, this literature does not seek to evaluate why such procedures should have come into existence, nor does it deal with the problem that more than one-fifth of the 1960 participation base outside the South had disappeared by 1976, despite significant marginal relaxations in the impact of registration rules between those two dates. But it identifies nevertheless a significant and measurable component of the problem.

Certain other writings, especially during the 1950s and early 1960s, not only accepted both the low participation rate and the heavy class skew, but in fact celebrated it as part of a "politics of happiness"—pragmatic, low-keyed politics in a contented middle-class political culture. [7] In the wake of the events which convulsed American politics from 1965 to 1974, such views have understandably tended to go out of fashion. Moreover, the current decline in turnout approaching all-time lows is closely associated chronologically—and perhaps causally—with an even steeper and well-documented decline in the public's affective support for national political leaders and institutions. [8] The reasons for electoral abstention almost certainly vary with the specific historical situation. But even without the present atmosphere of distrust, hostility, and bafflement which appears to dominate public opinion, it requires an exceptionally distorted view of democratic procedure to accept with equanimity both the extreme class skewing of participation and its policy implications.

In sum, it is the argument of this essay that the decay in participation during this century has been real, that the high levels of democratization during the nineteenth century were also real, and that the decay—an essentially unique property of modern American politics—is largely the artifact of political decisions in a context of uncontested hegemony. In what follows, we shall first establish several comparative benchmarks, then examine the history of American electoral participation in some detail, and finally evaluate the contemporary situation.

I. Comparisons with Other Countries Today

A major theme of the literature of comparative electoral politics is the existence of a close link between party organization and other politically relevant social organizations, and the mobilization of voters.[9] It is virtually axiomatic that organizations penetrating and mobilizing the American working classes are much feebler than they typically are in Europe. Gunnar Myrdal has gone so far as to comment that the United States has the most disorganized social infrastructure (or, if one prefers, the largest *Lumpenproletariat*) to be found in any advanced industrial society.[10] Table 1 contrasts contemporary Swedish and American turnout patterns by occupational class.

The data in Table 1 are unambiguous. Turnout in Sweden is essentially invariant along class lines, and is extremely high in each category. In the United States, there is a massive class skew in turnout. The Swedish turnout ratio between manual workers and propertied middle-class voters is 1.03 to 1 in favor of the latter; in the United States, this ratio was 1.42 to 1 in 1968 and 1.65 to 1 in 1976. Even more extreme American skews can be found when cross-tabulating educational and occupational levels. Where such cross-tabulation can be performed in 1972 the turnout rate among white male laborers with a grade-school education was 40.9 percent compared with 86.6 percent among people in managerial occupations and with a degree—a ratio of 2.12 to 1. This class skew also shows up in the 1976 survey among adults who have never voted in elections. Among white males, 6 percent of the propertied middle classes reported that they never voted, compared with 13.5 percent of the subaltern middle classes ("white collar" salaried workers), 20.2 percent of craftsmen and service workers, and 30.4 percent of people in lower working-class occupations. While race differences are most often commented about in discussions of turnout in America, in fact class differences are greater.[11]

Two other points should be made about Table 1. Turnout patterns in Sweden and elsewhere in Europe have not only been very high but also invariant from election to election in recent decades. This reflects the capacity of the Social Democrats and other parties to penetrate and mobilize the lower classes, and two rules of the electoral game which facilitate mass participation in elections. The first of these is automatic state registration of voters, a practice universal in one form or another in every Western democratic system except for the United States. The second is proportional representation, which essentially eliminates "wasted votes" and the potential turnout-depressing effects of "safe" seats in the first-past-the-post representation systems like the American or the British.

In the United States the combination of personal-registration and first-past-the-post balloting is no doubt an important contributing factor in depressing the participation rate. But it should be noted that their contribution is marginal at best. Moreover, there has been a notable relaxation of barriers to the franchise since the early 1960s in the whole country. Yet this has not been associated with increased participation (except in the South) but with declining participation. In contemporary America, turnout is not only low, but also highly variable. The primary explanation for this must be found not so much in structural factors (which in any case are not without political causes) but in politics itself. What is it about? How relevant is electoral politics in the United States to the latent or manifest needs of the lower classes?

Table 1

Voting Participation in Sweden, 1960,
and in the United States, 1968 and 1976,
by Broad Occupational Category

Socio-occupational classification	Voting, Sweden, 1960 %	Voting, USA		Difference between Sweden and USA:	
		1968 %	1976 %	1968 %	1976 %
Propertied middle class (professional, managerial farm owners)	89.6	81.7	76.9	− 7.9	12.7
Non-propertied ("white-collar") middle class[1]	90.4	77.4	70.4	−13.0	−20.0
Subtotal: middle class	90.0	79.9	73.6	−10.1	−16.4
Craftsmen, foremen[2]	93.3	66.9	58.0	−26.4	−35.3
Workers (incl. farm labourers)[3]	87.0	57.5	46.7	−29.5	−40.3
Working class	87.4	62.0	52.3	−25.4	−35.1
Total turnout from survey	86.6	67.8	59.2	−18.8	−27.4

[1] The occupational categories are not quite the same as between the countries. Nonpropertied "white collar" (salaried employees) includes two categories in the US and three in Sweden.

[2] Craftsmen, foremen. In the US this has been expanded in this table to include also service employees. For the craftsman-foreman category alone in the US, the turnouts were 68.6 percent in 1968 and 56.1 percent in 1976, with differences with Sweden of −24.7 in 1968 and −37.2 in 1976.

[3] Workers (including farm labourers). In the Swedish sample, this includes two categories: all non-craftsman blue-collar workers and farm labourers. In the American case, it includes three categories: operatives, labourers (except farm) and farm labourers. It should also be noted that the Swedish survey contains a substantial category of people not in the labour force (independents, members of families), with a turnout rate of 75.5 percent, reducing the overall to 86.6 percent.

Sources: Sweden, 1960: Statistisk Arsbok for Sverige, 1964, p. 380. Based on a 1/30th sample of total voting-age population. United States, 1968: US Bureau of the Census, Current Population Reports, Series P-20, No. 192 (2 December 1969), Voting and Registration in the Election of November 1968, p. 22; 1976 ibid., Series P-20, No. 322 (March 1978), Voting and Registration in the Election of November 1976, pp. 63-64.

As with class, so with age. It is well-known that younger voters in the United States participate much less than those of middle age. But this is not an inexorable law. A review of American participation rates in the nineteenth century makes it clear that class differentials in participation then must have been much closer to the contemporary Swedish example than to the current American situation. The same considerations apply to age stratification in voting participation. If the authentic aggregate turnout rate is 90 percent or better, it is trivial to show that the participation of the youngest age cohorts varies by a few percent from middle-aged people. An obvious comparative case involves two elections held at the same time (1972) in the United States and West Germany, both of which had enfranchised 18-year-olds since their last general election. In Germany, the ratio between the participation rate of the 18 to 20-year-old age group and the highest-turnout group (50 to 59) is 1.11 to 1. In the United States, the ratio between the participation of the newly-enfranchised and the highest-participation group (45 to 54) is 1.47 to 1. (See Table 2.)

Table 2

Turnout Rates by Age: United States, 1972,
West Germany, 1972

	United States				W. Germany		
Age group	M %	W %	Total %	Age group	M %	W %	Total %
18-20	47.7	48.8	48.2	18-20	85.0	84.3	84.6
21-24	49.7	51.7	50.7	21-24	83.9	85.0	84.4
25-29	57.6	58.0	57.8	25-29	87.6	88.8	88.2
30-34	62.1	61.7	61.9	30-34	90.4	91.3	90.8
35-44	65.9	66.7	66.3	35-39	92.4	92.3	92.3
				40-44	93.4	92.8	93.1
45-54	72.0	69.9	70.9	45-49	94.5	93.5	93.9
				50-59	95.2	93.3	94.1
55-64	72.4	69.2	70.7	60-69	94.5	92.2	93.2
65-74	73.1	64.3	68.1				
75 & over	65.9	49.1	55.6	70 & over	90.2	83.3	85.9
Total	64.1	62.0	63.0	Total	91.4	90.2	90.8
Actual turnout, % of potential electorate			55.7				91.1

Sources: US Bureau of the Census, Current Population Reports, *Population Characteristics*, 'Voting and Registration in the Election of November 1972, Series P-20, No. 253 (October 1973). W. Germany: Statistisches Bundesamt, *Statistisches Jahrbuch 1975 für die Bundesrepublik Deutschland*, p. 143.

With an aggregate turnout rate of 91 percent, the maximum age-cohort gap in German turnout is less than 10 percent. With an aggregate survey turnout rate of 63 per cent. With an aggregate survey turnout rate of 63 per cent (7 percent over-reporting), the maximum age-cohort gap in American turnout is nearly 23 percent. This point is supported by the age-stratified data in *The Changing American Voter* which stresses the magnitude of rejection of political parties among the youngest age cohorts. [12] We conclude that in addition to a massive failure in political *incorporation* of the lower classes, there is today an almost equally massive failure in political *socialization* of the young into participation in the American electoral process.

II. The Evolution of Voting Participation in the United States

The Nineteenth Century   In general, there is a great and irreducible difference between American participation rates in the nineteenth and twentieth centuries. The United States was the first major Western country to adopt substantially universal male suffrage.[13] A major comparative distinction exists between the situation in the United States in this period and in most other Western political systems. In the latter, it was not until the period 1885–1918 that full enfranchisement of the adult male population was accomplished. In all cases, the struggle to expand or to contain the franchise was intensely, and explicitly political. It was closely linked with the emergence of socialist mass movements whose first demand, naturally, was for class equality in political participation.

As the European franchise was broadened under this kind of pressure, the simple, often dualistic, competition between middle-class "parties of notables" was immensely complicated by the entry of socialist—and in some cases, notably Ireland and Austria— nationalist mass movements. The transition to the European party systems which we take for granted today was by no means a smooth or gradual process. In some countries (notably Germany, Italy and Spain) it was derailed by Fascist counter-revolutions. In Britain it led to a highly volatile multiparty system which came to pivot on the Irish question, and toward a civil war which was averted only by the international explosion of August 1914. Britain's problem was settled (at least for the next 50 years) only by the separation of southern Ireland from the British polity in 1921.

In the United States, on the other hand, matters were far different. First, as J. R. Pole has demonstrated, the proportion of adults legally able to participate in electoral politics was generally very large even in the colonial era, and especially so by contempo- rary British standards.[14] Secondly, the period from 1818 to 1830 was marked by a very rapid elimination of old property barriers to universal white male suffrage in virtually all states where these had existed except for Louisiana, Rhode Island and South Carolina. This "constitutional revolution" was not associated with the emergence of mass move- ments hostile to the foundations of the economy or the state. It occurred at a time when four-fifths of the population lived in rural areas. Moreover, with the sole if important exception of the issue of black participation in the electoral system, the reform was not only speedily carried through but almost instantly won universal acceptance. Even in the antebellum South this was very largely the case. So long as the institution of slavery was not threatened by organized electoral movements elsewhere in the country, participation and the closeness of interparty competition reached heights fully comparable with those found elsewhere at the same time. If, after 1860 and 1877, Southern cultural norms turned away from democracy, it seems fair to say that this happened because there was no way to preserve it without accepting the presence of large numbers of blacks in the active electorate.

These differences are largely explicable by the difference between what Louis Hartz calls the American "fragment culture" and the much more complex European "matrix."[15] This "fragment culture" has involved a consensus about the nature of the political economy, the organization of the political system, and the place of religion in public life which was and is quite absent in any European context, even the British. Put another way, the United States is a very conspicuous example of *uncontested hegemony*. If one were to find a single term which might describe this hegemony most concisely, it would be *liberal capitalism*: a consensual value-system based on support for private property, and political democracy. The primordial value is that of *self-regulation* extended to the individual level; hence, for example, the enduring vitality of Western movies in the popular culture. In Europe, on the other hand, the hegemony of the middle classes (the bourgeoisie) has been anything but uncontested. They have had to fight a two-front war against organized traditionalist social forces (the church, the nobility, and to a large extent the peasantry), and subsequently against a socialism which seeks the speedy or eventual replacement of capitalism.

These differences are fundamental, and have enormous ramifications. With regard to democratization and the suffrage, it is enough to make a few points. First, in the United States there was a paucity of traditionalist social forces threatened by, and resisting mass enfranchisement. Second, unlike Europe, the propertied classes in the United States accommodated themselves both speedily and effectively to the democratic dispensation, since it rapidly became clear that the democracy which came into being offered no serious threat to themselves or their property. Third, substantially full democratization occurred—radically differently from Europe—well before the onset of urbanization and concentrated industrial capitalist development, which was to create a sensation of acute vulnerability among the propertied classes of the industrial Northeast by the end of the century.

Fourth, as Hartz suggests, the absence of effective organized opposition to the liberal-capitalist consensus involved a significant blurring of ideas and of alternatives. So far as popular participation was concerned, property-holding barriers to the ballot-box were removed quickly and easily. By the end of the nineteenth century, the growth of huge ethnically polyglot urban "masses" led to the creation of personal-registration legislation—ostensibly, at least, to combat corruption, i.e., stuffing the ballot box. This legislation was not only created, but varied extremely widely in its incidence and effects (like all other electoral legislation) from state to state and locality to locality. Moreover, it too was accepted consensually: it is very hard to find any critical literature of political science on this subject until as late as the 1960s.[16]

In Europe and other democratic political systems, on the other hand, the burden of registering electors is universally borne, in one way or another, by the state. There are two obvious reasons for this. First, the epic struggles over the state, lasting several centuries, had produced a "hard" or "internally sovereign" state with elaborate and prestigious bureaucracies. The sheer physical competence required for the state to enroll voters was in place. Second, struggles among social groups produced great clarity about the political uses to which electoral legislation could be put by those in power, and an insistence that individuals (especially of lower and dependent classes) not be burdened by cumbersome procedures which might easily lead to their abstention. In the United States, on the other hand, personal registration appears to have come into being as beyond organized political criticism because it fits so well with the underlying, hegemonic ideology. The other side of the coin of individual self-regulation is individual responsibility: if an individual wants to vote, it is up to him to prove to the electoral officials that he is legally qualified to do so.

Finally, one may speculate that political parties could develop their organizational capacities to penetrate and mobilize an individualistic electorate only up to a point. Maurice Duverger points out that American parties have a "very archaic general structure" compared with newer types of mass parties in the European context.[17] If so, an essential reason for this is that these newer parties reflect a *collectivist* organizational capacity which cannot strike root in the United States so long as the consensual ideology of liberal capitalism retains its uncontested hegemonic position. So long as the demographic structure and the political economy were of American nineteenth-century type, the traditional major parties could and did mobilize very effectively indeed. In the radically different social and economic conditions of today, their mobilization capacity would almost inevitably be seriously impaired: neither their organizational form nor their leadership are geared to do so, and the cultural conditions for a serious effort along those lines do not exist.

The most notable point about nineteenth-century participation is its rapid growth with the spread of organized, mass-based democratic politics in the 1830s. One case among many which could be chosen is Connecticut's presidential vote between 1820 and 1844. (See Table 3.)

Table 3

Classic Mobilization in the Jacksonian Period:
the Case of Connecticut

Year	Voting %	Non-voting %	Of Potential Electorate Jacksonian (Dem.) %	Opposition %	Other %
1820	7.6	92.4	6.4 (Monroe)		1.2
1824	14.9	85.1	—	11.8 (Adams)	3.1 (Crawford)
1828	27.2	72.8	6.6	20.6 (Adams)	—
1832	46.0	54.0	16.0	25.2 (Clay)	4.7 (Wirt)
1836	52.3	47.7	26.5 D	25.8 W	—
1840	75.7	24.3	33.6	42.0	0.1
1844	80.0	20.0	36.9	39.1	2.4 (Liberty)

The process of growth in this period took extremely diverse forms from state to state. By the early 1840s, a moderate to very full mobilization had occurred in most states. It is possible to give a modal description. Essential to the new parties of this period was their use of a variety of devices to get voters to the polls. Throughout most of the nineteenth century, party identification was obviously much more complete throughout the voting population, and much more intense, than it is today. This meant, typically, that parties could not expect very many conversions from already-active opposition voters, and that they could not count upon a large pool of free-floating independent voters. Propaganda, torchlight parades, and other activities were designed to secure a maximum turnout of their own voters, since that was normally the way to win elections. This accounts, among other things, for the creation of Tammany's Naturalization Bureau in 1840, since it was already clear to this organization that most immigrants, if naturalized in time for the election as required by New York law, would vote the Democratic ticket. The resultant turnout rates in closely contested states like New York throughout this period, or Indiana from 1860 on, were truly awesome. (See Table 4.)

In this period there were effectively no personal-registration statutes or other significant barriers to the franchise in most states. What amounted to freehold or property qualifications survived in Louisiana and South Carolina until the Civil War, and in Rhode Island until after 1888. In a few states (Massachusetts, Connecticut and Rhode Island), anti-Irish sentiment led by the American ("Know-Nothing") party resulted in the adoption of literacy qualifications of varying effectiveness in the mid-1850s.

Similarly, the conduct of elections was very largely a party matter. Printed tickets were typically produced by the parties and distributed to their voters—initially, before the election, but toward the end of the century on election day near the polls. Such tickets, of course, immensely simplified the act of voting for the plethora of candidates and offices which are elective in the complex American system. They could be and often were "scratched" by voters dissatisfied with one or more of the candidates on the printed ticket. It was possible in effect to cast a "split ticket" under this system; but in general, it facilitated staight-ticket voting, reflecting the intense partisanship of the age.

In a great many jurisdictions, the act of voting itself was at best only semi-secret: often, separate ballot urns were maintained for the supporters of each candidate. This kind of system could and did lend itself to abuse on occasion. But typically this occurred when a party organization was willing to terrorize or bribe officials belonging to the opposition (as well as the police). This sort of thing was episodic. Well-known cases include the Placquemines Parish frauds of 1844, which helped Polk win the Presidency, and the New York frauds of 1868, when the Tweed Machine produced turnouts of well over 100 percent in many election jurisdictions, helping Seymour carry New York state by exactly 10,000 votes, it was said, in order for a leading city politician to win an election bet! But Jensen is obviously right: these cases were episodic rather than the norm.[18] Normally, it would seem that the system worked without excessive ballot-box stuffing because in the rural areas of North and West people knew each other and because in the cities the two parties had every incentive to watch each other. Moreover, each organization's cadres had an extremely precise idea of just how many troops the other army had.

In general, turnout rates reached their historic high in the United States during the last quarter of the nineteenth century. The broad reason for this is obvious. The most traumatic collective experience through which Americans have ever passed was the Civil War (and, for Southerners, the reconstruction which followed the war). In many respects, it was, as Barrington Moore has argued, the "last capitalist revolution" in modern world history,[19] and it partook of many of the characteristics of revolution—not only in the South. The Civil War produced a much higher tax of men than did World War II. Using as a benchmark the total male population 21 and over, about two-fifths served in the Union army, and probably somewhat more than half in the Confederate army, compared with about one-third of the age and sex group during World War II. Even more dramatic were the differentials in casualty rates: 18.0 percent of those who served in the Union army died during the war, while another 13.8 percent were wounded. The Confederate toll was still more ghastly: about 34 percent in its army died, and another 26 percent were wounded. By comparison, only 1.1 percent of all those who served in World War II died, and another 1.6 percent were wounded.

In retrospect, the most important collective tasks of our party system were the creation of the political preconditions for this conflict and, then, its political management.[20] In view of the magnitude of this trauma and the fundamental issues at stake in it, it is hardly surprising that in the North the quality and quantity of party organizational effectiveness reached levels never seen before or since. In the wartime era, the trauma in the South was vastly greater, because of the victors' requirement of incorporating the just-freed black population into the electorate. In this esoteric—almost "third world"— context, its effects were to destroy any long-term stable basis for electoral competition, and to encourage the white population to get rid of the region's black voters.

Another concomitant of the Civil War period was the shift toward urbanization and concentrated industrial capitalism which achieved a temporary maximum velocity during the 1880s. (1) Devotion by most Americans to the premises of our uncontested hegemony—self-regulation and business in the broader sense of the term—continued after the Civil War as it did before. In politics, this was manifested in the increasingly machine-dominated character of party organizations, fuelled both by the rapid increase in the concentrated power of money and by the growth of dependent immigrant urban populations which were used effectively as electoral cannon-fodder. (2) The growth of the "new" capitalist and the "new" political boss, along with the "new", i.e., post-1882 immigration, led to a massive sense of loss—in cultural values, prestige and status— among older-stock middle-class elements. The forces promoting this alienation eventu- ally produced a reaction with major consequences for the electoral mechanism and for representation itself. (3) The shift toward new industrial-urban concentrations of power produced many of the same social-issue strains among farmers, and massive economic dislocation as well. These were byproducts not only of general processes by which rural areas were subordinated to the industrial-capitalist city, but of public policy too. The Civil War had left an enormous public debt behind, and this was largely funded by inflation. The twin objectives of Treasury policy under both parties from 1865 to the 1890s were to shrink the money supply, returning to and then defending an implicit gold standard; and to retire the national debt. The result was a generation-long deflation which was particularly damaging to Southern and Western cash-crop farmers because they were so often undercapitalized and in debt. The stage was thus set for a massive agrarian insurrection against the new capitalist order. The extraordinary anxieties which defenders of that order displayed during the crisis of the 1890s becomes somewhat more explicable when it is recalled that an absolute majority of the work-force was employed in agriculture until about 1879, and nearly a majority until after 1900.

The political explosion which struck the United States was ignited in this highly- politicized and mobilized setting. Just how comparatively full this mobilization was can be gauged from Table 4, which provides mean turnout values by state for the 1874-1892 period and, for contrast, "stable" turnout patterns of the 1952-1970 era and the shrunken rates of the 1970s.

The first and obvious thing to note about the 1874-1892 period is that aggregate presidential turnouts in the non-Southern states were then about as high as they are today in such high participation European countries as Norway and Sweden, and higher than in Britain, France or Canada. Indeed, turnouts in these areas of the country were higher for off-year congressional elections during this period than they were for the Presidency in the 1952-1970 period—to say nothing of later figures.

Secondly, on the whole, the most densely-populated states were also those with the highest turnouts.[21] Among the 14 states whose mean presidential turnout rates ranged from 80.1 percent to 92.7 percent (roughly equivalent to a range from France to Italy in contemporary Europe), only two—Iowa and Kansas—could be described as overwhelm- ingly rural. Of the ten largest cities in the United States in the 1890 census, eight were in states whose mean presidential turnout was 80 percent or greater during this period. The South was already moving toward the extremely low turnouts of the succeeding era (six of its eleven states fall in the lowest quartile), a move only consolidated shortly after 1900. Outside the South, the peripheries, and especially the frontier areas, tended to have the lowest turnout rates. (Table 5 provides a sense of this concentration of participation in the most densely-populated and socio-economically developed parts of the country—and what has happened on this dimension more recently.)

Both the relative and absolute drop off from presidential to off-year congressional participation was significantly smaller in all parts of the country in the last quarter of the nineteenth century than it has ever been since. For example, the relative presidential/off-

Table 4

Changes in Electoral Participation by
State, United States, 1874-1978

Rank State (1874-1892)	1874-1892 (Mean) Presidential %	1874-1892 (Mean) Off-year congressional %	1952-1970 (Mean) Presidential %	1952-1970 (Mean) Off-year congressional %	1972-1978 (Mean) Presidential %	1972-1978 (Mean) Off-year congressional %
1 Ind.	92.7	83.5	73.5	59.9	60.6	43.2
2 N.J.	92.2	76.6	69.6	49.7	59.0	37.5
3 Ohio	92.1	76.8	67.1	48.7	56.0	38.4
4 Iowa	91.8	73.4	72.9	49.0	63.9	43.0
5 N.H.	89.7	83.0	74.7	53.8	61.6	41.3
6 N.Y.	89.0	68.4	66.0	49.5	53.3	34.9
7 W.Va.	87.5	72.6	74.2	50.5	61.5	34.3
8 Ill.	86.1	67.4	73.4	54.2	61.8	37.2
9 N.C.	84.5	67.3	51.8	28.8	43.5	26.6
10 Conn.	82.8	69.7	74.8	61.2	64.1	47.1
11 Pa.	82.7	70.5	66.7	54.8	55.4	41.2
12 Md.	81.4	65.3	56.1	37.7	50.3	30.5
13 Wis.	81.3	64.4	69.6	50.1	64.1	41.4
14 Kans.	80.1	66.6	67.6	50.3	59.5	43.5
15 Mo.	78.2	64.9	68.7	42.3	57.6	39.7
16 Fla.	76.6	67.9	49.4	25.1	50.1	29.0
17 Va.	76.4	54.2	37.6	22.5	46.8	28.3
18 Ky.	76.3	45.6	56.8	30.7	51.2	25.4
19 Del.	76.1	65.8	72.7	56.1	61.0	39.6
20 Mont.	74.2	70.0	70.8	61.9	66.2	53.3
21 Nev.	73.9	73.4	62.5	50.9	49.9	40.6
22 Calif.	73.4	65.1	65.9	53.1	55.7	40.0
23 Vt.	73.3	56.2	67.2	53.5	58.3	39.3
24 Me.	73.2	70.1	66.1	49.2	63.9	49.9
25 Tenn.	72.7	54.9	49.1	28.0	47.1	33.5
26 Texas	72.3	54.9	43.2	20.5	46.5	20.9
27 Mass.	71.8	58.2	71.7	54.7	61.6	41.3
28 Mich.	71.5	63.3	68.7	51.3	58.8	40.3
29 S.D.	70.7	80.4	75.3	61.5	67.4	56.7
30 Minn.	70.3	60.3	72.8	58.5	69.7	47.7
31 Wash.	67.3	48.2	69.4	50.2	61.7	36.7
32 Neb.	66.1	55.2	67.6	50.3	56.3	42.9
33 Ore.	64.9	70.2	69.0	55.0	62.0	48.9
34 Idaho	63.1	67.0	76.4	63.0	62.7	49.4
35 Ala.	62.2	47.0	34.4	25.4	45.7	23.2
36 Ark.	61.4	34.9	44.3	36.9	50.4	32.4

Table 4 (continued)

Rank State (1874-1892)	1874-1892 (Mean) Presidential %	Off-year congressional %	1952-1970 (Mean) Presidential %	Off-year congressional %	1972-1978 (Mean) Presidential %	Off-year congressional %
37 S.C.	58.2	54.8	34.0	19.9	40.4	23.2
38 N.D.	56.6	66.4	73.8	55.4	69.3	51.1
39 Colo.	55.4	51.4	69.7	52.9	61.1	44.5
40 La.	54.6	49.7	44.7	17.6	47.7	22.5
41 R.I.[1]	52.5	26.4	73.0	59.0	62.6	44.2
42 Ga.	48.9	30.6	37.2	19.5	40.6	21.6
43 Miss.	48.3	35.3	31.6	16.7	47.9	26.6
44 Wyo.	47.7	49.1	70.6	60.5	61.7	50.2
Admitted since 1892:						
Ariz.			52.6	41.1	49.0	36.1
N.M.			60.9	50.9	57.4	43.2
Okla.			63.3	40.9	56.6	32.4
Utah			78.4	63.1	69.2	51.6
Alaska			53.4	43.6	50.5	40.3
Hawaii			55.0	47.4	49.7	42.3
North and West[2]	85.4	70.8	68.5	52.6	58.4	40.3
Non-South	84.5	69.2	68.0	51.2	58.0	39.5
Border	79.1	60.3	63.2	39.7	54.9	32.3
South	65.6	49.9	42.6	23.3	46.1	25.7
USA	78.5	64.7	62.0	44.5	55.1	36.0

[1]Rhode Island: freehold qualification for voting until 1892.
[2]Regions: Border: Ky., Md., Okla. Mo., W. Va.; South: Ala., Ark., Fla., Ga., La., Miss., N.C., Tenn., Texas, Va.; Non-South: North and West plus Border. North and West: all states not in South and Border.

year decline in the Northern and Western states was 17.1 percent then, compared with 23.8 percent in 1952-1970 and 31.0 percent in 1972-78. Turnouts of 80 to 90 percent are prima facie evidence that the contemporary American class skew did not then exist in such areas. A similar assumption seems warranted about the absence of an age skew as well. (Cf. Tables 1-2.)

Quite a different pattern emerges when we compare that mobilized universe with the patterns of 1952-1970 and 1972-1978; the latter reinforcing the characteristics of the former. Drop-off rates between presidential and off-year elections are uniformly higher in every comparable state during the second period than during the first, except for the very special case of Rhode Island. In some cases, especially in the Southern and Border states, they are very much larger, even absolutely, despite the notable overall shrinkage in the active electorate as measured by presidential turnouts. The political effects of this shrinkage at the state level may be magnified significantly by another development: the wholesale movement of state gubernatorial elections for four-year terms to off-years. Granted current participation patterns, this typically means that the chief state executive

Table 5

The Long-term Shift away from the Metropole:
Number of Representatives in States
in Top Turnout Quartile, 1874-1976 (Presidential)

Period	Range of turnout, top quartile	No. of representatives	% of total	Mean no. of reps. per state
1874-1892	82.7-92.7	158	44.4	14.4
1894-1910	81.5-91.7	154	39.4	14.7
1912-1930	67.7-77.8	120	27.6	10.0
1932-1950	71.0-78.4	90	20.7	7.5
1952-1976	62.0-69.7	77	17.7	6.4
1972-1976	62.0-69.7	46	10.6	3.8

officer (and most other elective state officials) will be chosen by one-third to two-fifths of the potential electorate.

Another and most suggestive change can be seen in the distribution of states in the top and bottom quartiles. The movement in the bottom quartile is perfectly straightforward. In the 1874-1892 period, this quartile was a mixture of some Southern states,[22] Rhode Island (which uniquely maintained a freehold qualification for voting until after 1888), and frontier states of the West.

Movements in the top quartile are in some respects more interesting and are certainly less well-known. With the sole exceptions of North Carolina and West Virginia, the 1874-1892 top quartile was concentrated in the emerging "metropole" of the country, and included the four most populous states: Illinois, New York, Ohio, and Pennsylvania. By 1952-70 the only American "megastate" to qualify in the top quartile turnout is Illinois. To it must be added Connecticut, Rhode Island and Indiana within the ex-metropole; the other nine are Plains, Mountain, and Pacific states. Table 5 graphically demonstrates the shift in the top turnout quartile's distribution toward smaller and, on the whole, sparsely-populated peripheral regions of the country.

The Disappearing American Electorate, 1896-1930: Social Crisis and Political Response   The late nineteenth-century electorate we have been describing was fully mobilized. Its participation was the fruit of several generations of effective work by America's traditional, party organizations. But it presented dangers for elites, chronic and growing irritation among old-stock middle-class elements who saw themselves between the hammer of corporate giantism and the anvil of machine corruption, and serious impediments to the realization of technocratic and bureaucratic ambitions. The great socio-economic crisis of the 1890s appeared to demonstrate that this electorate was not only large but might also be a mortal danger to emergent hegemonic interests.

The United States was unique in that it had a fully operating set of mass-democratic institutions and values before the onset of industrial-capitalist development.[23] In every other industrializing nation of the 1850–1950 period, modernizing elites were effectively insulated from mass pressures. In most of the West this insulation was accomplished by the *régime censitaire* or other formal devices for keeping lower classes out of electoral politics, supplemented in some cases by ingenious *trasformismo*-type manipulation and corruption of both electorates and of legislature. In the Communist world, insulation involved dictatorship and the use of elections as devices of acclamation for the regime rather than choice. In today's third world, a mixture of the two—coupled with the entry of the Army where "necessary" as an ultimate control—generally prevails.

Since the processes of capitalist development can be exploitative, harsh, and even brutal, it is not surprising that so wide a range of devices has been employed to prevent modernizing elites being overthrown by an outraged population, and that the quest for such insulation has been universal. This was a problem with particular urgency in the American context, because of the relative breadth of popular participation, and because so many participants were agrarian. Alexander Hamilton's policy, from beginning to end, betrays preoccupation with an overriding question: How can one find a legitimate way to win mass acquiescence for measures designed to promote the creation of what Madison, Monroe, and others quite correctly called "empire" and to accumulate movable capital? It is hardly surprising that Jefferson suspected Hamilton of harboring dictatorial designs. It is still less surprising that the turn-of-the-century Progressives—particularly those of a technocratic-corporatist bent—revered Hamilton as their hero and rejected Jefferson as a tribune of all the backward agrarian forces in American society. [24]

How, then, does one tame a fickle, numerous, and dangerous electorate without outright overthrow of the engrained democratic tradition in American politics? It is not suggested that any of our corporate elites or the organic intellectuals and politicans who supported them at the turn of the century ever put the question in such nakedly self-conscious terms. Still more doubtful it is that what happened to participation and the nature of the party system in this period was the result of a conspiracy among elites who knew just what they wanted and how to get it—though localized conspiracies abounded, chiefly in the South, where the stakes were higher and the social structure primitive.

The questions to ask ourselves, then, are these. What was done? Against whom was it done? What was the convergence of interests making it possible to do things at all? What were the effects of what was done? And finally, why was what was done so rapidly and fully legitimated that it remained beyond criticism for more than a half-century or even today?

We may begin by identifying schematically the major targets of legislative changes affecting elections and their opponents.

Whether or not elites conspired, the pattern of political change which emerged during the first third of this century functioned as though its proponents and beneficiaries agreed on a number of points which are scarcely in accord with participatory-democratic political theory. (1) The greater preliminary hurdles which a potential voter had to cross in order to vote, the fewer voters there would be. (2) These hurdles would be easily cleared by people in the native-stock middle classes, would not exist at all in small towns and rural areas, would be serious impediments to urban lower-class voting, and would be virtually impassable for Southern blacks. (3) Political parties were dangerous anachronisms when it came to giving cities efficient, expert government. They were to be abolished where possible (especially at the urban level), and were elsewhere to be heavily regulated by the state. In particular, their monopoly over nominations would be stripped from them, so that "the people" (between 5 and 35 percent of the potential electorate as a rule) could choose candidates in direct primaries. (4) Close partisan competition was generally undesirable, though for different reasons as between the South (where a quasi-absolute prohibition of party competition developed) and the North and West. Desirable or not, it was substantially abolished down through 1932 in the South and in vast reaches of the North from Pennsylvania to California.

The basic legal devices which were adopted—particularly the device of personal registration—without question contributed to the massive decline in voter participation after 1900. In the extreme case of the South, the result was that by the mid-1920s, presidential turnout had declined to about 18 percent of the potential electorate, while in the off-year congressional election of 1926 only 8.5 percent of the South's potential voters actually went to the polls. Participation fell in the North and West as well, but very unevenly. How much of this was attributable to these rules-of-game changes? In an earlier study, I concluded that in the period prior to the enfranchisement of women (nationally adopted in 1920) no more than one-third of the decline could be attributed to these causes alone.[25] It is possible from recent Ohio data to give a more precise estimate of the effect of introducing personal-registration requirements on the participation rate.

Ohio is a state, like many others, where until 1977 the basic electoral law prescribed personal registration in counties of a certain size, and allowed local option in all other counties. In some counties, registration applied only to one or two small towns, with the rural areas having no such requirement for voting. In the period from 1960 to 1976, a significant number of counties shifted from non-registration to registration status. It is therefore possible to derive a relatively good estimate of the effects of registration by comparative analysis (see Table 6).

Table 6

**Turnouts in Ohio Counties,
1960__1976 by Registration Category***

| | | Turnout | | | | |
Category type: registration began	No. of counties	1960 %	1964 %	1968 %	1972 %	1976 %
Before 1960	28	69.0	64.0	62.3	57.7	57.1
Before 1964	5	75.5	60.4	57.9	54.6	53.8
Before 1968	4	77.7	72.1	63.3	57.9	58.3
Before 1972	10	79.2	72.3	69.3	59.9	59.0
Before 1976	5	79.5	72.7	70.6	63.7	57.1
Never	23	79.8	73.0	70.0	65.8	71.4

*Does not include counties with partial registration coverage during this period.

Taking the transitions in each group but subtracting the year-on-year turnout change for full-registration counties yields a differential of 6.1 percent. Another approach is a straightforward year-on-year comparison between those counties fully covered and those never covered across the period. Not surprisingly, this yields the highest general differential of 10.0 percent, though it provides no basis for estimating possible turnout differentials arising from the rurality of the 23 counties which do not have registration as a requisite for voting. Still another way of analyzing the data in Table 6 is to estimate the positive deviation in pre-registration turnout in each category with "before" and "after" experience. This produces a positive deviation of 7.8 percent, which—when one attempts such crude controls for the downward movement in turnout—seems perhaps to be the most accurate estimate of the three. It is worth noting that all of these measures, except the simple comparison between full and non-registration counties, are at their maximum in 1960, the election with the highest overall turnout rate. Equally noteworthy, a substantial decline in turnout occurred across the board between 1960 and 1968. In those counties with personal registration throughout the period under review, this decline was 6.7 percent. In those where this requirement did not exist at any time, the decline was 9.8 percent between 1960 and 1968, i.e., prior to the enfranchisement of the 18-20 age group.

Rosenstone and Wolfinger conclude that if the laws of all states were brought into conformity with the registration statutes of the most permissive states, the estimated increase in turnout would be 9.1 percent.[26] It could be assumed that a fully automatic state-enrollment system of the type normally found in other Western nations would eliminate any residual burdens associated with these laws, and add several more points to the estimated increase. The analysis of our Ohio data would suggest that the latter condition (approximated, of course, by a situation in which no registration is required at all for voting) would increase turnout by a rather small figure, that is, by between 7 and 9 percent. Applied to the states of North and West for the 1952-1970 period (see Table 4), this latter estimate would yield a mean presidential turnout in the 75 to 77 percent range. This is a considerable improvement, but would still leave unaccounted for half of the difference between the actual 1952-1970 average turnout and the 85.4 percent of the 1874-1892 average. Moreover, such estimates are implicitly static in character. They give no information about the causes of the marked decline in turnout after 1960 shown in the bottom two rows of Table 6. Nor do they, for example, explain why turnout declined in New York City by a full 21.3 percent (34 percent of the 1960 electoral base) from 1960 to 1976, despite continuity or marginal liberalization of electoral law.

Viewed over the long run, the same considerations apply to expansions of the size of the electorate—notably to the enfranchisement of women, which was legally completed in 1920. There is no doubt at all that the enfranchisement of women initially reduced sharply the participation rate. This too, however, appears to have varied widely in accordance with the extent of political mobilization (or "socialization") prevailing in a given society at the time of enfranchisement. It is well known that women participated much less than men, especially in ethnically polyglot cities, from the time of enfranchisement until the 1928 election, which involved the issue of Al Smith's Catholicism, and substantially less than men thereafter down to the early 1950s, when contemporary survey data becomes available. Thus, in his pioneering study, *Political Behavior*,[27] H.L.A. Tingsten reports a female participation rate immediately after enfranchisement of 61.8 percent in Sweden (1919), 68.1 percent in New Zealand (1896) and 82.1 percent in Austria (1919). This meant that female participation trailed male turnout by 7.1 percent in the first case, 7.8 percent in the second, and 4.9 percent in the third. The data in the United States is largely limited to Chicago, where separate returns by sex were published for the 1916-1920 period. Without going into exhaustive analysis of this case, it is enough to report that the 1916 turnout in Chicago was 77.1 percent of estimated potential electorate among men and 47.3 percent among women, a sex differential of 29.8 percent.[28]

Such data makes it very easy—indeed, too easy—to assume that the post-1928 mobilization of women and other previously non-participating groups was in some sense the overwhelmingly dominant electoral "cause" of the New Deal realignment. The issues

involved are much more complex than that, though the importance of these mobilizations cannot be denied.[29] Secondly, there is an interesting implication in the 1976 finding
that the participation differential between men and women had virtually disappeared. In
the historical context, the turnout rates in 1976 and 1978 mean that while women are
turning out somewhat more than fifty years ago, men are participating vastly less, perhaps
by a factor of 20 percent or more.

Thus, by the end of World War I, an essentially oligarchic electoral universe had
come into being, with a hegemonic sectionalism and the disappearance of socialism as an
even marginal electoral force. Table 7 reveals the magnitude of the transformation.
Essentially, a political system which was congruent with the hegemony of laissez-faire
corporate capitalism over the whole society had come into being. This system rested on
two non-competitive party hegemonies and upon a huge mass of non-voters.

Table 7

The Achievement of Normalcy: Turnouts in
the North and West, 1880-90 and 1920-30

Year	President %	Congress %	Drop off %
1880	87.6	86.8	
1882		71.4	18.5
1884	84.9	84.2	
1886		71.6	15.7
1888	86.4	87.7	
1890		71.3	17.5
1920	56.3	53.5	
1922		42.8	24.0
1924	57.4	52.4	
1926		39.7	30.8
1928	66.7	61.6	
1930		43.7	34.5

This implies, of course, that an American electorate had come into being: that is,
one heavily skewed toward the middle classes *in the absence of an organizable socialist
mass movement capable of mobilizing lower-class voters.* This is implicit in a comparison
of contemporary turnout rates with those prevailing in the normalcy era. Individual-level
data for the 1920s is, naturally, extremely fragmentary, but, such as it is, it supports the
inference. Tingsten reports one study of 1925 which focussed on the small and
overwhelmingly native-stock city of Delaware, Ohio.[30] This study found a turnout rate of
86 percent among the local upper class (corporate and banking elites), compared with 63
percent among the "mass of industrial workers." Since, as it happens, personal registration
requirements were not imposed there until 1965, this class gap in the 1920s supports the
view that the interaction of social change and organizable political alternatives, rather
than rules change, was *primarily* responsible for what happened to American electoral
participation after 1900. Where one finds a disappearance or even reversal of this class-
structured turnout pattern during the 1920s—and one does find such—cases—the

inversion can be linked directly to the existence and motivations of political machines able to deliver votes as need arose.[31]

Incomplete Remobilization and the (So-called) New Deal Revolution   The "system of 1896" was composed of a series of mutually reinforcing parts, bound together by a common belief in the corporate-capitalist path to economic development and individual affluence. It was destroyed by the Depression which undermined its ideological and operational base, laissez faire. The emergence of the Democrats as the new majority party was associated with a relatively huge mobilization of population groups which had not voted in the 1920s.[32] The examination of registration by party in San Francisco in the 1928-1940 period illuminates this transition (see Table 8).

Table 8

Mobilization and Conversion in the
New Deal Period: the Case of San Francisco,
1928-1940

Year	Estimated potential electorate	Non-registered	Percentage of potential electorate		
			Dem.	Registered Rep.	Misc., decl. to state
1928	393,600	35.7	19.1	41.9	3.3
1930	401,933	43.1	8.4	46.2	2.3
1932	410,200	33.3	30.5	34.5	1.7
1934	418,500	25.1	38.9	34.0	2.0
1936	426,800	25.9	47.0	25.5	1.6
1938	435,100	21.7	50.7	25.7	1.9
1940	443,386	12.9	56.2	29.1	1.8

If we were to make two most unrealistic assumptions—that all conversions and mobilizations favoured the Democrats only and that the electorate was wholly stationary during this twelve-year period—we could conclude that the 56 percent Democratic registration of 1940 had the following origins in the 1928-30 period; 14 percent Democratic, 15 percent Republican, 26 percent non-registered, and 1 percent miscellaneous. Obviously these are in no way the true figures. But in a city where growth was comparatively tightly constrained, they suggest something of what happened. It is not off the mark to suggest that about three-fifths of the accretions to the Democratic registration pool came from the mobilization of people not registered before, and about two-fifths from Republican conversions.

But if remobilization formed a central part of constructing a nationwide Democratic majority in the 1930s, there are important parts of the story which are less frequently emphasized. In the first place, one extremely important component of the "system of 1896" not only survived the New Deal era but was actually reinforced: the "solid South," composed of eleven ex-Confederate states retained their antipartisan, antiparticipatory structure until after 1950. The pro-Democratic thrust of the New Deal realignment drastically weakened what was left of the Republican opposition in the few states—like Tennessee and North Carolina—where it had been relatively strong in the preceding period. Turnouts in these states, as in the Border states where similar realignments occurred, fell subsequently below the levels reached in the 1920s. Moreover, the ascendancy of the Democratic party nationally entailed normal Democratic majorities in both houses of Congress. Granted the salience of seniority and the effects of occasional Republican sweeps in the North (as in 1946 and 1952), the result was that Democratic ascendancy nationally meant Southern ascendancy in Congress. As events after 1938 were to demonstrate, this involved a critical limitation on the reformist potential of the New Deal until well into the 1960s.

Earlier we saw that the turnout patterns of the late nineteenth century involved both very high levels of mass mobilization and extremely stable levels as well. (See Table 7.) By contrast, the period between 1940 and 1950 showed major fluctuations in turnout and the post-1970 period a precipitous decline from already mediocre levels. Thus, while turnout in the North and West reached 58.6 percent in the congressional elections of 1938 and 73.7 percent in the presidential election of 1940, participation skidded to 43.2 percent in 1942 and 48.4 percent in 1946, while by 1948 only 62.2 percent of the Northern-Western electorate bothered to vote for President. Certainly neither war nor women's suffrage can be held accountable for the low turnout in the latter two elections.[33] One is led to suspect instead that the replacement of "Dr. New Deal" by "Dr. Win-the-War" may have had something to do with this. The off-year election of 1938 was marked by a turnout which has never since been equalled outside the South, a turnout fully 18 percent higher than the 38.0 percent voting in 1978.

The Contemporary Period: 1952 to the Present   From many aspects of contemporary electoral participation, we will select three major themes: (1) regional change involving civil rights and the South; (2) longitudinal change in the Northern and Western states, especially the recent decline in participation to historically low levels; (3) certain attributes of voters and non-voters in the mid-1970s.

(1) As we have indicated, the New Deal "revolution" in voting participation almost wholly bypassed the South, whose elites had long since set up the oligarchic conditions epitomized by the 1.5 percent turnout rate in the South Carolina gubernatorial election of 1925. This extraordinary regional deviation from democratic norms was enforced by a dense network of exclusionary legislation and—especially in the early years of this system—by the widespread use of extralegal violence. This unfinished business was finally taken in hand in the Civil Rights Acts of 1965 and 1970. In the black-belt areas of worst electoral repression, local authorities were simply bypassed and federal registration machinery set up to enroll voters. More generally, abolition of such barriers to the franchise as literacy and poll-tax requirements opened the sluice-gates throughout the region. It should be stressed that these laws came at the end of a process of development rather than at the beginning. The crumbling of the Solid South and the urbanization of the electorate had already brought considerable mobilization by the early 1950s; these laws completed the job. As a result, there was a major improvement in Southern turnout—from abysmally low levels—between 1948 and 1970, followed thereafter by stagnation or decline. (See Table 9).

(2) Civil rights acts significantly lowered access thresholds outside the South too, for example, reducing residency requirements in presidential elections to 30 days and suspending literacy tests in those non-Southern states (like New York) which had them. Table 10 should be read bearing in mind that since the early 1960s a number of states have simplified the registration process to make the act of voting easier than it was in 1960.

Table 9

Mandated Remobilization:
Southern Turnouts, 1948-1978

| | | Percentage of potential electorate voting for: | | |
| | | US House, Presidential | US House, | |
Year	President	years	Off-years	Drop off
1948	24.6	21.2		
1950			12.4	49.6
1952	38.5	32.2		
1954			16.1	58.2
1956	36.6	29.2		
1958			15.1	58.7
1960	41.2	33.6		
1962			24.0	41.7
1964	45.6	39.3		
1966			29.0	36.4
1968	51.0	41.5		
1970			32.2	34.9
1972	44.9	39.3		
1974			25.1	44.1
1976	47.6	41.8		
1978			26.3	44.7

Overall, the participation rate in these states was stable between 1950 and 1966, with a mean in presidential elections of 69.6 percent, in congressional elections held in presidential years of 66.7 percent and in off-year congressional elections of 53 percent. Thereafter a substantial decline occurred, bringing the latest rates down to 57.2 percent, 53.4 percent, and 38.6 percent respectively. By 1976, 21.4 percent of the 1960 active-electorate base was not voting; by 1978, 29.4 percent of the 1962 active-electorate base was no longer participating. The general enfranchisement of the 18-20 age group in 1971 does not begin to account for the magnitude of these declines. Analysis of the Census Bureau participation surveys by age cohorts makes it clear that the addition of this cohort has depressed post-1971 presidential turnout by not more than 1.5 percent, leaving nine-tenths of the drop from 1960 to 1976 unaccounted for.

Decline in voting participation outside the special mandated case of the South has been nearly universal since 1960, but it has proceeded at very different rates, both in terms of social stratification and geography. As Table 11 shows, the lower the social class the more rapid the decline, both in presidential and off-year elections.

A complementary pattern of decline emerges along geographical lines when comparing participation rates in the early 1960s with the late 1970s. To take an extreme local case, New York City in 1976 reached its lowest turnout rate in 150 years, at 42.1 percent of the potential electorate, compared with a 72.6 percent turnout in 1940 and 63.4 percent as late as 1960.[34] Much of this effects the influx of non-white dependent populations whose turnout rates are extremely low, and also in decline. But there are

Table 10

Surges, Declines and Decays: Turnouts in
the Northern and Western States, 1948-1978

		Percentage of potential electorate voting for:		
Year	Presidential	US House, Presidential years	US House, Off-years	Drop off
1948	62.2	59.8		
1950			52.8	15.1
1952	71.1	68.2		
1954			51.4	27.7
1956	68.4	65.6		
1958			53.8	21.3
1960	71.7	68.2		
1962			54.7	23.7
1964	67.3	64.9		
1966			52.3	22.3
1968	64.1	60.7		
1970			50.7	20.9
1972	59.7	56.8		
1974			41.9	29.8
1976	57.2	53.4		
1978			38.6	32.5

broader issues at work. Thus, for example, turnout in white assembly districts for the 1977 mayoral election appears to have reached a low without precedent since the first mayor was elected in 1834.

On a national basis, the relative rate of decline in states from 1962 to 1978 shows marked geographic concentrations. As might be expected, the quartile of states with smallest losses or actual gains in this 16-year interval include nine of the Southern states plus Missouri, Maine, and Oregon. The bottom quartile is heavily concentrated in the urbanized states of the East and near Midwest from Massachusetts to Illinois; two other very large states (Ohio and California) show attrition rates not much smaller than these. If one rearranges the analysis to deal with non-Southern states only, the top quartile of states (relative declines of 2.9 to 18.8) shows a mean of 4.9 House members per state, and 13.5 percent of all non-Southern House members. The bottom quartile, on the other hand (relative declines from 1962 to 1978 of between 32.2 and 41.4) has a mean of 14.9 House members per state, and 45.6 percent of all non-Southern congressional representation. This bottom quartile contains both states which have traditionally had very strong party organization (e.g., Illinois, Indiana, and West Virginia), and those with weak or very weak organizations (e.g., Massachusetts and Washington).

(3) Chronologically, this is a period during which very large and well-documented changed occurred in individual political cognitions and responses to political stimuli. So large and substantively important were these changes that they led to a complete rewriting of *The American Voter* since 1964, and to a growing crisis of explanatory paradigms

Table 11

Class Differentials in Abstentions:
Turnout Rates by Occupation, United States, 1966-1974

| | Presidential years | | | | Off years | | | |
Categories	1968 %	1972 %	Shift %	Norm-alized shift** %	1966 %	1974 %	Shift %	Norm-alized shift** %
Propertied middle class	81.7	79.7	—2.0	—2.4	69.8	59.8	—10.0	—14.3
Dependent middle class	77.4	72.8	—4.6	—5.9	64.9	50.3	—14.6	—22.5
Upper working class	66.9	60.4	—6.5	—9.7	55.8	41.1	—14.7	—26.3
Lower working class	57.5	49.5	—8.0	—13.9	46.2	33.7	—12.5	—27.1
Middle class	79.9	76.5	—3.4	—4.3	67.9	55.3	—12.6	—18.6
Working class	62.0	55.0	—7.0	—11.3	51.0	37.4	—13.6	—26.7
USA, Census/ CPS Survey	67.8	63.0	—4.8	—7.1	55.4	44.7	—9.7	—19.3
USA, Aggregate data*	60.7	55.7	—5.0	—8.2	45.3	37.1	—8.2	—18.1

*Off-year aggregate data: House elections only. Total turnouts (including those for Governor, Senator, etc.) typically 1.5 to 2 percent higher.

**Calculated as the shift as a proportion of the actual participation rate at time 1.

Classifications of occupations:

Propertied middle class: professional, managerial, farm owners
Dependent middle class: clerical, sales
Upper working class: craftsmen & kindred workers, service workers
Lower working class: operatives, labourers, farm labourers

within the voting-behavior research community as a whole.[35] In the 1964-1976 period, as issue-polarization dramatically rose, the salience of political parties and their acceptability to wide strata of the mass public steeply declined. This decay of party was associated with a marked fragmentation of electoral response along office-specific lines, yielding a multi-tiered structure of electoral alignments. So far as congressional elections are concerned, the chief aggregate change of the past fifteen years has been the emergence of a dominant incumbency effect as a significant "cue" to electoral decision as the collective, cross-district bonds of party deteriorated.[36]

Borrowing from the work of Anthony Downs and other rational-choice theorists, it could be argued that (a) party is a particularly vital aggregate short-cut device for calculating utilities among those who have little other information to rely on; (b) access to politically-relevant information is strongly class-skewed in a capitalist society; (c) therefore, the disappearance of party as a meaningful vehicle for calculating utilities is likely to result not only in increasing abstention generally, but also to an increase in abstention among those who already vote least. On the other hand, a different analytical tradition would suggest that the rise in abstention is not only chronologically but causally associated with stimuli which have produced growing waves of alienation with politics, politicians, and political institutions among the public.

Arthur T. Hadley suggests another view even though he fails to take class variables into account.[37] Hadley observes that alienated voters—so similar to the alienated segment of non-voters in attitudes and other characteristics—might well provide the basis for even further large-scale increases in abstentions under the right circumstances. What, then, discriminates? It appears that the most powerful single attitudinal variable is a question about the respondent's attitude toward his or her personal life: does a respondent believe that luck determines most of what happens to him or her, or is one's life susceptible of personal control through planning? Those who believe that their lives are largely determined by chance will tend to be non-voters, those who believe otherwise will tend to vote.

This singular finding has an a priori fit with an argument in survey-research analysis: it is not differentials in individual political trust that divide voters from non-voters, but differentials in their sense of political efficacy. Those who believe that nothing they can do will make much difference, will tend to vote less often than those with similar demographic characteristics but a sense of political efficacy.

Since the late 1960s that internal composition of the non-voter population has changed as the pool of non-voters has grown. The classic formulation of the early survey-research studies—non-voters are people who are essentially "out of it" politically—is no longer remotely adequate to describe this pool. Finally, if we assume even that the proportion of politically inefficacious or luck-oriented people has remained constant within the non-voter pool since, say, 1968 (and much more so if we assume that this component has increased) we are left with the following naked proposition: *The structure of political choices offered the electorate in the United States, and the major decisions made by political elites, have together produced more and more baffled ineffective citizens who believe that chance rules their world.* This not only implies the long-term paralysis of democracy, but also a rapid speed-up of this paralysis in the most recent period of our history.

Conclusion

It has long been argued that American politics is not organized in class-struggle terms. At the most, social class is one among a wide variety of competing variables explaining voters' decisions. This conventional wisdom is very largely right. Lack of explicit class-consciousness among the large majority of the population is an essential linchpin of uncontested hegemony in the United States. But in that case, it would be logical to suppose that the "real" class struggle, the point at which class polarization is most salient, is not found in the contests between Democrats and Republicans in the active electorate, but *between* the active electorate as a whole *and* the non-voting half of the adult population as a whole. As in nineteenth-century Europe, there is a major difference in American today between le pays légal and le pays réel. That difference was razor-sharp in Europe a century ago, but is blurred and indeed nearly invisible in the United States. In America, it is possible to devote a whole book to the problem of non-voting without seriously addressing the class issue at all.

Given a large and enduring comparative deficiency in political consciousness among Americans, what difference does it make?

One set of objections arises from the evident collision between the realities of the case and the postulates of democratic theory. The current and until now fruitless debates in Congress about electoral-law reform are part of the characteristically obscure but never-ending struggle about the first principles of electoral democracy. This struggle has continued in the United States for decades after its counterparts elsewhere were concluded.[38] Comparative analyses make it clear that there are significant and conservative implications for the shape of American public policy.[39]

But one may also take a position much closer to that of *Realpolitik* in international relations. Giovanni Sartori, himself no left-wing ideologue, has restated a well-known axiom of politics.[40] Political parties and large-scale mass participation in politics appear to be functional requisites of a modern state. First, they provide a means of channeling demands and socializing adult citizens into the possibilities and limits of political action in a given system. Second, they provide a means of communication or linkage between rulers and ruled, reducing the great distance which otherwise can produce popular alienation from government. Third, parties and participation are not only important to rulers as means to penetrate the society for purposes of government; they are also essential feedback mechanisms through which the rulers can gain legitimacy for themselves, their policies, and their rule. But it should be emphasized that there is a price for all this. That price is the creation of mass party organizations and the shaping of public policies and policy conflicts in the terms meaningful to the electorate, and particularly to those living in the lower half of a class society.

Quite different conditions now prevail in the United States today. The channels to which Sartori refers are in an advanced state of decay. With this decay has come an explosion of highly intense, narrowly-focussed sectoral demands on political elites. This rancourous *hyper*pluralism coexists with a steep decline in mass participation from relatively low levels, and a decline in popular support for governing elites. In the process, the state is seriously impaired at a time when the longer-term interests of the political economy—both at home and abroad—require its strengthening. It is therefore hardly surprising that the media has discovered a "governability crisis" in the 1970s. But this "crisis," whatever it is, has not come into being because of the immoderate demands of fickle and inconstant masses. It has come into being because of a contradiction, now becoming increasingly evident, between the maintenance of uncontested hegemony on one hand and the requirements of the modern state for coherence, stability, and legitimacy on the other.

The problem of participation in the United States today probably cannot be resolved within the existing framework of organizable political alternatives. It is structural in origin, and a major change in political consciousness would be needed to overcome it. But the shape of electoral law clearly makes a difference. Personal registration requirements did not descend from the skies. They were made by men, and are now defended by men who see no particular advantage to themselves in making it easier for ordinary Americans to get to the polls. Their abolition and replacement by automatic state-enrollment procedures is only a first step, but a necessary one.

We simply do not know with any great clarity what it would take to bring the missing adults, 40 million or more of them, back into the active American electorate. Presumably, political structures would have to be developed for the representation of interests which are now feebly or not at all represented in electoral politics. This could not be accomplished without fundamental changes in political consciousness and equally fundamental challenges to things which upper- and upper-middle-class Americans believe to be sacrosanct. The United States appears to be moving into an historical era during which, at some point, uncontested hegemony will cease to exist. If so, that stability of the regime will be more secure if organized channels for representing the interests of the lower half of the population have come into being.[41] This point, to which Sartori is justly sensitive, is precisely identified by E. E. Shattschneider:

A greatly expanded popular base of political participation is the essential condition for public support of the government. This is the modern problem of democratic government. The price of support is participation. The choice is between participation and propaganda, between democratic and dictatorial ways of *changing consent into support, because consent is no longer enough.*[42]

Notes

1. For good discussions of the European cases, see Seymour M. Lipset and Stein Rokkan (eds.), *Party Systems and Voter Alignments* (New York: Free Press, 1967), and Stein Rokkan, *Citizens, Elections, Parties* (New York: David McKay, 1970). An early long-range review of American turnout, in which the developmental "movie" runs backwards, is contained in Walter Dean Burnham, "The Changing Shape of the American Political Universe," *American Political Science Review*, (1965): 7-28.

2. The most complete contemporary analysis thus far is Sidney Verba and Norman Nie, *Participation in America: Political Democrary and Social Equality* (New York: Harper & Row, 1972). See also the controversy between the present author and Professors Philip E. Converse and Jerrold G. Rusk: "Theory and Voting Research: Some Reflections on Converse's 'Change in the American Electorate'," *American Political Science Review*, 68 (1974): 1002-1023; comments by Converse and Rusk, ibid., 1024-1049; and author's rejoinder, ibid.:1050-1057.

3. Cf. Philip E. Converse's contribution, "Change in the American Electorate," (ch. 8), in Angus Campbell and Philip E. Converse (eds.), *The Human Meaning of Social Change* (New York: Russell Sage, 1972), and the present author's discussion in "Theory and Voting Research," op. cit.

4. For example, Richard Jensen has observed that "The myth of massive corruption so cleverly conceived that it cannot be detected is a ghost story . . . By nineteenth-century standards, American or European, the midwestern elections were quiet, decorous affairs—hard-fought, but basically honest." Richard Jensen, *The Winning of the Midwest* (Chicago, 1971): 35-36.

5. Converse, op. cit. Similar reliance on rules changes as a sufficient explanation of post-1900 change in turnout rates is to be found in Rusk, "Comment," op. cit.; and, though not directly related to the turnout question, Rusk raises interesting collateral issues in "The Effect of the Australian Ballot on Split-Ticket Voting: 1876-1908," *American Political Science Review*, 64 (1970): 1220-1238.

6. Steven J. Rosenstone and Raymond E. Wolfinger, "The Effect of Registration Laws on Voter Turnout," *American Political Science Review*, 72, (1978): 22-45.

7. The phrase is Heinz Eulau's; but the locus classicus is probably Seymour M. Lipset, *Political Man* (New York: Doubleday, 1960): 179-263.

8. The most recent installment of this story is found in *Public Opinion*, 1 (2) (May/June 1978), p. 23.

9. The work of Stein Rokkan and his associates, op. cit., is particularly helpful. See also Dieter Nohlen, Bernhard Vogel et al., *Die Wahl der Parlamente*, Vol. 1 (Europa), (Berlin: Walter de Gruyter, 1969).

10. Gunnar Myrdal, *Challenge to Affluence* (New York: Pantheon, 1963), esp. pp. 92-123. Myrdal comments that " . . . it is fatal for democracy, and not only demoralizing for the individual members of this under-class, that they are so mute and without initiative, and that they are not becoming organized to fight for their interests" (p. 39).

11. There is a well-known general tendency for blacks to participate less than whites at all income levels. Thus, in 1976 the racial stratification by income was:

1976 Income Level	Whites		Blacks	
	Registered %	Voted %	Registered %	Voted %
Under $5,000	57.7	46.2	54.2	41.7
$5,000-9,999	62.6	54.2	58.5	48.8
$10,000-14,999	68.8	61.4	63.3	54.7
$15,000-24,999	76.9	71.2	69.9	64.6
$25,000 and over	83.4	77.8	77.6	73.1
Total (including not reported)	68.7	61.4	59.1	49.5

But the importance of social-class related factors for the turnout of both racial groups is obvious. In this connection, it should be noted that 32.5 percent of black respondents reported incomes of less then $5,000, compared with 13.2 percent of whites. US Bureau of the Census "Voting and Registration in the Election of November 1976," p. 66.

12. Norman H. Nie, Sidney Verba, and John R. Petrocik, *The Changing American Voter*, (Cambridge: Harvard University Press, 1976): 59-73.

13. Samuel P. Huntington, *Political Order in Changing Societies* (New Haven: Yale University Press, 1968), pp. 122-133; J. R. Pole, *Political Represenation in England and the Origins of the American Republic* (Berkeley: University of California Press, 1966), especially pp. 172-213.

14. Pole, ibid., Appendix II, "Voting Statistics in America": 543-564.

15. Louis Hartz, *The Liberal Tradition in America* (New York: Harcourt, Brace, 1955); cf. also his articulated theory of the "fragment culture" in Louis Hartz (ed.), *The Founding of New Societies* (New York: Harcourt, Brace & World, 1964): 3-122.

16. But note Dudley O. McGovney, *The American Suffrage Medley* (Chicago: University of Chicago Press, 1949).

17. Maurice Duverger, *Political Parties* (New York: Wiley, 1961): 21-22, 217-220.

18. Jensen, op. cit., ch. 2.

19. Barrington Moore, Jr., *Social Origins of Dictatorship and Democracy* (Boston: Beacon Press, 1966): 111-155.

20. See the important article by Eric McKitrick, "Party Politics and the Union and Confederate War Efforts," in William N. Chambers and Walter Dean Burnham (eds.), *The American Party Systems* (New York: Oxford University Press, 1967, 1975): 117-151.

21. Rhode Island was in a class by itself. It retained an essentially freeholder suffrage qualification until after 1888, and the last vestiges of its peculiar *régime censitaire* electoral law were not removed until 1928. It is, therefore, the only state in the union to show a longitudinal upward trend in voter participation from the mid-nineteenth century to the 1952-1970 period.

22. V. O. Key, Jr., *Southern Politics in State and Nation* (New York: Knopf, 1949). See especially Part Five, "Restrictions on Voting," pp. 531-663, for a comprehensive discussion of the full range of suffrage-restricting devices then in place in the ex-Confederate states. Mean Southern presidential turnouts from 1912 to 1928 were 24.8 percent; from 1932 to 1948, 25 percent; from 1952 to 1968, 42.6 percent.

23. The basic argument is made, if rather crudely, in Burnham, "The Changing Shape of the American Political Universe," op. cit.

24. This is a chief theme of the so-called "Bible of Progressivism," Herbert Croly's *The Promise of American Life* (New York: Macmillan, 1909).

25. Burnham, "Theory and Voting Research," op. cit.

26. Rosenstone and Wolfinger, op. cit., pp. 33, 41. These authors also argue that movement toward a "most permissive" standard would enlarge the electorate without changing its internal composition very much. This of course is true, granted both the social structure and the very large but still marginal numbers involved. It would be somewhat less true on the assumption that the class differential in participation, at whatever aggregate level of turnout, were to disappear altogether.

Comparison of the male labour-force categories in Table 12 in terms of their share of the total adult male population on one hand, and 1972 reported Census Bureau turnouts on the other, would give the following:

Category	Percentage of population 1972	Percentage of active electorate 1972	Discrepancy
Propertied middle class	31.6	38.1	+6.5
Dependent middle class	13.2	14.9	+1.7
Middle class total	44.8	53.0	+8.2
Upper working class	28.3	26.5	−1.8
Lower working class	27.0	20.6	−6.4
Working class total	55.2	47.0	−8.2

A shift toward full equality of participation along class lines—certainly not a matter of registration law alone, as we argue here—would thus produce marginal but not inconsequential changes in the aggregate class composition of the active electorate.

27. H. L. A. Tingsten, *Political Behavior* (London: King, 1937): 10-78.

28. The Chicago data make clear the truth of the axiom that if people go to the trouble of registering, the probability is high that they will vote. Male registration in 1916 was 82.7 percent of estimated potential electorate, female registration was 51.1 percent, a discrepancy of 31.6 percent. Subsequent data for 1920 and 1924 are essentially identical. In 1928, however, male registration was 80.5 percent, while female registration rose to 64.2 percent, closing the gap to 16.3 percent. It would appear that very similar results were obtained in Philadelphia.

29. See e.g., Samuel Lubell, *The Future of American Politics* (New York Harper, 1952), which concentrates its attention on the influx from 1928 on of formerly nonparticipant foreign-born and foreign-stock voters; and Kristi Anderson, "Generation, Partisan Shift, and Realignment: A Glance back to the New Deal," in Nie et al., *The Changing American Voter*, op cit.: 74-95.

30. Tingsten, op cit.: 157-158.

31. Detailed data analysis can normally pick up such cases without difficulty. Thus, in the 1902 gubernatorial election, eight notoriously machine-controlled wards of Philadelphia produced a turnout rate of 105.3 percent, with 85.4 percent of their vote going to the machine's candidate (this turnout was 37.5 percent higher than in Pennsylvania as a whole). Again, in the 1926 Republican gubernatorial primary, the turnout in these largely proletarian, "river" wards was 60.1 percent (30.2 percent higher than in the state as a whole); and the organization's candidate got 96.7 percent of the votes case in these wards.

32. Anderson, op. cit.; David F. Prindle, "Turnout: An Historical Investigation," doctoral dissertation, Massachusetts Institute of Technology, 1977.

33. The contrast between the turnouts in the "war elections" of 1918 and 1942 on one hand, and that of 1862 on the other, is striking. Despite the intensity of the demographic effort involved in the Civil War, and despite the fact that laws in many states did not permit soldiers in the field to vote, 68.8 percent of the estimated potential (exclusively male) electorate voted in the North and West in the 1862 election. The all-time high turnout in any off-year election was reached in 1866 (75.8 percent in North and West), reflecting the intense struggle then going on between Andrew Johnson and the radical Republicans over Reconstruction policy.

34. The basic methodology employed in the construction of the population-base denominators for turnout estimates is explained in detail in the author's note, "Voter Participation in Presidential Elections, by State, 1924-1968," in Bureau of the Census, *Historical Statistics of the United States, Colonial Times to 1970*, vol. II (Washington: Government Printing Office, 1975): 1067-1069. For the most recent period, problems exist not only with census undercounts of the

"underclass population," but with the identification of aliens in 1960 and in some jurisdictions in 1970. For 1970, an exclusion of those aliens counted can be made for New York City, and a proportionate approximation made for 1960 in constructing the denominator. The undercount problem involving "underclass" (especially nonwhite) adults is a more serious one. See David M. Heer, (ed.), *Social Statistics and the City* (Cambridge: Joint Center, 1968). It almost certainly means that the turnouts reported for New York City and other central-city areas are substantially *higher* than the true rates of participation: though one wonders how much lower one can go than the 24.7 percent of estimated adult population voting for president in 1976 in Shirley Chisholm's Brooklyn district (CD 12).

35. The study referred to is, of course, Nie et al., *The Changing American Voter*, op cit. In addition to the controversies referred to in notes 2 and 3 above, the pardigm crisis is reflected in a recent exchange of views: on one side, the Michigan CPS group, Arthur H. Miller et al., "A Majority Party in Disarray: Policy Polarization in the 1972 Election," *American Political Science Review*, 70 (1976): 753-778; and on the other, Samuel Popkin et al., "Comment: What Have You Done for Me Lately? Toward an Investment Theory of Voting," ibid.: 779-805.

36. Cf. the extensive discussion of this phenomenon and its background in Morris P. Fiorina, *Congress: Keystone of the Washington Establishment* (New Haven: Yale Fastback, 1976); and also, Walter Dean Burnham, "The 1976 Election: Has the Crisis Been Adjourned?" in W. D. Burnham and Martha Weinberg (eds.), *American Politics and Public Policy* (Cambridge: MIT Press, 1978), esp.: 14-21.

37. Arthur T. Hadley, *The Empty Polling Booth* (Englewood Cliffs: Prentice-Hall, 1978).

38. The fullest recent discussion of the philosophical issues involved in this obscure struggle is found in my "A Political Scientist and Voting-Rights Litigation: The Case of the 1966 Texas Registration Statute," *Washington University Law Quarterly*, 1971 (1971): 335-358.

39. Douglas A. Hibbs, Jr., "Political Parties and Macroeconomic Policy," *American Political Science Review*, 71 (1977): 1467-1487. This study demonstrates that American macroeconomic policy is much more sensitive to inflation (a particular concern among middle- and upper-status voters), and much less sensitive to unemployment (of particular concern among working-class voters) than is the case in European political contexts.

40. Giovanni Sartori, *Parties and Party Systems*, Vol. 1 (Cambridge: Cambridge University Press, 1976): 39-51.

41. This point is thoroughly discussed in a pioneering work which needs more professional attention than it has thus far received: the chapter by William McPhee and Jack Ferguson, "Political Immunization," in William McPhee et al., *Public Opinon and Congressional Elections* (Glencoe: The Free Press, 1962): 155-179.

42. E. E. Schattschneider, *The Semisovereign People* (New York: Holt, Rinehart and Winston, 1960): 109.

2.6

Political Parties, Political Mobilization, and Political Demobilization

MARTIN SHEFTER

Election laws and voting turnout are only two of the factors that comprise a working system of political parties. Another, and very important, set of factors relates to the internal characteristics of political parties themselves—whether they are centralized or not; how much they rely on ideology, or on political patronage, to motivate their adherents; the extent of elite direction of parties, and so forth. In this essay Martin Shefter discusses American political parties from the standpoint of these characteristics, focusing particularly on the question of precisely when it behooves a political party to try to mobilize and involve people in the political process—and whom.

The conduct of electoral politics in nations with formally democratic institutions is influenced by forces on the "supply side" as well as the "demand side" of the electoral market—that is, by the character of a nation's parties and the preferences of those elites whose views party leaders find it necessary to take into account, as well as by the opinions and attitudes of voters. Political parties not only establish the alternatives among which voters choose on election day, they also influence the level of popular mobilization—or demobilization—in a nation's politics. This essay analyzes the conditions that influence whether or not strong, broadly based party organizations will be constructed in a nation early in the democratic era, and some of the subsequent circumstances that contribute to the persistence or decay of the party organizations established at this crucial juncture of a nation's political history.

Electoral Mobilization, Mass Organization, and the Emergence of Parties

In seeking to understand the conditions that lead to the emergence of strong, broadly based party organizations, it is useful to distinguish between two types of parties.[1] The first, which may be called "externally mobilized" parties, are founded by leaders who do not occupy positions of power within the existing regime, and who seek to bludgeon their way into the political system by mobilizing and organizing a mass constituency. Most of the socialist parties in Europe fall into this category. The second, which may be termed "internally mobilized" parties, are founded by leaders who do occupy positions of power in the prevailing regime and who undertake to mobilize a popular following behind themselves, either because they seek to secure their hold over the government in the face of a challenge by an externally mobilized party, or because a major cleavage develops within the nation's governing class and each side seeks to overwhelm its opponents by appealing for popular support. The major political parties in American history, and most conservative and centrist parties in Europe, were founded in these circumstances.

In the sections below I will argue that the leaders of both of these types of parties will mobilize and organize an extensive popular following only if they must overcome substantial opposition to gain or retain power and they lack other means of accomplishing this end.

Externally Mobilized Parties   There are a number of strategies that outsiders can pursue to gain control over, or entry into, a political system. The wealthy can bribe public officials; soldiers can stage coups; students and intellectuals can riot, agitate, propangan-dize, conspire, and engage in acts of terrorism. Workers and peasants can go to the barricades or stage jacqueries; they can strike or withhold their crops; and they can demonstrate to gain the franchise, and vote as a bloc if they succeed in obtaining it.

The fewer resources any group of outsiders commands, the more it will have to rely upon the weight of numbers to achieve its political demands, and hence it will depend upon mobilizing and organizing as large a proportion of its potential supporters as possible to make its weight felt. This would explain why the mass parties of Europe were organized "from the Left," as Maurice Duverger observes.[2] Parties that sought to gain political and social rights for the working class or small farmers had to aggregate the resources of large numbers of people to finance their activities, and had to rely upon collective actions (the most dramatic being the general strike) to bring pressure to bear to gain their demands.

A second condition influencing the strength of externally mobilized parties is the amount of resistance the party must overcome to win a measure of power. The stronger the regime an externally mobilized party confronts, the more determined are incumbent leaders to exclude the group in question, and the fewer the allies the party enjoys within the regime, the stronger and more broadly based must be the organization the party constructs if it is to succeed in forcing its way into the political system.

The German Social Democratic party of the late nineteenth century is a case in point. The German socialists found it necessary to construct a strong party organization because they faced substantial resistance, and could count upon the support of few allies, in their efforts to secure representation for the working class.[3] The black civil rights movement in the United States during the late 1950s and early 1960s is a contrasting case. Blacks during this period were excluded from the political system in the South, much as workers and peasants who failed to meet property requirements were excluded from the *regimes censitaires* of pre–World War I Europe. To dramatize their demands for civil and political rights, black leaders organized civil rights groups, staged demonstra-tions, and often were compelled to endure intimidation and violence. The chief function of these demonstrations, however, was not to impose sanctions directly upon their targets; rather, they were efforts to mobilize whites who were allied with the civil rights movement or who could be induced to support its demands.[4] Because blacks enjoyed such support, they neither had to rely upon their own resources to finance their activities, nor were they compelled to organize a separate political party to gain a voice in the Congress and the executive branch. But for the very reason that they could draw upon the resources and the support of such allies, the civil rights groups and the black political parties they did establish mobilized only a small proportion of their potential constituency, and as organizations they proved to be rather weak and often short-lived.

Internally Mobilized Parties   Elites who occupy positions of authority within a regime, like outsiders who are seeking to gain entry into that regime or to overthrow it, will construct a strong, broadly based party organization only to the extent that it is necessary for them to do so in order to gain, retain, or exercise power. As was indicated earlier, incumbent elites might find it necessary to appeal for popular support to sustain their position if they are challenged by an externally mobilized party, or if a deep cleavage develops within the governing class and one or both sides undertakes to mobilize outside supporters in an effort to overwhelm its rival.[5] In both these instances, however, incumbents may respond to these threats without embarking upon an all-out campaign of mass mobilization and organization; in particular, they may proceed to repress their rivals, or they may seek to smooth over incipient conflicts or to contain the very process of mobilization itself so as to forestall the emergence of an ever-widening spiral of mobilization and countermobilization, organization and counterorganization. The best way to understand the conditions that lead incumbent elites to pursue a full-scale strategy of mass mobilization and party building is to turn this question on its head, and ask what would prevent their relying upon one of these alternative courses of action.

Restraints on coercion. The most obvious way for incumbent elites to respond to challenges to their position is, of course, to repress their opponents. For any one of a number of reasons, however, they may not be in a position to do this, or they may find it to be less in their interest to embark upon a strategy of repression in dealing with their rivals than a strategy of countermobilization. In the first place, the regime in question may not command a repressive apparatus its rulers can use to crush their opponents. Incumbent elites may find themselves in this situation because the military forces at their command simply are not strong enough relative to those at the disposal of their opponents to enable them to overawe the opposition. A major reason, for example, that the Federalist administration did not attempt to crush the Republican opposition Jefferson and Madison were organizing——the response that Alexander Hamilton, among others, advocated—was that the United States army of the 1790s was no larger than the militia that the Republican stronghold of Virginia easily could raise.[6] Alternately, incumbent elites may find themselves unable to crush their opponents because they could not count upon the loyalty of the repressive apparatus they do command were they to attempt to put down the opposition of the day.[7]

A second major reason why incumbent elites may pursue a strategy of countermobilization rather than one of demobilization in dealing with their opponents is that international considerations or foreign powers may preclude their pursuing the harsher course of action. These considerations go a long way toward explaining why, despite the fragility of democratic traditions in Germany, Japan, and Italy, the conservatives who came to power in these countries in the late 1940s sought to outmobilize, rather than to crush, the major working class parties that challenged their rule. The United States, which as an occupying power and later a creditor and military protector of these regimes enjoyed enormous leverage over them, simply would not have tolerated any other policy. Or, to phrase this more precisely, these regimes resorted only to those repressive measures—outlawing the Communist Party in Germany and Japan, efforts to split the labor movement and to expel peasants from illegally occupied land in Italy—that the Allied powers, and especially the United States, would tolerate.

The third and perhaps most important reason why incumbent elites may pursue a strategy of countermobilization rather than demobilization in dealing with their opponents is that they require the cooperation of these opponents (and of the social groups their opponents are seeking to mobilize) to accomplish their own goals, especially to deal with threats from abroad. A nation seeking to mobilize the manpower, industrial production, and money that modern warfare requires cannot risk conscription riots, labor strife, and high rates of tax avoidance, and these forms of resistance are less likely to occur the more firmly attached the population is to the regime that is calling for these sacrifices. It was for this reason that the final wave of popular enfranchisement occurred in the West as Europe was plunging into World War I.[8]

Collusion. Incumbent elites can avoid the necessity of constructing a strong and broadly based party organization not only by repressing their opponents, but also by coming to terms with them. By so doing they can interrupt the chain of events which, if allowed to proceed, leads internally mobilized parties to bring ever larger numbers of voters into the political arena. That chain, as indicated above, proceeds as follows: A sharp cleavage on questions of major importance polarizes the political class; the losers in this conflict, in an effort to reverse that outcome, undertake to mobilize popular support for their cause, thereby threatening to swamp their opponents at the polls or to make it difficult for them to govern in the face of popular turbulence; to meet this threat politicians on the other side seek to establish a mass base for themselves; and in this way the parties come to construct stronger and more broadly based party organizations. Under the appropriate conditions, however, this process of competitive mobilization and party-building can be aborted.

The conditions that provide party leaders with a strong incentive to collude with one another to contain the process of popular mobilization are similar to those that encourage business firms to restrict price competition and nation-states to restrict military competition: Each side recognizes that it cannot destroy the other, and it fears that unrestrained competition will lead to their mutual destruction or at least will impose intolerable costs on each of them.[9] In the case of political parties total victory is out of the question when each party enjoys a solid base of support within some segment of the electorate. And party leaders will regard the effort to rally additional voters to their side as terribly dangerous if they fear that the entry of new groups into the political system will lead the existing parties to be swamped by the new voters, or if incumbent leaders fear that pursuing such a strategy will lead them to lose control over their own party.

Incumbent politicians are especially unlikely to enter into a process of competitive mobilization if the deepest line of cleavage within the political system runs along geographic (as opposed to class or sectoral) lines, and the nation's institutions allocate seats in the legislature (or votes in an electoral college) to geographically defined constituencies. If each party controls a geographic bastion—be it a set of cities, provinces, or states—then it has little incentive to maximize the turnout of voters within its domain because it will not thereby increase its representation in the legislature. And if each party sees little hope in winning votes in the opposition's bastion, then it will have no incentive to attempt to undercut its rival by invading the opposition's domain.

Very roughly speaking, this state of affairs existed in the United States between the elections of 1896 and 1932. During this period the South was solidly Democratic, and the Republicans enjoyed firm majorities in most (though not all) Northern states. Therefore, the Republicans abandoned the effort to win any congressional seats or electoral votes in the Southern states, and the Democrats made only a token effort to compete in many Northern states. And for this, among other reasons, the level of electoral mobilization in the United States during this period declined quite dramatically from the plateau it had achieved during the period 1840-1896.[10]

Political leaders will abstain from pursuing a strategy of mobilization and party-building not only if the lines of cleavage within the political system fail to encourage such a strategy, but also if they fear that the entry of new voters into the political system will lead to their mutual destruction. It was just such a (well-grounded) fear among the political classes of the nations of Southern Europe—Portugal, Spain, and Italy—during the last decades of the nineteenth century and the first decade of the twentieth, which goes a long way to explaining why, despite the existence of formally democratic institutions, political leaders colluded with one another to restrict the mobilization of new voters into the electoral arena, and consequently why mass-based party organizations failed to emerge in these nations during this period.

The regimes governing the nations of Southern Europe in the late nineteenth century were grounded upon coalitions of landowners and industrialists, and pursued policies that were highly beneficial to these coalition partners, and provided precious few benefits to anyone else.[11] Regimes pursuing policies that served the interests of such a narrow segment of the population would have found it difficult to survive in the presence of party competition. Moreover, active competition for the votes of the peasantry had the potential of undermining the harsh system of labor control upon which landowners depended. Rather than engaging in a strategy of competitive mobilization and party-building, then, the leaders of the national parties developed a set of mechanisms for alternating in power, and/or inducing deputies who nominally belonged to the opposition party to vote for the government of the day.[12]

Finally, if incumbent politicians are to contain the process of popular mobilization, they must have some means of maintaining themselves in power short of building a mass-based party organization; moreover, the participation of groups that are excluded from the regime must in one way or another be limited or deflected. Again, the nations of Southern Europe during the late nineteenth and early twentieth centuries can be cited as examples. Italy, Spain, and Portugal had adopted the institutions of the Napoleonic state, and as was true of the Second Empire in France, the government of the day was able to use the prefectorial system to "make" elections. The benign side of this system involved funneling patronage through this structure to local landlords or creditors, who in turn would distribute it to their clients. On the other side, however, local bosses or *caciques* could with utter impunity rely upon violence to deal with the recalcitrant because the judicial system was entirely under the control of the central government and closed its eyes to such election practices. This system of electoral management was so reliable that in the case of Spain the official government gazette was able to report accurately the results of elections before they were actually held![13] These narrowly based regimes only could survive, however, so long as politically excluded groups did not join in a concerted attack upon them. When the regimes' opponents did join forces, the liberal system collapsed and order was restored only when an authoritarian dictator seized power.

In short, even in nations with formally democratic institutions, incumbent political leaders can remain in power without building strong, mass-based party organizations if: (a) the lines of cleavage within the political class are not so deep or of such a character as to induce them to embark upon a strategy of mobilization; (b) the leaders of the existing parties have reason to fear that the entry of new groups into the political system will lead to their mutual destruction; (c) politicians are able to rely upon institutions other than parties to mobilize political support; and (d) the politically excluded groups are divided or can be intimidated.

The spiral of mobilization and party building. The converse of these propositions indicates the conditions under which political leaders will build strong, broadly based party organizations. In the first place, politicians will have an incentive to embark upon a strategy of mass mobilization and party-building if a serious cleavage opens up within the political class which divides it along functional or sectoral lines, and which political leaders cannot readily compromise or smooth over. The challenge of an externally mobilized party that politicizes the issues of religion, culture, or social class also can lead incumbent elites to respond with a strategy of countermobilization and counterorganization. The last three decades of the nineteenth century and the first of the twentieth witnessed a burst of competitive party-building in Northern Europe because precisely such cleavages were generated by the extension of state power into new realms of life and into the peripheral regions of the nation, and by the growth of international trade during that era.[14]

Political leaders will respond to these challenges by pursuing a strategy of mobilization and countermobilization only if they are confident that they will not be displaced and that the political and economic power of the classes with which they are allied will not be completely destroyed in the process. There are a number of circumstances under which this will occur or ways this can be accomplished. Incumbent politicians may agree to restrict the authority of elected officials so that they and their elite allies will not be displaced from key government positions. In Great Britain, for example, where a proposal for civil service reform had been roundly defeated in 1854, another proposal was passed without arousing any opposition whatever immediately upon the heels of the suffrage extension of 1867. The insulation of the civil service from the influence of party politics assured Britain's traditional governing classes that lower middle class and working class politicians would not be able to use patronage to build an independent base for themselves, and that the grip the aristocracy and upper middle class held upon positions of leadership in the Liberal and Conservative parties, the cabinet, and the higher civil service would not be loosened.[15] Alternately, party leaders may strive to exclude potentially threatening issues from the arena of electoral politics. The very politicians who were responsible for building the world's first mass-based party organizations—the leaders of the Democratic and Whig parties in the United States—attempted in a variety of ways over a twenty-year period to exclude the question of slavery from the national political arena, an issue which they correctly perceived would shatter their parties.[16]

Another precondition for incumbent leaders' pursuing a strategy of party building and political mobilization is that no single public or private institution so completely overshadow all others in civil society that politicians are able to maintain themselves in power simply by allying themselves with it; for in that event they would have no incentive to undertake the hard work involved in building a structurally autonomous party organization. This is one reason why political struggles took the form of competitive party-building more often in nations that industrialized early than in late industrializers or nations in the periphery of the world economy.[17] The economies of late industrializers and peripheral nations are commonly dominated by a few large corporations, banking combines, or the state itself; and where this is so, politicians are likely to be able to withstand challenges by drawing on the organizational and material resources of these corporations. Where this alternative is not available, the only way that politicians may be able to link themselves to a popular base and mobilize electoral support is to build an organization for this very purpose—that is, a mass based party organization.

Finally, incumbent political leaders are likely to respond to challenges to their rule by building strong, broadly based party organizations only if they are not in a position to rely upon intimidation to deal with their opponents. This will be true if a regime requires the active loyalty, rather than merely the sullen acquiescence, of its citizenry to accomplish the goals of its rulers. Such was the case in Northern Europe in the late nineteenth and early twentieth century, where the integrity of international boundaries was far from assured, and where political leaders sought to foster rapid industrialization. Statesmen who were prepared to take a leap in the dark and deal with their opponents by attempting to outmobilize them quickly discovered that this is a more effective strategy of political stabilization than a policy of repression and demobilization. The very process of channeling political participation through party organizations and the institutions of representative government contains it, and reduces the probability that it will take violent forms and be directed against the regime itself.[18]

Subsequent Developments

The circumstances of a party's origins can have enduring consequences for the strength of the organization it constructs and the breadth of its popular base. If the leaders of a regime come to power by constructing a broadly based party organization, or respond to the initial challenge they face from a mass based party organization by pursuing a strategy of countermobilization and counterorganization, the party organization they build is likely thereafter to play a major role in their nation's politics for two reasons. First, the party organization they construct to meet these early challenges will be at hand to meet whatever subsequent challenges they face to their rule, and the subsequent problems they confront in governing the regime they now control. Secondly, to the extent that these rulers are dependent upon their party to maintain themselves in power, they will have an incentive to use their positions of authority to further strengthen the party.

History does not, however, come to an end with the entry of the masses onto the political stage. The ties binding voters to the party that brought them (or their grandparents) into the political system can be shattered if that party proves itself to be utterly incapable of protecting their way of life during a depression or a period of inflation. The social dislocation of wartime mobilization or postwar demobilization can have a similar effect. And finally, millennarian expectations arising from religious revivals or foreign revolutions also can lead to changes in mass political behavior.[19]

Similarly, elites may for one of a number of reasons abandon the political parties with which they once had been allied, and come to advocate changes in political arrangements they once had supported or at least tolerated. Businessmen who once were allied with a political machine, for example, may desert it if in an effort to retain mass support it lives beyond its means and in the process accumulates a large public deficit. Urban machines that behave in this way may ultimately be unable to borrow funds to finance their deficits, and national political parties that live beyond their means can generate severe balance-of-payments difficulties, rampant inflation, and eventually serious social turmoil. As this occurs the business interests that once had supported the party in question are likely to abandon it, and to insist that a program of reform and retrenchment be adopted. It is just such a sequence of events that commonly led to the formation of business-dominated reform movements in American cities during the late nineteenth century, and that more recently has led businessmen, higher civil servants, and army officers to support military coups against civilian regimes in a number of Third World nations.[20]

Finally, mass based party organizations may be subject to external challenges they are unable to withstand or to internal strains that seriously undermine their strength. Among these are the emergence of new forms of organization and new media of communication which permit politicians to mobilize popular followings apart from older political structures. The rise of television, the emergence of professional campaign firms, and the development of computer based mass mailing operations have enabled candidates for elective office in the United States to appeal to voters apart from, and in opposition to, old-line party organizations.[21] Finally, mass based party organizations may be seriously weakened from within, so to speak, if they are unable to maintain control over their cadres. This is an especially severe problem for parties that attract cadres by holding out to them the prospect of obtaining positions or promotions in the civil service, for this system can be undermined if the civil servants form labor unions to protect their interests against the politicians who helped them get their jobs in the first place.

Developments that loosen the ties binding voters, elites, and cadres to old parties provide political entrepreneurs with the opportunity to piece together a new governing coalition. Any effort by such entrepreneurs to bring about major political changes, however, is likely to precipitate major political struggles. And the higher the stakes in such struggles, the more likely it is that each side will pull out the stops and attempt to rally all the allies it can find to support its cause—including allies who exercise control over the means of production, administration, and, in the extreme case, violence. As groups that normally remain on the sidelines are drawn into the struggle and as conflicts spill outside normal institutional channels, the political situation becomes increasingly unstable and its outcome difficult to predict. Nonetheless, it remains true that the better organized and the more broadly based were the parties constructed by politicians prior to the reformist challenge, the stouter the defense they will be able to mount on behalf of existing institutional arrangements. This is because a well organized and broadly based party is less likely than a weaker one to suffer massive defections or to collapse in the face of the various strains and challenges mentioned above, and consequently its leaders will be able to retain a political base for resisting the political forces that rally against them.

In sum, the party organizations that are constructed when a mass electorate is first mobilized into politics are not immune to subsequent challenge or change. Subsequent developments may lead to the emergence of political forces that conclude that their interests can best be served not by working through the existing party system but by attacking that system broadside—by seeking to reform (or destroy) the existing parties or to alter the relationship between them and other public institutions. Parties that mobilized a very broad popular base and constructed a strong organization early in the democratic era are in the best position to withstand such challenges. But there are challenges that even strong parties cannot withstand without suffering defections. And the outcome of a full-scale battle may be uncertain and the fight itself can impose costs on both sides. For this reason party leaders have an incentive to come to terms with their opponents. Such deals are arranged by granting forces that challenge the old parties some control over a portion of the governmental apparatus. By this means the forms of party politics may be preserved, while the domain of the old party system is diminished. In the United States during the twentieth century this process has occurred in several guises: reforming the civil service, and creating independent agencies not directly subject to the control of elected officials; forging a bipartisan consensus in the realm of foreign policy, and protecting national security secrets; and, not least, defending the prerogatives of the judiciary, and upholding rights that, it is claimed, are constitutionally protected. It is precisely such processes that have contributed to the decay of political parties and the demobilization of the electorate in the United States.

Notes

1. Maurice Duverger, *Political Parties* (London: Methuen & Co. Ltd, 1959), pp. xxiii–xxxviii; Samuel P. Huntington, *Political Order in Changing Societies* (New Haven, Conn.: Yale University Press, 1968), pp. 417–419.

2. Duverger, *Political Parties*, p. xxvii.

3. See, e.g., Guenther Roth, *The Social Democrats in Imperial Germany* (Totowa, N.J.: Bedminster Press, 1963).

4. Michael Lipsky, "Protest as a Political Resource," *American Political Science Review* 57 (December, 1968): 1144–1158.

5. Huntington, *Political Order*, pp. 415–416.

6. Richard Hofstadter, *The Idea of a Party System: The Rise of Legitimate Opposition in the United States, 1780–1840* (Berkeley and Los Angeles: University of California Press, 1969), p. 109.

7. Theda Skocpol, "A Critical Review of Barrington Moore's *Social Origins of Dictatorship and Democracy*," *Politics and Society* 4 (Fall 1973): 1–34.

8. Benjamin Ginsberg, *The Consequences of Consent* (Reading, Mass.: Addison-Wesley, 1982), p. 16.

9. This formulation was developed in the course of discussions with Benjamin Ginsberg.

10. Walter Dean Burnham, "The System of 1896: An Analysis," in Paul Kleppner, ed., *The Evolution of American Electoral Systems* (Westport, Conn.: Greenwood Press, 1981).

11. See, e.g., Raymond Carr, *Spain, 1808–1939* Oxford: University Press, 1966), p. 394; Denis Mack Smith, *Italy: A Modern History* (Ann Arbor, Mich.: University of Michigan Press, 1959), chap. 15.

12. James Kurth, "Industrial Change and Political Change: A European Perspective," in David Collier, ed., *The New Authoritarianism in Latin America* (Princeton, N.J.: Princeton University Press, 1979), pp. 335–337.

13. Gerald Brenan, *The Spanish Labyrinth* (Cambridge: Cambridge University Press, 1960), p. 5.

14. Seymour M. Lipset and Stein Rokkan, "Cleavage Structures, Party Systems, and Voter Alignments: An Introduction," in idem., eds., *Party Systems and Voter Alignments* (New York: The Free Press, 1967), pp. 1–64; Peter Gourevitch, "International Trade, Domestic Coalitions, and Liberty: Comparative Responses to the Crisis of 1873–96," *Journal of Interdisciplinary History* 8 (1977): 281–313.

15. Martin Shefter, "Party and Patronage: Germany, England, and Italy," *Politics and Society* 7 (1977): 403-452.

16. Eric Foner, *Politics and Ideology in the Age of the Civil War* (New York: Oxford University Press, 1980), chap. 3.

17. James R. Kurth, "The Political Consequences of the Product Cycle: Industrial History and Political Outcomes," *International Organization* 33 (Winter 1979): 1–34.

18. Adam Przeworski, "Institutionalization of Voting Patterns, or Is Mobilization the Source of Decay?" *American Political Science Review* 69 (March 1975): 49–67.

19. See, e.g., Paul E. Johnson, *A Shopkeeper's Millennium: Society and Revivals in Rochester, New York, 1815–1837* (New York: Hill and Wang, 1978); Samuel P. Huntington, *American Politics: The Promise of Disharmony* (Cambridge: Harvard University Press, 1981); Charles Maier, *Recasting Bourgeois Europe* (Princeton, N.J.: Princeton University Press, 1975), part I.

20. Martin Shefter, "New York City's Fiscal Crisis: The Politics of Inflation and Retrenchment," *The Public Interest* 48 (Summer 1977): 98–127; Collier, *The New Authoritarianism in Latin America*, passim.

21. Benjamin Ginsberg, "Electoral Politics and the Redistribution of Political Power," delivered at the 1983 Annual Meeting of the American Political Science Association, Chicago, Ill., September 1–4, 1983.

What Have You Done for Me Lately?
Toward an Investment Theory of Voting

SAMUEL POPKIN, JOHN W. GORMAN
CHARLES PHILLIPS, JEFFREY A. SMITH

In his book The Responsible Electorate V. O. Key went against the dominant trend of voting analysis of his day by observing that in an electoral system where "buncombe" is provided to the prospective voter as "information," then buncombe will almost certainly be the voter's product in the electoral marketplace. Most of the normative judgments about what constitutes rational voter behavior do, in the end, rest on critical assumptions about what the voter ought to do. The model of the citizen-voter, a key element of pluralist models of democracy, indicates that citizens ought to be informed on a wide variety of issues, and are "irrational" or "uninformed" when they are not. Contrarily, the model advanced by Anthony Downs (in an essay in this collection) contends that because the acquisition of political information is costly, and because voters will use shortcuts to acquire information where possible, the lack of information is perfectly "rational" from an individual point of view. In this essay, Samuel Popkin, John W. Gorman, Charles Phillips, and Jeffrey A. Smith rework the Downsian model in an analysis of the 1972 presidential election. They criticize the citizen-voter and ideological voter models for a number of deficiencies and provide a picture of an instrumentally oriented, "rational" investor-voter.

> A resuscitation of the assumptions buried under the gravestones
> "hence," "therefore," "because" and the like will often reveal that
> the explanation offered is poorly bounded or downright
> unacceptable.
>
> Karl Popper

A Majority Party in Disarray: Policy Polarization in the 1972 Election, by Arthur H. Miller, Warren E. Miller, Alden S. Raine and Thad A. Brown, the latest Survey Research Center/Center for Political Studies quadrennial election study offers a portrait of the American electorate which is in stark contrast with that which emerges from *The American Voter*, the classic product of the SRC's researches into voting behavior.[1] In effect, the authors of the latest version now declare the original account to be—in one of the more memorable phrases of recent political discourse—inoperative. [. . .]

Reprinted with permission from the *American Political Science Review*, Vol. 70, No. 3 (September 1976), "Comment," pp. 779–805 (with deletions). Copyright 1976 by the American Political Science Association.

The findings of "Majority Party" are in stark contrast to previous SRC/CPS findings. They state that, for the first time in 20 years, issues were more potent than party as a determinant of the vote (p. 770), that a "spectacular change in the quality of mass attitudes towards questions of public policy" (p. 754) has occurred and that voters are now becoming ideological. (p. 766) Repeatedly, in numerous passages of their paper the authors of "Majority Party" describe changes in the nature of the electorate or the nature of voting a change from party and candidate to ideology and issues, and claim an increased ideological content to the act of voting. The basis for these claims of change lies in comparisons with the findings of past Survey Research Center studies, but these past studies employed different *models*, *methods*, and *standards*. Since, when we compare the old and new models, the changed model produces massively different results for 1972 than does the older model for 1972, can anyone suppose it would produce the same results for 1964 or 1952? To arrive at these new findings, the authors of "Majority Party" have introduced a model of voting that differs distinctly from the traditional model of voting that Survey Research Center analysts have used since the early 'fifties. This new model—and its associated methods and standards—generates conclusions about the 1972 election radically different from those produced for 1972 by the old "American Voter" model. The "American Voter" model and the school of voting research based on it have their roots in group theory. But now, in order to account for findings which the "American Voter" model cannot explain, the authors of "Majority Party" have incorporated ideas into their model from what is often described as the economic-rational school of voting research, exemplified by the work of Anthony Downs.[2] Yet in trying to repair the older model the authors have adopted those parts of Downs's work primarily concerned with the nature of policy voting and the aggregation of individual preferences into one-dimensional "ideological space." Some of these concepts are ill-suited to the study of actual voting because they fail to take into account the context of American politics; in other cases, they are simply incorrect as originally formulated. A different aspect of Downs's work which we will emphasize here is the analysis of the costs of information with its implications for the role of informational shortcuts and the origins and nature of issue concerns. [. . .]

The Investor-Voter

The massive differences between the findings of "Majority Party" and the findings of earlier SRC studies are not only due to changes in the American electorate; they reflect changes in the models, methods and standards by which voters are assessed. Such differences call for a careful re-examination of past studies for a comparison of the two approaches. We contend that both approaches are flawed, that neither can provide a consistent explanation of American voting, and that a new approach to the study of voting is needed, an approach which takes a different view of the voter and a different view of politics.

To that end, we will propose a view of voting that sees the voter as an investor and characterizes each vote as *an investment in one or more collective goods made under conditions of uncertainty with costly and imperfect information.*

Elections are by their nature collective enterprises; both the outcome of the election and the subsequent performance of the government are collective goods for the entire electorate. Given the size of the electorate and the privacy of the voting act, there are great incentives for the individual to abdicate the responsibility for the outcome to others, certainly to a greater extent than would be the case if his vote were decisive. The collective aspect of elections reduces the value of the vote in so far as it affects the provision of collective goods, and consequently makes the expected returns from investment in voting decisions small relative to the opportunity costs of such investment.

An instrumental voter applies information relevant to the choice between alternatives, i.e., information which bears upon the expected returns to the voter of the election of particular candidates. The accumulation of information always involves the expenditure of resources by individuals. These costs are directly affected by the quality of the information available; the problem of assessing the credibility of information; the difficulty of distinguishing between campaign rhetoric and actual position statements; the question of interpretation of vague positions; the difficulty of assigning responsibility for collective outputs; and simple gaps in the available information. Under such conditions, we would expect voters to employ information cost-saving devices, such as party and ideological labels and demographic characteristics of the candidates, and to be satisfied with incomplete information.

If the voter is viewed as an investor, an account of the 'fifties, 'sixties, and 'seventies is possible within the framework of a single model. The roots of such an approach, which is developed in the remainder of this paper, lie in the work of Anthony Downs.

We will elaborate the implications of this approach by examining four critical aspects of voting and illustrating the problems of both the old SRC theory and the newer theories of "Majority Party." In so doing we will begin to develop the notion of an instrumental investor-voter, drawing upon Downs but modifying his ideas for the American context and correcting him in those places where he is wrong. The four aspects of voting are the cost of information, the role of parties, the role of candidates and the role of ideology.

Information Costs   The accumulation of information involves the expenditure of resources, if only the time required for its procurement, analysis and evaluation. Since information is costly, voters will obtain only limited amounts. There are, of course, individuals who find politics so fascinating that they will inform themselves even when they have no personal interest in or cannot affect the outcome of a political event. In general, however, the investor-voter will be informed when he:

(1) Is able to apply "free" information, i.e., information gathered for other purposes which is also applicable to the vote decision.

(2) Is immediately and personally affected by a particular issue, e.g., a student estimating the draft as part of his career plans.

An investor-voter model which incorporates the understanding that information is costly leads to expectations about the voter which differ from those of the SRC, or citizen-voter, model. Whereas citizen-voters are expected to have well-developed opinions about a wide range of issues, a focus on information costs leads to the expectation that only some voters—those who must gather the information in the course of their daily lives or who have a particularly direct stake in the issue—will develop a detailed understanding of any issues. Most voters will only learn enough to form a very generalized notion of the position of a particular candidate or party on some issues, and many voters will be ignorant about most issues. The investor-voter will use partisan and ideological labels as practical solutions to the problem of costly information.

Whereas the citizen-voter model gives interest in politics causal priority over issue concern, consideration of information costs reverses the direction of causality; political involvement becomes a product of the perception of the individual stakes and costs involved.

Thus, while the citizen-voter model assumes that the individual's level of political involvement is invariant during adult life and is internal to the individual, i.e., unaffected by changes in the political context,[3] the investor-voter model predicts that involvement will vary as the voter's life situation changes and as he responds to new opportunities and political events.

How well informed should we expect the voter to be? Previous SRC studies of voting have graded the voter against an exacting standard. The (ideal) voter-citizen was expected to hold informed opinions on all the crucial issues of the day and to exhibit a high level of interest in politics. When the voters of the 'fifties were found not to meet these standards, it was assumed that the problem lay with the voter. Specifically, a low level of political information, narrow range of expressed issue concerns, lack of perceived party differences, and lack of interest were traced to a lack of education.

When voters were shown to be issueless in the 'fifties, the standard used in order to ascertain whether or not a voter was issue-oriented was very different from the one used today: "If a person goes on record in favor of leaving electric power production to private industry, but has no idea what the Administration is doing about the question, we may deduce that his opinion is not based on substantial familiarity with the subject. He has an opinion but knows so little about the topic as to deprive the opinion of significance for his subsequent political behavior." The application of this standard led to rather pessimistic conclusions about voters: "An example of public indifference to an issue that was given heavy emphasis by political leaders is provided by the role of the Taft-Hartley Act in the 1948 election. . . . Almost seven out of every ten adult Americans saw the curtain fall on the Presidential election of 1948 without knowing whether Taft-Hartley was the name of a hero or a villain."[4]

"Majority Party" bases its findings of heightened issue orientation upon very different standards. As noted above, in the 1972 questionnaire format, voters were allowed to express general preferences rather than precise policy choices on particular items of legislation. It was just such generalized preferences or concerns that were so strongly disparaged in past writings. In the 'fifties, when Campbell reported that "there were no great questions of policy which *the public* saw as dividing the two parties," he meant that instead of being concerned about well-defined issues and items of legislation, people cared about the "mess in Washington and the stalemate in Korea."[5] By changing standards, "Majority Party" leaves unresolved how many of our "new" voters by the more stringent standards of the past, knew whether Cooper-Church was a fast-food chain or a rock group.

Few voters can be expected to have issue opinions which are sufficiently detailed to satisfy the stringent standards of earlier SRC studies. Because gathering and digesting such details about the fate of specific bills and particular administration programs is a costly process, we expect the only voters to bear the cost will be those who need the details for other than voting purposes: e.g., a farmer who needs to know about trade legislation in order to determine what proportions of his land should be planted in what crops.

Voters do, however, acquire much political information in the course of their daily lives. Such information then helps voters to form political opinions and make vote decisions. It is not surprising that voters make use of such "free" information and feel most comfortable dealing with political choices in terms of these "mundane" life experiences, and there is no need to ignore such "gut" voting as a subject of serious analysis.

Philip Converse, in discussing his interviewing experience, provides some support for this aspect of the voter-investor model. He notes that many respondents show clear discomfort when asked certain survey questions and that there seems to be a pattern to this discomfort: "I should make very clear that such events were rare to nonexistent when questions dealt with the immediate terms of the respondent's life, such as whether the respondent was satisfied with his housing or how he would feel about blacks moving in next door. But they began to mount significantly in questions concerning politics, and hit something of a maximum on the national issue items of the structured kind . . ."[6]

Usable political information is acquired in the process of making individual economic decisions: housewives learn about inflation of retail prices, homebuyers find out the trends in mortgage loan interest rates, and owners of stocks follow the Dow-Jones averages. On the basis of this information, voters can gauge the economy, and apply this data when they vote. In the past, SRC analyses discarded such economic views as insignificant. And even in 1972, when the SRC transformed its measure of issue concern to a more realistic "gut-level" general issue preference, they still failed to ask voters their impressions of and prognosis for the national economy, asked no questions about taxes, inflation and unemployment, and thus failed to tap significant levels of voter concern and information about economic issues.

The citizen-voter model assumes that a well-educated electorate will be a well-informed electorate: "The educated citizen is attentive, knowledgeable and participatory and the uneducated citizen is not."[7] However, as "Majority Party" points out, while there has been an enormous increase in the educational level over the past two decades, the proportion of people caring who wins the election has not increased and there is no reason to believe that knowledge about specific legislation has increased either. The investor-voter model suggests that it is the amount of "free" daily life information and invididual need to know—motivation rather than just education level—which explains how informed about issues voters will be.

Given the cost of gathering information solely for the purpose of the vote decision, we should not expect issue consensus within parties. Where candidates are engaged in assembling a coalition of output-oriented voters, it is to be expected that people in every coalition will be ignorant of the candidate's stand in many areas not central to their primary concerns. Without sorting the voters into "issue publics" on the basis of the salience of various issues to them, one cannot expect to find high levels of interest or of information. Similarly, within every coalition there will be people who disagree with the candidate or party stand in some area and still support the candidate or party. It is not essential that in 1964 a black Democratic voter whose primary concern is civil rights support or even be familiar with Lyndon Johnson's Vietnam policy in order to qualify as an issue-oriented voter. We ought not to be surprised if we find that the most vocal advocates or opponents of busing or of the Vietnam war are totally ignorant about farm price support policy or revenue-sharing distribution criteria.

This emphasis on the conditions under which voters will inform themselves about issues brings the notion of issue publics to the forefront of public opinion and voting research. As Converse has noted: "We have come a step closer to reality when we recognize the fragmentation of the mass public into a plethora of issue publics."[8]

The investor-voter model assumes that voters have issue interests but expects those interests to be generalized because of the cost of information. Where such issue interests are related to vote decisions, they need not be relegated to insignificance simply because they are lacking in detail. An individual facing a choice situation like voting, where the number of alternatives is limited, need only gather enough information to determine which alternative is preferable. Any expenditure of resources for additional information which does not have a high probability of changing his preference is superfluous. Thus, a generalized notion of the position of a particular candidate or party will usually prove

SAMUEL POPKIN ET AL.

sufficient for the vote decision. This suggests that a proper criterion for evaluating issue-orientation is the existence of relationships between issue position and vote decision, not a judgment about the "richness" of the voter's expression of his issue interest.[9]

Because information is costly, most voters will save time and energy by using informational shortcuts to the vote decision. In this way we can explain the widespread reliance on party identification and ideological labels. So long as the actions of candidates appear consistent with the generalized notion the voter attaches to a particular label, the voter is able to save considerable costs associated with keeping track of all the various activities of government. By employing such a cost-saving strategy, the voter does not sacrifice his basic issue-orientations; he simply deals with them in a more economical way.

The citizen-voter and investor-voter perspectives have strikingly different implications for evaluating the voters' level of participation and involvement. According to the citizen-voter model, voter apathy and general levels of interest, involvement, and participation depend solely on education and internal motivation. The SRC precluded the possibility that voter behavior was a realistic response to the actual political context rather than an expression of internal psychological states.

For example, Converse equated voter involvement with comprehension: "We tend to use involvement as a surrogate for comprehension because it is a fair assumption that there is a high correlation between involvement (motivation to attend to information about matters political) and breadth of comprehension about what is going on in politics."[10] Furthermore, involvement is defined operationally as concern over the outcome of the election and interest in the campaign.[11] The implicit assumption of this linkage is that there are always meaningful differences between the parties or candidates for all to see. Given these assumptions, if a person does not care who wins, he obviously does not comprehend politics.

In the investor-voter model, interest, involvement, and participation depend on the voter's calculation of the individual stakes and costs involved in the election; included in this calculation are the voter's issue concerns and his estimates of his opportunities for participation. As a result, much of the stigma of "apathy" is transferred from the voter to the electoral system.

The SRC also assumed that the major barriers to participation were internal to the individual. In 1960 they stated, "The greater impact of restrictive electoral laws on Negroes is, in part at least, a function of the relatively low motivational levels among Negroes."[12] The increase of participation among black voters in the 1960's is, of course, a clear example of a situation where political participation as well as political interest and involvement, rather than being fixed expressions of individual motivation, responded instead to an increase in investment opportunities and a legal decision by Congress to reduce the cost (or more aptly, to provide subsidies to aid blacks in paying the costs) of voting.

Political Parties   The difference between the investor-voter approach and the SRC approach is sharply illustrated when views of political parties and party identification are compared. For the SRC, party identification was attachment to a group:

> In characterizing the relation of the individual to party as a psychological identification we invoke a concept that has played an important if somewhat varied role in psychological theories of the relation of individual to individual or of individual to group. We use the concept here to characterize the individual's

affective orientation to an important group-object in his environment. Both reference group theory and small group studies of influence have converged upon the attracting or repelling quality of the group as the generalized dimension most critical in defining the individual-group relationship and it is this dimension that we will call identification.[13]

This concept of party as affective group identification devoid of political policy content is different from that presented by Downs, for whom parties constitute "ideal teams" that attempt to gain elective positions through an appeal to the voters which is based on a platform that is composed of issue positions.[14] This perspective emphasizes an instrumental rather than an affective relationship between voter and party. The most useful way to conceptualize party for this purpose is as a coalition of voters coordinating their efforts to pursue a set of collective goods. While the coalition may exhibit a great deal of stability over time, the basis of the attachment of each individual to the party is instrumental, which is to say that affective attachment depends on rewards received.

The view one holds of the relationship between individual and party has a significant impact on how one sees the voting act. The person who sees an affective relationship interprets the casting of a vote as primarily an act of group loyalty. On the other hand, the person who sees an instrumental relationship finds that the vote is cast as a contribution to a set of collective goods. It follows from the instrumental view that when a voter uses party label as a principal determinant of his vote preference, the label is used as an informational shortcut.

It is important to note the coalitional structure of parties. While there may at times be widespread agreement within a party on general goals, there is no reason to assume that all voters have the same priorities and saliences. Viewing political parties as coalitions of minorities has two important implications for voting research. First of all as noted earlier, the multiplicity of group and individual interests suggests that one should not expect consensus of attitudes across a number of issues within the party. There also is no logical inconsistency in the attitudes of a black Democrat who is pro-civil rights and anti-labor or even any logical reason to suppose such an individual experiences any significant crosspressure when casting a vote for a Democrat. Furthermore, seeing the parties as coalitions of minorities makes it illogical to assume that any significant number of voters should be able to locate the party on some hypothetical "continuum" that summarizes party positions for all issues.

The authors of "Majority Party" summarize the role of parties as it developed in the work of the SRC during the 'fifties when they state, " . . . Party identification has a predisposing effect that forces images of candidates and attitudes on issues to be consistent with party attitudes which in turn are the factors that directly affect the vote decision." (p. 769) In this view of party, there is no instrumental component to membership, no feedback from party performance to party support, and no serious consideration of autonomous interests or values by which voters might judge—even roughly—the performance of their party and occasionally reconsider their support.

A review of the literature shows that many assumptions about party loyalty and the absence of instrumental relationships that are commonly supposed to rest on empirical SRC "findings" are without foundation. They were read into the data or were assumed at the time of the earlier studies on the basis of group theory. One assumption that illustrates this problem is clearly stated in *The Voter Decides*: " . . . Our concept of party identification leads us to *assume* that a person who associates himself strongly with a party will conform to what he sees to be party standards and support party goals."[15] This notion of party identification as a psychological force on the individual to conform to standards and support party goals found expression in the cold-war view of the Communist party and what might be called the "loyalist" model of the party member as party follower, following every twist and turn of the party line. Obviously, issue agreement or support for a party's positions was simply the result of following the party line; belonging to a party exerted considerable influence on an individual "to conform to what he sees as party standards."[16]

Yet the original empirical evidence for "willingness to conform" to party positions is not very strong. In 1952, for example, less than 40 per cent of self-identified "strong" Democrats and "strong" Republicans felt that they would vote for their party's candidate even if they didn't like him or agree with him; less than 60 per cent of the "strong" identifiers even felt that a person should vote for the same party for President and for Congress.[17]

A more important assumption was that party identification was actually a psychological hindrance to issue voting. In *The American Voter*, an analysis of farmers revealed "spectacular links between simple economic pressures and partisan choice."[18] An investor-voter explanation of these "spectacular links" would follow these general lines: The collective nature of the vote means that there is low incentive for an individual to collect information solely to cast one of many millions of votes. Farmers, however, gather the information on their own businesses in great detail—not because they are better citizens than urban laborers, for example, but because they are independent managers and the information necessary for management is directly related to government policy in many cases. Laborers, not being economic managers and thus not collecting the information for their daily use, would be more likely to rely on past performance, using party label as an informational shortcut.

How does *The American Voter* explain the "spectacular links" its authors observed? The spectacular links exist because farmers have weaker partisan identification than laborers, and thus are "psychologically free to march to the polls and vote the rascals out . . ."[19]

Two arguments buttressed the contention of *The American Voter* that there was no causal relationship between party identification and the instrumental goals of the voters:[20]

(1) The lack of congruence within parties on the central issues of the day.

(2) The belief that allegiances had formed early and endured over time.

Yet a lack of congruence within parties is hardly proof that there is no issue-based switching from party to party. There is no reason to expect congruence on every issue unless one assumes that all voters have exactly the same issue preferences and saliences and the same information. A voter without concerns in a particular area would seldom gather information on that area.

Moreover, party allegiances over time are not as stable as had previously been assumed. Between 1956 and 1960, certainly not regarded as a period of dynamic or unprecedented change, one out of every four persons in an SRC panel survey shifted his or her allegiance on a Democrat-Independent-Republican scale.[21] In addition, one out of three people who stated his identification as "strong" Democrat or "strong" Republican, no longer so identified himself four years later, and one out of twelve voters changed parties.

Furthermore, it is an empirical fact that the "weight" attached to party performance varies from election to election; even if there were no switching from party to party, the weight the voters accord to party in the complex of factors in the decision calculus varies according to party performance and according to variations in information possessed by the voters.

The large amount of movement found on panel surveys between partisan strength categories means *it no longer follows that* "responsiveness of the vote decision to short-term partisan forces varies inversely with the mean strength of party identification."[22] Instead, Democrats become strong Democrats when they strongly intend to vote Democratic or agree strongly with the Democratic position on an issue. In other words, there is feedback from issues and performance to partisan identification. Strength of partisanship is a running tally of current party assessment.

The existence of feedback and shifting changes in the strength of partisan identification, contradicts a fundamental assumption behind the Normal Vote, namely that the vote can be separated into long term and short term forces where the short term forces are the "response to transient election circumstances which do not materially affect the abiding division of party loyalties."[23]

In fact, the analysis of the 'fifties provides considerable evidence of "feedback" from performance affecting party image in voting. The traditional associations between the Republican party and the Depression and between the Democratic party and war have been the subject of much comment in voting research. Even these associations, however, do not appear to have been immutable in the minds of the voters. Stokes et al. in analyzing the 1956 election note that " . . . four years of Republican prosperity destroyed the major party of a fourteen-to-one margin the Democrats had had in the partisanship of these responses. After haunting the Republicans in every election since 1932, memories of the 'Hoover Depression' had receded at least temporarily as a direct force in American politics."[24]

On the other hand, the experience of the first four years of the Eisenhower Administration amplified and reinforced another set of associations. It was found that ". . . references to war and peace in 1952 were pro-Republican or anti-Democratic by a ratio of greater than seven to one. By 1956, the virtual disappearance of comments favorable to the Democrats or hostile to the Republicans had increased the ratio five times."[25]

By 1968, the election that seems to have provoked a re-examination of past theory, an important caveat appeared in discussions of party in the SRC election study: " . . . in the moment of truth in the polling booth, party allegiance seems the most relevant cue for many voters *if conditions permit it to be used.*"[26] The authors of "Majority Party" offer yet another statement of the role of the party:

> During a period of issue consensus or strong alignment between issue orientation and traditional partisan division, party ties can be expected to have a significant impact, both directly and as a predisposing agent, on the vote decision. However, during periods when questions of policy attain new levels of public salience and divide the population in a fashion that is orthogonal to traditional partisan differences, other political stimuli, such as new candidates and especially candidates associated with the new issues, may become relatively more important in explaining of voting behavior . . . (p. 770).

In other words, sometimes party and issues will be correlated and sometimes they will not. Apparently, what the authors of "Majority Party" wish us to believe is that when issues correlate with party, people are following the party line—as in the "loyalist" model—and issues do not matter. But now that issues do not correlate, they do matter.

A much stronger and clearer statement is needed. If partisan attachment were "affective" and "psychologically predisposing," as the SRC theory of voting originally postulated, orthogonality would not have developed. If orthogonality has developed, the theory is wrong. Indeed, it is notable that while the party has been discussed as a "group" and party identification as "willingness to conform," when the authors of "Majority Party" introduce "liberal-conservative" measures, they are beginning to employ significantly different terminology. To be a liberal, a moderate, or a conservative is to have a " . . . simple policy yardstick by which the Presidential candidates were evaluated with respect to the voters' own policy orientation." (p. 776)

If the liberal/moderate/conservative labels are now to be treated as yardsticks, then why not also treat party as a yardstick and reject the notion of party as a psychologically given group identification with no instrumental content?

Candidates   The structural context in which voters are operating is as crucial to their actual behavior as is the costliness of information and the attendant use of informational shortcuts. There are crucial differences between the American political system and the idealized world which Anthony Downs was modeling. These differences affect both how well the system can be expected to respond to voters' preferences, *ceteris paribus*, and where the voters themselves will focus their attention.

Downs explicitly assumes an "ideal team" party that behaves as if it is a single, unified point. Furthermore, he implicitly assumes that the parties have equal ability to carry out the programs they advocate. American parties do not even approximate these assumptions. The American federal system is characterized by widely dispersed patronage centers, local primaries, local fund raising and national party organizations which have few resources at their disposal.[27] In this context voters will rely less on party and party platforms and more on candidate assessments. In addition, voters will use different criteria for evaluating challengers and incumbents.

The American political system is a system that vests power in a single individual who has no formal ties to his party. The unity of the executive branch, the separation of the executive and legislative branches, and the weakness of the American party system combine to give the American president a degree of power and independence unknown in a parliamentary system, and certainly not envisioned in a Downsian "ideal-team" system. This causes the investor-voter to focus on the presidential candidate rather than just the party, since the party is an unreliable cue for predicting the performance of individual candidates.

In the American system, party labels are poor predictors of actual output because:

(1) The independence of the party member from the party means that a party candidate is free to adhere or not to the party platform, and further, that a candidate might conceivably adhere to the platform for purposes of election but follow a different course in office.

(2) With a multiplicity of offices and levels of government, assessing individual credit or blame for the total party output becomes important, but very difficult.

(3) Finally, where parties are coalitions of minorities, it is to be expected that the relative strength of different groups within the party will vary over time, with consequent effects on the party output. [. . .]

Ideology [28]   Anthony Downs said that under conditions of costly information and uncertainty, voters would apply an ideology—or yardstick—to the problem in order to reduce their costs. At one point, the authors of "Majority Party" adopted the "yardstick" metaphor for their liberal/moderate/conservative measure, a metaphor with which we agree. The authors, however, have then elaborated on the idea to produce the conclusion that " . . . the 1972 race could be labeled 'ideological' " (abstract).

The authors further indicate that they found evidence of an "increase in the ideological nature of public opinion" (p. 768). This seems to be a different use of the word "ideological." Do the authors of "Majority Party" mean perhaps that yardsticks are used more than in the past? It is doubtful that "yardstick" could be substituted in either of the quoted passages and still retain the intended meaning.

Whereas Downs argued that voters employ ideology as a *substitute* for information, Philip Converse argued that the use of a single dimension of issue evaluation like the liberal-conservative continuum required "relatively full information."[29] Thus, because the American electorate exhibited low levels of political information, ideology would not be a major factor in American politics. Or, in other words, the American electorate was too uninformed to be Downsian. Ideology was transformed from an information cost-saving device into a criterion for telling when a voter was using relatively informed, sophisticated reasoning, and the use of ideology came to be seen as a sign of growth and enlightenment.

Despite this important difference in the two conceptions of ideology, the authors of "Majority Party" have adopted notions about the implications of ideology which were originally formulated by Downs; they adopt these notions directly from Downs's work without reference to the corrections and modifications which have appeared since 1957. A major and incorrect Downsian assumption is that all the various "yardsticks" a voter might employ would aggregate over the electorate to a one-dimensional issue space, as in the traditional notions of left-right or liberal-conservative continua. Donald Stokes, in a critique of Down's spatial modeling of party competition, pointed out that voters, in fact, use multiple dimensions for evaluation of issues and argued that the multidimensional issue space itself was a variable to be studied rather than assumed.[30] When issues are not single-peaked, or when different issues have different salience for different voters, or when there is more than one issue or when abstention is high, there is no reason to expect party convergence to a "central" position and indeed there may not even be a "center." The important and enduring aspect of Down's work—his focus on information costs— remains vital to understanding politics, but it is necessary to move away from simple notions of convergence.

The SRC's search for ideology was motivated not only by a desire to find "good citizens" but also by the belief that the existence of a unidimensional structure had major implications for the political system. "If an electorate responds to public affairs in terms of one or a few well-defined and stable ideological dimensions on which there is little movement of opinion, political controversy will be relatively tightly bounded and the possibilities of party maneuver—and alteration in office—relatively circumscribed."[31] Downs also made this argument for a two-party system.[32] He assumed that voters always vote for the party closest to their position on the continuum. If voters were symmetrically distributed along this single dimension and the parties or candidates engaged in vote-maximizing strategies, then both parties would converge on the center of the continuum. Neither party would have an incentive to deviate from the center because, by doing so, it would increase the distance between itself and some of its centrist constituents, thus throwing the election to the opposition. The implications for the political system were

(1) that each party would adopt an ideologically consistent platform or set of issue positions which could be designated by a point on a one-dimensional issue space

(2) that there exists a unique, vote-maximizing platform

(3) that this platform is located at the center of the issue space

(4) that the platforms of the two parties would, therefore, converge toward stable points near the center or median, *ceteris paribus*. [. . .]

Conclusion

On one point, we are in total agreement with the authors of "Majority Party": a fresh approach to the study of voting is needed. The disagreement is on what that approach should be. The authors of "Majority Party" claim to have found a "new" voter, whose increased education is changing the basis of his vote from parties and candidates to issues and ideology. The authors of "Majority Party" have crossed the line in the debate between those who see voting as based on candidates, parties, and psychological motivations and those who see it as based on issues, ideology, and rational choice. Yet when crossing the line, they have failed to recognize that the dichotomy was false in the first place. It was produced by mistaken standards and theories used in analyzing the whole body of SRC election studies.

The authors of "Majority Party" gloss over the discontinuity of their work with the past by implying that the voters, rather than the theory, have changed (i.e., that the voters have outgrown the framework in which *The American Voter* placed them). Where previously voters were too uninformed to be Downsian, education has now enabled them to behave in a sophisticated way. We want to state plainly that we see the old theories as inapplicable not because they are outdated, but because they were wrong: the standards they applied to the voter were misleading and the tests they applied faulty.

In particular, the old theories were wrong about the nature of party, seeing the affective and ignoring the instrumental. They were wrong about the invariance of interest and involvement over a life-time. They were wrong when they assumed that there was little feedback from party performance to party identification. They were wrong when they assumed that voters took their cues from party and candidate lines and ignored cues from their daily lives and self-interest. More than anything that we can say, the events of the 1960s proved them wrong: the changes of party, the growth of black participation, the success of issue-based protest movements in toppling at least one president from within his own party, and certainly the rise of George Wallace—perhaps even the rise of George McGovern.

The authors of "Majority Party" are almost always wrong, or at least without foundation, when they talk about "change" but use a new proximity model; the new findings on 1972 are produced by new instruments, and where direct comparisons are possible the new and old instruments do not agree. "Majority Party" is wrong, for example, when it argues that candidates have decreased rather than increased in importance.

Moreover, the new "Majority Party" approach to voting is misguided in several important respects. It is wrong about ideology—particularly when it sees the use of ideology as a manifestation of sophistication rather than as a cost-saving device. It is also wrong about the relation between candidate and issues. For example, it is a mistake to imply, as they do, that the voter will take the promise of proximity on issues in lieu of predictions of actual performance, and it is wrong for them to portray candidate concerns as antithetical to issue concerns, elements to be neutralized so that issues can shine through. And finally, the authors of "Majority Party," in their rush to modernize, have erred by embracing parts of the Downsian model which are either inapplicable to the American political system or simply wrong.

Rather than attempt patchwork revisions as the authors of "Majority Party" have done, one must challenge the old theories at their core—their view of the American voter. Using concepts from group theories and standards based on democratic ideals, the old theories developed expectations, hypotheses, and more than a few normative judgments—in particular, placing all the onus for apathy or poor performance on the voter and reifying "consistency." The authors of "Majority Party," while incorporating other methods, do not seriously challenge the old view of the voter.

As we suggest, one fresh approach may begin with the idea that the voter is using his vote as an investment in one or more collective goods, made under conditions of uncertainty with costly and imperfect information. As an investor the voter is concerned with outputs, and because the outputs are collective goods, there is incentive to be a free-rider and pass the responsibility to others to inform themselves. Combined with the costliness of information, this leads to the use of informational cost-saving devices like party, ideology or demographic characteristics and an expectation that voters will be most informed when information is "free" or when it is obtained not to prepare for voting but for use in daily life. Combined with the weak nature of the American party system and the power of the President, this leads to a focus on the candidate himself and not just on his party. As an investor, the voter is concerned not with abstract policies of the candidate, but rather with what the candidate can be expected to "deliver" and, thus, the voter looks for signs of competence. [. . .]

We have discussed three different models of the American voter: the original SRC model for the citizen voter, the more educated, ideological "Downsian" voter of "Majority Party," and our investor-voter. The differences in the models are summed up by the main question they suggest is in the minds of the voters. The old SRC model suggests that the voter asks, "Where do my affections lie?" The "Majority Party" revised model suggests that the voter asks, "What promises are closest to my ideals?" We instead suggest that the American voter goes beyond affect and promises to ask, "What have you done for me lately?"

Notes

1. Arthur H. Miller, Warren E. Miller, Alden S. Raine, and Thad A. Brown, "A Majority Party in Disarray: Policy Polarization in the 1972 Election," *American Political Science Review*, 70 (September 1976). Angus Campbell, Philip E. Converse, Warren E. Miller, and Donald E. Stokes, *The American Voter* (New York: John Wiley & Sons, 1960).

2. Anthony Downs, *An Economic Theory of Democracy* (New York: Harper & Row, 1957).

3. Campbell, "Voters and Elections: Past and Present," p. 746. See also Philip E. Converse, "The Concept of the Normal Vote," in *Elections and the Political Order*, ed. Angus Campbell, Philip Converse, Warren Miller, and Donald Stokes (New York: Wiley, 1966), pp. 9-39.

4. Campbell et al., *The American Voter*, p. 172-173.

5. Campbell, "Voters and Elections . . ." p. 752.

6. Philip E Converse, "Comment: The Status of Non-attitudes," *American Political Science Review* 68 (June 1974), 650.

7. Phillip E. Converse, "Change in the American Electorate," in *The Human Meaning of Social Change*, ed. Angus Campbell and Philip Converse (New York, Russell Sage Foundation, 1972), p. 324.

8. Philip Converse, "The Nature of Belief Systems in Mass Publics," in *Ideology and Discontent*, ed. David Apter (Glencoe, Ill: Free Press, 1964), p. 245.

9. Michael Shapiro, "Rational Political Man: A Synthesis of Economic and Social-Psychological Perspectives," *American Political Science Review*, 63 (December 1969), 1106-1119.

10. Philip E. Converse, "Information Flow and the Stability of Partisan Attitudes," in *Elections and the Political Order*, ed. Campbell et al., pp. 138-139.

11. Campbell et al., *The American Voter*, pp. 102-103.

12. Campbell et al., *The American Voter*, p. 279.

13. Campbell, et al., *The American Voter*, p. 121, emphasis added.

14. Downs, *An Economic Theory of Democracy*, p. 26.

15. Angus Campbell, Gerald Gurin, and Warren Miller, *The Voter Decides* (Evanston, Ill.: Row, Peterson, 1954). p. 107. Emphasis added.

16. See for example Angus Campbell and H. C. Cooper, *Group Differences in Attitudes and Votes: A Study of the 1954 Congressional Election* (SRC, 1956), p. 95, as cited in Peter B. Natchez, "Images of Voting: The Social Psychologists," *Public Policy* 17 (Summer 1970) 564. This paper was aided by Natchez's stimulating analysis.

17. Campbell et al., *The Voter Decides*, pp. 95-96.

18. Campbell et al., *The American Voter*, p. 430.

19. Ibid., p. 430.

20. Ibid., pp. 185-186.

21. SRC 1956-58-60 panel reported by John C. Pierce and Douglas D. Rose, "Non-attitudes and American Public Opinion: The Examination of a Thesis," *APSR* 68 (June 1974), 626-650, esp. p. 632.

22. Converse, "The Concept of a Normal Vote," p. 21.

23. Converse, "Religion and Politics: 1960," p. 101 in *Elections and the Political Order*.

24. Stokes et al., "Components of Electoral Decision," p. 373.

25. Ibid., p. 375.

26. Converse et al., "Continuity and Change in American Politics . . . " p. 1099 (emphasis added).

27. R. Mayhew, *Congress: The Electoral Connection* (New Haven: Yale University Press, 1974).

28. The arguments in this section are, for the most part, distilled from recent work by Joe A. Oppenheimer, and Norman Frohlich. See Joe A. Oppenheimer, "Relating Coalitions of Minorities to the Voters Paradox, or Putting the Fly in the Democratic Pie," paper given at the 1972 meeting of the Southwest Political Science Association, San Antonio, Texas, March 30-April 1, 1972; Joe A. Oppenheimer, "Some Political Implications of 'Vote Trading and Voting Paradox: A Proof of Logical Equivalence': A Comment," *American Political Science Review* 69 (September 1975): Norman Frohlich and Joe A. Oppenheimer, *Modern Political Economy* (Englewood Cliffs, N.J.: Prentice Hall), Chapter 7.

29. Converse, "The Nature of Belief Systems in Mass Publics," p. 227.

30. Stokes, "Spatial Models of Party Competition,"

31. Campbell et al., *The American Voter*, p. 550.

32. For the sake of simplicity, the authors will always assume two parties or two candidates in this analysis.

2.8

Money and Power:
The New Political Economy
of American Elections

BENJAMIN GINSBERG

The last decade has brought about significant changes in American electoral politics, including the public funding of presidential campaigns, for which a candidate must poll 5 percent of the national vote in order to qualify, and the proliferation of so-called political action committees, or PACs. These changes in the legal constraints on campaign financing have gone hand-in-hand with the introduction of new campaign techniques based on the electronic media and the ersatz "personal contact" made possible by computerized direct mailings. The anomic and perhaps even anemic quality of such campaigns stands in sharp contrast to the precinct-by-precinct canvassing, torchlight parades, and mass rallies of the nineteenth century, when electoral participation reached record levels. The smiling faces of handsome astronauts and actors are now worth more at the polls than an intellectual grasp of the issues. Taken in this sense, the continuing plunge in participation rates may be a tribute to the good taste, if not the good sense, of the average (non)voter. In this essay, Benjamin Ginsberg traces the history and impact of changes in campaign techniques and technology, concluding that current trends have biased electoral politics toward right-wing candidates.

Over the past three decades, sophisticated communications technology has supplanted mass organization as the ultimate weaponry of American electoral conflict. Until the mid-twentieth century, electoral contests were dominated by party coalitions capable of deploying huge armies of workers to mobilize voters. Organization has not become politically irrelevant. But declines in party strength, coupled with increases in the potency and availability of the new technology, have led competing groups in the 1980s to shift their reliance from large-scale organization to computers, opinion survey analyses, and electronic media campaigns directed by small staffs of public relations experts. This change in the character of competitive political practices is, in some respects, analogous to the transformation of military technology over the past century. The enormous infantry armies that dominated World War I battlefields have given way in importance to powerful modern weapons systems operated from electronic command posts by small groups of technicians.

The displacement of organizational methods by the new political technology is sometimes seen merely as a matter of changing "campaign styles." But this change is, in essence, a shift from labor- to capital-intensive competitive electoral practices and has the most far-reaching implications for the balance of power among contending political groups. Labor-intensive organizational tactics allowed parties whose chief support came from groups nearer the bottom of the social scale to use the numerical superiority of their forces as a partial counterweight to the institutional and economic resources more readily available to the opposition. The capital-intensive technological format, by contrast, has given a major boost to the political fortunes of those forces—usually found on the political right—whose sympathizers are better able to furnish the large sums now needed to compete effectively. Indeed, the new technology permits financial resources to be more effectively harnessed and exploited than was ever before possible. As a result, the significance of the right's customary financial advantage has been substantially increased. Money and the new political technology, not some spontaneous "shift to the right" by mass public opinion, were the keys to the stunning successes scored by conservative Republicans in 1978 and 1980, and the Republicans' surprisingly strong showing during what amounted to an economic depression in 1982.

Clearly, their greater capacity to employ the new campaign techniques no more guarantees victory in every race to parties and factions speaking for the relatively well-to-do, than did superior numbers and organization ever mean that the political formations representing the relatively worse-off would always succeed. Obviously, a variety of factors, including especially the performance of the domestic economy and the state of America's foreign involvements, will inevitably have an impact on electoral outcomes. Nevertheless, the new technology loads the electoral dice in favor of the right. The expanding role of the new electoral techniques means that over the coming decades, groups closer to the political left will increasingly find themselves engaged in a species of political warfare that they are poorly equipped to win. The supersession of organization by the new technology may prove to be the functional equivalent of a critical electoral realignment, substantially redistributing power and profoundly transforming political possibilities in the United States.

The "Will of the People": Cause or Effect?

Students of American politics, like members of the public-at-large, typically presume that popular support determines electoral outcomes. It is because of this presumption that the academic voting literature focuses so intently upon voters' beliefs and their social, psychological, and demographic correlates. Obviously, citizens' votes do formally determine election results. But, this formal power does not mean that voters are the decisive actors on the electoral stage. First and most obvious, the mass electorate's power to decide is constrained by the alternatives it is offered. The electorate's options are defined by the interests, parties, and candidates vying for power, not by voters themselves. Opposing groups are certainly free to take voters' preferences into account but, often enough, other factors play a more significant role in determining what possibilities will be proposed to the electorate.[1]

More important, however, voters' choices are often results rather than causes of successful electoral efforts. The voter-centered perspective of the electoral literature is based on the implicit assumption that voters' opinions are formed and electoral choices made more or less independently of the efforts of contending forces to mobilize mass support. This assumption is a political counterpart of the concept of the autonomy of consumer preference in neoclassical economic theory and is vulnerable to the same criticism that many economists have directed at that notion.[2] Consumers' preferences and choices often are consequences of successful merchandising efforts and reflect the market power of competing firms more than the exogenous or autonomous judgments of individuals. By the same token, voters' opinions and choices are often—albeit not always—products of the efforts of contending groups to build mass followings, and mainly reflect these groups' relative capacity to achieve a measure of visibility, to communicate cogent appeals, and to offer voters solidary and material incentives sufficiently compelling to secure their allegiance. As Schumpeter once put it, "The will of the people [is ultimately] the product not the motive power of the political process."[3] Perhaps all voters cannot always be convinced of all things. But, it is significant that in a variety of national and historical settings individuals with very similar social origins and life conditions have been recruited by political forces that differed substantially from one another in aims and methods. Conversely, individuals whose social origins and personal circumstances have been very different, frequently have been persuaded to join the political camps of the same or very similar parties.[4] Of course, once they are established (to employ another helpful economic analogy), consumer preferences can sometimes be "sticky" with respect to short-term market incentives. Brand loyalty is the classic example. Established electoral preferences may be similarly resistant to change. The durability of partisan attachments in the United States, for example, is well known. But, over time, citizens' preferences are frequently protean and malleable—witness the instances in which parties and candidates have gradually been able to convince large groups to shift their political allegiances across enormous ideological chasms.[5]

The ability of competing forces to contact, rally, and maintain mass followings—their political "market power"—is heavily dependent upon the social and economic resources they are able to deploy in the electoral arena. Effective electoral competition requires substantial financial, institutional, educational, and organizational assets. When groups that lack economic means or access to major social institutions compete for electoral support with groups in possession of such resources, the outcome, as critics of pluralist theories like to point out, is seldom in doubt.

In general, changes in the relative economic power and social resources of competing interests are, sooner or later, followed by political readjustments. Historically, major economic and social transformations in the United States have triggered political aftershocks in the form of critical electoral realignments. These realignments have functioned to redistribute political authority in a manner that reflected the new economic and social balance. In the contemporary American political setting, the supersession of mass electoral organization by new political technologies does not precisely represent a change in the underlying distribution of resources among opposing political interests. This transformation of electoral formats does, however, substantially alter the relative importance of two key political resources—money and personnel—and, as a result, the relative power of the groups possessing each. The likely product of this change, too, is the eventuality that Schumpeter envisaged, a change in the manifest expression of the popular will.

From Organization to Technology

For more than a century and a half, organization was the most potent weapon available to contending electoral forces. Political parties in nineteenth-century Europe, most notably the German SPD, built elaborate partisan machinery, enrolled hundreds of thousands of dues-paying members, and molded these adherents into disciplined political battalions. The leading American electoral machines of the nineteenth and early twentieth centuries could mobilize tens of thousands of patronage employees for political work. On a day-to-day basis, party functionaries maintained close contact with voters and their families, if necessary assisting constituents with personal, financial, and legal problems while at the same time learning their views and securing their trust. During election campaigns the party machines deployed their forces to trumpet the candidates' virtues, rally popular support, and bring the faithful to the polls. In terms of their organization, size, and behavior, the competing parties resembled nothing so much as armies of foot soldiers on the march—regiments of party workers engaging the enemy in a street-by-street, house-by-house struggle to maximize electoral support. Victory generally went to the party with the most energetic and best-drilled legions. Before the turn of the century, politicians even thought in military terms, conceiving elections as battles between huge opposing armies and their generals.[6]

Quite obviously mass organization is a political technique that can be used by groups espousing any viewpoint or representing any social or economic interest. In the United States both Democrats and Republicans constructed political machines; in Europe socialists, liberals, conservatives, and others organized for political action. But, although it can be used by any sort of group, organization is not a neutral political tactic. The construction of strong, permanent mass organization has most often been a strategy pursued by groups that must aggregate the energies and resources of large numbers of individuals to counter their opponents' superior material means or institutional standing. During the course of European political history, disciplined and coherent party organizations were generally developed first by groups representing the political aspirations of the working classes. Parties, Duverger notes, "are always more developed on the left than on the right because they are always more necessary on the left than on the right."[7] In the United States, the first mass party was built by the Jeffersonians as a counterweight to the superior social, institutional, and economic resources that could be deployed by the incumbent Federalists. In a subsequent period of American history, the efforts of the Jacksonians to construct a coherent mass-party organization were impelled by a similar set of circumstances. Only by organizing the power of numbers could the Jacksonian coalition hope to compete successfully against the superior resources commanded by its adversaries. Precisely these efforts at party building, it may be recalled, led to the Jacksonian era's famous controversies over the use of a "spoils system" for staffing federal administrative posts and Jackson's practice of depositing federal funds in "pet" state banks. The spoils system obviously meant the appointment of loyal party workers to the national bureaucracy. The pet banks were controlled by individuals with close ties to the party.

In both the United States and Europe, the political success of party organizations forced their opponents to copy them in order to meet the challenge. It was, as Duverger points out, "contagion from the left" that led politicians of the center and right to attempt to build strong party organizations. These efforts were sometimes successful. In the United States, for example, the Whigs carefully copied the organizational techniques devised by the Jacksonians and were able to win control of the national government in the famous "hard cider" campaign of 1840. But, even when groups nearer the top of the social scale responded in kind to organizational efforts by their inferiors, the net effect nonetheless was to give lower class groups an opportunity to compete on a more equal footing. In the absence of coherent mass organization, middle- and upper-class factions almost inevitably had a substantial competitive edge over their lower-class rivals. Even if both sides organized, the net effect was still to erode the relative advantage of the well-off. Parties of the right, moreover, were seldom actually able to equal the organizational coherence of the working-class opposition. As Duverger and others have observed, middle- and upper-class parties generally failed to construct organizations as effective as those built by their working-class foes, who typically commanded larger and more easily disciplined forces.[8] Of course, even the superior organization of the left did not fully offset the variety of social and economic resources available to groups on the right. But, its organizational advantages nevertheless gave the left an opportunity to compete on a much more equal footing than would otherwise have been possible.

Erosion of Organizational Strength

The advantages derived by the left from organizational tactics often led centrist and right-wing politicians to the conclusion that an organized, partisan politics posed a serious threat to the established social order and to their own political power. George Washington's warning against the "baneful effects of the spirit of party" was echoed by the representatives of social, economic, and political elites in many nations who saw their right to rule challenged by groups able to organize the collective energies and resources of mass publics.

Opposition to party was the basis for a number of the institutional reforms of the American political process promulgated at the turn of the century during the so-called "Progressive era." Many Progressive reformers were undoubtedly motivated by a sincere desire to rid politics of corruption and to improve the quality and efficiency of government in the United States. But, simultaneously, from the perspective of middle- and upper-class Progressives and the financial, commercial, and industrial elites with which they were often associated, the weakening or elimination of party organization promised to have a number of other important political functions. The enervation of party would mean that power could more readily be acquired and retained by the "best men," i.e., those with wealth, position, and education. The weakening of party organization, moreover, would have the effect of denying access to power to reformers' political opponents, who, indeed, relied heavily on party organization. Not coincidentally, Progressive reforms were aimed especially at the destruction of the powerful urban machines built by the representatives of lower-class and ethnic voters.

The list of anti-party reforms of the Progressive era is a familiar one. The Australian ballot reform took away the parties' privilege of printing and distributing ballots and introduced the possibility of split-ticket voting. The introduction of nonpartisan local elections eroded grass-roots party organization. The extension of "merit systems" for administrative appointments stripped party organizations of their vitally important access to patronage and thus reduced their ability to recruit workers. The development of the direct primary reduced party leaders' capacity to control candidate nominations. The reforms obviously did not destroy political parties as entities but, taken together, they did substantially weaken party organizations in the United States. After the turn of the century, the organizational strength of American political parties gradually diminished. American party organizations, as a result, entered the twentieth century with rickety substructures. And, as the use of civil service, primary elections, and the other Progressive innovations spread during the period between the two world wars, the strength of party organizations continued to be eroded. By the end of World War II, political scientists were already beginning to bemoan the absence of party discipline and "party responsibility" in the United States.[9]

This erosion of the parties' organizational strength set the stage for the introduction of new political techniques. These new methods represented radical departures from the campaign practices perfected during the nineteenth century. In place of manpower and organization, contending forces began to employ intricate electronic communications techniques to woo electoral support. The new political technology includes five basic elements.

1. *Polling*. Surveys of voter opinion provide the information that candidates and their staffs use to craft campaign strategies. Candidates employ polls to select issues, to assess their own strengths and weaknesses as well as those of the opposition, to check voter response to the campaign, and to determine the degree to which various constituent groups are susceptible to campaign appeals. In recent years, pollsters have become central figures in most national, state, and local campaigns.

2. *The broadcast media*. Extensive use of the electronic media, television in particular, has become the hallmark of the modern political campaign. By far the most commonly used broadcast technique is the 30- or 60-second television spot advertisement—such as Lyndon Johnson's famous "daisy girl" ad—which permits the candidates's message to be delivered to a target audience before uninterested or hostile viewers can cognitively, or physically, tune it out. Television spot ads and other media techinques are designed to establish candidate name identification, to create a favorable image of the candidate and a negative image of the opponent, to link the candidate with desirable groups in the community and to communicate the candidate's stands on selected issues. These spot ads can have an important electoral impact. Generally, media campaigns attempt to follow the guidelines indicated by candidates' polls. Thus, media ads are particularly aimed at constituency groups that are, according to poll data, especially amenable to the candidate's blandishments or whose loyalties are especially in need of reinforcement. At the same time, advertisements seek to tap especially salient electoral sentiments, again, as identified by poll data. One observer notes that the broadcast media are so central to modern campaigns that most other candidate activities are tied to their media strategies.[10] For example, a sizeable percentage of most candidates' newspaper ads are now used mainly to advertise radio and television appearances. Other candidate activities are designed expressly to stimulate television news coverage. For instance, incumbent senators running for reelection or for higher office almost always sponsor committee or subcommittee hearings to generate publicity. In recent years, Senate hearings on hunger, crime, health, and defense have been used mainly to attract television cameras. Similarly, a number of candidates have found that walking the streets of the South Bronx could lead to useful news coverage.

3. *Phone banks*. Through the broadcast media, candidates communicate with voters *en masse* and impersonally. Phone banks allow campaign workers to make personal contact with hundreds of thousands of voters. "Personal" contacts of this sort are thought to be extremely effective. Again, poll data serve to identify the groups that will be targeted for phone calls. Computers select phone numbers from areas in which members of these groups are concentrated. Staffs of paid or volunteer callers, using computer-assisted dialing systems and prepared scripts, then place calls to deliver the candidate's message. The targeted groups are generally those identified by polls as either uncommitted or weakly committed, as well as strong supporters of the candidate who are contacted simply to encourage them to vote.

4. *Direct mail*. Direct mail serves both as a vehicle for communicating with voters and as a mechanism for raising funds. The first step in a direct mail campaign is the purchase or rental of a computerized mailing list of voters deemed to have some particular perspective or social characteristic. Often sets of magazine subscription lists or lists of donors to various causes are employed. A candidate interested in reaching conservative voters, for example, might rent subscription lists from *National Review, Human Events,* and *Conservative Digest*. Or, a candidate interested in appealing to liberals might rent

subscription lists from *The New York Review of Books* or *The New Republic*. Considerable fine-tuning is possible. After obtaining the appropriate mailing lists, candidates usually send pamphlets, letters, and brochures describing themselves and their views to voters believed to be sympathetic. Different types of mail appeals are made to different electoral subgroups. Often the letters sent to voters are personalized. The recipient is addressed by name in the text and the letter appears actually to have been signed by the candidate. Of course, these "personal" letters are written and even signed by a computer.

5. *Professional public relations.* Modern campaigns and the complex technology upon which they rely are typically directed by professional public relations consultants. Virtually all serious contenders for national and state-wide office retain the services of professional campaign consultants. Increasingly, candidates for local office, too, have come to rely upon professional campaign managers. For example, a number of candidates for municipal office in New York City in 1982 retained consulting firms. Consultants offer candidates the expertise necessary to conduct accurate opinion polls, produce television commercials, organize direct mail campaigns, and make use of sophisticated computer analyses. Some consulting firms specialize in particular aspects of campaigning. Tarrance Associates, for example, specializes in polling; Richard Vigurie specializes in direct mail; Rothstein-Buckley and Roger Ailes concentrate on the broadcast media. A growing number of firms, though, like Spencer-Roberts, Napolitan Associates and DeVries and Associates, will direct every aspect of an electoral effort.[11] A "full-service" firm will arrange

> advertising campaigns for radio, television and newspapers, including layout, timing and the actual placing of advertisements; public relations and press services, including the organization of public meetings, preparation and distribution of press releases and statements and detailed travel arrangements for the candidate; research and presentation of issues, including preparation of position papers, speechwriting and arranging for consultations between candidates and outside experts in appropriate areas of public policy; fund-raising solicitations, both by mail and through testimonial dinners and other public events; public opinion sampling to test voter response to the campaign and voter attitudes on major issues; technical assistance on radio and television production, including the hiring of cameramen and recording studios for political films and broadcasts; campaign budgeting assistance designed to put campaign funds to the best possible use; use of data processing techniques to plan campaign strategy based on computer evaluations of thousands of bits of information; and mobilization of support through traditional door-to-door campaigns and telephone solicitation of voters.[12]

Most professional consultants prefer to work for one party or for candidates with a particular ideology. Matt Reese, for example, generally works for Democratic candidates; Stuart Spencer consults for Republicans; Richard Vigurie serves as a fund raiser for candidates of the new right. Many firms, however, do not limit themselves to candidates of any one persuasion. While David Garth, for example, is best known for his work for liberal Democrats, Garth's firm will conduct campaigns for Republicans—under the supervision of Garth's partner, Ronald Maiorana, a former press secretary for Nelson Rockefeller. A major New York City firm, Dressner, Morris, and Tortorello, will gladly assist any candidate willing to pay the appropriate fees. Richard Morris, one of the firm's partners, declares, "We're not a political club, we're a business."[13]

Several of the components of this "new" political technology were, of course, developed long before World War II. Professional public relations firms first became involved in electoral politics in 1934, when the firm Whittaker and Baxter helped to defeat Upton Sinclair's Socialist candidacy in the California gubernatorial race of that year. Primitive opinion polls were used in American elections as early as 1824, and relatively sophisticated surveys were employed extensively during the 1880s and 1890s.[14] But, after World War II, the introduction of television and the computer provided the mechanisms that became the electronic heart of the modern campaign. These electronic innovations coincided with a growing realization on the part of politicians and activists that the capacity of traditional party organizations to mobilize voters had greatly diminished. As this realization spread, a small number of candidates began to experiment with new campaign methods. The initial trickle of political innovators became a flood when politicians observed that the new campaign techniques were generally more effective than the more traditional efforts that could be mounted by the now debilitated party organizations.

In a number of well-publicized congressional, senatorial, and gubernatorial campaigns during the postwar years, candidates using the new campaign methods decisively defeated rivals who continued to rely on the older organizational techniques. The successful campaigns mounted by Richard Nixon in the 1948 California Senate race, Jacob Javits in his 1948 New York congressional race, and Winthrop Rockefeller in the 1964 Arkansas gubernatorial contest were very visible examples of the power of technology. The flood of technologically oriented campaigns became a deluge after 1971. The Federal Elections Campaign Act of that year prompted the creation of large numbers of political action committees (PACs) by a host of corporate and ideological groups. This development increased the availability of funds to political candidates—conservative candidates in particular—which meant in turn that the new technology could be used more extensively. Initially, the new techniques were employed mainly by individual candidates who often made little or no effort to coordinate their campaigns with those of other political aspirants sharing the same party label. For this reason, campaigns employing the new technology sometimes came to be called "candidate-centered" efforts, as distinguished from the traditional party-coordinated campaign.

However, nothing about the new technology precluded its use by political party leaders seeking to coordinate a number of campaigns. In recent years party leaders, Republicans in particular, have learned to make good use of modern campaign technology. The difference between the old and new political methods is not that the latter are inherently candidate-centered while the former is strictly a party tool; the difference is, rather, a matter of the types of political resources upon which each method relies.

Money and Electoral Politics

The displacement of organizational methods by the new political technology is, in essence, a shift from labor- to capital-intensive competitive electoral practices. Campaign tasks that were once performed by masses of party workers and a modicum of cash now require fewer personnel but a great deal more money, to operate the polls, computers, and other electronic paraphernalia upon which the new political style depends. Of course, even when manpower and organization were the key electoral tools, money had considerable political significance. Indeed, nineteenth-century American patronage machines could neither have built nor have maintained their huge campaign establishments without the boodle they arrogated from a variety of sources including the public treasury. In effect, machine politics functioned as a primitive form of public funding of election campaigns. Nevertheless, the chief resource of nineteenth-century politics was manpower—the sympathizers, loyalists, functionaries, and activists who staffed the party organization and operated its electoral machinery. Ostrogorski, for example, estimates that as many as 2.5 million individuals were employed in political work during the 1880s.[15] Modern campaigns, by contrast, depend heavily on money. Each element of the new political technology is enormously expensive. This expense is reflected in the immense cost of the 1980 and 1982 American national elections. Senate candidates in 1980 spent some $476 million while candidates for the House of Representatives spent another $120 million. The two major presidential candidates received and spend $60 million in public funds and, in addition, at least another $13.7 million was spent on the presidential race by various independent groups supporting Ronald Reagan. Some estimates place the total cost of the 1980 campaigns at over $1 billion.[16] The 1982 off-year races were also extremely expensive. In 1982, according to the Federal Election Commission (FEC), Senate candidates spent approximately $114 million, while candidates for the House of Representatives spent a total of $176 million. Another $103 million was spent by independent groups supporting various candidates. Certainly, manpower is not irrelevant to modern political campaigns. Candidates continue to utilize the political services of tens of thousands of volunteer workers. Nevertheless, the new technology has made money the key political resource.

Traditional, labor-intensive campaign techniques worked to the advantage of the political left. The new, capital-intensive campaign format, however, clearly serves the interests of the political right. Almost invariably, groups and forces on the right have superior access to the massive financial resources needed to make effective use of the new technology. During the 1980 elections, for example, according to the Federal Election Commission, the Republican party was able to raise and spend approximately five times the sum available to its Democratic opponent—$170 million for the Republicans in federal, state, and local races, compared with some $35 million for the Democrats. In the same year, the Democratic congressional campaign committee was able to raise only $750 thousand while its Republican counterpart spent some $3 million. The Democratic senatorial campaign committee spent $800 thousand while the Republicans raised and spent $5.5 million. The Democratic National Committee spent $15 million, while the Republican National Committee spent some $73 million. At the same time, independent conservative groups such as the National Conservative Political Action Committee and the Fund for a Conservative Majority spent some $14 million on behalf of the Reagan candidacy. These same "new right" groups also spent several million dollars on behalf of a number of Republican senatorial candidates. Neither the Carter campaign nor the campaigns of Democratic legislative candidates were able to secure comparable support. In 1982 the Democratic and Republican senatorial campaign committees each raised and spent approximately $600 thousand. While the Democratic congressional campaign committee was able to spend only $1 million, its Republican counterpart raised and spent some $4.6 million. At the same time, the Republican National Committee outspent the Democratic National Committee by a factor of 5—$14.7 million for the Republicans versus only $2.9 million for the Democrats. Independent conservative groups raised enormous quantities of money in 1982: NCPAC accumulated $10 million; Jesse Helms's National Conservative Club raised $9.7 million; the Fund for a Conservative Majority amassed approximately $3 million. All told, however, these groups spent less than $1 million on 1982 electoral contests. Presumably, much of the remainder is earmarked for the 1984 presidential primaries and general election.[17]

Before 1980, Democratic candidates had been able to rely on two key sources of financial support to counter the Republicans' fund-raising abilities. First, many corporate donors who preferred the Republicans nevertheless contributed heavily to Democratic campaigns on the presumption that the great majority of incumbents—who were, of course, mainly Democrats—would win reelection no matter what efforts might be made to defeat them. Second, organized labor traditionally contributed heavily enough to the Democrats to partially offset business and conservative support for the Republicans. The value to the Democrats of incumbency was reduced in 1980 when a large number of corporate donors came to realize that with sufficient funds and the new technology, previously unassailable Democratic incumbents might be defeated. Midway through the 1980 race, many corporate political action committees halted virtually all their contributions to Democratic incumbents and redoubled their efforts on behalf of the Republicans.[18]

In 1982 Democratic incumbents—especially those generally deemed to be holding safe seats—had little difficulty raising money. Indeed, on the average, Democratic incumbents raised and spent only $35,000 less than incumbent Republicans. Nevertheless, the funds raised by incumbent Democrats for their own races could never fully offset the electoral impact of the Republican national party's 5–1 spending edge vis-à-vis the Democrats. In essence, Democratic funds were raised and spent mainly in the districts already most likely to be carried by a Democrat. The funds available to the Republicans at the national level, by contrast, could be used in contests where infusions of cash could have the most telling effects. Thus, Democratic incumbents, the Democrats most likely to win anyway, generally had a comfortable funding edge vis-à-vis their Republican challengers. In contests involving an incumbent Democrat and a Republican challenger, the average amount spent by the Democratic candidate was $240,000 while the average Republican expenditure was some $90,000 less—$150,000.

The Republican party, for its part, invested its funds, first, to protect Republican incumbents. Republican incumbents, as a result, were able to outspend their Democratic challengers by an average margin of nearly $140,000—$275,000 for the Republicans to $137,000 for the Democrats. Second, the Republicans directed their funds to contests involving open seats. In 60 percent of all contests for open seats, Republican candidates outspent their Democratic rivals. The average Republican margin was $78,000—$297,000 for the Republicans to $219,000 for the Democrats. Finally, the Republicans focused on races that were likely to be close. It is, of course, in close races that spending can matter most. Seventy percent of the eighty-eight 1982 congressional races in which the final margin of victory was five percent or less were won by the candidate who spent the most. In 75 percent of these races, Republican candidates outspent their Democratic opponents. On average, the Republican spending advantage was $110,000—$375,000 for the Republicans compared with $265,900 for the Democrats. This difference helps to explain why 50 percent of the close races in 1982 were won by Republicans (as against 38 percent of all congressional races in that year).

The significance of labor support for the Democrats also decreased substantially in 1980. During that election, 318 labor unions formed political action committees. But, for the first time, their number was overshadowed by the 1,226 corporate political action committees that took part in the race. In 1982 the number of labor PACs declined to 228, but the total amount contributed by labor groups increased 47 percent to more than $20 million. This expansion of labor's efforts, however, was more than offset by the opposition. In 1982 the number of PACs affiliated with corporations increased to 1,310 and their total contribution level rose 36 percent to $29.3 million. These corporate PACs were joined by 520 "trade, membership and health" committees—groups such as the

American Medical Association and the National Realtors Association. These committees contributed $22.8 million in 1982. The realtors alone gave $2 million to congressional and senatorial candidates. At the present time, labor unions and corporations as well as trade associations are feverishly organizing political action committees. However, since there are some 50 thousand corporations and thousands of trade associations in the United States, compared with only a few hundred labor unions, the opportunity for expanded corporate and trade involvement would appear to be much greater than the possibility of an increased financial effort by organized labor.

Innovation from the Right

This portrayal of the new political technology as the weapon of the right is reinforced by an examination of the history of American campaign practices. Just as the organizational format that dominated nineteenth-century electoral politics was generally pioneered by the left, the trail for the newer technological format was largely blazed by conservative forces. Indeed, groups on the right often saw the new technology as a means of employing their superior financial resources to compensate for their historic organizational deficiencies. In some respects, the most interesting example of technological innovation by the right is the very oldest component of the "new" technology—polling.

Historically, the introduction of polling was, in fact, detrimental to the political fortunes of the social formations that represented the interests and aspirations of the working classes. Polling erodes one of the major competitive advantages that has traditionally been available to lower-class groups and parties—a knowledge of mass public opinion superior to that of their middle- and upper-class opponents. The inability of bourgeois politicians to understand or sympathize with the needs of ordinary people is, of course, the point of one of the favorite morality tales of American political folklore, the misadventures of the "silk stocking" candidate. And, indeed, office-seekers from Easy Street often find it difficult to communicate with voters on Cannery Row.

But more important than social proximity is the matter of organization. The superior coherence and discipline of their mass organizations gave parties of the left a more accurate and extensive view of the public's mood than could normally be acquired by their less well organized opponents. In western Europe, the "branch" style of organization evolved by working-class parties in the nineteenth century gave them direct access to the views of a nation-wide sample of ordinary citizens. In the United States, the urban political machines that mobilized working-class constituencies employed armies of precinct workers and canvassers. Among their other duties, these functionaries were responsible for learning the preferences, wants, and needs of each and every voter living within an assigned precinct or election district. Through its extensive precinct organization, the urban machine developed a capacity to understand the moods, and thus to anticipate and influence the actions, of hundreds of thousands of voters.

The advent of polling eroded the advantage that social proximity and organization had given working-class parties in the competition for mass electoral support. Of course, any sort of political group can use an opinion survey. But, historically, polling has been particularly valuable to parties and candidates who lacked disciplined organizations and whose own social roots did not offer many clues to the desires of ordinary voters. Part of the historical significance of polling is that it represented a major element in the response of the right to the left's twin advantages—greater organizational coherence and social consanguinity with ordinary citizens. In the United States, systematic political polling was initiated during the second half of the nineteenth century. Most of the early polls were sponsored by newspapers and magazines affiliated with conservative causes and middle- and upper-class political factions. The conservative *Chicago Tribune* was a major promoter of polls during this period. Prior to the critical election of 1896, the *Tribune* polled some 14,000 factory workers and purported to show that 80 percent favored McKinley over William Jennings Bryan.[19] Many of the newspapers and periodicals that made extensive use of political polling in the nineteenth-century were linked with either the Mugwumps or the Prohibitionists—precisely the two political groupings whose members might be least expected to have much firsthand knowledge of the preferences of common folk. During the 1896 campaign the Mugwump *Chicago Record* spent more than $60,000 to mail postcard ballots to a random sample of one voter in eight in twelve midwestern states; 328,000 additional ballots went to all registered voters in Chicago. The Democrats feared that the *Record* poll was a Republican trick and urged their supporters not to participate.[20] Other prominent members of the Mugwump press that frequently sponsored polls before the turn of the century included the *New York Herald*, the *Columbus Dispatch*, the *Cincinnati Enquirer*, the *Springfield* (Massachusetts) *Republican*, and the *Philadelphia Times*.[21]

In the early years of the twentieth century, many of the major polls were affiliated with groups on the political right. The Hearst newspapers, for example, polled extensively. *Fortune* magazine published widely read polls. The *Literary Digest*, which, of course, sponsored a famous presidential poll, was affiliated with the Prohibitionists.[22] The clientele of most of the major pre-World War II pollsters—Gallup, Roper, and Robinson, for example—was heavily Republican, reflecting both the personal predilections of the pollsters and relative capacities of Democrats and Republicans of the period to understand public opinion without the aid of complex statistical analysis.[23] In recent years, the use of political polling has become virtually universal. Nevertheless, the polling efforts of groups on the political right have been far more elaborate and extensive than those of other political factions. Appropriately enough, according to a recent report, Ronald Reagan and his advisors have relied more heavily and extensively on polling for their political information than any previous national administration.[24]

What is true of polling is also true of most of the other elements of the new political technology. The use of these methods, sometimes adopted by the left, as well, has been pioneered and perfected by groups on the political right.[25] Even when right-wing forces were not the first actually to use a particular technique, conservative groups were usually the ones fully to exploit and develop its potential. Thus, direct-mail fundraising was first used extensively in a presidential race by George McGovern. However, the political use of direct mail has been expanded and perfected by conservative groups. For example, Richard Vigurie, the chief fundraiser of the new right, has assembled a mailing list of more than 30 million individuals interested in conservative causes. Liberal Democrats are generally far behind Vigurie and other right-wing fundraisers in terms of the quality and sophistication of their techniques.[26]

Money, Technology, and Political Power

By the mid-1980s, of course, parties and candidates of every political stripe were using the new political techniques. Nevertheless, the forces of the political right have continued to be the chief devotees and principal beneficiaries of the new campaign methods. Indeed, the ascendancy of the capital-intensive technological format has meant that the balance of political power has shifted—perhaps decisively—in favor of the right. First, because of their superior access to financial resources, groups on the right will undoubtedly continue to be able to make more extensive use of the electronic media, polls, phone banks, and the other elements of the new technology. As the new political technology continues to supplant the older organizational format that generally favored the left, the political advantage will shift more and more markedly toward the right.

At the same time, the new technology permits the superior financial resources of the right to be more effectively harnessed and more fully exploited than was ever before possible. Money was always an important campaign asset, but was seldom seen as the critical factor in electoral competition.[27] The introduction of the new technology, however, was to money what the invention of the internal combustion engine was to oil—a development that substantially increased the utility and importance of this resource by permitting a fuller utilization of its inherent potential. Prior to the advent of the new political technology, money alone did not give political contenders the capacity to mount potent campaigns. No mechanism existed that could simply and directly translate financial resources into political effectiveness. With the new political technology, however, candidates can directly harness their financial resources to contact large numbers of voters, elicit electoral opinion, encourage supporters to go to the polls, and generally perform the tasks necessary to a successful campaign. Thus, in essence, the chief consequence of the new technology has been to make the traditional financial advantage of the right a much more significant political factor.

Money, more than some attitudinal shift to the right on the part of the electorate, was the key to Republican electoral success in 1978 and 1980. In 1978 the Republicans netted 14 House seats and 3 Senate seats. In 1980 the Republicans added 33 House seats and won control of the Senate by adding 12 more seats. These Republican successes were attributed by the press to the increased conservatism of the mass electorate. Interestingly enough, however, there seems to have been little or no empirical relationship between Republican electoral success and changes in voters' ideological perspectives in 1978 and 1980. As a number of analysts have begun to point out, Republican electoral success during this period cannot easily be explained in terms of prior shifts in the electorate's ideological or policy preferences.[28]

Republican success during these year was, however, associated with the GOP's financial lead over the Democrats. In 1978, according to FEC data, the Republicans spent an average of $283,000 in the 21 districts they took from the Democrats. The average expenditure across all congressional races in 1978 was only $106,000. In 1980 the Republicans outspent the Democrats in 26 of the 37 districts that moved from Democratic to Republican hands. On average, the Republicans outspent the Democrats by $60,000—$325,000 to $265,000 in these 37 districts. The average candidate expenditure across all districts in 1980 was some $200,000. It is especially significant that the Republican gains of 1978 and 1980 were not erased during the depression-year election of 1982. In that year the Republicans were able to hold their losses to a mere 24 congressional seats and to retain control of the Senate, despite the nearly 11 percent unemployment rate that might have been expected to result in a Republican debacle. What is particularly interesting is that in 1982 only 18 of the total of 58 congressional districts that the Republicans captured from the Democrats in 1978 and 1980 were retaken by the Democrats. Again, the Republican funding advantage figured prominently in the GOP's capacity to hold its gains. Republican candidates outspent their Democratic opponents in 51 of the 58 races in question. The average Republican expenditure in these races was $340,000, nearly $75,000 more than the average Democratic expenditure of $266,000.

Redistribution of Political Power?

These Republican successes cannot be seen simply as short-term electoral phenomena. Rather, they reflect a fundamental change in the underlying strength of political forces in the United States. The marriage of money and the new technology has given the forces of the political right a significant—perhaps a decisive—competitive edge. The full extent of the competitive advantage now enjoyed by the right is perhaps best illustrated by the historic reversals that occurred in a number of congressional districts in 1978 and 1980. In both years, the Republicans captured a sizeable number of districts that had been Democratic strongholds for decades. In 1978 the Republicans captured a total of 21 congressional districts that had been held by the Democrats. Several of these were long-standing Democratic bastions. The Arkansas 2nd had not been won by a Republican since 1870; the Georgia 6th had never been held by a Republican since its creation in 1844; the South Carolina 4th not since 1874. In addition to these southern districts, the Republicans captured the California 34th, held by the Democrats since its creation in 1962; the Iowa 2nd, held by the Democrats since 1962; the New York 1st, Democratic since 1958; the Ohio 19th, Democratic since 1934; and Pennsylvania's 4th and 15th, held by the Democrats in every election since their creation in 1934 and 1958. In addition, the Republicans were able to increase their level of voter support by 10 percent or more in another 21 districts that remained Democratic. Several of these had been held by the Democrats since the turn of the century.

In 1980 the Republicans captured 37 previously Democratic districts. Five of these 37 districts had been Democratic since the 1960s, four since the 1950s, five since the 1940s, two since the 1930s, and two since the nineteenth century. Two districts, the North Carolina 6th and the Texas 8th, had never previously been held by a Republican. In another 28 districts that were won by the Democrats, the Republicans increased their voting margin by 10 percent or more. Three of these districts had been held by Democrats since the 1920s, three since the turn of the century, and four during the entire period of their existence.

In 1980 the Republicans, of course, also won control of the Senate. Several of the newly elected Republican senators were the first Republicans from their states in decades—Jeremiah Denton, Alabama's first Republican senator since 1868; Paula Hawkins, Florida's second Republican since 1868; Mack Mattingly, Georgia's first since 1871; John East, North Carolina's second since 1868; and Slade Gorton, Washington's first since 1946.

In the course of American political history, major changes in the relative strength of competing political forces have led to partisan realignments—changes in the distribution of voter attachments to the party organizations that mobilized the electorate for political competition. The capacity of Republicans to penetrate and hold significant positions in what had been traditional Democratic strongholds is indicative of an ongoing shift in the relative power of competing political forces in the United States. This change in the balance of power has not yet produced a realignment of electoral coalitions of the classic sort. Partisan realignments reflected the fact that political parties were the chief actors on the electoral stage and chief foci for voters' attention. The present-day change in the underlying strength of American political forces is a result precisely of the displacement of political party organizations by new mechanisms of electoral mobilization. Few voters develop strong ties to public relations firms. As a result, the contemporary reorientation of electoral forces has been what might be called an "apartisan realignment"—a reorientation of electoral forces not yet distinguished by the formation of strong new partisan loyalties. Of course, there remains the intriguing possibility that disciplined national party institutions might ultimately emerge from the new politics. To the extent that campaign funds come to be controlled by parties rather than individual candidates, the national parties might have the means of imposing a measure of discipline on legislators and other office holders. The Republican National Committee is already the source of a good deal of funding for Republican candidates, and the Democratic National Committee is seeking to follow suit for its own partisan adherents. Indeed, legislative reforms are occasionally proposed that would require the channeling of a greater proportion of campaign funds through the parties. The result of such a development could well be a revival of partisan politics—though still a capital-intensive, rather than the more labor-intensive politics once associated with organized parties.

Whatever the future possibilities, in terms of its implications and consequences the present apartisan realignment is not so different from the more fully partisan reorientations of the past. Since the seminal work of V. O. Key in the 1950s, analysts of political change in the United States have focused on realignments of voters as the "mainspring," to use Burnham's phrase, of American politics. Yet, in an important sense, realignments of voters have never been the mainsprings but have always been epiphenomenal—effects more than causes of shifts in the balance of political power in the United States. Partisan realignments of voters have been the tips of the iceberg. The iceberg itself has always been the emergence of powerful new economic interests or social forces that changed the balance of power among contending groups and interests. The voter realignment of the 1930s, for example, was a reflection and reinforcement rather than a cause of the emergence of powerful new economic and social interests that linked themselves to the Democratic party.[29] Major changes in the behavior and attitudes of voters reflect, register, and reinforce rather than cause such shifts in the underlying distribution of political resources and power.[30]

Today, the shift in the underlying balance of political power favors the forces of the right. Obviously, these forces will not win every election. Perhaps Ronald Reagan will be defeated in 1984. Nevertheless, given the new capital-intensive, technological format of American electoral politics, the right is likely to be the dominant electoral force in the United States for the forseeable future. Already, this ascension of the right has had major policy consequences—a curtailment of many of the programs associated with the Great Society and partial erosion of some programs originating with the New Deal as well.[31] More can be expected as the right increases its hold on the structure of the state. Indeed, given the central role now played by the national government in the United States, this contemporary shift in the distribution of political power, once consolidated, could be the most significant in American history. The vaunted anti-state bias of the right in America seldom prevents conservatives from taking full advantage of their opportunities to control the levers of state power. In practice, if not in principle, American conservatives disagree with their liberal counterparts mainly about how—not whether—the state's power should be used. Ronald Reagan made this very clear from the first day of his administration. In his inaugural address he declared: "Now so there will be no misunderstanding, it is not my intention to do away with government. It is, rather, to make it work."[32] It would, therefore, be ironic but not surprising if the political forces that claim to speak for tradition, stability, and above all, limited government continued to use their control of the state to seek the most far-reaching changes in American politics and society.

Notes

1. This is one of the major points of what has come to be called the "issue voting" literature. See, for example, Benjamin Page, *Choices and Echoes in Presidential Elections*, (Chicago: University of Chicago Press, 1978).

2. The relationship between these economic and political assumptions is discussed in Martin Shefter, "Party and Patronage: Germany, England, and Italy," in *Politics and Society* 7, no. 4 (1977), p. 409.

3. Joseph Schumpeter, *Capitalism, Socialism, and Democracy*, (New York: Harper, 1950), p. 263.

4. Thus, as Shefter observes, southern Italian peasants who migrated to northern Italian cities were recruited by the Socialist and later the Communist party while their cousins who migrated to American cities became the mainstays of conservative patronage machines. See Shefter, "Party and Patronage," p. 407. In the same vein, conservative parties in all the western democracies have generally been able to recruit large numbers of working class voters to stand alongside their middle class coutrymen. See, for example, Robert McKenzie and Allan Silver, *Angels in Marble*, (Chicago: University of Chicago Press, 1968). In general, parties that rely on material rather than solidary incentives are likely to construct the most heterogeneous constituencies. The classic example is, of course, the nineteenth-century American patronage machine.

5. For example, the Basque peasantry, which had been a bastion of conservative Catholicism and reactionary Carlism at the turn of the century, generally supported the Loyalist cause during the Spanish Civil War and is, of course, a base of support for radical Socialism today. See Gerald Brenan, *The Spanish Labyrinth*, (New York: Cambridge University Press, 1960), especially Ch. 9.

6. For an account of the "militarist style" of American campaigns during this period, see Richard Jensen, *The Winning of the Midwest*, (Chicago: University of Chicago Press, 1971), Ch. 6.

7. Maurice Duverger, *Political Parties*, (New York: Wiley, 1954), p. 426.

8. *Ibid.*, Ch. 1.

9. The classic statement is the report of the American Political Science Association's Committee on Political Parties, "Toward a More Responsible Two-Party System," *American Political Science Review*, 44 (September 1950), Supplement.

10. Richard A. Joslyn, *The Mass Media and Election Campaigns*, (Reading, MA: Addison-Wesley, forthcoming 1984).

11. For a discussion of the character of the various consulting firms, see William J. Lanouette, "The Selling of the Candidates 1978," in *National Journal*, (November 4, 1978), pp. 1772–1777.

12. Quoted in Joslyn, forthcoming.

13. Frank Lynn, "Political Consultants' Campaign Role is Expanded," *The New York Times*, (March 28, 1982).

14. See Richard Jensen, "American Election Analysis," in Seymour Martin Lipset (ed.), *Politics and Social Sciences*, (New York: Oxford, 1969).

15. Ostrogorski, *Democracy and the Organization of Political Parties*, (New York: Macmillan, 1902), p. 285.

16. See, "Election Tab: A Billion Dollars, and Rising," *U.S. News and World Report*, (December 15, 1980).

17. Adam Clymer, "PAC Gifts to Candidates Rose 45% in Latest Cycle," *The New York Times*, (April 29, 1983).

18. See John Felton and Charles W. Hucker, "Business Groups Gave GOP a Late Windfall," *Congressional Quarterly Weekly Report*, (November 11, 1978). Also, Glen Maxwell, "At the Wire, Corporate PACs Come Through for the GOP," *National Journal*, (February 3, 1979).

19. Jensen, "American Election Analysis," p. 229.

20. *Ibid.*, pp. 229–230.

21. For a dicussion of newspaper polls see Claude Robinson, *Straw Votes*, (New York: Columbia University Press, 1932), Ch. 4.

22. Jensen, "American Election Analysis," p. 238.

23. See Michael Wheeler, *Lies, Damn Lies, and Statistics*, (New York: Liveright, 1976), especially Ch. 3.

24. See Rich Jaroslovsky, "New-Right Cashier," *Wall Street Journal*, (October 6, 1978), p. 1. On Reagan's use of polls, see B. Drummond Ayres, Jr., "GOP Keeps Tabs on Nation's Mood," *The New York Times*, (November 16, 1981).

25. Epstein has called this phenomenon, "contagion from the right." See Leon Epstein, *Political Parties in Western Democracies*, (New York: Praeger, 1967), p. 257.

26. Jaroslovsky, p. 1. Also, Larry J. Sabato, *The Rise of Political Consultants*, (New York: Basic Books, 1981), p. 222.

27. See, for example, Alexander Heard, *The Costs of Democracy*, (Chapel Hill, NC: The University of North Carolina Press, 1960), Ch. 2. Also, Overacker, Ch. 4.

28. See, for example, Arthur H. Miller and Martin Wattenberg, "Decision-Making Dilemmas in the 1980 Election: Choosing the Lesser of Two Evils," in Benjamin Ginsberg (ed.), *Do Elections Matter?* (Reading, MA: Addison-Wesley, 1983).

29. See Thomas Ferguson, *Critical Realignment: The Fall of the House of Morgan and the Origins of the New Deal*, (New York: Oxford, forthcoming). Also, Thomas Ferguson, "Elites and Elections," in Ginsberg (ed.), *Do Elections Matter?*.

30. For a fuller analysis of the relationship between elections and the underlying distribution of power in society, see Benjamin Ginsberg, *The Consequences of Consent: Elections, Citizen Control, and Popular Acquiescence*, (Reading, MA: Addison-Wesley, 1982), Ch. 4. See also Kenneth Prewitt and Alan Stone, *The Ruling Elites*, (New York: Harper, 1973), Ch. 7.

31. For an account of the Reagan administration's social policies, see Frances Fox Piven and Richard A. Cloward, *The New Class War*, (New York: Pantheon, 1983).

32. "President Reagan's Inaugural Address," quoted in *The New York Times*, (January 21, 1981).

2.9

Congressional Responses to the Twentieth Century

SAMUEL P. HUNTINGTON

As Madison made clear in Federalist paper No. 10, the American system of federal government was designed with the intention of making sweeping, decisive reform difficult to enact. The American constitutional form of government is thus often seen as having a bias toward "doing nothing," which tends to favor the status quo. This stems from the ability of various groups to protect their respective interests through close association with any one of the several branches of the government. Whereas in European parliamentary systems a majority in parliament guarantees a political party control over the government as a whole, in the United States control over the Congress has no such effect, and may only lead to a stalemate between Congress and the Executive Branch, or the Judiciary. It has therefore become a truism of American politics that interest groups that fail to obtain what they want lament congressional "obstructionism." This complaint issues from the conservative or the liberal wing of American politics, depending on the issue. There is some truth, too, to the charge that the government's tendency toward deadlock denies it the ability to act decisively except in severe emergencies, as during the Civil War. In this essay, Samuel P. Huntington explores the nature of the different constituencies that have grown up around the executive and legislative branches of the government in this century, and the potential problems arising therefrom.

Congress is a perennial source of anguish to both its friends and its foes. The critics point to its legislative failure. The function of a legislature, they argue, is to legislate and Congress either does not legislate or legislates too little and too late. The intensity of their criticism varies inversely with the degree and dispatch with which Congress approves the President's legislative proposals. When in 1963 the Eighty-eighth Congress seemed to stymie the Kennedy legislative program, criticism rapidly mounted. "What kind of legislative body is it," asked Walter Lippmann, neatly summing up the prevailing exasperation, "that will not or cannot legislate?" When in 1964 the same Eighty-eighth Congress passed the civil rights, tax, and other bills, criticism of Congress correspondingly subsided. Reacting differently to this familiar pattern, the friends of Congress lamented its acquiescence to presidential dictate. Since 1933, they said, the authority of the executive branch—President, administration, and bureaucracy—has waxed, while that of Congress has waned. They warned of the constitutional perils stemming from the permanent subordination of one branch of government to another. In foreign and military policy, as well as domestic affairs, Congress is damned when it

Reprinted from *Congress and America's Future* (David Truman, ed.), pp. 6–38 (with deletions). Copyright 1973 by Prentice-Hall, Inc. Reprinted with permission from The American Assembly.

acquiesces in presidential leadership (Tonkin Gulf Resolution, 1964) and also when it attempts to seize the initiative (Mansfield Resolution, 1971). At the same time that it is an obstructive ogre to its enemies, Congress is also the declining despair of its friends. Can both images be true? In large part, they are. The dilemma of Congress, indeed, can be measured by the extent to which congressional assertion coincides with congressional obstruction.

This paradox has been at the root of the "problem" of Congress since the early days of the New Deal. Vis-à-vis the executive, Congress in an autonomous, legislative body. But apparently Congress can defend its autonomy only by refusing to legislate, and it can legislate only by surrendering its autonomy. In the past, there has been a familiar pattern: Congress balks, criticism rises, the clamoring voices of reformers fill the air with demands for the "modernization" of the "antiquated procedures" of an "eighteenth century" Congress so it can deal with "twentieth century realities." The demands for reform serve as counters in the legislative game to get the President's measures through Congress. Independence thus provokes criticism; acquiescence brings approbation. If Congress legislates, it subordinates itself to the President; if it refuses to legislate, it alienates itself from public opinion. Congress can assert its power or it can pass laws; but it cannot do both.

Legislative Power and Institutional Crisis

The roots of this legislative dilemma lie in the changes in American society during the twentieth century. The twentieth century has seen: rapid urbanization and the beginnings of a postindustrial, technological society, the nationalization of social and economic problems and the concomitant growth of national organizations to deal with these problems; the increasing bureaucratization of social, economic, and governmental organizations; and the sustained high-level international involvement of the United States in world politics. These developments have generated new forces in American politics and initiated major changes in the distribution of power in American society. In particular, the twentieth century has witnessed the tremendous expansion of the responsibilities of the national government and the size of the national bureaucracy. In 1901, the national government had 351,798 employees or less than $1\frac{1}{2}$ percent of the national labor force. In 1971 it had 5,637,000 employees, constituting almost 7 percent of the labor force. The expansion of the national government has been paralleled by the emergence of other large, national, bureaucratic organizations: manufacturing corporations, banks, insurance companies, labor unions, trade associations, farm organizations, newspaper chains, radio-TV networks. Each organization may have relatively specialized and concrete interests, but typically it functions on a national basis. Its headquarters are in New York or Washington; its operations are scattered across a dozen or more states. The emergence of these organizations truly constitutes, in Kenneth Boulding's expressive phrase, an "organizational revolution." The existence of this private "Establishment," more than anything else, distinguishes twentieth-century America from nineteenth-century America. The leaders of these organizations are the notables of American society: they are the prime wielders of social and economic power.

Adaptation Crises These momentous social changes have confronted Congress with an institutional "adaptation crisis." Such a crisis occurs when changes in the environment of a governmental institution force the institution either to alter its functions, affiliation, and modes of behavior, or to face decline, decay, and isolation.

Crises usually occur when an institution loses its previous sources of support or fails to adapt itself to the rise of new social forces. Such a crisis, for instance, affected the Presidency in the second and third decades of the nineteenth century. Under the leadership of Henry Clay the focal center of power in the national government was in the House of Representatives; the congressional caucus dictated presidential nominations; popular interest in and support for the Presidency were minimal. The "Executive," Justice Story remarked in 1818, "has no longer a commanding influence. The House of Representatives has absorbed all the popular feelings and all the effective power of the country." The Presidency was on the verge of becoming a weak, secondary instrumental organ of government. It was rescued from this fate by the Jacksonian movement, which democratized the Presidency, broadened its basis of popular support, and restored it as the center of vitality and leadership in the national government. The House of Commons was faced with a somewhat similar crisis during the agitation preceding the first Reform Bill of 1832. New social groups were developing in England which were demanding admission to the political arena and the opportunity to share in political leadership. Broadening the constituency of the House of Commons and reforming the system of election enabled the House to revitalize itself and to continue as the principal locus of power in the British government.

In both these cases a governmental institution got a new lease on life, new vigor, new power, by embodying within itself dynamic, new social forces. When an institution fails to make such an alignment, it must either restrict its own authority or submit to limitations upon its authority imposed from outside. In 1910, when the House of Lords refused to approve Lloyd George's budget, it was first compelled by governmental pressure, popular opinion, and the threat of the creation of new peers to acquiesce in the budget and then through a similar process to acquiesce in the curtailment of its own power to obstruct legislation approved by the Commons. In this case the effort to block legislation approved by the dominant forces in the political community resulted in a permanent diminution of the authority of the offending institution. A somewhat similar crisis developed with respect to the Supreme Court in the 1930s. Here again a less popular body attempted to veto the actions of more popular bodies. In three years the Court invalidated twelve acts of Congress. Inevitably this precipitated vigorous criticism and demands for reform, culminating in Roosevelt's court reorganization proposal in February of 1937. The alternatives confronting the Court were relatively clear-cut: it could "reform" or be "reformed." In "the switch in time that saved nine," it chose the former course, signaling its change by approving the National Labor Relations Act in April 1937 and the Social Security Act in May. With this switch, support for the reorganization of the Court drained away. The result was, in the words of Justice Jackson, "a failure of the reform forces and a victory of the reform."

Congress's Response   Each of these four institutional crises arose from the failure of a governmental institution to adjust to social change and the rise of new viewpoints, new needs, and new political forces. Congress's legislative dilemma and loss of power stem from the nature of its overall institutional response to the changes in American society. This response involves three major aspects of Congress as an institution: its affiliations, its structure, and its functions. During the twentieth century Congress gradually insulated itself from the new political forces which social change had generated and which were, in turn, generating more change. Hence the leadership of Congress lacked the incentive to take the legislative initiative in handling emerging national problems. Within Congress power became dispersed among many officials, committees, and subcommittees. Hence the central leadership of Congress lacked the ability to establish national legislative priorities. As a result, the legislative function of Congress declined in importance, while the growth of the federal bureaucracy made the administrative overseeing function of Congress more important. These three tendencies—toward insulation, dispersion, and oversight—have dominated the evolution of Congress during the twentieth century.

Affiliations: Insulation from Power

Congressional Evolution   Perhaps the single most important trend in congressional evolution for the bulk of this century was the growing insulation of Congress from other social groups and political institutions. In 1900 no gap existed between congressmen and the other leaders of American society and politics. Half a century later the changes in American society, on the one hand, and the institutional evolution of Congress, on the other, had produced a marked gap between congressional leaders and the bureaucratically oriented leadership of the executive branch and of the establishment. The growth of this gap can be seen in seven aspects of congressional evolution.

(1) *Increasing tenure of office*. In the nineteenth century few congressmen stayed in Congress very long. During the twentieth century the average tenure of congressmen has inexorably lengthened. In 1900 only 9 percent of the members of the House of Representatives had served five terms or more and less than 1 percent had served ten terms or more. In 1957, 45 percent of the House had served five terms or more and 14 percent ten terms or more. In 1897, for each representative who had served ten terms or more in the House, there were 34 representatives who had served two terms or less. In 1971 the ratio was down almost to equality, with 1.2 members who had served two terms or less for each ten-termer.[1] In the middle of the nineteenth century, only about half the representatives in any one Congress had served in a previous Congress, and only about one-third of the senators had been elected to the Senate more than once. By the second half of the twentieth century, close to 90 percent of the House were veterans, and almost two-thirds of the senators were beyond their first term. The biennial infusion of new blood had reached an all-time low.

(2) *The increasingly important role of seniority*. Increasing tenure of congressmen is closely linked to increasingly rigid adherence to the practices of seniority. The longer men stay in Congress, the more likely they are to see virtue in seniority. Conversely, the more important seniority is, the greater is the constituent appeal of men who have been long in office. The rigid system of seniority in *both* houses of Congress is a product of the twentieth century.

In the nineteenth century seniority was far more significant in the Senate than in the House. Since the middle of that century apparently only in five instances—the last in 1925—has the chairmanship of a Senate committee been denied to the most senior member of the committee. In the House, on the other hand, the Speaker early received the power to appoint committees and to designate their chairmen. During the nineteenth century Speakers made much of this power. Committee appointment and the selection of chairman were involved political processes, in which the Speaker carefully balanced factors of seniority, geography, expertise, and policy viewpoint in making his choices. Not infrequently prolonged bargaining would result as the Speaker traded committee positions for legislative commitments. Commenting on James G. Blaine's efforts at committee construction in the early 1870s, one member of his family wrote that Blaine "left for New

Table 1

Veteran Congressmen in Congress

Congress	Date	% Representatives elected to House more than once	% Senators elected to Senate more than once
42nd	1871	53	32
50th	1887	63	45
64th	1915	74	47
74th	1935	77	54
87th	1961	87	66
92nd	1971	88	65

Sources: Figures for representatives for 1871–1915 are from Robert Luce, *Legislative Assemblies* (Boston: Houghton Mifflin Company, 1924), p. 365. Other figures were calculated independently. I am indebted to Emily Lieberman for assistance in updating these and other statistics in this essay.

York on Wesnesday. He had cotton and wool manufacturers to meet in Boston, and, over and above all, pressure to resist or permit. As fast as he gets his committees arranged, just so fast some after-consideration comes up which overtopples the whole list like a row of bricks."[2] Only with the drastic curtailment of the powers of the Speaker in 1910 and 1911 did the seniority system in the House assume the inflexible pattern which it has today. Only twice in the years after the 1910 revolt—once in 1915 and once in 1921—was seniority neglected in the choice of committee chairmen.

In the 1960s seniority came under increasing criticism within Congress and some small steps away from it were taken. In 1965 the House Democratic caucus stripped two southern congressmen of their committee seniority for supporting Barry Goldwater in 1964. One of them, John Bell Williams of Mississippi, had been a member of the House since 1947 and was the second-ranking Democrat on the Committee on Interstate and Foreign Commerce. In 1967 a select House committee recommended punishing Representative Adam Clayton Powell by, among other things, taking away his seniority and hence his position as chairman of the Committee on Education and Labor. The House, however, instead voted to deny Mr. Powell a seat in the Ninetieth Congress. In 1971 the House Republican and Democratic caucuses decreed that the selection of committee chairmen should be subject to caucus approval; the Democratic caucus then approved as chairmen those who would have been chairmen by seniority. Nor was a serious effort made to change the seniority system in the Legislative Reorganization Act of 1970. These events suggest that the system will remain but that deviations from it (at least in the House) will occasionally occur and will be accepted as legitimate.

(3) *Extended tenure: a prerequisite for leadership.* Before 1896 Speakers, at the time of their first election, averaged only 7 years' tenure in the House. Since 1896 Speakers have averaged 23 years of House service at their first election. In 1811 and in 1859 Henry Clay and William Pennington were elected Speaker when they first entered the House. In 1807 Thomas Jefferson arranged for the election of his friend, William C. Nicholas, to the House and then for his immediate selection by the party caucus as floor leader. Such an intrusion of leadership from the outside would now be unthinkable. Today the Speaker and other leaders of the House and, to a lesser degree, the leaders of the Senate are

legislative veterans of long standing. In 1971 46 House leaders averaged over 23 years' service in the House while 40 leading senators averaged 17 years of senatorial service. The top House leaders (Speaker, floor leaders, chairmen and ranking minority members of Ways and Means, Appropriations, and Rules Committees) averaged 26 years in the House and 8 in leadership positions in 1971. Top Senate leaders (President *pro tem.*, floor leaders, chairmen, and ranking minority members of Finance, Foreign Relations, and Appropriations Committees) averaged 23 years of service in the Senate and 11 in leadership positions. Increasing tenure means increasing age. In the nineteenth century the leaders of Congress were often in their thirties. Clay was 34 when he became Speaker in 1811; Hunter, 30 when he became Speaker in 1839; White, 36 at his accession to the Speakership in 1841; and Ore, 35 when he became Speaker in 1857. In contrast, Rayburn was 58 when he became Speaker, Martin 63, McCormack 71, and Albert 62. In 1971 the top leaders of the House averaged 63 years, those of the Senate 69 years.

(4) *Leadership within Congress: a one-way street.* Normally in American life becoming a leader in one institution opens up leadership possibilities in other institutions: corporation presidents head civil agencies or become cabinet officers; foundation and university executives move into government; leading lawyers and bankers take over industrial corporations. The greater one's prestige, authority, and accomplishments within one organization, the easier it is to move to other and better posts in other organizations. Such, however, is not the case with Congress. Leadership in the House of Representatives leads nowhere except to leadership in the House of Representatives. To a lesser degree, the same has been true of the Senate. The successful House or Senate leader has to identify himself completely with his institution, its mores, traditions, and ways of behavior. "The very ingredients which make you a powerful House leader," one representative has commented, "are the ones which keep you from being a public leader."[3] Representatives typically confront a "fourth-term crisis": if they wish to run for higher office—for governor or senator— they must usually do so by the beginning of their fourth term in the House. If they stay in the House for four or more terms, they in effect choose to make a career in the House and to forswear the other electoral possibilities of American politics. Leadership in the Senate is not as exclusive a commitment as it is in the House. But despite such notable exceptions as Taft and Johnson, the most influential men in the Senate have typically been those who have looked with disdain upon the prospect of being anything but a United States Senator. Even someone with the high talent and broad ambition of Lyndon Johnson could not escape this exclusive embrace during his years as majority leader. In the words of Theodore H. White, the Senate, for Johnson, was "faith, calling, club, habit, relaxation, devotion, hobby, and love." Over the years it became "almost a monomania with him, his private life itself."[4] Such "monomania" is normally the prerequisite for Senate leadership. It is also normally an insurmountable barrier, psychologically and politically, to effective leadership outside the Senate.

(5) *The decline of personnel interchange between Congress and the Administration.* Movement of leaders in recent years between the great national institutions of the establishment and the top positions in the administration has been frequent, easy, and natural. This pattern of lateral entry distinguishes the American executive branch from the governments of most other modern societies. The circulation of individuals between leadership positions in governmental and private institutions eases the strains between political and private leadership and performs a unifying function comparable to that which common class origins perform in Great Britain or common membership in the Communist party does in the Soviet Union.

The frequent movement of individuals between administration and establishment contrasts sharply with the virtual absence of such movement between Congress and the administration or between Congress and the establishment. The gap between congressional leadership and administration leadership has increased sharply during this century. Seniority makes it virtually impossible for administration leaders to become leaders of Congress and makes it unlikely that leaders of Congress will want to become leaders of the administration. The separation of powers has become the insulation of leaders. Between 1861 and 1896, 37 percent of the people appointed to posts in the President's cabinet had served in the House or Senate. Between 1897 and 1940, 19 percent of the Cabinet positions were filled by former congressmen or senators. Between 1941 and 1963, only 15 percent of the cabinet posts were so filled. Former congressmen received only 4 percent of over 1,000 appointments of political executives made during the Roosevelt, Truman, Eisenhower, and Kennedy administrations.[5] In 1963, apart from the President and Vice-President, only one of the top 75 leaders of the Kennedy administration (Secretary of the Interior Udall) had served in Congress. The Nixon administration was somewhat more hospitable to legislators, but in 1971 only 4 of its 75 top leaders (apart from the President) had congressional experience.

Movement from the administration to leadership positions in Congress is almost equally rare. In 1971 only one of 84 congressional leaders (Senator Anderson) had previously served in the President's cabinet. Those members of the administration who do move on to Congress are typically those who have come to the administration from state and local politics rather than from the great national institutions. Few congressmen and even fewer congressional leaders move from Congress to positions of leadership in national private organizations, and relatively few leaders of these organizations move on to Congress. Successful men who have come to the top in business, law, or education naturally hesitate to shift to another world in which they would have to start all over again at the bottom. In some cases, establishment leaders also consider legislative office simply beneath them.

(6) *The social origins and careers of Congressmen.* Congressmen are much more likely to come from rural and small-town backgrounds than are administration and establishment leaders. A majority of the senators holding office between 1947 and 1957 were born in rural areas. Of the 1959 senators 64 percent were raised in rural areas or in small towns, and only 19 percent in metropolitan centers. In contrast, 52 percent of the presidents of the largest industrial corporations grew up in metropolitan centers, as did a large proportion of the political executives appointed during the Roosevelt, Truman, Eisenhower, and Kennedy administrations. The contrast in origins is reflected in fathers' occupations. In the 1950s, the proportion of farmer fathers among senators (32 percent) was more than twice as high as it was among administration leaders (13 percent) and business leaders (9 to 15 percent).[6]

Of perhaps greater significance is the difference in geographical mobility between congressmen and private and public executives. Forty-one percent of the 1959 senators, but only 12 percent of the 1959 corporation presidents, were currently residing in their original hometowns. Seventy percent of the presidents had moved 100 miles or more from their hometowns but only 29 percent of the senators had done so.[7] In 1971 over two-fifths of the leaders of Congress but only 13 percent of administration leaders were still living in their places of birth. Seventy-five percent of the congressional leaders were living in their states of birth, while 62 percent of the administration leaders had moved out of their states of birth. Fifty-nine percent of administration leaders had moved from one region of the country to another, but only 16 percent of congressional leaders had similar mobility.

Table 2

Geographical Mobility of National Leaders (in %)

	Congressional leaders		Administration leaders		Political executives	Business leaders
	(1963) $N=81$	(1971) $N=86$	(1963) $N=74$	(1971) $N=75$	(1959) $N=1,865$	(1952) $N=8,300$
None	37	43	11	13	14	40
Intrastate	40	35	19	25		
Interstate, intraregion	5	8	9	3	10	15
Interregion	19	14	61	52	73	45
International	0	0	0	7	3	0

Sources: "Political Executives" in W. Lloyd Warner, et al., *The American Federal Executive*, p. 332; business leaders, W. Lloyd Warner and James C. Abegglen, *Occupational Mobility in American Business and Industry*, p. 82; congressional and administration leaders, independent calculation. Geographical mobility is measured by comparing birthplace with current residence. For administration leaders, current residence was considered to be last residence before assuming administration position. The nine regions employed in this analysis are defined in Warner et al., pp. 42-43. See note 6.

During the course of this century the career patterns of congressmen and of executive leaders have diverged. At an earlier period both leaderships had extensive experience in local and state politics. In 1903 about one-half of executive leaders and three-quarters of congressional leaders had held office in state or local government. In 1971 the congressional pattern had not changed significantly, with 71 percent of the congressional leaders having held state or local office. The proportion of executive leaders with this experience, however, had dropped drastically. The proportion of administration leaders who had held state or local office was still less than half that of congressional leaders, although it had gone up to 31 percent from 17 percent in 1963. When coupled with the data presented earlier on the larger number of former congressmen in the Nixon administration than in the Kennedy administration, these figures suggest a slight shift in recruitment toward local politics and away from the national establishment for the former as compared to the latter.

In recent years, congressional leaders have also more often been professional politicians than they were earlier: in 1903 only 5 percent of the congressional leaders had no major occupation outside politics, while in 1963, 22 percent of the congressional leaders had spent almost all their lives in electoral politics. Roughly 90 percent of the members of Congress in recent years, it has been estimated, "have served apprenticeship in some segment of our political life."[8]

The typical congressman may have gone away to college, but he then returned to his home state to pursue an electoral career, working his way up through local office, the state legislature, and eventually to Congress. The typical political executive, on the other hand, like the typical corporation executive, went away to college and then did not return home but instead pursued a career in a metropolitan center or worked in one or more national organizations with freqent changes of residence. As a result, political executives have become divorced from state and local politics, just as the congressional leaders have become isolated from national organizations. Congressional leaders, in short, come up

Table 3

Experience of National Political Leaders
in State and Local Government (in %)

Offices held	Congressional leaders			Administration leaders		
	1903	1963	1971	1903	1963	1971
Any state or local office	75	64	71	49	17	31
Elective local office	55	46	37	22	5	4
State legislature	47	30	42	17	3	9
Appointive state office	12	10	16	20	7	12
Governor	16	9	5	5	4	7

through a "local politics" line while executives move up through a "national organization" line.

The differences in geographical mobility and career patterns between congressional
and administration leaders reflect two different styles of life which cut across the usual
occupational groupings. Businessmen, lawyers, and bankers are found in both Congress
and the administration. But those in Congress are more likely to be small businessmen,
small-town lawyers, and small-town bankers. Among the 66 lawyers in the Senate in
1963, for instance, only 2—Joseph Clark and Clifford Case—had been "prominent
corporation counsel[s]" before going into politics.[9] Administration leaders, in contrast, are
far more likely to be affiliated with large national industrial corporations, with Wall Street
or State Street law firms, and with New York banks.

(7) *The provincialism of congressmen.* The absence of mobility between Congress and
the executive branch and the differing backgrounds of the leaders of the two branches of
government stimulate different policy attitudes. Congressmen have tended to be oriented
toward local needs and small-town ways of thought. The leaders of the administration and
of the great private national institutions are more likely to think in national terms.
Analyzing consensus-building on foreign aid, James N. Rosenau concluded that congressmen typically had "segmental" orientations while other national leaders had "continental" orientations. The segmentally oriented leaders "give highest priority to the
subnational units which they head or represent" and are "not prepared to admit a
discrepancy between" the national welfare and "their subnational concerns." The
congressman is part of a local consensus of local politicians, local businessmen, local
bankers, local trade union leaders, and local newspaper editors who constitute the
opinion-making elite of their districts. As Senator Richard Neuberger noted: "If there is
one maxim which seems to prevail among many members of our national legislature, it is
that local matters must come first and global problems a poor second—that is, if the
member of Congress is to survive politically." As a result, the members of Congress are
"isolated" from other national leaders. At gatherings of national leaders, "members of
Congress seem more conspicuous by their absence than by their presence." One piece of
evidence is fairly conclusive: of 623 national opinion-makers who attended ten American
Assembly sessions between 1956 and 1960, only 9 (1.4 percent) were members of
Congress![10]

The difference in attitude between segmentally oriented congressmen and the other, continentally oriented national leaders are particularly marked in those areas of foreign policy (such as foreign aid) which involve the commitment of tangible resources for intangible ends. But they have also existed in domestic policy. The approaches of senators and corporation presidents to economic issues, Andrew Hacker found, were rooted in "disparate images of society." Senators were provincially oriented; corporation presidents "metropolitan" in their thinking. Senators might be sympathetic to business, but they thought of business in small-town, small-business terms. They might attempt to accommodate themselves to the needs of the national corporations, but basically they were "faced with a power they do not really understand and with demands about whose legitimacy they are uneasy." As a result, Hacker suggests, "serious tensions exist between our major political and economic institutions . . . . There is, at base, a real lack of understanding and a failure of communication between the two elites."[11]

"Segmental" or "provincial" attitudes are undoubtedly stronger in the House than they are in the Senate. But they have also existed in the Senate. Despite the increased unity of the country caused by mass communications and the growth of "national as distinguished from local or sectional industry," the Senate in the 1950s was, according to an admiring portraitist, "if anything progressively less national in its approach to most affairs" and "increasingly engaged upon the protection of what is primarily local or sectional in economic life."[12]

For both House and Senate these local patterns are being challenged and in some degree undermined by the nationalizing impact of the media and the geographical extension of party competition.[13] Yet within Congress old ideas, old values, and old beliefs linger on. The structure of Congress encourages their perpetuation. The newcomer to Congress is repeatedly warned that "to get along he must go along." To go along means to adjust to the prevailing mores and attitudes. The more the young congressman desires a career in the House or Senate, the more readily he makes these adjustments. The country at large has become urban, suburban, and metropolitan. Its economic, social, educational, and technological activities are increasingly performed by huge national bureaucratic organizations. In the 1960s these developments were only beginning to make themselves felt in Congress, as gradually younger and more adventurous congressmen took the initiative in challenging the old ways. On Capitol Hill the nineteenth-century ethos of the small town, the independent farmer, and the small businessman slowly wanes behind the institutional defenses which developed in this century to insulate Congress from the new America.

Defects in Representation   In the twentieth century the executive branch grew in power vis-à-vis Congress for precisely the same reason that the House of Representatives grew in power vis-à-vis the executive in the second and third decades of the nineteenth century. It became more powerful because it had become more representative. Congress lost power because it had two defects as a representative body. One, relatively minor and in part easily remedied, dealt with the representation of people as individuals; the other, more serious and perhaps beyond remedy, concerned the representation of organized groups and interests.

Congress was originally designed to represent individuals in the House and governmental units—the states—in the Senate. In the course of time the significance of the states as organized interests declined, and popular election of senators was introduced. In effect, both senators and representatives now represent relatively arbitrarily-defined territorial collections of individuals. This system of individual representation has suffered from two inequities. First, of course, is the constitutional equal representation of states in the Senate irrespective of population. Second, in the House, congressional districts have varied widely in size and may also be gerrymandered to benefit one party or group of voters. For much of this century the net effect of these practices was to place the urban and the suburban voter at a disadvantage vis-à-vis the rural and small-town voter. The correction of this imbalance moved rapidly ahead, however, following the Supreme Court decisions (*Baker v. Carr*, 1962; *Wesberry v. Sanders*, 1964) mandating equal size for districts. As a result of the Court action, there was a net shift of between 10 and 19 districts from predominantly rural to predominantly urban during the 1960s.[14] The application of the new standards to the 1970 census population, it has been estimated, should result in 291 metropolitan districts in 1972 compared to 254 in 1962. Of these 129 would be suburban districts compared to 92 such districts in 1962. Central city representation, on the other hand, will drop to 100 congressmen from 106 in 1962 and a peak of 110 in 1966.[15] As Milton Cummings notes:

> In all this there is a very considerable irony. The battle for greater urban representation in the House in the 1950s and 1960s was often accompanied by rhetoric stressing the need to help the central cities, who, it was asserted, were penalized by rural overrepresentation. Now that the one-man/one-vote doctrine is being implemented, however, it is the suburbs, not the central cities, that stand to gain the most.[16]

The overall membership of the House will thus be increasingly metropolitan and suburban. Adherence to seniority, however, means that the leadership of the House will remain southern rural and northern urban for some years to come.

The second and more significant deficiency of Congress as a representative body concerns its insulation from the interests which have emerged in the twentieth century's "organizational revolution." How can national institutions be represented in a locally-elected legislature? In the absence of any easy answer to this question, the administration has tended to emerge as the natural point of access to the government for these national organizations and the place where their interests and viewpoints are brought into the policy-making process. In effect, the American system of government is moving toward a three-way system of representation. Particular territorial interests are represented in Congress; particular functional interests are represented in the administration; and the national interest is represented territorially and functionally in the Presidency.

Every four years the American people choose a President, but they elect an administration. In this century the administration has acquired many of the traditional characteristics of a representative body that Congress has tended to lose. The Jacksonian principle of "rotation in office" and the classic concept of the Cincinnatus-like statesman are far more relevant now to the administration than they are to Congress. Administration officials, unlike congressmen, are more frequently mobile amateurs in government than career professionals in politics. The patterns of power in Congress are rigid. The patterns of power in the administration are flexible. The administration is thus a far more sensitive register of changing currents of opinion than is Congress. A continuous adjustment of power and authority takes place within each administration; major changes in the distribution of power take place at every change of administration. The Eisenhower administration represented one combination of men, interests, and experience, the Kennedy-Johnson administration another, and the Nixon administration yet a third. Each time a new President takes office, the executive branch is invigorated in the same way that the House of Representatives was invigorated by Henry Clay and his western congressmen in 1811. A thousand new officials descend on Washington, coming fresh from the people, representing the diverse forces behind the new President, and bringing with them new demands, new ideas, and new power. Here truly is representative government along classic lines and of a sort which Congress has not known for decades. One key to the "decline" of Congress lies in the defects of Congress as a representative body.

Structure: The Dispersion of Power in Congress

The influence of Congress in our political system thus varies directly with its ties to the more dynamic and dominant groups in society. The power of Congress also varies directly, however, with the centralization of power in Congress. The corollary of these propositions is likewise true: centralization of authority within Congress usually goes with close connections between congressional leadership and major external forces and groups. The power of the House of Representatives was at a peak in the second decade of the nineteenth century, when power was centralized in the Speaker and when Henry Clay and his associates represented the dynamic new forces of trans-Appalachian nationalism. Another peak in the power of the House came during Reconstruction, when power was centralized in Speaker Colfax and the Joint Committee on Reconstruction as spokesmen for triumphant northern radicalism. A third peak in the power of the House came between 1890 and 1910, when the authority of the Speaker reached its height and Speakers Reed and Cannon reflected the newly established forces of nationalist conservatism. The peak in Senate power came during the post-Reconstruction period of the 1870s and 1880s. Within Congress, power was centralized in the senatorial leaders who represented the booming forces of the rising industrial capitalism and the new party machines. These were the years, as Wilfred Binkley put it, of "the Hegemony of the Senate."

Specialization Without Centralization   Since its first years, the twentieth century has seen no comparable centralization of power in Congress. Instead, the dominant tendency has been toward the dispersion of power. This leaves Congress only partially equipped to deal with the problems of modern society. In general, the complex modern environment requires in social and political institutions *both* a high degree of specialization and a high degree of centralized authority to coordinate and to integrate the activities of the specialized units. Specialization of function and centralization of authority have been the dominant trends of twentieth-century institutional development. Congress, however, has adjusted only half-way. Through its committees and subcommittees it has provided effectively for specialization, much more effectively, indeed, than the national legislature of any other country. But it has failed to combine increasing specialization of function with increasing centralization of authority. Instead the central leadership in Congress has been weakened, and as a result Congress lacks the central authority to integrate its specialized bodies. In a "rational" bureaucracy authority varies inversely with specialization. Within Congress authority usually varies directly with specialization.

The authority of the specialist is a distinctive feature of congressional behavior. "Specialization" is a key norm in both House and Senate. The man who makes a career in the House, one congressman has observed, "is primarily a worker, a specialist, and a craftsman—someone who will concentrate his energies in a particular field and gain prestige and influence in that." "The members who are most successful," another congressman concurred, "are those who pick a specialty or an area and become real experts in it."[17] The emphasis on specialization as a norm, of course, complements the importance of the committee as an institution. It also leads to a great stress on reciprocity. In a bureaucracy, specialized units compete with each other for the support of less specialized officials. In Congress, however, reciprocity among specialists replaces coordination by generalists. When a committee bill comes to the floor, the non-specialists in that subject acquiesce in its passage with the unspoken but complete understanding that they will receive similar treatment. "The traditional deference to the authority of one of its committees overwhelms the main body," one congressman has observed. "The whole fabric of Congress is based on committee expertise. . . ." Similarly, in the Senate "a large number of highly specialized experts generally accept each other's work without much criticism."[18] Reciprocity thus substitutes for centralization and confirms the diffusion of power among the committees.

History of Dispersion The current phase of dispersed power dates from the second decade of this century. The turning point in the House came with the revolt against Speaker Cannon in 1910, the removal of the Speaker from the Rules Committee, and the loss by the Speaker of his power to appoint standing committees. For a brief period, from 1911 to 1915, much of the Speaker's former power was assumed by Oscar Underwood in his capacities as majority floor leader and chairman of the Ways and Means Committee. In 1915, however, Underwood was elected to the Senate, and the dispersion of power which had begun with the overthrow of the Speaker rapidly accelerated.

During the first years of the Wilson administration, authority in the Senate was concentrated in the floor leader, John Worth Kern, a junior senator first elected to the Senate in 1910. Under his leadership the seniority system was bypassed, and the Senate played an active and creative role in the remarkable legislative achievements of the Sixty-third Congress. Conceivably the long-entrenched position of seniority could have been broken at this point. "If the rule of 'seniority' was not destroyed in 1913," says Claude G. Bowers, "it was so badly shattered that it easily could have been given the finishing stroke."[19] Kern, however, was defeated for re-election in 1916, seniority was restored to its earlier position of eminence, and the power which Kern had temporarily centralized was again dispersed. Except for a brief reversal in the 1930s, this process of dispersion has intensified over the years. This is, it has been argued, the natural tendency of the Senate, with centralizing moves usually requiring some outside stimulus. In the late 1960s "important institutional positions" were "being dispersed ever more widely. . . ." As a result, "Virtually all senators acquire substantial legislative influence." The pattern is not even one of "decentralization"; it is one of "individualism."[20]

Thus since 1910 in the House and since 1915 in the Senate the overall tendency has been toward the weakening of central leadership and the strengthening of the committees. Most of the "reforms" which have been made in the procedures of Congress have contributed to this end. "Since 1910," observed the historian of the House in 1962, "the leadership of the House has been in commission. . . . The net effect of the various changes of the last 35 years in the power structure of the House of Representatives has been to diffuse the leadership, and to disperse its risks, among a numerous body of leaders."[21] The Budget and Accounting Act of 1921 strengthened the appropriations committees by giving them exclusive authority to report appropriations, but its primary effects were felt in the executive branch with the creation of the Bureau of the Budget. During the 1920s power was further dispersed among the Speaker, floor leaders, Rules, Appropriations, Ways and Means chairmen, and caucus chairman. In the following decade political development also contributed to the diffusion of influence when the conservative majority on the Rules Committee broke with the administration in 1937.

The dispersion of power to the committees of Congress was intensified by the Legislative Reorganization Act of 1946. In essence, this act was a "committee reorganization act" making the committees stronger and more effective. The reduction in the number of standing committees from 81 to 34 increased the importance of the committee chairmanships. Committee consolidation led to the proliferation of subcommittees, now estimated to number about 250. Thus the functions of integration and coordination which, if performed at all, would previously have been performed by the central leadership of the two houses, were now devolved on the leadership of the standing committees. Before the reorganization, for instance, committee jurisdictions frequently overlapped, and the presiding officers of the House and Senate could often influence the fate of a bill by exercising their discretion in referring it to committee. While jurisdictional uncertainties were not totally eliminated by the act, the discretion of the presiding officers was drastically curtailed. The committee chairman, on the other hand, could often influence the fate of legislation by manipulating the subcommittee structure of the committee and by exercising his discretion in referring bills to subcommittees. Similarly, the intention of the framers of the Reorganization Act to reduce, if not eliminate, the use of special committees had the effect of restricting the freedom of action of the central leadership in the two houses at the same time that it confirmed the authority of the standing committees in their respective jurisdictions. The Reorganization Act also bolstered the committees by significantly expanding their staffs and by specifically authorizing them to exercise legislative overseeing functions with respect to the administrative agencies in their field of responsibility.

The act included few provisions strengthening the central leadership of Congress. Those which it did include in general did not operate successfully. A proposal for party policy committees in each house was defeated in the House of Representatives. The Senate subsequently authorized party policy committees in the Senate, but they did not become active or influential enough to affect the legislative process significantly. The act's provision for a Joint Committee on the Budget which would set an appropriation ceiling by February 15 of each year was implemented twice and then abandoned. In 1950 the appropriations committees reported a consolidated supply bill which cut the presidential estimates by $2 billion and was approved by Congress two months before the approval of the individual supply bills of 1949. Specialized interests within Congress, however, objected strenuously to this procedure, and it has not been attempted again. The net effect of the Reorganization Act was thus to further the dispersion of power, to strengthen and to institutionalize committee authority, and to circumscribe still more the influence of the central leadership. The Legislative Reorganization Act of 1970, a far more modest measure than that of 1946, reinforced these tendencies. It did not deal with seniority and none of its provisions was designed to strengthen central leadership. To the extent that it was implemented, its effects were, indeed, to disperse power still further within committees by reducing the prerogatives of the chairmen.

In the years after the 1946 reorganization, the issues which earlier had divided the central leadership and committee chairmen reappeared in each committee in struggles between committee chairmen and subcommittees. The chairmen attempted to maintain their own control and flexibility over the number, nature, staff, membership, and leadership of their subcommittees. Several of the most assertive chairmen either prevented the creation of subcommittees or created numbered subcommittees without distinct legislative jurisdictions, thereby reserving to themselves the assignment of legislation to the subcommittees. Those who wished to limit the power of the chairman, on the other hand, often invoked seniority as the rule to be followed in designating subcommittee chairmen. In 1961 31 of the 36 standing committees of the House and

Senate had subcommittees and in 24 the subcommittees had fixed jurisdictions and significant autonomy, thus playing a major role in the legislative process. In many committees the subcommittees go their independent way, jealously guarding their autonomy and prerogatives against other subcommittees and their own committee chairman. "Given an active subcommittee chairman working in a specialized field with a staff of his own," one congressional staff member observes, "the parent committee can do no more than change the grammar of a subcommittee report."[22] In the Senate after World War II the predominant influence in legislation shifted from committee chairmen to subcommittee chairmen and individual senators. Specialization of function and dispersion of power, which once worked to the benefit of the committee chairmen, now work against them.

Position of Central Leaders The Speaker and the majority floor leaders are the most powerful men in Congress, but their power is not markedly greater than that of many other congressional leaders. In 1959, for instance, thirteen of nineteen committee chairmen broke with the Speaker to support the Landrum-Griffin bill. "This graphically illustrated the locus of power in the House," one congressman commented. "The Speaker, unable to deliver votes, was revealed in outline against the chairmen. This fact was not lost on Democratic Members."[23] The power base of the central leaders has tended to atrophy, caught between the expansion of presidential authority and influence, on the other hand, and the institutionalization of committee authority, on the other.

At times individual central leaders have built up impressive networks of personal influence. These, however, have been individual, not institutional, phenomena. The ascendancy of Rayburn and Johnson during the 1950s, for instance, tended to obscure the difference between personal influence and institutional authority. With the departure of the Texas coalition their personal networks collapsed. "Rayburn's personal power and prestige," observed Representative Richard Bolling, "made the institution *appear* to work. When Rayburn died, the thing just fell apart."[24] Similarly, Johnson's effectiveness as Senate leader, in the words of one of his assistants, was "overwhelmingly a matter of personal influence. By all accounts, Johnson was the most personal among recent leaders in his approach. For years it was said that he talked to every Democratic senator every day. Persuasion ranged from the awesome pyrotechnics known as 'Treatment A' to the apparently casual but always purposeful exchange as he roamed the floor and the cloakroom."[25] When Johnson's successor was accused of failing to provide the necessary leadership to the Senate, he defended himself on the grounds that he was Mansfield and not Johnson. His definition of the leader's role was largely negative: "I am neither a circus ringmaster, the master of ceremonies of a Senate nightclub, a tamer of Senate lions, or a wheeler and dealer. . . ."[26] The majority leadership role was uninstitutionalized and the kindly, gentlemanly, easygoing qualities which Mansfield had had as Senator from Montana were not changed when he became majority leader. The power of the President has been institutionalized; the powers of the congressional committees and their chairmen have been institutionalized; but the power of the central leaders of Congress remains personal, *ad hoc*, and transitory.

In the House the dispersion of power has weakened the central leadership and strengthened committee and subcommittee chairmen. The latter, products of the seniority system, are normally legislative veterans of long standing. In the Senate, on the other hand, the more widespread dispersion of power within a smaller body has produced a more egalitarian situation in which freshmen senators are often able to take the initiative on important issues of particular concern to them or on which they have developed special expertise. The dispersion of power in the Senate, in short, has tended to open up that body to new and outside influences while in the House it has had the reverse effect.

In both houses, however, the dispersion of power makes obstruction easy and the development of a coherent legislative program difficult. Congress cannot play a positive role in the legislative process so long as it lacks a structure of power which makes positive leadership possible. During the last decades of the nineteenth century, for instance, the Speakers of the House centralized power, exercised personal leadership, and played an innovative role in policy. In subsequent years, in contrast, the Speakers "lost or gave away powers" and what initiative there was in policy came from the executive branch.[27] So long as the Speaker remains, in Bolling's words, "a weak King surrounded by strong Dukes," the House cannot organize itself to lead: "A strong Speaker is crucial to the House. He is the indispensable man for its legislative and political health, education, and welfare."[28] The same is true of the majority leader in the Senate. Perpetuation there of the dispersion of power, on the other hand, means that there is "no general plan for bringing bills to the floor in a given order or at a given time"; the legislative process as a whole becomes "highly segmented"; and the prospects for organized institutional reform are very low.[29]

Function: The Shift to Oversight

Loss of Initiative The insulation of Congress from external social forces and the dispersion of power within Congress have stimulated significant changes in the functions of Congress. The congressional role in legislation has largely been reduced to delay and amendment; congressional activity in overseeing administration has expanded and diversified. During the nineteenth century Congress frequently took the legislative initiative in dealing with major national problems. Even when the original proposal came from the President, Congress usually played an active and positive role in reshaping the proposal into law. "The predominant and controlling force, the centre and source of all motive and of all regulative power," Woodrow Wilson observed in 1885, "is Congress. . . . The legislative is the aggressive spirit."[30] Since 1933, however, the initiative in formulating legislation, in assigning legislative priorities, in arousing support for legislation, and in determining the final content of the legislation enacted has clearly shifted to the executive branch. All three elements of the executive branch—President, administration, and bureaucracy—have gained legislative functions at the expense of Congress. Today's "aggressive spirit" is clearly the executive branch.

In 1908, it is reported, the Senate, in high dudgeon at the effrontery of the Secretary of the Interior, returned to him the draft of a bill which he had proposed, resolving to refuse any further communications from executive officers unless they were transmitted by the President himself.[31] Now, however, congressmen expect the executive departments to present them with bills. Eighty percent of the bills enacted into law, one congressman has estimated, originate in the executive branch. Indeed, in most instances congressmen do not admit a responsibility to take legislative action except in response to executive requests. Congress, as one senator has complained, "has surrendered its rightful place in the leadership in the lawmaking process to the White House. No longer is Congress the source of major legislation. It now merely filters legislative proposals from the President, straining out some and reluctantly letting others pass through. These days no one expects Congress to devise the important bills."[32] The President now determines the legislative agenda of Congress almost as thoroughly as the British cabinet sets the legislative agenda of Parliament. The institutionalization of this role was one of the more significant developments in presidential-congressional relations after World War II.[33]

Loss of Policy Control   Congress has conceded not only the initiative in originating legislation but—and perhaps inevitably as the result of losing the initiative—it has also lost the dominant influence it once had in shaping the final content of legislation. Between 1882 and 1909 Congress had a preponderant influence in shaping the content of 16 (55 percent) out of 29 major laws enacted during those years. It had a preponderant influence over 17 (46 percent) of 37 major laws passed between 1910 and 1932. During the constitutional revolution of the New Deal, however, its influence declined markedly: only 2 (8 percent) of 24 major laws passed between 1933 and 1940 were primarily the work of Congress.[34] Certainly its record after World War II was little better.

The loss of congressional control over the substance of policy was most marked, of course, in the area of national defense and foreign policy. At one time Congress did not hesitate to legislate the size and weapons of the armed forces. During the 1940s and 1950s this power—to raise and support armies, to provide and maintain a navy—came to rest firmly in the hands of the executive. Is Congress, one congressional committee asked plaintively in 1962, to play simply "the passive role of supine acquiescence" in executive programs or is it to be "an active participant in the determination of the direction of our defense policy?" The committee, however, already knew the answer:

> To any student of government, it is eminently clear that the role of the Congress in determining national policy, defense or otherwise, has deteriorated over the years. More and more the role of Congress has come to be that of a sometimes querulous but essentially kindly uncle who complains while furiously puffing on his pipe but who finally, as everyone expects, gives in and hands over the allowance, grants the permission, or raises his hand in blessing, and then returns to the rocking chair for another year of somnolence broken only by an occasional anxious glance down the avenue and a muttered doubt as to whether he had done the right thing.[35]

Congressional Reassertion   This image of Congress accurately summarizes its role in foreign and military policy from the mid-1940s to the mid-1960s. In the late 1960s, however, the winds of change began to blow and congressional groups attempted to reassert their historical role in these areas of policy. The critics of United States involvement in Indochina, particularly those in the Senate Foreign Relations Committee, as well as those more generally concerned about the extent of the United States role in world affairs, moved to challenge Presidential leadership on foreign policy in two key areas. One concerned the size and equipment of the armed forces. In 1969 the Senate came only one vote short of cancelling funds for the administration's anti-ballistic missile system and did compel or induce several significant changes in the nature of that program. In 1971 Congress wrote a limitation on the size of the army which compelled the administration to cut back United States military strength more rapidly than it would have preferred. Congress is now likely to veto major weapons systems and to impose restrictions on the overall size of the armed forces in ways which it never did for twenty years after World War II. The "day is over," as one defense-minded congressman has stated, when a "member of Congress would hesitate to vote against anything proposed by the Joint Chiefs of Staff because he might be subject to the charge of being soft on communism."[36]

The second area in which Congress has seemed to assert a new role concerns the commitment and use of military force. This area, however, is further removed than men and weapons from the traditional control of Congress. As of the spring of 1972, Congress's bark in this field was much more noticeable than its bite; congressional resentment at Presidential power was outrunning congressional reassertion of legislative power. In two instances in 1969 and 1970, Congress legislated prohibitions on the use of funds to support United States ground combat forces in Laos, Thailand, and Cambodia—after the executive branch had stated it had no intention of introducing such forces or was in the process of withdrawing them. Although comparable limitations were proposed on the use of United States forces in Vietnam, these were not approved when the administration opposed them. On a broader front, Congress did move cautiously to redefine in general terms the conditions under which the President could involve United States military forces in armed conflict, the Senate approving such legislation in the spring of 1972. These manifestations of Congress's unhappiness with the profligate commitment of United States troops abroad without its approval undoubtedly introduced greater caution into executive behavior. The actions of Congress during the Johnson and Nixon administrations also indicated, however, a desire to avoid a constitutional showdown with the executive on these issues.

These presidential–congressional differences over foreign policy illustrate one way in which Congress can play a more positive or innovating policy role. Congressional assertion, we have argued, is normally manifested through congressional obstruction. If, however, the President and executive agencies continue to pursue overall foreign policy objectives which have become obsolete or dated, congressional efforts to obstruct or to veto these policies can lay the basis for policy innovations. In the 1940s and 1950s, the executive had the initiative in foreign policy, and Congress consequently had either to acquiesce or to obstruct. In the late 1960s and early 1970s, the executive was often less concerned with initiation in foreign policy than with the maintenance of past policies (most dramatically and concretely revealed, for instance, in the insistence of both the Johnson and Nixon administrations on the maintenance of United States military strength in Europe). Unable to produce new policies itself, Congress could by objecting to the continuation of old policies, facilitate the innovation of new ones. In this sense, congressional "negativism" might lead to policy "positivism."

Overseeing Administration   The overall decline in the legislative role of Congress in the twentieth century has been accompanied by an increase in its administrative role. The modern state differs from the liberal state of the eighteenth and nineteenth centuries in terms of the greater control it exercises over society and the increase in the size, functions, and importance of its bureaucracy. Needed in the modern state are means to control, check, supplement, stimulate, and ameliorate this bureaucracy. The institutions and techniques available for this task vary from country to country: the Scandinavian countries have their *Ombudsmen;* Communist countries use party bureaucracy to check state bureaucracy. In the United States, Congress has come to play a major, if not the major, role in this regard. Indeed, many of the innovations in Congress in recent years have strenghtened its control over the administrative processes of the executive branch. Congressional committees responded with alacrity to the mandate of the 1946 Reorganization Act that they "exercise continuous watchfulness" over the administration of laws. Congressional investigations of the bureaucracy have multiplied: each Congress during the period between 1950 and 1962 conducted more investigations than were conducted by *all* the Congresses during the nineteenth century.[37] Other mechanisms of committee control, such as the legislative veto and committee clearance of administrative decisions, have been increasingly employed. "Not legislation but control of administration," as Galloway remarks, "is becoming the primary function of the modern Congress."[38] In discharging this function, congressmen uncover waste and abuse, push particular projects and innovations, highlight inconsistencies, correct injustices, and compel exposition and defense of bureaucratic decisions.

Constituency Service   In performing these activities, Congress is acting where it is most competent to act: it is dealing with particulars, not general policies. Unlike legislating, these concerns are perfectly compatible with the current patterns of insulation and dispersion. Committee specialization and committee power enhance rather than detract from the effectiveness of the committees as administrative overseers. In addition, as the great organized interests of society come to be represented more directly in the bureaucracy and administration, the role of Congress as representative of individual citizens becomes all the more important. The congressman more often serves their interests by representing them in the administrative process than in the legislative process. The time and energy put into this type of representation undoubtedly varies widely from one congressman to another. "The most pressing day-to-day demands for the time of Senators and Congressmen," according to Hubert Humphrey, "are not directly linked to legislative tasks. They come from constituents."[39] Sixteen percent of one sample of House members listed the "Errand Boy" function as their primary activity; 59 percent listed it as second to their legislative work. Another group of House members was reported to spend 25 to 30 percent of their time and 50 percent of the time of their Washington staffs on constituency service. One freshman representative, however, estimated that half of his own time and two-thirds of that of his staff were devoted to constituent service. Senatorial staffs apparently spend about twice as much time on constituency service and oversight as they do on legislative matters.[40] In performing these services congressmen are both representing their constituents where they need to be represented and checking up on and ameliorating the impact of the federal bureaucracy. Constituent service and legislative oversight are, in some measure, two sides of the same coin. Both are functions which no other public agency is as well qualified as Congress to perform. Responding to needs unmet elsewhere, Congress plays an increasingly important role as the representative of the interests of unorganized individuals and as the stimulant, monitor, corrector, and overseer of a growing federal bureaucracy.

Adaptation or Reform

Insulation makes Congress unwilling to initiate laws. Dispersion makes Congress unable to aggregate individual bills into a coherent legislative program. Constituent service and administrative overseeing eat into the time and energy which congressmen give legislative matters. Congress is thus left in its legislative dilemma where the assertion of power is almost equivalent to the obstruction of action. What then are the possibilities for institutional adaptation or institutional reform? [. . .]

Adaptation and Reform: Redefining Function   [One] way out of Congress's dilemma involves not the reversal but the intensification of the recent trends of congressional evolution. Congress has a legislative dilemma because opinion conceives of it as a legislature. If it gave up the effort to play a major role in the legislative process, it could, quite conceivably, play a much more positive and influential role in the political system as a whole. Representative assemblies have not always been legislatures. They had their origins in medieval times as courts and as councils. An assembly need not legislate to exist and to be important. Indeed, some would argue that assemblies should not legislate. "[A] numerous assembly," John Stuart Mill contended, "is as little fitted for the direct business of legislation as for that of administration."[41] Representative assemblies acquired their legislative functions in the seventeenth and eighteenth centuries; there is no necessary reason why liberty, democracy, or constitutional government depends upon their exercising those functions in the twentieth century. Legislation has become much too complex politically to be effectively handled by a representative assembly. The primary work of legislation must be done, and increasingly is being done, by the three "houses" of the executive branch: the bureaucracy, the administration, and the President.

Far more important than the preservation of Congress as a legislative institution is the preservation of Congress as an autonomous institution. When the performance of one function becomes "dysfunctional" to the workings of an institution, the sensible course is to abandon it for other functions. In the 1930s the Supreme Court was forced to surrender its function of disallowing national and state social legislation. Since then it has wielded its veto on federal legislation only rarely and with the greatest of discretion. This loss of power, however, was more than compensated for by its new role in protecting civil rights and civil liberties against state action. This is a role which neither its supporters nor its opponents in the 1930s would have thought possible. In effect, the Court used the great conservative weapon of the 1930s to promote the great liberal ends of the 1960s. Such is the way skillful leaders and great institutions adapt to changing circumstances.

The redefinition of Congress's functions away from legislation might involve, in the first instance, a restriction of the power of Congress to delay indefinitely presidential legislative requests. Constitutionally, Congress would still retain its authority to approve legislation. Practically, Congress could, as Walter Lippmann and others have suggested, bind itself to approve or disapprove urgent presidential proposals within a time limit of say, three or six months. If thus compelled to choose openly, Congress, it may be supposed, would almost invariably approve presidential requests. Its veto power would become a reserve power like that of the Supreme Court if not like that of the British Crown. On these "urgent" measures it would perform a legitimizing function rather than a legislative function. At the same time, the requirement that Congress pass or reject presidential requests would also presumably induce executive leaders to consult with congressional leaders in drafting such legislation. Congress would also, of course, continue to amend and to vote freely on "nonurgent" executive requests.

Explicit acceptance of the idea that legislation was not its primary function would, in large part, simply be recognition of the direction which change has already been taking. It would legitimize and expand the functions of constituent service and administrative oversight which have become so important in recent decades. However isolated it might be from the dominant social forces in society, Congress could still capitalize on its position as the representative of the unorganized interests of individuals. It would become a proponent of popular demands against the bureaucracy rather than the opponent of popular demands for legislation. It would thus continue to play a major although different role in the constitutional system of checks and balances.

A few years ago a survey of the functioning of legislative bodies in 41 countries concluded that parliaments were in general losing their initiative and power in legislation. At the same time, however, they were gainng power in the "control of government activity."[42] Most legislatures, however, are much less autonomous and powerful than Congress. Congress has lost less power over legislation and gained more power over administration than other parliaments. It is precisely this fact which gives rise to its legislative dilemma. If Congress can generate the leadership and the will to make the drastic reform required to reverse the trends toward insulation, dispersion, and overseeing, it could still resume a positive role in the legislative process. If this is impossible, an alternative path is to eschew the legislative effort and to adapt itself to discharge effectively those functions of constituent service and bureaucratic control which insulation and dispersion do enable it to play in the national government.

Notes

1. George B. Galloway, *History of the United States House of Representatives* (House Document 246, Eighty-seventh Congress, First Session, 1962), p. 31; T. Richard Witmer, "The Aging of the House," *Political Science Quarterly*, 79 (Dec. 1964), pp. 526-541. See Nelson Polsby, "The Institutionalization of the U.S. House of Representatives," *American Political Science Review*, 62 (March 1968), pp. 144-68, for documentation in historical detail for the House of Representatives of several of the trends posited here and analysis of them according to criteria of institutionalization (autonomy, coherence, complexity) which I elaborated in "Political Development and Political Decay," *World Politics*, 17 (April 1965), pp. 386-430.

2. Gail Hamilton, *Life of James G. Blaine*, p. 263, quoted in DeAlva S. Alexander, *History and Procedure of the House of Representatives* (Boston: Houghton Mifflin, 1916), p. 69. On the development of the House seniority system, see Michael Abram and Joseph Cooper, "The Rise of Seniority in the House of Representatives," *Polity*, 1 (Fall 1968), pp. 52-85, and Nelson Polsby, Miriam Gallaher, and Barry Spencer Rundquist, "The Growth of the Seniority System in the U.S. House of Representatives," *American Political Science Review*, 63 (Sept. 1969), pp. 787-807. For the operation of the system, see, in general, Barbara Hinckley, *The Seniority System in Congress* (Bloomington: Ind. Univ. Press, 1971).

3. Quoted in Charles L. Clapp, *The Congressman: His Work as He Sees It* (Washington: Brookings Institution, 1963), p. 21.

4. Theodore H. White, *The Making of the President, 1960* (New York: Atheneum Press, 1961), p. 132.

5. See Pendleton Herring, *Presidential Leadership* (New York: Farrar and Rinehart, 1940), pp. 164-65 for figures for 1861-1940; figures for 1940-1963 have been calculated on same basis as Herring's figures; see also Dean E. Mann, "The Selection of Federal Political Executives," *American Political Science Review*, 58 (March 1964), p. 97.

6. See Andrew Hacker, "The Elected and the Anointed," *American Political Science Review*, 55 (Sept. 1961), pp. 540-41; Mann, *ibid.*, 58 (March 1964), pp. 92-93; Donald R. Matthews, *U.S. Senators and Their World* (Chapel Hill: Univ. of N.C. Press, 1960), pp. 14-17; W. Lloyd Warner *et al.*, *The American Federal Executive* (New Haven: Yale Univ. Press, 1963), pp. 11, 56-58, 333; W. Lloyd Warner and James C. Abegglen, *Occupational Mobility in American Business and Industry* (Minneapolis: Univ. of Minn. Press, 1955), p. 38; Suzanne Keller, "The Social Origins and Career Patterns of Three Generations of American Business Leaders" (Ph.D. dissertation, Columbia Univ., 1953), cited in Wendell Bell, Richard J. Hill, and Charles R. Wright, *Public Leadership* (San Francisco: Chandler Press, 1961), p. 106. Leroy N. Rieselbach has noted that congressmen in the 1950s and 1960s were not more rural or small-town in their birthplaces than the population of the country as a whole in 1900 and 1910. "Congressmen as 'Small Town Boys': A Research Note," *Midwest Journal of Political Science*, 14 (May 1970), pp. 321-30. His argument, however, involves a quite different question from that argued here which concerns not the representativeness of congressmen compared to the general population, but rather the similarity or difference in background of congressional and other elites.

7. Hacker, *op. cit.*, p. 544. For further analysis of the limited geographical mobility of representatives, see Roger H. Davidson, *The Role of the Congressman* (New York: Pegasus, 1969), pp. 54-59.

8. Davidson, *Role of the Congressman*, p. 54.

9. Andrew Hacker, "Are There Too Many Lawyers in Congress?" *New York Times Magazine*, January 5, 1964, p. 74.

10. James N. Rosenau, *National Leadership and Foreign Policy* (Princeton: Princeton Univ. Press, 1963), pp. 30-31, 347-350.

11. Hacker, *op. cit.*, pp. 547-49.

12. William S. White, *Citadel* (New York: Harper & Bros., 1956), p. 136.

13. See John S. Saloma III, *Congress and the New Politics* (Boston: Little, Brown, 1969), pp. 68-69.

14. Authorities vary on the exact impact of the Court decisions on the rural-urban balance in Congress, but they generally agree that it was less than had been anticipated. See Saloma, *Congress and the New Politics*, pp. 77-87; Andrew Hacker, *Congressional Districting: The Issue of Equal Representation* (Washington: Brookings Institution, rev. ed., 1964).

15. Richard Lehne, "Shape of the Future," *National Civic Review*, 58 (Sept. 1969), pp. 351-55.

16. Milton C. Cummings, Jr., "Reapportionment in the 1970's: Its Effects on Congress," in Nelson W. Polsby, ed., *Reapportionment in the 1970's* (Berkeley: Univ. of Cal. Press, 1971), p. 222.

17. Clapp, *op. cit.*, pp. 23-24.

18. Clem Miller, *Member of the House* (New York: Scribner's, 1962), p. 51; Randall B. Ripley, *Power in the Senate* (New York: St. Martin's Press, 1969), p. 172.

19. Claude G. Bowers, *The Life of John Worth Kern* (Indianapolis: Hollenback Press, 1918), p. 840.

20. Ripley, *Power in the Senate*, pp. 15-16, 53, 77, 185.

21. Galloway, *op. cit.*, pp. 95, 98, 128.

22. George Goodwin, Jr., "Subcommittees: The Miniature Legislatures of Congress," *American Political Science Review*, 56 (Sept. 1962), pp. 596-601.

23. Miller, *op. cit.*, p. 110.

24. Quoted in Stewart Alsop, "The Failure of Congress," *Saturday Evening Post*, 236 (December 7, 1963), p. 24.

25. Ralph K. Huitt, "Democratic Party Leadership in the Senate," *American Political Science Review*, 55 (June 1961), p. 338.

26. *Congressional Record* (Nov. 27, 1963), pp. 21, 758 (daily ed.).

27. Randall B. Ripley, *Party Leaders in the House of Representatives* (Washington: Brookings Institution, 1967), pp. 16-17.

28. Richard Bolling, *Power in the House: A History of the Leadership of the House of Representatives* (New York: E. P. Dutton, 1968), p. 29.

29. Ripley, *Power in the Senate*, pp. 13-14.

30. Woodrow Wilson, *Congressional Government* (Boston: Houghton Mifflin, 1885), pp. 11, 36.

31. George B. Galloway, *The Legislative Process in Congress* (New York: Crowell, 1955), p. 9.

32. Abraham Ribicoff, "Doesn't Congress Have Ideas of Its Own?" *Saturday Evening Post*, 237 (March 21, 1964), p. 6.

33. Richard E. Neustadt, "Presidency and Legislation: Planning the President's Program," *American Political Science Review*, 49 (Dec. 1955), pp. 980-1021.

34. Lawrence H. Chamberlain, *The President, Congress, and Legislation* (New York: Columbia Univ. Press, 1946), pp. 450-52.

35. House Report 1406, Eighty-seventh Congress, Second Session (1962), p. 7.

36. Representative George H. Mahon, *Washington Post*, Dec. 27, 1969, quoted in Francis O. Wilcox, *Congress, The Executive, and Foreign Policy* (New York: Harper & Row, 1971), p. 135.

37. Galloway, *op. cit.*, p. 166.

38. *Ibid.*, pp. 56-57.

39. Hubert H. Humphrey, "To Move Congress Out of Its Ruts," *New York Times Magazine* (April 7, 1963), p. 39.

40. See Davidson, *Role of the Congressman*, pp. 97-107; Saloma, *Congress and the New Politics*, pp. 183-89; Clarence D. Long, "Observations of a Freshman in Congress," *New York Times Magazine* (December 1, 1963), p. 73; Ripley, *Power in the Senate*, pp. 189-95.

41. John Stuart Mill, "On Representative Government," *Utilitarianism, Liberty, and Representative Government* (London: J. M. Dent), p. 235.

42. Inter-Parliamentary Union, *Parliaments: A Comparative Study on Structure and Functioning of Representative Institutions in Forty-One Countries* (New York: Praeger, 1963), p. 398.

2.10

The Reformation of American Administrative Law

RICHARD B. STEWART

Welfare state regulation of economic and social life has posed a potentially fatal challenge to traditional understandings of the "rule of law." In the United States those understandings derive both from classical liberalism's claim to a separation of public and private power and from attention to the specific ordering devices for government decision-making and the administration of justice (e.g. "separation of powers" doctrine and the requirements of "due process") which are canonized in the American constitution. Regulation poses problems on both fronts. It introduces explicitly social concerns and constraints into the transactions of private property owners, and it does so in a way that disturbs expectations of a pristine separation of judicial, executive, and legislative functions, coupled with a case-by-case formalized adjudication of individual disputes.

Nowhere is this rupture of received understandings more evident than in administrative law itself, i.e., the law that putatively governs the behavior of administrative agencies. Performing a multiplicity of functions and diverse regulatory tasks, and commonly acting pursuant to deliberately vague legislative mandates, administrative agencies have repeatedly been assailed for violating strictures on the separation of powers and for performing their functions through a process of highly discretionary group-directed decision-making incompatible with the procedural and substantive claims of individual justice.

Richard Stewart's article on "The Reformation of American Administrative Law" is concerned with describing and criticizing one particular response to the continuing problems of administrative legitimacy, namely the judiciary's implicit endorsement of an "interest representation" model of administrative process. Faced with a manifest lack of consensus on substantive issues, and unable to articulate adequate procedural guidelines or rulemaking requirements for administrative agencies, courts have recently resorted to attempts to widen the range of interests represented in administrative proceedings. The interest representation strategy has been pursued chiefly through decisions sharply scaling back the threshold requirements for standing and participation in agency decision-making, although it has sometimes taken the more ambitious form of structuring positive incentives to participation. This is the "reformation" of Stewart's title. In the preliminary discussion excerpted here, Stewart takes up the development that first gave that reformation impetus, namely the apparent inability to thematize administrative process through traditional understandings of law.

Reprinted with permission from *Harvard Law Review*, Vol. 88, No. 8 (June 1975), pp. 1667-1711 (chapters I and II, with deletions). Copyright © 1975 by the Harvard Law Review Association.

There is now general agreement about the necessity for delegated
legislation; the real problem is how this legislation can be
reconciled with the processes of democratic consultation, scrutiny
and control.

ANEURIN BEVAN

I. The Traditional Model and the Problem of Discretion

A. The Traditional Model   Our inquiry into the traditional model of American
administrative law begins with the developments generated by the regulation of private
business conduct which commenced on a broad scale in the latter part of the nineteenth
century. The direct control by state, and then federal, administrative officials of rates,
services, and other practices, first of railroads and then of a wide variety of other
enterprises, grew so pervasive and intrusive that it could not be justified by reference to
past executive practices. Accordingly, a body of doctrines and techniques developed to
reconcile the new assertions of governmental power with a long-standing solicitude for
private liberties by means of controls that served both to limit and legitimate such power.
During the period 1880-1960 a coherent set of principles emerged. Though not fully
applicable to every exercise of administrative power, this body of doctrine has nonetheless
enjoyed such widespread acceptance that it may be termed the traditional model of
administrative law. Its essential elements are:

(1) *The imposition of administratively determined sanctions on private individuals
must be authorized by the legislature through rules which control agency action.* With the
possible exceptions of military and foreign affairs functions and times of national
emergency, the Constitution recognizes no inherent administrative powers over persons
and property. Coercive controls on private conduct must be authorized by the legislature,
and, under the doctrine against delegation of legislative power, the legislature must
promulgate rules, standards, goals, or some "intelligible principle" to guide the exercise of
administrative power.

The doctrine against delegation appears ultimately to be bottomed on contractarian
political theory running back to Hobbes and Locke, under which consent is the only
legitimate basis for the exercise of the coercive power of government.[1] Since the process of
consent is institutionalized in the legislature, that body must authorize any new official
imposition of sanctions on private persons; such persons in turn enjoy a correlative right
to repel official intrusions not so authorized. These principles would, however, be
deprived of all practical significance were the legislature permitted to delegate its
lawmaking power in gross.[2] Choices among competing social policies would be made by
non-elected executive officials. Moreover, the absence of meaningful statutory controls
on agencies would deprive citizens of effective protections against the abusive exercise of
administrative power; the legislature could not exercise continuous supervision of all
agency actions, and without a guiding statutory directive the courts would have no
benchmark against which to measure assertions of agency power.

The requirement that agencies conform to specific legislative directives not only
legitimates administrative action by reference to higher authority, but also curbs officials'
exploitation of the governmental apparatus to give vent to private prejudice or passion. At
the same time, private autonomy is secured in two ways by such a requirement. First, it
promotes formal justice by ensuring that the governmental sanctions faced by an
individual are rule-governed, which facilitates private avoidance of sanctions and allows
interaction with the government on terms most advantageous to the individual. Second,

on contractarian premises, the requirement ensures that sanctions have been validated by a governmental authority to which the individual has consented and therefore the restraints imposed by the threat of sanctions may be viewed as self-imposed.[3]

(2) *The decisional procedures followed by the agency must be such as will tend to ensure the agency's compliance with requirement (1).* If agencies may exercise delegated powers only in accordance with legislative directives, and if effective limitation on administrative power is not to be more theoretical than real, agency procedures must be designed to promote the accurate, impartial, and rational application of legislative directives to given cases or classes of cases. Thus where the facts that would justify governmental action are disputed and important liberty or property interests are at stake, a hearing is generally required in which the person whose interests are threatened has the opportunity to present evidence and challenge the factual and legal bases for the agency's action. Moreover, the agency must normally decide the matter on the basis of the record developed at the hearing through factfindings supported by substantial evidence and the reasoned application of legislative directives to the facts found.

(3) *The decisional processes of the agency must facilitate judicial review to ensure agency compliance with requirements (1) and (2).*

(4) *Judicial review must be available to ensure compliance with requirements (1) and (2).* To ensure that administrative sanctions are imposed only in accordance with general legislative rules, judicial review is not a logical necessity. The combination of legislative supervision, popular opinion, and bureaucratic tradition might conceivably be adequate to ensure a tolerable degree of agency compliance with legislative directives. But such a view would rest on assumptions that with us appear too optimistic. Judicial review is normally available as an additional assurance that agencies not exceed their authorized powers. As a further corollary, agency decisional processes and findings must be adequate to permit the judge to ascertain with reasonable assurance whether the legislative directive was correctly observed in each case.[4]

The traditional model of administrative law thus conceives of the agency as a mere transmission belt for implementing legislative directives in particular cases. It legitimates intrusions into private liberties by agency officials not subject to electoral control by ensuring that such intrusions are commanded by a legitimate source of authority—the legislature. Requiring agencies to show that intrusions on private liberties have been directed by the legislature provides a rationale for judicial review and also serves to define the appropriate role of the courts vis-a-vis the agencies. The court's function is one of containment; review is directed toward keeping the agency within the directives which Congress has issued. On the other hand, this conception of the reviewing function implies that the court is to pass upon only those matters as to which the statute provides ascertainable direction; all other issues of choice, whether general or interstitial, are for the agency. By subjecting agency impositions of sanctions to judicial review in order to ensure compliance with legislative directives, the traditional model of administrative law also seeks to mediate the inconsistency between the doctrine of separation of government powers and the agencies' conspicuous combination of various lawmaking and law-enforcing functions. To the extent that the separation of powers doctrine is construed as demanding only that the exercise of power by one organ of government be subject to check by some other governmental body, the traditional model furnishes such a check through the judiciary.

B. The Problem of Discretion   Vague, general, or ambiguous statutes create discretion and threaten the legitimacy of agency action under the "transmission belt" theory of administrative law.[5] Insofar as statutes do not effectively dictate agency actions, individual autonomy is vulnerable to the imposition of sanctions at the unruled will of executive officials, major questions of social and economic policy are determined by officials who are not formally accountable to the electorate, and both the checking and validating functions of the traditional model are impaired. However, rather than being the exception, federal legislation establishing agency charters has, over the past several decades, often been strikingly broad and nonspecific, and has accordingly generated the very conditions which the traditional model was designed to eliminate.

So long as administrative power was kept within relatively narrow bounds and did not intrude seriously on vested private interests, the problem of agency discretion could be papered over by applying plausible labels, such as "quasi-judicial" or "quasi-legislative," designed to assimilate agency powers to those exercised by traditional governmental organs. But after the delegation by New Deal Congresses of sweeping powers to a host of new agencies under legislative directives cast in the most general terms, the broad and novel character of agency discretion could no longer be concealed behind such labels.

Defenders flaunted the breadth of the discretion afforded the new agencies by Congress, maintaining that such discretion was necessary if the agencies were to discharge their planning and managerial functions successfully and restore health to the various sectors of the economy for which they were responsible. Given the assumption that the agencies' role was that of manager or planner with an ascertainable goal,[6] "expertise" could plausibly be advocated as a solution to the problem of discretion if the agency's goal could be realized through the knowledge that comes from specialized experience. For in that case the discretion that the administrator enjoys is more apparent than real. The policy to be set is simply a function of the goal to be achieved and the state of the world. There may be a trial and error process in finding the best means of achieving the posited goal, but persons subject to the administrator's control are no more liable to his arbitrary will than are patients remitted to the care of a skilled doctor. This analysis underlay the notion that administrators were not political, but professional, and that public administration has an objective basis.[7] It also supported arguments by New Deal defenders that it would be unwise for the Congress to lay down detailed prescriptions in advance, and intolerably inefficient to require administrators to follow rigid judicial procedures.

However, many lawyers remained unpersuaded, and attacked the delegation of broad discretion to administrators as violative of the principles of separation of powers and formal justice which the traditional model was designed to serve. In theory the traditional model might have been effectively used to curtail the discretionary exercise by agencies of broadly delegated powers through a rigorous application of the non-delegation doctrine to require greater specificity in legislative directives. This solution, however, proved unworkable because of difficulties in implementing the doctrine and because of the institutional hazards involved in persistent, wholesale invalidation by courts of broad legislative directives. Instead, the courts, reacting in part to the Administrative Procedure Act and its history, turned to a number of alternative (and more enduring) techniques to control the exercise of administrative discretion.

First, by undertaking a more searching scrutiny of the substantiality of the evidence supporting agency factfinding and by insisting on a wider range of procedural safeguards, the courts have required agencies to adhere more scrupulously to the norms of the traditional model. This judicial stance has promoted more accurate application of legislative directives. Additionally, more rigorous enforcement of procedural requirements, such as hearings, may have influenced agencies' exercise of their discretion and may have served as a partial substitute for political safeguards by, for example, facilitating input from affected interests. These developments may also have reduced effective agency power by affording litigating tools to resistant private interests and by providing judges with an additional basis for setting aside decisions.

A second technique which was developed to control the broad discretion granted by New Deal legislation was the requirement of reasoned consistency in agency decision-making. Under this doctrine, an agency might be required to articulate the reasons for reaching a choice in a given case even though the loose texture of its legislative directive allowed a range of possible choices. Courts might also impose the further requirement that choices over time be consistent, or at least that departures from established policies be persuasively justified, particularly where significant individual expectation interests were involved. Again, these requirements were not directly addressed to the substance of agency policy.[8] Their aim was, and is, simply to ensure that the agency's action is rationally related to the achievement of some permissible societal goal, and to promote formal justice in order to protect private autonomy. Yet these requirements may also have an impact on the substance of agency policy. A requirement of reasoned consistency may hobble the agency in adapting to new contingencies or in dealing with an individual case of abuse whose basis is not easily susceptible to generalized statements, and such a requirement may provide additional tools for litigants resisting agency sanctions and for judges seeking procedural grounds for setting aside dubious decisions.

Third, courts began to demand a clear statement of legislative purpose as a means of restraining the range of agency choice when fundamental individual liberties were at risk. A paradigm example is *Kent v. Dulles*, where Congress had made an apparently unrestricted grant of discretion to the President and Secretary of State to issue passports, and the Secretary had denied passports to persons with alleged Communist associations or sympathies. Stressing that a constitutionally protected "liberty" of travel was involved, the Court held that broad delegations of power would be construed narrowly in such cases and that, since Congress had not specifically authorized a refusal to issue passports on the grounds here asserted, the refusal was invalid. The technique has since been utilized in a variety of contexts to protect important individual interests where the agency had followed questionable procedures or dubious substantive policies. The technique is more discriminating than the non-delegation doctrine; it substitutes tactical excision for wholesale invalidation.[9]

These various techniques, which matured in the twenty years after the enactment of the APA, were well adapted to selective application, and could be utilized to trim agency powers without intruding upon the major bulk of delegated authority implicit in a statutory scheme. Through adroit application of these control techniques, an uneasy truce between administrators and judges developed into working accommodation.

C. The Problem of Discretion Renewed   Today it is obvious that this working compromise has come unstuck. Judicial review once again "gives a sense of battle." Criticism of agency policies is widespread and vociferous.

One strand of this criticism has focused on the assertedly unlawful and abusive exercise of administrative power in areas where the traditional model had seldom applied and the private interests most directly at stake had not enjoyed its protections. These areas include interests in the continuation of advantageous relations with the government (such as the receipt of welfare benefits and eligibility to bid on government contracts) that had not been regarded as within the realm of legally protected liberty or property, and interests in avoiding sanctions imposed by agencies (such as prison authorities and school officials) that had hitherto been accorded considerable immunity from judicial review. Critics have asserted that such interests represent an important aspect of private autonomy and that they are at least as deserving of protection against unauthorized official power as traditional liberty and property interests. The obvious solution is the extension of the traditional model to protect these additional classes of private interests.

A second theme of contemporary criticism of agency discretion has been the agencies' asserted failure affirmatively to carry out legislative mandates and to protect the collective interests that administrative regimes are designed to serve. The possibility of such failure was no concern of the traditional model, which was directed at protecting private autonomy by curbing agency power. It was simply assumed that agency zeal in advancing the "unalloyed, nonpolitical, long-run economic interest of the general public" would be assured by the professionalism of administrators or by political mechanisms through which the administrative branch would "eternally [refresh] its vigor from the stream of democratic desires."

Experience has withered this faith. To the extent that belief in an objective "public interest" remains, the agencies are accused of subverting it in favor of the private interests of regulated and client firms. Such a "devil" theory at least holds out the possibility of redemption. However, we have come not only to question the agencies' ability to protect the "public interest," but to doubt the very existence of an ascertainable "national welfare" as a meaningful guide to administrative decision. Exposure on the one hand to the complexities of a managed economy in a welfare state, and on the other to the corrosive seduction of welfare economics and pluralist political analysis, has sapped faith in the existence of an objective basis for social choice.

Today, the exercise of agency discretion is inevitably seen as the essentially legislative process of adjusting the competing claims of various private interests affected by agency policy. The unravelling of the notion of an objective goal for administration is reflected in statements by judges and legal commentators that the "public interest is a texture of multiple strands," that it "is not a monolith," and "involves a balance of many interests." Courts have asserted that agencies must consider all of the various interests affected by their decisions as an essential predicate to "balancing all elements essential to a just determination of the public interest."

Once the function of agencies is conceptualized as adjusting competing private interests in light of their configuration in a given factual situation and the policies reflected in relevant statutes, it is not possible to legitimate agency action by either the "transmission belt" theory of the traditional model, or the "expertise" model of the New Deal period. The "transmission belt" fails because broad legislative directives will rarely dispose of particular cases once the relevant facts have been accurately ascertained. More frequently, the application of legislative directives requires the agency to reweigh and reconcile the often nebulous or conflicting policies behind the directives in the context of a particular factual situation with a particular constellation of affected interests. The required balancing of policies is an inherently discretionary, ultimately political procedure. Similarly, the "economic manager" defense of administrative discretion—under which discretion was bound by an ascertainable goal, the state of the world, and an applicable technique—has been eroded by the relatively steady economic growth since World War II, which has allowed attention to be focused on the perplexing distributional questions of how the fruits of affluence are to be shared. Such choices clearly do not turn on technical issues that can safely be left to the experts.

The sense of uneasiness aroused by this resurgence of discretion is heightened by perceived biases in the results of the agency balancing process as it is currently carried on. Critics have repeatedly asserted, with a dogmatic tone that reflects settled opinion, that in carrying out broad legislative directives, agencies unduly favor organized interests, especially the interests of regulated or client business firms and other organized groups at the expense of diffuse, comparatively unorganized interests such as consumers, environmentalists, and the poor. In the midst of a "growing sense of disillusion with the role which regulatory agencies play," many legislators, judges, and legal and economic commentators have accepted the thesis of persistent bias in agency policies. At its crudest, this thesis is based on the "capture" scenario, in which administrations are systematically controlled, sometimes corruptly, by the business firms within their orbit of responsibility, whether regulatory or promotional. But there are more subtle explanations of industry orientation, which include the following:

First. The division of responsibility between the regulated firms, which retain primary control over their own affairs, and the administrator, whose power is essentially negative and who is dependent on industry cooperation in order to achieve his objectives, places the administrator in an inherently weak position. The administrator will, nonetheless, be held responsible if the industry suffers serious economic dislocation. For both of these reasons, he may pursue conservative policies.

Second. The regulatory bureaucracy becomes "regulation minded." It seeks to elaborate and perfect the controls it exercises over the regulated industry. The effect of this tendency, particularly in a regime of limited entry, is to eliminate actual and potential competition and buttress the position of the established firms.

Third. The resources—in terms of money, personnel, and political influence—of the regulatory agency are limited in comparison to those of regulated firms. Unremitting maintenance of an adversary posture would quickly dissipate agency resources. Hence, the agency must compromise with the regulated industry if it is to accomplish anything of significance.

Fourth. Limited agency resources imply that agencies must depend on outside sources of information, policy development, and political support. This outside input comes primarily from organized interests, such as regulated firms, that have a substantial stake in the substance of agency policy and the resources to provide such input. By contrast, the personal stake in agency policy of an individual member of an unorganized interest, such as a consumer, is normally too small to justify such representation. Effective representation of unorganized interests might be possible if a means of pooling resources to share the costs of underwriting collective representation were available. But this seems unlikely since the transaction costs of creating an organization of interest group members increase disproportionately as the size of the group increases. Moreover, if membership in such an organization is voluntary, individuals will not have a strong incentive to join, since if others represent the interests involved, the benefits will accrue not only to those participating in the representation, but to nonparticipants as well, who can, therefore, enjoy the benefits without incurring any of the costs (the free rider effect). As a somewhat disillusioned James Landis wrote in 1960, the result is industry dominance in representation, which has a "daily machine-gun like impact on both [an] agency and its staff" that tends to create an industry bias in the agency's outlook.

These various theses of systematic bias in agency policy are not universally valid. Political pressures and judicial controls may force continuing agency adherence to policies demonstrably inimical to the interests of the regulated industry, as in the case of FPC regulation of natural gas producer prices. Moreover, the fact that agency policies may tend to favor regulated interests does not in itself demonstrate that such policies are unfair or unjustified, since protection of regulated interests may be implicit in the regulatory scheme established by Congress. Nonetheless, the critique of agency discretion as unduly favorable to organized interests—particularly regulated or client firms—has

sufficient power and verisimilitude to have achieved widespread contemporary acceptance.

The traditional model provides scant assistance in dealing with the problem of
agencies' failure to exercise discretion under broad statutory directives so as to discharge
their responsibilities equitably and effectively. The traditional model is an essentially
negative instrument for checking governmental power; it does not touch "the affirmative
side" of government "which has to do with the representation of individuals and interests"
and the development of governmental policies on their behalf. Thus the protections of
the traditional model have normally applied only to formal agency proceedings eventuat-
ing in sanctions on regulated firms. Those interests that have assertedly been disregarded
by the agencies—notably beneficiaries of the administrative scheme—have not been
subject to sanctions and thus have normally not been entitled to invoke the protections of
the traditional model. Many of the policy decisions most strongly attacked by agency
critics—the failure to prosecute vigorously, the working out of agency policy by negotiation with regulated firms, the quiet settlement of litigation once initiated—take place
through informal procedures where the traditional controls have not normally applied.

In view of the traditional model's apparent impotence to redress asserted bias in the
exercise of agency discretion, critics have sought alternative solutions. Part II of this
Article will examine the most promising among these alternatives, and explore their
limitations at the level both of principle and practical application. The ultimate problem
is to control and validate the exercise of essentially legislative powers by administrative
agencies that do not enjoy the formal legitimation of one-person one-vote election.

II. Alternative Responses to the Problem of Agency Discretion

A number of solutions have been suggested to deal with the problems of systematic bias
and agency "failure" in the existing process of administrative decisionmaking. Among
these alternatives are: deregulation and abolition of agencies; enforcement of the doctrine
against delegation of legislative power; a requirement that agencies crystallize their
exercise of discretion through standards; and adoption of allocational efficiency as a
substantive yardstick for agency decisions.

The first three of these alternatives seek to legitimate policy outcomes by reference to
the institutional processes that produce them: respectively, the market, the legislature,
and a revised process of agency decisionmaking. The criterion of allocational efficiency is
a surrogate process solution in that it seeks to replicate the results that would be achieved
through market exchange if imperfections in the market could be eliminated. This resort
to process solutions is predictable when faith in objective standards for social choice has
etiolated and the problem of decision is viewed as the accommodation of potentially
conflicting private interests. In such a context, specification (and legitimation) of policy
outcomes can only be accomplished by adopting a given (and authoritative) procedure for
resolving the disparate private interests at stake. Each of the four alternatives offers some
promise in ameliorating the perceived shortcomings in agencies' exercise of discretion in
policy choice. But none approaches a complete solution, and they are in considerable
degree mutually inconsistent.

A. Abolition of Agencies: The Return to the Market A short answer to the
problem of agency discretion is to abolish the agency and remit the agency's functions to
the private market economy (perhaps supplemented by court-enforced liability rules).
This solution is frequently proposed as a means of promoting allocational efficiency and
private autonomy.

In working terms, allocational efficiency consists in the maximization, given existing resources, of the total output of goods and services so that no more of any one commodity can be produced without producing less of some other commodity.[10] Critics of regulation urge that, even though unregulated markets are characterized by various imperfections which hinder the attainment of allocational efficiency, administrative agencies often function even more imperfectly because they utilize regulatory controls that restrict competition among firms and limit consumer choice.[11] Critics charge that, at best, administrative regulation is completely ineffective, and thus a waste of resources, or that the agency's task could be better carried out by the courts.

The deregulation argument based on allocational efficiency has undoubted merit with regard to particular administrative regimes. For example, reduction of entry and price controls in the transportation sector seems most desirable. But dismantling administrative agencies is not a prescription of universal validity. Even advocates of deregulation favor some minimum of regulation to ensure a competitive market structure and acknowledge the necessity for governmental provision of public goods such as dams, roads, and national defense. An official apparatus is also needed to raise governmental revenues and to redistribute income in accordance with political dictates. The discharge of even such a minimum level of governmental function would, however, require a sizeable administrative bureaucracy enjoying considerable discretion.

Moreover, even if we limit our perspective to administrative regulation of private business conduct other than anticompetitive practices, sound analysis would not support wholesale abolition.[12] What is required in each particular case is a detailed assessment of the likely imperfections of given markets as contrasted with the operation of regulatory or promotional regimes. While some such studies have made a persuasive case for deregulation in fields such as price control of natural gas production, it is doubtful that one can generalize from these cases to other areas of regulation.

There are many categories of cases where administrative regulation seems clearly warranted by considerations of allocational efficiency. For example, some administrative control of bona fide natural monopolies seems inescapable. Collectively managed controls may also be necessary to deal effectively with many types of economic externalities. While the problems of air and water pollution might theoretically be dealt with entirely through private liability rules administered by the courts, the difficulties and drawbacks involved in implementing such a scheme[13] have led responsible observers to endorse centralized and specialized administrative direction as an essential element in dealing with the problems of environmental degradation. And in a complex industrial society permeated by technological changes with significant second and third order consequences, one may responsibly come to the same judgment in many other fields.

A second category of cases, such as FCC control over entry and programming in broadcasting, presents a less compelling, but still respectable, case for regulation. The finite nature of the radiomagnetic spectrum and the problem of broadcast interference call for some system of allocating frequencies. However, a program of regulation through licensure, directed in part at program content, is not inevitable. Periodic auctions of broadcast licenses, or the creation of transferable property rights in the spectrum, are allocational alternatives that might better serve existing viewer tastes without the troublesome prospect of governmental control over program content. But there are countervailing considerations. The preference-shaping impact of television on audiences, especially children, may afford a ground for governmental regulation based on considerations independent of allocational efficiency. The limited number of channels may generate a "bunching" effect, concentrating programming content into areas desired by large groups with congruent interests, leaving significant segments of the population without service.

Moreover, the "fairness doctrine" implicates larger social concerns that might not necessarily be served adequately by alternatives to regulation. The choice between regulation and alternatives geared to market mechanisms is thus fairly debatable, as it may often be where the activity in question has significant preference-shaping or distributional effects.

In a third category of cases, the arguments for deregulation are compelling. Entry and pricing controls for motor carriers and, to a lesser degree, transportation in general are good examples. But in such cases the capacity of the judiciary to facilitate the adoption of sounder policies may be limited. To be sure, the judges could and should construe more narrowly the margins of regulatory authority where the case for its further extension is doubtful, but legislative actions will be required to accomplish any major degree of deregulation. Those groups benefiting from regulatory regimes that limit competition have a strong vested interest in continuing the status quo and may often be more vocal and better organized than the more diffuse interests that may benefit from abolition. The agency marked for extinction will fight abolition relentlessly. Accordingly, even in those cases where analysis supports deregulation, prudence may sometimes dictate a "second best" solution of rendering more tolerable the exercise of a degree of administrative discretion that ought ideally to be abolished.

In addition to the economic argument for deregulation, it has been asserted that substituting the private market for administrative regulation would advance private autonomy by replacing official discretion with the impersonal rules of market exchange.[14] But this libertarian argument for deregulation likewise does not justify wholesale dismantling of our administrative apparatus. Whatever the abstract appeal of such arguments, deregulation may in practice merely lead to a transfer of discretionary power over policy from administrative agencies to large and highly organized private interest groups. In a world characterized by concentrations of economic and social power, a regime of private ordering may simply mirror disparities between organized and unorganized interests, and a measure of administrative intervention may therefore be necessary to counterbalance such disparities. The imperfections of the private market are not always the lesser of two evils. Deregulation, while an important principle, is not a universal prescription.

B. Reviving the Doctrine Against Delegation   A second potential solution to the problem of administrative discretion would be more precise legislative formulation of directives to agencies. If the legislature were to specify in detail the policies to be followed by administrators, the traditional model would operate to reduce the effective range of administrative discretion. Choice among competing interests and social values would be exercised by the presumptively most responsive governmental body rather than by nonelected bureaucrats.

The nondelegation doctrine grows out of the contract notion of government based on consent, and is premised on the belief that discretionary power is, in effect, political power which must be limited to the politically responsible organs of government. Responsible administrative decisionmaking, therefore, can only be ensured by precise legislative directives. These considerations, together with dissatisfaction over the discretionary policy choices made by administrators, have recently led commentators, including Professor Theodore Lowi and Judge Skelly Wright, to advocate vigorous judicial enforcement of the nondelegation doctrine to prohibit broad legislative delegations to agencies.[15] Professor Lowi, for example, calls for judicial extension of "the still valid but universally disregarded *Schechter* rule" to declare "invalid as unconstitutional any delegation of power to an administrative agency that is not accompanied by clear standards of implementation."

While the courts might in some cases more carefully limit broad legislative delegations through statutory construction, any large-scale enforcement of the nondelegation doctrine would clearly be unwise. Detailed legislative specification of policies under contemporary conditions would be neither feasible nor desirable in many cases, and the judges are ill-equipped to distinguish contrary cases.

In many government endeavors it may be impossible in the nature of the subject matter to specify with particularity the course to be followed. This is most obvious when a new field of regulation is undertaken. Administration is an exercise in experiment. If the subject is politically and economically volatile—such as wage and price regulation—constant changes in the basic parameters of the problem may preclude the development of a detailed policy that can consistently be pursued for any length of time. These limitations are likely to be encountered with increasing frequency as the federal government assumes greater responsibility for managing the economy.

In addition, there appear to be serious institutional constraints on Congress' ability to specify regulatory policy in meaningful detail. Legislative majorities typically represent coalitions of interests that must not only compromise among themselves but also with opponents. Individual politicians often find far more to be lost than gained in taking a readily identifiable stand on a controversial issue of social or economic policy. Detailed legislative specification of policy would require intensive and continuous investigation, decision, and revision of specialized and complex issues. Such a task would require resources that Congress has, in most instances, been unable or unwilling to muster. An across-the-board effort to legislate in detail would also require a degree of decentralized responsibility that might further erode an already weak political accountability for congressional decisions.[16] These circumstances tend powerfully to promote broad delegations of authority to administrative agencies. Moreover, quite apart from these factors, one may question whether a legislature is likely in many instances to generate more responsible decisions on questions of policy than agencies.[17]

Finally, there are serious problems in relying upon the judiciary to enforce the nondelegation doctrine. A court may not properly insist on a greater legislative specification of policy than the subject matter admits of. But how is the judge to decide the degree of policy specification that is possible, for example, in wage and price regulation when it is initially undertaken? How does he decide when knowledge has accumulated to the point where additional legislative specification of policy is now possible? What if the political situation is such that the legislative process cannot be made to yield any more detailed policy resolution? How does the judge differentiate such cases from those where the legislature is avoiding its "proper" responsibilities?[18] Such judgments are necessarily quite subjective, and a doctrine that made them determinative of an administrative program's legitimacy could cripple the program by exposing it to continuing threats of invalidation and encouraging the utmost recalcitrance by those opposed to its effectuation. Given such subjective standards, and the controversial character of decisions on whether to invalidate legislative delegations, such decisions will almost inevitably appear partisan, and might often be so.

This is not to deny the possibility of a more modestly conceived judicial role in policing legislative delegation of discretionary choices to agencies. Courts have applied policies of clear statement to construe narrowly statutory delegations that infringe important individual interests. Were policies of clear statement applied in the context of economic and social administration, Congress would at least have to take a fresh look at the agency's mandate before its powers were extended.[19] Accordingly, a policy of narrow construction of statutory delegations might usefully be followed,[20] but adoption of such a policy would hardly represent the large-scale revival of the nondelegation doctrine envisaged by Professor Lowi and Judge Wright. Obtaining greater specificity in regulatory statutes is essentially a political problem, and even if judges were to hazard a more venturesome approach, any remotely tolerable application of the nondelegation doctrine would be limited to gross instances of legislative irresponsibility. As Professor Lowi himself admits, a very substantial residuum of discretion would remain.

C. Structuring Administrative Discretion   A third possible response to the problems created by broad legislative delegation is to acknowledge the large discretion enjoyed by agencies and to require that it be exercised in accordance with consistently applied general rules. This alternative is responsive to the ideal of formal justice: that government interference with important private interests be permitted only accordance with rules known in advance and impartially applied. *"La liberté consiste a ne dependre que des lois."*

By eliminating ad hoc official discretion, formal justice enables individuals to adjust their own conduct to avoid sanctions or to treat with the government on terms they regard as the most advantageous. Substituting general rules for ad hoc decision also tends to ensure that officials will act on the basis of societal considerations embodied in those rules rather than on their own preferences or prejudices, and increases the likelihood that the contents of the policies applied will be consistent with the preferences of a greater number of citizens. All of these effects taken together promote a general sense of individual and social security.

To the extent that agencies exercise uncontrolled discretion, there is an absence of formal justice. The traditional model of administrative law seeks to promote formal justice by requiring that agency action conform to legislative directives. Where the applicable statutes are vague or ambiguous, or grant broad powers to the agency, however, the protections and sense of formal justice provided by the traditional model may be rendered largely illusory. In response to this problem Professor Davis has argued that the dangers posed by broad statutes can to a large extent be avoided if courts require agencies themselves to adopt rules that narrow discretion. This proposal seeks to reconcile the need for (as well as the inevitability of) generous delegations of power to the agencies with the desire for predictability and consistency in governmental policies. However, Professor Davis also recognizes that the value of formal justice may frequently be outweighed by the need for flexible and effective administration. Since rules of varying degrees of specificity may impose different levels of restraint on discretion, he asserts that the ultimate objective is "to locate the optimum degree of structuring in each respect for each discretionary power." In order to reach this goal, Professor Davis contends that the courts must in each case "determine what discretionary power is necessary and what is unnecessary."

This test might, however, leave a good deal of residual discretion in the very areas where its exercise has occasioned concern. More seriously, it would place an impossible burden on the courts. The difficulties in judicial enforcement of such a standard are closely analogous to those presented by the doctrine against delegation of legislative power that Professor Davis so roundly criticizes. When an agency resists adoption of any rule, or declines to make a vague rule more specific, how is the judge to determine whether its position is justified? The field in question and the state of relevant knowledge may not permit a more specific rule. The political situation may be too mixed or fluid to allow a firm policy to crystallize. Moreover, the formulation of meaningful rules may require a considerable expenditure of agency resources that might be better utilized elsewhere. In light of these considerations, the degree of specificity in a rule must ordinarily be determined by the agency.

Courts may properly seek to promote the purposes of formal justice by demanding more complete articulation of the grounds for agency action, whether accomplished through rulemaking or adjudication, and should police the agencies' choice between rulemaking and adjudication for abuse of discretion. But the notion that judges can and should attempt to "locate the optimum degree of structuring in each respect for each discretionary power" is unrealistic and unwise. Since judges would often lack the facts or experience necessary to ascertain the extent of agency ability to specify policy in greater detail, such a standard would largely turn on subjective judgments, and would pose a debilitating threat to agency programs which could chill needed policy initiatives.

Even if it were possible to constrain agency action by rules so that formal justice would be achieved, the implementation of such a program could not in itself solve the problem of asserted bias in agencies' discretionary policy choices. Formal justice merely dictates the manner in which discretion is exercised, not its substance, and is indifferent to the wisdom, fairness, or efficacy of the policy chosen. But much contemporary criticism of administrative discretion is directed precisely at the content of administrative policy. Concededly, formal justice may indirectly affect policy outcomes. Stiffened requirements of formal justice may weaken agency effectiveness by draining resources and affording opponents new litigating weapons. Requiring agency policy to be crystallized in a rule rather than camouflaged in a series of case-by-case rationalizations may promote more careful decisions and facilitate public and legislative supervision. But the magnitude of these latter effects is subject to question. Many agency opinions still read as exercises in rationalization. Widely scattered, unorganized individuals with a minute stake in agency policy are unlikely to be galvanized into fighting units by a somewhat clearer exposition of those policies. Experience under the National Environmental Policy Act (NEPA) suggests, for example, that the beneficial impact on agency policy of procedural adjustments may be quite marginal. Professor Joseph Sax has gone so far as to assert that:

> I know of no solid evidence to support the belief that requiring articulation, detailed findings or reasoned opinions enhances the integrity or propriety of administrative decisions. I think the emphasis on the redemptive quality of procedural reform is about nine parts myth and one part coconut oil.

This is too extreme. A requirement that agencies articulate and consistently pursue policy choices may have only a modest effect on outcomes, but it can serve as a useful, selective judicial tool to force agency reconsideration of questionable decisions and to direct attention to factors that may have been disregarded. A "total" program of "structuring" every facet of agency discretion would not, however, be worth the price. Moreover, while formal justice is valuable for its own sake, it is alone not an adequate solution to the problem of agency discretion.

D. Substantive Rules for Agency Discretion   The "expertise" rationale for agency discretion is based on the supposition that the administrator's task is to realize a discernible goal—for example, the economic health of a given industry—and that objective rules to achieve the goal can be discovered and implemented. However, the very difficulty that gives rise to the most serious contemporary issues regarding administrative discretion is the absence of agreement on any such single overriding goal. The dominant view is that administrative goals are (or should be) mixed or that, in the absence of any general consensus on a single goal, they must be accepted as mixed. Administration is therefore a process of accommodating various competing social interests.

Despite this problem—indeed, in large part because of it—economic analysis has frequently been advocated as a source of substantive rules for determining administrative policy. Under this theory, the goal of administration is the maximization of the output of goods and services in the economy. This goal is to be implemented through agency rules which mimic, insofar as possible, the allocation of goods and services that would be produced in a perfectly competitive economic market. Since the conditions for allocative optimization are assertedly knowable, agency performance can be measured and controlled by its conformity with the requirements of economic efficiency. Mimicry of the market is, nonetheless, a solution to agency discretion that is procedural in principle since the market itself is a procedural solution to the problem of allocating goods and services. Such a solution has merit in some contexts; however, a requirement that administrators seek to maximize allocational efficiency falls short of providing a complete solution to the problem of agency discretion for a number of reasons.

First. Because applied economics is an art that requires discretionary judgments to be made in selecting the proper universe for analysis, defining and measuring the relevant variables, and resolving the complications of second, third, and fourth order effects generated by possible policy choices, no single policy solution will generally be indicated to be clearly correct.[21] More frequently, there will be respectable economic arguments for a number of quite different alternatives. Even in the case of entry and price regulation in natural monopoly industries, where the market analogue is most readily apparent and applicable, these discretionary elements are many. The indeterminacy becomes far more acute in fields of regulation, such as those relating to environmental quality, that are more remote from market analogues. Therefore, although economic analysis is undoubtedly a powerful and useful tool for assessing administrative policy choices, a rule requiring administrators to select policies which will secure allocational efficiency will, in practice, leave administrators considerable discretion.

In addition, there may be serious distortions in the process of reducing a wide range of economic and social impacts to the quantifiable terms that are necessary in order to apply the yardstick of allocational efficiency. The very process of quantification may import systematic bias through a tendency to "dwarf soft variables." The values in question—such as environmental and aesthetic amenities or human life and health—may lack market analogues. Surrogate measures for such values are normally tied to "hard" indices that have their own "dwarfing" potential, and may obscure features such as the sense of community in a neighborhood threatened by large-scale development. It may be possible to enrich our methods of analysis to meet these difficulties, but a considerable degree of tunnel vision may be inevitable given the fact that methods of administrative decision must be fitted to the capacities of ordinary men.

Second. Economic analysis normally assumes that choices among alternatives are to be made by reference to the population's existing preferences for goods and services. These preferences are normally assumed to be fixed; however, our present choices among goods and services will affect our future preferences because tastes and values are shaped by experience. Preference-shaping effects are often minimal in private consumption choices, but they may be significant for governmental decisions because of the large absolute amount of resources which may be affected, their pervasive long-term character, and the fact that the process of choice is collective rather than individual. These characteristics, together with the efforts of affected agency and client interests to maintain and expand programs once initiated, often invest governmental programs with a self-generating, self-fulfilling dynamic.

These dynamic characteristics pose serious problems for proposals that agency policies be selected through economic analysis. Uncertainty is created as to whether the choices should be based on existing preferences or the alternative sets of future preferences that would be generated by other policies that might be chosen. Because policy choice may affect preferences, administrators must at least address the question of whether policy choices should be based on individuals' actual preferences at any given time, or whether such preferences should be discounted, in order to give weight either to the preferences individuals might develop if they were well-informed, or to normative judgments that certain preferences should be encouraged or discouraged. [22]

It is far from obvious that government policies should in principle be addressed solely to "consumers' " existing preferences. Congress in practice—and often in disregard of the advice of proponents of the economic allocation model[23]—frequently adopts policies, such as making transfer payments in kind (food stamps, housing) rather than in cash, that seem implicitly to reject the criterion of maximizing the satisfaction of existing preferences.[24] Whether these policies reflect a conclusion that existing choices will be made in ignorance, or the more "paternalistic" position that the collectivity can dictate the use of transfer payments as it sees fit, they suggest that Congress would not regard allocational efficiency as an invariably correct or appropraite principle of policy choice. Moreover, putting congressional judgments to one side, it is hardly self-evident that only existing preferences should "count." Economic analysis cannot ultimately resolve the question of which preferences to encourage or discourage, ignore or implement; but issues of just this sort are at the heart of many governmental choices.

Third. Economic analysis is unable to deal with distributional considerations, both because there is no economic criterion for "correct" wealth distribution and because "there is no objective basis for balancing . . . distributive benefits against allocative costs." Often it is simply assumed that the initial distribution of income is optimal and that any changes in distribution occasioned by the attainment of allocational efficiency will be costlessly corrected by other means, such as transfer payments authorized by the legislature, or that, given a series of administrative decisions, such changes will tend to cancel out.

These assumptions may be highly unrealistic. The initial distribution of income may be far from "optimal," and reform of the tax structure in response to changes in actual distribution or changes in view about fair distribution often comes slowly and in gross. It cannot be assumed that changes in the initial distribution resulting from administrative decision will inevitably cancel out or be corrected by legislative action. Quite apart from limitations in congressional resources, a centralized system for redressing the cumulative distributional effects of many individual administrative decisions might prove unworkable because such effects are often interstitial and not easily quantified. In many cases, therefore, administrators must deal with the distributional consequences of agency decisions or no one will.

Moreover, discussion by economists of questions of distributional equity and their relation to allocational efficiency has typically been framed in terms of the aggregate distribution of income; analysis developed in such a global perspective may, however, be of little assistance where distributional effects must be considered in the context of numerous, uncoordinated administrative decisions. The possibility of developing distributional weights that could be utilized in the context of uncoordinated decisions has been explored, but such proposals have serious flaws and the whole concept has been sharply criticized.

Additionally, economists' analyses of distributional issues are often of little help in the context of administrative decisions because such analyses are typically framed in terms of distribution among all individuals in society ranked vertically according to net income or wealth, and ignore other distributional axes—horizontal, geographical, or temporal—that have great importance in the administrative context. Moreover, considerations of justice may dictate distribution to each individual of a minimum amount of some specified commodities, such as healthful air or assistance in the defense of criminal litigation. These considerations suggest that the question of distributional equity is far more complex than many economists have allowed, exacerbating the problem of resolving conflicts between allocational efficiency and distributional equity.

The inability of economic analysis to resolve distributional issues is especially pertinent in the case of discretion exercised by agencies whose mission is creating a more equitable distribution of scarce resources, such as public housing. The government statute may provide little guidance when, as is often the case, the demand for such resources exceeds the supply. It would plainly be contrary to the basic purposes of the public housing program, however, to apply market principles to deal with housing scarcity. No simple alternative principle, such as priority of application, income, number of children, or racial balance is obviously compelling. In these circumstances, economic analysis may provide some assistance in understanding the consequences of alternative choices for housing markets, but it cannot resolve the basic decisional problem.

Fourth. Economic analysis appears unable to accommodate process values. Decision is a function of a centralized decision-maker's measurement of alternative outcomes. No direct participation in the process of decision by those affected is required; indeed, the political tug and pull arising from participation might well threaten the impartiality and rationality of the decisional process. Yet administrative decisionmaking is sharply criticized as remote, impersonal, and unresponsive to the concerns of those affected. Some mechanism for broader participation, direct or representative, may accordingly be desirable in order to enhance the public acceptability of resulting policies and foster that sense of involvement in, and responsibility for, government which is itself a good.

The significance of these limitations in economic analysis will vary considerably from case to case, depending on the nature of the governmental functions involved and the importance of relevant considerations other than allocational efficiency. One might conceive of a spectrum of agency activities arranged in terms of the primacy of allocational efficiency as an appropriate goal of decision. One extreme category would include the regulation of natural monopolies or concentrated oligopolies, where the fundamental goal ought to be allocational efficiency. Market factors or their analogues may be developed as the basis for decision with relative ease and the shaping of consumer preferences and distributional factors may be disregarded to the same extent as essentially similar problems in standard competitive markets. To the extent that departures from allocational efficiency are sought—as in the case of air fare cross-subsidies to underwrite service to small towns—one can pinpoint net economic costs and force hard consideration of the justification of, for example, forcing long haul passengers to subsidize such short haul passengers. It is just this sort of exacting scrutiny which is sorely needed in many regulatory contexts.

A middle category would include fields less analogous to private markets—for example, environmental protection or food and drug regulation—where distributional and preference shaping issues have greater importance, the limitations of economic analysis may be more apparent, and the impetus for some process of representation of affected interests more urgent. Economic analysis may, however, be extremely useful in underscoring the relevance of allocational efficiency and the costs of departures from it, and in identifying the least expensive way to achieve given goals.

The other polar category would encompass the distribution of scarce "welfare" resources, such as public housing, in which allocational efficiency is unlikely to play more than a subsidiary role, and a quasi-political process of decision may be more appropriate.

But even if we consider only those administrative decisions where considerations of allocational efficiency should predominate, we are still faced with a problem of implementation. Experience suggests that Congress is unlikely to replace broad agency delegations with a specific command to maximize allocational efficiency. The suggestion that agencies would pursue more economically efficient policies if economists were appointed as commissioners may be somewhat naive when one considers the prevalence of economic experts on both sides of many major regulatory and antitrust controversies, the fact that possession of a professional degree is not a guarantee of excellence, and the importance of other factors in agency decisions. Reliance on reviewing courts to promote greater allocational efficiency in agency policies likewise appears misplaced.

Specialized advocacy is a potential, albeit incomplete, answer to these difficulties. The creation of a specialized, high-level government advocate to provide agencies with sound economic analysis in selected cases has been suggested. Such advocacy might be justified as necessary to ensure representation of the diffuse interests of those individuals who would gain from the adoption of allocationally efficient policies. But if allocational efficiency is not accepted as the sole criterion of agency policy, should not other diffuse interests also enjoy representation? The principle of advocacy for the unrepresented is not easily confined, and a system of representation for a broad range of affected interests may be inimical to the adoption of efficient policies.

The principle of allocational efficiency thus displays both theoretical and practical infirmities, and fails to provide an all-embracing solution to problems of agency choice. Even if there is no single generally appropriate principle for agency decisionmaking (and no other single principle can match allocational efficiency in power and generality), it is nonetheless conceivable that a "correct" mix of values and corresponding decisional rules could be identified for each discrete field of government administration. Even if such rules existed, they would not be obvious from the statute or *ex hypothesi* there would be no problem of discretion. In such circumstances, one might doubt the ability of judges to divine such rules or their willingness to enforce them against the agencies. Instead, one would be remitted to faith in the specialized experience of administrators to discover and implement the "correct" rules; but this is the very faith of which we have become disabused.

Notes

1. Commentators have stressed the textual basis in Article I of the Constitution for the doctrine against delegation. See T. Cooley, *A Treatise on the Constitutional Limitations Which Rest upon the Legislative Power of the State of the American Union* 116–17 (1868). However, once it is acknowledged that some delegations of legislative power are permissible, see, e.g., American Trucking Ass'ns, Inc. v. United States, 344 U.S. 298, 309–12 (1953), the textual argument is substantially less useful as a guide to decision.

2. It may be argued that the legislature has agreed to accord an agency discretion, and therefore the members of society have consented to the agency's exercise of discretion. But to speak of legislative "agreement" may be misleading; broad delegation is more often a function of political standoff or legislative incapacity. More fundamentally, the process and results of decisionmaking may differ significantly between the agency and the legislature. Thus consent to a legislative resolution of disputed questions of social policy does not fairly imply consent to the remission of such questions to

the legislature's agency. See E. Freund, *Administrative Powers over Persons and Property* 220–21 (1928).

3. See J. Rawls, A *Theory of Justice* 7–22, 118–83 (1971); J.-J. Rousseau, *The Social Contract*, Book I, chs. V, VI. Private autonomy may thus be defined as individual freedom of choice constrained only by rule-governed sanctions authorized through procedures to which an individual would consent. See J. Locke, *The Two Treatises of Government*, Book II § 22 (P. Laslett ed. 1960). *See also Kennedy, "Legal Formality," 2. J. Legal Stud. 351 (1973). In addition to facilitating an* individual's calculated satisfaction of his various interests, freedom from constraints other than those imposed through procedures to which one would consent may be viewed as a good in itself.

4. Requirements (such as a hearing on the record) designed to promote accurate agency application of legislative directives will also facilitate judicial review, but reviewing courts have imposed on agencies additional requirements—such as detailed findings—for the explicit purpose of facilitating judicial review.

5. Discretion has two sources. First, the legislature may endow an agency with plenary responsibilities in a given area and plainly indicate that within that area its range of choice is entirely free. Second, the legislature may issue directives that are intended to control the agency's choice among alternatives but that, because of their generality, ambiguity, or vagueness, do not clearly determine choices in particular cases.

There is a third possible source of discretion, namely legislative preclusion of judicial review of agency action. However, where the legislature has laid down directives for agency action, it has presumably intended that the agency follow such directives. Governmental officials are not free to disregard the law simply because judicial enforcement mechanisms are not available. See Dworkin, "The Model of Rules," 35 *U. Chi. L. Rev.* 14, 32–34 (1967). Some writers on administrative law unfortunately do not distinguish the question of the lawful scope of administrative discretion from the question of the administrator's de facto freedom of choice. See, e.g., K. David, *Discretionary Justice* 4 (1969).

6. Two basic types of directives may be distinguished: rules and goals. See R. Unger, *Knowledge and Politics* (1975); M. Weber, *On Law in Economy and Society* (Rheinstein ed., 1954), at xl-xlii; Kennedy, supra note 3. A rule directs agency disposition of some classes of cases without resort to intermediate premises. See, e.g., Addion v. Holly Hill Fruit Prods., Inc., 322 U.S. 607 (1944). A goal provides that a given condition is to be obtained or value maximized. In order to decide a particular case, it is necessary to know the likely effects of the various alternatives on the realization of the goal specified and make a prudential judgment as to which alternative is best calculated to achieve the designated objective. See, e.g., Federal Aviation Act of 1958, § 102(f), 49, U.S.C. § 1302(f) (1970) (development of civil aeronautics). There are mixed cases, of course, as where a rule is applied by reference to some presumed goal it is to serve. See, e.g., Board of Governors v. Agnew, 329 U.S. 441 (1947). See also Kennedy, supra note 3.

7. For a brief history of the idea that public administrations is an apolitical science, see M. Vile, *Constitutionalism and the Separation of Powers* (1967), at 277–80. See also authorities cited in Freedman, "Crisis and Legitimacy in the Administrative Process," 27 *Stan. L. Rev.* 1041, 1057 n.74 (1975).

8. The agency's articulation of reasons may, however, be an essential prelude to a reviewing court's determination that the choice made is so plainly unreasonable on the particular facts as to constitute an abuse of discretion. Citizens Ass'n of Georgetown, Inc. v. Zoning Comm'n, 477 F.2d 402, 408 (D.C. Cir. 1973); Environmental Defense Fund, Inc. v. Ruckelshaus, 439 F.2d 584, 596–98 (D.C. Cir. 1971). Invalidation of agency action as an abuse of discretion should itself be viewed as part of the court's central function of confining agency action within the bounds of legislative directives, for it is logical to imply in a legislative delegation of discretion a directive that it be rationally exercised.

9. A concern that administrative intrusions on private interests be explicitly authorized through the consensual mechanism of the legislature underlies both the clear statement requirement and the doctrine against delegation. The clear statement technique could be thought of as operating on a sliding scale: the more vital the individual liberty infringed, the more explicit must be the expression of consent.

10. There will be numerous sets of commodities with varying proportions of particular goods and services which meet this condition. The particular set produced will reflect consumer preferences as expressed through purchases within existing market structures and the existing distribution of income. Deregulation, which will change the market structure in which goods are traded, is thus likely to have interacting allocational and distributional effects.

11. Administrative limitations on entry and prices are most frequently attacked as inefficient economically. See, e.g., The President's Advisory Council on Executive Organization, A *New Regulatory Framework: Report on Selected Independent Regulatory Agencies* (1971). But cf. Kitch, Isaacson & Kasper, "The Regulation of Taxicabs in Chicago," 14 *J. Law & Econ.* 285 (1971). It has also been argued that health and safety regulation may impair economic efficiency. See Peltzman "An Evaluation of Consumer Protection Legislation: The 1962 Drug Amendments," 81 *J. Pol. Econ.* 1049, 1068–90 (1973). But see Green & Moore, "Winter's Discontent: Market Failure and Consumer Welfare," 82 *Yale L. J.* 903, 904 n.4 (1973).

12. Some advocates of deregulation would abolish selected agency functions while actually extending others. For example, in Green & Nader, "Economic Regulation vs. Competition: Uncle Sam the Monopoly Man," 82 *Yale L. J.* (1973), the authors propose to abolish, or at least greatly curtail, the scope of administrative regulation over entry and pricing in particular sectors (such as transportation) but advocate expanded regulation in such areas as consumer protection, occupational health and safety, and the environment. As Professor Winter correctly points out, there is no a priori line dividing malign market regulation from benign health and welfare regulation. Both types of regulation limit market competition, restricting the goods and services that can be offered for consumer choice. The decision whether to maintain regulation in a given field must be determined on the basis of a particularized assessment of the likely gains from regulation versus the probable losses from restricting competition, and cannot be made by assuming that certain broad categories of regulation are inevitably beneficial or malign.

13. Some of the more obvious difficulties with exclusive reliance on private liability rules are as follows: (A) the diffuse nature of the harm caused and the operation of the free rider effect may result in an absence of adequate incentives for the invocation of private liability rules; (B) judicially applied liability rules may not be effective in dealing with degradation caused by the interplay of effects resulting from the conduct of many actors; (C) judicial remedies may not provide adequate prophylaxsis against future degradation, particularly where long term, highly diffused effects are involved or where planning activities such as land use zoning are required; (D) specialized knowledge may be required; (E) differing applications by judges and juries of liability rules may have distorting effects on competition; (F) it may be difficult to secure adequate representation of the interests of future generations. See generally J. Krier, *Environmental Law and Policy* 221–23 (1971). But cf. R. Nozick, *Anarchy, State and Utopia* 79–81 (1974) (suggesting the use of protective associations to allow collective action to surmount the need for administrative control).

14. See F. von Hayek, *The Constitution of Liberty* 12–13 (1960). Compare R. Nozick, supra, at 149-294. The private market may be seen not only as the most perfect regime of liberty (as defined by Hayek) but also as a perfect system of decisional representation, in that each individual's preferences are automatically translated into effective demands on appropriate resources. However, under this system an individual's preferences are effectively weighted by the wealth at his command. In practice, actual regimes of private ordering have produced substantial differences in wealth and other differences in bargaining power that may distort the effect of asserted "impersonal" rules and lead to domination of some groups by others. See Kennedy, supra note 3, at 377–91 (discussing implications for the legal system).

15. See T. Lowi, *The End of Liberalism* 297–98 (1969). Judge Wright believes that the revival of the nondelegation doctrine would be an important step in controlling agency discretion, although he recognizes the difficulty in developing workable criteria to differentiate between permissible and impermissible delegations. Other critics, such as Judge Friendly, assert the desirability of more specific legislative directives to agencies, but are quite vague as to how this goal is to be accomplished. Judge Friendly seems to rest on the hope that the legislature can be expected to respond to exhortations by judges, commentators, and the public to give greater direction to policy delegations. But in view of the limited legislative capacity or incentive for specific delegation,

exhortation appears hardly to be sufficient. At the other extreme, Professor Davis takes the view that it is both unrealistic and unnecessary to expect greater specification of policy from the legislature.

16. The same basic criticisms apply to proposals for a greatly strengthened oversight role for Congress. The legislature lacks the resources to discharge such a role. Even if such resources were provided, there would necessarily be an effective delegation of authority that would raise troubling questions about the political responsibility of oversight decisions. Indeed, such questions already exist concerning the limited oversight role Congress presently assumes. While there are examples of effective and politically responsible congressional oversight, there are perhaps an equal or greater number of contrary examples. And the same basic difficulties attend proposals to strengthen Congress' control over the exercise of administrative discretion that require administrative regulations to be laid before the legislature for approval or disapproval or provide for a veto of agency action by legislative action short of enacting a statute. See authorities discussed in W. Gellhorn & C. Byse, *Administrative Law: Cases and Comments* 122–27 (6th ed. 1974). All of these proposals suffer from the defect of assuming that Congress can responsibly accomplish through other means what it cannot achieve through legislation.

17. That legislative specification of policy is no guarantee of wisdom is indicated by criticism of the detailed provisions of the 1970 Clean Air Amendments. See Jacoby & Steinbruner, "Salvaging the Federal Attempt to Control Auto Pollution," 21 *Public Policy* 1 (1973). Moreover, while administrative agencies have been criticized as unduly responsive to wealth and to organized interests, see T. Lowi, supra note 15, at 87–89, such criticisms might equally be applied to the legislature, see Sofaer, "Judicial Control of Informal Discretionary Adjudication and Enforcement," 72 *Colum. L. Rev.* 1293, 1306 & n.63 (1972) (instances of "farsighted" agency action blocked by "Congress acting in the service of special interests"); cf. E. Freund, note 2, at 221–22 (suggesting that whether the legislature is actually a more responsive or safer respository of regulatory power than administrative agencies must be a matter of pure speculation).

18. Even where seemingly precise standards are provided, the translation of such standards into operational realities may involve such large measures of discretion that their practical effect in retraining agency choice may be extremly limited. See, e.g., Yakus v. United States, 321 U.S. 414 (1944); United States v. Rock Royal Co-op., Inc., 307 U.S. 533 (1939).

19. Inertia and limitations in resources might preclude meaningful congressional reassessment in every case where agency authority is narrowly construed, but given current criticism of agencies' performances, such a consequence may be beneficial in many, perhaps most, cases.

20. Unfortunately, courts often do just the opposite, broadly construing administrative powers in cases where the justification for broadened powers is dubious. However, National Cable Television Ass'n, Inc. v. United States, 415 U.S. 336 (1974), gives some indication of judicial willingness to force legislative reconsideration of broad delegating statutes by applying a narrowing construction to them.

21. In response it may be argued that the degree of refinement in the analysis need not be pushed beyond the point where the costs of the analysis threaten to exceed its likely benefits. But such a procedure would underscore the importance of (debatable) simplifying assumptions, and introduces an increased degree of uncertainty and possible error in the results. However, the problem of complexity may be equally present in any other model for decisionmaking where the model remains that of the single rational decisionmaker.

22. It might be argued that while governmental policy choices may indeed have an effect on preferences, administrators should disregard such effects in making their decisions. Not only are such effects difficult to gauge, but the very lack of consensus on goals that gives rise to the problem of agency discretion in policy choices and provokes resort to the economic model may mean that administrators will lack any manageable criteria for dealing with such effects. In these circumstances it may be the better part of valor to mimic the competitive market by defining allocation efficiency in terms of present preferences. However, the problems generated by preference-shaping effects are sufficiently important to deserve thoughtful exploration.

23. See, e.g., M. Friedman, *Capitalism and Freedom* 178–79, 191–92 (1962).

24. If the achievement of allocational efficiency by reference to the present preferences of transfer payment recipients were the sole criterion, transfer payments should not be made through,

for example, food stamps, because recipients might prefer to utilize equivalent cash payments to obtain commodities other than food. Economic analysis may enable us to approximate the loss in consumer satisfaction, given existing preferences, among those who would rather spend additional income on commodities other than food. However, it cannot tell us whether we should encourage a choice in consumption preferences for food either on grounds of outright paternalism or by way of compensating for imperfect information on the part of consumers.

Flagellating the Federal Bureaucracy

MORRIS P. FIORINA

Taken as an aggregate, the Federal Government and its bureaucracies constitute an imposing—and some would say oppressive—whole. An infinite number of examples of government inefficiency and waste are readily available to politicians who "run against the government" while attempting to be elected a part of it. But the bottom line always remains: constituencies and costs. Bureaucracies are created and maintained through specific sets of interests: one person's "over-regulation" is another's "vital interest." In short, while it may be easy to say that the whole of the bureaucratic apparatus is too expensive and too burdensome, the political reality is that the parts are likely to have active constituencies working on their behalf. In this essay, Morris P. Fiorina outlines the major theories of bureaucratic development and sketches the broad form of the byzantine interconnections between Congress, constituencies, and government agencies.

Only a decade ago, flagellating the federal bureaucracy was primarily a conservative Republican solidarity rite. Today, representatives of every political persuasion are fighting over the whip. In the mid-1960s the country elected a Democratic president committed to a federally built Great Society. In the mid-1970s the country elected a Democratic president who claimed that he was not then nor had he ever been a part of the federal establishment. In 1980 the citizenry rejected that Democratic president in favor of a Republican who explicitly promised to get government off their backs.

Political leadership in the United States usually reduces to the ability to discern which way the tide is flowing and avoid inundation by it. The Republican party of 1980 found itself well situated to catch the wave, though we may debate whether this reflects Republican acumen—even persuasion—or merely forty-odd years of political habit. Meanwhile, some Democrats paddle furiously to overtake the crest (e.g., Senator Paul Tsongas), while others tread the backwater in the hope that the tide will soon reverse (e.g., Senator Edward Kennedy). The waves have been forming for some time, but we should be cautious in attempting to pinpoint their source. For every rightward trend on public-opinion data, there exist seemingly related data which show no trend or even a touch of leftward movement. There is little evidence of any general conservative mandate—the American people are not in the habit of granting mandates, they lean more towards probation. And a realigning election? There have been two or three in American history, but those who dwell on such things should reread "The Boy Who Cried Wolf."

What public opinion data over the past two decades do show is a rather steady and large-scale disillusionment with the operation of American government. There is little or

Published by permission of Transaction, Inc., from *Society*, Vol. 20, No. 3, pp. 66-74 (with deletions). Copyright © 1983 by Transaction, Inc.

no desire to eliminate major federal commitments (with the exception of foreign aid). Nor does the public massively reject government regulation. What the public has increasingly come to reject is the manner in which programs are designed, implemented, and administered. For example, since 1958 the Center for Political Studies (CPS) of the University of Michigan has asked repeatedly in its election studies, "Do you think people in the government waste a lot of money we pay in taxes, waste some of it, or don't waste very much of it?" Between 1958 and 1978 the proportion of the population giving the answer "waste a lot of it" increased from a minority of 43 percent to an overwhelming majority of 77 percent. During the same period CPS has asked, "Do you feel that almost all of the people running the government are smart people who usually know what they are doing?" Over the twenty-year period the proportion of the population choosing the "don't know what they're doing" response increased from 37 to 51 percent. The literature abounds with similar indications of loss of confidence in government institutions and their operation, though not with the basic idea of a significant government role in the economy and society.

The growing unhappiness with the operation of government should come as no surprise. By any standard, government's impact on the citizen has increased significantly during the past generation. Not only does the public sector now take a considerably larger share of national income and employ a larger fraction of the work force, but the regulatory process impinges on a much broader range of ordinary activities. Other things being equal, the average citizen now has a much higher probability of experiencing a real or perceived infringement of his or her activities than was the case a generation ago. Moreover, over and above their personal experiences, citizens are deluged with information about government failures, chiefly those involving the bureaucracy. Senator William Proxmire bestows his Golden Fleece amid much fanfare, Ralph Nader and other watchdogs level their charges in press releases and at public hearings, investigative reporters publish their exposés of government wrongdoing and/or incompetence. In recent years the informed citizen would have come across the following disturbing examples of bureaucratic irresponsibility and/or excess, as well as innumerable others similar to them.

Example 1: Wasteful Bureaucrats. Every September, the last month of the federal government's fiscal year, wasteful spending prevails in government bureaucracies. In 1978, for example, the Pentagon contracted for $187,631 of construction work on a base the Army had decided to close. At approximately the same time, the Youth Conservation Corps purchased 1,000 pairs of riding chaps, 4,000 pairs of gloves, and 181 chain saws for a YCC camp with 300 enrollees. A Senate subcommittee concluded that wasteful purchases total at least $2 billion a year. Federal purchase agents often face intense pressure from their superiors to accelerate year-end spending. According to Harry Anderson, in a 1980 issue of *Newsweek*, a procurement officer with the Law Enforcement Assistance Administration, who testified that efforts to halt two especially wasteful year-end contracts were actively discouraged, subsequently found his staff cut and his office moved three times.

Example 2: Deceptive Bureaucrats. According to a 1979 article in the *Los Angeles Times*, more than 7 million people are paid with federal funds, despite the fact that official statistics place the government's civilian work force at approximately 2.9 million. Hundreds of thousands of workers in government-created agencies are excluded from the monthly statistics of the Civil Service Commission, as are millions of "outside" workers who are paid by the government under a variety of contracts and grants. In recent years officials have responded to critics of big government by maintaining that the federal work force has remained largely stable despite the rapid growth of the federal budget; in the same period, the number of state and local employees tripled as s result of the growth in federal programs.

Example 3: Disingenuous Bureaucrats. According to Alan Murray in a 1980 issue of *Congressional Quarterly Weekly Report*, bonus programs for federal employees were allowing some top-level bureaucrats to earn salaries far above the congressionally imposed ceiling of $50,112. At NASA, for example, more than half its 427 career senior executives were pushed over the pay cap with bonuses ranging from $2,000 to $20,000. All this was done in accordance with the law and government personnel regulations; Congress had authorized such bonuses in 1978, hoping to promote government productivity. "What Congress intended, apparently, was that only the crème de la crème would receive bonuses," said NASA personnel director Carl Grant, "but that is not what the law says." While Carl Grant denied that the bonus system was a way to circumvent the pay cap, Congresswomen Gladys Spellman disagreed, further charging that some bonuses were being used by high-level "cliques" that planned to distribute the annual awards among themselves in a rotating basis.

Example 4: Crooked Bureaucrats. In 1978, evidence of massive fraud and abuse—including false claims for benefits and services, collusion among contractors, and bribery of officials—in the operations of the General Services Administration were uncovered in hearings held by the Senate Governmental Affairs Federal Spending Practices Subcommittee. Bob Livernash, in the *Congressional Quarterly Weekly Report*, related that results of a study by the General Accounting Office (GAO) suggested that similar problems existed in other federal agencies; Elmer B. Staats, Comptroller General and head of the GAO, cited Justice Department estimates that up to $25 billion of the $250 billion the government spends annually in federal assistance programs may be lost through fraud or abuse.

Example 5: Paternalistic Bureaucrats. Columnist James Kilpatrick, in a 1980 issue of the *Los Angeles Times*, reported on and criticized a recently issued regulation of the Environmental Protection Agency mandating a certain level of permissible noise by compacting garbage trucks. Commented Kilpatrick, "Costs and benefits to one side, this petty, stupid, nit-picking regulation based almost entirely on gauzy conjectures as to 'sleep and activity interference' offers one more instance of a bureaucracy that has gone berserk."

Example 6: Crazy (?) Captive (?) Bureaucrats. Bruce Johansen described, in *Heavy Duty Trucking Magazine*, a case that spent over five years in litigation. Olympia and Chehalis, two towns in Washington, are 21 miles apart via interstate highway. The Interstate Commerce Commission (ICC), which regulates trucking routes and cargoes, told the Puget Sound Truck Lines that its drivers could travel between Olympia and Chehalis only through the city of Aberdeen, making the distance 120 miles, 99 more than the direct route. The route problem originated on the late 1960s after Puget Sound (licensed to carry goods between Seattle, Olympia, and Aberdeen) purchased South Bend Transfer (licensed to haul between Aberdeen, Chehalis, and Portland, Oregon). The company joined the two routes into a potentially lucrative one between two major markets, Seattle and Portland. To save time, money, and gasoline consumption, Puget Sound began using the direct route. Competing truckers, who would have had an advantage if Puget Sound had to take the wayward route, complained to the ICC and the case went to court.

After persistent exposure to reports like the preceding, it is no wonder that the average citizen thinks "a lot" of his tax money is wasted by officials who "don't know what they're doing." (Or worse yet, by officials who know exactly what they're doing—robbing him!) A critical question of our time, however, is whether that average citizen eventually comes to believe that a lot of his tax money is wasted in government activities which are *in principle* doomed to failure. The longer the stream of government failures to which the citizen is exposed, the more probable this eventuality. And while libertarians may gleefully anticipate a future era in which citizens have lost all belief in the efficacy of government action, they should consider that the alternative to the social democratic state is not necessarily the exchange economy of the optimistic individualist philosophers. Rather, the alternative instruments of resource allocation might just as well be the club and the gun of pessimistic Hobbesians.

The point of view in this article is reformist rather than revolutionary. Examples like the six presented should arouse curiosity, not outrage. Why do so many bureaucratic failures exist, and what can be done about them? The examples presented, and the myriad others which could be cited, are not simply specific manifestations of a single general phenomenon called bureaucratic failure. It is important to recognize that there are numerous varieties of bureaucratic failure, that they have different primary sources, and that they require different remedies. In particular, while the varieties illustrated in Examples 1 and 4—wasteful and crooked bureaucrats—undoubtedly cost the polity billions of dollars and are perhaps the most visible and outrageous offenders to the citizenry, they probably represent the most straightforward cases to diagnose and cure. Bureaucratic failures such as those illustrated in Examples 2, 3, 5, and 6 are undoubtedly more costly, more complex, and more difficult to deal with. For these failures are not primarily bureaucratic failures; rather, they are aspects of more general political failures. And it is these which most threaten the well-being of the country.

The concept of bureaucratic failure presumes a particular viewpoint on the part of the analyst—a public-interest, or general-interest, viewpoint. Since these terms submit to no very precise formulation, I propose a simple working definition of bureaucratic failure. If an ideologically mixed bag of observers consensually reject or condemn a bureaucratic rule, practice, decision, or other behavior when the latter is described in the abstract (e.g., without identifying whether the bureaucracy is HHS or DOD), then we have a good candidate for the category of bureaucratic failure.

Varieties of Failure

Most instances of bureaucratic failure fall into two broad classes. The first class includes those practices which conflict with widely accepted notions of good government. Example 1, which illustrates waste and extravagance, falls into this category, as does Example 4, which illustrates good old-fashioned graft. Generally speaking, this class of bureaucratic failures contains those more easily and noncontroversially identified, and more remediable than those of the second class. Graft eventually will out, and indictments will result. Waste is frequently exposed, and while procedural tinkering is no panacea, it can alleviate the worst cases. In addition, the bright light of public exposure and the resulting political pressure usually have at least a temporary salutary effect.

The second class of bureaucratic failures consists of those practices and activities which conflict with the explicit goals of the authorizing legislation and/or the legislative intent behind it. Example 2 details a widely used means of evading explicit employment ceilings. Example 3 reports an apparent deflection of the intent of Congress: the NASA official admits that his department has not administered the program as intended, but maintains that no law had been violated. Example 6 describes an apparent bureaucratic perversion of the intent of the authorizing legislation.

Some instances of the second class are as easily identified and noncontroversial as those of the first. Congress took action to alter the executive bonus situation (Example 3), which clearly violated the intent of the original law. Other instances create greater difficulty. The goals of the authorizing legislation may be rather vaguely stated, an important element in Theodore Lowi's indictment of American government in *The End of Liberalism*. If so, inconsistency with the authorizing legislation is something that lies in the eye of the beholder. Mr. Kilpatrick most emphatically rejects the finding that the noise of garbage compactors "jeopardizes health and welfare." Others may disagree and offer plausible reasons why the matter should not be left to local ordinance. Sometimes legislative goals may actually be contradictory, in which case the bureaucracy is condemned to act in a manner partially inconsistent with legislative intent. This has been a charge commonly leveled at legislation in the area of economic regulation. Perhaps most seriously, we may observe bureaucratic activity openly acknowledged as inconsistent with the intent of Congress as a whole, but consistent with the desire of a segment of Congress holding particular importance for the relevant agency. Such cases move us out of the area of bureaucratic failure and into the area of more broadly defined political failure.

Different types of bureaucratic failure draw sustenance from different sources. Any exploration of the wide-ranging literature on bureaucracy will uncover at least three general explanations for the failures bureaucracies exhibit. The first, the Imperfect Bureaucrat explanation, focuses on the personal qualities and characteristics of bureaucrats. This explanation has two variants. The more extreme variant, the Evil Bureaucrat, crops up frequently in popular commentary and in material published by various citizens' groups. Nader's organization, for example, often seems to suggest that government is rife with material corruption. In addition to outright bribery charges (e.g., Example 4), there are numerous intimations of technically legal but morally corrupt behavior—acceptance of material favors, incestuous ties among present government employees, previous government employees, and future private employers, and conflicts of interest (e.g., Example 3). This variant holds that bureaucrats are too often not as good as the rest of us.

Sources of Failure

The less extreme variant might be termed the Insufficiently Dedicated Bureaucrat. According to this variant, bureaucrats lead harder lives than most. Material rewards are poor, public opprobrium is common, and even private satisfaction in a job well done is problematic because the nature of the enterprise makes one's individual contribution hard to trace. If the Evil variant holds that bureaucrats are not as good as the rest of us, the Insufficiently Dedicated variant holds that they should be better than the rest of us, but are not.

Imperfect Bureaucrat views seldom appear in the academic literature, for social science favors explanations which treat political actors as no better or worse than anyone else. Thus, the roots of bureaucratic failure are not sought in human imperfection, but in more general conditions which lead ordinary humans to behave imperfectly. A now dated explanation might be called the "structural" view, which focuses on badly designed governmental organizations. In the older literature in public administration, one finds condemnations of duplications of efforts, overlapping jurisdictions, blurred lines of responsibility, lack of central control, and so forth. In essence, if the bureaucracy were organized according to what were perceived as sound business principles, bureaucratic failure could be largely overcome. This view, however, is now passé, and has given way to more sophisticated views that place incentives in the forefront.

The third view of bureaucratic failure is an umbrella explanation, variants of which appear in the literatures of the several disciplines which address the subject of bureaucracy. For lack of a better term, let us call the third view the Discrepant Incentives explanation. In general, this explanation focuses on the slippage between how the ideal bureaucracy functions in an ideal world and how real bureaucracies function in the here and now. The source of the slippage is located in the discrepant incentives faced by those who people the bureaucracy. These individuals often have little or no incentive to behave in a manner consistent with the ideal account. Thus, economists assume that bureaucrats are no worse than the rest of us, but, in fact, just like the rest of us—self-serving. Outright illegality is no great (theoretical) problem; when uncovered it is punished in the private and public sectors alike. But whereas the private sector turns self-serving behavior to societal advantage through the hidden hand of the market, the public sector produces no such happy outcome. The bureaucrats' personal rewards are only remotely connected to the public costs and benefits of the bureau's activities. Only if public-sector actors were to behave in an other-serving manner would they produce favorable societal outcomes (if then), and they have no more incentive to behave in such fashion than the rest of us. [. . .]

Scholars as disparate as economists and sociologists are in general agreement on the root cause of bureaucratic failures: individual bureaucrats face incentives which are unrelated to, if not incompatible with, the efficient and faithful implementation and administration of the law. To be sure, major differences appear once we move beyond this general position. Sociologists place more weight on intangible goals (e.g., status, peer approval) relative to material rewards than do economists. The literatures differ, too, on the subject of intentionality. Sociologists speak of the "internal dynamics of organizations" as if these had an existence at least partially independent of the individuals in the organization. Happenstance and history also play a nontrivial role in sociological analysis. In contrast, economists emphasize the conscious pursuit of goals (if not conspiracy). To take an extreme example, George Stigler says in essence that only naïve academics believe that the general interest ideal should bear any relation to the special interest reality of economic regulation, that the regulatory process is of, by, and for the regulatees, and that the high-minded sentiments of the authorizing legislation were purely symbolic and known to be so at the time. The literatures also differ greatly in their treatment of institutions. Much of the economic literature models the pursuit of private interests through a relatively undifferentiated political process. The sociological literature places greater emphasis on institutional forms. The political science literature and to some extent the public choice literature also pay heed to institutions. The latter can shape incentives, or at least the behavior by which individuals pursue their ends, though the public choice literature, in particular, recognizes that institutions themselves, especially informal ones such as norms and standard operating procedures, are the reflections of incentives faced by those who originated them. In this view, private incentives affect both the structure and activity of the bureaucratic process.

Insofar as we are concerned with the redress of bureaucratic failures, differences like the preceding are of major importance. From the standpoint of the institutionally sparse model of Stigler, one type of proposal for reform of the regulatory process might naturally arise. From the standpoint of the institutionally richer model of William Niskanen, another type of reform might seem more obvious. And from the standpoint of the socially rich model of the sociologists, yet another variety of reform might appear appropriate.

In order to make any claims about the likely efficacy of structural reforms now in the air, let alone propose any new ones, we must ascertain whether such reforms will get at the root of the problem—the inconsistent incentives facing those involved in bureaucratic failures. Thus, we must consider in greater depth the incentive problems thought to underlie the kinds of bureaucratic failures illustrated in all six examples. Many of these incentive problems originated in Congress, or, more broadly, in the American electoral system. Thus, properly speaking, they are not bureaucratic failures at all, but congressional failures. Because of this, as we shall see, prospects for structural reform are poor.

We have defined bureaucratic failure as the consensual judgment that a bureau or agency is not accomplishing its manifest goals as efficiently as possible. As an explanation for bureaucratic failure, we have identified insufficient incentives for bureaucrats to carry out efficiently the manifest goals of the bureau, and/or the existence of strong incentives to behave in a manner inconsistent with the efficient pursuit of the bureau's manifest goals. Let us now take a closer look at these various and sundry incentives.

Perverse Incentives

Economists long ago pointed out the differences between the incentive structure faced by private-sector providers of private goods and public-sector providers of public goods. Bureaus and agencies are not profit-making entities. Thus, their performance is not judged by the usual private-sector standards. Indeed, for many agencies it is difficult to make even rough estimates of the overall benefits and costs of their activities. How are public goods like national security and wilderness preservation to be valued? And while the direct costs of bureaucracy might be tabulated fairly easily, the indirect costs are another matter.

As a result of these fundamental differences, the standard analysis continues, bureaucratic managers' rewards are not based on the "bottom line." Their remuneration consists of a fixed salary, which is for all practical purposes guaranteed regardless of the performance—however roughly evaluated—of their agency or bureau. These managers have little personal material incentive to avoid inefficient operations, since they cannot appropriate any of the savings more efficient operations might produce. In fact, the standard analysis continues, matters are probably worse. Public-sector managers' rewards (tangible, such as salary and perks: and intangible, such as status and power) vary with both the size (employment and budget) and importance (i.e., power) of the agencies. Thus, there are positive incentives to increase agency work forces, budgets, and missions. Not only is there no incentive to operate efficiently, there are compelling incentives to operate inefficiently.

The standard analysis regards other bureaucratic characteristics as derivatives of this perverse incentive structure. A bold decision which proves well advised will produce little more than a pat on the back, whereas one which proves ill advised may have real costs in terms of promotion prospects (and occasionally in terms of perks). Similarly, detailed rules and excessive adherence thereto reflect the determination to cover one's flanks. In general, the "conservatism" of bureaucracy is attributed to the lack of positive incentive for initiative vis-à-vis negative incentive to minimize risk and avoid responsibility. And, of course, the standard analysis recognizes that self-selection may reinforce the asymmetry of incentive. Those individuals who lack initiative and thrive in highly structured settings may be disproportionately attracted to and successful in bureaucracies.

The standard analysis undoubtedly captures a part of the explanation of bureaucratic failure in the federal government (e.g., parts of Example 1 through 4). But there are certain questions it fails to illuminate. Most obviously, why do bureaucrats ever take bold, controversial actions? Why did the Federal Trade Commission provoke the 96th Congress into legislative retaliation? Even if such cases are dismissed as deviant, other questions remain. If internal bureaucratic incentives are all wrong, why not change them? It is not sufficient to mention Civil Service; the law could be changed. And even if it were not, why should the federal government rely so heavily on service-providing and regulatory bureaucracies as instruments of public policy? There are others; why are they not used more often?

William Niskanen begins with the standard analysis, but appends to it a second major consideration. Not only is a bureaucrat's personal remuneration not directly linked to the benefit-cost ratio of his agency's programs and activities; in addition, a bureau's revenues are similarly unlinked. The typical government bureau receives a large part, if not all, of its revenues in the form of an appropriation or grant from the legislature. Thus, bureaus and their political sponsors engage in a bilateral exchange relationship. The sponsor is not satisfied with the private market outcome, else there would be no program. The agency is prepared to design and administer a program—for a price. The sponsor wishes to buy cheap, the agency wishes to sell dear, and the game begins. Various asymmetries characterize the game. The bureau has much more accurate knowledge of its production function than the sponsor, and based on past experience can estimate what price the legislative market will bear. Thus, the typical bureau's position is that of a monopoly supplier with some degree of ability to exploit a passive sponsor (e.g., Example 2). Niskanen models this situation insightfully. His general conclusion is that the bilateral exchange between legislature and bureaucracy results in an oversupply of publicly provided goods and services.

Niskanen's seminal analysis has spawned an extensive literature. These derivative analyses typically modify some part or another of the original structure of the model, and report specific conclusions somewhat different from those in the original. For our purposes, the basic finding of the model is what matters, and that finding is common to the many variations on the main theme. Even when we presume nothing in the way of internal bureaucratic dynamics, bureaucratic politics, the nature of bureaucratic personalities, or whatever, we still find an important variety of bureaucratic failure—inefficient supply of public services—which arises purely from the interaction between bureaucratic and legislative institutions. The finding is simple, stark, and discouraging.

The literature stimulated by Niskanen's work is almost completely theoretical. Part of the reason for its generally positive reception lies in the existence of an extensive literature in political science which is consistent with the outlines of Niskanen's conclusions. As mentioned earlier, the political science literature on bureaucracy draws heavily from sociological formulations which emphasize organizational dynamics and bureaucratic politics. But there is another large literature which treats the bureaucracy as a component of larger policy processes, a literature which contains numerous case studies consistent with, though more complex than, the simple model of bilateral exchange. The central concept of this latter literature is that of the "policy subsystem," also called "subgovernment" or "iron triangle." The three elements of such triangles are a government bureau, its constituency (i.e., the consumers of its services or activities), and the congressional committees or subcommittees with jurisdiction over the bureau. These three components of a policy subsystem engage in trilateral exchange: congressmen nurture the bureau, the bureau services its constituencies, and the constituencies provide political support for the congressmen. Much of this literature focuses on public-policy failure, but given the perspective just advanced, such failures are not hung solely on the bureaucracy. In fact, upon considering the legally subordinate position of the bureaucracy and the politically supplicant position of the bureau's constituency, the "subgovernment" literature attributes a large part of policy failure to the Congress.

After reading accounts like those presented in the six examples, the outraged citizen asks: "Why doesn't Congress do something besides publicize and recommend!" The student of Congress replies: "Because there's no such thing as Congress; there are only two Houses, four party caucuses, 300-odd committees and subcommittees, and ultimately 535 members." Congress generally does little besides investigate and recommend, because, in the end, one congressman's bureaucratic failure comes too close to another congressman's bread and butter. That this argument should need further repeating at this stage in our history is amazing; but it does, so let us consider it one more time.

Representatives and senators are elected from geographically defined districts which only by chance are microcosms of the nation as a whole. Our representatives are no worse than the rest of us, but no better either. Thus, they regard themselves as principally responsible to those who control their personal fates, namely subgroups in their geographically defined districts. Congressmen comprehend the national interest only when it is translated into local dialects.

As David Mayhew has persuasively argued, the complicated formal and informal structure of Congress facilitates the typical member's efforts to please his district and thus win re-election. For our purposes, the most important element of the congressional structure is the committee system and the practices which surround it. In a society like ours, there is much to be said for a division of labor. If members separate into small groups, specialize in a particular program area, and respect each other's areas of expertise, will we not get better law than if the entire Congress tries to participate on an equal footing in all policy areas? Certainly that is the belief underlying traditional justifications of the committee system and its supporting structure of informal norms like apprenticeship, specialization, and reciprocity (the notion that members not on a committee should refrain from interfering in the business of that committee). The justification would be more persuasive if congressmen were elected at large, or if committees were selected randomly from the membership of the full body. In either case, there would be little reason to believe that small, specialized committees would make decisions greatly different from those the entire chamber would make if equally well informed.

Obviously, however, such conditions do not hold. Not only does each member have a locally colored perception of the national interest, but the committee assignment process generally allows members to join those committees whose subject matter is of greatest interest (i.e., political importance) to them. If these interested members then develop programs and oversee agencies in a relatively autonomous fashion, should we really expect a government which unequivocally serves the general interest? Or should we expect a government which generously subsidizes commercial agriculture, the Teamsters, government employees, defense contractors, or whatever one's favorite special interest? The relevant committee may be well aware that money is being wasted, but at least it is being wasted by their people and on their people.

Are we to believe that members of relevant appropriations subcommittees (Example 2) really were unaware of the submerged iceberg of federal payrolls? Is it unduly cynical to suggest that they tacitly approved a means of evading employment ceilings imposed by their colleagues?

Are we to believe that the EPA promulgated regulations (Example 5) which were really beyond its congressional overseers' wildest dreams? Is it not likely that the Democratic members of the Senate Environment and Public Works Committee had a broader concept of "jeopardy to health and welfare" than does Mr. Kilpatrick?

Are we to believe that members of the Commerce Committees and the relevant appropriations subcommittees really were unaware of the economic impact of ICC regulation of the trucking industry (Example 6)? Is it unduly cynical to agree with Mayhew that, "there is every reason to believe that the regulatory agencies do what Congress wants them to do."

Even when an agency clearly violates the intent of its congressional masters, the reactions are illuminating. In Example 3, for example, it sounds as if Congresswoman Spellman, who then chaired the Compensation and Employee Benefits Subcommittee of the Post Office and Civil Service Committee, might go howling for bureaucratic scalps. Not so. The article goes on to report that Spellman, a vigorous defender of federal employees, favored elimination of the federal pay cap, rather than enforcement: "I think it's a silly way to deal with the problem."

In the end, many of our bureaucratic failures seem to have a large element of congressional failure underlying them. Wasteful, deceptive, disingenuous, paternalistic, and captive bureaucrats work in harmony with wasteful, deceptive, disingenuous, paternalistic, and captive congressmen. To a considerable extent the former reflect the latter. The bureaucrats catch a disproportionate share of the public relations flak, while the congressmen appropriate a disproportionate share of the political credit, in return for which they shelter the bureaucrats. Various special interests provide the motive force and are paid handsomely for their labors, but the more general interests of American citizens get short shrift under such a system.

Reforming the Structure?

Political science professors are by nature cautious about structural reform. To some extent their caution reflects knowledge of numerous reforms whose unintended and unanticipated consequences were fully as bad as the objects of reforms. And to some extent their caution simply reflects the old saw, "If it ain't broke, don't fix it." Why dissipate resources on structural reform campaigns that will not solve the targeted problems even if successful? Reformers should recognize that the day-to-day processes of the government reflect equilibria of political forces. If all the politically significant actors in a given program or policy area are reasonably happy with the state of that area, then structural reform is not likely to succeed, and if it does, it is not likely to make much difference. There simply are not that many cases of devilishly deceptive bureaucrats pulling the wool over congressional eyes, though some congressmen would like us to believe that. There are, however, many cases in which congressmen voluntarily don wool blinders.

The brutal fact is that only a small minority of our 535 congressmen would trade the present bureaucratic structure for one which was an efficient, effective agent of the general interest—the political payoffs of the latter are lower than those of the former. Congressional talk of inefficient, irresponsible, out-of-control bureaucracy is typically just that—talk—and when it is not, it usually refers to agencies under the jurisdiction of other congressmen's committees. Why do reformers continually ignore the fact that Congress has all the power necessary to enforce the "people's will" on the bureaucracy? The Congress can abolish or recognize an agency. The Congress can limit or expand an agency's jurisdiction, or allow its authority to lapse entirely. The Congress can slash an agency's appropriations. The Congress can investigate. The Congress can do all of these things, but individual congressmen generally find reasons not to do so.

Congressmen themselves are increasingly aware of the contradictions between their individual interests and their constitutional responsibilities. Not surprisingly, structural reform in Congress itself has been their preferred solution. In an attempt to increase congressional oversight of the bureaucracy, special oversight subcommittees have been established, but while the sheer volume of oversight activity has increased (why be a subcommittee chairman without holding a hearing now and then), we await research showing that the quality or effectiveness of the oversight has improved. Skepticism is justified because the structural reform does not touch the problem Seymour Scher identified long ago: insufficient incentives to oversee in the systematic way desired by reformers. Not only are other uses of congressional time more politically profitable, but, as Scher points out, oversight can be dangerous. A subcommittee might blunder onto a smoothly functioning subgovernment and thereby provoke the ire of colleagues and interest groups. And, of course, in their own bailiwicks, congressmen feel that oversight can best be done in an informal, personal, and confidential manner.

Another structural reform which has attracted much attention in Congress is the class of proposals labeled "sunset." Recent reports indicate that this is an idea whose time has come and gone. Even so, notice that sunset is an attempt to force Congress to exercise powers it already has. If Congressmen had any compelling incentive to scrutinize the operations of agencies and the impacts of programs, they would do so without sunset and/ or special oversight subcommittees. The incentive is not there, and sunset will not change that.

Any structural reforms that would make a difference are so radical as to horrify the average citizen. To have an impact a structural reform must change incentives. What kind of reform, then, would change the incentives which underlie the congressional–bureaucratic failures here discussed? The most obvious one would involve a change in the electoral system. Proportional representation would break the link between geographic district and congressman, and thus allow the latter to hear the general interest a bit more clearly. So would single-member district elections with districts composed of randomly selected social security numbers rather than geographic areas. One can say a great deal for and against such proposals, but in view of their total infeasibility, one need not bother. [. . .]

Creative intellects can propose structural reforms from now till doomsday, but those reforms that would significantly change the incentives facing congressmen and bureaucrats will stand little chance of adoption, even if political analysts can marshal no major negative arguments against them. The political forces underlying existing equilibria will understandably block any structural reform capable of destroying these equilibria. Unfortunately, such equilibria arise from fundamental features of our constitutional system; only structural reforms aimed at that level can make much of a difference.

References

Cutler, Lloyd. "To Form a Government." *Foreign Affairs* 59 (1980): 126-44.
Mayhew, David. *Congress: The Elected Connection*. New Haven; Yale University Press, 1974.
Niskanen, William. *Bureaucracy and Representative Government*. Chicago: Aldine-Atherton, 1971.
Scher, Seymour. "Conditions for Legislative Control." *Journal of Politics* 25(1963): 526-51.
Stigler, George. "The Theory of Economic Regulation." *Bell Journal of Economics and Management Science* 2(1971): 3-21.

3

PERFORMANCE

Policies, Outcomes, Directions

Having examined how the basic structures of advanced industrial states constrain political action, and how specific institutions and processes have functioned in the American system, we now turn to a consideration of the state–market nexus in operation and then attempt to discern some trends in the development of the system. Accordingly, the first readings in this section focus on a number of especially pertinent policy areas. David R. Cameron examines the peculiar American experience of recurrent economic recessions; Lester M. Salamon and John J. Siegfried attempt to identify and explain certain patterns in corporate taxation; and James R. Kurth looks at U.S. weapons policy. Papers by Peter Alexis Gourevitch, Alan Stone, and Immanuel Wallerstein situate the national political economy within the world economy. Finally, Adam Przeworski and Michael Wallerstein and Claus Offe examine the prospects for endurance or collapse of the system that has been the subject of this book.

3.1

The Politics and Economics
of the Business Cycle

DAVID R. CAMERON

Within the American business community it is a truism that "big labor" is responsible for a host of ills, ranging from industry's lack of competitiveness to inflation. Because wages are continually going up, it is said, prices must be raised also. It follows that, if inflation is to be stopped, recessionary policies—with all their obvious and hidden costs (unemployment, increased incidence of alcoholism, child abuse, suicide, etc.)—are needed to break the power of labor unions at the bargaining table.

In this essay David R. Cameron picks up where Michal Kalecki, in Part 1 of this collection, left off. Cameron gathers and examines data from many industrial countries on labor-management conflict in search of an explanation of why some countries (in particular, the United States) have frequent bouts of inflation and unemployment-creating recessions while some Western European countries, including many with politically strong labor movements, have been relatively untroubled by such storms.

In the four decades since World War II, the U.S. economy has oscillated sharply between good times and bad, between periods of high growth and periods of recession, between periods of accelerating inflation and rising unemployment.[1] While the New Deal and, in particular, the wartime experience during the 1940s greatly expanded the role of the Federal government in the economy and provided it with instruments for countercyclical macroeconomic policy, the United States nevertheless has continued to experience the peaks and troughs of the business cycle. More important, it has experienced, relative to the other advanced capitalist nations, frequent recessions and a long-term secular trend of increasing unemployment. As Andrew Shonfield wrote in *Modern Capitalism*:

> the American case was exceptional in the postwar Western world. It was accompanied by many features which had no parallel elsewhere—notably a rising level of unemployment and a declining level of business investment. . . . The evidence suggests that a continuing "recession psychology" in the United States has been a major reason for the contrast between American and West European economic experience in recent years. . . . There have been more recessions in the United States than in Western Europe, and they have been allowed to go further before the government intervened decisively to boost demand.[2]

If it was true in the 1960s, when Shonfield wrote his classic work, that the United States exhibited a "continuing recession psychology," that characterization is even more accurate today. In the past dozen years, the United States has experienced four major recessions and two of these, in 1973–75 and 1981–82, produced the largest decreases in production and employment since the 1930s (see Table 1). This essay offers an explanation of the American experience of recurrent boom and bust, growth and recession, inflation and unemployment. The explanation is simultaneously economic and political—economic in that it concentrates on the interests and behavior of the two major economic groupings in capitalist society; political in that it considers how government has responded to the articulation of those interests.

Table 1

Recessions in the United States, 1948-1982

Date	Duration (months)	President (Party) at beginning of recession	Increase in % unemployed
November 1948 –October 1949	12	Truman (Dem.)	2.1 ('49)
July 1953 –May 1954	11	Eisenhower (Rep.)	2.6 ('54)
August 1957 –April 1958	9	Eisenhower (Rep.)	2.5 ('58)
April 1960 –February 1961	11	Eisenhower (Rep.)	1.2 ('61)
December 1969 –November 1970	12	Nixon (Rep.)	2.4 ('70,71)
November 1973 –March 1975	17	Nixon (Rep.)	3.6 ('74,75)
January 1980 –July 1980	7	Carter (Dem.)	1.3 ('80)
July 1981 –November 1982	17	Reagan (Rep.)	2.6 ('81,82)

The explanation presented here views the cyclical movement of an economy, recessions and inflationary booms, and the magnitude of those peaks and troughs as a reflection of the relative power of, and ongoing conflict between, the major economic groups in society—a conflict that centers on a struggle for income. The recurrent booms and slumps are viewed as indicative of the relative influence at various moments of organized labor, industrial capital, and financial capital in the unending struggle for larger shares of the national income. We take the American pattern of relatively frequent recession to reflect the relative power of the groups and classes whose long-run interests are served by recurrent recessions. To suggest that such groups might exist may seem quite perverse; there are undoubtedly many who would prefer to believe that recessions "just happen" and are unintended, rather than deliberately induced to attain certain benefits. However, we shall demonstrate that such is not the case—in particular, that American business collectively benefits in the long run from recurrent recessions (in spite of the obvious fact that innumerable businesses suffer immensely in the short run, from recessions). In this regard, our analysis resembles that of Boddy and Crotty:

> That profits are lowest during the recession has often been the basis for arguing that it is preposterous to claim that corporations want a recession. Indeed, they would like to avoid it. Yet the recession is a necessary condition for achieving the highly profitable first phase of the expansion and for avoiding the highly unprofitable consequences of sustained full employment. Historically, recessions have also provided the political context within which the state has granted new fiscal incentives to capital.[3]

And insofar as the argument more generally portrays macroeconomic outcomes as the products of an on-going conflict among economic groups and classes, it is quite compatible with Kalecki's view of the "political business cycle":

> In the slump, either under the pressure of the masses, or even without it, public investment financed by borrowing will be undertaken to prevent large scale unemployment. But if attempts are made to apply this method in order to maintain the high level of employment reached in the subsequent boom a strong opposition of "business leaders" is likely to be encountered. . . . Lasting full employment is not at all to their liking. The workers would "get out of hand". . . . Moreover, the price increase in the upswing is to the disadvantage of small and big *rentiers* and makes them "boom tired." In this situation a powerful block is likely to be formed between big business and the *rentier* interests, and they would probably find more than one economist to declare the situation was manifestly unsound. The pressure of all these forces, and in particular of big business . . . would most probably induce the Government to return to the orthodox policy of cutting down the budget deficit. A slump would follow. . . .[4]

After presenting an analysis of the cyclical dynamics of the U.S. economy, we shall consider why some nations appear to be able to avoid the American pattern of sharp oscillation between inflation and recession and, in particular, the experience of frequent severe recession. After comparing the extent to which other advanced capitalist nations have maintained employment, the essay concludes with a discussion of some of political reasons why they have been able to do so, even during the world economic crisis of the 1970s and 1980s.

Unemployment and Inflation in the United States

During the postwar era the United States experienced sharp oscillations in macroeconomic performance. As Figure 1 demonstrates, both inflation and unemployment moved in a quite erratic pattern over a considerable range. In some years, such as 1949 and 1955, prices actually decreased, while in others they increased by more than 10 percent; in some years less than four percent of the civilian work force was unemployed, while in other unemployment approached 10 percent.[5]

Unemployment   Considering first the trend line for unemployment in Figure 1, at least four important facts appear:

(1) There were two, and only two, periods when the economy was operating with

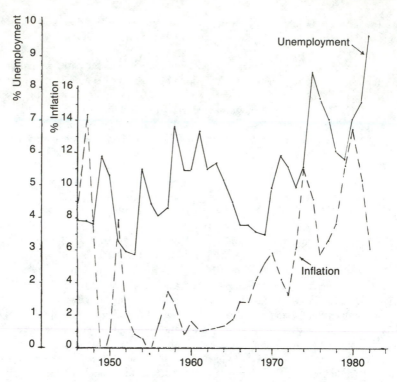

Figure 1. Unemployment and inflation in the United States, 1946–82.

little surplus labor, as reflected in an unemployment rate substantially under 4 percent. The two periods were 1951–53 and 1966–69. In both, the United States was involved in war in Asia—in Korea in the early 1950s and in Vietnam beginning in the mid-1960s.[6] That war is an essential element of American macroeconomic performance will hardly surprise those familiar with the experience of the 1930s and 1940s. For example, it was not until 1941, the year in which the United States entered World War II, that the rate of unemployment dropped back into single digits after the Great Depression, and a perusal of the data on rates of unemployment for those decades suggests that involvement in war was far more consequential than the New Deal for its reduction.[7] It is not facetious to say, then, that if the United States has a full-employment policy, it is war.

(2) Recessions, accompanied by the sharp upsurge in unemployment, typically occur *after* a period of acceleration in the rate of change in prices. (For the timing of recessions, using the initial and last months determined by the dating committee of the National Bureau of Economic Research: see Table 1.) Thus, the recession that began in late 1948 was preceded by a dramatic surge in prices in 1946 and 1947. Likewise, the 1953–54 recession occurred after a steep increase in prices in 1951 and the existence of inflationary pressures in 1952 and 1953 (which were suppressed by price controls). Similarly, the recessions of 1957–58, 1970, 1973–75, and 1980 were all foreshadowed by sharp increases in prices.

(3) Recessions, and the sharp increases in unemployment that they produced, were more likely to occur when Republicans occupied the White House. Table 1 indicates that although Democratic and Republican Presidents were in office for nearly identical

lengths of time during the 35 years after 1947 (17 years for the Democrats, 18 years for Republicans), six of the eight postwar recessions occurred while Republicans held the office. As Table 2 indicates, there is a consistent relationship between the partisanship of the President and the magnitude of increase in unemployment and occurrence of recession. The initiation of a recession and the increase in unemployment that accompanies recession were considerably more likely when Republicans were President. Those recessions typically began in the year after election (1953, 1957, 1969, 1973, 1981), while the two Democratic Presidents presided over election-year recessions (and suffered the consequences).[8]

Table 2

Politics and Recession in the United States, 1948-82

	Increase in % unemployed	Year in which recession began
Year of presidential election	—.14	.15
Democratic president	—.28	—.27

Note: These data represent Pearson product-moment correlations between values for pairs of variables measured for 1948-82. The left-hand measures are dummy variables: year of presidential election = 1, rest = 0; Democratic President = 1, Republican = 0.

(4) The pattern of recurrent recessions in the United States in the postwar era has produced a long-term secular increase in the rate of unemployment. That is, the rate of unemployment is always greater (except when the nation is involved in war) after a recession than before a recession. In other words, the unemployment that is created in a recession is not fully reabsorbed in the subsequent "recovery." Some of the unemployed become permanently unemployed and some of the sectors hardest hit by the recession (e.g., steel and autos in the 1970s and 1980s) lose jobs permanently. Accompanying the long secular upswing in the nonrecession rate of unemployment, the peak rate of unemployment in each recession has increased.

The Consequences of Unemployment   Undoubtedly the most significant consequence of unemployment is the impact on individuals' lives. A growing body of research has identified a close relationship between recession and the unemployment that accompanies it and an increase in the aggregate incidence of marital difficulties, child abuse, mental illness, and suicide, and those policymakers who deliberately institute deflationary policies that generate recession and unemployment bear the responsibility for the suffering, illness, and death that can be directly attributed to recession.[9]

In terms of the economic well-being of those who retain their jobs through a recession, the effects of recession and the accompanying sharp increase in unemployment are less severe but nevertheless distinct. Figure 2 presents two of the more important consequences for wage earners. The figure arrays the rate of unemployment during the postwar period with (1) the level of strike activity[10] and (2) the rate of change in adjusted hourly earnings of production and nonsupervisory workers.[11]

In regard to strikes, we note that the sheer magnitude of strike activity drifted downward in the 1950s and 1960s from the record level of 1946, moved upward in the

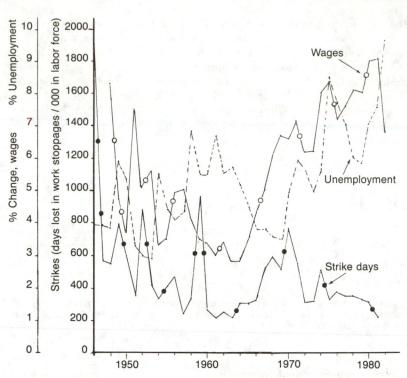

Figure 2. Unemployment, strikes, and wages in the United States, 1946–81.

late 1960s, and after 1970 drifted downward again, reaching the lowest level of the postwar period in 1981. While both unemployment and strike activity varied widely over time, it does appear that strike activity increased in times of relatively full employment (e.g., 1952, 1967-69) as well as in several nonrecession years, and decreased during and immediately after recessions. In particular, the series of recurrent recessions in the 1950s and the 1970s were followed by long-term decreases in strike activity. We can conclude, then, that one important consequence of recession, and especially of a series of recessions, is a diminution of organized labor's ability and/or interest in using its ultimate weapon—the strike—against employers.

If recessions dampen the aggregate level of strike activity by creating a large pool of potential "scab" laborers who can replace striking workers and by increasing the fear of job loss among would-be strikers, they also—partly because of those effects on workers—reduce the magnitude of the increases in wages that workers ask for, and receive. Figure 2 demonstrates that although the relationship between the level of unemployment and the rate of change in money wages is far less perfect than a good Phillipsian might assume,[12] the rate of change has usually dropped somewhat in the wake of recessions—for example, in 1949-50, 1954-55, 1958-59, 1960-61, 1971, and 1982. (Conversely, Figure 2 also indicates that money wages tended to increase relatively rapidly in periods of relatively full employment—especially in the war-generated near-full employment of 1951-53 and 1965-69.) In short, in the wake of recessions wage earners become less willing to use the strike against employers and more willing to accept reductions in the rate of increase in

pay. In other words, recessions dampen the economic militance, and instead increase the
quiescence, of wage earners.

What is the consequence of recession-induced labor quiescence? Figure 3 suggests
the answer. That figure compares the trend lines during 1948-82 in the rate of profits of
U.S. nonfinancial corporations and in employee compensation as a proportion of all
national income.[13] The strong relationship between the trend lines in the rate of
profitability and the proportion of national income received by wage earners (r = −.77)
suggests that business and labor are indeed engaged in a distributional struggle for
income. The long downward trend in the rate of profit between the end of World War II
and the early 1970s, and the long upward trend in employee compensation until 1970,
indicate that wage earners—taken in the broadest sense of the term (and quite distinct
from industrial workers and unionized workers, who composed only a small fraction of
that category)—were improving their economic situation relative to that of the owners of
industrial capital.[14] Just as interesting as the direction of the long-term trends in corporate
profitability and employee compensation is the suggestion in Figure 3 that the movement
in the trend lines has been largely generated by the two episodes of war-related boom and
the series of recessions that followed each boom. Figure 3 indicates that substantial
improvements in wage earners' share of national income were confined to two periods—
1951-53 and 1966-70. These were, of course, the two periods of involvement in Asian
war, during which the economy was booming and unemployment was driven to record
postwar lows. Figure 3 also indicates that it was during those periods—and presumably
because businesses were forced, by the tightness of labor markets, to bid up the price of
labor—that the rate of profit experienced its most pronounced declines. Outside those two
periods, the trend lines in corporate profitability and employee income remained more or
less flat, indicating that industrial capital and labor were, to some extent, stalemated in
their distributional struggle with each other.

If industrial capital and labor were stalemated, in terms of distributional *outcomes*, in

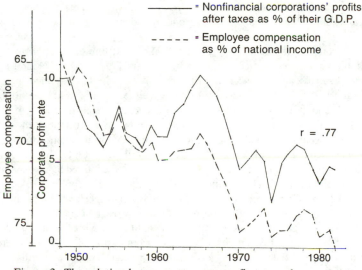

Figure 3. The relation between corporate profit rate and
compensation of employees.

the nonwar years, they were nonetheless fully involved in a distributional *struggle*, and recessions played an essential role in that struggle. Figure 3 suggests that the major reason why the rate of profit did not continue to drop in the nonwar years, and why, conversely, the proportion of employee income did not continue to increase, was the frequent occurrence of recession. Before each recession the rate of profit experienced a decline and the proportion of income received by wage earners increased; after each recession the rate of profit increased and wage earners' share of income decreased. It is not too far-fetched, then, to see recessions—especially a string of recessions such as occurred in the 1950s and again in the 1970s and early 1980s—as devices by which the owners and managers of industrial capital improve their economic situation at the expense of wage earners. If that is true, then it is also true, as Kalecki surmised, that capitalists may very well benefit from recession. And if that is true, then it is also true that the existence of a "continuing recession psychology" in the United States, and the nation's frequent experience of recession must reflect the relative power of capital and, conversely, the relative weakness of labor.[15]

Inflation   Having noted that most of the several American postwar recessions occurred after episodes of rapid acceleration in the rate of change in prices (especially when Republicans occupied the White House), an understanding of why the United States manifests a "continuing recession psychology" would seem to depend on understanding why inflation occurs (and why, in addition, Republicans are apparently more averse to inflation than Democrats).

What causes inflation? One might think the answer is obvious: Inflation occurs because the sellers of products, services, and labor are able to raise their price to buyers of products, services, and labor. At the most general level, this answer is true; it does not, however, provide a great deal of assistance in understanding the *dynamics* of the American political economy because it does not explain why the rate of change in prices varies over time and thus why recessions are instituted at certain times and not others. In order to understand these dynamics, we must, of necessity, search for an answer in the political and economic life of the nation—in the fiscal and monetary policy of government and the impact of that policy on the economy and on American labor and business.

The Causes of Inflation: Fiscal Policy   The trend line of inflation in Figure 1 reveals four major surges in prices in the postwar era—in 1947, 1951, 1974, and 1979-80. The latter two, of course, reflect in part the impact of the OPEC price increases of 1973-74 and 1979-80—the former to punish the West for its support of Israel in the Yom Kippur War (and also in order to restore OPEC's declining real income),[16] the latter to reflect the temporary loss of Iran's supply to the world. As important as these distinct episodes were, what is especially interesting about the trend in inflation is the suggestion that the rate of change in prices began to accelerate well before OPEC began to raise the price of oil. In particular, the data in Figure 1 suggest that the United States experienced a long gradual upward acceleration in the rate of change after the early 1960s.

Why did the inflation rate in the United States begin to accelerate in the mid-1960s? Figure 4 suggests that at least part of the answer may involve the Federal government and its fiscal policies. Figure 4 arrays the rate of unemployment with the magnitude of the surplus or deficit of the Federal government, as a proportion of G.N.P.[17] There is no economic theory that claims that budget deficits are inherently and always inflationary; to the extent that the deficits of government increase in size in bad times and decrease in good times—that is, are countercyclical—they presumably have no discernible effect on

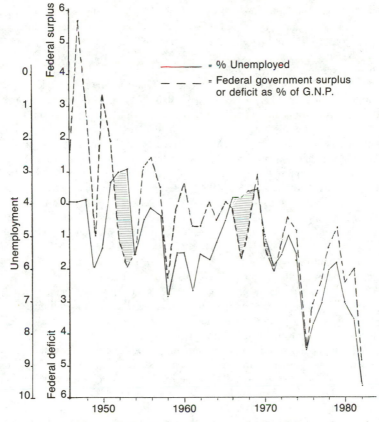

Figure 4. Magnitude of deficit of federal government and rate of unemployment in the United States, 1946–82.

inflation. On the other hand, if deficits are incurred during a period of full capacity utilization and high employment, they may contribute to "excessive" consumption and investment; in other words, they may "overstimulate" the economy by providing too much demand and thereby lead sellers to raise prices and buyers to willingly pay those prices. Figure 4 indicates that two such periods of high-employment deficits occurred after World War II, in 1952-53 and in 1965-67 and 1969-70. During both the United States was involved in a land war in Asia.

The deficits in the mid-1960s were not large compared to those of the 1950s and 1970s. Nevertheless, Figure 4 suggests that fiscal policy during the Johnson Administration was badly out of "sync" with the performance of the economy, that a purely "neutral" fiscal policy would have produced a surplus equal to perhaps one or two percent of G.N.P. rather than deficits, and that the actual policy therefore "overstimulated" the economy. Why did the U.S. government fail to dampen, through budget surpluses, the inflationary tendencies that would inevitably be produced by fiscal stimulation in an economy that was at the peak of its postwar boom—in part because the nation was embroiled in another war? In retrospect, the Johnson Administration's fiscal mismanagement can be attributed to four factors:

(1) President Johnson was eager, for electoral reasons, to enact John F. Kennedy's

much-delayed tax legislation and did so in 1964, in spite of the fact that by then the economy was in a sustained boom and experiencing the highest rates of economic growth and capacity utilization and the lowest rate of unemployment in the postwar period. In other words, a Federal tax cut was implemented although it was no longer needed and, in fact, should have been replaced with an *increase* in taxes.[18]

(2) Johnson's desire to win the 1964 presidential election by a landslide and thereby move out of the shadow of his predecessor and establish a mandate for his Administration meant that he was not at all averse to providing voters a significant reduction in income taxes in the midst of a booming economy. An analysis reported elsewhere[19] investigated whether fiscal policy in the United States has been excessively expansionary—in the sense of increasing the deficit, increasing expenditures, and/or decreasing revenues more than would occur if policy were fiscally "neutral"—in election years. Over the nine presidential election years from 1948 through 1980, excessive fiscal stimulation occurred in only two of the nine election years—1948 and 1964. In those two elections, and only in those two, the incumbent was an unelected Democrat seeking to hold the office. In both years, the primary means of fiscal stimulation was a significant reduction in personal income taxes.

(3) The rapid escalation of the U.S. military involvement in Vietnam in 1965—certainly not foreseen when Kennedy's advisers proposed a tax cut in the early 1960s and perhaps not anticipated even when the tax cut was enacted in 1964—added literally tens of billions of dollars in government spending and provided an additional budget stimulus at precisely the moment when the economy was reaching its postwar peak in terms of capacity use, rate of growth, and unemployment.[20]

(4) The unpopularity of the war in Vietnam—the expenditures for which accounted for the fiscal overstimulation in 1966–68—coupled with Johnson's desire to remain popular and win election to a second, full term, caused him to delay introduction of legislation, proposed by his economic advisers, that would raise taxes. The legislation was not introduced until late in 1967, more than two years after the commitment of large numbers of troops and materiel to the war. And it was not signed into law until well after the President's "defeat" in the New Hampshire primary and his subsequent withdrawal from the campaign.

The cumulative effect of the Johnson Administration's fiscal and foreign policies (and one cannot talk about one without the other) can be seen by turning again to Figure 1. For more than a half-decade prior to 1965 the United States had experienced a very low rate of inflation. But that pattern was broken in 1965, and in the next four years the nation experienced a rapid acceleration of inflation. It was that acceleration in the rate of change of prices in 1965–70 that initiated the enduring inflation of the 1970s and early 1980s. Thus, if one wishes to explain why the United States experienced persistent inflation over the past two decades, one must look to events that preceded by at least a half-decade those of August 1971, when President Nixon terminated the convertibility of dollars into gold, and those of late 1973–74, when OPEC responded to the Yom Kippur War and the erosion of its "real" dollar income by raising oil prices. One must go back, instead, to the fiscal policies of the Johnson Administration. For reasons having to do with electoral and international politics, that Administration produced a relatively large economic stimulus just as the economy moved as close as it ever had in the postwar era (and closer than it ever would in later years) to full employment.

The Causes of Inflation: Wages, Productivity, and Profits   The discussion in the previous section suggests that the fiscal policy of the Federal government in the late 1960s was at least partially responsible for the long-term acceleration in inflation. However, while "demand-pull" inflation may well have been operative then in the United States, the experience of the more recent period—here as well as in other nations in the advanced capitalist world that suffered high rates of inflation while also experiencing high levels of unemployment, low rates of economic growth, and considerable excess capacity— suggests that inflation can not be attributed simply to excessive demand in an economy operating near full capacity and full employment. The simultaneous experience of inflation and economic stagnation suggests, instead, that inflation derived from factors quite independent of demand and that it was, to an increasing degree, "cost-push" rather than "demand-pull."

In this section and the next, we present an alternative explanation to one that concentrates on government as irresponsible manager of demand. The alternative explanation satisfies, we believe, Gordon's criterion for a theory of inflation:

> The central task of a comprehensive theory of inflation is the identification of the sources of differences in the rate of inflation . . . across time in particular countries, and across countries at a given time.[21]

The explanation is an alternative in that it attributes inflation (and thus recession) not simply and completely to the misguided policies of government but, instead, to the inherent dynamics of a capitalist economy. The explanation views inflation, and also other macroeconomic outcomes such as recession and unemployment, as reflections of the relative power of business and labor[22]—that is, as the product of a perpetual, never-ending struggle between major economic groups seeking to maintain and expand their shares of national income. If, as we argued above, recessions are the aggregate result of thousands of attempts by individual businessmen to dampen their labor costs in a period of economic militancy by labor and declining profitability, inflation reflects (at least in part) the successful attempt of certain segments of labor—in particular, labor that is organized and in sectors dominated by oligopolistic or monopolistic firms that can set prices and can pass along increased costs to buyers—to push up wages.

The most important cost in any advanced capitalist economy is the compensation of employees, i.e., wages, salaries, and fringe benefits. To give but one example, by the early 1980s total compensation in the United States was equivalent to about 61 percent of G.N.P.—that is, about twice the magnitude of total government spending.[23] Therefore, if one wishes to elaborate a cost-centered explanation of inflation, rather than one that emphasizes government's management (or mismanagement) of demand, it is logical to investigate the impact on inflation of changes over time in compensation. Figures 5 and 6 provide time series data for the United States since 1948 on annual rates of change in compensation as well as in "productivity" (defined as the change in output per unit of labor[24]) and inflation. Figure 5 presents the relationship between changes in compensation and productivity; Figure 6 presents the relationship between the difference in those two rates of change and the rate of inflation.

Figure 5 indicates that a yawning gap developed after the mid-1960s between the rates of change in compensation and productivity. There was a period, in the early 1960s, when labor (defined as broadly as possible) received increases in compensation that were "warranted" by the increases in productivity. But since then, throughout the 1970s and into the 1980s, annual increases in compensation have far exceeded increases in productivity. Thus, in the early 1980s compensation increased by about eight to ten percent a year although productivity gains were negligible.

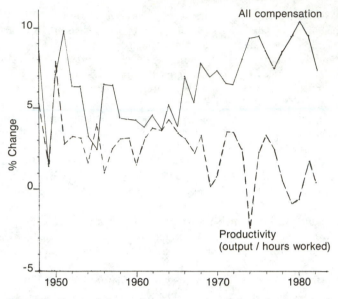

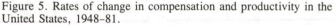

Figure 5. Rates of change in compensation and productivity in the
United States, 1948–81.

What is the consequence of the large gap between the rates of change in compensation and productivity? If compensation per hour increased only as much as output per
hour worked, the cost of wages and salaries per unit of output would not increase. Instead,
it would remain constant. But if aggregate compensation in the economy increased more
rapidly than output per hour, as it did after 1965, then the labor-based cost of each unit of
output would also increase. That being the case, sellers of the goods and services provided
by this labor would have to either pay the additional cost out of profits or pass it along to
consumers in the form of higher prices (or both). Since the former hardly seems
rational—or possible over the long term—the increased cost of each unit of output must
eventually appear in prices.

Figure 6 presents the relationship between the disparity in the rates of change in
compensation and productivity and the rate of inflation. The relationship is very close
over the entire postwar period ($r = +.88$ for 1948–82) and even stronger for the period
since 1960 ($r = +.95$). As strong as it is, however, the relationship in Figure 6 does not
necessarily indicate a causal link between the compensation–productivity gap and
inflation. The increases in compensation could have *followed* previous increases in prices,
reflecting the attempt of employees to catch up with inflation in order to maintain their
"real" incomes. If that were the case, we would still lack an explanation of why the rate of
change in prices accelerated in the first place. In order to infer that the compensation–
productivity gap caused inflation (rather than vice versa), it is necessary to demonstrate
that increases in compensation, relative to productivity, *preceded* increases in the rate of
change in prices.

The sequence of changes in compensation and inflation in Figure 6 supports an
inference that the acceleration in the rate of change in prices in the United States after
1965 was indeed caused by the growing disparity between the rates of change in
compensation and productivity. Each of the three major accelerations in the rate of

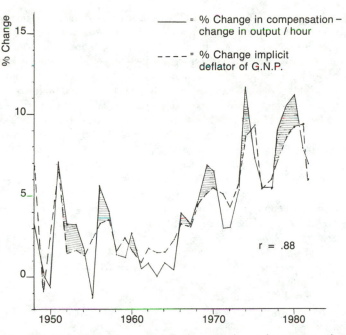

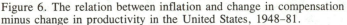

Figure 6. The relation between inflation and change in compensation minus change in productivity in the United States, 1948–81.

change in prices—in 1966–70, 1973–74, and 1978–80—occurred as compensation increased sharply, relative to productivity. And more important for the inference of causation, in each of those periods the compensation–productivity gap increased at a *faster* rate than prices, in effect pulling up the rate of change in prices in its wake. (Note the shaded areas in Figure 6.)

What, if anything, can be inferred about the relations between the major economic groupings in American society from the data in Figures 5 and 6? To answer this question, it is important to recast our discussion of compensation, productivity, and prices in terms of shares of national income—specifically, the shares that go to capital, in the form of profits, and to labor, in the form of compensation. When the rate of change in compensation is precisely equal to the rate of change in productivity and prices, the porportions of national income going to capital and labor remain unchanged. If the increase in compensation is *less* than the increase in productivity and inflation, the aggregate share of national income received by labor decreases, since, in terms of real income, business receives a disproportionate share of the additional output per unit of labor. Conversely, the aggregate share of national income received by business increases. On the other hand, if the increase in compensation is *greater* than the combined increase in productivity and prices, labor's share of income increases, since—again in terms of real income—labor receives a disproportionately large share of the additional output per unit of labor. As a result, the aggregate share of national income received by business decreases.

The shaded areas of Figure 6 indicate years in which the increase in compensation *exceeded* the increase in productivity plus the increase in prices. In those years—1952–53,

1956–57, 1960, 1966–70, 1974, and 1978–80—labor's share of national income increased. In other years—most notably, 1950, 1955, 1959, 1961–65, 1971–72, and 1975—compensation increased less than productivity and prices and labor's share of income decreased. Under what circumstances do the shares of income fluctuate, to either the advantage of labor or that of business? In answering the question, we come back to Kalecki's notion of the "political business cycle": Compensation is most likely to increase more rapidly than productivity and prices (thus increasing labor's share of income) when the rate of unemployment is relatively low, labor markets are tight, and labor's collective bargaining power is therefore relatively strong. There were only three periods in the United States after World War II when increases in compensation exceeded those in productivity and prices for three or more years in a row. Although different in many ways, the three periods—1951–53, 1966–70, and 1978–80—were alike in one way: In comparison with the years before and after, they were periods of decreasing unemployment—periods, that is, when employment, if not high, was nevertheless approaching a localized peak and when, as a result, labor's collective bargaining power was presumably increasing and relatively high, in large part because labor markets were relatively tight. (They were also periods that began while the White House was controlled by the Democrats—a party that is not *of* labor, but is nevertheless closer than its opponent to the labor movement and more concerned with unemployment.[25])

What is the response in the economy to the expansion of labor's share of income during periods of relatively high employment? The answer is apparent—not only in the Kaleckian argument but in the data presented earlier in Figures 1 and 3, 5 and 6. Each period of rapid increase in compensation, and expansion of labor's share of income, was marked by a sharp drop in the rate of corporate profitability. Each period was accompanied by a sharp acceleration in the rate of change in prices. Each period was ultimately followed by recession—or, more accurately, by a *series* of recessions. Thus, the wage push of 1951–53 was followed by the recession of 1954, that of 1956–57 by the sharp recession of 1958, that of 1960 by the recession of 1960–61, that of 1966–70 by the recession of 1970–71, that of 1973–74 by the recession of 1974–75, and that of 1978–80 by the recessions of 1980 and 1981–82. (While the three periods of wage push began during Democratic administrations, we recall that all but one of the post-push recessions began while the Republican party controlled the White House.)

If it is true that each period of sustained wage push and declining profitability was inexorably followed by a recession that reversed the trends in compensation and profits, it is nevertheless unclear precisely how those reversals came about. The microeconomic view implicit in our account thus far would seem to portray recessions as the aggregate consequence, perhaps unintended, of a vast number of individual firm-level decisions by industrial capitalists about employment, production, and profitability. As plausible as that view may seem, it ignores the role of a fundamental intermediary in the economy—one that has a strong interest in dampening inflation and plays a central role in bringing about the reversals in employment, wages, and profitability. That interest is financial capital.

Unlike industrial capital (if it is possible to speak of such inclusive segments), financial capital is concerned with maintaining the value of the dollar, maintaining thereby the value of its loans and assets. It tends to favor price stability, balanced budgets, domestic contraction, scarce money (which inevitably causes the price of its assets—interest rates on money—to rise), reductions in imports, balance-of-payments surpluses, and a strong dollar (in order to maintain the value of its overseas loans and assets). This material interest in price stability stands in marked contrast to the interest of industrial capital (especially industry that produces for domestic and overseas markets, in contrast to multinational firms that have much of their production abroad and that therefore share many of the interests of financial capital). Domestically-producing industry tends, unlike financial capital and international industry, to favor domestic expansion, increased consumption, demand stimulation (even if through budget deficits), easy money, and low interest rates.

The fact that the U.S. economy tends to display a greater propensity to price stability, tight money, and a strong dollar than to domestic expansion, demand stimulation, and a cheap dollar attests to the *relative* influence, *within* the capitalist class, of finance and international industry and the *relative* weakness of domestic industry.[26] This variation in the economic and political strength of the several segments of American capital reflects the transformations of the last century in the U.S. economy—the shift from a nineteenth-century "newly industrializing country" to one that replaced Britain after World War II as the dominant economic, political, and military power in the world. With the erosion of Britain's role as "hegemon" and the ascendance after the war of the United States to that position, the economic and political influence of U.S. firms involved in international finance and industry increased relative to that of domestic industry. With the development of the Bretton Woods system of international trade and finance (marked by the creation of the dollar as a reserve currency pegged to gold, the International Monetary Fund, the General Agreements on Trade and Tariffs) and the numerous military alliances that maintained the system, the United States became committed to free trade and the unimpeded flow of capital—a commitment that reflects the material interests of those sections of American capital that were involved in, and dominating, the international economic system. As a result, U.S. economic policy accepted the steady inflow of imports that took markets from domestic producers, the steady outflow of capital that deprived the economy of funds that might have contributed to domestic growth and employment, and the overvaluation of the dollar that maintained the value of assets owned abroad while contributing to the loss of export markets and domestic markets. With these commitments—which are, we should note, entirely "natural" for any nation that enjoys a dominant position in the world economy—U.S. macroeconomic policy came to emphasize price stability over growth and employment. And much as Britain became wedded to a "stop–go" policy in the late years of its dominance, in the period after World War I, in order to preserve the value of the pound and its foreign assets, the United States came in the postwar period to exhibit a characteristic pattern of "stop–go" in which frequent recessions were instituted, usually with a tight money policy, in order to maintain price stability and an overvalued dollar.[27] In short, the aversion to inflation that had always existed among industrial capitalists, for reasons having to do with the effect of wage increases on profits outlined above, was supplemented with the aversion to inflation of another distinct segment of capital—that involved in finance and international industry—which became increasingly important after World War II.

Figure 7 presents the trend lines in three rates that are of central concern to financial capital. Along with the rate of change in consumer prices, the figure includes the average annual discount rate for member-bank borrowings from the Federal Reserve Bank and the prime rate of commercial banks.[28] The figure demonstrates one of the major mechanisms by which recessions have come into being, especially the recessions of the 1960s, 1970s, and 1980s. We observe a sharp increase in interest rates in the boom that typically occurs before each recession. Clearly, a contributing factor in the rise of prices that occurred in the late 1960s, early 1970s, and late 1970s was the rise in the price of money, as demand for money, like that for other goods, rose and allowed suppliers to raise the price. The figure demonstrates that as significant as the increases in the Federal Reserve's discount rate were, the prime rates of commercial lenders increased even more rapidly. As a result, a spread typically opened up between the two rates—a spread that represented increased rates of profit for commercial banks. Thus, while the profits of industrial firms are typically dropping in the late stages of a sustained expansion, the profits of financial interests are typically rising. Eventually, the two interests—that of industrialists wishing to restore profit margins, that of financiers wishing to maintain their high rates of interest— combine and produce a recession, which reverses the downward trend in the profitability of nonfinancial firms and, by dampening the rate of inflation, actually *increases* the "real" interest rate received by financial interests.

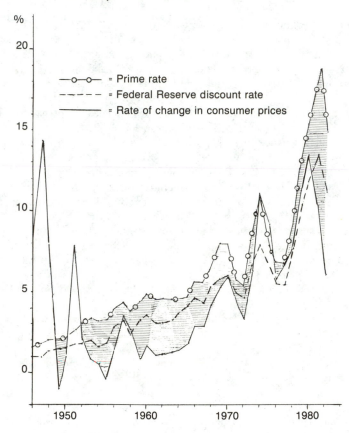

Figure 7. Interest rates and inflation in the United States, 1948–81.

Are recessions—the troughs of the business cycle—simply undesired, unanticipated, and randomly timed episodes, produced by the fiscal and/or monetary mismanagement of government? Or do they play an important role in a capitalist economy, do they occur at certain quite predictable periods, are they deliberately created in order to serve certain interests in the economy, and are they in some sense necessary for the continued well-being of capitalism? In short, are recessions an inherent and essential ingredient of capitalist economics?

The data presented here suggest that recessions are not simply randomly timed episodes of governmental mismanagement. To understand why recessions should be regarded not as the unintended consequence of misguided economic policy but, instead, as events that produce long-term economic gain for business, consider again the data in Figures 1–3, 5, and 6. Taken together, the data suggest that recessions occur at quite predictable periods—after prolonged periods of wage push, made possible by tight labor markets, that expand labor's share of income, reduce the aggregate rate of profitability in several successive years, and, as a by-product, cause the rate of change in prices to increase. The data also suggest that although both business and labor suffer in the midst of a recession—the former through low profits, the latter through high unemployment—the longer-term effects are more beneficial to business. Unemployment dropped back to its pre-recession levels after only two of the eight postwar recessions (those of 1949 and 1960–61), and then only because of protracted booms produced by the wars in Korea and Vietnam. Otherwise, unemployment remained higher after each recession than it had been before. (Hence the long secular increase in the rate of unemployment over the postwar period noted in Figure 1.) Largely because of that increase in unemployment, productivity increased dramatically in each post-recession recovery. At the same time, the sharp increase in unemployment during the recesion—on average, about two percent in each one—dampened wage demands. Thus, we observe sharp decreases in the rate of change in compensation in 1949, 1954–55, 1958–59 and 1960–61, 1971–72, 1976–77, and 1981–82. The smaller increase in compensation that labor typically accepts during and after a recession, together with the increase in productivity during the period immediately after a recession, as output expands with a smaller work force, causes a drop in the rate of change in prices. This drop is a measure of the extent to which business, with the assistance of government (for example, by contributing to the onset of recession by a tight money policy), succeeds in reversing the previous trends in the shares of income received by business and labor. Thus, it is in the years immediately after each recession that business experiences the sharpest increases—in fact, the *only* increases—in the rate of profitability! In short, by weakening labor's bargaining power, reducing labor costs and increasing productivity (thereby reducing the rate of inflation), and reversing the downward slide in profitability, recessions serve the longer-term *collective* interest of business (although, obviously, not the short-term *individual* interest of each businessman, since many of them suffer losses and/or bankruptcy).

What, then, can we conclude about the recurrent experience of recession in the U.S. economy? Are recessions simply the unintended by-products of misguided fiscal and monetary policy? Or are they instituted deliberately in order to further certain specific material interests? Given the temporal relationship between changes in wages, changes in profitability, and the onset of recession, it would be an exercise in naivete to believe that recessions are simply undesired, unanticipated, and randomly timed episodes, produced by the fiscal and/or monetary mismanagement of government. Recessions evidently play as an important role in the U.S. economy and occur at certain quite predictable periods—and for quite obvious reasons that involve the material interests of those who control major segments of the economy. Indeed, insofar as recessions dampen the militance of labor, reduce the rate of increase in employee compensation, restore the rate of profitability for industry, and increase the "real" interest received by finance, they appear to be necessary for the continued well-being of a capitalist economy.[29]

The American Experience in Comparative Perspective

Must all nations suffer the macroeconomic oscillations between boom and bust that are generated by the perpetual struggle between the major economic groups of capitalist society? Must all experience, as the United States so frequently has in the postwar era, periodic surges in prices and declines in profit rates, followed by economic slump? Must they incur the enormous human cost of high unemployment in order to stabilize prices? Or can they attain price stability without bludgeoning labor with depression-level unemployment as in the United States? And if some nations can attain price stability without increasing the enormous human costs associated with unemployment, what are the political conditions that allow them to escape the apparently inevitable trade-off beween price stability and full employment?

Table 3 demonstrates that while all of the advanced capitalist nations experienced some increase in unemployment over the last two decades, not all experienced as much unemployment as the United States, either in terms of the average rate or the increase in the rate from the mid-1960s to the early 1980s.[30] Nor did all nations experience the same degree of cyclical volatility or oscillation in unemployment, as reflected in the standard deviation and the average annual first-order change in the rate of unemployment. Fourteen of the eighteen nations had lower average rates of unemployment over the eighteen years between 1965 and 1982, nine had lower first-order increases in unemployment between 1965-67 and 1980-82, and between seven and thirteen (depending on the measure) experienced less oscillation in the rate of unemployment. Some nations with lower average rates of unemployment than the United States over the eighteen years experienced large increases between the mid-1960s and early 1980s—for example, West

Table 3

Unemployment in Eighteen Nations, 1965-82

	Average 1965-82	% of Total Labor Force Unemployed		
		Increase, 1965-67 to 1980-82	Standard deviation 1965-82	Average annual change, 1965-82
Switzerland	0.2	0.3 (0.0 to 0.3)	0.2	0.1
Japan	1.6	0.9 (1.3 to 2.2)	0.4	0.1
Austria	1.8	0.7 (1.9 to 2.6)	0.5	0.2
Norway	1.8	0.5 (1.6 to 2.1)	0.3	0.3
Sweden	2.1	0.9 (1.6 to 2.5)	0.5	0.4
W. Germany	2.2	3.9 (0.6 to 4.5)	1.7	0.5
Netherlands	3.2	6.5 (1.0 to 7.5)	2.5	0.6
Finland	3.6	3.5 (1.9 to 5.4)	1.8	0.9
Australia	3.7	4.5 (1.7 to 6.2)	2.0	0.4
France	3.8	5.5 (1.7 to 7.2)	1.9	0.4
Denmark	4.1	7.3 (1.4 to 8.7)	3.0	0.8
Britain	5.1	7.8 (2.6 to 10.4)	2.9	0.9
Belgium	5.2	8.9 (2.1 to 11.0)	3.4	0.7
Spain	5.4	11.3 (2.4 to 13.7)	4.2	0.9
United States	5.7	4.1 (3.9 to 8.0)	1.7	0.8
Canada	6.2	5.0 (3.6 to 8.6)	1.9	0.7
Ireland	6.3	3.4 (4.8 to 8.2)	1.4	0.6
Italy	6.4	2.8 (5.4 to 8.2)	1.1	0.5

Germany, the Netherlands, Belgium, France, Denmark, Britain, and Spain. But other nations—most notably, Switzerland, Japan, Austria, Norway, and Sweden—enjoyed virtually full employment throughout the two decades, experienced very little increase in unemployment, and, moreover, experienced very little of the cyclical oscillation in unemployment that is observed in the United States.

The suggestion that some nations have largely avoided the American experience of high and increasing unemployment and sharp cyclical oscillations in the economy becomes even more intriguing when one considers Figure 8. That figure arrays the average rate of unemployment during 1965-82 with the increase in the average rate of change in consumer prices between 1965-67 and 1980-82.[31] It reveals that, contrary to the cross-national implication to be drawn from the Phillips curve,[32] the nations with the highest rates of unemployment had the *highest* rates of inflation (defined here in terms of acceleration in the rate of change in prices) and, conversely, the nations with relatively full employment had the *lowest* increases in the rate of change in prices. Some nations, such as Switzerland, Japan, and Austria, experienced the best of both worlds—full employment *and* price stability. Other nations, most notably, Italy and Ireland but also, in varying degrees, France, Britain, Canada, and the United States, experienced the *worst* of both worlds—high rates of unemployment throughout the period *and* relatively large increases in the average rate of change in prices.

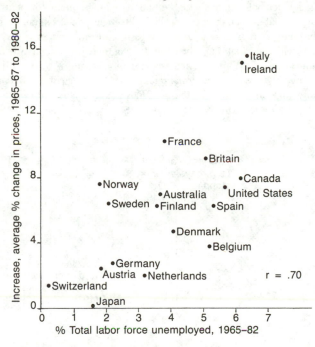

Figure 8. Unemployment and inflation in eighteen nations, 1965-82.

Why were some nations apparently able to maintain relative price stability during the 1970s and early 1980s without resorting to the American anti-inflationary policy of frequent recession and the high and increasing unemployment associated with frequent recession? Why were some nations, for example Switzerland, Japan, Austria, Sweden, and Norway, able to limit the increase in prices between the mid-1960s and early 1980s to single digits without forsaking near-full employment? And what, if anything, does that imply about the distributional struggle between, and relative power of, capital and labor in those nations, compared with the situation in the United States? Such questions demand extensive analysis and it would be foolhardy to attempt to offer complete answers in the closing paragraphs of this essay.[33] Furthermore, the very nature of the small group of countries that have managed to defy a Phillipsian trade-off between employment and price stability—including, as it does, large nations and small, nations in which the work force is highly unionized and organized in powerful labor confederations and others in which most of the work force is unorganized and grouped in weak confederations, and nations that have been dominated by Social Democratic and Labor parties as well as nations in which such parties are weak or excluded from power—guarantees that any generalization will be subject to qualification.

In spite of the inevitable caveats and qualifications that must accompany any generalization about the sources of cross-national variation in inflation and unemployment, it is nevertheless possible to identify several consequential attributes that have allowed some nations to avoid the American experience of price stabilization through frequent recession and high and increasing unemployment. Figure 9 suggests a few of those attributes and helps one understand why some nations escaped the supposedly unavoidable trade-off between price stability and full employment while others, including the United States, suffered both relatively high inflation *and* high unemployment.

Figure 9 suggests that the variation across the eighteen advanced capitalist nations in the magnitude of increase in average rate of change in consumer prices is very closely associated (r = .93) with the variation in the magnitude of increase in the hourly earnings of workers in manufacturing.[34] While not necessarily demonstrating a "wage-push" model of inflation, the extremely close cross-national relationship does suggest that the acceleration in the rate of change in prices after the mid-1960s was associated with, and possibly causally related to, the increase in the rate of change in wages (as our earlier analysis

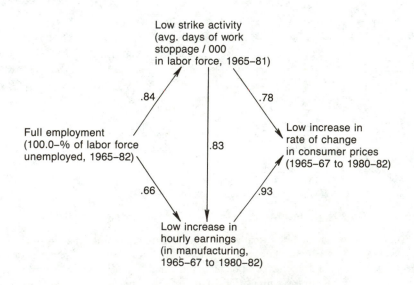

Figure 9. The relation of rate of unemployment, strike activity, increase in earnings, and increase in prices in eighteen nations, 1965–82.

suggested was the case in the United States at certain periods). Figure 9 also suggests that the cross-national variation in the magnitude of the change in the average rate of change in earnings is very closely associated (r = .83) with a measure of the cross-national variation in strike activity.[35] These data indicate, then, that the nations that experienced high levels of strike activity throughout the period experienced large increases in the rate of change of earnings and consumer prices. Conversely, the nations in which strike activity was, on average, relatively low experienced relatively small increases (or even decreases) in the rate of change in earnings, and thus relatively small increases in the rate of change in consumer prices.

   Why was labor quiescent in some nations—quiescent in the sense of manifesting a relatively low level of strike activity and obtaining relatively small increases in the rate of change in earnings—and economically militant in others, using the strike to push for relatively large increases in wages? Figures 9 and 10 suggest an answer—one that helps us account for the initially paradoxical occurrence of price stability and full employment in some nations and inflation and high unemployment in others. These figures reveal that the cross-national variation in strike activity and acceleration in earnings is very closely associated with the level of unemployment. The nations that maintained virtually full employment throughout the period were the ones in which the average rate of change in earnings increased by the *smallest* amount (r = .66). And they were the nations in which the average level of strike activity was *lowest* over the eighteen years (r = .84). In other words, labor quiescence, which was apparently a necessary precondition for price stability, depended in turn on the maintenance of full employment. As Figure 10

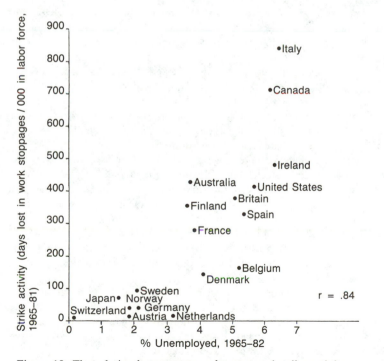

Figure 10. The relation between unemployment and strike activity in eighteen nations, 1965–82.

demonstrates, Switzerland, Japan, Norway, Sweden, West Germany, Austria, and the Netherlands were the only nations that managed to maintain the long-term average rate of unemployment at or below three percent. They were also the only nations in which the average rate of strike activity was less than 100 days. As a result of this abstinence from using its ultimate weapon in the distributional struggle with capital, labor experienced relatively small increases in earnings (in spite of the existence of tight labor markets) and these nations thus experienced price stability *in spite of* near-full employment. Conversely, all the nations in which average unemployment exceeded four percent experienced at least 150 days of strikes per thousand workers, and all but one of those in which unemployment exceeded five percent experienced more than 300 days of strike activity. Included in this latter group of nations—nations in which most workers were unorganized but in which those who were organized were militant in the sense of using the strike to push for wage increases—are Italy, Canada, Ireland, Britain, and the United States. In these nations, the organized segment of the labor movement struck frequently, in spite of the high and increasing rate of unemployment, in order to promote its short-term economic interests. In so doing, it not only maintained and accentuated the considerable wage differentials that already existed between organized and unorganized labor but also contributed to the acceleration in the rate of change in prices, thereby providing an incentive for employers to shed more labor.

The relationships presented in Figures 9 and 10 suggest that the simultaneous occurrence of price stability and full employment in some nations and inflation and unemployment in others reflects a complex causal relationship between the two, in which the relative quiescence or economic militance of labor plays a critical intermediary role. Where full employment is maintained, labor is relatively quiescent and thus earnings, and prices, increase at only a modest rate. Where unemployment is relatively high, labor is militant and thus earnings, and prices, increase by relatively large amounts. In the latter case, those increases in earnings and prices provide employers a rationale for further increases in unemployment, just as the modest increases in earnings and prices in the former case provide sufficient profits to dampen the labor-shedding tendencies of employers. In both cases, there exists an implicit trade-off between the immediate economic gains of organized workers and the longer-term likelihood of jobs for all workers; in some countries, where labor is economically militant, it opts for the former; in others, where labor is quiescent, it opts for the latter, and in so doing allows the nation to experience relatively full employment *and* price stability.[36]

The analysis presented here suggests that some nations have in fact avoided the American experience of accelerating inflation *and* high and rising unemployment, and the tendency to fight inflation with unemployment. They have done so by maintaining price stability, in large part because of the quiescence of labor movements that valued the maintenance of full employment more highly than large increases in wages in the short term. That being the case, it is perhaps appropriate to conclude this discussion by asking what political and social factors are most likely to produce enduring full employment and labor quiescence, in contrast to the predominantly Anglo-American pattern of high unemployment and labor wage militance.

Table 4 presents correlations between several political and social attributes in the eighteen nations and the measures of long-term employment and labor quiescence. These attributes include the average proportion of the labor force that is unionized; the extent to which collective bargaining takes place on an industry-wide or economy-wide basis; the extent to which leftist parties governed during the eighteen years; the extent of the power of labor confederations to intervene in collective bargaining, the extent to

Table 4

Political and Social Correlates of Full Employment
and Labor Quiescence in Eighteen Nations, 1965-82

	Full employment (100 − % unemployed)	Low strike activity (1/days lost per 000)
Avg. % labor force, union members	.16	.20
Scope of collective bargaining	.29	.34
Leftist party control of government	.44	.47
Labor confederation power in collective bargaining	.44	.51
Organizational concentration of the labor movement	.51	.61
Works councils and schemes of co-determination	.51	.67

which the labor movement is organized in a few broad industry-wide unions grouped in a single confederation or, conversely, in a large number of unions, many of which are craft or skill-based; and, finally, the extent to which works councils and schemes of co-determination exist.[37] Table 4 reveals that enduring full employment and labor quiescence—the two factors that enabled some nations to experience relatively small increases in prices and unemployment in the last two decades—were only modestly associated with the extent of unionization and a wide scope of collective bargaining. But both were quite strongly associated with the extent of leftist party control of government, the power of labor confederations in collective bargaining, the existence of a highly concentrated labor movement marked by the presence of relatively few unions grouped in one or a few confederations, and, finally, the existence of works councils and schemes of co-determination. All of these attributes of labor's power—its inclusiveness, its ability to speak with a single voice in collective bargaining, its organizational coherence, its representational role within enterprises, and its affiliation with the government—are not, of course, enough to alter the fundamental nature of the capitalist economy and the inherent imbalance of power between capital and labor. But where labor has possessed those attributes it has at least been able to avoid the fate experienced in countries, such as the United States, where labor is weak: It has been able to avoid participating in an interminable struggle over shares of income that produces inflation at one stage and, soon thereafter, one more in a series of recurrent, unemployment-creating recessions. Such "power resources" have not transformed capitalism,[38] but they have enabled labor, in Scharpf's words, "to effectively disengage employment opportunities from the development of the capitalist economy."[39] That obviously has not produced, and has little prospect of producing, a transition to socialism. But, given the enormous costs of high unemployment, it is—from the vantage point of the United States—a very significant achievement.

Notes

1. An earlier version of this argument was originally prepared as the concluding section of "Taxes, Spending, and Deficits: Does Government Cause Inflation?" in Charles Maier and Leon Lindberg, eds., *The Politics of Inflation and Economic Stagnation* (Washington, D.C.: The Brookings Institution, 1984). For their comments and suggestions, the author wishes to thank Gosta Esping-Andersen, Thomas Ferguson, John Goldthorpe, Peter Katzenstein, Robert Keohane, Peter Lange, Fritz Scharpf, and Susan Woodward.

2. Andrew Shonfield, *Modern Capitalism* (London: Oxford, 1969), pp. 61, 62.

3. Raford Boddy and James Crotty, "Class Conflict and Macro-Policy: The Political Business Cycle," *The Review of Radical Political Economics*, Vol. 7 (Spring 1975), p. 10.

4. Michal Kalecki, "Political Aspects of Full Employment," *The Political Quarterly* (October-December 1943), pp. 329-30. Kalecki's view was hardly novel, even four decades ago. Wesley Mitchell made a similar argument in 1913 in *Business Cycles* (California, 1913), republished in 1941 as *Business Cycles and Their Causes*. See, in addition, Michal Kalecki, *Selected Essays on the Dynamics of the Capitalist Economy* (Cambridge, 1971); Arthur F. Burns and Wesley C. Mitchell, *Measuring Business Cycles* (National Bureau of Economic Research, 1947); Joseph Schumpeter, *Business Cycles*, 2 Vol. (McGraw Hill, 1939); and Robert A. Gordon and Lawrence R. Klein (eds.), *Readings in Business Cycles* (Irwin, 1965).

5. The data contained in Figure 1 and subsequent Figures for the United States are reported in *Economic Report of the President, February 1983* (Washington, D.C.: U.S.G.P.O., 1983). Employment is reported in Table B-29, and inflation in Table B-55.

6. The U.S. involvement in Vietnam began, of course, much earlier—shortly after the defeat of the French at Dien Bien Phu in 1954 (and lasted much later, into the mid-1970s). In terms of substantial troop commitments, however, the involvement began in the summer of 1965 when Lyndon Johnson approved the military's first large request for troops (205,000).

7. See Table B-29 of the *Economic Report of the President, February 1983*.

8. We should note, however, that the 1948-49 recession did not begin until November 1948. It seems unlikely, therefore, that Truman's difficulty in winning can be attributed to the recession. On the other hand, Carter's defeat—especially insofar as it derived from defections of working class voters in heavily industrialized states—surely can be so attributed. For a discussion of the 1980 election, see Thomas Ferguson and Joel Rogers, eds., *The Hidden Election: Politics and Economics in the 1980 Presidential Campaign* (New York: Pantheon, 1981), especially the chapters by Ferguson and Rogers, Walter Dean Burnham, and Gerald Epstein.

9. See M. Harvey Brenner, *Mental Illness and the Economy* (Cambridge: Harvard, 1973) and M. Harvey Brenner, "Estimating the Social Costs of National Economic Policy: Implications for Mental and Physical Health and Criminal Aggression," Prepared for the Joint Economic Committee of the Congress of the United States (Washington, D.C.: U.S.G.P.O., 1976).

10. Strike activity is defined in terms of the number of days of work stoppage per thousand members of the total labor force, excluding those work stoppages which involve fewer than six employees or last for less than one day. The data from which the rate of strike activity was calculated are reported in *Statistical Abstract of the United States*, 1982/83 and earlier years.

11. The data are reported in Table B-38 of the *Economic Report of the President, February 1983*.

12. See A. W. Phillips, "The Relation Between Unemployment and the Rate of Change of Money Wage Rates in the United Kingdom, 1861-1957," *Economica* Vol. 25 (1957), pp. 283-99.

13. The rate of profit is calculated after taxes and inventory valuation and capital consumption adjustments, as a proportion of the gross domestic product of those corporations. The profit rates are calculated from data presented in Table B-12 of the *Economic Report of the President, February 1983*. Employee compensation includes wages, salaries, and employers' contributions for social insurance and to private pension, health, and welfare funds. The proportions are calculated from data presented in Table B-21 of the *Economic Report of the President, February 1983*.

14. For a discussion of the secular trend of declining profitability, see William D. Nordhaus, "The Falling Share of Profit," *Brookings Papers on Economic Activity* (1:1974), pp. 169-208; Martin Feldstein and Lawrence Summers, "Is the Rate of Profit Falling?" *Brookings Papers on Economic*

Activity (1:1977), pp. 211-27; and Thomas E. Weisskopf, "Marxian Crisis Theory and the Rate of Profit in the Post-War U.S. Economy," *Cambridge Journal of Economics*, Vol. 3 (December 1979), pp. 341-378.

15. This argument is hardly surprising, of course. For one discussion of the "privileged position" of business, see Charles E. Lindblom, *Politics and Markets* (New York: Basic Books, 1977).

16. Because OPEC was paid in dollars, its "real" income decreased through the late 1960s and early 1970s as inflation reduced the value of the dollar. And after 1971, when Nixon closed the "gold window" at the Treasury and terminated the Bretton Woods system of fixed exchange rates pegged to the dollar and to gold, the OPEC nations suffered a substantial reduction in the real value of oil revenues.

17. Calculated from data in Tables B-1 and B-75 of the *Economic Report of the President, February 1983*.

18. For a discussion of the fiscal policy of the Johnson Administration—a policy that was made as much *against* as with the advice of the Council of Economic Advisers—see Arthur Okun, *The Political Economy of Prosperity* (Washington, D.C.: Brookings, 1970). Okun served as a member of the Council between 1964 and 1968 and as chairman in 1968-69. For a discussion of macroeconomic policy in the early 1960s by another former member of the Council, see James Tobin, *The New Economics One Decade Older* (Princeton: Princeton, 1974). Also, see Herbert Stein, *The Fiscal Revolution in America* (Chicago: Chicago, 1969), Ch. 15-17.

19. David R. Cameron, "Elections and the Economy," unpublished manuscript, 1984.

20. See Okun, *The Political Economy of Prosperity*, Ch. 3; and Tobin, *The New Economics One Decade Older*, Ch. 2.

21. Robert J. Gordon, "The Demand for and Supply of Inflation," *Journal of Law and Economics*, December 1975, p. 808.

22. For a theoretical and empirical discussion of the relative power of business and labor in the advanced capitalist nations, see Walter Korpi, *The Democratic Class Struggle* (London: Macmillan, 1983), Ch. 3 and 8.

23. Calculated from data in Tables B-1 and B-21 of the *Economic Report of the President, February, 1983*.

24. The data are reported in Table B-41 of the *Economic Report of the President, February 1983*. We should note that the measure of productivity is not entirely satisfactory, since it includes only one of the several factors of production in the denominator. Increases in output may depend to a much greater degree on the amount of capital invested than on the amount of hours worked by employees. In addition, of course, the measure of output is highly problematic as an indicator of the product of large sectors of the economy such as government, hospitals, universities, etc.

25. See Edward Tufte, *Political Control of the Economy* (Princeton: Princeton, 1978), p. 75.

26. Note the emphasis on the word *relative*. We are *not* suggesting that American industry is weak. It is weak only relative to finance and the large multinational segment of industry; certainly relative to labor, industry has been, and remains, very strong.

27. See Peter Katzenstein, "Conclusion," in Katzenstein, ed., *Between Power and Plenty* (Madison: Wisconsin, 1978) for a discussion of the difference in foreign economic policy between the United States and Britain, in which international financial and industrial interests were strong and which favored a stable although overvalued dollar or pound, and France, West Germany, and Japan, in which domestic industrial producers—including exporters—were relatively stronger and which as a result were more likely to favor an undervalued currency. For a discussion of how the decline in Britain's imperial order contributed to the characteristic pattern of "stop-go" policy and slow growth—an experience that is analogous in many ways to that of the United States after World War II—see David R. Cameron, "Creating Theory in Comparative Political Economy: On Mancur Olson's Explanation of Economic Growth," presented at the Annual Meeting of the American Political Science Association, Chicago, 1983.

28. The data are reported in Table B-67 of the *Economic Report of the President, February 1983*. See also the analysis of Fed Policy in Gerald Epstein, "Domestic Stagflation and Monetary Policy: The Federal Reserve and the Hidden Election," in Ferguson and Rogers, *The Hidden Election*.

29. The argument presented here is, of course, quite compatible with Schumpeter's notion

of "the perennial gale of creative destruction" in capitalist society. See Joseph A. Schumpeter, *Capitalism, Socialism and Democracy* (Harper and Row, 1950), Ch. 7 (quoted at p. 84).

30. The data on unemployment have been standardized by calculating all unemployed as a proportion of the total labor force. Data are reported in Organisation for Economic Co-operation and Development, *Labour Force Statistics, 1960-71* (Paris: O.E.C.D., 1973) and subsequent volumes, including *Quarterly Supplements*.

31. The data are reported in O.E.C.D., *Economic Outlook*, 33 (July 1983) (Paris: O.E.C.D., 1983), p. 167.

32. See Phillips, "The Relation Between Unemployment and the Rate of Change of Money Wage Rates in the United Kingdom, 1861-1957." For a cross-national analysis that finds a trade-off between unemployment and inflation analogous to that of the Phillips curve, see Douglas A. Hibbs, Jr., "Political Parties and Macroeconomic Policy," *American Political Science Review*, Vol. 71 (December 1977), p. 1472.

33. For such an analysis, see Fritz Scharpf, "Strategy Choice, Economic Feasibility and Institutional Constraints as Determinants of Full-Employment Policy During the Recession," in John Goldthorpe, ed., *Order and Conflict in Western Capitalism* (forthcoming).

34. The data on hourly earnings are reported in O.E.C.D., *Economic Outlook*, and O.E.C.D., *Main Economic Indicators*.

35. The measure of strike activity is comparable to that presented earlier for the United States. It consists of the average over the seventeen years between 1965-81 (the last year for which data are available) in the number of days lost in work stoppages per thousand members of the labor force. The data are reported in International Labour Organisation, *Yearbook of Labour Statistics, 1981*, and earlier volumes. For a discussion of these data, see David. R. Cameron, "Social Democracy, Corporatism, and Labor Quiescence in Advanced Capitalist Society," in Goldthorpe, ed., *Order and Conflict in Western Capitalism*. Also, see Korpi. *The Democratic Class Struggle*, Ch. 8.

36. For an elaboration, see Cameron, "Social Democracy, Corporatism, and Labor Quiescence in Advanced Capitalist Society." See, also, Adam Przeworski and Michael Wallerstein, "The Structure of Class Conflict in Democratic Capitalist Societies," *American Political Science Review*, Vol. 76 (June 1982).

37. For a detailed discussion of these measures, see Cameron, "Social Democracy, Corporatism, and Labor Quiescence in Advanced Capitalist Society."

38. On "power resources," see Korpi, *The Democratic Class Struggle*, Ch. 2, 3.

39. Scharpf, "Strategy Choice, Economic Feasibility and Institutional Constraints as Determinants of Full-Employment Policy During the Recession," p. 11.

Economic Power and Political Influence: The Impact of Industry Structure on Public Policy

LESTER M. SALAMON and JOHN J. SIEGFRIED

It has been a cliché of politics since biblical times that "money surpasseth all things" in providing the means to achieve political ends. Though this general point is almost universally admitted, the controversies are numerous as to when and where financial means are decisive in a political conflict, and to what end they are used. The following study by Lester M. Salamon and John J. Siegfried starts with the assumption that corporations have both the means and the motivation to be involved in the political process. By establishing a "Tax Avoidance Rate" index, they show that firm size, industry size, and other organizational factors have a statistically demonstrable influence on an outcome that is presumably of vital interest to a firm: its effective tax rate.

F ew questions are as important to an understanding of American democracy as the relationship between economic power and political influence.[1] Yet few questions have received so many disparate answers from scholars and pundits alike. While few students of the subject would deny that corporations have unusual resources for political action, there is considerable disagreement over the extent of their success in bringing these resources to bear in the policy process. Depending on which examples one chooses, in fact, it is possible to conclude that American corporations are either politically impotent or politically omnipotent, with infinite variations in between. Some writers see in the extensive interchanges between corporate and governmental elites, the frequent success of corporate lobbying in both legislative and administrative realms, and the widespread pattern of private expropriation of public authority sufficient evidence to support Woodrow Wilson's charge that "the masters of the government in the United States are the combined capitalists and manufacturers of the United States."[2] But others stress the alternative sources of power in the political process and the nonpolitical activities that can absorb the energies and attention of the economic elite.[3] [. . .]

Industry Structure and Political Influence: The Theory

In general terms, two broad sets of factors shape the impact that an economic sector has on public policy: first, the nature of the political system; and second, the structure of the economic sector itself. The first of these helps define the political system's susceptibility to

Reprinted from the *American Political Science Review*, Vol. 71, No. 4 (December 1977), pp. 1026-43 (with deletions). Copyright 1977 by the American Political Science Association.

economic influences; the second helps determine the ability of a particular industry to take advantage of that susceptibility. While other factors—like skill, luck, timing, and leadership—also play important roles, these two set the broad parameters of the relationship between economic and political power, and therefore offer the most fruitful subjects for systematic analysis. Let us examine each in turn.

The Political Process   Perhaps the defining characteristic of the American political system is its permeability to outside pressures. Through voting, congressional testimony, campaign finance, and a host of additional means, the political system offers relatively easy access by citizens to the central policy-making process on a regular basis. While this relative permeability raises the possibility of broad public control of governmental policy *à la* pure democratic theory, however, it also raises the paradoxical possibility of translating disproportionate economic power into disproportionate political influence in a way that can frustrate broad public control. Three aspects of the political system in particular facilitate this translation.

The first of these concerns the maldistribution of incentives for political action, what might be termed the "free rider problem." As numerous democratic theorists have noted, political involvement is, like any other investment, contingent upon the expectation of a reasonable rate of return on invested resources. But since each individual consumer-taxpayer (or small firm) typically bears only a small portion of the costs and enjoys only a small share of the benefits from public programs, he surely has the incentive to spend the energy, time, and resources needed to influence the policy. For other political actors, like large corporations, however, the potential benefits and costs of government action are sizeable enough to make political involvement a rational investment. The consequence is a gross disparity in the incentives for political involvement that works to induce the citizen-taxpayer toward passivity while stimulating the large corporation toward political activism. In his essay on *The Logic of Collective Action*, Mancur Olson provides a general theory of political activism in just these terms, arguing that groups with larger numbers can be expected to be less effective in securing collective goods than those with fewer members because

> a collective good is, by definition, such that other individuals in the group cannot be kept from consuming it once any individual in the group has provided it for himself. Since an individual member thus gets only part of the benefit of any expenditure he makes to obtain more of the collective good, he will discontinue his purchase of the collective good before the optimal amount for the group as a whole has been obtained. In addition, the amounts of the collective good that a member of the group receives free from other members will further reduce his incentive to provide more of that good at his own expense. Accordingly, *the larger the group, the farther it will fall short of providing an optimal amount of a collective good* [emphasis in original].[4]

Not only does Olson's theory suggest a difference in incentives for political activism between consumer-taxpayers and the corporate sector generally, however, it also suggests a basis for expecting variations in incentives *within* the corporate sector itself because of differences in the economic structure of different industries. It is this aspect of the free rider concept we will test below.

Not only are the *incentives* for political involvement grossly disparate, but so is the distribution of politically relevant *resources*. Large-scale corporate enterprises have important political advantages by virtue of their control over sizeable quantities of several crucial political resources: money, expertise, and access to government officials. These resources are frequently direct outgrowths of the enterprises' regular economic activities, which, in the age of the "new industrial state," frequently put the enterprise in intimate contact with scores of government officials on a day-to-day basis. By contrast, the typical consumer-taxpayer has only one resource regularly at his command: the vote. While the electoral process theoretically gives the mass of unorganized citizens a mechanism to remedy whatever inequities arise from the struggle of organized groups without incurring the costs associated with more direct political action, things rarely work out so smoothly in practice. [. . .]

What makes this maldistribution of *incentives* and *resources* for political action so important is the highly fragmented character of the policy process in American government, which plays directly into the hands of those with organized resources focused on particular policy issues. Part of this fragmentation is dictated by constitutional provisions establishing a government of "separated institutions sharing powers."[5] But part of it grows out of the more informal arrangements these institutions have developed to process their workload. The classic example of this fragmentation is the pervasive decentralization of power in the U.S. Congress. Long ago legislators discovered that they could hold their own in the interinstitutional donnybrook that is the American political system only by channeling legislative business through specialized committees run by politically independent legislators with long tenure in the Congress. In pursuit of institutional viability, therefore, decision-making authority was fractionated into numerous relatively autonomous chunks. [. . .]

The consequences of this pattern of governmental decision making are profound. Instead of a single integrated policy process, what emerges is a series of individual, and largely independent, "policy subsystems" linking portions of the bureaucracy, their related congressional committees, and organized clientele groups in a symbiotic state of equilibrium.[6] The key to policy-making power, therefore, is access not to the political system generally but to these well-insulated and highly structured subsystems. Voter-taxpayers can occasionally gain access to the overall political system. Effective access to the subsystems, however, is typically confined to those with the expertise, resources, and influence to provide stable sources of support to key subsystem actors over extended periods of time.

Further complicating the job of the activist citizen is the predominance of administrative over legislative decision making in modern government. The theory of separation of powers notwithstanding, the bureaucracy performs crucial legislative and judicial as well as administrative functions in American government. The vast bulk of legislation considered by Congress originates in the bureaucracy, and it is the bureaucracy that makes the most potent input into the legislative process thanks to its control of information. In addition, statute law (law passed by Congress) is overwhelmed by the far greater volume of administrative law produced by the bureaucracy in the course of interpreting congressional intent. As a former commissioner of the Federal Communications Commission has put it:

> While the Courts handle thousands of cases each year and Congress produces hundreds of laws each year, the administrative agencies handle hundreds of thousands of matters annually. The administrative agencies are engaged in the mass production of law, in contrast to the Courts [and Congress], which are engaged in the handicraft production of law.[7]

This predominance of administrative rule-making puts a premium on technical expertise and on the ability to follow the complex evolution of administrative decision making. Far from expanding presidential power *per se*, the expansion of administrative rule making really contributes to the influence of the private subsystem actors who alone have the resources to retain Washington legal counsels and research staffs to analyze relevant agency decisions and respond to them effectively. The very structure of governmental decision making, like the maldistribution of incentives and resources, thus facilitates the translation of economic power into political influence.

Economic Structure and the Political Process   If the maldistribution of incentives and resources for political action, and the structure of the policy process facilitate the translation of economic power into political influence, the economic structure of particular industries helps determine which ones are in the best position to take advantage of this opportunity.   But which aspects of economic structure are most germane? What types of differences among industries are most relevant in explaining variations in their levels of political influence?

To answer these questions, it is necessary to turn to the literature on industrial organization and to evaluate this literature in the light of political science findings about the effectiveness of various corporate pressure group tactics.[8] What emerges most clearly from such an evaluation is the hypothesis that *firm size* , the average size of firms in an industry, is the most important aspect of economic structure so far as the implications for political influence are concerned. Much of the concern about conglomerates and rising aggregate concentration in the American economy, in fact, grows out of the fear that large firms wield not just disproportionate economic power, but also disproportionate political influence,[9] for a variety of reasons. In the first place, to the extent that public policies deliver benefits proportional to the size of the firm (which is the case, for example, with the income tax system), then the larger the firm the greater the incentive to participate in politics, for reasons suggested by Olson. But larger firms not only have greater incentives to participate in politics, they also have larger resources with which to do so. Kaysen[10] and Edwards[11] have both suggested that economic power is an important source of political power, either directly, through campaign finance, or indirectly, through the purchase of expertise to generate information instrumental in the policy process and liaison agents to transmit this information to the relevant policy makers. A National Industrial Conference Board study found that large firms tended to represent their legislative views more frequently than did smaller firms.[12] By the same token, Bauer, Poole, and Dexter found that firm size is an important determinant of the political activity of executives, since the executives of large firms could afford the luxury of hiring staffs and taking the time to inform themselves about policy issues.[13]

What makes the absolute size of available resources, and hence firm size, so important politically is the fact that political involvement has certain fixed costs attached to it (we will call this the "threshold problem"). Like a single pain-reliever commercial, corporate political activity is likely to produce little payoff unless sustained over a period of time and spread over a variety of policy-making arenas. Since small firms can rarely sustain these high fixed costs, they are generally constrained to channel their political involvement more extensively through trade associations, with all the intra-organizational differences, lack of control, and consequent weakening of influence that carries with it.[14]

Access to economic resources is not the only political asset arising from larger firm size. Also important is the prestige typically accorded individuals who reach the command posts of the larger corporate enterprises, a prestige that is transferable into political influence through the numerous advisory committees and personal contacts that bind the worlds of business and government together. Equally important is the larger pool of expertise potentially available to the larger firms, and, on some occasions, the larger number of employees and stockholders who can be mobilized (or threatened to be mobilized) for political action. Other things being equal, therefore, we hypothesize that an industry containing large firms will have greater political influence than an industry of the same size but composed of more numerous small firms. At the same time, we expect this influence to be mitigated somewhat by the visibility of large firms and the consequent dangers they face of attracting adverse public attention. [. . .]

Federal Corporate Income Tax Rates: Empirical Test I   Under the federal income tax laws in effect at the time for which we collected our data, all firms were required to pay 52 per cent of their taxable income in taxes. However, the Internal Revenue Code includes numerous "special' tax provisions (such as the investment credit, the special capital gains rate, the surtax exemption for income under $25,000, the depletion allowance, etc.) that reduce the effective tax rate below this 52 per cent level. For each of the 110 "minor industries" for which tax data were available, we computed the effective average tax rate produced by these special tax provisions.[15] Our dependent variable, then, is the deviation of this effective tax rate from the 52 per cent rate. This "tax avoidance rate" measures the success with which an industry has reduced its tax burden below the standard 52 per cent rate thanks to the operation of the "special provisions" in the code. As shown in Table 1, the tax avoidance rate varied from a high of 35.8 per cent for the Miscellaneous Nonmetallic Minerals industry to a low of 3.9 per cent for the Newspaper industry. [. . .]

To test our hypotheses about the political impact of variations in economic structure, we converted each of our dimensions of economic structure into measurable terms and tested its impact on the Tax Avoidance Rate, using multiple regression techniques to control for the impact of the other factors in the model. Table 2 below summarizes the results of this analysis, along with the measurement used for each variable, and the relationship hypothesized on the basis of our theory. (Table 3 records the simple correlation between each of our independent variables and the Tax Avoidance Rate.)

Firm size: The first thing that emerges from this table is that the hypothesized relationship between firm size and political influence, which formed the heart of our inquiry, is supported by the data. As noted in the table, firm size was measured by taking the asset size of that firm which accounts for the median asset dollar in an industry. When this factor was tested for its effect on the corporate Tax Avoidance Rate, while controlling for the effects of our four other measures of economic structure, the results were statistically significant and in the expected direction. A one per cent increase in firm size was found to be associated with a .08 per cent increase in the Tax Avoidance Rate. Even though it is difficult to evaluate the practical importance of this degree of change, it is nevertheless significant to have validated this hypothesis empirically across so large a number of observations.

Industry size: Unlike the firm size variable, the industry size variable seems to have little significant impact on the Tax Avoidance Rate. Industry size was measured in terms of total employment, which allowed us to tap the political influence represented by employee dependence on the industries that employ them. As noted, we had theoretical reasons to expect a positive relationship between industry size and tax avoidance, on grounds that larger industries had more resources with which to overcome the threshold problem and greater number of potential supporters among voters. But we also had reason to expect a negative relationship, on the grounds that larger industries would encounter

Table 1

1963 Tax Avoidance Rates for Industries with Rates More than
One Standard Deviation from the All-industry Mean
(Mean = 12.6, Standard Deviation = 6.82)

IRS "Minor Industry" Code	Industry Description	Tax Rate Avoidance (Percentage)
1498	Miscellaneous Nonmetallic Minerals	35.8
1100	Coal Mining	33.8
2912	Petroleum Refining with Extraction	32.2
3330	Nonferrous Primary Metals	30.5
3662	Electronic Components	28.2
1310	Crude Petroleum Natural Gas and Liquids	27.9
1410	Stone and Gravel	27.6
2870	Agricultural Chemicals	27.2
2911	Petroleum Refining without Extraction	27.0
2091	Vegetable and Animal Oils	25.5
3098	Miscellaneous Plastic Products	23.7
2410	Logging, Lumber, and Basic Wood Products	21.0
1020	Copper, Lead, Zinc, Gold, Silver Ores	20.9
2010	Meat Products	20.2
3198	Leather Tanning and Finishing	19.5
2070	Confectionary Products	5.8
3530	Construction, Mining, Material Handling Machinery	5.6
3611	Electrical Transmission and Distribution Equipment	5.6
3260	Pottery	5.4
3698	Electrical Machinery, N.E.C.	5.4
2212	Broad Woven Fabric Mills, Man-Made Fibers	5.0
3560	General Industry Machinery	4.9
2640	Converted Paper and Paperboard Products	4.6
2100	Tobacco Manufactures	4.1
2611	Pulp Mills	4.1
2711	Newspapers	3.9

the "free rider" problem more severely. Therefore, we subjected this hypothesis to a more rigorous, two-tailed significance test. The results suggest that the "free rider" hypothesis is the more accurate one—a finding that makes sense in light of the many competing interests that vie for the voter patronage of industrial workers. On tax matters in particular, it seems more likely that employees will support a position contrary to that of management, especially if they are unionized, since unions recognize that taxes not paid by business will result either in a reduction of public services or an increase in other taxes. But the observed negative relationship, though consistent with our earlier hunch, is too weak to give us more than 90 per cent confidence that it did not occur merely by chance.

Market concentration: In the case of *market concentration,* the results show a

Table 2

Relationship Between Tax Avoidance Rate and
Five Aspects of Economic Structure,
110 IRS "Minor Industries"

Variable	Measurement	Hypothesized Sign[a]	Regression Coefficient	t-ratio
Firm Size	Asset size of firm which accounts for the median asset dollar in an industry	+	.084**	2.42
Industry Size	Employees	+/—	—.095	—1.72
Market Concentration	Percent of sales accounted for by four largest firms	+/—	—.512**	—2.94
Profit Rate	Net income plus interest as % of assets	+/—	—.301*	—2.46
Geographical Concentration	Index based on distribution of employees across states; higher values indicate more concentration	+/—	—.017	—0.15

[a]A positive sign indicates that we hypothesize a direct relationship between the independent and dependent variables. A positive and negative sign signifies that we have found theoretical reasons to expect either a direct or indirect relationship. In such cases, we subject our results to a two-tailed significance test.

*Statistically significant at the .05 level.

**Statistically significant at the .01 level.

R^2 (coefficient of determination) = .158.

Fisher's F statistic = 3.892*.

Standard error of the estimate = .465.

Number of observations = 110.

Table 3

Mean and Standard Deviation of Independent Variables
and Correlation with Tax Avoidance Rate

Independent Variables	Mean	Standard Deviation	Simple Correlation with TAR
Firm Size (F)	$166 million	$368 million	.060
Industry Size (I)	223,500 employees	225,900 employees	—.050
Market Concentration (C)	39.62%	14.34%	—.176
Profit Rate (R)	11.15%	5.46%	—.189
Geographical Dispersion (D)	.1401	.0742	.007

significant impact on the Tax Avoidance Rate, but in a direction opposite to what we originally expected. Market concentration was calculated on the basis of the proportion of all industry shipments accounted for by the four largest firms in the industry.[16] We hypothesized that market concentration would be associated with a high level of political influence, since concentrated industries could expect to avoid the "free rider" problem more easily than nonconcentrated industries. At the same time, we noted that highly concentrated industries would face some disabilities in exercising political influence as a result of their fears about arousing public attention and what we called the "wear-out-your-welcome" problem. As is apparent from Table 2, this latter argument is the one that finds support in the evidence. A one per cent increase in market concentration is associated with a .512 per cent decrease in Tax Avoidance Rates. One reason for this finding could be that our measure of market concentration does not capture the "free rider" problem as accurately as a simple measure of the number of firms in an industry, which is already partially accounted for in the industry size variable. Indeed, with the "free rider" and higher profit rate aspects of market concentration factored out (which is what our controls for firm size, industry size, and profit rate essentially do), it is understandable that the independent effect of market concentration on the successful exercise of political power is negative.

Profit rate: The profit rate variable also turns out to be negatively related to success at tax avoidance. Profit rate is defined here as the ratio of net income plus interest to total industry assets, where net income is calculated by taking reported taxable income and adding to it the items excluded from reported taxable income thanks to the special tax provisions. On the basis of the available literature, we suggested that industries with higher profits would be most effective politically because of their access to more substantial resources and the greater incentive they would have to reduce taxes on their profits. Yet, we also noted that such industries had a strong incentive to abstain from efforts to lower their effective average tax rates for fear that extensive political involvement might draw attention to the favorable market environment responsible for their high returns and thus invite government regulation. In addition, we suggested that such firms, having achieved their profit objectives, might be pursuing other objectives that are inconsistent with the pursuit of political influence.

The significant negative relationship between profit rate and Tax Avoidance Rate recorded in Table 2 suggests that these latter arguments are more accurate. Profit rate does have a significant impact on the successful exercise of political influence as measured here, but for reasons associated with the favorable-market-environment-more-to-lose hypothesis, not the higher-profits-more-resources-more-to-gain hypothesis.

Geographical concentration: Of all the measures of economic structure used here the geographical concentration factor turns out to have the least discernible impact. Geographical concentration was measured by an index based on the distribution across states of employment in each of the 110 Census-defined industries.[17] The more concentrated the employment of the industry in a few states, the larger the concentration index.

We hypothesized that since a highly concentrated industry would have the greatest success in attracting the attention of at least one set of legislators, it could be assured of having its interests represented in the political process. Here, too, however, an alternative hypothesis also made sense, namely that the more dispersed an industry the more access it could expect to have in the political process. The data reported in Table 2 do not provide sufficient evidence to favor either argument. However, it could be that both factors are at work, but that their approximately equivalent impacts cancel out in our empirical test.

Taken together, the five dimensions of economic structure incorporated in our model explain 16 per cent of the variation in corporate tax avoidance rates, and do so at a confidence level exceeding 95 per cent. For a model seeking to explain so complex a phenomenon over so large a cross-section of observations, this is an encouraging result. What it suggests is that variations in economic structure do affect the success of various industries in securing public benefits (or avoiding public costs), even though such variations explain only a portion of this success. Beyond this, our findings suggest the feasibility of testing the widely hypothesized link between economic structure and political influence in a more systematic, empirical fashion than has been done in the past. In this regard, our discovery of a positive relationship between firm size and Tax Avoidance Rates is particularly significant, since it suggests an empirical base for the long-standing argument that antitrust policy is necessary to avoid not just undue concentra-tions of economic power but also threatening concentrations of political power.

This latter conclusion is further substantiated, moreover, when we take the analysis one step further and examine variations in tax avoidance *within* industries, not just variations among them. For this purpose, we examined the petroleum refining industry in particular, calculating the tax avoidance rates for categories of firms within this industry grouped by asset size.[18] Table 4 below records the results of this analysis. What it shows is that the very largest oil refiners, in particular the integrated "majors," have been best able to take advantage of the special tax provisions that affect business in general and the petroleum industry in particular.[19] This finding supports the results of our cross-industry analysis reported above. Not only do industries with larger firm sizes have larger tax avoidance rates, but also the larger firms within those industries do better than the smaller ones.

Before we can have confidence in any of these tentative conclusions, however, it is necessary to determine whether they are peculiar to the federal income tax arena. Accordingly, we turn our attention to an aspect of state policy to determine whether the economic structure/political influence hypothesis finds empirical support there as well.

Table 4

Tax Avoidance Rates (TAR)
for Petroleum Refining Industry, 1967

Asset Size Class ($1,000,000)	TAR_1	TAR_2
5-10	14.3	14.8
10-25	0.2	8.2
25-50	14.5	14.5
50-100	13.0	13.2
100-250	34.8	35.4
Over 250	27.9	42.3

TAR_1 = 0.52 — (tax liabilities/"true" accounting profits), treating foreign taxes entirely as a substitute for U.S. taxes; foreign tax credit not a "special" provision.

TAR_2 = 0.52 — (tax liabilities — foreign tax credit /"true" accounting profits), treating the foreign tax credit as a "special" tax provision.

State Gasoline Excise Tax Rates: Empirical Test II   In assessing the impact of economic structure on state politics and policy, it is necessary to alter the mode of analysis somewhat. Instead of focusing on industry-by-industry variations in policy impact, the focus here must be on state-by-state variations. What we have done, therefore, is to identify a range of policy that exists in all the states, and then examine state variations in that policy in terms of state-by-state variations in the strength and structure of the economic sectors most affected by it.

The motor fuel excise tax is an excellent candidate for this kind of scrutiny. Every state has such a tax, and the tax rate varies significantly from state to state. In twenty-eight of the states, motor fuel excise tax receipts are "dedicated" to highway construction by constitutional amendment. Not surprisingly, major oil firms have not opposed increases in motor fuel excise tax rates in these states, since these taxes construct highways that ultimately help to increase the demand for gasoline. However, in twenty-two of the states, where motor fuel tax receipts are not dedicated to highway construction, the oil companies have generally lobbied against such increases.[20]

Since state policy making has traditionally been considered even more vulnerable than federal policy making to private interest pressure,[21] we expect significant relationships between state-by-state variations in petroleum industry economic structure and state motor fuel excise tax policies, both the policies on "dedication" and the policies on tax *rates*. Of particular concern are the impacts of two dimensions of state petroleum industry structure: first, the overall size of this industry in the state, measured as a share of state personal income; and second, the extent to which large firms dominate this industry within the state. Based on earlier hypotheses about the impact of economic structure on political influence, we hypothesize, first, that states in which the petroleum industry is large will be more likely to dedicate their motor fuel excise taxes to highway construction than is the case for states without large petroleum industries; and second, that among nondedication states—those that do not dedicate motor fuel excise taxes to highways—the motor fuel excise tax rate will vary indirectly with both the overall size of the petroleum industry in the state and the dominance of large firms within the industry. This latter hypothesis, which suggests that motor fuel excise tax rates will be lower where the petroleum industry is both large and dominated by large firms, reflects the industry's opposition to special taxes on its products when the resulting revenue is not tied to highway construction. In the case of the dedication states, where the petroleum industry has taken a generally neutral stance towards proposed increases in motor fuel excise tax rates (because these taxes are earmarked for further highway expenditures that can be expected to boost gasoline sales), we hypothesize little relationship between our two measures of industry structure and motor fuel excise tax rates.

To test these relationships, we developed measures of the overall size of the petroleum industry in each state and the degree of dominance of large firms within this industry in each state. The first of these measures was computed as the ratio of the value added by the petroleum industry in each state to the personal income of the state. The second was computed as the ratio of the number of firms greater than a fixed employment size to the total number of firms in the industry in each state.[22] In both cases, we computed our indices separately for the crude oil production and petroleum refining segments of the petroleum industry. This was done because there is reason to believe refiners are relatively more interested in excise taxes than crude oil producers, both because a relatively greater proportion of refinery products go into motor fuel production and because a much larger proportion of refinery products are consumed at home, in the states where the refineries are located.

Table 5

Distribution of States Cross-Classified
by Motor Fuel Excise Tax Dedication
and Size of Industry in State

Size of Petroleum Industry	Dedicate Motor Fuel Taxes to Highway Construction		Do Not Dedicate Motor Fuel Taxes to Highway Construction	
	Number of States	Percent of Row	Number of States	Percent of Row
Petroleum refining				
Large[a]	7	(78%)	2	(22%)
Small[b]	21	(51%)	20	(49%)
Crude oil production				
Large[a]	9	(60%)	6	(40%)
Small[b]	19	(54%)	16	(46%)

[a]Greater than one percent of state personal income.

[b]Less than or equal to one percent of state personal income.

To assess the validity of the first hypothesis, i.e., that states with large petroleum industries are more likely to dedicate their motor fuel taxes to highway construction because of the political clout of this industry in state politics, we grouped the states in terms of two factors: whether they contain large or small petroleum industries, and whether or not they dedicate their motor fuel excise taxes to highway construction. The results, reported in Table 5, generally support our hypothesis. Almost four-fifths of the states where petroleum refining accounts for a substantial share of state personal income dedicate their motor fuel taxes to highway construction, compared to only one-half of the states where the overall size of the petroleum refining industry relative to the overall state economy is small. A similar relationship holds with respect to the crude production industry, but there the disparity is much narrower (60 versus 54 per cent), which is what our hypothesis suggested.

To test the impact of firm size and relative industry size on the *level* of state motor fuel excise tax rates, a somewhat more complex analysis was necessary. Like other state revenues, gasoline taxes too may respond more to the availability of income or the general effective demand for public services in a state than to oil industry lobbying. In fact, several political scientists have demonstrated a substantial relationship between state income levels and state governmental expenditures.[23] Since there was reason to expect that the *relative* size of the petroleum industry in a state would vary with the size of the state's economy, it was necessary to introduce controls to verify that our economic structure variables are not really proxies for these overall income variables. In particular, we utilized two control variables, first, the ratio of total state governmental revenues to total state personal income (which measures the state's preference for public vs. private consumption and thus the effective demand for revenues); and second, the state's per capita income (which measures the supply of wealth available). Multiple regression techniques were then applied to determine the impact of these economic structure and control variables on the level of state excise tax rates for all states, and for dedication and nondedication states separately.

Table 6

Relationship Between State Motor Fuel Excise Tax Rates and Petroleum Industry Economic Structure

Regression model for:	Constant	Refining Industry		Crude Oil Industry		Controls		R^2 (proportion of variance explained)
		Overall size[a]	Large firm dominance[b]	Overall size[a]	Large firm dominance[c]	State tax effort[d]	State per capita income	
All 50 States	8.537	−0.423* (−2.78)	−1.295* (−2.54)	+0.046 (2.02)	+1.936 (0.41)	−0.065 (−1.54)	−0.010 (−0.03)	.291
22 Nondedication States	8.290	−0.414 (−0.88)	−1.963* (−2.77)	+0.070 (1.15)	2.816 (0.08)	−0.093 (−1.75)	0.251 (0.65)	.454
28 Dedication States	7.543	−0.370 (−0.43)	−.518 (−0.93)	0.024 (0.17)	3.024* (2.31)	0.044 (0.31)	−0.183 (−0.73)	.283

(Figures shown are partial regression coefficients [B] with t-ratios in parentheses.)

*Statistically significant at the .05 level.

[a]Value added by refining or crude industry in state as a percentage of state personal income.
[b]Number of refineries with greater than 250 employees as a percentage of total number of refineries in state.
[c]Number of crude oil and natural gas establishments with greater than 100 employees as a percentage of total number of crude and natural gas establishments in state.
[d]Total state government revenues as a percentage of state personal income.

The results of these tests, recorded in Table 6, substantially confirm our hypotheses about the relationship between industry economic structure and the successful exercise of political influence. For all fifty states, the structure of the petroleum refining industry is significantly related to the level of motor fuel excise tax rates in precisely the direction hypothesized: tax rates are lower where the petroleum refining industry is large and where it is dominated by large firms. By contrast, no significant relationships were found between tax rates and crude oil industry structure, which is consistent with our argument that crude oil producers are less interested in motor fuel tax rates than are refiners.[24] By the same token, the controls for state tax effort and per capita income showed no significant relationship to motor fuel tax rates, suggesting that the economic *structure* of a state may be more important in explaining significant policy differences than aggregate levels of state economic activity. Altogether, our model accounted for close to 30 per cent of the variation in state motor fuel tax rates among the fifty states, most of it as a result of the impact of the refining industry structure variables.

A comparison of the results for the twenty-two nondedication states to those for the twenty-eight dedication states lends further support to these conclusions. As expected, our economic structure/political influence model is far more successful in explaining tax rate variations in the nondedication states, where the industry lobbied against tax rate increases, than in the dedication states, where it did not. Particularly noteworthy is the operation of our refining industry firm size variable, which is significantly negatively related to the tax rate in the twenty-two nondedication states but not in the dedication states. Evidently, where the large refiners flex their political muscles (the twenty-two nondedication states), they have considerable success. Here is important additional support, therefore, for the firm size/political power hypothesis outlined at the outset of this article.

This finding is even more noteworthy in view of the absence of any statistically significant relationship between motor fuel tax rates and the state per-capita income variable that other researchers have identified as an important determinant of state policy. But these researchers did not control for the economic structure variables we have argued are most relevant politically. Interestingly, the per-capita income variable is not even consistently related to the tax rate in the expected direction. The same is true, moreover, of the state tax effort variable, which, far from having a significant impact on motor fuel excise tax rates, is also not even related to the tax rate in the expected direction in two out of the three tests.

In summary, it appears that states with substantial oil refining industries are more likely to dedicate motor fuel tax revenues to highway construction. Similarly, in those states where no such dedication occurs and where the petroleum industry has consequently made political efforts to keep tax rates low, industry success has been a function of the size of the firms in the industry in the state: the larger the firms, the greater the success in keeping motor fuel tax rates low. The results of this test of the relationship between economic structure and political influence in the area of state tax policy thus lend support to the results of our earlier test in the area of federal income tax policy, especially with regard to the political influence flowing from large firm size.

Summary and Conclusions

Despite its tentative and partial character, the evidence presented in this study lends empirical credence to the notion that the structure of the American corporate economy has important implications for the operations of the American political system at both state and federal levels. Especially striking are the positive relationships discovered between firm size and industry success in avoiding both federal corporate income taxes and state excise taxes. To the extent that political power is reflected in such actual policy outcomes, we can therefore say that larger firm size does indeed seem to yield greater political power. Also interesting are the findings suggesting that larger industries (as opposed to larger firms) are less successful politically, which supports the "free rider" hypothesis advanced by Mancur Olson, since larger industries in general have more firms than smaller industries. In addition, we found evidence that industries which are most visible and most fearful of government intervention because of their attractive (i.e., concentrated) market structure of profitability are more inclined to avoid (or are less successful at mounting) political influence efforts aimed at reducing their tax burdens.

Beyond these immediate substantive conclusions, however, the work summarized here also has broader methodological and theoretical implications because of what it suggests about the feasibility of a comprehensive empirical approach to analyzing the relationship between economic structure and political power, a relationship that is vital to the future of American democracy. For too long now, political scientists have contented themselves with imperfect case study approaches to this question, ignoring the insights available in the economics literature that make it possible to identify measurable aspects of economic structure and thus to undertake more systematic testing of hypotheses.[25] While we are fully aware of the special strengths of the case study approach and the limitations of our own, we believe that the relationship between economic and political power will not be fully understood until the findings of particular case studies can be compared with the results of more comprehensive and systematic empirical research of the sort reported here. Given the importance that an understanding of this relationship holds for the structure of the American political system, and the implications it has for the shaping of public policies, it is our hope that the analysis offered here will help open the way for the progress on the systematic, empirical side of this research strategy that is so clearly needed.

Notes

1. This point is argued convincingly in: Henry Kariel, *The Decline of American Pluralism* (Stanford: Stanford Univesity Press, 1961); Grant McConnell, *Private Power and American Democracy* (New York: Alfred A. Knopf, 1966); Theodore Lowi, *The End of Liberalism* (New York: W. W. Norton and Company, Inc., 1969); Robert A. Dahl, "Business and Politics: A Critical Appraisal of Political Science," in Robert A. Dahl, Mason Haire, and Paul F. Lazarsfeld, *Social Science Research on Business: Product and Potential* (New York: Columbia University Press, 1959), pp. 3, 44; Robert A. Dahl, *After the Revolution* (New Haven, Conn.: Yale University Press, 1970); Edwin M. Epstein, *The Corporation in American Politics* (Englewood Cliffs, N.J.: Prentice-Hall, Inc., 1969).

2. Woodrow Wilson, *The New Freedom* (New York: Doubleday, 1913), p. 57. See, for example: C. Wright Mills, *The Power Elite* (New York: Oxford University Press, 1956); G. William Domhoff, *Who Rules America?* (Englewood Cliffs, N.J.: Prentice-Hall, 1967); Floyd Hunter, *Community Power Structure* (Chapel Hill: University of North Carolina Press, 1953); Robert S. Lynd and Helen M. Lynd, *Middletown in Transition* (New York: Harcourt, Brace, Jovanovich, 1937); Morton Mintz and Jerry Cohen, *America, Inc.* (New York: The Dial Press, 1971); Philip M. Stern, *The Great Treasury Raid* (New York: Random House, 1967); Mark Green, *The Closed Enterprise System*. Ralph Nader's Study Report on Antitrust Enforcement (New York: Grossman Publishers, 1972); Fred R. Harris, "The Politics of Corporate Power," in *Corporate Power in America*, ed. Ralph Nader and Mark J. Green (New York: Grossman Publishers, 1973), pp. 25–44; Theodore Lowi, *The End of Liberalism*.

3. See, for example: Robert A. Dahl, *Who Governs?* (New Haven: Yale University Press, 1961); Raymond Wolfinger, *The Politics of Progress* (Englewood Cliffs, N.J.: Prentice-Hall, 1974); David B. Truman, *The Governmental Process: Political Interests and Public Opinion*, Second Edition (New York: Alfred A. Knopf, 1971); Raymond Bauer, Ithiel de Sola Poole, and Lewis Dexter, *American Business and Public Policy* (New York: Atherton Press, 1963).

4. Mancur Olson, *The Logic of Collective Action, Public Goods and the Theory of Groups* (Cambridge Mass.: Harvard University Press, 1965), p. 35.

5. Richard Neustadt, *Presidential Power*, Signet Edition (New York: The New American Library, 1964), p. 42.

6. On the concept of "policy subsystems," see J. Leiper Freeman, *The Political Process* (New York: Random House, 1965); Lee J. Fritschler, *Smoking and Politics* (New York: Appleton-Century Crofts, 1969).

7. Quoted in Lee J. Fritschler, *Smoking*, p. 94.

8. We are indebted here to Edwin Epstein, *The Corporation in American Politics* (Englewood Cliffs, N.J.: Prentice-Hall, Inc., 1969), particularly pp. 67-111 for an excellent review of patterns of corporate political involvement.

9. See, for example, Carl Kaysen, "The Corporation: How Much Power? What Scope?" in *The Corporation in Modern Society*, ed. E. S. Mason (Cambridge, Mass.: Harvard University Press, 1959), p. 99; Kaysen asserts: "The market power which large absolute and relative size gives to the giant corporation is the basis not only of economic power but also of considerable political and social power of a broader sort." According to Senator Fred Harris: "In any area, the size of a big corporation can be translated into political strength." Harris, "Politics of Corporate Power," p. 39. Ronald H. Coase writes that "if policy is to be based on 'fear of size,' it is surely desirable to discover what is really feared, whether it results from size, and whether this comes about in all circumstances or only in some" [*Congressional Record* (June 16, 1969)].

10. Kaysen, "The Corporation."

11. Corwin D. Edwards, "Conglomerate Bigness as a Source of Power," *Business Concentration and Price Policy* (Princeton, N.J.: Princeton University Press, 1955), pp. 331-352.

12. National Industrial Conference Board, *The Role of Business in Public Affairs*, Studies in Public Affairs, No. 2 (New York: National Industrial Conference Board, Inc., 1968), p. 8.

13. Bauer, Poole, and Dexter, *American Business and Public Policy*, p. 227.

14. Commenting on the relative advantages of having a full-time firm representative in Washington and working through a trade association, Corwin Edwards notes: "While some smaller business interests make a comparable showing through associations set up for the purpose, the experience of a Washington official is that small companies generally find out what is happening too late and prepare their case too scantily to be fully effective where their interests conflict with those of large companies." Edwards, "Conglomerate Bigness," p. 347.

15. The effective average tax rate is the ratio of actual tax liabilities to estimated "true" accounting net income, which is the industry's reported income plus the amount it was able to exclude from its reported income because of the special provisions in the Internal Revenue Code. For a detailed description of the effective average tax rate see John J. Siegfried, "Effective Average U.S. Corporation Income Tax Rates," *National Tax Journal*, 27 (June, 1974), 245-259.

16. To compute this variable for each "minor industry," we employed the concentration ratios provided for the Census Bureau's more narrowly defined Standard Industrial Classification of firms. These concentration ratios for the SIC industries were then aggregated, using a weighted average based on employment, to derive the concentration ratios for the "minor industries" which the SIC firms comprise.

17. This index consists of the sum (across states) of the squared share of total industry employment located in each state in 1963. An index of this type is sensitive to both the number of states in which an industry has employees and the distribution of employees among these states. Fewer states or a more unequal distribution will cause the index to rise. Squaring the shares weights the large employment states (and hence the more important states) more heavily in the index.

18. Those firms having less than five million dollars of assets were excluded because many of them showed deficits, and we were not able to remove these effects from the data. Furthermore,

firms with less than five million dollars in assets are not representative firms in the petroleum refining industry.

19. For a more detailed discussion of the petroleum industry within the framework developed here, see: Lester M. Salamon and John J. Siegfried, "The Relationship Between Economic Structure and Political Power: The Energy Industry," in *Competition in the Energy Industry*, ed. Thomas D. Duchesneau (Cambridge, Mass.: Ballinger, 1975).

20. Information provided by Mr. William Haga, representative of major oil company interests in the State of Tennessee. Since 1971 some major oil companies have taken a position of not opposing gasoline taxes which are used for nonhighway purposes if they are dedicated instead to mass transit purposes. Not all companies currently take this position. Since our empirical test is for 1967, however, this change in policy will not affect our hypothesis. Furthermore, we are seeking to discover evidence of general relationships between economic structure and political decision making, and consequently the relevance of our analysis is not diminished by a change in the policy of some oil companies.

21. On the permeability of state legislatures to special interest pleading, see: Terry Sanford, *Storm over the States* (New York: McGraw-Hill Book Company, 1967).

22. The index was computed for crude petroleum using 100 employees as the cutoff size and for petroleum refining using 250 employees as the cutoff size. These sizes were chosen on the basis of data availability and to provide sufficient variation in the explanatory variables constructed from them. 1967 *Census of Manufactures* data were used.

23. Thomas R. Dye, *Politics, Economics, and the Public: Policy Outcomes in the American States* (Chicago: Rand McNally, 1966); Richard Dawson and James A. Robinson, "Inter-Party Competition, Economic Variables, and Welfare Policies in the American States," *Journal of Politics*, 25 (May, 1963), 265–289; Charles F. Cnudde and Donald J. McCrone, "Party Competition and Welfare Policies in the American States," *American Political Science Review*, 63 (September, 1969), 959–966; Ira Sharkansky and Richard Hofferbert, "Dimensions of State Policy," in *Politics in the American States: A Comparative Analysis*, Second Edition, ed. Herbert Jacob and Kenneth N. Vines (Boston: Little, Brown and Company, 1971). Sharkansky and Hofferbert have been most comprehensive in their treatment of economic variables, examining no fewer than 15 separate variables. Though they include items as diverse as value added by manufacturing and the number of telephones per 1,000 population, however, they do not include variables measuring the structure of different industries that would make it possible to test hypotheses about the impact industry structure (e.g., firm size, market concentration) has on political influence. Yet these are the hypotheses most often generated by students of the economic aspects of political power.

24. Several alternative explanations for this lack of relationship might also apply. In the first place, the result might reflect relatively less success at influencing policy on motor fuel tax rates because of lower concentration and the associated higher organizational costs of lobbying even though crude producers have a similar desire for lower rates. Furthermore, the data used to measure the share of activity of this sector in each state also included natural gas production. Although natural gas production and crude production are highly correlated across states, the additional variation produced by the inclusion of natural gas production (which does not go toward motor fuels) may be the source of the absence of an effect of this variable on the gasoline excise tax rate.

25. Two recent exceptions to this point, focusing on the trade policy area are: C. P. MacPherson, "Tariff Structures and Political Exchange," Ph.D. Dissertation, Department of Economics, University of Chicago (December, 1972); and J. J. Pincus, "Pressure Groups and the Pattern of Tariffs," *Journal of Political Economy*, 83 (August, 1975), 757–778.

3.3

International Trade, Domestic Coalitions and Liberty: Comparative Responses to the Crisis of 1873-1896

PETER ALEXIS GOUREVITCH

The period of free trade that has prevailed since the end of World War II is a historical anomaly. The role of tariffs in structuring the development of markets and technologies has generally been at the forefront of world politics, from the very inception of international capitalism down through the present day. But, with the postwar adoption of the Bretton-Woods agreement and the GATT (General Agreement on Tariffs and Trade), the saliency of protectionist issues tended to recede from front-page headlines to the more recondite arenas of the business sections and financial tabloids. By 1971-73, however, there were indications that the decline of the relative economic power of the United States diminished the prospects for the continued dominance of international free trade policy. By the 1980s it was clear to everyone that with the upsurge of international competition in such sectors as automobiles, steel, oil refining, and chemical production, the question of protective tariffs and related issues of employment, national security, and economic theory had once again made their way to the forefront of the political arena. The sense of urgency and high stakes that attends these debates may seem new, but in important respects it is rather a return to the political climate of decades past. The following essay by Peter Alexis Gourevitch sets forth with remarkable clarity the importance and pervasiveness of tariff politics at a crucial period in the evolution of the modern world industrial order.

For social scientists who enjoy comparisons, happiness is finding a force or event which affects a number of societies at the same time.[1] Like test-tube solutions that respond differently to the same reagent, these societies reveal their characters in divergent responses to the same stimulus. One such phenomenon is the present world-wide inflation/depression. An earlier one was the Great Depression of 1873–1896.[2] Technological breakthroughs in agriculture (the reaper, sower, fertilizers, drainage tiles, and new forms of wheat) and in transportation (continental rail networks, refrigeration, and motorized shipping) transformed international markets for food, causing world prices to fall. Since conditions favored extensive grain growing, the plains nations of the world (the

Reprinted from *The Journal of Interdisciplinary History*, VIII (1977), 281-313, with permission of *The Journal of Interdisciplinary History* and the MIT Press, Cambridge, Massachusetts. Copyright © 1977 by The Massachusetts Institute of Technology and the editors of *The Journal of Interdisciplinary History*.

United States, Canada, Australia, Argentina, and Russia) became the low cost producers. The agricultural populations of Western and Central Europe found themselves abruptly uncompetitive.[3]

In industry as well, 1873 marks a break. At first the sharp slump of that year looked like an ordinary business-cycle downturn, like the one in 1857. Instead, prices continued to drop for over two decades, while output continued to rise.[4] New industries—steel, chemicals, electrical equipment, and ship-building—sprang up, but the return on capital declined. As in agriculture, international competition became intense. Businessmen everywhere felt the crisis, and most of them wanted remedies.

The clamour for action was universal. The responses differed: vertical integration, cartels, government contracts, and economic protection. The most visible response was tariffs. Table 1 classifies countries according to the mix of tariffs adopted after 1873.

Table 1

Tariff Levels in Industry and Agriculture

	High Tariffs on Industry	Low Tariffs on Industry
High Tariffs on Agriculture	France, Germany, Italy	Austria-Hungary
Low Tariffs on Agriculture	Australia, United States Canada	Great Britain, Argentina

Although the economic stimuli were uniform, the political systems forced to cope with them differed considerably. Some systems were new or relatively precarious: Republican France, Imperial Germany, Monarchical Italy, Reconstruction America, Newly-Formed Canada, Recently Autonomous Australia. Only Britain could be called stable. Thirty years later when most of these political systems had grown stronger, most of the countries had high tariffs. The importance of the relation between the nature of the political system and protection has been most forcefully argued by Gershenkron in *Bread and Democracy in Germany*. The coalition of iron and rye built around high tariffs contributed to a belligerent foreign policy and helped to shore up the authoritarian Imperial Constitution of 1871. High tariffs, then, contributed to both world wars and to fascism, not a minor consequence. It was once a commonly held notion that free trade and democracy, protection and authoritarianism, went together. Table 2 relates tariff levels to regime types.

These basic facts about tariff levels and political forms have been discussed by many authors.[5] What is less clear, and not thoroughly explored in the literature, is the best way to understand these outcomes. As with most complex problems, there is no shortage of possible explanations: interest groups, class conflict, institutions, foreign policy, ideology. Are these explanations all necessary though, or equally important? This essay seeks to probe these alternative explanations. It is speculative; it does not offer new information or definitive answers to old questions. Rather, it takes a type of debate about which social scientists are increasingly conscious (the comparison of different explanations of a given phenomenon)[6] and extends it to an old problem that has significant bearing on current issues in political economy—the interaction of international trade and domestic politics.

Table 2

Political Systems and Tariff Levels

Tariffs/Regimes		Parliamentary	Authoritarian
Industrial	Agricultural		
High	High	France	Germany
High	Low	United States, Canada, Australia	
Low	High		Austria-Hungary
Low	Low	Argentina, United Kingdom	

The paper examines closely the formation of tariff policy in late nineteenth-century Germany, France, Britain, and the United States, and then considers the impact of the tariff policy quarrel on the character of each political system.

Explaining Tariff Levels

Explanations for late nineteenth-century tariff levels may be classified under four headings, according to the type of variable to which primacy is given.

1. *Economic explanations.* Tariff levels derive from the interests of economic groups able to translate calculations of economic benefit into public policy. Types of economic explanations differ in their conceptualization of groups (classes vs. sectors vs. companies) and of the strategies groups pursue (maximizing income, satisficing, stability, and class hegemony).[7]

2. *Political system explanations.* The "statement of the groups" does not state everything. The ability of economic actors to realize policy goals is affected by political structures and the individuals who staff them. Groups differ in their access to power, the costs they must bear in influencing decisions, prestige, and other elements of political power.[8]

3. *International system explanations.* Tariff levels derive from a country's position in the international state system. Considerations of military security, independence, stability, or glory shape trade policy. Agriculture may be protected, for example, in order to guarantee supplies of food and soldiers, rather than to provide profit to farmers (as explanation 1 would suggest).[9]

4. *Economic ideology explanations.* Tariff levels derive from intellectual orientations about proper economic and trade policies. National traditions may favor autarchy or market principles; fadishness or emulation may induce policy makers to follow the lead given by successful countries. Such intellectual orientations may have originated in calculations of self-interest (explanation 1), or in broader political concerns (explanation 2) or in understandings of international politics (explanation 3), but they may outlive the conditions that spawned them.[10]

These explanations are by no means mutually exclusive. The German case could be construed as compatible with all four: Junkers and heavy industry fought falling prices, competition, and political reformism; Bismarck helped organize the iron and rye coalition; foreign policy concerns over supply sources and hostile great powers helped to create it; and the nationalist school of German economic thought provided fertile ground for protectionist arguments. But were all four factors really essential to produce high tariffs in Germany? Given the principle that a simple explanation is better than a complex one, we may legitimately try to determine at what point we have said enough to explain the result. Other points may be interesting, perhaps crucial for other outcomes, but redundant for this one. It would also be useful to find explanations that fit the largest possible number of cases.

Economic explanation offers us a good port of entry. It requires that we investigate the impact of high and low tariffs, both for agricultural and industrial products, on the economic situation of each major group in each country. We can then turn to the types of evidence—structures, interstate relations, and ideas—required by the other modes of reasoning. Having worked these out for each country, it will then be possible to attempt an evaluation of all four arguments.

Germany

Economic Explanations   What attitude toward industrial and agricultural tariffs would we predict for each of the major economic groups in German society, if each acted according to its economic interests? A simple model of German society contains the following groups: small peasants; Junkers (or estate owners); manufacturers in heavy, basic industries (iron, coal, steel); manufacturers of finished goods; workers in each type of industry; shopkeepers and artisans; shippers; bankers; and professionals (lawyers, doctors). What were the interests of each in relation to the new market conditions after 1873?

Agriculture, notes Gerschenkron, could respond to the sharp drop in grain prices in two ways: modernization or protection.[11] Modernization meant applying the logic of comparative advantage to agriculture. Domestic grain production would be abandoned. Cheap foreign grain would become an input for the domestic production of higher quality foodstuffs such as dairy products and meat. With rising incomes, the urban and industrial sectors would provide the market for this type of produce. Protection, conversely, meant maintaining domestic grain production. This would retard modernization, maintain a large agricultural population, and prolong national self-sufficiency in food.

Each policy implied a different organization for farming. Under late nineteenth-century conditions, dairy products, meats, and vegetables were best produced by high quality labor, working in small units, managed by owners, or long-term leaseholders. They were produced least well on estates by landless laborers working for a squirearchy. Thus, modernization would be easier where small units or production already predominated, as in Denmark, which is Gerschenkron's model of a modernizing response to the crisis of 1873. The Danish state helped by organizing cooperatives, providing technology, and loaning capital.

In Germany, however, landholding patterns varied considerably. In the region of vast estates east of the Elbe, modernization would have required drastic restructuring of the Junkers' control of the land. It would have eroded their hold over the laborers, their dominance of local life, and their position in German society. The poor quality of Prussian soil hindered modernization of any kind; in any case it would have cost money.[12] Conversely, western and southern Germany contained primarily small- and medium-sized farms more suited to modernization.

Gerschenkron thinks that the Danish solution would have been best for everyone, but especially for these smaller farmers. Following his reasoning, we can impute divergent interests to these two groups. For the Junkers, protection of agriculture was a dire necessity. For the small farmers, modernization optimized their welfare in the long run, but in the short run protection would keep them going; their interests, therefore, can be construed as ambivalent.

What were the interests of agriculture concerning industrial tariffs? Presumably the agricultural population sought to pay the lowest possible prices for the industrial goods that it consumed, and would be opposed to high industrial tariffs. Farmers selling high quality produce to the industrial sector prospered, however, when that sector prospered, since additional income was spent disproportionately on meat and eggs. Modernizing producers might therefore be receptive to tariffs and other economic policies which helped industry. For grain, conversely, demand was less elastic. Whatever the state of the industrial economy, the Junkers would be able to sell their output provided that foreign sources were prevented from undercutting them. Thus, we would expect the Junkers to be the most resolutely against high industrial tariffs, while the smaller farmers would again have a less clearcut interest.

Neither were the interests of the industrial sector homogenous. Makers of basic materials such as iron and steel wanted the producers of manufactured products such as stoves, pots and pans, shovels, rakes, to buy supplies at home rather than from cheaper sources abroad. Conversely the finished goods manufacturers wanted cheap materials; their ideal policy would have been low tariffs on all goods except the ones that they made.

In theory, both types of industries were already well past the "infant industry" stage and would have benefited from low tariffs and international specialization. Indeed, German industry competed very effectively against British and American products during this period, penetrating Latin America, Africa, Asia, and even the United States and United Kingdom home markets.[13] Low tariffs might not have meant lower incomes for industry, but rather a shift among companies and a change in the mix of items produced.

Nevertheless, tariffs still offered certain advantages even to the strong. They reduced risk in industries requiring massive investments, like steel; they assured economies of scale, which supported price wars or dumping in foreign markets; and to the extent that cartels and mergers suppressed domestic production, they allowed monopoly profits. Finally, iron and steel manufacturers everywhere faced softening demand due to the declining rate of railroad building, not wholly offset by shipbuilding.[14] As we shall see, steelmen were in the vanguard of protectionist movements everywhere, including Britain (their only failure).

All industrialists (except those who sold farm equipment) had an interest in low agricultural tariffs. Cheap food helped to keep wages down and to conserve purchasing power for manufactured goods.

The interests of the industrial work force were pulled in conflicting directions by the divergent claims of consumer preoccupations and producer concerns. As consumers, workers found any duties onerous, especially those on food. But as producers, they shared an interest with their employers in having their particular products protected, or in advancing the interests of the industrial sector as a whole.

Shippers and their employees had an interest in high levels of imports and exports and hence in low tariffs of all kinds. Bankers and those employed in finance had varied interests according to the ties each had with particular sectors of the economy. As consumers, professionals and shopkeepers, along with labor, had a general interest in keeping cost down, although special links (counsel to a steel company or greengrocer in a steel town) might align them to a high tariff industry.

This pattern of group interests may be represented diagrammatically. Table 3 shows each group's position in relation to four policy combinations, pairing high and low tariffs

Table 3

Interests of Different Groups in Relation to
Industrial and Agricultural Tariffs (Germany)

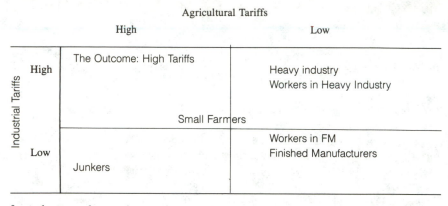

		Agricultural Tariffs	
		High	Low
Industrial Tariffs	High	The Outcome: High Tariffs Small Farmers	Heavy industry Workers in Heavy Industry
	Low	Junkers	Workers in FM Finished Manufacturers

for industry and agriculture. The group's intensity of interest can be conveyed by its placement in relation to the axis: closeness to the origin suggests ambiguity in the group's interest; distance from the intersection suggests clarity and intensity of interest.

Notice that no group wanted the actual policy outcome in Germany—high tariffs in both sectors. To become policy, the law of 1879 and its successors required trade-offs among members of different sectors. This is not really surprising. Logrolling is expected of interest groups. Explanation 1 would therefore find the coalition of iron and rye quite normal.

Nevertheless, a different outcome—low tariffs on both types of goods—also would have been compatible with an economic interest group explanation. Logrolling could also have linked up those parts of industry and agriculture that had a plausible interest in low tariffs: finished goods manufacturers, shippers and dockworkers, labor, professionals, shopkeepers, consumers, and farmers of the West and South. This coalition may even have been a majority of electorate, and at certain moments managed to impose its policy preferences. Under Chancellor Georg von Caprivi (1890-1894), reciprocal trade treaties were negotiated and tariffs lowered. Why did this coalition lose over the long run? Clearly because it was weaker, but of what did this weakness consist?

Political Explanations   One answer looks to aspects of the political system which favored protectionist forces at the expense of free traders: institutions (weighted voting, bureaucracy); personalities who intervened on one side or another; the press of other issues (socialism, taxation, constitutional reform, democratization); and interest group organization.

In all these domains, the protectionists had real advantages. The Junkers especially enjoyed a privileged position in the German system. They staffed or influenced the army, the bureaucracy, the judiciary, the educational system, and the Court. The three class voting system in Prussia, and the allocation of seats, helped over-represent them and propertied interests in general.

In the late 1870s, Bismarck and the emperor switched to the Protectionist's side. Their motives were primarily political. They sought to strengthen the basic foundations of the conservative system (autonomy of the military and the executive from parliamentary pressure; a conservative foreign policy; dominance of conservative social forces at home; and preservation of the Junkers). For a long time, industry and bourgeois elements had fought over many of these issues. Unification had helped to reconcile the army and the middle classes, but many among the latter still demanded a more liberal constitution and economic reforms opposed by the Junkers. In the 1870s Bismarck used the *Kulturkampf* to prevent a revisionist alliance of Liberals, Catholics, and Federalists. In the long run, this was an unsatisfactory arrangement because it made the government dependent on unreliable political liberals and alienated the essentially conservative Catholics.[15]

Tariffs offered a way to overcome these contradictions and forge a new, conservative alliance. Industrialists gave up their antagonism toward the Junkers, and any lingering constitutionalist demands, in exchange for tariffs, anti-Socialist laws, and incorporation into the governing majority. Catholics gave way on constitutional revision in exchange for tariffs and the end of the *Kulterkampf* (expendable because protection would now carry out its political function). The Junkers accepted industry and paid higher prices for industrial goods, but maintained a variety of privileges, and their estates. Peasants obtained a solution to their immediate distress, less desirable over the long run than modernization credits, but effective nonetheless. Tariff revenues eased conflicts over tax reform. The military obtained armaments for which the iron and steel manufacturers received the contracts. The coalition excluded everyone who challenged the economic order and/or the constitutional settlement of 1871. The passage of the first broad protectionist measure in 1879 has aptly been called the "second founding" of the Empire.[16]

Control of the Executive allowed Bismarck to orchestrate these complex trade-offs. Each of the coalition partners had to be persuaded to pay the price, especially that of high tariffs on the goods of the other sector. Control of foreign policy offered instruments for maintaining the bargain once it had been struck. Indeed, Wehler, following the tradition of Kehr, stresses the primacy of domestic preoccupations as the basis of Bismarck's foreign policy.[17] The Chancellor used imperialism, nationalism, and overseas crises to obscure internal divisions, and particularly, to blunt middle-class criticism. Nationalism and the vision of Germany surrounded by enemies, or at least harsh competitors, reinforced arguments on behalf of the need for self-sufficiency in food and industrial production, and for a powerful military machine.[18] "From the early 1880's, imperialism became an ideological force for integration in a state which lacked stabilizing historical traditions and which was unable to conceal sharp class divisions beneath its authorization cloak."[19]

The protectionists also appear to have organized more effectively than the free-traders. In the aftermath of 1848, industry had been a junior partner, concerned with the elimination of obstacles to a domestic German free market (such as guild regulations and internal tariffs). Its demands for protection against British imports were ignored.[20] Up to 1873, "the most powerful pillars of the Prussian-German state, the great landowners, the representatives of the wholesale trade, the majority of the Prussian Chamber of Deputies and of the German Parliament (Reichstag), and the central bureaucracy all stood opposed to protective tariffs."[21] The boom of the 1860s greatly increased the relative importance of the industrialists. After 1873, managers of heavy industry, mines and some of the banks formed new associations and worked to convert old ones: in 1874 the Association of German Steel Producers was founded; in 1876, the majority of the Chambers of Commerce swung away from free trade, and other associations began to fall apart over the issue.[22] These protectionist producers' groups were clear in purpose, small in number, and intense in interest. Such groups generally have an easier time working out means of common action than do more general and diffuse ones.[23] Banks and the state provided coordination among firms and access to other powerful groups in German society.

The most significant of these powerful groups—the Junkers—became available as coalition allies after the sharp drop in wheat prices which began in 1875. Traditionally staunch defenders of free trade, the Junkers switched very quickly to protection. They organized rapidly, adapting with remarkable ease, as Gerschenkron notes, to the ère des foules. Associations such as the Union of Agriculturalists and the Conservative Party sought to define and represent the collective interest of the whole agricultural sector, large and small, east and west. Exploiting their great prestige and superior resources, the Junkers imposed their definition of that interest—protection as a means of preserving the status quo on the land. To legitimate this program, the Junker-led movements developed many of the themes later contained in Nazi propaganda: moral superiority of agriculture; organic unity of those who work the land; anti-Semitism; and distrust of cities, factories, workers, and capitalists. "With grain culture stands and falls German agriculture; with German agriculture stands and falls the German Reich."[24]

The alternative (Low/Low) coalition operated under several political handicaps. It comprised heterogeneous components, hence a diffuse range of interests. In economic terms, the coalition embraced producers and consumers, manufacturers and shippers, owners and workers, and city dwellers and peasants. Little in day to day life brought these elements together, or otherwise facilitated the awareness and pursuit of common goals; much kept them apart—property rights, working conditions, credit, and taxation. The low tariff groups also differed on other issues such as religion, federalism, democratization of the Constitution, and constitutional control of the Army and Executive. Unlike the High/High alliance, the low tariff coalition had to overcome its diversity without help from the Executive. Only during the four years of Caprivi was the chancellor's office sympathetic to low tariff politics, and Caprivi was very isolated from the court, the kaiser, the army, and the bureaucracy.[25]

Despite these weaknesses, the low tariff alliance was not without its successes. It did well in the first elections after the "refounding" (1881), a defeat for Bismarck which, Wehler argues, drove him further toward social imperialism. From 1890, Caprivi directed a series of reciprocal trade negotiations leading to tariff reductions. Caprivi's ministry suggests the character of the programmatic glue needed to keep a low tariff coalition together: at home, a little more egalitarianism and constitutionalism (the end of the antisocialist laws); in foreign policy, a little more internationalism—no lack of interest in empire or prestige, but a greater willingness to insert Germany into an international division of labor.

International System Explanations   A third type of explanation for tariff levels looks at each country's position in the international system. Tariff policy has consequences not only for profit and loss for the economy as a whole or for particular industries, but for other national concerns, such as security, independence, and glory. International specialization means interdependence. Food supplies, raw materials, manufactured products, markets become vulnerable. Britain, according to this argument, could rely on imports because of her navy. If Germany did the same, would she not expose her lifeline to that navy? If the German agricultural sector shrank, would she not lose a supply of soldiers with which to protect herself from foreign threats? On the other hand, were there such threats? Was the danger of the Franco-British-Russian alliance an immutable constituent fact of the international order, or a response to German aggressiveness? This brings us back to the Kehr-Wehler emphasis on the importance of domestic interests in shaping foreign policy. There were different ways to interpret the implications of the international system for German interests: one view, seeing the world as hostile, justified protection; the other, seeing the world as benevolent, led to free trade. To the extent that the international system was ambiguous, we cannot explain the choice between these competing foreign policies by reference to the international system alone.

A variant of international system explanations focuses on the structure of bargaining among many actors in the network of reciprocal trade negotiations. Maintenance of low tariffs by one country required a similar willingness by others. One could argue that Germany was driven to high tariffs by the protectionist behavior of other countries. A careful study of the timing of reciprocal trade treaties in this period is required to demonstrate this point, a type of study I have been unable to find. The evidence suggests that at least in Germany, the shift from Caprivi's low tariff policy to Bernhard Bülow's solidarity bloc (protection, naval-building, nationalism, antisocialism) did not come about because of changes in the behavior of foreign governments. Rather, the old Bismarckian coalition of heavy industry, army, Junkers, nationalists, and conservatives mobilized itself to prevent further erosion of its domestic position.

Economic Ideology   A fourth explanation for the success of the protectionist alliance looks to economic ideology. The German nationalist school, associated with Friedrich List, favored state intervention in economic matters to promote national power and welfare. Free trade and laissez-faire doctrines were less entrenched than they were in Britain. According to this explanation, when faced with sharp competition from other countries, German interests found it easier to switch positions toward protection than did their British counterparts. This interpretation is plausible. The free trade policies of the 1850s and 1860s were doubtless more shallowly rooted in Germany and the tradition of state interventionism was stronger.

All four explanations, indeed, are compatible with the German experience: economic circumstances provided powerful inducements for major groups to support high tariffs; political structures and key politicians favored the protectionist coalition; international forces seemed to make its success a matter of national security; and German economic traditions helped justify it. Are all these factors really necessary to explain the protectionist victory, or is this causal overkill? I shall reserve judgement until we have looked at more examples.

France

The French case offers us a very different political system producing a very similar policy result. As with Germany, the causes may explain more than necessary. The High/High outcome (Table 1) is certainly what we would expect to find looking at the interests of key economic actors. French industry, despite striking gains under the Second Empire and the Cobden-Chevalier Treaty, was certainly less efficient than that of other "late starters" (Germany and the United States). Hence manufacturers in heavy industry, in highly capitalized ones, or in particularly vulnerable ones like textiles had an intense interest in protection. Shippers and successful exporters opposed it.[26]

Agriculture, as in Germany, had diverse interests. France had no precise equivalent to the Junkers; even on the biggest farms the soil was better, the labor force freer, and the owners less likely to be exclusively dependent on the land for income. Nonetheless, whether large or small, all producing units heavily involved in the market were hard hit by the drop in prices. The large proportion of quasi-subsistence farmers, hardly in the

market economy, were less affected. The prevalence of small holdings made modernization easier than in Prussia, but still costly. For most of the agricultural sector, the path of
least resistance was to maintain past practice behind high tariff walls.

As we would expect, most French producer groups became increasingly protectionist
as prices dropped. In the early 1870s Adolphe Thiers tried to raise tariffs largely for
revenue purposes but failed. New associations demanded tariff revision. In 1881, the
National Assembly passed the first general tariff measure, which protected industry more
than agriculture. In the same year American meat products were barred as unhealthy.
Sugar received help in 1884, grains and meats in the tariffs of 1885 and 1887. Finally,
broad coverage was given to both agriculture and industry in the famous Méline Tariff of
1892. Thereafter, tariffs drifted upwards, culminating in the very high tariff of 1910.[27]

This policy response fits the logic of the political system explanation as well.
Universal suffrage in a society of small property owners favored the protection of units of
production rather than consumer interests. Conflict over nontariff issues, although
severe, did not prevent protectionists from finding each other. Republican, Royalist,
Clerical, and anti-Clerical protectionists broke away from their free-trade homologues to
vote the Méline Tariff.[28] Méline and others even hoped to reform the party system by
using economic and social questions to drive out the religious and constitutional ones.
This effort failed but cross-party majorities continued to coalesce every time the question
of protection arose and high tariffs helped reconcile many conservatives to the Republic.[29]

In France, protection is the result we would expect from the international system
explanation: international political rivalries imposed concern for a domestic food supply
and a rural reservoir of soldiers. As for the economic ideology explanation, ideological
traditions abound with arguments in favor of state intervention. The Cobden-Chevalier
Treaty had been negotiated at the top. The process of approving it generated no mass
commitment to free trade as had the lengthy public battle over the repeal of the Corn
Laws in Britain. The tariffs of the 1880s restored the *status quo ante*.

Two things stand out in the comparison of France with Germany. First, France had
no equivalent to Bismarck, or to the state mechanism which supported him. The
compromise between industry and agriculture was organized without any help from the
top. Interest groups and politicians operating through elections and the party system came
together and worked things out. Neither the party system, nor the constitution, nor
outstanding personalities can be shown to have favored one coalition over another.

Second, it is mildly surprising that this alliance took so long to come about—perhaps
the consequence of having no Bismarck. It appears that industry took the lead in fighting
for protection, and scored the first success. Why was agriculture left out of the Tariff of
1881 (while in Germany it was an integral part of the Tariff of 1879), when it represented
such a large number of people? Why did it take another eleven years to get a general bill?
Part of the answer may lie in the proportion of people outside the market economy; the
rest may lie in the absence of leaders with a commanding structural position working to
effect a particular policy. In any case, the Republic eventually secured a general bill, at
about the same time that the United States was also raising tariffs.

Great Britain

Britain is the only highly industrialized country which failed to raise tariffs on either
industrial or agricultural products in this period. Explanation 1 appears to deal with this
result quite easily. British industry, having developed first, enjoyed a great competitive
advantage over its rivals and did not need tariffs. International specialization worked to
Britain's advantage. The world provided her with cheap food, she supplied industrial

products in exchange and made additional money financing and organizing the exchange. Farmers could make a living by modernizing and integrating their units into this industrial order. Such had been the logic behind the repeal in the Corn Laws in 1846.[30]

Upon closer inspection, British policy during the Great Depression seems less sensible from a materialist viewpoint. Conditions had changed since 1846. After 1873, industry started to suffer at the hands of its new competitors, especially American and German ones. Other countries began to substitute their own products for British goods, compete with Britain in overseas markets, penetrate the British domestic market, and erect tariff barriers against British goods. Britain was beginning that languorous industrial decline which has continued uninterrupted to the present day.[31]

In other countries, industrial producers, especially in heavy industry, led agitation for protection in response to the dilemma of the price slump. Although some British counterparts did organize a Fair Trade league which sought protection within the context of the Empire (the policy adopted after World War I), most industrialists stayed with free trade.

If this outcome is to be consistent with explanation 1, it is necessary to look for forces which blunted the apparent thrust of international market forces. British producers' acceptance of low tariffs was not irrational if other ways of sustaining income existed. In industry, there were several. Despite Canadian and Australian tariff barriers, the rest of the Empire sustained a stable demand for British goods; so did British overseas investment, commercial ties, and prestige. International banking and shipping provided important sources of revenue which helped to conceal the decline in sales. Bankers and shippers also constituted a massive lobby in favor of an open international economy. To some degree, then, British industry was shielded from perceiving the full extent of the deterioration of her competitive position.[32]

In agriculture, the demand for protection was also weak. This cannot be explained simply by reference to 1846. Initially the repeal of the Corn Laws affected farming rather little. Although repeal helped prevent sharp price increases following bad harvests, there was simply not enough grain produced in the world (nor enough shipping capacity to bring it to Europe) to provoke a major agricultural crisis. The real turning point came in the 1870s, when falling prices were compounded by bad weather.[33] Why, at this moment, did the English landowning aristocracy fail to join its Junker or French counterpart in demanding protection? The aristocrats, after all, held a privileged position in the political system; they remained significantly overrepresented in the composition of the political class, especially in the leadership of Parliament; they had wealth and great prestige.

As with industry, certain characteristics of British agriculture served to shield landowners from the full impact of low grain prices. First, the advanced state of British industrial development had already altered the structure of incentives in agriculture. Many landowners had made the change from growing grain to selling high quality foodstuffs. These farmers, especially dairymen and meat producers, identified their interest with the health of the industrial sector, and were unresponsive to grain growers' efforts to organize agriculture for protection.

Second, since British landowners derived their income from a much wider range of sources than did the Junkers, the decline of farming did not imply as profound a social or economic disaster for them. They had invested in mining, manufacturing, and trading, and had intermarried with the rising industrial bourgeoisie.[34] Interpenetration of wealth provided the material basis for their identification with industry. This might explain some Tories' willingness to abandon protection in 1846, and accept that verdict even in the 1870s.[35]

If repeal of the Corn Laws did not immediately affect the British economy it did profoundly influence politics and British economic thought in ways, following the logic of explanations 2 and 4, that are relevant for explaining policy in the 1870s. The attack on the Corn Laws mobilized the Anti-Corn Law League (which received some help from another mass movement, the Chartists). Over a twenty year period, the League linked the demand for cheap food to a broader critique of landed interest and privilege. Its victory, and the defection of Peel and the Tory leadership, had great symbolic meaning. Repeal affirmed that the British future would be an industrial one, in which the two forms of wealth would fuse on terms laid down for agriculture by industry. By the mid-1850s even the backwoods Tory rump led by Disraeli had accepted this; a decade later he made it the basis for the Conservative revival. To most of the ever larger electorate, free trade, cheap food, and the reformed political system were inextricably linked. Protection implied an attack on all the gains realized since 1832. Free trade meant freedom and prosperity. These identifications inhibited the realization that British economic health might no longer be served by keeping her economy open to international economic forces.[36]

Finally, British policy fits what one would expect from analysis of the international system (explanation 3). Empire and navy certainly made it easier to contemplate dependence on overseas sources of food. It is significant that protection could be legitimated in the long run only as part of empire. People would do for imperialism what they would not do to help one industry or another. Chamberlain's passage from free trade to protection via empire foreshadows the entire country's actions after World War I.[37]

United States

Of the four countries examined here, only the United States combined low-cost agriculture and dynamic industry within the same political system.[38] The policy outcome of high industrial tariffs and low agricultural ones fits the logic of explanation 1. Endowed with efficient agriculture, the United States had no need to protect it; given the long shadow of the British giant, industry did need protection. But despite its efficiency (or rather because of it) American agriculture did have severe problems in this period. On a number of points, it came into intense conflict with industry. By and large industry had its way.

Monetary policy. The increasing value of money appreciated the value of debt owed to Eastern bankers. Expanding farm production constantly drove prices downward, so that a larger amount of produce was needed to pay off an ever increasing debt. Cheap money schemes were repeatedly defeated.

Transportation. Where no competition among alternative modes of transport or companies existed, farmers were highly vulnerable to rate manipulation. Regulation eventually was introduced, but whether because of the farmers' efforts or the desire of railroad men and other industrialists to prevent ruinous competition—as part of their "search for order"—is not clear.[39] Insurance and fees also helped redistribute income from one sector to the other.

Tariffs. The protection of industrial goods required farmers to sell in a free world market and buy in a protected one.

Taxation. Before income and corporate taxes, the revenue burden was most severe for the landowner. Industry blocked an income tax until 1913.

Market instability. Highly variable crop yields contributed to erratic prices, which could have been controlled by storage facilities, government price stablization boards, and price supports. This did not happen until after World War I.

Monopoly pricing practices. Differential pricing (such as Pittsburgh Plus, whereby goods were priced according to the location of the head office rather than the factory) worked like an internal tariff, pumping money from the country into the Northeast. The antitrust acts addressed some of these problems, but left many untouched.

Patronage and pork-barrel. Some agrarian areas, especially the South, fared badly in the distribution of Federal largesse.[40]

In the process of political and industrial development, defeat of the agricultural sector appears inevitable. Whatever the indicator (share of GNP, percentage of the work force, control of the land) farmers decline; whether peasants, landless laborers, family farmers, kulaks, or estate owners, they fuel industrialization by providing foreign exchange, food, and manpower. In the end they disappear.

This can happen, however, at varying rates: very slowly, as appears to be the case in China today, slowly as in France, quickly as in Britain. In the United States, I would argue, the defeat of agriculture as a *sector* was swift and thorough. This may sound strange in light of the stupendous agricultural output today. Some landowners were successful. They shifted from broad attacks on the system to interest group lobbying for certain types of members. The mass of the agricultural population, however, lost most of its policy battles and left the land.

One might have expected America to develop not like Germany, as Moore suggests (although that was certainly a possibility) but like France: with controlled, slower industrial growth, speed sacrificed to balance, and the preservation of a large rural population.[41] For it to have happened the mass of small farmers would have to have found allies willing to battle the Eastern banking and industrial combine which dominated American policy-making. To understand their failure it is useful to analyze the structure of incentives among potential alliance partners as was done for the European countries. If we take farmers' grievances on the policy issues noted above (such as money and rates) as the functional equivalent of tariffs, the politics of coalition formation in the United States become comparable to the equivalent process in Europe.

Again two alliances were competing for the allegiance of the same groups. The protectionist core consisted of heavy industry, banks, and textiles. These employers persuaded workers that their interests derived from their roles as producers in the industrial sector, not as consumers. To farmers selling in urban markets, the protectionists made the familiar case for keeping industry strong.

The alternative coalition, constructed around hostility toward heavy industry and banks, appealed to workers and farmers as consumers, to farmers as debtors and victims of industrial manipulation, to the immigrant poor and factory hands against the tribulations of the industrial system, to farmers as manipulated debtors, and to shippers and manufacturers of finished products on behalf of lower costs. Broadly this was a Jackson-type coalition confronting the Whig interest—the little man versus the man of property. Lower tariffs and more industrial regulation (of hours, rates, and working conditions) were its policies.

The progressive, low tariff alliance was not weak. Agriculture employed by far the largest percentage of the workforce. Federalism should have given it considerable leverage: the whole South, the Midwest, and the trans-Mississippi West. True, parts of the Midwest were industrializing, but then much of the Northeast remained agricultural. Nonetheless the alliance failed: the explanation turns on an understanding of the critical realignment election of 1896. The defeat of populism marked the end of two decades of intense party competition, the beginning of forty years of Republican hegemony, and the turning point for agriculture as a sector. It will be heuristically useful to work backwards from the conjuncture of 1896 to the broader forces which produced that contest.

The battle of 1896 was shaped by the character and strategy of William Jennings Bryan, the standard bearer of the low tariff alliance.[42] Bryan has had a bad historical press because his populism had overtones of bigotry, anti-intellectualism, archaicism, and religious fundamentalism. Politically these attributes were flaws because they made it harder to attract badly needed allies to the farmers' cause. Bryan's style, symbols, and program were meaningful to the trans-Mississippi and Southern farmers who fueled Populism, but incomprehensible to city dwellers, immigrants, and Catholics, to say nothing of free-trade oriented businessmen. In the drive for the Democratic nomination and during the subsequent campaign, Bryan put silver in the forefront. Yet free coinage was but a piece of the populist economic analysis and not the part with the strongest appeal for nonfarmers (not even the most important element to farmers themselves). The city dweller's grievances against the industrial economy were more complex. Deflation actually improved his real wages, while cheap money threatened to raise prices. In the search for allies other criticisms of the industrial order could have been developed, but Bryan failed to prevent silver from overwhelming them.

Even within the agrarian sector, the concentration on silver and the fervid quality of the campaign worried the more prosperous farmers. By the 1890s, American agriculture was considerably differentiated. In the trans-Mississippi region, conditions were primitive; farmers were vulnerable, marginal producers: they grew a single crop for the market, had little capital, and no reserves. For different reasons, Southern agriculture was also marginal. In the Northeast and the Midwest farming had become much more diversified; it was less dependent on grain, more highly capitalized, and benefited from greater competition among railroads, alternative shipping routes, and direct access to urban markets. These farmers related to the industrial sector, rather like the dairymen in Britain, or the Danes. Bryan frightened these farmers as he frightened workers and immigrants. The qualities which made him attractive to one group antagonized others. Like Sen. Barry Goldwater and Sen. George McGovern, he was able to win the nomination, but in a manner which guaranteed defeat. Bryan's campaign caused potential allies to define their interests in ways which seemed incompatible with those of the agricultural sector. It drove farmers away rather than attracting them. Workers saw Bryan not as an ally against their bosses but as a threat to the industrial sector of the economy of which they were a part. To immigrants, he was a nativist xenophobe. Well-to-do Midwestern farmers, Southern Whigs, and Northeast shippers all saw him as a threat to property.

The Republicans, on the other hand, were very shrewd. Not only did they have large campaign funds, but, as Williams argues, James G. Blaine, Benjamin Harrison, and William McKinley understood that industrial interests required allies the support of which they must actively recruit. Like Bismarck, these Republican leaders worked to make minimal concessions in order to split the opposition. In the German coalition the terms of trade were social security for the workers, tariffs for the farmers and the manufacturers, guns and boats for the military. In America, McKinley, et al., outmanoeuvred President Grover Cleveland and the Gold Democrats on the money issue; when Cleveland repealed the Silver Purchase Act, some of the Republicans helped pass the Sherman Silver Purchase Act. The Republican leaders then went after the farmers. Minimizing the importance of monetary issues, they proposed an alternative solution in the form of overseas markets: selling surpluses to the Chinese or the Latin Americans, negotiating the lowering of tariff levels, and policing the meat industry to meet the health regulations Europeans had imposed in order to keep out American imports. To the working class, the Republicans argued that Bryan and the agrarians would cost them jobs and boost prices. Social security was never mentioned—McKinley paid less than Bismarck.

In 1896, the Republican candidate was tactically shrewd and the Democratic one was not. It might have been the other way around. Imagine a charismatic Democrat from Ohio, with a Catholic mother, traditionally friendly to workers, known for his under-standing of farmers' problems, the historical equivalent of Senator Robert Kennedy in the latter's ability to appeal simultaneously to urban ethnics, machine politicians, blacks, and suburban liberals. Unlikely but not impossible: had he existed, such a candidate would still have labored under severe handicaps. The difference between Bryan and McKinley was more than a matter of personality or accident. The forces which made Bryan the standard bearer were built into the structure of American politics. First, McKinley's success in constructing a coalition derives from features inherent in industrial society. As in Germany, producers' groups had a structural advantage. Bringing the farmers, workers, and consumers together was difficult everywhere in the industrial world during that period. In America, ethnic, geographic, and religious differences made it even harder.

Second, the industrialists controlled both political parties. Whatever happened at the local level, the national Democratic party lay in the firm grip of Southern conservatives and Northern businessmen. Prior to 1896, they wrote their ideas into the party platforms and nominated their man at every convention. The Gold Democrats were not a choice but an echo. Even the Republicans thought so: after the election of 1892, Andrew Carnegie wrote to Henry Clay Frick: "Well we have nothing to fear and perhaps it is best. People will now think the Protected Manufacturers were attended to and quit agitating. Cleveland is a pretty good fellow. Off for Venice tomorrow."[43] A Bryan-type crusade was structurally necessary. Action out of the ordinary was required to wrest the electoral machine away from the Gold Democrats. But the requirements of that success also sowed seeds for the failure of November 1896.

Why, in turn, did the Industrialists control the parties? The Civil War is crucial. At its inception, the Republican party was an amalgam of entrepreneurs, farmers, lawyers, and professionals who believed in opportunity, hard work, and self-help; these were people from medium-sized towns, medium-sized enterprises, medium-sized farms. These people disliked the South not because they wished to help the black race or even eliminate slavery, but because the South and slavery symbolized the very opposite of "Free Soil, Free Labor, Free Men."[44] By accelerating the pace of industrialization, the Civil War altered the internal balance of the Party, tipping control to the industrialists. By mobilizing national emotions against the South, the Civil War fused North and West together, locking the voter into the Republican Party. Men who had been antibusiness and Jacksonian prior to 1860 were now members of a coalition dominated by business.[45]

In the South, the Old Whigs, in desperate need of capital, fearful of social change, and contemptuous of the old Jacksonians, looked to the northern industrialists for help in rebuilding their lands and restoring conservative rule. What would have been more natural than to have joined their northern allies in the Republican party? In the end, the hostility of the Radical Republicans made this impossible, and instead the Old Whigs went into the Democratic Party where they eventually helped sustain the Gold Democrats and battled with the Populists for control of the Democratic organization in the South.

There were, then, in the American system certain structural obstacles to a low-tariff coalition. What of economic ideology (explanation 4) and the international system (explanation 3)? Free trade in the United States never had the ideological force it had in the United Kingdom. Infant industries and competition with the major industrial power provided the base for a protectionist tradition, as farming and distrust of the state provided a base for free trade. Tariffs had always been an important source of revenue for the Federal government. It is interesting that the "Free Soil, Labor and Men" coalition did not add Free Trade to its program.

Trade bore some relation to foreign policy. The whole thrust of Williams' work has been to show how American involvement with the world was shaped by the quest for markets, first for agricultural products, then for industrial. Nonetheless, it is hard to see that the international political system determined tariff policy. The United States had no need to worry about foreign control of resources or food supply. In any case the foreign policy of the low tariff coalition was not very different from the foreign policy of the high tariff coalition.

In conclusion, four countries have been subjected to a set of questions in an attempt to find evidence relevant to differing explanations of tariff levels in the late nineteenth century. In each country, we find a large bloc of economic interest groups gaining significant economic advantages from the policy decision adopted concerning tariffs. Hence, the economic explanation has both simplicity and power. But is it enough? It does have two weaknesses. First, it presupposes a certain obviousness about the direction of economic pressures upon groups. Yet, as the argumentation above has sought to show, other economic calculations would also have been rational for those groups. Had farmers supported protection in Britain or opposed it in Germany and France, we could also offer a plausible economic interpretation for their behavior. The same is true for industrialists: had they accepted the opposite policy, we could find ways in which they benefited from doing so. We require an explanation, therefore, for the choice between two economic logics. One possibility is to look at the urgency of economic need. For protectionists, the incentive for high tariffs was intense and obvious. For free traders, the advantages of their policy preference, and the costs of their opponents' victory, were more ambiguous. Those who wanted their goals the most, won.

Second, the economic explanation fails to flesh out the political steps involved in translating a potential alliance of interest into policy. Logrolling does take some organization, especially in arranging side payments among the partners. The iron–rye bargain seems so natural that we forget the depth of animosity between the partners in the period preceding it. To get their way, economic groups had to translate their economic power into political currency.

The political structures explanation appears to take care of this problem. Certain institutions and particular individuals helped to organize the winning coalition and facilitate its victory. Looking at each victory separately, these structures and personalities bulk large in the story. Yet viewed comparatively, their importance washes out. Bismarck, the Junkers, the authoritarian constitution, the character of the German civil service, the special connections among the state, banking, and industry—these conspicuous features of the German case have no equivalents elsewhere. Méline was no Bismarck and the system gave him no particular leverage. Mobilization against socialism did not occur in the United States, or even in Britain and France. Yet the pattern of policy outcomes in these countries was the same, suggesting that those aspects of the political system which were *idiosyncratic* to each country (such as Bismarck and regime type) are not crucial in explaining the result. In this sense the political explanation does not add to the economic one.

Nonetheless, some aspects of the relation between economic groups and the political system are *uniform* among the countries examined here and do help explain the outcome. There is a striking similarity in the identity of victors and losers from country to country:

producers over consumers, heavy industrialists over finished manufacturers, big farmers over small, and property owners over laborers. In each case, a coalition of producers' interests defined by large scale basic industry and substantial landowners defeated its opponent. It is probable, therefore, that different types of groups from country to country are systematically not equal in political resources. Rather, heavy industrialists and landowners are stronger than peasants, workers, shopkeepers, and consumers. They have superior resources, access to power, and compactness. They would have had these advantages even if the regimes had differed considerably from their historical profiles. Thus a republicanized or democratized Germany would doubtless have had high tariffs (although it might have taken longer for this to come about, as it did in France). A monarchist France (Bourbon, Orleanist, or Bonapartist) would certainly have had the same high tariffs as Republican France. An authoritarian Britain could only have come about through repression of the industrialists by landowners, so it is possible a shift in regime might have meant higher tariffs; more likely, the industrialists would have broken through as they did in Germany. Certainly Republican Britain would have had the same tariff policy. In the United States, it is possible (although doubtful) that without the critical election of 1896, or with a different party system altogether, the alternation between protectionist Republicans and low tariff Democrats might have continued.

Two coalitions faced each other. Each contained a variety of groups. Compared to the losers, the winners comprised: (1) groups for which the benefits of their policy goal were intense and urgent, rather than diffuse; (2) groups occupying strategic positions in the economy; and (3) groups with structurally superior positions in each political system. The uniformity of the winners' economic characteristics, regardless of regime type, suggests that to the extent that the political advantages derive from economic ones, the political explanation is not needed. The translation of economic advantage into policy does require action, organization, and politics; to that extent, and to varying degrees, the economic explanation by itself is insufficient. It is strongest in Germany, where the rapidity of the switch from free trade to protection is breathtaking, and in France where economic slowness made the nation especially vulnerable to competition. It works least well for Britain where the policy's advantages to the industrialists seem the least clear, and for the United States, where the weakness of agriculture is not explicable without the Civil War. Note that nowhere do industrialists fail to obtain their preferences.

In this discussion, we have called the actors groups, not classes, for two reasons. First, the language of class often makes it difficult to clarify the conflicts of interest (e.g., heavy industry vs. manufacture) which exist within classes, and to explain which conception of class interest prevails. Second, class analysis is complex. Since interest group reasoning claims less, and works, there is no point in going further.[46]

The international system and economic ideology explanations appear the least useful. Each is certainly compatible with the various outcomes, but has drawbacks. First, adding them violates the principle of parsimony. If one accepts the power of the particular economic-political explanation stated above, the other two explanations become redundant. Second, even if one is not attracted by parsimony, reference to the international system does not escape the difficulty inherent in any "unitary actor" mode of reasoning: why does a particular conception of the national interest predominate? In the German case, the low tariff coalition did not share Bismarck's and Bülow's conception of how Germany should relate to the world. Thus the international system explanation must revert to some investigation of domestic politics.

Finally, the economic ideology explanation seems the weakest. Whatever its strength in accounting for the Free Trade Movement of the 1850s and 1860s, this explanation cannot deal with the rapid switch to protection in the 1870s. A national culture argument cannot really explain why two different policies are followed within a very short span of time. The flight away from Free Trade by Junkers, manufacturers, farmers, and so on was clearly provoked by the price drop. For the United Kingdom, conversely, the continuity of policy makes the cultural argument more appropriate. Belief in free trade may have blunted the receptivity of British interest groups toward a protectionist solution of their problems. The need for the economic ideology explanation here depends on one's evaluation of the structure of economic incentives facing industry: to whatever extent empire, and other advantages of having been first, eased the full impact of the depression, ideology was superfluous. To whatever extent industry suffered but avoided protection, ideology was significant.[. . .]

These observations on the political consequences of the tariff debate are clearly speculative. What has interested me from the beginning is the linkage between the broad struggle for domination in society and the more specific policy problem posed by the drop in prices. The two once seemed, in my view, to be different sides of the same coin: the tariff levels and the coalitions which supported them would stand or fall on this issue. If the coalition were defeated, the tariff levels would change; if the coalition could not defend its tariff level, it would then collapse. Now they seem much more independent.

The character of the political system may have little impact on the content of various policies. This paper has explored the relation for only one case: tariffs in the late nineteenth century. Policy issues are to some extent neutral mediums, able to take on widely varying tints. Regimes of quite different types may use the same policy as proof of their superiority, efficacy, or legitimacy.[47] The precise impact that policy has on regime type depends on historical context. Its effects may last long after the policy has become obsolete or abandoned. Some may see this as evidence of the derivative and dependent character of politics. To me, it suggests the originality and independence of politics.

Notes

1. I particularly want to thank James Kurth, and also Richard Gordon, Lisa Hirshman, Peter Katzenstein, Charles Kindleberger, Charles Maier, Barrington Moore, Jr., Thomas Naylor, Joseph Nye, Victor Perez-Diaz, and Martin Shefter.

2. The literature on the nature of the Great Depression is enormous. See David Landes, *The Unbound Prometheus* (Cambridge, Mass., 1969); S. B. Saul, *The Myth of the Great Depression* (New York, 1969); Walt W. Rostow, *The British Economy of the Nineteenth Century* (Oxford, 1948); Hans Rosenberg, "The Depression of 1873–1896 in Central Europe," *Journal of Economic History*, XIII (1943), 58-73; Joseph Schumpeter, *Business Cycles* (New York, 1939).

3. See Alexander Gerschenkron, *Bread and Democracy in Germany* (New York, 1966); Michael Tracy, *Agriculture in Western Europe* (London, 1964); J. D. Chambers and G. E. Mingay, *The Agricultural Revolution 1750–1880* (London, 1966).

4. Landes, *Unbound Prometheus*, 191–194; Eric J. Hobsbawm, *Industry and Empire* (New York, 1968).

5. The most useful treatments remain those written over twenty years ago: Gerschenkron, *Bread and Democracy*; Rosenberg; Charles P. Kindleberger, "Group Behavior and International Trade," *The Journal of Political Economy*, LIX (1951), 30–46.

6. On the problem of alternative explanations of the same phenomena see James Kurth, "A Widening Gyre: The Logic of American Weapons Procurement," *Public Policy*, XIX (1971), 373–405; *idem*, "American Hegemony: A Thicket of Theories," paper read at a Canadian Political Science Association meeting, 1971; Graham Allison, *Essence of Decision* (Boston, 1971).

7. E. E. Schattschneider, *Politics, Pressure Groups and the Tariffs* (Hamden, 1963); Richard

Caves, "The Political Economy of Tariff Structures," W. A. Mackintosh Lecture, Queen's University (1975), mimeo.

8. Gerschenkron's explanation seems to be of this type.

9. See allusions to this type of argument in Gerschenkron and in Benjamin Brown, *The Tariff Reform Movement in Britain, 1884–1895* (New York, 1943).

10. See Charles P. Kindleberger, "The Rise of Free Trade in Western Europe, 1820–1875," *Journal of Economic History*, XXXV (1975), 20–55.

11. See Gerschenkron, *Bread and Democracy, passim*; Einas Jensen, *Danish Agriculture: Its Economic Development* (Copenhagen, 1937). A third alternative was emigration or urbanization, which happened everywhere, but took time as a way of solving the crisis.

12. Although access to capital was probably not a problem for the Junkers, who could make use of the "Hypothekenbanken" and the "Reifeinsenkassen." George Garvy, in litt., March, 1975.

13. See Derek Aldcroft, "Introduction: British Industry and Foreign Competition," in Aldcroft (ed.), *British Industry and Foreign Competition* (London, 1968), 11–36.

14. Rostow, *British Economy*; Landes, *Unbound Prometheus*.

15. Arthur Rosenberg, *Imperial Germany* (Boston, 1964); A. J. P. Taylor, *The Course of German History* (New York, 1946).

16. Rosenberg, *Imperial Germany*, 1–72.

17. Hans-Ulrich Wehler, "Bismarck's Imperialism, 1862–1890," *Past & Present*, 48 (1970), 119–155. This is a summary of his important *Bismarck und der Imperialismus* (Köln, 1969); Eckhart Kehr, *Schlachtflottenbau und Parteipolitik* (Berlin, 1930); idem, *Der Primat der Innenpolitik* (Berlin, 1965).

18. Naval building, so important to the steel industry, was superfluous for the autarchy policy since a self-sufficient Germany would not have to import.

19. Wehler, "Bismarck's Imperialism," 143.

20. Theodore Hamerow, *Restoration, Revolution and Reaction* (Princeton, 1958).

21. Helmut Böhme, "Big Business Pressure Groups and Bismarck's Turn to Protectionism, 1873–79," *The Historical Journal*, X (1967), 218–236. This is an abridgement of *Deutschlands Weg zur Grossmacht* (Köln, 1966). See also Hartmut Kaelble, *Industrielle Interessenpolitik in der Wilhelminischen Gesellschaft* (Berlin, 1967); Hans-Jürgen Puhle, *Politische Agrarbewegungen in Kapitalistischen Industriegesellschaften: Deutschland, USA und Frankreich im 20.Jahrhundert* (Göttingen, 1975).

22. Böhme, "Big Business," 223–231. See also Ivo Lambi, *Free Trade and Protection in Germany, 1868–1879* (Wiesbaden, 1963).

23. Mancur Olson, *The Logic of Collective Action* (New York, 1965).

24. Gerschenkron, *Bread and Democracy*, 54–58. On corporatist arguments and peasant organizations see Suzanne Berger, *Peasants against Politics* (Cambridge, Mass., 1972).

25. J. Alden Nichols, *Germany after Bismarck: The Caprivi Era* (New York, 1958); Sarah Tirrell, *German Agrarian Politics after Bismarck's Fall* (New York, 1951).

26. Thomas Kemp, *Economic Forces in French History* (London, 1971); C. P. Kindleberger, *Economic Growth in Britain and France* (Cambridge, Mass., 1967).

27. Eugene Golob, *The Méline Tariff* (New York, 1944); J. H. Clapham, *Economic Development of France and Germany* (Cambridge, Mass., 1968; 4th ed.); M. Augé-Laribé, *La politique agricole de la France de 1880 à 1940* (Paris, 1950); Michael Tracy, *Agriculture in Western Europe* (London, 1964).

28. Sanford Elwitt, *The Making of the Third Republic: Class and Politics in France, 1868–1884* (Baton Rouge, 1975), 230–272.

29. John McManners, *Church and State in France* (London, 1972); Stanley Hoffmann, "Paradoxes in the French Political Community," in Stanley Hoffmann et al., *In Search of France* (Cambridge, Mass., 1963).

30. See works cited by Aldcroft, Landes, Rostow, Saul, and Hobsbawn. Also J. H. Clapham, *An Economic History of Modern Britain* (Cambridge, 1950); P. J. Perry (ed.), *British Agriculture 1875–1914* (London, 1973).

31. See especially Hobsbawm, *From Industry to Empire*.

32. See Brown, *Tariff Reform*; Leland Hamilton Jenks, *The Migration of British Capital* (New York, 1927); S. B. Paul, *Studies in British Overseas Trade 1870–1914* (Liverpool, 1971).

33. Chambers and Mingay, *The Agricultural Revolution*; C. S. Orwin and E. H. Whelman, *A History of British Agriculture, 1846–1919* (London, 1963; 2nd ed.).

34. F.M.L. Thompson, *English Landed Society in the 19th Century* (London, 1963); Barrington Moore, Jr., *Social Origins of Dictatorship and Democracy* (Boston, 1966).

35. It is interesting that the literature on Britain concentrates not on why there was no restoration of protection in the 1870s but whether and why agriculture did a poor job modernizing; one of the reasons offered by those who think that it was poorly done is the same as that given in the German case—the concentration of ownership eliminated the middling farmer needed to do the job.

36. Paul Smith, *Disraelean Conservatism and Social Reform* (London, 1967); Robert Blake, *Disraeli* (New York, 1966).

37. "Yet as an imperialist movement, Fair Trade was suspect. The league was never quite able to overcome the impression that many of its members were merely stowaways on the good ship Empire because their own protectionist ship had little prospect of making port." Brown, *Tariff Reform*, 89; "Men became protectionist usually because they wanted to secure their bread and butter; but often because they were Conservatives and wanted ammunition to snipe at Liberals; often because they believed in the empire; and sometimes, indeed because they revered their grandfathers or were members of the Church of England." *Ibid.*, 102.

38. It would be interesting to compare the responses of the plains countries, exploring the consequences of having different types of industrial "presences" (strong domestic capital, foreign capital, shippers and bankers), in the United States, Russia, Argentina, Canada, Australia, and elsewhere. See Theodore H. Moran, "The Development of Argentina and Australia: The Radical Party of Argentina and the Labor Party of Australia in the Process of Economic and Political Development," *Comparative Politics*, III (1970), 71-92. It would also be stimulating to apply the categories of specialized function in the world economy, such as that of the core, semicore, and periphery, worked out by Immanuel Wallerstein and others. Britain could pursue free trade because she was the core country; the others had to protect. This works in a broad way, but is less useful in matters of timing, especially in explaining why it took Britain so long to react after losing its hegemony. I am grateful to Wallerstein and George Niosi for their comments during a discussion at McGill University, 1975. See Immanuel Wallerstein, *The Modern World-System* (New York, 1974); Tom Naylor, "The Rise and Fall of the Third Commercial Empire of the St. Lawrence," in Gary Teeple (ed.), *Capitalism and the National Question in Canada* (Tronto, 1972): Tom Naylor, *The History of Canadian Business, 1867-1914* (Toronto, 1975), 2 v.

39. Robert Weibe, *The Search for Order 1877-1920* (New York, 1967).

40. The Compromise of 1876 which put Hayes in the White House had less to do with the end of Reconstruction, which was ending anyway, than with the desire by Southerners to obtain patronage and a railroad through the Southwest. See C. Van Woodward, *The Origins of the New South* (Baton Rouge, 1951); Gabriel Kolko, *The Triumph of Conservatism* (Glencoe, 1963); *idem.*, *Railroads and Regulation* (Princeton, 1965); William Appelman Williams, *Roots of the Modern American Empire* (New York, 1969). See also Frank Taussig, A *Tariff History of the United States* (New York, 1931).

41. Moore, *Social Origins*, 111-155.

42. C. Van Woodward, *Reunion and Reaction* (Boston, 1961); *Tom Watson: Agrarian Rebel* (New York, 1938); Paul Glad, *McKinley, Bryan and the People* (Philadelphia, 1964); John Hope Franklin, *Reconstruction* (Chicago, 1961).

43. Letter of Nov. 8, 1892, cited in Joseph Wall, *Andrew Carnegie* (New York, 1970), 569.

44. Eric Foner, *Free Soil, Free Labor, Free Men* (Oxford, 1970).

45. Walter Dean Burnham, *Critical Elections and the Mainsprings of American Politics* (New York, 1970); James L. Sundquist, *Dynamics of the Party System* (Washington, 1973).

46. I wish to thank Janice Stein, Jean Laux, Albert Legault, and Lynn Mytelka for their comments on this point made at a conference in Montreal, 1975.

47. The relation between policy content and regime types ought to be elucidated by comparative policy studies. See Arnold J. Heidenheimer, "The Politics of Public Education, Health, and Welfare in the U.S.A. and Western Europe: How Growth and Reform Potentials Have Differed," *British Journal of Political Science*, III (1973), 315-340.

Capitalism, Case Studies, and Public Policy: Trade Expansion Legislation Re-examined

ALAN STONE

Foreign trade legislation is supremely important to the workings of the political economy, and American social scientists have frequently used detailed case studies of particular pieces of tariff legislation to provide the basis for more ambitious claims about the general nature of public policy formation in the United States. One much studied piece of legislation that has been used in this way is the Kennedy administration's 1962 Trade Expansion Act. In this essay Alan Stone re-examines the background of the Act, and offers an account at odds with virtually all the leading interpretations both of the origins of the legislation and of what its passage should tell us about policy formation generally, from Raymond Bauer, Ithiel de Sola Pool, and Lewis Dexter's classic American Business and Public Policy (1963) to William Domhoff's sharp attack on their work in his The Higher Circles (1970). Stone also takes issue with Theodore Lowi's related efforts, which rely prominently on the Bauer, Pool, and Dexter study, to fashion a general typology of public policy formation. Adopting what he describes as a non-mechanical Marxist approach, Stone argues that scholars have not only misunderstood the specific dynamics of the Kennedy administration's trade legislation initiatives, but have misunderstood as well the persistent importance of impersonal economic constraints and the shifting demands of capitalist economic development in setting the outer boundaries of public policy decisions in general.

Introduction: Tariff and Public Policy Generalization

The tariff, probably more than any other public policy area, has triggered theories for which analysts have claimed more general applicability. We may begin with E. E. Schattschneider's justly famous 1935 account of the bargaining process between interest group lobbyists and government over the enactment of the Hawley-Smoot Tariff during the Hoover Administration; it is no exaggeration to state that many of our received conceptions of lobbying activity stem from that work.[1] The work of Schattschneider and other students of public policy employing a similar framework provided the raw material for David Truman's brilliant pluralist synthesis in *The Governmental Process*.[2]

Tariff policy during the Eisenhower presidency provided the next set of major generalizations about American public policy. The first important study, it should be noted, was used by its authors—Bauer, Pool, and Dexter—to explain not only policy during Eisenhower's presidency, to which almost all of the collected data pertains, but, to a lesser extent, to President Kennedy's Trade Expansion Act of 1962, as frequent text references indicate.[3] In any event, the authors concluded that "the stereotype of pressure politics, of special interests effectively expressing themselves and forcing politicians either to bow to their dictates or to fight back vigorously," is essentially false.[4] They maintained that business leaned "over backward not to exert pressure" and that political actors were "utterly unaware of pressure campaigns directed against them." Insofar as this case study is taken as typical of policy process, then, the necessary conclusion is that the "relative power of big business in American politics has declined in the past fifty years."[5] The notion of "big business" is analytically of limited value; it has neither the unity of interest nor the cohesion to be considered as a single-minded interest in political life.

The Bauer, Pool, and Dexter study provided Theodore J. Lowi with an opportunity to develop a plausible hypothesis, purporting to explain virtually all case studies of American public policy. Employing a highly original and influential framework, Lowi divided policies into three basic categories—distributive, regulatory, and redistributive—from which an analyst is able to probabilistically predict the primary units involved in the process of policy formation, relations among these units, and the relative importance of Congress and the executive branch in forming the most important portions of the statute. Thus, in the case of redistributive policies (those that operate on the economic environment as a whole) such as macroeconomic policies, the primary units are peak associations or their equivalents, the relations among these units are largely ideological, and the executive branch plays a legislative role. In regulatory policies (those that impose limits on the discretion of groups) the principal actors are trade associations, their relations are characterized by bargaining, and Congress plays a creative role; while in the case of distributive (or subsidy) policies, the primary units are single firms or small numbers, the characteristic relations between actors are logrolling, and congressional committees are the major arenas of activity.

In applying this scheme to tariff legislation, Lowi concluded that, with the advent of the Trade Expansion Act, foreign trade legislation, which at one time was distributive, had now become regulatory. For this reason, Lowi surmised, the high degree of lobbying activity by firms found in a study of earlier tariff policy was absent in conjunction with the Trade Expansion Act; tariff had largely become a regulatory policy in 1962, with only residues of the older, disaggregated style of tariff making. Congress, not committees, became stage center and trade groups (textiles, railroads, etc.), not individual firms or small segments of industries, became major actors in crucial events.[6]

Then, in 1970, G. William Domhoff, writing as an intellectual descendant of C. Wright Mills, purported to show in a brief three pages that the "pluralist" interpretation of the 1962 Trade Expansion Act allegedly offered by Bauer, Pool, and Dexter was incorrect.[7] However, Domhoff's characterization of the original study is inaccurate, since Bauer, Pool, and Dexter go to some lengths to show that interest groups—the key actors in an orthodox pluralist analysis—played little part in the decision-making process. Rather, the heart of Bauer, Pool, and Dexter's thesis is that Congress was able to develop the particulars of the Trade Expansion Act relatively free of constraints and pressure imposed by narrow outside interests. In contrast, the great value of Domhoff's analysis of the 1962 statute was in pointing out the major role played by the executive branch in shaping and developing the legislation. Domhoff went to great pains to portray the key decision makers of the statute as members of the "power elite." But Domhoff did not explore: (1) whether and how the key decision makers felt themselves to be part of the "power elite"; (2) why the decision was of particular importance to a power elite—was it simply because it concerned foreign policy? and (3) whether the decision needed the involvement of a power elite to lead to the same substantive result. In general, Domhoff has examined a number of case studies of public policy decisions, attempting to point out that they were made by a power elite that in turn is dominated by an upper class. But, after following his case studies, one has no unifying sense of which public policies are of concern to the power elite, which are not, and why. We do not know what the options of the power elite were, and why they chose what they did. Nor can we understand how and why policies (such as pollution regulations) are sometimes adopted that are at odds with the profit-maximizing motivations of big business, presumably the major interest for which the power elite renders its decisions.

In summary, then, a great deal of public policy analysis has converged on the subject of foreign trade legislation, but without allowing us to draw implications that are broader than the conclusion reached about the case studied. If Schattschneider and Bauer *et al.* could at best do no more than draw conclusions about specific cases at given times, then Lowi has been able to do no more than supply a plausible hypothesis that a large number of additional case studies can only strengthen, not confirm. That is, if Lowi were to find, say, 100 additional cases confirming his threefold scheme, it still does not follow that the next 200 cases will conform to the scheme. Nor does the threefold scheme, in itself, explain either the changes in the politics of policy formation or the substance of policy content. For example, why (assuming that Lowi's and Domhoff's characterizations are correct) did tariff policy move from a subsidy policy during the Hoover presidency through a regulatory policy during the Eisenhower presidency to a highly centralized policy in the Kennedy Administration? None of the schemes discussed adequately explains the transition. Nor, to take a more current set of examples, can we understand, simply on the basis of any of these theories, why energy policy making was transformed from a highly decentralized process in the early 1960s to one initiated in the highest reaches of the executive branch during the 1970s. The substance of what follows will consider the Trade Expansion Act of 1962 in an attempt to provide a framework for policy studies that will allow generalization without being reductionist and also comprehend change over time.

Capitalism, Case Studies, and Public Policy

My intention very simply is to avoid the "constant diversion from the objective structures and laws of the system to the personal motivations of their agents."[8] It is a commonplace that we live in a capitalist society, but the inferences from that fact, the stage of capitalism in which a particular society is located, its functional requisites, and the implications that follow from the development of these conceptions are rarely developed.[9] But the starting point of public policy analysis is with these questions; once we have elaborated their implications, we may proceed to the various options among which policy makers may choose and to the roles of classes and groups. Thus, the stage of a particular capitalist society, and its functional requisites, imposes constraints on policy options and provides policy direction. Sometimes the constraints are loose and the options many, while at other times the choices are narrow. But until we ask these central questions, we cannot frame what the real choices are and we will tend to employ an overly voluntaristic conception of public policy making, whether our focus is on elites or on groups or on government agencies. In addition, the framework employed herein helps to explain why initiatives in policy making on decisions with broad consequences tend to become centralized in the hands of the executive branch and expert administrators, and does so without resorting to the unproved (perhaps unprovable) hypothesis of an integrated power elite.

Let us now turn to the 1962 Trade Expansion Act to apply this mode of analysis, placing American capitalism and its world position shortly before 1962 in perspective in order to understand the functions of the Trade Expansion Act.

Foreign Trade and the Balance of Payments

The last years of the Eisenhower presidency were characterized by a series of interrelated economic problems sufficiently serious and well known that one of President Kennedy's most important election slogans was "to get the country moving again." By some measures the United States was in a recession. By February 1961, the rate of unemployment reached 8 percent of the labor force and the gap between potential and actual GNP was $30–35 billion per annum. Rapid economic growth in Western Europe and Japan was contrasted with relative stagnation at home. Concomitant with domestic economic problems was America's worsening international economic status. In the words of one international economic affairs "insider":

> . . . the view that the United States had been endowed with a permanent international trade and payment advantage over the rest of the world had been abandoned by everyone. The new fear—of persisting U.S. deficit—was reinforced by the contrast between the spectacular rates of economic growth being achieved in Europe and relative stagnation at home. Given these signs and portents, there was more than usual unanimity—in the administration, the Congress and the American business community—that *something* needed to be done.[10]

A series of events accentuated the sense of impending crisis, of which the most dramatic was the gold crisis of October 1960. The run on gold during this period reflected declining international confidence in the dollar and the prospect of its devaluation. While the decline in U.S. gold stocks amounted to $1.7 billion from 1950 through 1957, the outflow between 1958 and 1960 alone shot up to $5.1 billion.[11] Again, the net outflow

---

Table 1

U.S. Balance of Payments ($ billions)

Period	Annual average amount
1950–56	−1.2
1957	+1.1
1958–59	−2.7
1960–64	−2.2

Source: Bank for International Settlements, *Annual Report, 1971*, as presented in Sidney E. Rolfe and James L. Burtle, *The Great Wheel* (see Note 12), p. 72.

---

of dollars rose to almost $4 billion in 1960, while the total balance of payments deficit from 1960 to 1964 averaged annually $2.2 billion, almost double the annual average of the 1950s.[12]

One of the important components of America's negative balance of payments—and the prospect of its getting worse—was defense outlays abroad, which amounted to $2.4 billion per annum between 1960 and 1964, or $.2 billion more than the total negative annual balance during those years. In accord with President Kennedy's new strategic doctrine of "flexible response," which called for upgrading of America's conventional and counterinsurgency capabilities, the probability was that overseas defense expenditures would grow significantly. In keeping with this posture, President Kennedy's fiscal 1962 defense expenditures were $5.9 billion more than President Eisenhower's request, and $6.4 billion above the fiscal 1961 appropriations.[13]

A second important development forming the backdrop of the Trade Expansion Act was the sharp rise of overseas investment by American firms, particularly by the so-called multinational companies.[14] Direct U.S. investment overseas had risen from $25 billion in 1957 to $36 billion in 1962. The principal American multinationals found during the 1950s that European tariff protection was sometimes effectively excluding their exports and, accordingly, they invested in Europe to circumvent tariff and other barriers. One factor accelerating this trend was the higher return on investment in Europe as compared to the United States.[15] Surveys of the top managements of large American business corporations indicated that investment of these firms in the European market would, if anything, accelerate. Typical is the statement of the then president of General Electric: "Regardless of economic or political ups and downs, the most rapidly expanding markets will be abroad in the next 25 years."[16]

Table 2

U.S. Merchandise Trade, 1960-63 ($ millions)

	1960	1961	1962	1963
Exports	19,650	20,107	20,779	22,252
Imports	14,744	14,519	16,218	17,011
Balance	4,906	5,588	4,561	5,241

Source: U.S. Department of Commerce, "Survey of Current Business," June 1972.

Given the prospective negative impact of "national security" and private foreign investment on America's balance of payments, and the probability of their negative impact increasing in the years following 1963, the principal item that could counterbalance them was merchandise export. "The view began to jell among economists that if the largest element of the U.S. payments position, merchandise trade, could be improved while the exodus of long-term multinational corporate or private portfolio investment could be kept in bounds, the American position might become increasingly tolerable."[17] Table 2 indicates the crucial importance of merchandise trade in countervailing the items contributing to a negative balance of payments.

Protecting America's favorable trade balance thus became a task extending well beyond the traditional concerns of tariff policy. Its implications extend into the realm of national security and the economic health of the nation. Trade expansion in 1962 and 1963 is best characterized by the Millsian term "important decision": it clearly related to war and peace, slump and prosperity.[18] Of equal importance, the major policy makers in the Kennedy Administration who designed the Act saw it in these terms. President Kennedy, for example, noted the worsening of America's balance of payments, which

> . . . turned a new spotlight on the importance of increasing American exports to strengthen the international position of the dollar and prevent a steady drain of our gold reserves. To maintain our defense, assistance and other commitments abroad . . . we must achieve a reasonable equilibrium in our international accounts by offsetting these dollar outlays with dollar sales.[19]

Again, two influential advisors on foreign economic policy—Will Clayton and Christian Herter—informed the Joint Economic Committee, in a report requested by the Committee, that "the United States must hold and add to its export markets, to pay for essential imports and to permit continuation of its heavy commitments abroad."[20]

Suppose we were to find that the Trade Expansion Act decision was largely made by members of Mills's "power elite" or Domhoff's "higher circles"; does this case study support these hypotheses? Not at all, for far more important than *who* made these decisions is the problem of *why* they were made in the form they were. Given the nearly universal consensus on America's internationalist foreign policy posture and the fact that the well-being of our great corporations *is* the well-being of our economic system,[21] only decision makers who radically differ with these constraining assumptions can offer significantly different alternatives. This does not mean, of course, that *all* choice is foreclosed, but rather that the range is narrowly compressed. The question of whether such "important" decisions are made by members of the power elite or persons of different background thus becomes secondary. The system has its own logic and to a very marked extent dictates "important" policy to decision makers irrespective of their own wills. One sees this, for example, in the behavior of Labour governments in the United Kingdom. Only a mind infected by paranoia would describe British Labourites as members of a power elite integrally tied to big business and the military—indeed the Labour Party is manifestly hostile to big business; yet Labour policies of cutting social welfare programs and holding down wage increases were not very different from those proposed by their Conservative counterparts.[22]

The range of choice exercised over such "important" decisions, whether through elite choice, interest-group activity, or public opinion, is thus dependent upon the constraints imposed by the socioeconomic system. The latter is the critical consideration, and, depending upon its intrinsic needs, policy options are wider or narrower. Thus, with respect to the core of a policy, there is no particular need for business groups to exert pressure on political decision makers. The latter—assuming that they are rational—know full well what the problems are, and share with outside interests a common framework within which to solve them. Interest group activity comes into play only after the central policy decision is made. Thus, policy with respect to such "important" issues is independent of the sociological characteristics of the policy makers who formulate the policies; yet, at the same time, as we shall see, the core of the policy is developed by a narrow circle, and interest groups play a significant role only in some of the aspects of the policy complementary to the core.

Let us now examine the genesis of the Trade Expansion Act to see how this process works.

The Trade Expansion Act and the Balance of Trade

In order to understand how the Trade Expansion Act attempted to reshape American foreign trade policy in response to new conditions, let us briefly review this policy area prior to the new statute. We begin with the Hawley-Smoot Tariff Act of 1930, which raised tariffs to their highest point in history.[23] This Act marked the high-water mark of congressional dominance over tariffs, for the 1934 Act amended the Hawley-Smoot Act by granting authority to the President to reduce tariffs by 50 percent in exchange for equivalent concessions from other countries. By 1945 most of the President's tariff-cutting authority was exhausted. Accordingly, Congress granted short-term tariff-cutting authority to the President in almost every other postwar year prior to the Trade Expansion Act.

Tariff negotiation under the extensions of the 1934 Act was extremely cumbersome, especially when compared to the method employed within the Common Market. The President was required to negotiate item-by-item instead of by groups of articles—the "linear method" employed by the Common Market and the 44 members of the G.A.T.T. (General Agreement on Tariffs and Trade.) Thus, it had taken American negotiators two years (1958–1960) just to draw up a list of items on which to bargain with the G.A.T.T. members.[24]

But far more important than the procedural difficulties in the negotiating process were the substantive problems raised by the formation and development of the European Economic Community (E.E.C.), which constituted one of the most important export markets for American merchandise as shown in Table 3.

As Table 3 demonstrates, not only was the E.E.C. a major market for exports but, more importantly, it appeared to be the most important U.S. market in terms of export growth potential. Moreover, the E.E.C.'s great importance in the balance-of-payments picture is shown in Table 4.

In 1957 E.E.C. members signed the Treaty of Rome, calling for the cutting of internal tariffs to signators. By the end of 1961 tariffs had been cut 30 percent and the future timetable called for additional cuts of 50 percent from the 1957 level by June 1962, and an additional 10 percent reduction by July 1963. Internal tariffs were scheduled to be

Table 3

U.S. Exports by Region (U.S.$ billions)

	Japan	LDCs	Canada	EEC
1958	1.0	8.1	3.5	3.9
1959	1.1	7.1	3.8	4.1
1960	1.5	7.7	3.8	5.7
1961	1.8	8.0	3.8	5.6
1962	1.6	8.3	4.1	5.9
1963	1.8	8.9	4.3	6.4

LDCs–less-developed countries.
EEC–European Economic Community.

Source: U.S. Congress, Senate, Committee on Finance, Staff Data and Materials on U.S. Trade and Balance of Payments, 93d Cong., 2d Sess., 1974, pp. 16-19.

Table 4

U.S. Balance of Payments by Region (U.S.$ billions)

Year	Japan	LDCs	Canada	EEC
1958	0.3	2.0	0.5	1.3
1959	0.1	0.8	0.4	0.4
1960	0.4	1.5	0.6	2.3
1961	0.7	2.0	0.5	2.3
1962	0.2	2.0	0.4	2.3
1963	0.3	2.3	0.4	2.6

Source: See Table 3.

removed by the beginning of 1967. Thus, U.S. businessmen and political leaders had considerable reason to be concerned about the prospect of declining trade balances due to E.E.C. external tariff barriers coupled with internal E.E.C. free trade. Not only was there the prospect of declining trade balances but, in addition, the possibility of not being in a position to sell to an expanding market. An influential report to the Joint Economic Committee noted:

The probable continuation, and even acceleration of the postwar rise in European living standards could well open up for U.S. exporters an expanding mass market for the wide variety of consumer durable and semidurable goods which the U.S. industry produces so efficiently. . . . That can happen [only if] the United States itself is prepared drastically to reduce its tariffs.[25]

President Kennedy emphasized that a new policy was necessary to prevent American sellers from being locked out of the lucrative West European markets.[26] Extremely flexible negotiating authority vested in the executive branch was obviously called for. If such negotiations resulted in mutual tariff reductions, administration officials calculated, U.S. businessmen would sustain a marked future advantage. Under-Secretary George Ball observed that the Common Market, with its "almost unlimited" growth potential, was "the kind of market best suited for American production. European industrialists have been accustomed to selling their products in small national markets. They have built their industrial plants with that in mind. . . . We alone in the free world have fully developed the techniques for mass production."[27] Further, administration officials judged that it would be many years before the E.E.C. countries would have either the capital or the large surpluses needed to make a major advance in American markets. Finally, these officials calculated that European demand would be particularly strong for those products that America had the capacity to supply in quantity, such as advanced machinery, complex products involving advanced technology, and consumer durables.[28]

Commerce Secretary Luther Hodges asserted on behalf of the Administration that America would continue to show great export surpluses in the face of tariff reductions because: (1) our economy was highly automated with the highest productivity in the world; (2) the United States had a 5-year lead in consumer-durable technology; (3) raw materials and capital financing were cheaper in the United States than in Europe; and (4) the United States had the most efficient marketing organization and merchandising techniques in the world.[29] On the other hand, failure to modernize our trade policy could be disastrous for American business. After noting that exports constituted about 8.7 percent of movable goods production in 1960 and 1961, Hodges stated: "As a business-man, I would say that the loss of a customer accounting for 8.5 percent . . . of sales would be for many companies the difference between operating at a profit and operating at a loss."[30]

Thus, in 1962 trade expansion was a policy area with implications too wide to be left in its important outlines to the bargaining and logrolling processes of Congress. It had to be developed by some central planning organization that could and would rise above the provincial interests, and a campaign had to be waged for it that would effectively tie Congress's hands and brand legislative opponents of the measure as irresponsible, if not worse. And as shown in the next section, the politics of the Trade Expansion Act and its major particulars were an executive innovation, with legislative and interest group activity filling in only those particulars about which the foregoing considerations permitted some flexibility.

The Politics of Trade Expansion

The genesis of the Trade Expansion Act can be traced to a pre-inaugural task force under the leadership of George Ball (who was to become Under-Secretary of State), which recommended a new trade program keyed to the development of the Common Market. After President Kennedy took office, Ball, Robert Schaetzel (a career State Department officer), and Howard Petersen (a Philadelphia banker appointed to head the Special Trade office) prepared versions of a trade expansion bill in the course of 1961. Ball, from the outset, wanted total reconstruction of foreign trade legislation; Petersen was initially willing to tinker with existing legislation, but very soon abandoned this notion as hopeless. The event that prompted Administration officials to press for the legislation was the United Kingdom's decision of July 31, 1961, to apply for Common Market membership.[31] One government foreign-trade insider declared: "The prospect of the United Kingdom and other EFTA countries joining the preferential Common Market . . . increased the urgency for the United States to act to forestall adverse effects on its commerce from European integration."[32]

In 1961, subsequent to the United Kingdom's announcement, a number of Administration spokesmen utilized speaking engagements to announce effectively that a major new foreign trade proposal was forthcoming. The official announcement of the proposal was made in President Kennedy's State of the Union message, and the text of the bill was sent to Congress on January 25, 1962, as the President's major legislative proposal in that year. The President's campaign for the bill was commensurate with its perceived importance. Extensive testimony before congressional committees was supplied by Hodges, Ball, Labor Secretary Goldberg, and Treasury Secretary Dillon. *Business Week* reported that the campaign was successful, there being little opposition to the bill, because "the U.S. faces a real challenge—the opportunity to expand export sales if we move toward freer trade, the certainty of losing markets in Europe if we don't."[33]

The authoritative *Congressional Quarterly Almanac*, describing the progress of the bill, observed that not only did prominent Republican figures back the bill, but many businessmen who supported the Republican Party had much to gain from the increased trade it was to bring about and so backed it. Most big businessmen who appeared at the hearings, as well as peak association and trade association executives, supported the bill for the reasons advanced by the Administration. Included among the active supporters were representatives of such multinational corporations as I.T.T. and United Fruit, the International Chamber of Commerce, whose Board of Trustees is virtually a Who's Who of large multinational companies, the American Bankers Association, the Council on Foreign Relations, the Commerce and Industry Association, and the Committee for Economic Development.[34]

Moreover, not only was there widespread support for the bill for the foregoing reasons; the intensive campaign mounted by the Administration tied the bill to U.S. military and economic commitments, the "fight against communism," etc., so that it became politically risky vigorously to oppose the bill. Not only was the "stick" used, but the "carrot" was employed as well. Organized labor supported the bill; other interests received special consideration from the Administration in connection with their problems. *Congressional Quarterly* quoted one informed observer who stated: "People learned that they could do better by going downtown to the White House than by trying to get special amendments in the bill."[35]

The picture of the process that led to the enactment of the Trade Expansion Act thus does not fit neatly into any of the aforementioned hypotheses advanced to categorize it. Contrary to Bauer, Pool, and Dexter, as well as the analyses that proceed from their data, Congress was not center stage of the processes and politics that took place; rather, the executive branch played the active role, with Congress playing a largely reactive and consensual role. Nor was the central issue framed in the classic terms of free trade and protectionism. Both the Act's proponents and its few opponents largely supported free trade, in view of the previously discussed advantage of this strategy. But, as the above examples show, the commitment to free trade was based upon a "come hell or high water" proviso. The statute itself reflected this by granting the President power to exclude any tariffs from tariff bargaining on grounds of defense requirements or "national interest." This effectively ruled out petroleum, lead, zinc, and other commodities from tariff negotiation. Finally, in an instance of serious injury to a domestic product, the President was empowered to raise tariffs to 50 percent of 1934 levels. In short, neither free trade nor protectionism was the overriding concern of policy makers "freely" choosing from among competing policies; rather, it was the constraints and limitations imposed by the needs to expand domestic output and increase or maintain our favorable trade balance.

But just as these structural limitations undermine the Bauer, Pool, and Dexter theory, so equally do they undermine the Mills–Domhoff elite perspective. It is of course true that some of the principal actors in these events—Hodges, Ball, Petersen, and Dillon—had business or business-related careers prior to their government service, but other important actors—Kennedy and Schaetzel, for example—did not. More importantly, the fruitless search for underlying motives that might be attributable to some of these people as members of a power elite ignores the way in which these actors thought and spoke about trade expansion. Given the widely shared ends of U.S. economic policy, the basic policy embodied in the Trade Expansion Act was a logical proposal, irrespective of the social background, career patterns, or interlocking associations of the policy makers. No evidence exists to show that these background factors had any direct input into the policy decision. Far more persuasive is the logic embodied in the policy, which motivated the responsible policy makers. In President Kennedy's words: "In the absence of authority to bargain down that [Common Market] external tariff, as the economy of the Common Market expands, our exports will not expand with it. They may even decline."[36]

Opposition to the bill did appear, but it was restricted to a few industries, which calculated that trade liberalization would adversely affect them, and to a few of the peripheral provisions of the legislation, most notably "adjustment assistance," which contemplated the provision of loans and financial aid to adversely affected firms as well as unemployment and retraining payments to workers. This provision, which was to operate jointly or alternatively with the traditional "escape clause" raising tariffs in the event of injury to an industry, was opposed by some on the ground that it might encourage unskillful negotiations.[37] But even among the opponents of this and other specific provisions, there was nearly unanimous acceptance of the fundamental principles and strategy underlying the bill. Accordingly, the Act passed the House 298–125 and the Senate 78–8, with most opponents objecting to particular provisions, not to the overriding principles.

The statute was well fashioned to achieve the aforementioned policy goals. Among its major provisions were:

(1) executive authority to reduce existing tariffs by 50 percent through reciprocal negotiations;

(2) special executive authority to eliminate through negotiations tariffs where the United States and the E.E.C. accounted for 80 percent or more of world exports of a product, excluding intra-E.E.C. and intra-communist block trade;

(3) executive authority to cut or eliminate tariffs or agricultural products that do not meet the 80 percent rule, provided the President finds that such action will maintain or expand U.S. exports of such products;

(4) executive authority to eliminate tariffs on products that were dutiable at 5 percent or less.

In addition to the provisions allowing tariff reduction negotiations, Section 252 authorized the President to retaliate against countries maintaining import restrictions that directly or indirectly burdened American commerce. An indirect burden on American commerce was perceived as a trade restriction imposed by the E.E.C. on a country that constituted an important export market. Thus, if the E.E.C. imposed restrictions on Latin American exports that could damage the economies of those nations, the United States could construe such an act as an indirect burden, since Latin American countries' capacities to import products from us would be reduced. In summary, then, the statute provided U.S. trade negotiators with the flexible instruments needed to assure expansion of U.S. exports.

Conclusion

Much policy analysis implicitly assumes that policy makers have a far wider range of choice than is actually the case. The constraints usually recognized are those imposed by political institutions and formalized processes, inasmuch as any bill must go through the legislative process before it carries the force of law. While such constraints on policy making clearly exist, they are hardly the only ones. Of at least equal, if not greater, importance are the constraints and demands imposed on policy makers by virtue of their roles as caretakers of the nation's economic system. In some instances this role propels policy makers toward one option only. In the instant case, policy makers would have to have been willing to overthrow the virtually universal consensual commitment to the economic health of America's business system, and the aggregation of the most important units in it, had they opted for a different policy direction.

The analysis of this policy issue suggests—at least in policy areas affecting the business system—that those who examine public policies would do well first to examine the constraints imposed by such structural factors *and then* to seek to understand the optional area beyond constraint. Obviously some policies involve a greater degree of freedom from structural constraint than others, but virtually every policy decision involves some degree of constraint. The analysis in this essay and the quotations from policy makers cited here suggest that this approach has the added merit of corresponding to how policy makers perceive their tasks.

Secondly, merely recognizing the problem to be solved does not necessarily suggest the means to achieve its solution. Assuming instrumental rationality, some situations suggest a wealth of past experience that can be employed to reduce the options to be examined. Such appears to have been the case in trade expansion. However, other situations may be far more ambiguous, in that they are either completely new situations in which there are no familiar cues, or contradictory situations in which different cues impel conflicting means.[38] In such situations the possible options are usually wider. Further, in "new" or "contradictory" situations, social background, career patterns, and interlocking associations may loom as far more important than in the instance where there is a reservoir of reasonable past experience. But even in the former cases there will probably be some constraints on action.

What I have sought to do here is avoid the reductionist traps of generalizing a theory of American public policy from one or even many case studies, by employing a marxian systemic framework in which the economic is given primacy, but not in a mechanistic manner. Policy makers are shown to have choices; but only after examining the policy problem within the context of a nation's stage of capitalism and its social formation can we determine what the range of choice is. If the policy problem is an important one with major, broad-ranging implications, as in the present case, the likelihood is that the major decisions will be made centrally within the executive branch (although the participation of important legislators within this context can not be ruled out). If, on the other hand, (1) a policy problem is relatively unimportant for the economy as a whole and (2) has few implications for other areas, and/or (3) the range of acceptable choices within the contextual needs of the capitalist social formation is wide, then we should look for the major influences on policy in interest-group, congressional, class and intra-class conflict. By looking at policies in this manner we can begin to see how, while policy makers support the requisites of the social formation, yet instances develop in which capitalist groups, even the class as a whole, lose—something a theory premised on the power elite hypothesis cannot do. At the same time, by looking at policy as the dependent variable, and the capitalist social formation, its development and contradictions, as the independent variable, we can see how the politics and the substance of a policy area change over time.

This is not to suggest that there cannot be differences in approach within this context, or that dissent—even vigorous dissent—is impossible. Rather, for policy makers (as opposed to policy critics), the capitalist social formation, its stage and contradictions, impose limits on the options that may be taken. Our attention should be focused first on an evaluation of these limits themselves, and not on policy alternatives or types in the abstract. In this respect, our analysis differs from descriptions based upon broad categories of public policy, of which Lowi's threefold scheme is the most notable example.

Notes

1. E. E. Schattschneider, *Politics, Pressures, and the Tariff* (Englewood Cliffs: Prentice-Hall, 1935).

2. David B. Truman, *The Governmental Process* (New York: Alfred A. Knopf, 1951). See p. 46 especially for a list of some of the most important of these studies.

3. Raymond Bauer, Ithiel de Sola Pool, and Lewis Dexter, *American Business and Public Policy* (New York: Atherton, 1968). See especially the index heading under Trade Expansion Act of 1962 for attempts to apply their findings to the Kennedy legislation.

4. *Ibid*, p. 484.

5. *Ibid*, p. 488.

6. Theodore J. Lowi, "American Business, Public Policy, Case Studies and Political Theory", *World Politics*, XVI (July 1964), pp. 677-715.

7. G. William Domhoff, *The Higher Circles* (New York: Random House, 1970), pp. 143-145. Domhoff did not reanalyze Bauer, Pool and Dexter's evidence on trade legislation during the Eisenhower presidency.

8. Ernesto Laclau, "The Specificity of the Political: The Poulantzas–Miliband Debate", *Economy and Society*, IV (February 1975), p. 89.

9. The best short analytical exposition of these conceptions is Oskar Lange, *Political Economy*, Volume I (Oxford: Pergamon Press, 1962), pp. 26-32. On the stages of capitalism notion see Werner Sombart, "Capitalism," *Encyclopedia of Social Sciences* (New York: Macmillan, 1930), 1930 ed., Vol. III, pp. 195-208 and Ernest Mandel, *Late Capitalism* (London: New Left Books, 1975), esp. Ch. 1.

10. John W. Evans, *U.S. Trade Policy* (New York: Harper & Row, 1967), pp. 5, 6. See also William Diebold, *The United States and the Industrial World* (New York: Praeger Publishers, 1972), pp. 32-34.

11. Bank for International Settlements, *Annual Report, 1971*, p. 17.

12. Sidney E. Rolfe and James L. Burtle, *The Great Wheel* (New York: McGraw Hill, 1973), pp. 79-81; and Ernest H. Preeg, *Traders and Diplomats* (Washington: Brookings Institution, 1970), p. 39.

13. Congressional Quarterly Service, *Congress and the Nation, 1945–1964* (Washington: Congressional Quarterly, 1965), pp. 311, 312.

14. Of the many books on multinational companies, the most indispensable is Mira Wilkins, *The Maturing of Multinational Enterprise* (Cambridge: Harvard University Press, 1974).

15. "Special Report—Multinational Companies," *Business Week* (April 20, 1963).

16. "For new opportunities: Now, the Word is Go Abroad," *U.S. News and World Report* (June 1, 1964).

17. Rolfe and Burtle, p. 81.

18. C. Wright Mills, "Comment on Criticism" in G. William Domhoff and Hoyt B. Ballard, *C. Wright Mills and the Power Elite* (Boston: Beacon Press, 1968), pp. 239-241.

19. U.S., Congress, House, Committee on Ways and Means, *Trade Expansion Act of 1962*, Committee Print, 87th Cong., 2d Sess., p. 2.

20. Fredrick J. Dobney (ed.), *Selected Papers of Will Clayton* (Baltimore: Johns Hopkins Press, 1971), p. 277.

21. See Morton S. Baratz, "Corporate Giants and the Power Structure," *Western Political Quarterly* (June 1956).

22. Perhaps the most important work illustrating this hypothesis in the context of specific policies is Richard Crossman, *The Diaries of a Cabinet Minister* (London: Hamish Hamilton, 1975). See, for example, the May 20, 1965 entry at p. 223.

23. The classic work on the tariff through 1930 is F. W. Taussig, *The Tariff History of the United States*, 8th Rev. ed. (New York: G. P. Putnam, 1931). For the subsequent period see Sidney Ratner, *The Tariff in American History* (New York: Van Nostrand, 1972).

24. Congressional Quarterly Service, *1962 Congressional Quarterly Almanac* (Washington: Congressional Quarterly Service, 1962), p. 256.

25. U.S., Congress, Joint Economic Committee, *The European Economic Community and the United States*, Joint Committee Print, 87th Cong., 1st Sess., p. 41.

26. See Jim F. Heath, *John F. Kennedy and the Business Community* (Chicago: University of Chicago Press, 1969), p. 87.

27. U.S., Congress, House, Committee on Ways and Means, *Trade Expansion Act of 1962, Hearings*, Part 2, 87th Cong., 2d Sess., p. 634.

28. *Ibid.*, Part 2, pp. 637-639, 818.

29. *Ibid.*, Part 1, pp. 79, 80, 85.

30. *Ibid.*, Part 1, p. 57.

31. Arthur Schlesinger, Jr., *A Thousand Days* (New York: Fawcett, 1965), pp. 771-774; *Business Week* (Aug. 19, 1961), p. 99; *Business Week* (Nov. 11, 1961); and Preeg, pp. 41, 44, 45.

32. Preeg, p. 41.

33. *Business Week* (March 31, 1962) p. 77. See also Preeg, pp. 46, 49, 50; and Heath, p. 89.

34. *Trade Expansion Act of 1962*, Part 2, pp. 1424-1426. See also R. Joseph Monsen and Mark W. Cannon, *The Makers of Public Policy* (New York: McGraw-Hill, 1965); and *1962 Congressional Quarterly Almanac*, p. 250.

35. *1962 Congressional Quarterly Almanac*, p. 250. See also *Business Week* (March 24, 1962), p. 32.

36. *Trade Expansion Act of 1962, Committee Print*, p. 6.

37. See, for example, U.S., Congress, Senate, Committee on Finance, *Trade Expansion Act of 1962, Hearings*, Part 3, 87th Cong., 2d Sess., p. 1273.

38. See Fred I. Greenstein, *Personality and Politics* (Chicago: Markham Publishing Co., 1969), pp. 50, 51.

3.5

Why We Buy the Weapons We Do

JAMES R. KURTH

Few areas of public policy are more fraught with consequences, both globally and domestically, than U.S. weapons procurement. In this essay, James R. Kurth begins by distinguishing four sorts of explanations for the pattern of that procurement that are offered by conventional literature—strategic, bureaucratic, democratic, and economic explanations—then tests these explanations against the major weapons decisions of the Kennedy, Johnson, and Nixon administrations. He develops in particular detail a variant on the industry-specific sort of economic explanation, featuring in his own construction "follow-on" and "bail-out" imperatives for government support of weapons producers. While this revised economic explanation illuminates many of the decisions in the procurement process, however, Kurth find it distinctly limited as a general theory of that process. It does not, for example, easily fit the U.S. decision to launch and continue with a major MIRV (multiple independently targetable reentry vehicles) missile program, where more explicitly strategic and bureaucratic explanations seem more plausible. Kurth concludes that no single available theory captures the complexity of the procurement process, and counsels explanatory eclecticism in understanding the mysteries of weapons development.

How can American weapons policy be explained? Why, for example, does the United States buy MIRV's, despite expert testimony about the grave dangers that these missiles will bring? With their high accuracy in targeting, their high number of warheads, and their high immunity to aerial surveillance, MIRV's can provoke a Russian fear of an American first strike against Russian land-based missiles. The Russians in turn will acquire their own MIRV's, perhaps leading again to "the reciprocal fear of surprise attack" and "the delicate balance of terror" of the 1950's. Why does the United States buy such costly aircraft as the F-111, with its frequent crashes and repeated groundings, the C-5A, with its mechanical and structural failures, and the B-1, said to be obsolete even before the first prototype is built? And why has the United States in recent months sharply increased its deliveries of other expensive military aircraft to underdeveloped countries, which in most cases do not need and cannot afford such equipment?

The problem with such questions about American weapons policy is not that there are no answers but that there are too many answers. Around MIRV, or around many cases of aircraft procurement by the U.S. military services, or around many cases of aircraft exports to the underdeveloped countries, there has grown up a cluster of competing explanations, a thicket of theories. Does MIRV, for example, result from rational

Reprinted with permission from *Foreign Policy* 11 (Summer 1973), pp. 33-56 (with deletions). Copyright 1973 by the Carnegie Endowment for International Peace.

calculations about Russian threats, or from reckless pursuit by weapons scientists and military bureaucrats of technological progress for its own sake, or from resourceful efforts by weapons manufacturers and their allies in Congress to maintain production and profits, or from some combination of these factors? More generally, we can distinguish in the academic and journalistic literature on weapons policy four broad types of explanations, each of which purports to account for the policy.

Strategic explanations, which are the explanations favored by the policy-makers and officials themselves, argue that weapons policy results from rational calculations about foreign threats or from the reciprocal dynamics of arms races.

Bureaucratic explanations see weapons policy as the outcome of competition between bureaucracies, especially the military services, and as the output of standard operating procedures within bureaucracies.

Democratic explanations see weapons policy as the outcome of electoral calculations by the President and by the members of Congress.

Finally, *economic* explanations see weapons policy as the result of the needs of the capitalist system or, in a less sweeping formulation, as the result of the needs of particular corporations in the aerospace industry.

Let us try to cut away at the thicket of theories that surrounds American weapons policy. My focus will be on those cases already mentioned—MIRV, F-111, C-5A, B-1, and the recent exports of military aircraft. But I will touch upon all of the major cases of aircraft and missile procurement by the U.S. government during the 1960's and 1970's, that is, during the Kennedy, Johnson, and Nixon Administrations.

Aircraft Procurement: Whys and Wherefores

The two most debated cases of manned aircraft procurement in the 1960's were the F-111 fighter-bomber and the C-5A jumbo transport. Both aircraft became famous, even notorious, because of "cost overruns," mechanical failures, prolonged groundings, and congressional investigations. Further, in June 1970 the Air Force awarded a contract to produce prototypes of a new, large, manned bomber, the B-1, which begins anew the numbering of the bomber series and which would go into operational deployment in the late 1970's. By that time, given the efficiency of strategic missiles and antiaircraft missiles, the new B-1 would be about as useful and about as obsolete as the first B-1 of the 1920's.

Why does the United States buy such aircraft? There are, of course, the official, strategic explanations: The F-111 is needed for a variety of tasks, such as tactical bombing, strategic bombing, and air defense; the C-5A is needed for massive airlifts of troops and supplies; and the B-1 is needed for strategic bombing and post-attack reconnaissance. But these explanations neglect the fact that the respective tasks can be performed by a variety of ways and weapons, and that these particular manned aircraft are not clearly the most cost-effective (to use the proclaimed criterion of Robert McNamara) way to do so.

Bureaucratic explanations are also possible: The F-111 is needed by the Tactical Air Command to preserve its power and prestige within the over-all balance of the military bureaucracies; the C-5A is needed similarly by the Military Airlift Command; and the B-1 is desired by the aging commanders of the Air Force and of the Strategic Air Command within it, who look back with nostalgia to their youth and to the manned bomber in which they rode first to heroic purpose and then to bureaucratic power.

But these explanations are not fully satisfactory: Neither the Tactical Air Command nor the Military Airlift Command is the strongest organization within the Air Force (the strongest is the Strategic Air Command), and probably neither of them could achieve such expensive programs as the F-111 and C-5A without allies. And even the powerful commanders of the Air Force and the Strategic Air Command could not achieve the B-1 on the basis of nostalgia alone, especially in a period of unusually sharp criticism of military spending and after the predecessor of the B-1, the B-70, had been cancelled as obsolescent by McNamara several years before.

An alternative explanation, more economic in emphasis and more general in scope, can be constructed, for these aircraft and perhaps for some other weapons systems also, by drawing some relations between two variables for the period since 1960: (1) aerospace systems which are military or military-related (i.e., military aircraft, missiles, and space systems) and (2) aerospace corporations which produce such systems.

Aerospace Systems   The major military aerospace systems produced at some time during the period from 1960 to 1973 have been the following, grouped according to six functional categories or production sectors: (1) large bombers: the B-52, B-58, and B-70 (only two prototypes of the B-70 were produced before it was cancelled); (2) fighter-bombers and fighters: the F-111, F-4, F-8, A-7, and F-14; (3) military transports: the C-130, C-141, and C-5A; (4) missile systems: Minuteman and Polaris and their MIRV successors or "follow-ons," Minuteman III and Poseidon; (5) anti-missile systems: ABM, including the Spartan and Sprint missiles; (6) space systems: the military-related Apollo moon program.

Major military aerospace systems presently planned for production in the mid or late 1970's are the B-1, which can be seen as a long-delayed follow-on to the cancelled B-70; the F-15, which will be a follow-on to the F-4; a lightweight fighter; an STOL transport; Trident or the Undersea Long-Range Missile System (ULMS), which will be a follow-on to Poseidon, and perhaps a super-MIRV, which will follow Minuteman III; and the military-related space shuttle program.

These add up to 24 major military or military-related aerospace systems for the 1960's and 1970's. For most of the 24, the procurement of the system has involved or will involve expenditures which amount to at least $3 billion and in some cases (for example, the B-1) as much as $15 billion.

Aerospace Corporations   In 1960, there were a large number of aerospace corporations which produced military aircraft, missiles, or space systems. Four stood out, however, in the sense that each received in fiscal year 1961 military and space "prime contracts awards" of some $1 billion or more: General Dynamics, North American, Lockheed, and Boeing. During the dozen years since, each of these four corporations has continued to receive normally each year $1 billion or more in military and space contracts, although Boeing occasionally has dropped below that amount, as did North American Rockwell in FY 1972. (North American changed its name in 1967 when it merged with a smaller company, Rockwell-Standard; the corporation again changed its name in 1973, to Rockwell International.)

In addition, some aerospace corporations which were minor contractors in 1960 expanded their military and space sales during the 1960's until they too reached the $1 billion level. McDonnell, which received military and space contracts of $295 million in FY 1961, greatly expanded its military sales, primarily with the F-4 Phantom, which was used extensively in the Vietnamese war. In 1967, McDonnell merged with Douglas, another minor contractor. In FY 1961, Douglas was awarded contracts of $341 million, much of which went to research and development programs for Skybolt, an air-to-surface missile cancelled in 1962, and for Nike Zeus, the first anti-missile; in FY 1966, the last year before the merger, Douglas was awarded contracts of $539 million. Since 1967, the merged corporation of McDonnell Douglas has normally received each year contracts of $1 billion or more. Grumman, another minor contractor in FY 1961 with contracts of $249 million, also greatly expanded its military and space sales, primarily with two large subcontracts awarded in the early 1960's, one for the aft fuselage of the F-111 and one for elements of the Apollo moon program. In 1968, Grumman also reached the $1 billion level.

Thus, there are now six aerospace corporations which produce military aircraft, missiles, or space systems and which each normally receive some $1 billion or more in military and space contracts each year; in FY 1972, General Dynamics, Boeing, Lockheed, McDonnell Douglas, and Grumman were each awarded contracts amounting to $1 billion or more; North American Rockwell was awarded some $900 million.

A seventh, smaller contractor should also be noted, the LTV Aerospace division of the conglomerate LTV, formerly Ling-Temco-Vought. LTV Aerospace is normally the next largest aircraft producer after the big six; it is also part of a conglomerate with annual sales—commercial as well as military—of more than $3 billion. Although it received less than $100 million in military and space contracts in FY 1961, LTV Aerospace also expanded its military sales in the 1960's, primarily with the A-7 Corsair, which, like the F-4 Phantom, was used extensively in the Vietnam war. In FY 1972, LTV Aerospace was awarded contracts of $410 million.

We should consider Lockheed, which is normally the largest military contractor, as having two main military divisions, Lockheed-Missiles and Space, located in California, and Lockheed-Georgia. Similarly, we can split McDonnell Douglas into its McDonnell division in Missouri and its Douglas division in California. There are thus nine major production lines.

Given these aerospace systems and aerospace corporations, two related but different economic explanations can be constructed, which we shall call the follow-on and the bail-out imperatives.

The Follow-on Imperative

We can chart the major military aerospace systems according to the production line to which the U.S. government awarded the contract and according to the years when major development or production phased in or out or is scheduled to do so. Some interesting patterns result (see Table 1).

About the time a production line phases out production of one major government contract, it phases in production of a new one, usually within a year. In the case of new aircraft, which usually require a development phase of about three years, the production line normally is awarded the contract for the new system about three years before production of the old one is scheduled to phase out. In the case of new missiles, the development phase usually is about two years. Further, in most cases, the new contract is for a system which is structurally similar while technically superior to the system being phased out, i.e., the new contract is a follow-on contract. (An exception is Apollo, but even here North American was NASA'S largest contractor before the Apollo contract was awarded; in the case of the B-1, the follow-on is one step removed from the B-70.)

A large and established aerospace production line is a national resource—or so it seems to many high officers in the armed services. The corporation's managers, shareholders, bankers, engineers, and workers, of course, will enthusiastically agree, as will the area's congressmen and senators.[1] The Defense Department would find it risky

Table 1

The Follow-on Imperative: Major Production Lines and Military Aerospace Systems

	General Dynamics	North American Rockwell	Boeing	Lockheed M & S	Lockheed Georgia	McDonnell	Douglas	Grumman	LTV Aerospace
1960	B-58	B-70	B-52; Minuteman	Polaris	C-130	F-4	Nike Zeus *d*	Miscellaneous	F-8
1961		Apollo *d* in	Minuteman buildup	Polaris buildup	C-141 *d* in				
1962	B-58 out / F-111 *d* in		B-52 out					F-111 *sub d* in	
1963								Apollo *sub d* in	
1964		B-70 out			C-141*p* in				A-7 *d* in
1965					C-5A *d* in		Nike Zeus out / Spartan *d* in		
1966	F-111 *p* in	Apollo *p* in	Minuteman III *d* in	Poseidon *d* in				F-111 *sub p* in / Apollo *sub p* in	F-8 out / A-7 *p* in
1967									
1968			Minuteman out / Minuteman III *p* in	Polaris out / Poseidon *p* in	C-141 out / C-5A *p* in				
1969		B-1 *d* in				F-15 *d* in		F-14 *d* in	
1970									
1971				Trident *d* in					
1972		Apollo out / Shuttle *d* in				F-4 out	Spartan *p* in	F-111 *sub* out / Apollo *sub* out / F-14 *p* in	
1973					C-5A out	F-15 *p* in			
1974	F-111 out / Lightweight fighter in?	B-1 *p* in	Minuteman III out / Super-MIRV or SST in?	Poseidon out / Trident *p* in?	STOL transport in?				A-7 out

d = development; *p* = production; *sub* = subcontract.

and even reckless to allow a large production line to wither and die for lack of a large production contract. This is especially so because for each of the aircraft production sectors (large bombers, fighters, and military transports), there are actually only a few potential production lines out of the nine major lines we have listed. Large bombers are likely to be competed for and produced by only General Dynamics, North American Rockwell, and Boeing; fighters and fighter-bombers by only General Dynamics, North American Rockwell, Boeing, McDonnell division, Grumman, and LTV Aerospace; and military transports by only Boeing, Lockheed-Georgia, Douglas division and, for small transports, Grumman. Thus, there is at least latent pressure upon the Defense Department from many sources to award a new major contract to a production line when an old major contract is phasing out. Further, the disruption of the production line will be least and the efficiency of the product would seem highest if the new contract is structurally similar to the old, in the same functional category or production sector, i.e., is a follow-on contract. Such a contract renovates both the large and established aerospace corporation that produces the weapons system and the military organization that deploys it.

This latent constraint or rather compulsion imposed on weapons procurement by industrial structure might be called the *follow-on imperative* and contrasted with the official imperative. The official imperative for weapons procurement could be phrased as follows: If strategic considerations determine that a military service needs a new weapons system, it will solicit bids from several competing companies; ordinarily, the service will award the contract to the company with the most cost-effective design. The follow-on imperative is rather different: If one of the nine production lines is opening up, it will receive a new major contract from a military service (or from NASA); ordinarily, the new contract will be structurally similar to the old, i.e., a follow-on contract.

The follow-on imperative can perhaps explain the production line and the product structure of 12 out of the 13 major contracts awarded from 1960 through 1972: (1) Minuteman III follow-on to Minuteman, (2) Poseidon follow-on to Polaris, (3) Trident follow-on to Poseidon, (4) C-141 follow-on to C-130, (5) C-5A follow-on to C-141, (6) A-7 follow-on to F-8; (7) F-14 follow-on to F-111 major subcontract, (8) F-15 follow-on to F-4, (9) Spartan follow-on to Nike Zeus, (10) space shuttle follow-on to Apollo, (11) F-111 after B-58 (superficially a less certain case, but the two planes are structurally similar, with the F-111 being a relatively large fighter-bomber and the B-58 being a relatively small bomber), (12) B-1 delayed follow-on to B-70. In regard to the 13th contract, Apollo, North American might have been predicted to receive the award: it was already NASA'S largest contractor.

The imperatives of the industrial structure are reinforced, not surprisingly, by the imperatives of the political system, as would be suggested by a democratic explanation. Six of the production lines are located in states which loom large in the Electoral College: California (Lockheed-Missiles and Space, North American Rockwell, and Douglas division of McDonnell Douglas), Texas (General Dynamics and LTV Aerospace), and New York (Grumman). The three others are located in states which in the 1960's had a senator who ranked high in the Senate Armed Services Committee or Appropriations Committee: Washington (Boeing; Henry Jackson), Georgia (Lockheed-Georgia; Richard Russell), and Missouri (McDonnell division of McDonnell Douglas; Stuart Symington).

It might be said, however, that one should expect most contracts to be follow-on contracts. Production of the original system should give an aerospace corporation a competitive edge in technical experience and expertise which will win for it the next system awarded in the same production sector. But in at least three major cases (the government has kept other cases secret), the Source Selection Board chose, on technical grounds, a different corporation than the one already producing a similar system; the contract became a follow-on contract only when the Board was overruled by higher officials. With the F-111, the original, technical choice was Boeing, rather than General Dynamics; with the C-5A, it was Boeing rather than Lockheed; and with Apollo, it was Martin rather than North American. More importantly, it is not always obvious that there should be any new system at all in an old production sector. This is especially the case because of the recent evolution of the six functional categories or production sectors. The aerospace systems within them or follow-on contracts are of course becoming progressively more complex and expensive, but they are also becoming progressively more dangerous strategically (MIRV), or operationally (F-111, F-14, and C-5A), or at best dubious (B-1, F-15, ABM, and the space shuttle).

The Bail-out Imperative

A related but inferior economic explanation can be constructed by looking at the annual sales, income, and employment figures for all seven (originally eight) aerospace corporations for the period 1960 to 1971 (at this writing, figures for 1972 are not yet available). Again, we can chart the major military aerospace systems according to the corporation to which the U.S. government awarded the contract and according to the years in which it did so. But this time we will also include in the table those years in which the corporation suffered either (1) a drop in sales of almost 10 percent or more from the previous year, (2) a deficit in income, or (3) a drop in employment of almost 10 percent or more from the previous year (see Table 2).

There have been many occasions when an aerospace corporation has experienced one or more of these three difficulties. In 12 cases, the U.S. government within the next year has awarded the corporation a new major military contract: (1) General Dynamics and the F-111 in 1962, (2) North American Rockwell and the B-1 in 1970, (3) North American Rockwell and the space shuttle in 1972, (4) Boeing and the Minuteman buildup in 1961, (5) Lockheed and the Polaris buildup and the C-141 in 1961, (6) Lockheed and the C-5A in 1965, (7) Lockheed and the development of Trident in 1971 (as well as a government guarantee of $250 million in bank loans), (8) McDonnell and the Air Force version of the F-4 in 1962, (9) Douglas and Skybolt in 1960, (10) McDonnell Douglas and the Johnson Administration's approval of the Sentinel ABM system, including Spartan, in 1967, (11) McDonnell Douglas and the Nixon Administration's approval of the Safeguard ABM system, including Spartan, in early 1969, (12) McDonnell Douglas and the F-15 in late 1969. In a 13th case, Ling-Temco-Vought was awarded the A-7 in February 1964, a little more than two years after its deficit year of 1961. These observations suggest that the government comes to the aid of corporations in deep financial trouble, that there is what might be called a *bail-out imperative*.

In three cases, each of them recent, the government has not awarded any new major contract to the afflicted corporation. General Dynamics did not immediately receive contract aid after its bad years of 1970 and 1971, although it is in a good position to receive large subcontracts for the space shuttle in 1973. (Similarly, General Dynamics did not immediately receive aid after 1960 but was awarded the F-111 in 1962.) Boeing did not immediately receive aid after 1969, but perhaps this was because the government planned for the SST to fill the gap in 1971; instead the SST was cancelled by Congress. Ling-Temco-Vought went through a series of deficit years beginning with 1969 and resulting from its conglomerate manipulation rather than from its aerospace production;

Table 2

The Bail-out Imperative: Corporate Financial Troubles and Military Aerospace Systems

	General Dynamics	North American Rockwell	Boeing	Lockheed	McDonnell	Douglas	Grumman	LTV Aerospace
1960	$27,000,000 deficit		9% employment drop	$43,000,000 deficit		$19,000,000 deficit; 25% emp. drop; Skybolt in		
1961	$143,000,000 deficit	Apollo in	Minuteman buildup	Polaris buildup; C-141 in	24% sales drop; 13% emp. drop	32% sales drop; 22% emp. drop		$13,000,000 deficit
1962	20% emp. drop; F-111 in				Air Force F-4 in		F-111 subcontract in	
1963	25% sales drop						Apollo subcontract in	
1964				17% sales drop				A-7 in
1965				C-5A in		Spartan in		
1966			Minuteman III in	Poseidon in		$28,000,000 deficit		
1967					McDonnell Douglas merger; Johnson ABM decision			
1968					11% employment drop			
1969		9% employment drop	13% sales drop; 15% employment drop	$33,000,000 deficit	Nixon ABM decision; 16% sales drop; 13% emp. drop; F-15 in		F-14 in	$38,000,000 deficit
1970	12% sales drop; $7,000,000 deficit; 22% emp. drop	10% sales drop; 22% employment drop; B-1 in	34% employment drop	$86,000,000 deficit; 13% employment drop	31% sales drop; 14% employment drop		16% sales drop; 21% employment drop	$70,000,000 deficit; 18% employment drop
1971	16% sales drop; 17% employment drop	10% emp. drop; 1972; space shuttle in 1972:	17% sales drop; 16% employment drop	12% emp. drop; $250,000,000 loan guarantee; Trident in			20% sales drop; $18,000,000 deficit	1% sales drop; $57,000,000 deficit; 24% emp. drop

it also did not receive contract aid. In three other cases, the government had just awarded the corporation a development contract for a major weapons system, which could be expected to revive the corporation as the system moved toward production (General Dynamics, 1963; McDonnell Douglas, 1970; and Grumman, 1970). Over-all, however, the bail-out imperative is a less general explanation than its follow-on counterpart: three major weapons systems have been awarded without an immediately preceding corporate crisis (Minuteman III, Poseidon, and the F-14). On the other hand, the bail-out imperative might have predicted the government's $250 million loan guarantee for Lockheed; the follow-on imperative would not.

The follow-on and bail-out imperatives may also explain part of the recent increase in U.S. exports of military aircraft to underdeveloped countries. As Table 1 indicates, Lockheed-Georgia has recently faced a severe problem, for it is phasing out production of its much-criticized C-5A. The production line needs a new major contract, but it is unlikely to receive one until the more unsavory aspects of the C-5A have faded from congressional memories. This is especially the case since Richard Russell, the powerful Senator from Georgia, died in 1971. The Nixon Administration has come to the rescue, however, through the device of increased exports. Readers may have already noted from Table 1 that the C-130 military transport has never been completely phased out of production at Lockheed-Georgia; throughout the last decade, a small number have continued to be produced, many of them for delivery to foreign countries. Now, with production of the C-5A phasing out, production of the C-130 is again building up. The Nixon Administration sent large numbers of C-130's to the South Vietnamese air force during the "peace is at hand" phase of November and December 1972, despite the fact that the South Vietnamese probably will not be able to maintain an aircraft with the C-130's complexity. The aircraft sent to South Vietnam were drawn from various military units, where they will be replaced by production from the Georgia plant. Further, C-130's form a large part of the recent contracting by Iran to buy $2 billion in military equipment from the United States, in what, according to the *New York Times*, "Defense Department officials describe as the biggest single arms deal ever arranged by the Pentagon."[2] The sales to Iran also include F-4's, and will assist McDonnell Douglas in the transition period before it reaches full production of the F-15.

The follow-on and bail-out imperatives at first glance might seem to explain not only cases of aircraft procurement and aircraft exports but also cases of missile procurement (the Minuteman and Polaris buildups of 1961-1964, the Spartan missile of the ABM, and, with the follow-on imperative, Minuteman III and Poseidon, which are the MIRV successors to Minuteman and Polaris). But an extension of the two imperatives from aircraft to missiles is not without problems.

First, a general point, the mere fact that a condition is present in many cases does not in itself demonstrate that it is important or salient in each of them. Alternative explanations may be less general but more real. This is especially likely with cases which are both strategically momentous and publicly debated, such as the Minuteman and Polaris buildup and the ABM. Elsewhere, I have analyzed these particular cases in non-economic terms.[3]

Second, in particular regard to MIRV, the two imperatives are insufficiently precise. Neither explains why highly accurate warheads as opposed to merely multiple ones (MIRV as opposed to MRV) were procured; economic needs would have been met equally well with a missile carrying either kind of warhead, and therefore economic needs alone do not explain the most important part, the "I" of MIRV. Consequently, there is a need to examine the case of MIRV on its own and in search of an alternative explanation.

MIRV Procurement: Bureaucrats and Technocrats

Why did the United States develop and deploy MIRV? The official explanation is again a strategic one, and the usual argument has been that MIRV is needed to penetrate Russian ABM systems. But this, like the economic explanations, does not explain why highly accurate, as opposed to merely multiple, warheads (MIRV instead of MRV) are needed. Nor does it explain why the United States continued to develop MIRV in the mid-1960's after the Russians limited their development of ABM, or why the United States continues to develop MIRV today after the SALT agreements to mutually limit ABM. A more accurate strategic explanation, suggested by censored congressional testimony, would argue that MIRV was developed in order to increase the U.S. capability to destroy Russian missiles:

Question by Senator Mike Mansfield (D-Mont.):

Is it not true that the U.S. response to the discovery that the Soviets had made an initial deployment of an ABM system around Moscow and probably elsewhere was to develop the MIRV system for Minuteman and Polaris?

Answer by Dr. John S. Foster, then Director of Defense Research and Engineering:

Not entirely. The MIRV concept was originally generated to increase our targeting capability rather than to penetrate ABM defenses. In 1961-62 planning for targeting the Minuteman force it was found that the total number of aim points exceeded the number of Minuteman missiles. By splitting up the payload of a single missile (deleted) each (deleted) could be programmed (deleted) allowing us to cover these targets with (deleted) fewer missiles. (Deleted.) MIRV was originally born to implement the payload split up (deleted). It was found that the previously generated MIRV concept could equally well be used against ABM (deleted).

Although Secretary of Defense McNamara had rejected a first-strike targeting doctrine, the Air Force commanders, formally his subordinates, had not. They preferred a first-strike doctrine, with its double implication that the United States could win a war with the Soviet Union and that the Air Force would have the prime role in doing so, to a second-strike doctrine, which implied that the United States could only deter a war and that the Air Force would be only an equal of the Navy in the task. Against McNamara, the Air Force commanders could not achieve an official first-strike targeting doctrine for the United States; with MIRV, however, they could achieve a real first-strike targeting capability for the Air Force. The initiation of MIRV in 1961-1962, then, can be explained by interservice rivalry and bureaucratic politics.

Further, the research and development of MIRV in the mid-1960's was of course highly classified. This kept knowledge of MIRV from Congress and the public as well as the Russians. Nor, in the early phases of the program, did Defense officials have any need to build support in Congress and the public for large expenditures of funds. As a result, the MIRV program faced no political opposition, and it quietly progressed in accordance with technical and bureaucratic procedures of research and development within Defense.

The MIRV program may have been reinforced by another round of bureaucratic politics in late 1966. McNamara was attempting to prevent the procurement of ABM but was meeting with the united opposition of the Joint Chiefs of Staff, supported by leading members of Congress. One of the main arguments of the proponents of ABM was that the Russians were going ahead with their own ABM system. One way for McNamara to neutralize this argument was to go ahead with an American offensive system with high penetration capabilities, i.e., MIRV. Thus, in late 1966, MIRV procurement may have been the price for ABM postponement. The price bought only a delay in ABM of less than a year.

The MIRV program continued to quietly progress in accordance with technical and bureaucratic procedures of research and development through 1967 and 1968. By the time the strategic implications of MIRV became public knowledge, it had already been tested, the production of Minuteman III and Poseidon missiles had already commenced, and the conversion of Polaris-launching submarines into Poseidon ones had already begun. Given this momentum generated by bureaucratic processes, the MIRV program could have been brought to a halt in 1969 or after only if the President or leading members of Congress had been willing to expend an extraordinary amount of political capital. And thus MIRV finally reached the point where bureaucratic pressures were reinforced by economic ones; where John Foster, the Director of Defense Research and Engineering, could make an economic argument against stopping the MIRV program before a congressional committee in 1970, much like our earlier argument about production lines:

> Another consequence of our stopping at this time would be financial. These programs I am discussing now have a number of years of research and development behind them and have also developed a significant production capability. . . . I do not see how we can justify the added expense that would be incurred as a result of keeping production capability on a standby.[4]

Further, once the United States had successfully tested MIRV, the Russians could not be sure that the United States had not also deployed it. The Russians probably then felt themselves compelled to develop, test, and deploy their own MIRV; the Russian program, in turn, reinforces the pressures behind the American one.

In summary, the procurement of MIRV, of highly accurate as well as multiple warheads, resulted from a developmental process over a relatively lengthy time. It is best explained by a combination of bureaucratic politics and bureaucratic processes: bargaining among different actors within the executive branch and standard procedures for research and development. Although the Minuteman III and Poseidon missile programs can be fitted into the broader economic framework formed by the follow-on imperative (but not by its bail-out counterpart), economic explanations do not capture the most important part of MIRV.

Bureaucratic politics may have structured another aspect of American missile procurement, that is, the close parallelism of the Air Force and the Navy programs. As Table 1 indicates, each service took the same steps at the same time: Minuteman and Polaris buildup in 1961, Minuteman III and Poseidon development in 1966, and production in 1968. Indeed, the first flight test for Minuteman III and the first flight test for Poseidon occurred on the same day, August 16, 1968. It is as if the two services had reached an agreement on rough equality, a "minimax" solution, in regard to their respective progress in the prestigious mission of strategic offense. If so, the recent funding for development of the Navy's Trident has imposed a considerable strain on the Air Force to achieve comparable funding for development of a super-MIRV or a mobile missile system.

The Trident program is important in another sense. Given the necessity to maintain an invulnerable nuclear deterrent, a long-range, submarine-launched missile system is clearly the most rational way to do so; for the next decade at least, its vulnerability to Russian attack will be much less than that of land-based missiles, even with such Air Force gimmicks as ever more hardened silos or putting missiles on railroad cars. The present development and eventual procurement of Trident, therefore, can readily be explained in strategic terms; Trident is one of the few American weapons systems initiated since 1960 for which the best explanation is the strategic explanation. Bureaucratic and economic interests are present, of course, and may insure that the rational, strategic choice will in fact result. But, over-all, Trident is a salutary reminder that not all cases of American weapons procurement can be reduced to bureaucratic and economic factors.

Cancellation and Compensation

Any satisfactory analysis of policy outcomes within an issue area must account not only for those outcomes which did occur but also those which, despite similar conditions, did not. In regard to aerospace weapons systems, an analysis must account for the two major cases of non-procurement or cancelled procurement in the period since 1960. These were the B-70 large bomber and the Skybolt air-to-surface missile, designed to be launched from large bombers. Superficially at least, economic explanations such as the follow-on and bail-out imperatives, and bureaucratic explanations stressing the dominant role of the bomber generals within the Air Force, would have predicted large-scale production of the B-70 and Skybolt.

Why did the United States cancel the B-70 and Skybolt? A strategic explanation, focusing on the vulnerability of the manned bomber and on its low cost-effectiveness versus Minuteman and Polaris, might seem quite sufficient (although similar strategic considerations have not been sufficient to bring about the cancellation of the B-1). Such strategic factors may have been reinforced by bureaucratic politics; that is, McNamara's determination to establish his authority over the military services and over the traditional autonomy of their procurement practices. A similar argument has been made to explain McNamara's insistence on commonality between the Air Force and the Navy versions of the F-111, another case which occurred at the same time, 1961-1962. Together, strategic and bureaucratic factors seem to account for the cancellations.

In the case of the B-70, however, cancellation came at the cost of compensation. First, as an account by Arthur Schlesinger suggests, the Air Force and its allies in Congress had to be compensated for the cancellation of the B-70 with a massive missile buildup, with its attendant costs of a Russian buildup and an arms race.[5] Second, as the follow-on imperative suggests, North American had to be compensated for the cancellation of the B-70 with another major contract, in this case the Apollo moon program.

The cancellation of Skybolt a year later does not seem to have exacted such a price. The Air force and its allies in Congress did not receive any obvious compensation (although one could imagine the continuation of the Minuteman buildup and of the MIRV program as part of an over-all compromise). Douglas, which was a minor contractor at the time, did not immediately receive another major contract comparable to Skybolt. This suggests that the compensation pattern for minor contractors (less than $500 million in military and space contracts per year) may be different than the pattern for major ones (more than $1 billion in military and space contracts per year) and that there may be a sort of class system for weapons contractors.

In summary, then, cancelled procurement is best explained by eclectic accounts. Strategic analysis and bureaucratic politics can enact a cancellation, but when a dominant military organization and a major aerospace corporation are involved, bureaucratic politics and economic imperatives will also exact a compensation. Such considerations would predict, for example, that any successful effort in the mid-1970's to cancel the B-1 would be confronted on the morrow of victory with a super-MIRV for the Strategic Air Command and more space shuttles for Rockwell International. [. . .]

Notes

1. See Les Aspin, "Games the Pentagon Plays," in *Foreign Policy*, Summer 1973.

2. The *New York Times*, February 22, 1973, p. 2.

3. James R. Kurth, "Aerospace Production Lines and American Defense Spending," in Steven Rosen, ed. *Testing the Theory of the Military-Industrial Complex* (Lexington, MA: D.C. Health & Co., 1973), chapter 6.

4. Hearings before the Subcommittee on Arms Control, Committee on Foreign Relations, U.S. Senate 91st Congress, June 4, 1970.

5. Arthur M. Schlesinger, Jr., *A Thousand Days* (Boston: Houghton Mifflin, 1965), pp. 499-500.

3.6

Friends as Foes

IMMANUEL WALLERSTEIN

For a generation after World War II the United States exerted virtually unquestioned dominance of the world political economy. Key to this dominance were the deep alliances between the U.S. and its chief trading partners and beneficiaries of military protection and economic assistance, Western Europe and Japan. Now, Immanuel Wallerstein argues, U.S. hegemony is in irreversible decline, and ever sharper rivalry defines relations among the great industrial powers. Old alliances are breaking apart, friends are becoming foes, and for U.S. policy makers the most difficult foreign policy decisions during the 1980s concern neither East-West relations nor North-South dealings, but the deep divisions that threaten the Western "community" itself. Wallerstein sketches the major issues splitting the Western powers. During the 1980s these centrally involve the problem of shifting the costs of economic decline onto industrial rivals ("who will export unemployment to whom") and the problem of positioning individual economies to benefit from the anticipated renewal of economic activity in the 1990s. That renewal will be led by high-tech innovations in microelectronics, biotechnology, and energy resources, and adapting to and gaining leadership in the new industries not only requires shifting costs among nation states but also, critically, within them. Wallerstein outlines the obstacles to such industrial innovation in the United States, and suggests as well a series of possible new alliances or more general pattern of realignment that might emerge out of the wreckage of the old system of U.S. hegemony. There is no sure path of such realignment, and for most of the world, neither its exact shape nor the fact of its occurrence may be of great consequence in the short term. But what is certain, Wallerstein argues, is that the coming period will be traumatic for citizens of the United States. As he observes, "Americans have spent the past 30 years getting used to the benefits of a hegemonic position, and they will have to spend the next 30 getting used to life without them."

T he year 1980 marks the midpoint in a global process: the steady erosion of the hegemonic position of the United States in the world-economy. The political keystone of this hegemony has been a strong alliance with Western Europe and Japan. Until 1967 the United States dominated the world military arena and political economy—including the markets of other industrialized countries—and Western Europe and Japan followed U.S. leadership willingly and completely. By 1990 the former allies will have parted company with the United States.

This process is not fortuitous, mysterious, or reversible. Roughly comparable

Reprinted with permission from *Foreign Policy* 40 (Fall 1980), pp. 119-31. Copyright 1980 by the Carnegie Endowment for International Peace.

declines in the capitalist world-economy have taken place twice before: Great Britain from 1873 to 1896; and, although this is less well-known, the United Provinces (the modern-day Netherlands) from 1650 to 1672. In each case, a nation of unquestioned supremacy fell to the lesser status of a very powerful state defending very central economic interests in the world-economy, but nonetheless one state amid several. And, in each case, in the decades following the loss of hegemony, the former predominant power continued to decline as a center of political-military strength and of high-profit enterprise, to the advantage of other states within the world-economy.

Such cyclical patterns—the rise and decline of hegemonic powers and the more frequent expansion and stagnation of the world-economy—exist within the framework of long-term secular trends that have been leading to a systemic crisis that transcends the immediate difficulties of the moment. These trends, characteristic of a capitalist world-economy, may be seen in the constant development of the division of labor in the world-economy as a whole and in the continued development of the interstate system.

For 400 years the development of the division of labor has involved a steady increase in the degree to which production has been mechanized, land and labor made into commodities purchasable on the market, and social relations regulated by contracts rather than by customary rules. This secular division of labor has proceeded in a step-like fashion that alternates 20-30 year periods of expansion with similar periods of contraction (sometimes called Kondratieff cycles, or A-phases and B-phases). Each A-phase of expansion has culminated in a major blockage of the world accumulation process, resulting in stagnation. And each B-phase of stagnation has been overcome by the further concentration of capital, the launching of new product cycles, the expansion of outer boundaries of the world-economy, and the expansion of effective demand—in short, by the spreading and deepening of the capitalist world-economy and the further polarization of distribution as measured globally and not within individual states.

The development of the interstate system has involved the elaboration and institutionalization of power in each of the member states, within the constraints of interstate rules that have become increasingly explicit. As the roles of the state machineries have become more prominent, the state has become even more the focus of antisystemic forces—social movements opposed to the basic mode of operation of the world-system—that have sought power in the name of socialist and nationalist ideologies. The strengthening of capitalist forces and the development of the world-economy itself have bred these antisystemic forces, whose own strength has increased significantly in the twentieth century.

A Mature Liberalism

This is the context within which the United States became the political center of global economic forces between 1945 and 1967. During that great postwar boom, despite the paranoia of American leaders and the constant clamor about national danger, there was no serious opposition in the world to U.S. hegemony. In the late 1950s, it was the communist world (with de-Stalinization) and not the West that was undergoing political crisis. The Soviet Union was easily contained; indeed, it was struggling to hold its own politically and economically, while it sought to rebuild militarily. Western Europe and Japan, the main beneficiaries of a massive creation of global effective demand via U.S. economic aid and military support, operated as virtual client states during the 1950s. Decolonization in Asia and Africa went smoothly, largely to the political advantage of the United States. And at home, the anticommunist political repression of the 1940s and

1950s (from President Truman's loyalty oaths to McCarthyism) seemed to stifle the dangerous social tensions of earlier periods.

The one major exception to complete U.S. hegemony was China, where the accession to power of the Communist party represented an effective overthrow of foreign domination and a radical alteration of China's position in the world-system.

For the most part, a generalized self-congratulatory contentment pervaded the United States during the Kennedy administration, evincing the liberalism of a mature hegemonic power and encouraging the growth of its offshoots—the Peace Corps, civil rights, and détente.

This liberal self-confidence explains the tremendous psychological shock experienced by U. S. political and business leaders in response to the events of 1967-1968: the currency and gold crises that marked the fall of the U.S. dollar from its pedestal; the Tet offensive against South Vietnam that revealed that a small Third World people could hold U.S. military power in check; the student–worker rebellions—such as those at Columbia University and in France—that showed that internal struggles within Western states were once again on the agenda.

In retrospect, the sudden explosions of 1967-1968 should not have been so surprising. The economic reconstruction of Western Europe and Japan created centers of competition with U.S.-based firms and contributed to the global overexpansion of world production. By concentrating on the military sphere, the Soviet Union had increased its military strength relative to that of the United States. At the same time, direct U.S. military intervention had severe financial and economic consequences for the United States. The steady decolonization of the world could not possibly remain a controlled and formal process; it would inevitably become more radical and spread to the Western industrialized, or core, countries themselves (to the "Third World within"). And the liberalism of the mature hegemonic power would retreat once its largess was rejected by oppressed groups asserting demands on their own terms.

All of a sudden, in 1967 the United States found itself in a B-Period, a period of decelerated growth. In the world-economy, the most significant result of this period of relative economic stagnation has been a striking decline in the competitiveness of U.S.-based production organizations compared with those located in Japan and Western Europe, excluding Great Britain. This relative decline is evident upon comparing growth rates, standards of living, capital investments as a percentage of gross national product, growth in productivity, capital-labor ratios, share in the world market, and research and development expenditures. The decline is also reflected in the relative strengths of currencies and in the rates of inflation and unemployment.

A second striking result of this B-phase has been the relocation of industry. On a world scale, this relocation involved the rise of the newly industrializing countries and the opening of free trade zones—the creation of the so-called new international division of labor. In general, the bargaining power of large semiperipheral countries such as Brazil and countries with key commodities such as the Organization of Petroleum Exporting Countries (OPEC) bloc has been greatly strengthened.

Acquiescense or Collusion

With respect to the changing world-economy, it is the OPEC price rises that have caught everyone's attention and that politicians and the press have transformed from consequence into cause. Two things should be noted about the oil price rises. First, they began in 1973, not in 1963 or 1953. The oil-producing countries did not suddenly become avaricious. Rather, in 1973 oil price rises became, for the first time, economically and politically possible, in large part because the global rise of industrial production entailed a vast increase in demand for current energy production. This overproduction in turn promoted competition among the core powers, thereby limiting their economic and military bargaining power. OPEC simply capitalized on this situation.

Second, the oil price rises met little opposition from the core states. This cannot be written off to political lassitude resulting from economic stagnation. There probably also existed U.S. acquiescence, even collusion. It is hard otherwise to account for the crucial support in 1973 for this policy by the Saudi and Iranian governments, without which there would have been no OPEC price rise. James Akins, former U.S. ambassador to Saudi Arabia, reported that the Saudis went along with the price rise only when they could not persuade the United States to put pressure on Iranian price demands.

The United States could have seen two short-run advantages in the 1973 oil price rise: a competitive boost relative to Western Europe and Japan because of their greater dependence in 1973 on imported oil; and the creation of financial bases for the shah and to a lesser extent the Saudis so they could serve as proconsuls for the United States, relieving in part the U.S. political and financial burden.

There are also long-run advantages for the core powers collectively in the oil price rises—advantages that probably outweigh any disruptive effects. In a situation of global stagnation, one key problem concerns possibilities for new industrial complexes of high-profit growth. One such complex could involve new energy sources and energy-saving devices. The first advantage, then, is that the higher cost of petroleum created a major incentive for this kind of complex. Former Secretary of State Henry Kissinger after all did talk of a floor for petroleum prices and not of a ceiling.

The second major advantage is that inflation itself can in fact lead to a considerable decline in the real wage bill of the core countries, redistributing surplus to owners in a form that is far more manageable than the bread lines of 1933.

German Chancellor Helmut Schmidt has spoken of the struggle for the world product, emphasizing only interstate allocations. This might better be called the world class struggle in which reallocations are being made within as well as between states. For example, if the oil-producing states have gained considerably in the last decade, it is scarcely the large oil multinationals that have lost. It is, rather, the middle and lower strata in both core and peripheral countries.

The decline of U.S. hegemony has had major effects on the interstate system as well. Alliances that emerged after World War II are collapsing. The Sino-Soviet split, begun in the 1950s but consecrated in the 1960s, did not necessarily serve the interests of the United States as a global power. The split made it impossible to consolidate stability through a political deal with the USSR and muddied irremediably ideological waters. And when the United States came to terms with China, Western Europe, and Japan could not simply maintain their old alliance with the United States, but were forced to reconsider all the options.

The Sino-Soviet split was liberating for national movements in the Third World. The split closed the books on the Communist International and forced liberation groups to move where they were under pressure to move anyway—to action that was autonomous of the world alliance system. Despite U.S.-Soviet détente, a de facto U.S.-Chinese alliance, and socialist wars in Southeast Asia, the 1970s saw a steady acceleration of revolutionary movements (southern Africa, Central America and the Caribbean, and the Middle East) rather than the reverse.

The West-West Conflict

The most difficult issues, however, that confront U.S. policy makers in the coming decades are neither East-West issues (notwithstanding Afghanistan) nor North-South issues (notwithstanding Iran). Rather they are West-West issues that are based on the great economic and therefore political threat of the two significant U.S. rivals, Western Europe and Japan. President Carter's handling of the crises in Afghanistan and Iran as well as his decision to develop the MX missile could be viewed as attempts to maintain U.S. political leadership in the West and regain economic supremacy via ideological pressure on U.S. allies. Indeed, the effort to constrain U.S. allies bids fair to become the priority concern of U.S. foreign policy.

What are the real problems facing the United States in this growing West-West conflict? There is the immediate problem of fending off the worst aspects of the economic decline of the 1980s. There is the more important, long-run concern of trying to profit maximally from the probable renewed economic expansion of the 1990s.

Because there will have to be major contraction in some centers of world production, the basic issue for the 1980s is who will export unemployment to whom. Thus far inflation has masked this issue, at least politically; but should a dramatic fall in world prices occur, minimizing the resultant economic damage will become a matter of survival for regimes throughout the West.

In the short run, the United States has two major mechanisms at its disposal. It can prop up technologically doomed industries (the Chrysler handout), which reduces unemployment in one sector at the expense of others and also diminishes the capital available for investment in industries that will make America competitive in the 1990s. In addition, it can increase military expenditures, also at the expense of long-run development.

For the 1990s the basic policy issue is who will gain the competitive edge in the new technologies of microelectronics, biotechnology, and energy resources. Success will be determined by an interlocking triplet of research and development innovations; reduction of real costs of production; and increased access to markets for the older sectors of production—formerly high-profit sectors, now medium-profit sectors—such as electronics, automobiles, and even computers.

What is happening today in industries such as steel, automobiles, and electronics is a double process. First, West European and Japanese firms are undercutting U.S.-based firms, even in the U.S. home market. Second, production processes are being broken up. Large parts of production chains are being moved to semiperipheral countries, including socialist countries, and the chains themselves are more likely to end in Western Europe and Japan rather than in the United States.

The structural causes of this massive shift in production centers outside the United States—a shift that is likely to accelerate sharply in the 1980s—are twofold. On the one hand, given larger and older U.S. industrial hardware, there are the higher costs of amortization of the overall plant. On the other, there is the higher U.S. wage bill. The real difference between U.S. costs of production and those of Western Europe and Japan does not lie in the wages paid a skilled mechanic. The political bargaining strength of workers is basically the same in all parts of the West. The real difference in costs—paid in part directly by companies, in part indirectly through government expenditures—lies in the salaries of the well-to-do middle stratum (i.e., professionals and executives).

It is not that the individual incomes of U.S. executives or professionals exceed those of their allied counterparts. In many cases, the opposite is true. Rather, it is that in the United States the well-to-do middle stratum is a significantly larger percentage of the total population. Hence, the social bill of the U.S. middle class is dramatically higher, and it is impossible for either the government or the large corporations to do anything about it.

An attack on these expenditures of a magnitude sufficient enough to make U.S.-based industry cost competitive again would entail higher political costs than anyone dares pay, especially because American political structures are heavily dominated by precisely those people whose incomes would have to be cut. It is therefore far easier for a multinational corporation to consider shifting its sites of production and research and eventually even its headquarters than to try to reduce costs directly. This has already begun to occur.

The process of disinvestment in the old industries will affect the research and development expenditures on the new ones by reducing both the U.S. tax and profit bases of U.S.-based companies. The markets for the new industries will be located primarily in the core countries themselves, but the markets for the older industries will be more world-wide. It will be important for producers to find fresh markets—zones whose expansion depends upon the products of these older industries. Such zones encompass the semiperipheral countries that are industrializing and that, even if they have their own plants and production sites, will need advanced machinery and hardware. The European Economic Community countries are up front in this effort in terms of their economic partnership with developing countries covered by the Lomé Convention. The largest likely market of 1980s and, to an even greater extent, of the 1990s will comprise the socialist countries. Behind the Sino-Soviet controversy lies a struggle to be this market in the most advantageous way possible. This is called catching up or modernizing.

European-Soviet Cooperation

Within this economic reality—this B-phase of stagnation—lie the bases for the realignment of alliances in the interstate system. In a sense, China jumped the gun by its dramatic and successful attempt to make an arrangement with the United States. It is no accident that this diplomatic turnabout was done with Richard Nixon, who represented those U.S. forces whose deep anticommunist ideology was not tightly linked to a commitment to a North Atlantic Treaty Organization alliance structure.

Japan, no doubt miffed by its exclusion from the very first diplomatic steps, quickly allowed its true interests to prevail in the Sino-Japanese reconciliation. Because of the strong, complementary economic interests of the two countries and the fundamental link of civilization (still a major factor in policy making), the reconciliation is even more important than the joint U.S.-Chinese Shanghai communiqué.

If the United States has moved in the direction of China, it is because such movement makes geopolitical, strategic sense. And given that during the 1970s the economic fruits of détente with the Soviet Union were clearly being garnered by Western Europe rather than by the United States, these strategic considerations seemed worth the risk.

In terms of the political economy of the world-system, Western Europe and the USSR have much to offer each other, both positively and negatively. Were the two sides to move slowly toward a de facto structure of cooperation that need not involve anything affirmative in the sphere of military alliances, the USSR could obtain the capital equipment it needs to improve its long-term relative position in the world-economy, thus meeting the most pressing demand of its own cadres. Of course, the Soviet Union would also thereby obtain security against any dangers (real or imagined) implied by the U.S.-Chinese structure of cooperation.

In conjunction with Western Europe—and probably not without it—the Soviet Union could also effectuate a significant breakthrough in economic links with the Middle East. This presumes that the USSR and Western Europe would be able to complete the Camp David process by an arrangement between Israel and the Palestine Liberation Organization. In addition, a Middle East agreement might partially defuse the Soviet Union's greatest internal danger point, the potentially higher consciousness of the central Asian Moslem peoples.

Moreover, an arrangement of this sort between the Soviet Union and Western Europe—in which the German Social Democratic Party would have to play a large part—could also discourage the revolt of Eastern Europe against the USSR. The uprisings in Prague during spring 1968 threatened the USSR in two ways. The idea of liberalization might spread eastward, particularly to the Ukraine. And Czechoslovakia might move out of the Soviet orbit, especially in economic terms, and into that of West Germany. In the context of West European-Soviet cooperation, the latter fear would become less relevant.

Such an arrangement could look equally attractive to Western Europe. The Soviet market would be opened in some meaningful sense to Western Europe-based industries. The resources of the Soviet Union would become available, at least over a crucial 20-30 year period. And the USSR and East European countries could serve as geographically convenient and politically constrained reservoirs of relatively cheap labor for participation in Western Europe's claims of production.

Furthermore, a solution to the East European question from the Soviet perspective is also a solution from the viewpoint of Western Europe. Cooperation would permit the reintegration of Europe—culturally, economically, and eventually politically—a development that has up to now been barred by Soviet military strength. In particular, cooperation would permit, at a minimum, the two Germanies to move closer toegether.

An amicable, working relationship with the Soviet Union would even have political advantages for Western Europe. Just as the USSR might not gain a breakthrough in the Middle East without Western Europe, so might the reverse be true. In addition, by guaranteeing a relatively strong position to West European firms during the difficult years of the 1980s, a structure of cooperation would insure the continuance of the high degree of social peace that Western Europe is currently enjoying. On the ideological front, it would also contain in part the USSR.

A New Hegemony?

Needless to say, the ideological sentiments on both sides remain very strong—but not unswerving. In the case of West Germany, ideological commitments have not changed, but their role has: In the 1950s and 1960s, West Germany's economic interests were served by emphasizing ideological commitments, whereas in the 1970s and the 1980s, these same economic interests are being advanced by playing down political beliefs.

Should this kind of realignment come about, the most indecisive power will be Great Britain, which faces difficulty no matter which way it turns. But in any West-West split, Britain will probably have to stay with the United States, if only because in the very important geopolitical struggle over southern Africa, British and American interests are closely linked. And in a world in which British markets are declining everywhere, southern Africa might be one of the last secure trading partners.

In this picture of potential realignments, what happens to the North-South struggle?

At one level, a realignment of the Northern powers along the lines suggested would create incredible ideological confusion in the South. At another level, it might lead to an ideological clarification. The process of disintegration of the world system, brought about by the cumulative strength of the world's antisystemic forces, cannot be controlled by the United States or the Soviet Union. Revolutions in, say, Honduras, Tunisia, Kenya, or Thailand are not primarily a function of geopolitical arrangements among the great powers. What realignments may bring about is a greater disillusionment among these revolutionary movements regarding the efficacy of achieving power via the control of individual state structures. After a century of detour, the emphasis may return to the importance of creating real worldwide intermovement links—ones that would cut across North-South and East-West boundaries. This is what is meant by ideological clarification.

And this is why even if the world-economy takes a major upturn in the 1990s and even if Western Europe begins to play the role of a new ascending hegemonic power, the world is not entering merely another cyclical moment of the present system. It is in this sense that the underlying, long-run systemic crisis of world capitalism may be more meaningful over the next 50 years. In the middle run, world capitalism will seem to recuperate: in the long run, it will be transformed fundamentally.

In the short run, however, the biggest traumas will be felt by the United States. Americans have spent the past 30 years getting used to the benefits of a hegemonic position, and they will have to spend the next 30 getting used to life without them. For the majority of the world, it may not make that big a difference. For that majority, the real question is not which nation is hegemonic in the present world-system, but whether and how that world-system will be transformed.

3.7

Democratic Capitalism
at the Crossroads

ADAM PRZEWORSKI and MICHAEL WALLERSTEIN

This essay invites attention as a comment both on technical economic theory and on the consequences of that theory's application for the social order of democratic capitalism. As the authors observe: "At one level we are discussing a question about an economic project that would constitute a reasonable and appealing alternative to both the policies of demand management and to the current wave of right-wing supply-oriented economics. But economic theories are rationalizations of the political interests of conflicting classes and groups, and should be treated as such. Behind economic alternatives lurk visions of society, models of culture, and thrusts for power. Economic projects entail political and social ones."

The "economic project" that concerns Przeworski and Wallerstein is the ongoing debate among economic policymakers about the rate of savings and investment in the U.S. economy. Many regard this as a bogus issue, or believe it can be addressed within the conventional Keynesian framework of demand manipulation. Przeworski and Wallerstein take exception to both views, but also oppose the prescriptive conclusions of those supply-side theorists who counsel higher profits and upward redistributions of income as the only solutions to the problem. Taking a lesson from the tax policies of such industrial rivals as West Germany and Japan, they outline an alternative economic strategy that uses the tax system to deliver higher levels of investment and greater income equality.

The "political and social project" that animates this debate concerns the fundamental organization of American society. Przeworski and Wallerstein view capitalist democracies like the United States as institutional compromises between capital and labor, forms of social organization in which "those who do not own the means of production consent to the institution of private ownership of capital stock while those who own productive instruments consent to political institutions that permit other groups to effectively press their claims to the allocation of resources and the distribution of output." For much of the twentieth century, Keynesian economic policy provided a foundation for such compromise. Even within the constraints imposed by popular representative institutions, capitalists profited from the maintenance of aggregate demand, and even within the constraints of capitalism, workers achieved an increased measure of material security. But now the U.S. economy is marked by the persistence of a set of problems that resist solution within the Keynesian framework. Keynesianism is in crisis, and that crisis threatens the continued viability of capitalist democracy as well. Much hangs in the balance, Przeworski and Wallerstein argue, for recent policy initiatives not only signal new directions for fiscal policy, but "constitute a project for a new society, a bourgeois revolution."

Reprinted with permission from *democracy*, Vol. 2, No. 3 (July 1982), pp. 52-68. Copyright © 1982 by The Common Good Foundation.

The ideology that orients the current right-wing offensive is in many ways a ghost of the 1920s: antistatist, emphasizing the hegemony of the entrepreneur, portraying popular consumption as inimical to national interests, and based on the belief in the rationality of the market and in the autonomous importance of money. Yet what is new in this ideology is the dominant role played by technical economic theory. In the 1920s, deflationary policies and the principles of the gold standard and of balanced budgets were justified as an accumulated wisdom derived from experience. The only abstract basis for these principles was the quantity theory of money. The ideological appeal was couched in terms of popular values, such as thrift, responsibility, and common sense. The spokesmen for this ideology were typically officials of the Treasury and the bankers. In the 1970s, in contrast, the justification is derived from seemingly technical theories: "monetarism," "*la nouvelle économie*," and "rational expectations" are all being offered as scientific reasons why everyone will be better off if the state withdraws from the economy and capitalists are allowed to accumulate without distributional considerations. Even the most naked program for an upward distribution of income—Reagan's economic policy—is masked as a "supply-side theory," with a concocted Laffer curve as its main theoretical mainstay.

It was Keynes who transformed macroeconomics from a frame of mind into a theory: a deductive method for analyzing the determinants of national income and for evaluating alternative policies. His followers constructed mathematical models of capitalist economies and described statistically particular economies in terms of these models. The new theory became the framework within which particular groups presented their interests as universal. It became the vehicle for the articulation of claims to hegemony and the language of economic policy. It is a lasting legacy of the Keynesian revolution that the terrain of ideological conflict has been conquered by technical economic theory.

While many people have subsequently claimed that the central principles of Keynesian economics had been presaged by Marx and some of his followers, in fact marxist economic theory has never been of economic importance for the left. Marx's theory provided a useful threefold analysis: first, capitalism is based on exploitation (the source of profit is surplus value); second, the private property of the means of production is the source simultaneously of the injustice and the irrationality of capitalism; third, the falling rate of profit is the source of crises. The theory has been politically useful only as a justification of revolutionary goals, specifically of the program of nationalization of the means of production. Marx's economics, even its most sophisticated version, is not a helpful tool for addressing workers' distributional claims within capitalism and it is useless as a framework for administering capitalist economies. It is easy to say "so what," but the fact is that all mass movements of the left historically have had to face precisely these tasks.

As a result, it has been the understanding of the capitalist economy and the policy recommendations provided by Keynesian economics that the left has embraced. But Keynesian economics is now badly tarnished. Two phenomena that have characterized much of the developed capitalist world since the early 1970s, a gradual increase in the rate of inflation and a gradual decline in the rate of growth, have proved remarkably unresponsive to the traditional interventions prescribed by Keynesian theory. Yet this deeply ingrained tradition perseveres, providing the basis for much of the left's current reactions to the conservative offensive. Many continue to insist that the supply of savings is not problematic, that demand is chronically insufficient, and that a redistribution of income, full-employment policies, and social spending are the only ways to get out of the current crisis. The problem is that such a response is no longer convincing. It represents a reaction of clinging to old ideas and old policies that the right claims, with some justification, have been tried and found wanting. An obstinate defense of policies associated with past failures abdicates the ideological terrain to the right and, we believe, is not necessary.

What, then, are the choices we face? At one level we are discussing a question about an economic project that would constitute a reasonable and appealing alternative both to the policies of demand management and to the current wave of right-wing supply-oriented economics. But economic theories are rationalizations of the political interests of conflicting classes and groups, and should be treated as such. Behind economic alternatives lurk visions of society, models of culture, and thrusts for power. Economic projects entail political and social ones.

The combination of democracy and capitalism constitutes a compromise: those who do not own instruments of production consent to the institution of the private ownership of capital stock while those who own productive instruments consent to political institutions that permit other groups to effectively press their claims to the allocation of resources and the distribution of output. It may be worth recalling that this compromise was deemed unfeasible by Marx, who claims that the "bourgeois republic" is based on a contradiction that renders it inherently unstable as a form of social organization. A combination of private ownership of the means of production with universal suffrage, Marx argued, must lead either to "social emancipation" of the oppressed classes utilizing their political power or to "political restoration" of the oppressing class utilizing its economic power. Hence, Marx held, capitalist democracy is "only the political form of revolution of bourgeois society and not its conservative form of life," "only a spasmodic, exceptional state of things . . . impossible as the normal form of society."

It was Keynesianism that provided the ideological and political foundations for the compromise of capitalist democracy. Keynesianism held out the prospect that the state could reconcile the private ownership of the means of production with democratic management of the economy. As Keynes himself put it: "It is not the ownership of the instruments of production which it is important for the state to assume. If the state is able to determine the aggregate amount of resources devoted to augmenting the instruments and the basic reward to those who own them, it will have accomplished all that is necessary."[1] Democratic control over the level of unemployment and the distribution of income became the terms of the compromise that made democratic capitalism possible.

The problem of the 1930s was that resources lay fallow: machines stood idle while men were out of work. At no time in history was the irrationality of the capitalist system more blatant. As families starved, food—already produced food—was destroyed. Coffee was burned, pigs were killed, inventories rotted, machines rusted. Unemployment was the central political problem of society.

According to the economic orthodoxy of the time, this state of affairs was simply a given and the only recourse was to cut the costs of production, which meant cutting wages and transfers. Some relief measures to assist the unemployed were obviously urgently required, but whether such measures were advisable from an economic point of view was at best controversial. In Great Britain the Labour government in fact proposed to reduce unemployment compensations: this was the condition for being bailed out by the IMF of the time, where "M" stood for the Morgan Bank. But in Sweden the Social Democratic Party, having won the election of 1932, broke the shell of the orthodox monetary policy. As unemployment climbed sharply with the onset of the Great Depression, they stumbled upon an idea that was truly new: instead of assisting the unemployed, the Swedish Social Democrats employed them. It was the beginning of the marriage of the left and Keynesian economics.[2]

Keynesianism provided the foundation for class compromise by supplying those political parties representing workers with a justification for holding office within capitalist societies. And such a justification was desperately needed. Ever since the 1890s, Social Democrats had thought that their irreversible electoral progress would culminate in an electoral majority that would allow them one day to enter into office and legislate their societies into socialism. They were completely unprepared for what ensued: in several countries Social Democratic, Labor, and Socialist parties were invited to form governments by default, without winning the majority that would have been necessary to pursue the program of nationalization but because the bourgeois parties were too divided to continue their traditional coalitions. Indeed, the first elected socialist government in the world was formed by the Swedish Social Democrats in 1920 just as they suffered their first electoral reversal. And once in office, socialists found themselves in the embarrassing situation of not being able to pursue the program of nationalization and not having any other program that would distinguish them from their bourgeois opponents. They could and did pursue ad hoc measures designed to improve conditions for their electoral constituency: the development of public housing, the institution of unemployment relief, the introduction of minimum wages, income and inheritance taxes, and old age pensions. But such measures did not differ from the tradition of conservative reforms associated with Bismarck, Disraeli, or Giolitti. Socialists behaved like all other parties: some distributional bias toward their own constituency but full of respect for the golden principles of the balanced budget, deflation, gold standard, etc.

Keynesianism suddenly provided working-class political parties with a reason to be in office. It appeared that there was something to be done, that the economy was not moving according to natural laws, that economic crises could be attenuated and the waste of resources and the suffering alleviated if the state pursued anticyclical policies of demand management. If the economy was producing at a level below its capacity, given the existing stock of capital and labor, a proper government policy could increase output until it approached the economy's full potential. The government had the capacity to close the "full-employment gap," to insure that there would be no unemployment of men and machines. Full employment became a realistic goal that could be pursued at all times.

How was this to be done? Here again Keynesian economics provided a technical justification for class compromise. The answer it provided was to increase consumption. In the Keynesian diagnosis, the cause of unemployment was the insufficiency of demand. Hence any redistribution of income downwards to people who consume most of it and any expansion of government spending will stimulate production and reduce unemployment.[3] Given the existing capital stock, the actual output can always be raised by increasing wages, transfers to the poor, and government spending, or by reducing taxes. Since raising output means augmenting the rate of utilization of resources, the same policies will diminish unemployment. Thus the distributional bias of the left toward their electoral constituency found a rationalization in a technical economic theory. As Léon Blum put it, "a better distribution . . . would revive production at the same time that it would satisfy justice."

But more was at stake. In the orthodox thinking, any demands by workers or the unemployed for higher consumption appeared as a particularistic interest, inimical to future national development. To increase wages or social services was to raise costs of production and to divert resources from the investment necessary for growth, accumulation of capital, and improved productivity. The welfare of the poor was a matter of private charity, not of economics. But in the Keynesian framework it is consumption that provides the motor force for production, and suddenly workers and the poor turned out to be the representatives of the universal interest. Their particularistic interest in consumption coincided with the general interest in production. The "people" became the hegemonic force in society. As Bertil Ohlin stated in 1938, "In recent years it has become obvious that . . . many forms of 'consumption'—food, clothing, housing, recreation— . . . represent an investment in the most valuable productive instrument of all, the people itself."[4] The terms of discourse became transformed.

Not all "Keynesian" positions are the same. One policy direction—warmly embraced by the radical left—focused on the redistribution of income toward wages and transfers. This is what happened in France in 1936. A more cautious, and more successful, policy consisted of manipulating government spending, taxation, and the money supply. The Swedish policy of 1932 was exclusively an "employment policy": it consisted of productive public employment financed by deficits and increased taxation. Wage rates did not increase in Sweden until 1938, well after the economy was out of the slump. In fact, the simple formal framework of Keynesian economics, as is found in modern macroeconomic textbooks, favors government spending over redistribution of income: the "multiplier" for government spending is greater than unity, while for wages and transfers it is less than unity. Hence, at least in principle, government spending more than pays for itself in increased production, while distribution of income partially hurts other components of demand.

In all of its forms, the Keynesian compromise consisted of a dual program: "full employment and equality," where the first term meant regulation of the level of employment via the management of demand, particularly government spending, and the latter consisted of the net of social services that constituted the "welfare state." The Keynesian compromise, therefore, came to consist of more than an active role for the government in macroeconomic management. As the provider of social services and regulator of the market, the state acted in multiple social realms. Governments developed manpower programs, family policies, housing schemes, income assistance nets, health systems, etc. They attempted to regulate the labor force by mixing incentives and deterrents to participation in the labor market. They sought to alter patterns of racial and regional disparities. The result is that social relations are mediated through democratic political institutions rather than remaining private.

At the same time, the Keynesian compromise became increasingly dependent upon economic concessions granted to groups of people organized as nonmarket actors. Politics turned into an interplay of coalitions among such groups, giving rise to corporatist tendencies of direct negotiation, either between organized groups—particularly labor and capital—under the tutelage of the government or between each group and the government. The allocation of economic resources became increasingly dominated by relations of political forces.

The compromise was tenable as long as it could provide employment and material security. Indeed, by most criteria of economic progress the Keynesian era was a success. Whether or not this was due to the efficacy of Keynesian economic policies or was merely fortuitous is a matter of debate. Nevertheless, output grew, unemployment was low, social services were extended, and social peace reigned. Until the late 1960s, Keynesianism was the established ideology of class compromise, under which different groups could conflict within the confines of a capitalist and democratic system. And, with the possible exception of Karl Rehn's 1951 program in Sweden and the Italian Communist Party's short-lived austerity policy of the mid-1970s, Keynesianism provided the only framework for such a compromise. The crisis of Keynesianism is a crisis of democratic capitalism.

Keynesian economics is demand economics. The supply of capital and the supply of labor are assumed to be constant. The supply of savings is determined endogenously: it always equals investment. As demand is stimulated, whether by government policies or exogenous events, production expands to match demand, income increases and so do savings until a new equilibrium is reached where savings again equals investment at a higher level of capacity-utilization. The level of output shifts to maintain the equality of savings and investment. Moreover, since the Keynesian problem is to bring the actual output to the potential level of the already existing capital stock, the accumulation of capital is ignored altogether, to the point where new investment is assumed to be nonnegative at the same time that the total stock of capital is assumed to be constant.

Keynesian economics is the economics of the "short-run," where the short-run is a situation rather than a period of time, in which cumulative changes of capital stock can be ignored. Given the Keynesian problem, this assumption is not unreasonable, but the effect is that this framework has nothing to say about the determinants of the potential level of output, about capital accumulation, or about productivity. The problem for Keynesian policies is always to close the gap between actual output and potential output, whatever the potential might happen to be.

Suppose for the moment that this problem has been solved and the economy is producing at its full potential. Since the already installed capital stock is now fully utilized, output cannot be increased without investment, that is, without new additions to the capital stock. In the demand view of the world, no longer Keynes's own but nevertheless very much "Keynesian," demand stimulation will still have the effect of increasing output, this time by "accelerating" investment.[5] Investors are assumed to make their investment decisions in order to increase production to match the expected future aggregate demand. Hence, the same government policies—spending, distribution of income, reduction of taxation—will continue to be effective, since by stimulating demand past the level of potential output the government will stimulate investment and economic growth.

But things look different when the supply of productive inputs is no longer taken to be fixed or passive. Now the question of whether the supply of savings is sufficient becomes problematic. The supply of savings available for investment is what is left from the total output after wages, transfers, and government expenditures have been subtracted. Hence the very measures designed to stimulate demand have the effect of reducing potential savings, that is, the savings that are available when the economy is running at its full potential.

As long as the economy operates below the full potential level there is no contradiction involved. The output determined by the level of aggregate demand is assumed not to be greater than the level possible given the already existing capital stock, and the supply of savings is not a constraint. Indeed, in such circumstances, savings are too high and the Keynesian remedies all involve a reduction of savings as a proportion of output. But when the economy is close to full employment the measures meant to increase aggregate demand and therefore to decrease aggregate saving have the effect of limiting the rate of growth of potential output. And since potential output is the ceiling for actual output, short-run demand stimulation turns out to have perverse effects for the long-run. When we encounter symptoms of insufficient investment—the stagnation of real wages, the decline of productivity, the obsolescence of plant and equipment—

demand management provides no solution. Indeed, the stimulation of demand accentuates the problem when the problem is the shortage of capital.

The supply side is the kingdom of the bourgeoisie. Here the bourgeoisie appears hegemonic: the realization of its interest in profits is a necessary condition for the improvement of the material conditions of everyone. Increased output requires investment, investment is financed by savings, savings are financed by profits. Hence profits are the condition for growth. From the supply side it is savings that provide the motor for accumulation and, as all studies show, workers do not save much. Increases in wages and transfers as well as "welfare" spending appear, therefore, as hindrances to growth. So does taxation of the wealthy and any form of government intervention that restricts profitability, even if such restrictions reflect social costs and negative externalities.

Clearly, such a rendition of the economic system is not particularly appealing to those who consume most of their incomes. The natural response of the left is to claim that the very problem of the supply of savings is a false one.[6] This is a response embedded in the Keynesian framework in which investment and growth are constrained by insufficient demand, not by available savings. But the response is wrong. The inadequate rate of investment in the U.S. did not suddenly appear in the recessions of the last ten years. Investment, capital accumulation, and growth of output per worker have been lower in the U.S. than in any major advanced capitalist economies, except for Great Britain, throughout the postwar period.[7] What is fallacious in the claims of right-wing economists is not the assertion that the supply of savings is insufficient to finance the desirable level of investment, but the argument that savings are insufficient because profits are too low.

True, the mere fact that the level of investment is inadequate does not imply that savings must be increased—at least if we accept the possibility that most of current investment may be socially wasteful, superfluous, or otherwise undesirable. The aggregate balance always hides qualitative alternatives. One bomber absorbs as much savings as would a modern mass-transit system for the city of Chicago. If investment is insufficient, there are many places to look for waste, and nonmilitary public expenditures would not necessarily be the first place selected by a rational observer.

But such a qualitative response is not sufficient. Moreover, it is not synonymous with an indiscriminate cry for a continued expansion of government spending, for supporting obsolete industries, and for an obstinate stimulation of demand. The problem of the supply of savings must be faced as such.

The historical experience of several countries demonstrates that growth can be generated without pernicious effects upon the distribution of income when governments actively influence the rate and the direction of investment and the supply of labor. The post war German "miracle," the rapid growth of Japan, and the apparent success of the Swedish Social Democrats in combining relatively fast growth of productivity with the most egalitarian distribution of income in the West demonstrate that there exists an alternative to demand-management as well as to profit-oriented, right-wing supply policies.

Although they have been pursued in somewhat different forms in several countries, these alternative supply-oriented policies have never been formalized in a theoretical framework. Indeed, the Swedish Social Democrats seem to have stumbled upon them in 1951 in a manner reminiscent of their discovery of deficit spending in 1932: mainly as a remedy to the problem of maintaining price stability under conditions of full employment.[8] Of the German post-1949 policies it is typically said that they were a discovery of bankers who behaved as if Keynes had never existed. Yet both the Germans and the

Swedes, along with a number of other countries, successfully pursued sustained programs consisting of public control over investment, elimination of inefficient industries, manpower policies designed to reduce structural unemployment, and expansion of the welfare system.

In order to understand abstractly these investment-oriented supply strategies, one must note first that in advanced capitalist economies productive investment is financed largely out of profit incomes. This implies that the rate of accumulation, that is, the ratio of the change in capital stock over total capital stock, is approximately equal to the product of two quantities: the rate of saving out of profits and the after-tax rate of profit.[9] For example, a 6 percent rate of growth could be accomplished by a saving rate of 60 percent combined with a rate of profit of 10 percent or, equivalently, by a saving rate of 30 percent combined with a rate of profit of 20 percent.

The crucial question is whether firms can be made to invest when the rate of profit is low. The argument of the right is that this situation is unfeasible, since without sufficient future rewards capitalists will not abstain in the present. Big business and the political forces that represent it always claim that the only way the volume of savings can be increased is by raising the after-tax rate of profit, an increase that is supposed to have two effects. First, given a constant rate of saving out of profits, either directly by firms or by the recipients of profit income, the aggregate volume of savings will rise in proportion to the increase in the aggregate volume of profits. Second, a higher rate of return is promised to induce a higher propensity to save out of profits. Giving more money to "those who save," in the words of the *Wall Street Journal*, will encourage them to save at a higher rate. Indeed, the central tenet of the new economics is that a redistribution of income in favor of profits is a necessary cost the society must bear in order to produce a higher rate of investment and economic growth. The policies of the right, therefore, are designed to increase the effective rate of profit by sharply reducing nominal rates of taxation of incomes derived from property, by cutting down nonmilitary public expenditures, by eliminating all of the profit-constraining regulation, and by limiting the right of workers to organize and strike. They offer in return the promise of increased investment, improvement of productivity, and an acceleration of growth.

Yet there are countries—those mentioned above among them—in which the rate of investment has been relatively high while the after-tax rate of profit has been relatively low. These are the countries in which governments sought to alter the terms of choice of private decision makers between consumption and investment through taxes, credits, and direct subsidies.

Let us concentrate on the use of the tax system. Consider all taxes levied on incomes derived from the ownership of capital. They typically include a personal income tax on earned income ("salaries" of top executives), a personal income tax on property income, a tax on wealth, and a corporate profit tax. Given any mixture of these incomes there exists some average nominal rate of taxation of the aggregate property income. At the same time, all western countries use the tax system as an instrument for stimulating investment: by a preferential treatment of capital gains, depreciation write-offs, investment credits, and grants. Given a mix of these different manners of investing, there exists again an average rate of investment relief, a rate that depends upon the rate of investment. Hence, the effective tax rate—the rate at which incomes from profits are in fact taxed—will be determined by the difference between the nominal rate of taxation and the rate of investment relief.

Let us now compare different tax systems. When the nominal tax rate on profits is low, the tax system has the effect of keeping the after-tax rate of profit high—independent of the rate of investment. Such a tax system rewards wealth, not investment. It may—although the evidence is at best mixed[10]—provide an incentive to invest, but it provides no assurance. It imposes no penalties on unproductive uses of profits. Hence, lowering the nominal rate of taxation of profits is the program of business. Owners of capital are then free to do whatever they find in their self-interest without any control.

But suppose that the nominal tax-rate on profits is high—*very* high—and the marginal rate of investment tax relief is also high, at least for some chosen types of investment.[11] Unproductive uses of profits are now being punished. People and firms that do not invest do not receive tax breaks. The terms of choice facing the owners of capital are altered, presenting the choice of investing in publicly designated directions or paying taxes. It is now in the interest of firms to invest.

Consider, again, the example of two societies that add to their capital stock and output at the rate of 6 percent per year: one with the after-tax rate of profit of 20 percent and the rate of investment of 30 percent, the other with the after-tax rate of profit of 10 percent and the rate of investment out of profits of 60 percent. As is illustrated in the table below, the distributional implications of these alternative patterns of growth are quite staggering. When accumulation is financed by a high rate of investment with a low rate of profit, Case B, the share of wages and government spending is much higher and the rate of consumption out of profit incomes much lower than Case A where accumulation is financed with a high rate of profit and a low rate of investment. The choice is brutally clear. The same rate of growth can be obtained in different ways. The question is simply who will pay the cost of accumulation: the wage-earners and unemployed or the owners of capital.

Hence, the problem of the supply of capital, that is, of investment and productivity, can be addressed without redistributing incomes upwards and dismantling government services—if the tax system is used to reward investment and discourage consumption of profit incomes. This kind of tax system satisfies three criteria. First, it delivers investment. Second, it does not place the burden of sacrifice on wage-earners and those dependent upon the government for survival. Third, if applied with qualitative criteria, it allows society to choose the directions of investment on the basis of criteria other than private profitability.

**Two Hypothetical Patterns of Capital Accumulation
at Six Percent Per Year
(Net incremental capital-output ratio is 2)**

	Case A	Case B
Rate of growth of output and capital stock	6%	6%
Net investment/output	12%	12%
Rate of profit	20%	10%
Rate of saving out of profits	30%	60%
Share of profits in output	40%	20%
Share of wages and government	60%	80%
Share of consumption out of profits	28%	8%

Investment + Wages and government + Consumption out of profits = 100%.

None of the above is intended to suggest, however, that democratic control over investment, exercised through the tax system, is a panacea. Decisions over the allocation of investment involve a number of trade-offs that are painful, as trade-offs are. We do not have consensual criteria by which to evaluate the choices presented by considerations of social effects, environment, health and safety, depletion of natural resources, and profitability. And in the absence of such criteria qualitative control over investment could lead to whimsical rule by government bureaucrats responding to political pressures. The exercise of discretion in investment policy makes it possible for firms (private and public) to succeed on the basis of influence within government bureaucracies rather than on the strict merits of their undertakings. And as long as market rationality remains the international criterion of efficiency in the allocation of resources, market critera tend to ultimately prevail under the pressure of international competition.

Moreover, the goals of economic growth and increased productivity are in conflict with the goal of protecting existing jobs. A policy that encourages labor-saving innovations, that refuses subsidies to inefficient producers or protection to obsolete industries, must be coupled with Swedish-style manpower programs of job-retraining and subsidies for labor mobility. But, as the Swedes discovered, such manpower policies are socially costly and may be politically intolerable.[12] Measures designed to make people move according to the shifting patterns of industry imply that families are uprooted, social ties are fractured, and even entire communities may die deserted by the breadwinners.

Yet a comprehensive, consistent system of public control over investment and income distribution opens the possibility for the realization of the original goal of the socialist movement, the goal that has been abandoned and perverted in its history, namely, reduction of the necessary labor time. It is ironic that, since the 1930s, full employment has been the predominant concern of the left. What in the middle of the nineteenth century used to be called "wage slavery" became the condition to be made universal. The working class has traveled a long road from seeking to abolish the wage relation to attempting to insure that none are excluded from it. As Rosa Luxemburg observed in 1906, workers had become an obstacle to technical change that would make possible their own liberation. Defense of obsolete plants and inefficient industries for the sake of maintaining jobs has been an almost irresistible stance to the left, with inevitable detrimental effects for economic welfare. The maintenance of full employment has turned into a major barrier to investment that would improve productivity, increase output, raise wages, and/or reduce working time.

The priority that the left has given to the creation of jobs is inevitable so long as a decent standard of living is contingent upon being employed. Only when a sufficient minimum income is guaranteed to all will the maintenance of full employment no longer be a necessary object of economic policy. A substantial degree of equality, then, is a precondition for a working-class-supported macroeconomic policy that would allow jobs to be lost for the sake of productivity growth that would not protect technologically backward plants and industries, that would encourage rather than block labor-saving innovations. But consider the rewards. At an annual rate of productivity growth of less than 3 percent, output per worker doubles in twenty-five years: within one generation we could reduce labor time by one half. Whether people would opt to use productivity gains to increase consumption or free time we do not know. But once the maintenance of full employment ceases to be a fetish, once decent life conditions are assured for everyone, this choice will be open.

In any society some decisions have a public impact while others have a private, or limited, effect. And in any society some decisions are made by the public while others are restricted to the private realm. Investment decisions—decisions to withhold a part of society's resources from current consumption and to allocate them to replace or augment the instruments of production—have an impact that is both general and long-lasting, that is, public. Yet the very institution of private property implies that they are a private prerogative. Control over investment is the central political issue under capitalism precisely because no other privately made decisions have such a profound public impact.

The program of the right is to let the type and quantity of investment be determined by the market. The market, after all, is an institution that coordinates private decisions and aggregates preferences. If the market is undistorted by monopolies, externalities, etc., and consumers are sovereign, the market aggregates private decisions in a way that corresponds to preferences of individuals as consumers. The decisions made by profit-maximizing investors will respond to the preferences of consumers concerning the atemporal and intertemporal allocation of resources. But the preferences to which the market responds are weighted by the amount of resources each individual controls. That an idealized "perfect" market matches aggregated consumer preferences for private goods efficiently is the first lesson of welfare economics. That aggregated consumer preferences reflect the distribution of income and wealth is an often neglected corollary.

A democratic political system constitutes another mechanism by which individual preferences are aggregated. If political competition is free of coercion and if voters are sovereign, then government policies will reflect the aggregated preferences of individuals as citizens. But as citizens individuals are weighted equally. Hence, the same set of individual preferences, for private as well as public goods, will normally yield a demand for a different allocation of resources when they are aggregated by political institutions rather than by the market.

Further, the market provides no guarantee that those whose consumption is most restrained in the present will reap the rewards of investment in the future. In any society some part of the current output must be withheld from consumption if production is to continue and consumption is to increase. What distinguishes capitalism is that investment is financed mostly out of profits, the part of the product withheld from wage-earners. It is upon profits that the renewal and enlargement of the capital stock depend. Hence, under capitalism, the presence of profits is a necessary condition for the improvement of material conditions of any group within the society. But it is not sufficient. Profits may be hoarded, consumed, exported, or invested badly. Even if capitalists are abstemious, efficient, and prescient, their market relation with workers ends as the cycle of production is completed and the wages are paid, and there is nothing in the structure of the capitalist system of production that would guarantee that wage-earners would be the ones to benefit from the fact that a part of the product is currently withheld from them as profit.

Any class compromise must, therefore, have at least two aspects: one concerning the distribution of income and the second concerning investment. If those who do not own capital are to consent voluntarily to the private property of the instruments of production, they must have a reasonable certainty that their material conditions would improve in the future as the result of current appropriation of profit by capitalists. Until recently, this compromise was rarely stated explicitly, for it is basically institutional: workers consent to the institution of private property of the instruments of production and owners of these instruments consent to political institutions through which other groups can effectively process their demands. Today, as trust in the compromise is eroding, workers are demanding more explicit commitments. As a recent report commissioned by the European Trade Union Confederation declared: "To accept the level of profits required for investments and to give companies a sound financial basis, workers will increasingly demand a say in decisions about investments and a fairer share of the income they generate."[13]

The current period, however, is the first moment since the 1920s in which owners of capital have openly rejected a compromise that involves public influence over investment and the distribution of income. For the first time in several decades, the right has an historical project of its own: to free accumulation from all the fetters imposed upon it by democracy. For the bourgeoisie never completed its revolution.

Just as it freed accumulation from the restraint of the feudal order, the bourgeoisie was forced to subject it to the constraint of popular control exercised through universal suffrage. The combination of private property of the means of production with universal suffrage is a compromise, and this compromise implies that the logic of accumulation is not exclusively the logic of private actors.

What is involved in the current offensive of the right is not simply a question of taxes, government spending, or even the distribution of income. The plans for relaxing taxation of profits, abolishing environmental controls, eliminating welfare programs, removing government control over product safety and conditions of work, and weakening the labor unions add up to more than reorientation of the economic policy. They constitute a project for a new society, a bourgeois revolution.

It is thus necessary to consider the following question: what kind of a society would it be in which accumulation would be free from any form of political control, free from constraints of income distribution, from considerations of employment, environment, health of workers, and safety of consumers? Such hypothetical questions have no ready-made answers, but let us speculate.

It would be a society composed of households and firms, related to each other exclusively through the market. Social relations would become coextensive with market relations and the role of the political authority would be reduced to defending the market from attempts by any group organized as nonmarket actors (i.e., other than households and firms) to alter the rationality of market allocations. Since social and political relations would be depoliticized, demands by nonmarket actors would find no audience. The tension between accumulation and legitimation would be overcome: accumulation would be self-legitimizing for those who benefit from it and no other legitimacy would be sought. As it has been said, "the government does not owe anybody anything."

Household income would depend solely upon the market value of the labor performed. Reproduction of the labor force would be reprivatized and the traditional division of labor within the household—between earners and nurturers—would be restored. Persons excluded from participation in gainful activities would have no institutional guarantee of survival. They might be isolated on "reservations," whether inner cities or depressed regions, where they could be forgotten or ignored.

Workers would be disorganized as a class. If wage bargaining is decentralized by law to the level of the firm (as it is now in Chile) and if the process of internationalization of production continues, the monopoly power of unions would be effectively broken. Workers would be controlled by a combination of decentralized co-optation by some firms, by repression oriented against monopoly power, and—most importantly—by the threat of unemployment.

All of these changes would represent a reversal of trends that we are accustomed to see as irreversible. Indeed, the picture we drew can be easily obtained by combining the trends of contemporary capitalism described by, say, E. H. Carr or Jürgen Habermas, and reversing them.[14] Economic relations would be depoliticized. Government economic planning would be abandoned. Legitimation would be left to the market. The "economic whip" would be reinstated as the central mechanism of political control.

Is such a society feasible? The Chilean experience demonstrates that it is feasible when accompanied by brutal repression, the destruction of democratic institutions, the liquidation of all forms of politics. At least in Chile—most observers agree—such a restructuring of the society could not have succeeded under democratic conditions, without the military dictatorship. But is it feasible without destroying formal democracy, without a "Chileanization" of capitalist democracies?

Where electoral participation has traditionally been high, where working-class parties enjoy electoral support, and where access to the electoral system is relatively open—in most Western European countries—the project of the right seems doomed to failure under democratic conditions. But in the United States, where about 40 percent of adults never vote, where parties of notables have a duopolistic control over the electoral system, and where the barriers to entry are prohibitive, one must be less sanguine about the prospects. For suppose that the project is economically successful, even if for purely fortuitous reasons, and beneficial for a sizeable part of the electorate, that the right captures both parties, and the offensive enjoys the support of the mass media. . . . Such a prospect is not totally farfetched.

Notes

1. John Maynard Keynes, *The General Theory of Employment, Interest, and Money* (New York: Harcourt, Brace, Jovanovich, 1964), p. 378.

2. In fact, the question whether the Swedish policies were an application of the ideas of Keynes or were developed autonomously, from Marx via Wicksell, continues to evoke controversy. See Bo Gustafsson, "A Perennial of Doctrinal History: Keynes and the 'Stockholm School,' " *Economy and History* 17 (1973): 114–128.

3. In theory there is another Keynesian instrument: increasing investment expenditures—and thus aggregate demand—by lowering interest rates. But the effect of nominal interest rates upon the level of investment proved empirically to be the weakest link of the Keynesian approach, a conclusion reached by Tinbergen in 1939. Therefore monetary policy was used in practice mainly to accommodate fiscal policy, that is, to prevent government deficits from driving up interest rates or to control inflation, but not to stimulate demand, at least not intentionally.

4. Bertil Ohlin, "Economic Progress in Sweden," *The Annals of the American Academy of Political and Social Science* 197 (1938): 5.

5. This theory of investment was first suggested by J. Maurice Clark, "Business Acceleration and the Law of Demand: A Technical Factor in Economic Cycles," *Journal of Political Economy* 25 (1917): 217–235. Its modern form is due to Hollis Chenery, "Overcapacity and the Acceleration Principle," *Econometrica* 20 (1952): 1–28.

6. See, for example, V. Perlo, "The New Propaganda on Declining Profit Shares and Inadequate Investment," *Review of Radical Economics*, Fall 1976; Paul Sweezy and Harry Magdoff, "Are Low Savings Ruining the U.S. Economy?" *Monthly Review* 7 (1980): 1–12, or, most recently, Emma Rothschild, "The Philosophy of Reaganism," *New York Review of Books*, April 15, 1982, pp. 19–26.

7. For a recent study, see John Kendrick, "Sources of Growth in Real Product and Productivity in Eight Countries, 1960–1978" (paper prepared for the Office of Economic Research, the New York Stock Exchange, New York, 1981).

8. Gösta Rehn, "The Problem of Stability: An Analysis and Some Policy Proposals," in Ralph Turvey, ed., *Wages Policy Under Full Employment* (London: William Hodge and Company, 1952).

9. Formally, $\Delta K/K = sP/K$, where K is the capital stock and ΔK its change, s is the rate of saving out of profit, P is the volume of profits, and P/K is the rate of profit.

10. "U.S. Economic Performance in a Global Perspective" (New York: New York Stock Exchange, 1981).

11. As Andrew Shonfield put it, referring to Germany, "To make the trick work, tax rates had

to be high. They were." *Modern Capitalism* (London: Oxford University Press, 1969), p. 282. And so were tax credits for investments: see Appendix IV.

12. For discussions of the problems encountered by the Swedish Social Democrats in the most ambitious attempt to date in a capitalist economy to shape the supply of both labor and privately owned capital through government policies, see Göran Ohlin, "The Changing Role of Private Enterprise in Sweden," in Karl Cerny, ed., *Scandinavia at the Polls* (Washington, D.C.: American Enterprise Institute, 1977), pp. 249–265; Robert Heilbroner, "Swedish Promise," *New York Review of Books* (December 4, 1980), pp. 33–36.

13. Günter Köpke, *Keynes Plus: A Participatory Economy* (Brussels: European Trade Union Institute, 1979), p. iv.

14. Edward H. Carr, *The New Society* (London: Oxford University Press, 1961); Jürgen Habermas, *Legitimation Crisis* (Boston: Beacon Press, 1975).

3.8

Competitive Party Democracy and the Keynesian Welfare State: Factors of Stability and Disorganization

CLAUS OFFE

Both Karl Marx and various proponents of classical liberalism argued (albeit for sharply different reasons) that capitalism and full representative democracy (understood as universal and equal suffrage) were incompatible. In the twentieth century, again on radically different grounds, both Lenin and various proponents of pluralist-elitist theory have argued for a necessary linkage between representative democracy and capitalist market society. Claus Offe pursues a question about representative democracy and capitalism not fully recognized by any of these contending traditions, viz. "which institutions and mechanisms regulate the extent to which the two can become incongruent in a given society, and what are the limits of such potential incongruity—limits, that is, which would constrain the range of potential variance of class power and democratically constituted political authority?"

Offe argues that the recent congruence of capitalism and representative democracy is due to the emergence of two central mediating principles—competitive mass party politics and the Keynesian welfare state (KWS)—but that there are reasons to believe that both of these principles and the organizations to which they gave rise are currently subject to substantial, perhaps irremediable strain. In Offe's analysis, the emergence of competitive mass party systems mitigates class conflict (and thus contributes to congruence) in three ways: (1) the requirements of electoral competition force working-class parties to deradicalize their ideology and to develop centralized bureaucratic organizational structures, staffed by professionals, with preoccupations often divergent from the membership base; (2) sustained orientation to the external political market devalorizes internal party debate, and hastens the deactivation of party members; (3) electoral competition encourages parties to pursue "product diversification" strategies of electoral appeal, but such "catch-all" strategies serve to undermine the collective identity of party members. Modern parties thus cease to be vehicles of class antagonistic programs. The KWS contributes to the democratic-capitalist congruence by establishing the basis for a viable compact or "accord" between workers and capitalists premised on demand maintenance, economic growth, and select programs of redistribution of the "tax dividend" of economic expansion.

Both mediating principles find themselves under sharp challenge, however. The reconciling potential of party politics is challenged by: (1) new social movements raising non-negotiable demands whose realization is seen by participants to be constitutive of moral and group identity, and thus not subject to compromise, accommodation (or, in claims to "autonomy," the further intrusions of state power); (2) the proliferation of corporatist modes of function-based interest representation; (3) the ever present attractions of authoritarianism. The KWS, on the other hand, has produced nearly limitless undesirable side-effects, while failing to address the supply-side problems of production/exploitation that have marked advanced industrial states since the middle 1970s. Pressures thus mount for the "disorganization" of capitalist democracy.

I. Introduction

Ⅰf we compare 19th century liberal political theory on the one side and classical Marxism on the other, we see that there is one major point of agreement of the two. Both Marx and his liberal contemporaries, such as J. S. Mill or de Tocqueville, are convinced that, in their contemporary societies, capitalism and full democracy (based on equal and universal suffrage) do not mix. Obviously, this analytical convergence was arrived at from diametrically opposed points of view: the classical liberal writers believed that freedom and liberty were the most valuable accomplishments of societal development which deserved to be protected, under all circumstances, from the egalitarian threats of mass society and democratic mass politics, which, in their view, would lead, by necessity, to tyranny and "class legislation" by the propertyless as well as uneducated majority.[1] Marx, on the other side, analyzed the French democratic constitution of 1848 as a political form that would exacerbate societal contradictions by withdrawing political guarantees from the holder of social power while giving political power to subordinate classes; consequently, he argued, democratic conditions could bring the proletarian class to victory and put into question the foundations of bourgeois society.[2]

From the 20th century experience of capitalist societies, there is a lot of evidence against this 19th century hypothesis concerning the incompatibility of mass democracy (defined as universal and equal suffrage plus parliamentary or presidential form of government) and bourgeois freedom (defined as production based on private property and "free" wage labor). The coexistence of the two is known as *liberal democracy*. To be sure, the emergence of fascist regimes in some of the core capitalist countries testifies to the continued existence of tensions and contradictions that prevail between the two models of economic organization and political organization, and to the possibility of the outbreak of such tensions under the impact of economic crises. But it is also true that most advanced capitalist countries have also been liberal democratic states throughout most of the 20th century and that "all major advanced bourgeois states are today democracies."[3] In view of this evidence and experience, ours is in some way a *problematique* that is the reverse of what the classical writers of both liberalism and Marxism concerned themselves with. While they *prognosticized* the incompatibility, we have to *explain* the *coexistence* of the two partial principles of societal organization. More precisely, we want to know (a) which institutional arrangements and mechanisms can be held responsible for the pattern of coexistence that proved to be solid beyond all 19th century expectations and (b) what, if any, the limits of such arrangements are. These limits, or failures of the working of mediating mechanisms, would be defined analytically as those points at which either capitalist societies turn non-democratic or democratic regimes turn non-capitalist. It is these two questions with which I will be concerned in this article. To put it schematically, the course of the argument starts from the problem of how we *explain* the compatibility[4] of the structural components of "mass polity" and "market economy," and then goes on to focus, on the level of each of these two structures, on the factors *contributing to* as well as

those putting into question such compatibility. This is done in the sequence of boxes (1)
(4) of the following schema:

	Factors maintaining stability	Factors paralyzing stability
Mode of democratic mass participation	(1)	(2)
Mode of economic steering (KWS)	(3)	(4)

To pose this question at all is to presuppose, in accordance with both Marx and Mill,
that there *is* some real tension between the two respective organizing principles of social
power and political power, market society and political democracy, a tension that must be
(and possibly cannot indefinitely be) bridged, mediated and stabilized. This is by no
means an undisputed assumption. For instance, Lenin and the Leninist tradition deny
that there is such tension. They assume, instead, that there is a prestabilized harmony of
the rule of capital and bourgeois democratic forms, the latter mainly serving as a means of
deception of the masses. Consequently, it does not make sense whatsoever to ask the
question of what makes democracy compatible with capitalism and what the limits of
such compatibility might be, because democracy is simply seen to be the most effective
and reliable arrangement of capitalist class dominance. "What is central to Lenin's
position is the claim that the very organizational form of the parliamentary democratic
state is essentially inimical to the interests of the working class," as one recent commenta-
tor has succinctly stated.[5] Plausible and convincing as this view can be taken to be if based
on the constitutional practise of Russia between 1905 and 1917, its generalization to the
present would have, among other and still worse political consequences, the effect of
grossly distorting and obscuring the very problematique which we want to discuss.[6]

The reciprocal distortion is the one promulgated by some ideologists of pluralist-
elitist democratic theory. They claim (or, more precisely, they used to claim in the fifties
and early sixties) that the tension between the principles governing capitalist market
society and political democratic forms had finally been eliminated in the American
political system. According to this doctrine, the class struggle on the level of bourgeois
society has been replaced by what Lipset calls "the democratic class struggle" which is
seen to make all social arrangements, including the mode of production and the
distribution of economic resources, contingent upon the outcomes of democratic mass
politics. The underlying logic of this analysis can be summarized in an argument like this:
"If people actually wanted things to be different, they simply would elect someone other
into office. The fact that they don't, consequently, is proof that people are satisfied with
the socio-political order as it exists." Hence, we get something like the inverse of the
Leninist doctrine: democracy is not tied to capitalism, but capitalism to democracy. Both
of these perspectives deny major tensions or incompatibilities between mass democracy
and the market economy.

Thus, both the Leninist and the pluralist-elitist conceptions of democracy are
missing the point that interests us here. The one dogmatically postulates total *dependence*
of democratic forms and procedures upon class power, while the other equally dogmatically postulates total *independence* of class and democratically constituted political power.
The question that is at the same time more modest and more promising in leading to
insights of both intellectual and practical significance is, however, this: which institutions

and mechanisms regulate the *extent* to which the two can become incongruent in a given society, and what are the *limits* of such potential incongruity—limits, that is, which would constrain the range of potential variance of class power and democratically constituted political authority?

Marketization of Politics and Politicization of the Private Economy   In what follows, I will argue that the continued compatibility of capitalism and democracy that was so inconceivable to both classical liberalism and classical Marxism (including Kautsky and the Second International) has historically emerged due to the appearance and gradual developments of two mediating principles, (a) political mass parties and party competition and (b) the Keynesian welfare state (KWS). In other words, it is a *specific version* of democracy, political equality and mass participation that is compatible with the capitalist market economy. And, correspondingly, it is a *specific type* of capitalism that is able to coexist with democracy. What interests us here are those specificities of the political and economic structures, the way in which their mutual "fit" is to be explained by the functions each of them performs, and furthermore the strains and tensions that affect those conditions of "fit."

Historically, each of those two structural components of "democratic capitalism" has largely taken shape in Europe either during or in the aftermath of the two World Wars; democracy through party competition after World War I and the Keynesian welfare state after World War II. Each of these two principles follows a pattern of "mixing" the logic of authority and the logic of the market, of "voice" and "exit" in Hirschman's terminology. This is quite obvious in the case of the Keynesian welfare state for which the term "mixed economy" is often used as a synonym. But it is no less true for the political sphere of capitalist society which could well be described as a "mixed polity" and the dynamics of which are often, and to a certain extent appropriately, described as the "oligopolistic competition" of political elites or political "entrepreneurs" providing public "goods."[7] The logic of capitalist democracy is one of mutual contamination: authority is infused into the economy by global demand management, transfers and regulations so that it loses more and more of its spontaneous and self-regulatory character; and market contingency is introduced into the state, thus compromising any notion of absolute authority or the absolute good. Neither the Smithean conception of the market nor the Rousseauan conception of politics have much of a counterpart in social reality. Thus, one of the ways in which compatibility is accomplished appears to be the infusion of some of the logic of one realm into the other, i.e., the notion of "competition" into politics and the idea of "authoritative allocation of values" into the economy.

Let us now consider each of the two links, or mediating mechanisms, between state and civil society in turn. Following the problematique developed before, we will ask two questions in each case. First, in what way and by virtue of which structural characteristics do political parties and the Keynesian welfare state *contribute to the compatibility of* capitalism and democratic mass politics. Second, which observable trends and changes occur within the institutional framework of both the "mixed economy" and the "mixed polity" that *threaten the viability* of the coexistence of capitalism and democracy?

II. Stabilization through Competitive Party Democracy

The widespread fear of the German bourgeoisie during the first decade of this century was that once the full and equal franchise was introduced together with parliamentary government, the class power of the working class would, due to the numerical strength of this class, directly translate into a revolutionary transformation of the state. It was the same analysis, of course, that inspired the hopes and the political strategies of the leaders of the Second International. Max Weber had nothing but sarcastic contempt for both these neurotic anxieties and naïve hopes. He was (together with Rosa Luxemburg and Robert Michels who conducted the same analysis with their own specific accents) among the first social theorists who understood (and welcomed) the fact that the transformation of class politics into competitive party politics implies not only a change of form, but a decisive change of content. In 1917, he stated that "amongst us, organizations like the trade unions, but also like the social democratic party, are a very important counterweight against the typically real and irrational power of street mobs in purely plebiscitary nations."[8] He expected that the bureaucratized political party together with the charismatic and demogogic political leader at its top would form a reliable bulwark to contain what he described as "blind mass rage" or "syndicalist insurrectionary tendencies."

Rosa Luxemburg's account of the dynamic of political mass organization differs only in its inverse evaluative perspective, not its analytical content. In 1906, she observed the tendency of working class organizations (i.e., unions and the party) to follow specialized strategies according to a tacit division of labor and of the organizations' leadership to dominate rather than serve the masses of the constituency. The tendency of the organizations' bureaucratic staff consists, according to Luxemburg, in a "great trend of rendering itself independent," "of specializing their methods of struggle and professional activity," "of overestimating the organization which becomes transformed into an end in itself and the highest good," "a need for rest," "a loss of general view of the overall situation," while at the same time "the mass of comrades are being degraded into a mass which is incapable of forming a judgment."[9] Biographically, politically and intellectually, Robert Michels absorbs and integrates the ideas of both Luxemburg and Weber by formulating, in 1911, his famous "iron law of oligarchy" in which the observation of empirical tendencies of organizations is transformed in the proclamation of an inexorable historical necessity.[10]

It is probably not too much to say that the 20th century theory of political organization has been formed on the basis of the experience and the theoretical interpretation of these three authors who, interestingly enough, arrived at widely divergent political positions at the end of their lives: Luxemburg died in 1919 as a revolutionary democratic socialist and victim of police murder, Weber in 1920 as a "liberal in despair," and Michels in 1936 as an ardent admirer and ideological defender of Mussolini and Italian fascism. In spite of the extreme diversity of their political views and positions, there is a strong common element in their analysis. This element can be summarized in the following way: as soon as political mass participation is organized through large scale bureaucratic organization (a type of organization, that is, which is presupposed and required by the model of electoral party competition and institutionalized collective bargaining), the very dynamic of this organizational form contains, perverts, and obstructs class interest and class politics in ways that are described as leading to opportunism (Luxemburg), oligarchy (Michels) and the inescapable plebiscitarian submission of the masses to the irrational impulses of the charismatic leader and his demagogic use of the bureaucratic party "machine" (Weber).

According to the common insight underlying this analysis, as soon as the will of the people is expressed through the instrumentality of the competitive party striving for government office, what *is* expressed *ceases* to be the will of the people and is instead transformed into an artifact of the form itself and the dynamics put into motion by the imperatives of political competition.

More specifically, these dynamics have three major effects. First, the deradicalization of the ideology of the party: to be successful in elections and in its striving for government office, the party must orient its programmatic stance towards the expediencies of the political market.[11] This means two things: first, to maximize votes by appealing to the greatest possible number of voters and consequently to minimize those programmatic elements that could create antagonistic cleavages within the electorate. Second, vis-à-vis other parties, to be prepared to enter coalitions and to restrict the range of substantive policy proposals to those demands which can be expected to be negotiable to potential coalition partners. The combined effect of these two considerations is to dissolve any coherent political concept or aim into a "gradualist" temporal structure or sequence, giving priority to what can be implemented at any given point in time and with the presently available resources, while postponing and displacing presently unrealistic and pragmatically unfeasible demands and projects. Also, the fully developed competitive party is forced by the imperatives of competition to equip itself with a highly bureaucratized and centralized organizational structure. The objective of this organization is to be present continuously on the political market, just as the success of a business firm depends in part upon the size and continued presence of its marketing and sales organization. The bureaucratic organization of the modern political party performs the tasks of (a) collecting material and human resources (membership dues, other contributions and donations, members, candidates), (b) disseminating propaganda and information concerning the party's position on a great number of diverse political issues and (c) exploring the political market, identifying new issues and monitoring public opinion and (d) managing internal conflict. All of these activities are normally executed by a professional staff of party officials who develop a corporate interest in the growth and stability of the apparatus that provides them with status and careers. This pattern of internal bureaucratization that can be found in parties of the right and the left alike, has two important traits. First, the social composition (as measured by class background, formal education, sex, occupation, age, etc.) of the party leadership, its officials, members of parliament, and government becomes more and more at variance both with the social composition of the population in general and the party's electoral base in particular. And second, the professionalization of party politics leads to the political dominance of professional and managerial party personnel who typically come, by their training and professional experience, from such backgrounds as business administration, public administration, education, the media, or interest organizations.

A second major consequence of this bureaucratic-professional pattern of political organization is the deactivation of ordinary members. The more the organization is geared toward the exploration of and adaptation to the external *environment* of the political market in what can be described as a virtually permanent electoral campaign, the less room remains for the determination of party policies by *internal* processes of democratic debate and conflict within the organization. The appearance of internal unanimity and consensus is what any competitive party must try to cultivate in order to become or remain attractive to voters, as a consequence of which internal division, factionalism and organized conflict to opinion and strategy are not only not encouraged, but rather kept under tight control or at least kept out of sight of the public in a constant effort to streamline the party's image and, as it were, to standardize its product. (It is tempting to compare, in this respect, the *practise* of some social democratic parties to the *theory* of the Leninist party, and I suspect we would find some ironic similarities.) The highly unequal importance of external and internal environments frequently becomes evident when the results of public opinion surveys, which today are routinely commissioned by the party leadership, suggest positions and strategies which are in conflict with declared intentions of party members who then, in the interest of "winning the next elections," are called upon to yield to political "reality."

The third characteristic of what Kirchheimer has called the modern "catch-all-party" is the increasing structural and cultural heterogeneity of its supporters. This heterogeneity results from the fact that the modern political party relies on the principle of "product diversification" in the sense that it tries to appeal to a multitude of diverse demands and concerns. This is most obvious in the case of social democratic and communist parties who have often successfully tried to expand their base beyond the working class and to attract elements of the old and new middle classes, the intelligentsia and voters with strong religious affiliations. The advantage of this strategy is quite obvious, but so is its effect of dissolving a sense of collective identity which, in the early states of both socialist and Catholic parties, was based on a cultural milieu of shared values and meaning.

It is easy to see why and how the three consequences of the organizational form of the competitive political party that I have discussed so far—ideological deradicalization, deactivation of members, erosion of collective identity—contribute to the compatibility of capitalism and democracy. Each of these three outcomes helps to contain and limit the range of political aims and struggles, and thus provides a virtual guarantee that the structure of political power will not deviate so far from the structure of socio-economic power as to make the two distributions of power incompatible with each other. "The party system has been the means of reconciling universal equal franchise with the maintenance of an unequal society," McPherson has remarked.[12] The inherent dynamic of the party as an organizational form which develops under and for political competition generates those constraints and imposes those "non-decisions" upon the political process which together make democracy safe for capitalism. Such "non-decisions" affect both the *content* of politics (i.e., what kinds of issues, claims, and demands are allowed to be put on the agenda) as well as the *means* by which political conflicts are carried out. The constraints imposed upon the possible content of politics are all the more effective since they are non-explicit, i.e., not based on formal mechanisms of exclusion (such as limitations of voting rights, or authoritarian bans on certain actors or issues), but rather constituted as artifacts and by-products of the organizational forms of universal political inclusion. This conclusion, of course, is strongly supported by the fact that no competitive party system so far has ever resulted in a distribution of political power that would have been able to alter the logic of capital and the pattern of socio-economic power *it* generates.

To avoid misunderstanding, I should emphasize that what I intend here is not a *normative* critique of the organizational form of the political party which would lead to the suggestion of an alternative form of political organization. Rather than speculating about the comparative desirability of anarchist, syndicalist, council-democratic, or Leninist models of either non-party or non-competitive party organization, let us now look at the future viability of this organizational form itself—its potential to construct and mediate, as it did in the post-war era, a type of political authority that does not interfere with the institutional premises of the capitalist economy. The question is, in other words, whether the institutional link that in most advanced capitalist countries has allowed capitalism and political democracy to coexist for most of the last 60 years is likely to continue to do so in the future. How solid and viable are the organizational forms that bring the "iron law" to bear upon the process of politics?

One way to answer this question in the negative would be to expect political parties to emerge which would be capable of abolishing the above-mentioned restrictions and constraints, thus leading to a challenge of class power through politically constituted power. I do not think that there are, in spite of Eurocommunist doctrines and strategies that have emerged in the Latin–European countries in the mid-seventies, and in spite of the recently elected socialist/communist government in France, many promising indicators of such a development. The other possibility would be a *disintegration of the political party as the dominant form of democratic mass participation* and its gradual replacement by other forms which possibly are less likely than party competition to lead to "congruent" uses of state power. As we are concerned with the prospects of competitive party democracy in the eighties, it might be worthwhile to explore this possibility a little further.

Causes of the Decline of the Party System as the Dominant Form of Mass Participation   It is well possible today to argue that the form of mass participation in politics that is channeled through the party system (i.e., according to the principles of territorial representation, party competition and parliamentary representation) has exhausted much of its usefulness for reconciling capitalism and mass politics. This appears to be so because the political form of the party is increasingly bypassed and displaced by other practices and procedures of political participation and representation. It is highly doubtful, however, whether those new and additional practices that can be observed in operation in quite a number of capitalist states will exhibit the same potential of reconciling political legitimation with the imperatives of capital accumulation that has been, at least for a certain period, the accomplishment of the competitive party system. Again, three points—referring in a highly schematic fashion to new social movements, corporatism and repression as phenomena—tend to bypass, restrict, and subvert the party system and its political practices and their reconciling potential.

First, in many capitalist countries, the new social movements which have emerged during the seventies are, for a number of reasons, very hard to absorb into the practices of competitive party politics. Such movements include ethnic and regionalist movements, various urban movements, ecological movements, feminist movements, peace movements, and youth movements. To a large extent, all of them share two characteristics. First, their projects and demands are based not on a collective contractual position on either goods or labor markets, as was the case, for instance, with traditional class parties and movements. Instead, their common denominator of organization and action is some sense of collective identity (often underlined by ascriptive and "naturalistic" conceptions of the collective "self" in terms of age, gender, "nation" or "mankind"). Closely connected with this is a second characteristic: they do not demand representation (by which their market status could be improved or protected) but, autonomy. In short, the underlying logic of these movements is the struggle for the defense of a physical and/or moral "territory," the integrity of which is fundamentally non-negotiable to the activists of these movements. For the purpose of this defense, political representation and parliamentary politics are often considered unnecessary (because what is requested of the state, as can be illustrated in the issues of abortion or nuclear energy, is not to "do something" but to "stay out"), or even dangerous, because the state is suspected of attempting to demobilize and disorganize the movement. To the extent such movements attract the attention and the political energies of people, not only individual political parties, but the traditional competitive party system as a whole will lose in function and credibility because it simply does not provide the arena within which such issues and concerns can possibly be processed. These "new social movements" are not concerned with what is to be created or accomplished through the use of politics and state power, but what should be saved from and defended against the state, and the considerations governing the conduct of public policy. The three most obvious cases of such movements, the peace movement, the environmental movement and various movements centered on human rights (e.g., of women, of prisoners, of minorities, of tenants) all illustrate a "negative" conception of politics trying to protect a sphere of life against the intervention of state (or state-sanctioned) policy. What dominates the thought and action of these movements is not a "progressive" utopia of what desirable social arrangements must be achieved, but a conservative utopia of what non-negotiable essentials must not be threatened and sacrificed in the name of "progress."

Second, many obeservers in a number of capitalist states have analyzed an ongoing process of deparliamentarization of public policy and the concomitant displacement of territorial forms of representation through functional ones. This is most evident in "corporatist" arrangements which combine the function of interest representation of collective actors with policy implementation vis-à-vis their respective constituencies.[13] The functional superiority of such corporatist arrangements, compared to both parliamentary-competitive forms of representation and bureaucratic methods of implementation, resides in their informal, inconspicuous, and non-public procedures and the "voluntary" character of compliance that they are said to be able to mobilize. Although the dynamics and limits of corporatist forms of public policymaking, especially in the areas of economic and social policies, are not of interest to us here, what seems to be clear is that there has been a trend toward such arrangements, most of all in countries with strong social democratic parties (such as in Europe, Sweden, the UK, Austria, and Germany) which has worked at the expense of parliament and the competitive party system. A number of Marxist and non-Marxist political scientists have even argued that "parliamentary representation on the basis of residence no longer adequately reflects the problems of economic management in a worldwide capitalist system," and that "a system of functional representation is more suited to securing the conditions of accumulation."[14]

Third, a constant alternative to free party competition is political repression and the gradual transformation of democracy into some form of authoritarianism. In an analytical sense, what we mean by repression is exclusion from representation. Citizens are denied their civil liberties and freedoms, such as the right to organize, demonstrate, and express certain opinions in speech and writing. They are denied access to occupations in the public sector, and the like. The expansion of police apparatuses and the practice of virtually universal monitoring and surveillance of the activities of citizens that we observe in many countries are indications of the growing reliance of the state apparatus upon the means of preventive and corrective repression. More important, in our context of discussing the limits of competitive party democracy, is one other aspect of the exclusion from representation. It is the de facto and/or formal limitation of competitiveness within the party sytem: be it by strengthening of intra-party discipline and the sanctions applied against dissenters; be it in the election campaigns from which substantive alternatives concerning the conduct and programmatic content of public policy often seem to be absent; be it finally on the level of parliament and parliamentary government where the identity of individual (and only nominally "competing") parties more and more often disappears behind what occasionally is called the "great coalition of the enlightened," inspired by some vague "solidarity of all democratic forces." Referring back to the economic methaphor used before, such phenomena and developments could well be described as the "cartelization" of political supply and the closure of market access.

If I am correct in assuming that the displacement of the role and political function of the competitive party system, as indicated by the emergence of new social movements, increasing reliance on corporatist arrangements, and self-limitation of the competitiveness of party systems is a real process that could be illustrated by many examples in numerous advanced (and not so advanced) capitalist states; and if I am also correct in assuming that the organizational form of the competitive political party plays a crucial role in making democratic mass participation compatible with capitalism, then the decline of the party system is likely to lead to the rise of less constrained and regulated practices of political participation and conflict, the outcomes of which may then have the potential of effectively challenging and transcending the institutional premises of the capitalist form of social and economic organization.

I have so far focused only on those limits of the "reconciling functions" of the organizational forms of mass democracy which consist in the weakening and more or less gradual displacement of the dominant role of political parties as mediators between the people and state power. But the picture remains incomplete and unbalanced as long as we concentrate exclusively on cases in which the "channel" of political participation that consists of party competition, elections and parliamentary representation is bypassed (and reduced in its legitimacy and credibility) by the protest politics of social movements or corporatist negotiations among powerful strategic actors, or where this channel is altogether reduced in significance by "repressive" mechanisms of exclusion.

The other alternative, alluded to before, consists not in a process of displacement and loss of relevance of the organizational form of political parties, but in the successful strategy of "self-transcendence" of the party moving from "political" to "economic" democracy. All models and strategies of *economic* democratization (beginning in the midtwenties in Austria and Germany and continuing through the current Swedish concepts of wage earner funds and the Meidner plan[15]) rely on the notion that the tension between the democratic principle of equal mass participation and the economic principle of unequal and private decisionmaking power could be put to use by instituting, by the means of electoral success and parliamentary legislation, democratic bodies on the level of enterprises, sectors of industry, regions, cities, and so on. The central assumption that inspires such strategies is that "democracy would explode capitalism (and) that the democratic state, because it could be made to represent the people, would compel entrepreneurs to proceed according to principles inimical to their own survival . . . The working class, as the spokesmen for the great, non-capitalist majority, would enforce the primacy of politics throughout the economy, as well as in politics per se."[16]

Although this alternative course of suspending the compatibility of democracy and capitalism is part of the programmatic objectives of almost all social democratic/socialist (and, increasingly, communist) parties in Europe (and even of some forces in North America), it has nowhere been carried out to the point where the private character of decisions concerning the volume, kind, point in time and location of investment decisions would have effectively been transformed into a matter of democratic control. In the early eighties, the European Left seems rather to be divided as to the strategic alternatives of trying to overcome the constraints of political democracy and its oligarchic organizational dynamics, either by supporting those "new social movements" and engaging in their politics of autonomy and protest, or to stick to the older model of economic democratization. Both tendencies, however, provide sufficient reason to expect a weakening of these organizational and political characteristics which so far have made democratic mass participation safe for capitalism. The extent, however, to which it becomes likely that competitive party democracy is either displaced by social and political movements and corporatist arrangements or is complemented by "economic democracy" will probably depend on the stability, growth and prosperity the economy is able to provide. Let us, therefore, now turn to the question of the organization of production and distribution and the changes that have occurred since Andrew Shonfield's classic *Modern Capitalism* came out in 1965.[17]

III. The Keynesian Welfare State and Its Demise

Let me now try to apply the analogous argument, in an even more generalized and schematic fashion, to the second pillar upon which, according to my initial proposition, the coexistence of capitalism and democracy rests, namely the Keynesian welfare state (KWS). The bundle of state institutions and practices to which this concept refers has been developed in western capitalism since the Second World War. Until the decisive change of circumstances that occurred after the mid-seventies and that was marked by OPEC price policies, the end of *détente,* and the coming to power of Thatcher in the UK and Reagan in the US (to mention just a few indicators of this change), the KWS has been adopted as the basic conception of the state and state practice in almost all western countries, irrespective of parties in government, and with only minor modifications and time lags. Most observers agree that its effect has been (a) an unprecedented and extended economic boom favoring all advanced capitalist economies and (b) the transformation of the pattern of industrial and class conflict in ways that increasingly depart from political and even revolutionary radicalism and lead to more economistic, distribution-centered and increasingly institutionalized class conflict. Underlying this development (that constitutes a formidable change if compared to the dynamics of the capitalist world system during the twenties and thirties) is a politically instituted class compromise or "accord" that Bowles has described as follows:

> [The accord] represented, on the part of labor, the acceptance of the logic of profitability and market as the guiding principles of resource allocation, international exchange technological change, product development, and industrial location, in return for an assurance that minimal living standards, trade union rights, and liberal democratic rights would be protected, massive unemployment avoided, and real incomes would rise approximately in line with labor productivity, all through the intervention of the state, if necessary.[18]

It is easy to see why and how the existence of this compact has contributed to the compatibility of capitalism and democracy. First, by accepting the terms of the accord, working class organizations (unions and political parties) reduced their demands and projects to a program that sharply differs from anything on the agenda of both the Third and the Second Internationals. After the physical, moral and organizational devastations the Second World War had left behind, and after the discredit the development of the Soviet Union had earned for communism, this change of perspective is not entirely incomprehensible. Moreover, the accord itself worked amazingly well, thus reinforcing a deeply depoliticized trust in what one leading German Social Democrat much later came arrogantly to call the "German Model" (*Modell Deutschland*)[19]: the mutual stimulation of economic growth and peaceful class relations. What was at issue in class conflicts was no longer the mode of production, but the volume of distribution, not control but growth, and this type of conflict was particularly suited for being processed on the political plane through party competition, because it does not involve "either/or" questions, but questions of a "more or less" or "sooner or later" nature. Overarching this limited type of conflict, there was a consensus concerning basic priorities, desirabilities and values of the political economy, namely economic growth and social (as well as military) security. This interclass, growth–security alliance does in fact have a theoretical basis in Keynes' economic theory. As applied to practical purposes of economic policymaking, it teaches each class to "take the role of the other." The capitalist economy, this is the lesson to be learnt from Keynesianism, is a positive-sum game. Therefore, playing like one would in a zero-sum game is against one's own interest. That is to say, each class has to take the interests of the other class into consideration: the workers profitability, because only a sufficient level of profits and investment will secure future employment and income increases; and the capitalists wages and welfare state expenditures, because these will secure effective demand and a healthy, well-trained, and well-housed working class.

The welfare state is defined as a set of legal entitlements providing citizens with claims to transfer payments from compulsory social security schemes as well as to state organized services (such as health and education) for a wide variety of defined cases of need and contingencies. The means by which the welfare state intervenes are thus bureaucratic rules and legal regulations, monetary transfers and professional expertise of teachers, doctors, and social workers. Its ideological origins are highly mixed and heterogeneous, ranging from socialist to Catholic–conservative sources; its character of resulting from ideological, political and economic interclass compromises is something the welfare state shares with the logic of Keynesian economic policymaking. In both cases, there is no fast and easy answer to the zero-sum question of who wins and who loses. For, although the primary function of the welfare state is to cover those risks and uncertainties to which wage workers and their families are exposed in capitalist society, there are some indirect effects which serve the capitalist class, too.

This becomes evident if we look at what would be likely to happen in the absence of welfare state arrangements in a capitalist society. We would probably agree that the answer to this hypothetical question is this: first, there would be a much higher level of industrial conflict and a stronger tendency among the proletariat to avoid becoming wage workers. Thus, the welfare state can be said to partially dispel motives and reasons for social conflict and to make the existence of wage labor more acceptable by eliminating parts of the risk that result from the imposition of the commodity form upon labor.[20] Second, this conflict would be much more costly in economic terms by its disruption of the increasingly complex and capital-intensive process of industrial production. Therefore, the welfare state performs the crucial function of taking part of the needs of the working class out of the class struggle and industrial conflict arenas, of providing the means to fulfill their needs more collectively and hence more efficiently, of making production more regular and predictable by relieving it of important issues and conflicts, and of providing, in addition, a built-in stabilizer for the economy by partly uncoupling changes in effective demand from changes in employment. So, as in the case of Keynesian doctrines of economic policy, the welfare state, too, can be seen to provide a measure of mutuality of interest between classes that virtually leaves no room for fundamental issues and conflicts over the nature of the political economy.

The functional links between Keynesian economic policy, economic growth and the welfare state are fairly obvious and agreed upon by all "partners" and parties involved. An "active" economic policy stimulates and regularizes economic growth; the "tax dividend" resulting from that growth allows for the extension of welfare state programs; at the same time, continued economic growth limits the extent to which welfare state provisions (such as unemployment benefits) are actually claimed. And the issues and conflicts that remain to be resolved within the realm of formal politics (party competition and parliament) are of such a fragmented, non-polarizing, and non-fundamental nature (at least in the areas of economic and social policy) that they can be settled by the inconspicuous mechanisms of marginal adjustments, compromise and coalition-building.

If all of this were still true, today's ubiquitous critiques and political attacks directed at Keynesianism, the welfare state and, most of all, the combination of these two most successful political innovations of the post-war era, would be plainly incomprehensible. They are not. As in the case of competitive political parties, these innovations and their healthy effects seem to have reached their limits today. While the integrative functions of the party system have partly been displaced by alternative and less institutionalized forms of political participation, the Keynesian welfare state has come under attack by virtue of some of its less desirable side effects and its failure to correct some of the ills of an economic environment that has radically changed, compared to the conditions that prevailed prior to the mid-seventies. Let us look at some of the reasons why there are very few people remaining—be they in academia or politics, on the Left or the Right—who believe that the Keynesian welfare state continues to be a viable peace formula for democratic capitalism.

My thesis, in brief, is this: while the KWS is an excellent and uniquely effective device to manage and control some socioeconomic and political problems of advanced capitalist societies, it does not solve all those problems. And the problems that can be successfully solved through the institutional means of the welfare state no longer constitute the most dominant and pressing ones. Moreover, this shift of *the socioeconomic problematique is in part an unintended consequence of the operation of the KWS itself*. The two types of problems to which I refer are the production/exploitation problem and the effective demand/realization problem. Between the two, a trade-off exists: the more effectively one of the two is solved, the more dominant and pressing the other one becomes. The KWS has indeed been able to solve, to a remarkable extent, the problem of macroeconomic demand stabilization. But, at the same time, it has also interfered with the ability of the capitalist economy to adapt to the production/exploitation problem as it has emerged ever more urgently since the mid-seventies. The KWS, so to speak, has operated on the basis of the false theory that the problems it *is* able to deal with are the only problems of the capitalist political economy, or at least the permanently dominant ones. This erroneous confidence is now in the politically and economically, equally painful process of being falsified and corrected.

To the extent the demand problem is being solved, the supply problem becomes wide open. The economic situation has changed in a way that lends strong support to conservative and neo-laissez-faire economic theory. Far from stimulating production any longer, the governmental practice of deficit spending to combat unemployment contributes to even higher rates of unemployment, by driving up interest rates and making money capital scarce and costly. Also (and possibly even worse), the welfare state amounts to a partial disincentive to work. Its compulsory insurance schemes and legal entitlements provide such a strong institutional protection to the material interest of wage workers that labor becomes less prepared and/or can be less easily forced to adjust to the contingencies of structural, technological, locational, vocational and other changes of the economy. Not only wages are "sticky" and "downwardly inflexible," but, in addition, the provisions of the welfare state have partly "decommodified" the interests of workers, replacing "status" for "contract," or "citizen rights" for "property rights" This change of industrial relations that the KWS has brought about has not only helped to increase and stabilize effective demand (as it was intended to), but it also has made employment more costly and more rigid. Again, the central problem on the labor market is the supply problem, how to hire and fire the right people at the right place with the right skills and, most important, the right motivation and the right wage demand. Concerning this problem, the welfare state is justifiably seen by business not to be part of the solution but, part of the problem.

As capital (small as well as big) has come to depend and rely on the stimulating and regularizing effects of interventionist policies executed on both the demand and supply sides, and as labor depends and relies on the welfare state, the parameters of incentives, motivations, and expectations of investors and workers alike have been affected in ways that alter and undermine the dynamics of economic growth. For capital and labor alike, pressures to adjust to changing market forces have been reduced due to the availability of state-provided resources that either help to avoid or delay adaptation or due to the expectation that a large part of the costs of adaptation must be subsidized by the state. Growth industries such as defense, civilian aircraft, nuclear energy, and telecommunications typically depend as much on markets created by the state (and often capital provided by the state) as stagnant industries (such as steel, textiles, and increasingly, electronics) depend on state protection and subsidized market shelters. Economic growth, where it occurs at all, has become a matter of political design rather than a matter of spontaneous market forces.

The increasing claims that are made on the state budget both by labor and capital, and both by the growing and the stagnant sectors of the economy, cannot but lead to unprecedented levels of public debt and to constant efforts of governments to terminate or reduce welfare state programs. But economic growth does not only become more costly in terms of budgetary inputs that are required to promote it, it also becomes more costly in terms of political legitimation. The more economic growth becomes "growth by political design," and the more it is perceived to be the result of explicit political decisions and strategies of an increasingly "disaggregated" nature (i.e., specified by product, industry, and location), the more governments and political parties are held accountable for the physical quality of products, processes and environmental effects resulting from such industrial policies. The widespread and apparently increasing concern with the physical quality of products and production, and the various "anti-productivist" and environmental political motives and demands that are spreading in many capitalist countries have so far mostly been interpreted in the social science literature either in objectivist terms ("environmental disruption") or in subjectivist categories ("changing values and sensitivities"). In addition, I suggest, these phenomena must be analyzed in terms of the apparent political manageability of the physical shape and impact of industrial production and growth, a perceived area of political decision—and non-decision—making that gives rise to a new arena of "politics of production." The outcomes of the conflicts in this arena, in turn, tend to cause additional impediments to industrial growth.

The strategic intention of Keynesian economic policy is to promote growth and full employment, the strategic intention of the welfare state to protect those affected by the risks and contingencies of industrial society and to create a measure of social equality. The latter strategy becomes feasible only to the extent the first is successful, thus providing the resources necessary for welfare policies and limiting the extent to which claims are made on these resources.

The combined effect of the two strategies, however, has been high rates of unemployment *and* inflation. At least, economic and social policies have not been able to check the simultaneous occurrence of unemployment and inflation. But one can safely say more than that. Plausible causal links between the KWS and today's condition of "the worst of both worlds" are suggested not only by conservative economic policy ideologues advocating a return to some type of monetarist steering of a pure market economy. They are equally, if reluctantly, accepted by the practice and partly by the theories of the Left. The relevant arguments are:

(1) The Keynesian welfare state is a victim of its success. By (partly) eliminating and smoothing crises, it has inhibited the positive function that crises used to perform in the capitalist process of "creative destruction."

(2) The Keynesian welfare state involves the unintended but undeniable consequence of undermining both the incentives to invest and the incentives to work.

(3) There is no equilibrating mechanism or "stop-rule" that would allow us to adjust the extension of social policy so as to eliminate its self-contradictory consequences; the logic of democratic party competition and the social democratic alliance with unions remains undisciplined by "economic reason."

While the latter argument is probably still exclusively to be found in the writings of liberal-conservative authors,[21] the other two can hardly be contested by the Left. Let me quote just one example of an author who clearly thinks of himself as a social democratic theoretician:

> It is unfortunate that those who wish to defend the welfare state . . . spend their energies persuading the public that the welfare state does not erode incentives, savings, authority or efficiency . . . What the Right has recognized much better than the Left is that the principles of the welfare state are directly incompatible with a capitalistic market system . . . The welfare state eats the very hand that feeds it. The main contradiction of the welfare state is the . . . tension between the market and social policy.[22]

It must not concern us here whether such blames and charges that today are ever more frequently directed against the KWS are entirely "true," or, in addition, partly the result of paranoid exaggerations or a conscious tactical misrepresentation of reality on the part of capital and its political organizations. For what applies in this context is a special version of a law known to sociologists as the "Thomas theorem": what is real in the minds and perceptions of people will be real in its consequences. The structural power position of the owners and managers and associational representatives of capital in a capitalist society is exactly their power to define reality in a highly consequential way, so that what is perceived as "real" by them is likely to have very real impacts for other classes and political actors.

Without entering too far into the professional realm of the economist, let me suggest two aspects of a potentially useful (if partial) interpretation of this change. One is the idea that the Keynesian welfare state is a "victim of its success," as one author has put it[23]: the side-effects of its successful practice of solving one type of macro-economic problem have led to the emergence of an entirely different problematique which is beyond the steering capacity of the KWS. The familiar arguments that favor and demand a shift of economic and social policymaking toward what has been named "supply-side economics" are these: the nonproductive public sector has become an intolerable burden upon the private sector, leading to a chronic shortage of investment capital; the work ethic is in the process of being undermined, and the independent middle class is being economically suffocated by high rates of taxation and inflation.

The other set of arguments maintains that, even in the absence of those economic side effects, the political paradigm of the KWS presently is in the process of definitive exhaustion due to inherent causes. The relevant arguments, in brief, are two. First, state intervention works only as long as it is not expected by economic actors to be applied as a matter of routine, and therefore does not enter their rational calculations. As soon as this happens, however, investors will postpone investment because they can be reasonably sure that the state, if only they wait long enough, will intervene by special tax exemptions, depreciation allowances or demand measures. The spread of such ("rational") expectations is fatal to Keynesianism, for to the extent it enters the calculations of economic actors, their strategic behavior will increase the problem load to which the state has to respond or at least will not contribute, in the way it had been naïvely anticipated, to resolving the unemployment (and state budget) problem. This pathology of expectations, of course, is itself known to (and expected by) actors in the state apparatus. It forces them to react either by ever higher doses of intervention or, failing that possibility for fiscal reasons, to give up the interventionist practice that breeds those very problems that it was supposed to solve. This would lead us to conclude that state intervention is effective only to the extent it occurs as a "surprise" and exception, rather than as a matter of routine.

A further inherent weakness of the KWS resides in the limits of the legal-bureaucratic, monetarized and professional mode of intervention. These limits become particularly clear in the areas of personal services, or "people-processing organizations," such as schools, hospitals, universities, prisons and social work agencies. Again, the mode of intervention generates the problems it is supposed to deal with. The explanation of this paradox is well-known: the clients' capacity for self-help—and, more generally, the system of knowledge and meaning generating such capacity—are subverted by the mode of intervention, and the suppliers of such services, especially professionals and higher level bureaucrats (who are in neo-conservative circles referred to as the "new class"), take a material interest in the persistence (rather than the solution) and in the continuous expansion and redefinition of the problems with which they are supposed to deal.[24]

Thus, for reasons that have to do both with its external economic effects and the paradoxes of its internal model of operations, the KWS seems to have exhausted its potential and viability to a large extent. Moreover, this exhaustion is unlikely to turn out to be a conjunctural phenomenon that disappears with the next boom of economic growth. For this boom itself is far from certain. Why is this so? First, because it cannot be expected to occur as the spontaneous result of market forces and the dynamics of technological innovation. Second, it apparently cannot be generated and manipulated either by the traditional tools of Keynesianism nor by its "monetarist" counterpart. Third, even to the extent it does occur either as an effect of spontaneous forces or state intervention, the question is whether it will be considered desirable and worthwhile in terms of the side-effects it inevitably will have for the "quality of life" in general and the ecology in particular. This question of the desirability of continued economic growth is also accentuated by what Fred Hirsch has called the "social limits to growth" by which he means the decreasing desirability and "satisficing potential" of industrial output, the use-value of which declines in proportion to the number of people who consume it.

IV. Conclusion

We have seen that the two institutional mechanisms on which the compatibility of the private economy and political mass participation rests—namely the mechanism of competitive party democracy and the paradigm of the Keynesian welfare state—have come under stress and strain, the order of magnitude of which is unprecedented in the post-war era. Limitations of space do not allow me to explore in any detail the interactive and possibly mutually reinforcing dynamics that take place between the two structural developments that I have sketched here.

One plausible hypothesis is that, as the political economy turns from a growth economy into a "zero-sum society,"[25] the institutional arrangements of conflict resolution will suffer from strains and tensions. These tensions are probably best described, using the conceptual paradigm of "organized capitalism" as a referent,[26] as threats of *disorganization*. Such threats are likely to occur on two levels: (a) on the level of interorganizational "rules of the game" and (b) on the level of the organization of collective actors. Under positive-sum conditions, it is not only a matter of legal obligation or traditional mutual recognition, but of the evident self-interest of each participant to stick to the established rules of interaction and negotiation. As long as one participates, one can be at least sure not to lose, to receive future rewards for present concessions, and to have one's claims respected as legitimate, since the process of growth itself provides the resources necessary for such compensation. Stagnation, and even more recession or expected no-growth conditions, destroy the basis for cooperative relations among collective actors; confidence, mutual respect, and reciprocity are put in question, and coalitions, alliances, and routinized networks of cooperation tend to be seen as problematic and in need of revision by the organizational elites involved. Crucial as these "social contracts"—i.e., subtle "quasi-constitutional" relations of trust, loyalty, and recognition of the mutual spheres of interest and competence—are in a complex political economy,[27] the interorganizational relations that are required for the management of economic growth tend to break down under the impact of continued stagnation. This is illustrated by growing strains within party coalitions, between unions and parties, employers' associations and governments, states and federal governments, all of which find the principle of "*sich auf die eigene Kraft verlassen*" (i.e., to engage in uncooperative strategies either because nothing appears to be gained from sticking to the rules and/or because relevant others are anticipated to do the same) increasingly attractive in a number of Western European political systems, including the European Community itself.

The second type of disorganization that follows from stagnation has to do with intraorganizational relations within collective actors such as trade unions, employers associations, and parties. Such organizations depend on the assumption shared by their members that gains achieved by collective action will be achieved at the expense of *third* parties, not at the expense of groups of members and in favor of other groups of members. As soon as this solidaristic expectation is frustrated, the representativeness of the organization is rendered questionable, and "syndicalist," "corporativist" or otherwise particularistic modes of collective action suggest themselves. The consequences of this internal disorganization of collective actors include either increasing "factionalism" of political and economic interests within the organization and/or a shrinking of the social, temporal, and substantive range of representation the organization is able to maintain.[28] The political and economic variants of the interclass accord that have gradually developed in all advanced capitalist states since the First World War and that have helped to make capitalism and democracy compatible with each other are clearly disintegrating under the impact of these developments and paradoxes.

Does that mean that we are back in a situation that supports the convergent views of Marx and Mill concerning the antagonism of political mass participation and (economic) freedom? Yes and no. Yes, because we have numerous reasons to expect an increase of institutionally unmediated social and political conflict, the expression of which is not channelled through parties or other devices of representation, and the sources of which are no longer dried up by effective social and economic policies of the state. But no, because there are strict limits to the analogy between the dynamics of "late" and "early" capitalism. One important limit derives from the fact that the forces involved in such conflicts are extremely heterogenous, both concerning their causes and socioeconomic composition. This pattern is remarkably different from a bipolar, "class conflict" situation which involves two highly inclusive collective actors who are defined by the two sides of the labor market. But, in spite of this highly fragmented nature of modern political conflict, its outcomes may well involve fundamental changes of either the economic or the political sphere of society, changes that have, for just a limited and short period of time, been inconceivable under the unchallenged reign of competitive party democracy and the Keynesian welfare state.

Notes

1. For instance, J. S. Mill's argument on the necessary limits of the extension of *equal* voting rights as developed in Ch. 8 of his *Considerations on Representative Government*. Oxford: Oxford Univ. Press.

2. This idea is stated in all three of Marx' major political writings on France, namely *Die Klassenkämpfe in Frankreich von 1848–1850* (1850), *Der achtzehnte Brumaire des Louis Bonaparte* (1852) and *Der Bürgerkrieg in Frankreich* (1871).

3. G. Therborn (1977). "The rule of capital and the rise of democracy," *New Left Review* 103:28.

4. This procedure is followed on the basis of the rather trivial, if not uncontroversial, idea that compatibility, stability, continuity or "self-reproductiveness" of any social system is not sufficiently accounted for in terms of its "inertia" or its presupposed "adaptive capacity," but can and must be explained as a *process* of reproduction in which integrative tendencies outweigh those of change or disruption. Cf. C.S. Maier (1981). "The two postwar eras and the conditions for stability in twentieth century Western Europe," *The American Historical Review* 86: 327–352.

5. B. Hindess (1980). "Marxism and parliamentary democracy," in A. Hunt (ed.), *Marxism and Democracy*, London: Lawrence and Wishart.

6. Lenin writes in *State and Revolution*: "The democratic republic is the best possible political shell for capitalism, and therefore capital, once in possession . . . of this very best shell, establishes its power so securely, so firmly, that no change of persons, of institutions, or of parties in the bourgeois democratic republic can shake it." Having in mind the Leninist tradition of thinking of the state as a mere reflection of socioeconomic power structures—and the corresponding theorem of the eventual withering away of the state after the revolution—the Italian political theorist Norberto Bobbio has rightly asked the question whether there is at all something like a "Marxist theory of the state" which would be conceptually equipped to grasp the "specificity of the political." Cf. N. Bobbio's contributions to *Il Marxismo e lo Stato*, Mondo Operaio Edizioni Avanti, Roma 1976; quoted after the German translation *Sozialisten, Kommunisten und der Staat*, Hamburg: VSA (1977), pp. 15–61.

7. It is only on the basis of *real* assimilation of the practices of political parties to market behavior that the "economic paradigm" in democratic theory (as formulated in the famous works of Schumpeter, Downs and Olsen) could become so plausible and influential.

8. Max Weber (1958). Gesammelte politische Schriften. Tübingen: Mohr, p. 392.

9. R. Luxemburg (1924). *Massenstreik, Partei und Gewerkschaften*, Gesammelte Werke Vol. 11, 163, 165, Berlin: Dietz.

10. Cf. R. Michels (1925). *Soziologie des Parteiwesens*, Stuttgart; W. J. Mommsen (1981). "Max Weber and Robert Michels," *Arch. Eur. Soc.* 22: 100–116; D. Beetham (1977). "From socialism to fascism: the relation between theory and practice in the work of Robert Michels," *Political Studies*, 25: 3–24, 161–181.

11. See the brilliant analysis of this problem by A. Przeworski (1980) "Social democracy as a historical phenomenon," *New Left Review* 122.

12. C. V. McPherson (1977). *The Life and Times of Liberal Democracy*. London: Oxford University Press, p. 69.

13. The most comprehensive account of recent theorizing and discussion on "corporatism" is P. C. Schmitter and G. Lehmbruch (eds.) (1979). *Trends Toward Corporatist Intermediation,* London: Sage.

14. B. Jessop (1980). "The transformation of the state in post-war Britain," in R. Scase (ed.) *The State in Western Europe.* London: Croom Helm, pp. 23–93.

15. Cf. for a detailed account of current Swedish debates on these plans and the debates surrounding them: U. Himmelstrand et al. (1981). *Beyond Welfare Capitalism?* London: Heinemann, esp. pp. 255–310.

16. D. Abraham (1982). " 'Economic Democracy' as a Labor Alternative to the 'Growth Strategy' in the Weimar Republic." Unpublished manuscript, Princeton, 16 ff.

17. A. Shonfield (1965). *Modern Capitalism: The Changing Balance of Public and Private Power.* London: Oxford University Press.

18. S. Bowles (1981). "The Keynesian Welfare State and the Post-Keynesian Political Containment of the Working Class." Unpublished manuscript, Paris, 12ff.

19. This slogan has since become a technical term, in comparative politics; cf. A. Markovits (ed.)(1982). *The Political Economy of West Germany. Modell Deutschland.* New York: Praeger.

20. For a detailed formulation of this argument see G. Lenhardt, and C. Offe (1977). "Staatstheorie und sozialpolitik politisch-soziologische erklärungsansätze für funktionen und innovationsprozesse der sozialpolitik," in: C. v. Ferber/ F. X. Kaufmann (Hrsg.) Sonderheft 19, der *Kölner Zeitschrift für Soziologie und Sozialpsychologie:* pp. 98–127.

21. See N. Luhmann (1981). *Politische Theorie in Wohlfahrtsstaat.* München; S. Huntington (1975). "The United States," in M. Crozier et al., *The Crisis of Democracy.* New York: NYU Press, pp. 59–118; B. Cazes (1981). "The welfare state: A double bind," in *The Welfare State in Crisis,* Paris: OECD, pp. 151–173. See also the powerful critique of the "economic reason vs. political irrationality" argument by J. Goldthorpe (1978). "The current inflation: Towards a sociological account," in F. Hirsch, and J. Goldthrope (eds.). *The Political Economy of Inflation.* London: Martin Robertson.

22. Quoted from a paper by G. Esping-Anderson, "The incompatibilities of the welfare state," *Working Papers for a New Society,* Jan. 1982.

23. See J. Logue (1979). "The welfare state—victim of its success," *Daedalus* 108 (4): 69–87; also R. Klein (1980). "The welfare state—a self-inflicted crisis?" *Political Quarterly* 51: 24–34.

24. On this problem of the new "service class" and its (partially converging) critique from the Left and the Right, see I. Illich (ed.) (1977). *Disabling Professions.* London: Marion Boyars; a penetrating and influential economic analysis of the rise of "unproductive" service labor is R. Bacon and W. Eltis (1976). *Britain's Economic Problem: Too Few Producers.* London: Macmillan.

25. See L. Thurow (1980). *The Zero-Sum Society. Distribution and the Possibilities for Economic Change.* New York: Basic Books.

26. See J. Kocka, "Organisierter kapitalismus oder staatsmonopolistischer kapitalismus. Begriffliche vorbemerkungen," in H. A. Winkler (ed.), (1974). *Organisierter Kapitalismus.* Göttingen: Vandenhoek.

27. Cf. E. W. Böckenförde (1976). "Die politische funktion wirtschaftlich-sozialer verbände," *Der Staat* 15: 457–483.

28. See, for the case of German and Italian unions. R. G. Heinze et al. (1981). "Einheitsprobleme der einheitsgewerkschaft (1982)," in *Soziale Welt* 32: 19–38; and M. Regini (1982). "Repräsentationskrise und klassenpolitik der gewerkschaften," *Leviathan* 10 (in press).

The Editors

THOMAS FERGUSON is an assistant professor of political science at the Massachusetts Institute of Technology, and the author of *Critical Realignment: The Fall of the House of Morgan and the Origins of the New Deal* (forthcoming). JOEL ROGERS is an assistant professor of political science at Rutgers University, and co-author (with Joshua Cohen) of *On Democracy: Toward a Transformation of American Society* (1983). Together Ferguson and Rogers edited *The Hidden Election: Politics and Economics in the 1980 Presidential Campaign* (1981). Their column "The Political Economy" appears in *The Nation*.

The Contributors

FRED BLOCK is associate professor of sociology, University of Pennsylvania. WALTER DEAN BURNHAM is professor of political science, Massachusetts Institute of Technology. DAVID R. CAMERON is associate professor of political science, Yale University. ANTHONY DOWNS is Senior Fellow at the Brookings Institution. MORRIS P. FIORINA is professor of government, Harvard University. BENJAMIN GINSBERG is associate professor of government, Cornell University. PETER ALEXIS GOUREVITCH is associate professor of political science, McGill University. SAMUEL P. HUNTINGTON is professor of government, Harvard University. The late MICHAL KALECKI (1899-1970) held research and academic positions in England and Poland and at the United Nations. KATHLEEN KEMP is associate professor of political science, Florida State University. JAMES R. KURTH is professor of political science, Swarthmore College. CHARLES E. LINDBLOM is professor of political science, Yale University. THEODORE J. LOWI is professor of government, Cornell University. CLAUS OFFE is professor of sociology, University at Bielefeld, West Germany. SAMUEL POPKIN is professor of political science, University of California, San Diego; JOHN W. GORMAN is an executive of Cambridge Reports International, Cambridge, Massachusetts; CHARLES PHILLIPS is assistant professor of political science, University of North Carolina; and JEFFREY A. SMITH is president of Opinion Analysts, Inc., Austin, Texas. ADAM PRZEWORSKI is professor of political science, and MICHAEL WALLERSTEIN is a visiting lecturer in political science, University of Chicago. LESTER A. SALAMON is director of the Center for Governance and Management Research, the Urban Institute, and JOHN J. SIEGFRIED is professor of economics, Vanderbilt University. MARTIN SHEFTER is associate professor of government, Cornell University. RICHARD B. STEWART is professor at the Harvard University Law School. GEORGE J. STIGLER is professor at the University of Chicago Graduate School of Business. ALAN STONE is associate professor of political science, University of Houston. IMMANUEL WALLERSTEIN is professor of sociology, State University of New York, Binghamton. JAMES Q. WILSON is professor of government, Harvard University.